1986

THE PHILOSOPHERS

THE PHILOSOPHERS

*Their Lives
and the Nature of their
Thought*

BEN-AMI SCHARFSTEIN

BASIL BLACKWELL · OXFORD

First published in Great Britain by
Basil Blackwell Publisher Ltd.
5 Alfred Street
Oxford OX1 4HB
England

British Library Cataloguing in Publication Data

Scharfstein, Ben-Ami
    The philosophers.
    1. Philosophers – Psychology
    I. Title
    101'.9   B68

ISBN 0-631-10311-2

Typeset in Great Britain by Preface Ltd., Salisbury, Wiltshire
Printed in the United States of America

To Ghela

Contents

"Mon *aveugle* confiance dans la clarté, dans la clarification."

Paul Valéry
Cahiers 1, Pléiade, 107

1
Persuasion

The first words of a book begin a long and possibly difficult adventure. The adventure I am now undertaking is an appraisal of my profession, philosophy, of my fellow professionals, the philosophers, and, finally, of myself, at least as a person who philosophizes. When I reflect on my motives for writing this book, I am inclined to give an answer that is good, I think, for philosophers in general, though much of it, coming here at the beginning, can be only preliminary.

My answer has three parts, all related to the human nature I have assumed we share with philosophers. I am writing this book, first, because I want to persuade you; secondly, because I feel that what I have to say is essentially true and important; and, thirdly, because after prolonged thought and equally prolonged delay, I feel the need to express myself on the subject.

I notice that in stating my answer I have already paired the subjective with the objective, as I mean to continue pairing them, and to pair, as well, the irrational with the rational. Joining the members of the one and the other pair, there is the *I*, which, as certainly as it is subjective, aspires to rise above mere subjectivity. This is the *I* that we know and do not know, depending on the notion of 'knowing' that we adopt, on our degree of understanding of ourselves, and on our closeness to or estrangement from ourselves. This is the omnipresent human *I* in which everything we feel, think, and do is joined, and which, if we are able and lucky enough, externalizes itself into a somehow detachable, *I*-transcending form.

Let me give a slow, separate explanation of each of the three parts of my answer, beginning with my attempt, or any attempt, to persuade. Persuasion, then, is the subject of this first chapter.

Persuasion as Mutuality and Disagreement

I want, of course, to persuade you; but the reasons for this desire are not all self-evident. I am writing with a certain anticipatory pleasure. I do not

1

know who you are. You are related to me only by these ribbons of printed words that speak for me in my physical absence and continue to speak in my voice after I am dead. As I set the words down, I find myself taking part in a subvocal conversation with myself, in which one of my voices plays your part, or the part of any philosophizing person not myself that it can assume. If what I say interests you, you in reality or in my mind, a common feeling begins to join us. If you approve of my ideas, you are indirectly approving of me, and I feel an immediate warmth towards you. Put otherwise, I am giving you the gift of my thoughts and you are giving me, in exchange, the gift of your interest. Our dislike of isolation may play some part in the exchange, but the pleasure of our mutuality, that of two separate but intersecting, sympathetic creatures, surely does.

Maybe you are persuasible. In spite of what I am about to say, I hope so. After all, lovers manage long spells of mutuality, not only of feeling but also of ideas; and the likeness of the ideas of husband and wife or parents and children shows that persuasion does, in some sense, take place. But we are not in love or married or related to one another like parent and child. As our conversation continues, I imagine that you, my partner, are still smiling, but beginning to disagree. As you state your disagreement, I may feel the hint of a physical tension. This tension, located in the diaphragm, is slightly painful, and I have learned that it may be a sign of anger, though I do not feel it as such. *You* may be unaware of my tension because you yourself may not share it. You may feel no more than the glow of a friendly intellectual conversation, especially if you are arguing as a professional on professionally familiar matters and if you take pleasure in intellectual duels.

Am I right in thinking that you will disagree with me? Why should I suppose that within a few minutes of conversation or a few paragraphs of print, you are likely to begin making mental reservations? What I am about to say strikes me as so evident that I have to make an effort to keep in mind that you are not already persuaded of its truth. All I want to do is to make a friendly characterization of philosophy and philosophers. So far as I know, my object is to understand, not to win intellectual victories; nor do I suppose myself in any way exempted from the difficulties in philosophizing that I mean to point out. Yet experience has taught me again and again that some of you (*you* now obviously in the plural) will disagree with me in principle, many of you with the way I express even the ideas on which we agree in principle, and all of you in at least some detail or other.

I can predict our disagreement, even if I smile as I write and you as you read these words. I *know* you cannot succeed in disputing the truth of what I have just said. To put it rather as the old paradox-makers did, if you agree with what I have just said on our predictable disagreement, then you agree that we will disagree later. If, on the other hand, you disagree that we will disagree, then my whole position is wrong, and we, of course, disagree fundamentally. And should you be impatient with such arguments and say, 'Nonsense, if only we are clear about our use of words, it is quite possible to agree with you both now and later,' I will answer, 'But you are already disagreeing with me even about my use of words. Besides, my infallible sign, my demon, my tenseness, says that we are opposed.'

I am therefore led to suppose that to understand one another, we must assume the likelihood of misunderstanding one another. To understand someone else, even on a purely intellectual level, is never easy for long. Intuitive openness to ideas and argumentative sharpness are by no means the same, and persuasibility and the desire to persuade are by no means equal. Those with the strongest desire to persuade, the criers of their own intellectual wares, are unlikely to yield to persuasion easily. If they do not ignore the persuasions of others, they cry out against them, for they are apt to be just as stubborn as their persuasive drive is strong. Among philosophers, it is true, reasons are usually given, but between the giving of reasons and the attainment of persuasion there is likely to be a considerable distance. In Wittgenstein's elliptical words:

'I said I would "combat" the other man—but wouldn't I give him reasons? Certainly; but how far do they go? At the end of reasons comes *persuasion*. (Think what happens when missionaries convert natives.)'[1]

Creative Resistance to Persuasion

But isn't it possible to argue and to persuade by logic alone? Of course; but outside of technically well-defined contexts, sheerly logical argument and persuasion seem to me rare, if, indeed, the idea of sheer logic outside of such contexts makes any sense. Every philosopher must have heard logicians arguing in loud, not to say passionate, tones, or seen them smiling (can it be with pleasure?) as they armed their logic with rhetorical rapiers or, more brutally, clubs.

It is obvious that even in professional arguments, more than objectively professional conclusions are at stake. Given the eagerness to win on the one side and the resistance to defeat on the other, professional competence may not be enough to ensure the understanding or the acceptance of even relatively simple points. There are capable and sometimes great scientists and philosophers who find it quite hard to understand others of their own profession. They have, that is, a natural resistance to ideas other than their own, so that no one persuades them, at least easily, except themselves. Lord Rayleigh, who won the Nobel prize for physics in 1904, took special pleasure in reducing confused scientific problems to basic intellectual order. His mind is said to have worked so efficiently that he often sent the solution of a problem to a journal for publication exactly as he had written it out for the first time. 'Nevertheless,' we are told, 'his mind was not swift and facile. He said that he never understood another person's experiment when it was explained to him for the first time.'[1]

Valéry, whom I have quoted before and will quote again, went so far as to say, 'Philosophy cannot suit anyone except the person who creates it, and even in him it is always in an inchoate stage,' the stage of always being born.[2] I would not like to accept these words without essential qualification; but there are good examples, not only of philosophers who are unable to understand others, but who recognize and admit this shortcoming. Let me give two examples, that of Leibniz and that of Kant.

In a letter written in 1675, Leibniz describes how the styles of philosophers such as Bacon and Gassendi attracts him, while those of such as Galileo and Descartes, which require 'deep meditation,' repel him. Finding it difficult, he explains, to follow closely written or geometrical arguments, he has been able to read Euclid only in the rapid way in which one reads history. He knows, he says, that this way is not good for Plato or Aristotle, or for Galileo and Descartes. Yet what he knows of Descartes comes almost entirely from popular books written by others. The explanation lies in his nature, he says:

> Personally, though I have always loved to think by myself, I have always found it hard to read books which one cannot understand without much meditation, for in following one's thoughts one follows a certain natural inclination and so gains profit with pleasure. One is violently disturbed, in contrast, when compelled to follow the thoughts of someone else.[3]

Kant, in a letter written when he was seventy, tells of the great difficulty he has in grasping the ideas of other philosophers. He attributes the difficulty to age and illness, which prevent him from thinking himself 'into the concatenation of ideas of another person' and so from forming a mature judgment of the other person's system.[4] But Kant's deafness to other philosophers was quite evident even in his prime.[5] Such is the testimony of a man who revered Kant and who, during nine years of Kant's prime, lives with him and served as his amanuensis. He says:

> Just at the time of his greatest maturity and strength of his understanding, as he worked on the critical philosophy, nothing was harder

for him than to think himself into the system of another. He could grasp the writings of even his opponents only with the most extreme effort, because it was impossible for him to extricate himself for only a limited time from his original system of thought. He admitted this himself and ordinarily gave his friends the task of reading for him, to inform him of the main results of the comparison of the content of alien systems with his own, and perhaps, on the same grounds, left to his students and friends the defence of his philosophy against the challenges of his opponents.[6]

Because Leibniz and Kant were genuinely creative philosophers, their difficulty in following others strikes me as natural and the explanations given for the difficulty as true. Their difficulty in following others is the obverse of their intensity of thought in their own directions and in response to their own needs. I think that these two examples are convincing enough, so I add only that of Husserl, of whom a level-headed disciple said:

> It was easier to discuss Husserl's ideas with him over the printed page than when confronted by his own irresistible monologue, his piercing glance riveted on his audience or on some point far off in space. For in discussion he would use questions and suggestions of others merely as stimulants to set the wheels of his own thought into ceaseless motion.[7]

Even apart from such creative resistance, a philosopher is naturally more difficult to persuade philosophically than a layman. He lives an intellectually competitive life, and to ask him to accept arguments without real resistance is like asking a chess player both to forego the pleasure of the game and to declare himself, all the same, to have been mated. In a sense, every other philosopher, even his ally, is his opponent, because, when their mutual opponent is absent, the allies' differences grow more apparent. The criticism levelled by an ally may strike as hard as that levelled by a member of the family, who resembles us, shares our sensitivities, knows our weak and sore spots, and enters into our lives in every way.

Persuasion of Others as Self-Persuasion

So far, persuasion has been seen as a form of attempted mutuality, disturbed, in the end, by resistance. This resistance expresses, among other things, our need to assert ourselves and not be swallowed up into the thought of someone else. Not to resist persuasion at all is to be intellectually non-existent, that is, not to have a particular individual existence. Because the need for individual existence or self-assertion is so strong intellectually in creative thinkers, it is likely to deafen them to whatever does not serve their own thought. But the resistance to

persuasion has still another cause. Philosophers and writers and their
likes may themselves be hard to persuade just because their persuasive
energies are directed against their own concealed doubts.

An instance or two may serve to make this last idea persuasive. The
most tragic one I know of is that, not of a philosopher, but of the
novelist, Virginia Woolf. As is well known, she experienced periods of
acute madness, and the fear of madness, which cast its shadow over all
her life, eventually prompted her suicide. It was apparently her fear of
madness that made her so sensitive to the reaction to her novels. 'She was
always conscious that, to the outside world' her novels 'might appear to
be mad, or worse still, that they really were mad.' The biographer who
makes this judgment recalls that in her diary of 1927 she wrote, 'Suppose
one woke and found oneself a fraud? It was part of my madness that
horror,' and then he continues, 'For her, therefore, a favorable notice was
more valuable than mere praise; it was a kind of certificate of sanity.'[1]

I do not know of any such extreme examples among philosophers; but
I think that the sometimes truculent self-assurance they have expressed
and their always stubborn attempts to persuade may have been meant to
still their own doubts. It will be shown that Descartes' self-assured
philosophizing was a response to his lack of self-assurance, which never
disappeared. A biographer of Hegel says that Hegel's disciples' 'faith
kindled his, and his strengthened theirs.'[2] Hegel himself says, 'The
individual needs public acceptance to prove the truth of what is as yet his
solitary concern; he needs to see how the conviction that is as yet
particular becomes general.'[3] Husserl alternated exuberant pride in his
philosophizing with 'near-despair and self-abasement,' was 'always
distressed' when a close student could not agree with him, and often
withheld or withdrew manuscripts from publication because of 'a feeling
of inadequacy to his task,' the reason he gave for not finishing his *Ideen*.[4]
When Wittgenstein sent a copy of his *Blue Book* to Russell, he added, in a
transparently ambivalent note, that he would be very pleased indeed if
Russell 'would get some mild enjoyment' out of the lectures, but, in his
words, 'If you don't read them *it doesn't matter at all*.'[5]

Bertrand Russell himself, as will later be described, was tempted to
commit suicide in his adolescence and suffered a profound fear of
inherited insanity. His cutting wit and external self-assurance concealed
an inward self he felt to be empty at its core. An intimate friend of his
later years says 'that he had in fact a powerful and profound need for
reassurance not only about the intellectual aspects of his life, but also
about the personal aspects . . . He certainly had a powerful and nagging
impulse to induce in other people his own impulses.'[6] As this friend tells
us, Russell's need for reassurance 'became urgent and almost painful'

after his current marriage broke up and after *Human Knowledge,* in which he had invested great hopes, was published. The inclusiveness of his demand for reassurance was astonishing, encompassing his writing style, his wit, and the extent and nature of his influence.[7]

Persuasive Presences: Philosophical Mentors and Saints

I do not know if the acuteness of Russell's need to persuade is representative of many philosophers, though I am sure that they all take the effort to persuade seriously and so may be said to display the need to persuade. Such persuaders, however, as philosophers come to be are not simply formed by the desire for distant communion, intellectual victory, or self-persuasion. They are also often formed in the image of authoritative figures, whether parents or parent-like teachers, whose behests they may be trying to carry out, or whose persons they may be trying to re-embody in themselves. They may also be formed by the persons they fall in love with; or by experiences of great intensity; or by an intense search for happiness. Even the experience of the power of reason itself may be a highly emotional one, giving the person who undergoes it an immediate, intense reward and promising him more such rewards in the future.

Let me go on by giving examples, in turn, of each of the kinds of formative influences I have mentioned. I omit only the influence of parents, to which I mean to devote particular attention later, and go on to teachers, beginning with the Greek philosophers, Socrates, Plotinus, and Proclus. That Socrates was extraordinarily attractive to his disciples, including Plato, need only be said. Plotinus, as his loving disciple, Porphyry tells us, searched for a philosophical mentor and grew depressed by his failure to find him, until an understanding friend 'sent him to Ammonius, whom he had so far not tried. He went and heard him, and said to his friend, "This is the man I was looking for." From that day on he stayed continually with Ammonius.'[1]

Plotinus, too, proved to be a magnetic philosopher-father, who inspired such devotion that 'many men and women of the highest rank, on the approach of death, brought him their children, both boys and girls, and entrusted them to him along with all their property, considering that he would be a holy and god-like guardian.'[2] Proclus, the great fifth-century systematizer of Neo-Platonism, who has been called 'the last creative mind in Greek philosophy,' was said to have been very handsome, vigorously healthy, and so eloquent 'that when he was speaking a radiance seemed to flow from him. According to his eulogist,

he exhibited all the virtues—physical, moral, political, ascetic, intellectual, and "theurgic" in a preeminent degree.' Sadly for those of us
who are philosophical, well-married, and love children, he was not only
ascetic, but attacked marriage and family life.[3]

I skip the Middle Ages, as I skip India and China, to all of which the
saintly philosophical mentor is an indispensable figure, and continue
with the philosophers of modern Europe, the real or apparent saintliness
or heroism of some of whom has been far more influential than is evident
from the prosaic biographical words allotted them in the usual history of
philosophy. Think of the Immanuel Kant who, in his lectures on
morality,

> ceased to be merely a speculative philosopher and became, at the same time,
> a spirited orator, sweeping the heart and emotions along with him, as well as
> satisfying the intelligence . . . He was almost worshipped by his students,
> who took every opportunity of letting him know it . . . People used to wait
> attentively to see him as he crossed the courtyard of the Albertinium on his
> way to the great lecture hall, for a meeting of the Senate or an academic
> ceremony.[4]

Schopenhauer, though he never knew Kant personally, regarded himself
as his true disciple and inheritor, while Nietzsche became for a time
Schopenhauer's disciple. On a later page I will cite Nietzsche's
discipleship as an example of conversion by way of a sudden,
overwhelming experience. Here I will retain Nietzsche's outburst of love
for Richard Wagner, whom he came to live with, serve, and regard as
father and mentor. On first acquaintance with Wagner, Nietzsche wrote
ecstatically, 'I have found a man who, like no one else, reveals to me the
image of what Schopenhauer calls "the genius" and who is quite
penetrated by' Schopenhauer's 'wonderful, heartfelt philosophy . . . In
him there rule such an unqualified idealism, such a deep and moving
humanity, and such a sublime seriousness of life.'[5] Even when
Nietzsche's love for Wagner turned to love-hate, he continued to express
his great debt to Wagner, of whom he said, 'I hold the rest of my human
relationships cheap.'[6]

It may be supposed that all this emotion of discipleship fits only
Germans, who have shown so great a capacity for Romantic
attachments; but the fact is that the emotion can overcome Englishmen
as well. To those who venerated him, G. E. Moore was surely the
philosopher-saint, while Wittgenstein was, one might say, the
philosopher-daimon. Russell, too, could inspire veneration. To speak of
the first of these first, I have read of 'the mute circle of seekers after truth
who sat puffing their pipes around the discreet shrine of G. E. Moore.'[7]
Moore impressed the critical Lytton Strachey

as being without question, really great . . . The passionate incandescent purity of his thought seemed to imbue and transfigure his countenance with a sublime beauty . . . Still slim in those days, Moore seemed indeed not of this miserable planet, but a prophet nourished with wisdom and goodness from some far-off mysterious source, enhaloed with transcendental illumination.[8]

Still another description says that in argument Moore's 'whole frame was gripped by a passion to confute error and expose confusion. To watch him at work was an enthralling experience . . . If the veneration his young admirers accord him almost matched that due a saint, we need not think that they were mistaken.'[9] Russell, who recalls the days when Moore was 'beautiful and slim, with a look almost of inspiration,' stresses a deeply passionate intellect and 'a kind of exquisite purity.'[10]

The old, famous, politically concerned Russell is said by his close, though problematic, disciple, Ralph Schoenman, to have had the 'combination of passionate rebellion and humor' that saved Schoenman and a small group of others from America's 'cruelty' and 'crassness.' These disciples were ironical when they said that Russell was their candidate for god, 'But we did,' Schoenman insists, 'worship him.'[11] For all his influence, however, Russell was not personally as impressive as Ludwig Wittgenstein, who seemed to many of his students to have the look and intensity of the paradigmatic philosopher.

> His face was lean and brown, his profile was acquiline and strikingly beautiful. His head was covered with a curly mass of brown hair . . . His look was concentrated, he made striking gestures with his hands as if he were discoursing. All the others maintained an intent and expectant silence.[12]

Wittgenstein's student, Alice Ambrose, suggests that she and his other students could not distinguish what they had gained from him philosophically from what 'his compelling personality made them feel they had gained.' She says that he was both difficult to his students and devoted to them.

> The intensity of his inner life and the compelling force of his own values communicated themselves to others and made demands for adjustment to him. But whoever has not experienced the directness of his gaze and the warmth of his reaction to small attentions is likely to underestimate this other side of his personality . . . What was important to him was philosophy, and the proper way of doing it; and his demand that others share his attitude and his standards was uncompromising. Doing philosophy was a moral matter for him.[13]

Love's Persuasions

At least some of the accounts I have been repeating express the not unerotic love of disciples for their teacher. But love can work more directly in making its philosophic conversions, as we see in the case of Socrates, the wonderful old exemplar of the personal and philosophical eros as one.[1] Perhaps Socrates, whom we respect, will make us indulgent with Hipparchia (*c.* 300 B.C.), who was converted to the Cynic philosophy when she fell in stubborn love with Crates, or indulgent with another Crates, a favourite of the head of the Academy, Polemo, to whose position he succeeded, and whose philosophy he shared in life, as, in death, he shared his tomb.[2]

Some modern philosophers have regarded their love for a woman as decisive, not only for their personal lives, but for their philosophies as well. Perhaps Schelling's Caroline fits this description. Certainly Comte's Clothilde does, and so does John Stuart Mill's Harriet, of whom more will be said in the pages devoted to Mill. The ability of love to exert intellectual effects and inspire conversions seems to me so obviously a commonplace of experience that I will add no more than the story told about himself by Herman Weyl (1885–1955), the eminent mathematician and philosopher of science. Weyl's Positivism, to which he had been led by his study of geometry, was vanquished by two successive loves. 'My peace of mind in positivism,' he writes, 'was shaken when I fell in love with a young singer whose life was grounded in religion and who belonged to a circle that was led philosophically by a well-known Hegelian. Partly because of my immaturity, but also because of this unbridgeable chasm in philosophical outlook, nothing of it. The shock, however, continued to work. It was not long afterward that I married a philosophy student, a disciple of Edmund Husserl, the founder of phenomenology, who was then working in Göttingen. So it came to be Husserl who led me out of positivism and once more to a freer outlook upon the world.'[3]

Axiomatic Experiences

Not only love, but any powerful experience can lead to or, in effect, constitute the conviction on which a whole philosophy is based. Such a conviction serves as a metaphysical assumption; but the word, 'assumption,' is inadequate to it, for unless it is displaced by an equally powerful experience, the philosopher or scientist who has accepted it can hardly reject it, and I should therefore prefer to speak of an 'axiomatic experience' or 'experiential axiom.'

To illustrate my meaning, I should like to recall philosophically decisive experiences in the lives of Descartes, Spinoza, Rousseau, Fichte, Nietzsche, James, Mach, and Russell.

Whoever is familiar with Descartes' biography will recall that the philosopher was inspired one memorable night by a series of three dreams. These will be commented on later, but the images they contained can at least be mentioned here, the terrifying phantoms, the 'sharp and piercing noise' he took for a clap of thunder, the mysterious dictionary, the anthology of Latin poetry, not to speak of the unknown man who presented him 'with some verses beginning with the words *Est et Non*.' Feeling that he was between an evil Genius and God, Descartes 'turned to God, praying to have His will revealed to him and that he would deign to enlighten and guide him in his search for truth. He next addressed himself to the Holy Virgin that he might commend to her this matter, which he judged to be the most important in his life.'[1]

To Descartes, the experience was not merely a series of dreams, but a revelation, which he interpreted optimistically, in keeping with the search he was already apparently undertaking for a generalized mathematical method, and in keeping with the philosophy that he was yet to create. While the other philosophers' experiences I mean to recall may not take so picturesque a form and do not conclude in prayer, they are of equal importance, I take it, in influencing the thought of each of the philosophers who underwent them.

Let me go on to Spinoza, who has left smoothed-over traces of a formative crisis in his life. In his *Treatise on the Correction of the Understanding,* he refers to an experience the depth of which we can sense though we do not know to what, exactly, Spinoza was referring. 'I saw myself,' he says, 'in the midst of a very great peril and obliged to seek a remedy, however uncertain, with all my energy: like a sick man seized with a deadly disease, who sees death before him if he does not find some remedy, is forced to seek it, however uncertain, with all his remaining hope, for in that is all his hope placed.'

The remedy Spinoza discovered, in principle not unlike that of the classic Yogis of India, was a change in the quality and the objects of his thought, from finite to infinite, from temporal to intemporal, because 'the love towards a thing eternal and infinite alone feeds the mind with pleasure, and it is free from all pain; so that it is much to be desired and to be sought with all our might.'[2]

Rousseau writes of a time when he was leafing through a journal and came on a question that had been posed by the Academy of Dijon. Suddenly, he says, his mind was dazzled, and confusing, inexpressibly disturbing crowds of ideas thronged his mind.

> Unable to continue breathing while walking, I let myself fall under one of the trees of the avenue, and I passed half an hour there in such agitation that when I got up I saw the whole front of my vest wet with my tears I had not felt myself shedding . . . All I could retain of these crowds of great truths which, in a quarter of an hour, illuminated me under that tree has been feebly distributed in my three principal writings, namely that first discourse, the one on inequality, and the treatise on education, which three works are inseparable, and form a single whole.[3]

While this description is, no doubt, rhetorically heightened, it is characteristic of Rousseau, and there is no reason not to take it as basically true to his experience. It is hard for those of us who are not subject to sudden awakenings or conversions to believe those who are. To me, at least, the strangeness of Rousseau's illumination is even exceeded by that of Fichte's conversion, in 1790, as the result of the reading of Kant's *Critique of Practical Reason*. Fichte testifies that the book filled his heart and mind, stilled his lust for work and his over-active imagination, and strengthened his mind. 'These were the happiest days I have ever experienced,' he writes; and he writes to Kant, 'The thought of you will always be my genius. . . .'[4]

Now Nietzsche. His attraction to Wagner has already been described. The way to Wagner had been prepared by an earlier intense experience, the reading of Schopenhauer's magnum opus, *The World as Will and Representation*. Nietzsche was then alone, he describes, as if suspended in air, without principles, hope, or a friendly memory. Then, one day, he came on Schopenhauer's book, which he found in a second-hand bookstore. In his own words:

> I do not know what demon whispered to me, 'Take this book home with you.' . . . I threw myself into the corner of the sofa with the newly-acquired treasure and began to allow that energetic, gloomy genius to take effect on me. Every line here cried out renunciation, denial, resignation, here I saw a mirror in which I beheld world, life, and my own nature in terrible grandeur. Here I saw the completely indifferent sun's eye of art, here I saw sickness and health, exile and refuge, hell and heaven.[5]

William James's critical experience came at the end of a long period of psychological and physical illness, which had brought him, he believed, to the edge of insanity. Attempting to take courage, he found an ally in the French philosopher, Charles Renouvier, whose definition of free will as the sustaining of a thought out of pure personal choice he decided to accept. He decided to exercise his freedom by, first of all, believing in it, believing in his individual reality and creative power. 'I will posit life (the real, the good),' he writes in his diary, 'in the self governing resistance of the ego to the world. . . .'[6]

The experience James underwent will be commented on later, in the context of his life. For the present it is enough to point out that it constitutes the experiential axiom of at least his doctrine of the 'will to believe.'

Ernst Mach, the physicist who was a father of the Logical Positivists, tells of a perceptual and emotional experience that obviously underlies much of his thought. At the age of fifteen, he had been deeply impressed by Kant's *Prolegomena*. But, he says,

the superfluity of the role played by the 'thing–in–itself' abruptly dawned upon me. On a bright summer day in the open air, the world with my ego suddenly appeared to me as *one* coherent mass of sensations, only more strongly coherent in the ego. Although the actual working out of this thought did not occur until a later period, yet this moment was decisive for my whole view.[7]

Bertrand Russell, too, had a conversion–experience, which became the lasting basis of his ethics. It occurred in 1901, when he found Mrs. Whitehead undergoing an attack of pain that cut her off from everyone. The effect on Russell was sudden and profound:

The sense of the solitude of each human soul suddenly overwhelmed me. Within five minutes I went through some such reflections as the following: the loneliness of the human soul is unendurable; nothing can penetrate it except the highest intensity of the sort of love that religious teachers have preached; whatever does not spring from this motive is harmful, or at best useless; it follows that a public school education is abominable, that the use of force is to be deprecated, and that in human relations one should penetrate to the core of loneliness in each person and speak to that.

Now Russell, 'become a completely different person,' changed from imperialist to pacifist; now, after years of concern for nothing but exactness and analysis, the sense of beauty suddenly filled him; now his interest in children was intense; and now he yearned, like the Buddha, to find a philosophy to make human life endurable. And though, he says, his supposed mystic insight faded and the habit of analysis reasserted itself, something of his experience always remained with him and lent a certain emotional tone to all his human relations.[8]

Euclidean Emotions

In speaking of axiomatic experiences, I have hardly distinguished between one form of experience and another and have required only that the experience should be deep and should in some way underlie the philosopher's subsequent thought. There is one sort of experience, however, that must be singled out, because it is that of the beauty and power of reason itself. In the early lives of philosophers and scientists there must have been many revelations of the great pleasure that reasoning can give in nothing other than its own exercise. The four instances I mean to give, from the lives of Thomas Hobbes, Blaise Pascal, Albert Einstein, and Bertrand Russell, are all responses to Euclidean geometry.

Hobbes is the subject of the following well-known story, told by his friend, John Aubrey:

> He was 40 years old before he looked on Geometry; which happened accidentally. Being in a Gentleman's library, Euclid's Elements lay open, and 'twas the 47 E. Libri I. He read the Proposition. By G—, says he, (he would now and then sweare an emphaticall Oath by way of emphasis) *this is impossible*! So he reads the Demonstration of it, which referred him back to such a Proposition; which proposition he read. That referred him back to another, which he also read. *Et sic deincips* and so on that at last he was demonstratively convinced of that truth. This made him in love with Geometry.[1]

Though developed late in life, Hobbes's love for mathematics was genuine and strong—Aubrey says that Hobbes used to draw lines on his thigh and, when in bed, on his sheets—and he came to the conclusion, which he honoured as best he could, that philosophy should be written in a geometrical style.

An equally well-known story is told about Pascal by his sister. Afraid that the satisfactions of mathematics would tempt the young Pascal away from the study of Latin and other languages, Pascal's father kept his own mathematics books closed and refrained from talking about the subject in the presence of his son. The young Pascal, his curiosity aroused, often begged his father to teach him mathematics, and once drew from his father the admission that mathematics was the means of making correct figures and of finding the proportions between them. Given this cue alone, the twelve-year-old began to draw geometrical figures in charcoal on the floor tiles, invented names for the figures, laid down axioms and (so says the sister) proceeded to make perfect demonstrations, going from one to the other until he arrived at the equivalent of the thirty-second proposition of Euclid's first book. He was rediscovering geometry, an act of genius that made his father cry with joy and relent a little, that is, allow his son to read Euclid during hours set aside for recreation.[2]*

From Pascal to Einstein. The age was the same. Einstein says that he experienced the wonder when he came on

> a little book dealing with Euclidean place geometry. . . . Here were assertions, as for example the intersection of the three altitudes of a triangle in one point, which—though by no means evident—could nevertheless be proved with such certainty that any doubt appeared to be out of the question. This lucidity and certainty made an indescribable impression upon me. That the axiom had to be accepted unproved did not disturb me. In any case it was quite sufficient for me if I could peg proofs upon propositions the validity of which did not seem to me to be dubious.[3]

From Einstein to Russell, the revelation again coming at about the same age. In Russell's own words:

> At the age of eleven, I began Euclid, with my brother as my tutor. This was one of the great events of my life, as dazzling as first love. I had not imagined that there was anything so delicious in the world. After I had learned the fifth proposition, my brother told me that it was generally considered difficult, but I had found no difficulty whatever. This was the first time it had dawned upon me that I might have some intelligence. From that moment until Whitehead and I finished *Principia Mathematica*, when I was thirty-eight, mathematics was my chief interest, and my chief source of happiness. Like all happiness, however, it was not unalloyed. I had been told that Euclid proved things, and was much disappointed that he started with axioms. At first I refused to accept them unless my brother could offer me some reason for doing so, but he said: 'If you don't accept them we cannot go on', and as I wished to go on, I reluctantly admitted them *pro tem*. The doubt as to the premises of mathematics which I felt at that moment remained with me, and determined the course of my subsequent work.[4]

It is interesting that Einstein found it easy and Russell hard to accept axioms without argument. This difference may help to explain why the one became a physicist and used mathematics as no more than a tool, while the other became a philosopher, ready to question everything and

---

*The psychologist, Jean Piaget, tells of a mathematician who chose his career because when a small boy he 'was counting some stones and he counted them from left to right and found there were ten. Then he counted them from right to left and, lo and behold, there were ten again. Then he put them in a circle and, finding ten again, he was very excited. He found, essentially, that the sum is independent of the order.' J. Piaget, 'Some Aspects of Operations,' in M. W. Peris, ed., *Play and Development* (New York: Norton, 1973), p. 23.

expend his energies in the attempt to clarify the nature of mathematics, which seemed to him to retain something unexplained and therefore arbitrary. Hence his need to base mathematics on logic, and hence, too, his later attempt to find the minimal necessary presuppositions for all science, implying, I think, that to recognize these presuppositions would be to rest in greater intellectual comfort or security. Ironically, it was this very attempt, in *Human Knowledge,* that so failed to persuade other philosophers that, as I have described, it seriously intensified Russell's self-doubt.

Persuasion for Mutuality

I want to end this chapter on persuasion somewhat as I began it, by emphasizing the philosopher's implicit need to come into contact with other persons. In this sense, his philosophy is his medium for mutuality. Spinoza says, quite openly, that his desire to persuade is part of the human search for perfection, which, to succeed, must persuade others to share the same thoughts:

> It is then part of my happiness that many others should understand as I do, and that their understanding and desire should be entirely in harmony with my understanding and desire; and in order to bring this to pass it is necessary to understand as much of nature as will suffice for the acquiring of such a nature, and moreover to form such a society as is essential for the purpose of enabling most people to acquire this nature with the greatest ease and security.[1]

In other words, without understanding, passed on by means of philosophical or, at least, rational persuasion, human mutuality is more difficult to achieve and human happiness therefore more remote. Therefore, to be happy, we must learn, organize society so that others can learn, persuade one another of the common therapeutic truth, and all be as one.

2
Truth (and Relevance)

Truth Plain, Plural, Pragmatic

At the beginning of this book, I gave a triple answer to the question why I was writing it. So far I have concentrated on the first answer, which is no more than that I should like to persuade you. This particular desire led to a discussion of the desire to persuade in general, especially among philosophers, and to the illustration of some of the non-rational ways in which philosophers have persuaded others and themselves been persuaded.

I now come to my second answer, that what I have to say is, I believe, true and important. On the truth and importance of understanding philosophers as simply and merely human I will not expatiate just here; my whole book must give whatever testimony it can. The point I want to emphasize here is that I believe whole-heartedly that there is an objective truth, and that an argument such as mine is a contribution, however modest, towards its attainment.

I am making this point emphatically because I am likely to be charged with a self-defeating relativism. Relativism may be entertaining, may deflate pretensions, and may express the defiance of those who feel themselves slighted; but a complete relativism is an intellectually impossible doctrine. Such a relativism makes the fixity of our meanings and our ability to communicate them quite incomprehensible; and it makes it impossible to argue for the truth of relativism itself, because to claim its own truth is, somehow, to privilege that truth and to contradict its basic claim that all statements are equally relative. In other words, the claim that relativism is true without limit implies a standard by which it is known to be true, just such a standard as unlimited relativism denies. But to say that unlimited relativism is an incoherent doctrine is not to say that a limited, so to speak, relative relativism, one that might be called 'pluralism,' or 'possibilism,' or 'fallibilism,' might not be as adequate a philosophical position as we could arrive at. I am attracted by what the Pragmatist, Charles Peirce, described as 'a contrite fallibilism, combined

17

with a high faith in the reality of knowledge, and an intense desire to find things out.'[1]

I cannot therefore deny that my belief in objective truths prevents me from seeing philosophy in a rather relativistic or pluralistic light. I claim, that is, that philosophy is a complex and doubtfully separable blend of the subjective and objective, so that it should be compared, not only with the exact sciences, but also with art. With all the limitations, which will later be stressed, of the sciences, I accept their conclusions much as does any other reasonable person. Let me put this in terms of the comparison of the different civilizations, which interests me seriously. In spite of the axiomatic geometry, the geometrical astronomy, and the logic of the Greeks, the exact grammar and the penetrating psychology of the Indians, and the philology, history, archaeology, and subtle aesthetics of the Chinese, it is clear to me that modern science is a unique human accomplishment, for which I feel the greatest respect and gratitude. It finally allows all human beings to pool their thought and to go beyond the limits of individual person and individual culture, each, in a characteristic way, partial, eccentric, and, above all, egocentric.

The respect and gratitude I feel towards science certainly encompass both mathematics and logic. In some sense they must lie behind or be embedded in our responses to the world. We are discovering them there, in our responses, just as we are discovering them in the cosmos, the particle, and whatever lies between these. Not only are mathematics and logic necessary to us, but they *are* us, they are constituents of our being. Certainly, then, I regard the law of contradiction and its companion law, of the excluded middle, as fundamental to our thought, though I agree that, for special purposes, we may have to qualify them, as, for example, in dealing with mathematical infinites. As I have implied in rejecting unlimited relativism, any general doubt cast on the law of contradiction is fatal to rational thought and fatal, in effect, to its own rationality as an objection to the law. Nothing of what I have said until now or will say in the future would make any sense to me if I did not believe in the objective truth as such and in our ability to approach it more or less closely. It is this very acceptance of the truth that helps to rid me of my qualms in admitting that everything I have said or will say is qualified by the same non-rational motives and modes of expression as those I attribute to philosophers in general. But although what I am saying does not belong as such to any science, theoretical or empirical, I regard my near-relativism, pluralism, or fallibilism with respect to philosophy, as itself empirically persuasive and more nearly true than simply absolutistic doctrines, which emphasize, not only that there is an absolute truth, but that their statement of it is absolutely true.

Regarding my pluralism as true, I do not regard it as subject to fundamental doubt. The word 'fundamental' conceals many problems, of course. I will allude to them soon, but I have no intention of facing them here in a prolonged or seriously analytical way, for they are not the direct subject of my book, but its necessary prolegomenon. In the psychological terms I will often use, I will say only that all my life I have had a strong personal conviction of the objectivity of truth. By my own mode of approach, I am therefore disqualified, I am afraid, from radical relativism. Yet experience has led me to see how subtly, deeply, and, nevertheless, qualifiedly people are different from one another; and this has led me to the common discovery that people take things differently, not simply because things are different in themselves, but because they are different from person to person. This discovery is no more than a variant of a truth long accepted in physics and astronomy, that a scientific observation and the theory in which it is embedded must be understood in terms of the instruments, techniques, and sub-theories by which the observation has been made. The world must be different to each of us, if only because we are different from each other; and yet, the world must be similar or even the same to us because we are similar to or the same as each other. In what ways we are different or similar or the same is a problem of which philosophy and the sciences are never rid. There are always areas of indecision between the extremes; and even the extremes are not always clear; and hence so many of our difficulties and pleasures in philosophy, science, and art. This, I am convinced, is our situation. That this conviction of mine is compatible with or even based on my early relations with my parents does not necessarily invalidate it or relativise it away. I say this knowing that I, like practically everyone else, regard myself as basically right in my major opinions—regard myself as right, but *know*, abstractly, that I cannot always be.

Before I continue, I should like to expand somewhat on the nature of my qualified relativism or pluralism in philosophy. I contend that philosophical positions cannot be and are not in fact judged by the standards of more or less exact science. Philosophical positions are therefore not subject, if I am right, to scientific standards of formulation, of use of evidence, or of openness to refutation. Strictly speaking, much in them is not subject to refutation at all. And because philosophies are compounded of an incompletely analysable amalgam of the subjective and objective, they are, to a degree difficult to analyse, personal, not only in their styles, but in their arguments and, of course, their conclusions. Even if we were to assume that an empirical science could prove its hypotheses beyond reasonable doubt, it is clear that philosophy, which is either, depending on one's point of view, sub-scientific or non-scientific in its theoretical arguments and use of evidence, cannot really *prove* anything.

I think that this near-relativism, when reasonably pursued, encourages a more reasonable understanding of philosophy and philosophers. The situation may be compared with that in painting or any other art. Some artists and critics have a vision so fixed that they can appreciate only one style of painting, while others, with a broader perspective, can appreciate why paintings are made at all and what qualities and standards inhere in the different styles of painting. The latter, more open, generous approach may pay for its broader sympathies by a reduced intensity; but it also expresses the desire to grasp the truth as a whole, and is in this sense, perhaps, the more intense. It refuses to lose anything. Furthermore, it tells us that in art, as, I think, in philosophy, understanding is not really separable from some modicum of psychological identification.

Although, as I have said, I cannot pursue this matter of the truth very far, to help the reader estimate my argument in the light of my conceptions or preconceptions, I should like to continue the explanation of why I think that the whole-hearted belief in the truth cannot free any particular expression of it from doubt. To this purpose, I will enlist the help of William James. He may never have succeeded in arriving at an unparadoxical understanding of the truth, but he stated the difficulty briefly and sharply:

> The 'absolutely' true, meaning what no further experience will ever alter, is that ideal vanishing-point towards which we imagine that all our temporary truths will some day converge . . . Meanwhile we have to live to-day by what truth we can get to-day, and be ready to-morrow to call it falsehood. Ptolemaic astronomy, euclidean space, aristotelian logic, scholastic metaphysics, were expedient for centuries, but human experience has boiled over those limits, and we now call these things only relatively true, or true within those borders of experience. 'Absolutely' they are false; for we know that those limits were casual, and might have been transcended by past theorists just as they are by present thinkers.

This statement by James is preceded by the well-known and once notorious sentences in which he tried to grasp the nature of the truth by means of his own Pragmatic criterion; ' *"The true",' to put it very briefly,'* he said,

> is only the expedient in the way of our thinking, just as 'the right' is only the expedient in the way of our behaving. Expedient in almost any fashion; and expedient in the long run and on the whole of course; for what meets expediently all the experience in sight won't necessarily meet all farther experience equally satisfactorily. Experience, as we know, has a way of *boiling over*, and of making us correct our present *formulas*.[2]

James's reaction to the dilemma he presents appears unsatisfactory to most philosophers, though in *The Meaning of Truth* he tries to refute the 'slanderous charge' that the Pragmatists deny real existence.[3] The burden James lays on the word 'expedient' appears too heavy for it to bear. Nevertheless, it is difficult to replace the Jamesian view with a fundamentally more satisfactory one. All kinds of philosophers are therefore, like all kinds of men, tempted to adopt it, even though it may be too problematic or too frightening for them to maintain for long. At least in relation to the proposition, 'There is a chair,' and at least in the privacy of a notebook, Wittgenstein, too, was ready to hazard, 'The proposition is true so long as it proves useful to me.'[4]

Truth and Pragmatism in Mathematics

The attractiveness and usefulness of the Pragmatists' view of truth can be given a dramatic illustration from the field of mathematics, that is, from the prolonged twentieth-century debate on the foundations of mathematics. The illustration is particularly apposite because mathematics has so often served philosophers as the ideal for an objectively true philosophy.

As everyone who has followed it knows, the debate on the foundations of mathematics has never come to any generally acceptable conclusion. The result may easily be taken to be that the absence of a conclusion has to serve as one, and even that the absence is an advantage. A standard, highly regarded book on the foundations of mathematics says:

> No unique and universally accepted way of reconstructing mathematics exists or is in view, and in this sense the foundational crisis is still in force . . . *Dealing with these foundations has, surprisingly enough, turned out to be not only a job that had to be undertaken for reasons of intellectual sincerity or philosophical meticulousness but something that was infinitely rewarding, and fruitful.*[1]

Having said this, the authors of the book then attack any mathematician who insists, for his own intuitive reasons, that only mathematical systems of a certain kind have the right to exist. They see no reason that compels anyone to believe that a unique solution will be discovered to the foundational problems of set theory, but they hope that 'the pragmatic criterion of acceptability' will keep the situation in mathematics from becoming chaotic. So long, they say, as the belief in the objective reality and uniqueness of the idea of set does not lead to dogmatic rejection of proposed set theories, 'it remains a harmless, and in a certain sense even helpful, metaphysical act of faith.' They oppose the mathematician who, 'in the name of some earthly or heavenly reality,' brandishes a criterion to disqualify all but his own favourite theory. 'There are many authors,' they conclude, 'who prefer perturbation out of freedom to tranquillity out of external coercion.'[2]

In spite of the words I have just quoted, I do not suppose that Pragmatism is a particularly natural attitude for mathematicians. Yet, as I have said, the book in question is highly regarded by mathematicians, who cannot regard the Pragmatic attitude it displays as totally implausible. Certainly, the book's agreement with James is striking— necessary as it may be, it says, to believe in the ideal, unique mathematical truth, *the* Set Theory, we know none such; but this combination of belief in principle with ignorance in fact may lend the ideal its fertility and provoke differences that extend and deepen mathematics.

The situation is such that a philosophical mathematician may even revive the idea that mathematics is an empirical science. 'Why do we not confess,' he may ask, 'that mathematics, like other sciences, is ultimately based upon, and has to be tested in, practice? . . . To declare mathematics a science having an empirical ground would not exclude the use of deductive methods, for many other empirical sciences use them successfully!'[3] From such a standpoint, attempts to solve mathematical problems are so many experiments, the success or failure of which reflects on the hypotheses and even the axioms they are related to. 'One should like to be open-minded and allow for the possibility of revoking or modifying our axioms if, for example, contradictions arise or the content of some axiom is rendered more precise by new findings.'[4] It is the empirical life of mathematics that changes the attitude of mathematicians and, in consequence, the nature of mathematics as they perceive it.

The Truth Is Certain but Vague

Now we arrive at what I will call 'James's dilemma,' which is that we may be quite sure of the truth in general, but that every one of its particular statements is subject to doubt. In a complex way, usefulness is the touchstone of the truth, but the relationship between usefulness and truth remains obscure. Perhaps a simple image will help to express how I see this: Theories that 'work' are like keys that open locks. But a lock can generally be opened, more or less well, by many keys, and even a refined lock can be opened by more than one key. Furthermore, a key that opens a lock can damage it, and locks, it should be remembered, can also be jimmied, and hinges can be removed, doors broken through, and so on—just as, to take the most obvious example, living organisms can be damaged or killed in the interests of some theory concerning their life.

Theories that 'work,' that is, in terms of the image, that open locks, are regarded as 'true.' Those that fit their respective locks more smoothly are regarded as more nearly true, or, if one prefers the truth to be exclusive, exclusively true. A difference or contradiction between theories is always intellectually disturbing, but it may be less important, in fact, than it seems. The reason is that the contradiction, whether apparent or real, may not be the feature that is relevant to the unlocking power of the key. Of course, we assume something common, likeness to an ideal key, to all the keys that open the same lock. We even assume something common to all keys that open all locks, which is their relationship to the truth—their notches have evidently been filed true enough to fit reality. But it is not clear that even if we succeeded in making the ideal key, we could recognize it, let alone prove it to be such. In any case, if nature is compared with a lock, it is a composite one, by which I mean that it is understood in terms of more than one principle or combination of principles, so that it is openable, more or less, by virtue of different key principles or modes of understanding, which may have no very obvious compatibility.*

Now, James's dilemma, the force of which I have tried to weaken by means of my image, is uncomfortable, but also useful. It is useful because it teaches us that even when a theory seems intellectually necessary and practically fruitful, it extends itself too far, it demands automatic acceptance, it grows old, it turns, very possibly, into a dogma. We have to be ready to move on to another idea, and another. At the risk of suggesting an impractical regress of doubts, I say that it is best to remain doubtful even of our pragmatically inspired doubt, because there are always possible flaws in the particular forms this doubt may take. We must always therefore both doubt and doubt doubt; and we must remember that dogmatism, too, can serve the truth, and that discovery requires intuition armed with faith. I know I am suggesting a humanly impossible combination of suspiciousness of our own certainties and brave adventuring in their service. This combination is the personified

---

*Speaking of contemporary biology, François Jacob says:

'In the study of living beings, history displays a pendulum movement, swinging to and fro between the continuous and the discontinuous, between structure and function, between the identity of phenomena and the diversity of beings. From these oscillations, the architecture of the living gradually emerges, revealed in ever deeper layers.' F. Jacob, *The Logic of Life* (New York: Random House (Vintage Books), 1976), p. 16.

equivalent of what I have been calling James's dilemma, which is clearly not James's alone, but that of all of us.

If we transpose the dilemma to philosophy, we may begin by saying that philosophy is inspired by the faith that the truth can be discovered and stated. With whatever qualifications, almost every philosopher agrees; but here agreement ends. It is shamefully easy to ask a series of questions that express one great doubt: If there is truth in philosophy, why cannot philosophers agree on it? How is it that their chronic disagreement leaves so many of them optimistic, not only in their belief that an objective truth exists, but in their belief that they, personally, can disclose it? And why does the truth tease us so much with its presence in its absence and absence in its presence? Or is this last not a reasonable question at all?

If we assume that a philosophy is a direct projection or a mirror–image of the truth, or, more cautiously, a somehow isomorphic representation of it, then every true philosophy must be consistent with every other true one; for we have long ago agreed to abide by the law of contradiction, which establishes that there is only one, non–contradictory truth. But if the mirror that reflects the truth has a peculiarly wavy surface, or if the isomorphism has peculiar local complications, then philosophies may easily appear inconsistent but not really be so; or they may really be inconsistent, but not in a way that is relevant to their power or truth.

I do not think that there is or can be a way of describing or analysing the world philosophically that can be satisfactory in general, no matter how sensitive, intelligent, well–educated, or logical the describer or analyst may be. It seems to me, on the contrary, that the more cohesive and detailed the description or analysis, the more evident the individual difference in reaction to it should be.

Yet there remains the one attractive, vague truth. I say 'vague,' because, of course, it remains resistant to clear, full exposure. The necessary truth is so necessarily vague that even the attempt to state its vagueness is necessarily vague. Such vagueness, in which I am now myself becoming entangled, is one of the basic characteristics, I think, of philosophy, as I will later do my best to explain; but I will not press the difficult issue of truth any further here, because I mean less to grapple with it than to expose the attitude that underlies my characterization of philosophers as human beings.[1]

Relevance Generally

If the truth philosophers search for is so far away, if we can never be sure of having found it, if it is, as I have been saying, vague, then the problem of relevance, too, is a difficult one. If we do not know just what or where the truth is, how can we know just what is relevant to its discovery? I ask this question not only because it is a difficult and natural one, but because I am proposing that the usual criteria of philosophy are now too narrow and should, at least sometimes, be replaced by broader ones. I would therefore like to consider the problem of relevance and ask what should or should not be judged relevant to the understanding of philosophy and philosophers.

I allow myself to begin this clarification of the idea of relevance with some words on myself. I hope that my readers will accept them as belonging to the inquiry we have begun together.

Throughout my professional life in philosophy, it has been my advantage and disadvantage that I have remained interested in many other fields—history, sociology, anthropology, psychology, literature, art, and the exact sciences, in the last of which my mathematical weakness confines me to a superficial understanding. I have a constant tendency, therefore, to consider philosophical problems in the light of these interests and to feel that the borderlines between the different subjects are artificial. At the time when I first studied philosophy in the United States, when John Dewey was still alive and Pragmatism was being taught here and there as a still-living option, such a wide range of reference did not necessarily seem unprofessional. Even today, a French philosopher may, without raising French professional eyebrows, bring all his knowledge, from whatever fields, to bear on a problem. The same may be true, though, I think, to a lesser degree, of a German philosopher. It appears to me, however, that most of the philosophical Frenchmen and Germans who use the data or reasoning of other fields to help them in their philosophizing affect a certain distance from these fields, a philosopher's depth as against a scientist's presumed shallowness. Most of them are also hostile to the kind of psychologizing I undertake, though something not unlike it has been fashionable in France for a number of years. Yet although I might be a sober American variant of a philosophical Frenchman or German, I can hardly be of the dominant kind of English or American philosophers, who live out their professional lives in greater intellectual abstemiousness, that is to say, in a more single-minded and technical devotion to philosophy in the strict, professional sense. They are professionally monogamous and, even in this age of promiscuity, must regard philosophers such as myself as promiscuous to no good end. When, therefore, I reason as if sociology, anthropology, psychology, and the rest, are able to contribute to the solution of philosophical problems, I am generally met with the accusation of irrelevancy. In an important sense, the accusation is justified, and I will not forget to put its justice to you as clearly and seriously as I can. But in a more important sense, the accusation is, I am convinced, unjustified. To argue this point, I will concentrate for a while on the problem of relevance in philosophy, at first in general, and then in particular relation to psychology. For the while, I will curb my use of biographical anecdotes—I will have to return to them later, for my argument is designed to be empirical.

The idea of relevance is always one of relationship. *The Shorter Oxford Dictionary* has two main definitions, the first, 'Bearing upon, connected with, pertinent *to*, the matter in hand,' and the second, a Scottish legal term, 'Legally pertinent or sufficient.' The idea necessarily involves a criterion of connection or pertinence. If our object is to understand philosophers (and, with them, philosophy), we must first ask what it is that we value in them. The question once answered, we have a criterion of connection, pertinence, or relevance.

Understanding a Philosopher

To suggest what we may value and therefore want to understand in a philosopher, I ask a preliminary series of questions:

Is a philosopher's value his discovery of solutions to problems we are interested in, so that we read him simply to know the solutions? Or are we more interested, not in his particular solutions, but in his ability as such to solve philosophical problems? If it is this ability that draws our interest, is it chiefly his philosophical acuteness (whatever *that* may consist in); or the information he can bring to bear on the problems; or the fertility that suggests many solutions; or the sheer novelty of his methods or solutions; or some optimal combination of all of these? Do we care most for the correctness, fluency, copiousness, or uniqueness of ideas? Or do we care for a peculiar philosophical sensitivity either to ideas or to the human condition? When we read or listen to philosophers, to what extent are we showing preferences for their interesting objectivity, their interesting acuteness, thier interesting grasp of ultimates, their interesting world-views, their interesting wisdom, or their interesting egocentricity? Or is there, perhaps, some special kind of rationality, different from everything I have mentioned, to which philosophers have privileged access? If it is the philosopher's particular business to think rationally or, as the old philosophers all wanted, to be rational (judge soundly, be sensible, sane, not foolish, absurd, or extravagant), is his rationality exercised mainly in the cultivation of efficiency of thought, irrespective of its end? Or is his rationality an intensive investigation of the best means to accomplish one's ends, irrespective of what they are? Or is it an intensive attempt to determine the best ends themselves? Or a special, not easily analyzed ability to judge soundly, be sensible, sane, not foolish, absurd, or extravagant, in words, in deeds, or in both?

I have said, innocently, that the answer to such questions should establish what it is that we want to understand; but the idea of 'understanding' has a great range of meanings or extensions, and many questions can be asked about it, too. Consider for instance, what it may mean to understand a geometrical problem, and how great a difference is made by the degree of restriction of the words, 'to understand.'

In what sense does one understand a geometrical problem when one can understand and reproduce its solution? Or when one can do not only this, but understand and reproduce the structure of the geometry in question—as Pascal, all by himself, reproduced a sequence of Euclid's propositions? Or does one understand the problem when one understands how geometries are constructed; or not only how they are constructed, but how they are related to other, non-geometrical forms of mathematics? Or when one can deal effectively with the (never finally settled) problems of the philosophy of mathematics? Or when one knows what goes on in the geometer's nervous system at the moment of his geometrizing? Or when one knows what, in the first place, makes individuals or societies interested in solving geometrical problems? Or when one can see what the solution in question will lead to mathematically? Or, to be absurdly unrestrictive, lead to in any way?

Some questions can naturally be asked about the understanding of anything; but I must now confine myself to the question, 'What does it mean to understand a philosopher?' I formulate the question in relation to him because he is the direct subject of my book; but my answer will aply to philosophy as well. The history of philosophy tells us that there are many possible answers to the question. Let me summarize a number of those that are often given, implicitly or explicitly. In my list, which I mean to be representative rather than exhaustive, there are six.

The first answer is that we understand a philosopher when we are able to respond intellectually, in ways that he might approve, to the sort of problems he was interested in. Such understanding depends on assimilation of the philosopher's attitudes and skills, or, in other words, on effective identification with his at least philosophical self. It is most earnestly practiced by his immediate faithful disciples.

The second answer is that we understand a philosopher when we are able to respond to problems by means of methods or principles taught or suggested by him, but not necessarily in ways that he would have approved. This is the answer typical of his more independent disciples or of eclectics, all of whom use him more freely than he might approve and in contexts that might seem to him foreign to his concerns.

The third answer is that we understand a philosopher when we are able to judge his arguments in terms of whatever facts, theories, or principles are judged to be best, quite independently of what the philosopher himself might have thought of them. For example, a biologist would be said to understand Aristotle when, having understood the text as such, he judged it in the light of contemporary biology. Similar examples might be those of a physicist judging Democritus; a Neo-Positivist, Bergson; an Existentialist, Carnap; or a linguistic analyst, an unabashed metaphysician—or vice versa.

The fourth answer is that understanding is the ability to place a philosopher in the history of philosophy or in the history of a particular philosophical problem, that is, the ability to reconstruct how the problem arose and how, in this context, the philosopher found and tried to solve it. One might try to define what his characteristic addition, emphasis, or originality was, and in what state he bequeathed the problem to his successors.

The fifth answer is that understanding is the ability to explain what human or social pressures made a philosopher set his philosophical problems and respond to them as he did. A biographer might try to give this kind of answer, and so might a sociologist.

The sixth, last answer is that to understand a philosopher is to see him as an intellectually creative person trying to give generally applicable, philosophical answers to questions that arose in him in particular, personal ways. This kind of answer is psychological and perhaps aesthetic. Like the economic, historical, and sociological answers, it is likely to emphasize that a philosopher's thought has not only an explicit, but also an implicit structure, an infra-structure. That is to say, the answerer looks for hidden assumptions, characteristic imagery, and characteristic sequences of ideas, in all of which he wants to identify a particular philosopher's tempos and moods, the resonance that marks the thought as his and no one else's.

The Ideal of Comprehensive Understanding

One possible response to so many questions and answers is the attempt to be comprehensive, to accept as many as practicable of the questions and respond to them with a synthesis of the answers. This is the encyclopedist's goal, which is often more useful than attractive; but if the synthesis is governed by some principle with genuine explanatory or integrative power, it can certainly be enlightening. Think of the analogy of the vector. One could regard a philosopher or philosophic idea or group of ideas as a kind of thought-motion in a certain direction, and then try to recompose the direction it takes as the effect of the meeting of different forces, logical, historical, social and personal. A rather more suggestive analogy, I think, is that of a hydraulic system. This system, no doubt, has an ideal description; but the system that exists in fact must be understood in relation to the peculiar and local nature of its pipes or channels—some of the fluid may be leaking away—the nature and degree of purity of the fluid, and the like. Philosophies are usually displayed as ideal systems, but they are not, in fact, ideal even by their own standards, and the confusion of ideal with real hampers the attempt to understand them.

Let me, however, abandon analogies and suggest instead what a reasonably complete understanding might include. Assuming that the philosophy in question is at least fairly comprehensive, it is likely to have been constructed of (a) the philosophical tradition available at the time of construction; (b) particular local variations of this tradition, as in the teachings of the local philosophers; (c) the facts, that is, what most reasonable persons are willing at the time to accept as established by means of ordinary perception, social experience, or science, whatever science may be at the time;[1] (d) logic or technically exact reasoning; (e) prevailing social circumstances, including those that force the philosopher to qualify by learning certain books or subjects and passing certain examinations, and, more generally, those that encourage acquiescence or revolt; (f) the particular situation and personality of the philosopher, including his need and ability to find intellectual mentors, his need for intellectual security, and his emotional attraction to certain premises and lines of argument.

It would not be difficult to analyze such factors more completely, but I think my point has been well enough made. Even, however, if a philosophy has been constituted of such factors, it does not follow that the philosopher himself wants to be understood in terms of them all. He usually prefers to consider only (c) and (d), that is, 'facts' and 'logic.' This preference expresses the philosopher's desire to be understood as he professionally understands himself, to be pictured, so to speak, from a dignified angle and in professional robes. A judge, he does not want to be judged by any laws except his own. Unfortunately for his desire, the factors that he so often prefers to ignore exert their effects all the same.

The Vagueness of Philosophical Relevance

In enumerating the factors that might be assembled to give a reasonably complete understanding of a philosopher, I am not merely trying to shield myself against the charge of narrow-mindedness that may be

made because I will concentrate on psychological factors and biographical evidence. I am, on the contrary, convinced that all the
factors are significant, and convinced that histories of philosophy ought
to do far more than string together analytical summaries of the
doctrines of philosophers. The strung-together histories are devitalized
by their complacent additiveness and their profoundly traditional
conception of their subject. They would become more accurate,
intelligible, and credible if they tried seriously to deal with the
evolution of philosophical ideas and idea-clusters, or to set philosophies
in their social and personal contexts.

Much as I would like to analyze the incompleteness, not to say
ingenuousness of the ordinary history of philosophy, I must stick to my
present theme and say of the comprehensive ideal only that it can never
be neutral. As Hegel and Dilthey show in practice, to gather, arrange,
and sum up points of view, one must have a point of view oneself. The
complexity of a summation is not able to free it of bias. Furthermore, the
ideal of comprehensiveness cannot really be put into practice. In saying
this, I do not mean to rule out encyclopedic accounts written by different
hands, but much of the unity they gain by their organization they lose by
the differences between the persons who write them. Nor do I mean to
rule out sketches of completeness, by which I mean, formulations of the
ideal and demonstrations of what it might lead to. But the virtue of a
sketch is precisely its sketchiness, and the attempt to be fully
comprehensive would end in a figurative and literal enormity. I therefore
want to use the ideal of a comprehensive understanding for one purpose
alone, which is to clarify the subjectivity of the notion of relevance.

Relevance is clearer in mathematics and logic. Their identity with their
own procedures is a kind of intellectual transparency. Their rules of
relevance are simply their rules. In other, less transparent fields, which
have not been or cannot be so exactly articulated, relevance is often
harder to see. It may be felt in practice, yet be on or even beyond the
periphery of consciousness. However, when a difficulty arises and it is
judged that some hardly known principle has been violated or some
customary procedure has been shown to be inadequate, conscious
attention is directed at this hardly known, unarticulated something. The
rules of relevance are then scrutinized and reassessed.

All thinking must have its rules of relevance, the ways in which it is
organized in view of the aims it is meant to reach. But the rules become
more obvious, more obviously organized, and more obviously directive
and confining, in the sciences, where claims to knowledge are laid bare
and anatomized. In the sciences, the rules are both strict and artificial, for
they require us to disregard much that in fact characterizes our

experience. We buy our ability to inquire intensively by narrowing and conventionalizing our concern and making it painstakingly explicit. At a given moment, many real complications are likely to be ruled out. The history of a science, like that of an art form, can be read as a series of changing contexts of relevance, which are its changing rules of attention and inclusion and exclusion. When schools of thought compete, as they do, for example, in psychology, the difference between them can be expressed in terms of their different contexts of relevance.

How does this apply to philosophy? Philosophy is organized like the sciences, in the form of problems to be solved; but its organization and problems are, I claim, more vague. The organization is, I think, implicitly hierarchical, so that some problems are supposed to be deeper than others, by which is meant that the solution of the deeper ones solves the shallower, but that the opposite is not the case. Philosophy, however, differs from the more exact sciences. In these sciences there is a history of problems solved, and the historic success or failure of the methods used to solve them is expressed in their rules of relevance, explicit or not. Unlike the sciences, philosophy does not have a history of problems solved. To put the matter more neutrally, to the extent that philosophy depends on science, it shares the solutions that have been arrived at; but to the extent that it remains independent, it remains, among the philosophers themselves, debatable both in principle and in detail. In the sense of solutions arrived at, not only is its future unknown, but its past, too, is unknown. That is, philosophers cannot reach any consensus on what solutions have been arrived at and how, therefore, at least in terms of progress towards solutions, the past of philosophy should be evaluated.

Perhaps I have been exaggerating. It is hard for me to judge, because the borderline between philosophy, literature, and science has so often been unclear. Not only is the separation of philosophy into these, its possible strands, problematic, but its separation might denature it, deprive it of its matrix-like quality, that in which everything can be found and extracted. From the standpoint of a science or a narrowly-defined art, philosophy is more like unworked ore than the metal that is refined from it. From the standpoint of the exact sciences— with all their imprecision—philosophy is and, I think, had better remain vague. This vagueness, of course, affects the nature of relevance in philosophy. In the exact sciences, you may not know very well at what target you are aiming, that is, what idea or technique will, by its success, prove relevant to the solution of your problem; but you have at least learned to aim by means of many past successes, which are the many targets that you or your forbears have hit. But if, as in philosophy, you are never more or less objectively sure of having hit any target, you cannot know how or at what to aim. You can shoot in a way that feels good to you, or you can imitate the way someone else is shooting; but then the activity is conducted for its own sake, for the sake of the company it allies you with, or for the sake of simply accidental hits. Not knowing how to shoot well, how can you know what is helpful, that is, relevant to really hitting targets? Either, then, philosophy is engaged in for the pleasure of philosophizing or of the company of other philosophers, or it aims at solving philosophical problems. If it aims at solving philosophical problems, it can aim only vaguely, and it cannot know whether the rules it adopts are really relevant to the hoped-for solutions.

The truth is, I must say, that my either-or is much too sharp to fit the reality; but relevance, like absolute truth, must remain vague to philosophers. To be conscious of this vagueness is, once again, to favour pluralism. Although I, too, should find it uncomfortable if all the context-dependent criteria of relevance were put on a par, I find it hard to deny that there are different criteria and only self-appointed judges to decide between them.

Consider relevance, then, in its actual vagueness. Each philosopher has his own tendencies or biases, each, consciously or not, builds his own idea of relevance into his philosophy, maps his recommended world, with boundaries his own imagination has marked and roads and bridges that his own judgment has approved. To shift to a different image, the philosopher makes up his own game with his own set of rules—he wants both himself and everybody else to do his own, the philosopher's, thing. Or, to speak without the help of images, he makes his assumptions or states his axioms and he explicates his concepts, all of which he manipulates according to rules he himself establishes. It is natural to try to grasp his thought in accord with his own standards of relevance, which may be called the local standards, but no less natural to adopt non-local standards and try to grasp him in a context different from that which he intends. Exact as the philosopher may be, his criteria cannot have the coercive exactness of mathematics or the empirical persuasiveness of an established empirical science. In such a situation, at once complex and vague, an observer may easily conclude that the philosopher's criteria of relevance are, at bottom, no more than what happens to interest him most philosophically. Of course, his criteria are affected by what he has learned of philosophers like himself, and he no doubt refines the criteria in accord with some philosophical tradition or other, with the demands of his professional colleagues, and with his own increasing sophistication; yet in the judgment of such a philosopher as Nietzsche, the criteria include the state of a philosopher's stomach, of such as Kierkegaard or Sartre, his sincerity and love-life, and of such as Jaspers, the spirit in which he meets extreme situations.

Conditions of Relevance: Time, Place, and Function

It may be helpful to linger here a while on some of the conditions of relevance, beginning with those that affect the very type of person to be designated a 'philosopher.' Surely, the conception of a philosopher has undergone changes in keeping with his changing functions and habitats, habitats that range from the Athenian gymnasium or market place to the Alexandrian Museum, the Hellenistic school or confraternity, the doctor's podium ('the Second Sophistic movement signals among other things an intensified general interest in the human body and its diseases'), the medieval university, the Renaissance court, the eighteenth-century salon, and the seventeenth- or eighteenth- or nineteenth- or twentieth-century university.[1] While Socrates had no formal profession and served no institutional function, and while his disciples listened to him for no ulterior motive, the medieval philosopher was a professional university teacher meant to educate the doctors, lawyers, and functionaries needed for the church and other institutions.[2] While Socrates neither commented on nor wrote books, the medieval philosopher studied prescribed texts and dictated books to his auditors. While Socrate's technique was a catch-as-catch-can amalgam of ironical flattery, brow-beating, and acute though not infrequently fallacious reasoning, the medieval philosopher's technique rested on the quoting of authorities, on syllogistic logic, of which Socrates had no formal awareness, and on a minutely formalized disputatiousness.

Now contrast the two types I have recalled, of Socrates and of an anonymous medieval, with an eighteenth-century philosopher.[3] Suppose we take a familiar philosopher, Kant, as our example. Unlike a medieval university teacher, he was required to lecture on many subjects, including mathematics, physics, geography, anthropology, and education. Furthermore, he was bound by the regulations of the Ministry of Education to certain textbooks, and his lectures were rarely, therefore, on his own philosophy, but on that of Wolff, Baumgarten, Meier, Achenwall, Eberhard, Feder, and others. As time went on, it is said, his lectures departed more from the textbooks on which they were, officially, a commentary—he did not so much read out the textbooks as comment on them extemporaneously. In any event, he took a great deal from his philosophical environment, including a sense of what was relevant. For example, he adopted both terms and ideas from Johann

Nikolas Tetens, who analyzed the constitutive factors of human knowledge and, like Kant, distinguished its matter from its form.

It is not my object to analyze Kant's sources, but only to say that we have inevitably forgotten what it was to be the philosopher Kant, just where and when he philosophized. If we ask why he used certain terms, arranged his ideas in certain ways, and posed and answered problems as he did, we may answer that he was sometimes only using the inheritance bequeathed by Wolff, Baumgarten, and others. Kant cannot be precisely grasped or his sense of relevance precisely clarified if we ignore his immediate philosophical environment.[4]

Conditions of Relevance: Professional Rivalry

Philosophers and philosophical schools form themselves by means of their clashes with rivals. The more prolonged and consistent the rivalry, the more similar the rivals are likely to become. The ancient Stoics and Epicureans, who were engaged in a prolonged, consistent rivalry, had different cosmologies and antithetical attitudes to pleasure and to freedom of the will, yet Stoic self-denial and Epicurean self-indulgence both turned out to lead to an abstemious theoretical calm. Each extension of the physics of one side and each of its epistemological refinements was countered by the other side, until both sides became nearly equal and opposite. Analogously, Indian philosophers would write long debates in dialogue form, with an interminably repeated 'They say' and 'We answer,' representing every attack and riposte they could imagine. In the European Middle Ages, Nominalists and Realists had the same intellectual standards, weapons, and jousts. In the seventeenth and eighteenth centuries, the Rationalists and Empiricists had diametrically-opposed theoretical standards, yet they were often quite similar. Whole pages of Locke, the Empiricist champion, are no more than a paraphrase of the most famous and characteristic pages of Descartes.[1] Picture-puzzle-like, every indentation in one of two long-competitive philosophies matches a projection in the other.

As an example of how an individual's rivalry, hate-like in its intensity, is compatible with intellectual dependence, one might cite Newton's relationship with Descartes. A careful researcher says:

> It would not be too strong to say that Newton eventually came to detest Descartes both as a physicist and a philosoper, his aversion to Descartes even extending to mathematics with his own well-known belief that a geometrical proof could only be regarded as well founded if presented in synthetic rather than analytic form. And yet in spite of Newton's strong, one

might say passionate, dislike of Descartes and all his works, there has always been a strong possibility that Newton was largely indebted to Descartes for the most important single element of his dynamics, the principle of inertia![2]

The strong possibility has become a near certainty. As the researcher points out, manuscripts have now been discovered that show his intimate acquaintance with Descartes' *Principia*, in which the principle of inertia is enunciated.

Briefly, professional rivalry helps to set the standards of philosophical relevance. An argument is taken to be relevant if it supports one's own position or weakens the position of one's rival. The decision on relevance is therefore the consequence of the decision to open and maintain a philosophical debate. Ideally, both sides should agree on what counts as relevant.

Conditions of Relevance: Leadership and Discipleship

The intellectual and other attractions of philosophical leaders have already been described. Around them there gather their sons, some more natural than others, some faithful, even after their father's death, others engaged in testing the limits of permissible variation of the principles their father lays down. Some of the sons will discover that their personal commitment clashes with their intellectual ambition, and just as the father may once have declared his independence of *his* father, so some of his sons declare their independence of him.[1]

In making these conventional–enough remarks, I have again minimized the sheerly intellectual element in the relationship between philosophical leader and disciple; but intellectual and non–intellectual attractions cannot, as I have said, be easily separated. As both leader and followers feel, loyalty is displayed, betrayal raises its perfidious head, missionaries are dispatched, and internecine struggles and external wars, involving prestige, position, and money, are waged.*

The story of the philosophical fathers and sons is tangled and sometimes sad, for their love may turn to indifference or hatred. From this standpoint it is sad to read about Descartes, Kant, or Husserl, all of

---

*The wars can be literal. In Athens of the fourth century A.D., the rivalry of 'sophists' could grow bloody. 'None of the sophists dared to present themselves in public to lecture, but limited their voices to their private auditoriums and had commerce with only quite young persons. In this way, they did not put their lives at stake, but fought for applause and acclamation alone.' Quoted from Eunapius, who studied in Athens in 362, in Proclus, *Théologie Platonicienne*, trans. H.D. Saffrey & L.C. Westerinck, vol. 1 (Paris: Les Belles Lettres, 1968), p. xxxix.

them, as I see it, lonely men. Hegel may have had a better time of it with his disciples.

I am not exaggerating. Let me recall the relationship of Descartes with his disciple, Henricus Regius, also called Henri le Roy (or, de Roy), professor of theoretical medicine and botany at the University of Utrecht.[2] Regius, an audacious, popular teacher, but a sometimes inept debater, became an enthusiastic exponent of the new, Cartesian philosophy, beginning with its version of the circulation of the blood, going on to its view of medicine as a whole, and then to its general position. His opponent was the relentless theologian, Gysbertus Voetius. Descartes, urging caution, set the example of a verbose courtesy, but in the privacy of a letter he was glad to point out that Regius's lessons in Cartesianism were leading Voetius to burst with rage.[3] Descartes came to call Regius, 'brother,' and Regius to show Descartes a worshipful affection. Because the philosophical battle had turned virulent and could, under prevailing conditions, become dangerous, the two philosophers, teacher and disciple, decided to live at some distance from one another. When Descartes, visiting France, increased the physical distance between them, the separation affected Regius, we are told, like the separation of soul from body.[4] In a letter to his 'dear master,' Regius wrote that if not for the duties that tied him to wife, children, and profession, he would follow him everywhere and attach himself to his person just as, he hoped, his heart would always remain attached to him.[5]

The friendship, however, began to sour. Both men presumed too much, Descartes in requiring that everything Regius wrote be approved by him, and Regius in his desire to be both Cartesian and independent. Descartes was especially rankled by the use Regius made of his, Descartes', theory of muscular contraction, which Regius both appropriated and misstated.[6] The interchanges between the two took on an acid tone. Regius wrote to Descartes that many men of intelligence and honour had told him that Descartes must be too intelligent to believe what he had publicly stated. Descartes, he added, was discrediting himself by promising clarity and certainty but publishing obscure, uncertain metaphysical doctrines. The doubts and shadows were multiplying, he said.[7]

The two men naturally broke with one another. Descartes wrote to correspondents to beware of Regius's *Foundations of Physics,* which would, he was afraid, cast discredit on him, for those who knew that Regius had hitherto loudly professed his friendship with Descartes and blindly followed all his opinions would now blame Regius's incoherence and errors on him.[8]

Now let me recall Kant as a philosophical leader, a role he played with considerable passion. In terms savouring of a military campaign, a fervent Benedictine disciple informed Kant that although people used to intrigue against Kantianism in Würzburg, from which the disciple was writing, Kantianism was now totally triumphant there, 'and no one dares to attack it.' The Austrian Emperor, he wrote, regarded the system as dangerous, and a Viennese professor who had lectured on it had lost his position; but many Austrians favoured and studied it, he heard, in secret. 'Alas,' he mourned, 'why must truth have to battle so many enemies before its voice is half heard!' He took comfort, however, in the perceptiveness of women and told Kant, 'You can't guess how enthusiastically young ladies and women are taken with your system and how eager they all are to learn about it. There are many women's groups here in Würzburg, where each is eager to outdo the others in showing knowledge of your system; it is the favourite topic of conversation.'[9]

Kant was sometimes willing to praise the good character of his opponents; but he ironized freely and was ready to make personal attacks. Thus he called Eberhard, whose assault on him was dangerous, 'an artificial man,' 'a real falsarius,' 'a metaphysical sleight-of-hand artist,' a deceitful man 'without a bit of sincerity,' 'made up of falsity,' and 'filled with invidious malice.' In the service of his struggle to uphold the 'critical philosophy,' Kant was quite capable of ruthless polemics.[10]

Grown old in battle, Kant praised those of his disciples who had remained loyal. 'You have until now been and will not regret having been steadfastly loyal to the critical philosophy,' he wrote, deploring the 'ludicrous passion for originality' that had misled some other disciples.[11] The truth was that Kant's more independent disciples were beginning to turn away from him. 'The most gifted apologists, Fichte, Reinhold, and Beck among them, worshipped by presuming to have a monopoly on understanding. Eventually each of them thought that nobody else understood Kant.'[12] Kant had regarded Leibniz as no more than a timid forerunner, but when Fichte, Reinhold, and Beck attempted to improve Kantianism and to cast Kant himself in the role of a forerunner, Kant felt betrayed. Fichte, he thought, was the worst among them, and he refused to have even his name pronounced in his hearing. In an open letter on Fichte's philosophy, he cited the proverb, 'May God save us from our friends—for our enemies we will watch out ourselves,' and he distinguished between his foolish and his treacherous disciples, those who speak the language of good will but are bent on the destruction of the good philosophers, '*our* destruction,' Kant said, and ended the letter in a burst of eulogy, not, of course, for his ephemeral self, but for his immortal philosophy:

> The critical philosophy must remain confident of its irresistible propensity to satisfy the theoretical as well as the moral, practical purposes of reason, confident that no change of opinions, no touching up or reconstruction into some other form, is in store for it; the system of the *Critique* rests on a fully secured foundation, established forever; it will be indispensable too for the noblest ends of mankind in all future ages.[13]*

After Kant, Hegel. Hegel had once appeared to be a disciple of Schelling, who said of him and the Hegelians, 'They eat my bread.' Hegel himself was fortunate in his disciples, among whom there were the loyal, able men who spread his teachings into many fields, issued an official journal, and defended the cause.

According to Hegel's friend and biographer, Rosenkranz, the disciples could be divided into three groups, the level-headed, the effusive, and the empty. 'The first,' he wrote, 'were the quiet but deep minds,' who went on to cultivate different fields of study. 'The second,' he wrote, 'were less scientific, but more poetic.' Enchanted, 'soon they began to celebrate a new Socrates in Hegel, soon, an Alexander of the world, soon, a speculative world-creating Brahma. In time such encomia were inflamed and heightened to the degree that Hegel was venerated, not indistinctly, as a philosophical world saviour.' The third group, wrote Rosenkranz, consisted of the empty, who could bestow shape upon themselves only by means of the system's magic wand. All three groups, he wrote, were as one in feeling 'they were participants in a great world-historical transformation,' the emotion of which exalted them not a little.[14]

After Hegel, we may go on to Husserl, and to the tragic distance he exemplified between master and disciple. Husserl revered his own teacher, Brentano, but he painfully abandoned him and went his own way. Holding the ideal of philosophy as a scientific and cooperative enterprise, he needed assistants and disciples. To break through the ring of his own ideas, he called on his assistant, Eugen Fink, to act the opponent, 'comparable to the "devil's advocate" in the proceedings for the canonization of a saint. But ultimately even in such attempts to "philosophize together" (*symphilosophein*) he always remained his only partner.'[15] A phenomenological yearbook was established by his disciples, but in the end 'he went so far as to declare that the yearbook

---

*In public, Fichte responded to Kant magnanimously, but in letters he denounced him as a timid, sophisticated old man, no more than 'a three-quarter brain' trying to perpetuate his 'leaden mediocrity,' but forced to end 'in vigorous self-prostitution.' Saner (see bibliographical notes p. 436), p. 157.

had become an institution aimed at annihilating the fundamental meaning of his own life work.'[16]

The bitterness of Husserl's accusation suggests that of a father accusing his sons of wanting to murder him. He was, repeatedly abandoned. His assistants during his last years, Ropohl, Landgrebe, and Fink, each learned to philosophize independently. Husserl once said 'that he always had to have Fink tell him what was in his [Husserl's] books.' Yet even this assistant, with his Husserlian memory and acuteness, who had acted as Husserl's spokesman and participated with him in a 'vast manuscript' on the phenomenology of time, came to believe that Husserl's philosophy was based on obscure presuppositions, showed bias, and was generally inadequate.[17]

The few examples I have given show how philosophical leaders arise and how disciples may collect around them like iron filings around a magnet. Groups form, enthusiasms flare, and the drama of advocacy, compliance, and revolt begins once more. This is the drama that establishes so much of the relevance of philosophical abstractions to philosophy as an individual passion and a social fact. As both, it polarizes thinkers and thought. In the early days of Dutch Cartesianism, for example, 'there was a time when each student who arrived at a renowned university or school, whatever the faculty in which he was enrolled, had to choose: for or against Descartes, that is, for the conservative or modern trend.'[18] Spinozism, which few dared to accept openly, inspired the more courageous thinkers of Holland, France, and England. To them, Spinoza's relevance was particularly his courage.[19] To Leibniz, on the contrary, Spinoza was relevant in demonstrating the abyss of sin into which a philosopher might fall. Leibniz therefore defined himself by studying Spinoza, with whom he had philosophical traits in common, and gradually moving away from him, until, in the end, he both feared and despised him.[20]

Kantianism polarized thought in a different way. The response to it may be gauged quantitatively.

All told, more than 2,000 essays and books pro and con, by some 700 authors, were printed in the last twenty years of Kant's life. The trade fair catalogues were overflowing with books for, about, and against Kant. Everybody who philosophized in Germany felt obliged to take sides and did so to the best of his ability, whether in a simple document of thinking along Kantian lines, in an attempted popularization, in a supposed complementation, or in a critique.[21]

The fact is that the relation between philosophical leaders and disciples, the drama of individual compliance and revolt, and of group formation, clash, dispersal, and re-formation, has constituted much of our intellectual life. By means of the drama, intellectual attitudes are renewed and society provided with intellectual directions in which to move. The disciples echo and magnify the powerful thinkers around whom they have gathered. Thanks to his disciples, Descartes entered the universities of Holland and the salons and even the religious orders of France. Thanks to them, his philosophy became medicine, physics, theology, grammar, sexual ethics, and an *Art of Living Happily According to the Principles of M. Descartes.*[22] Thanks to the Hegelians, Hegelianism divided, not only into right and left, but into theology, law, political thought, esthetics, linguistics, and history. I will not attempt to suggest the fructifying influence of Locke's philosophy or, just now, of Kant's. But philosophical mentor and disciple help to keep intellectual life from stagnating. They give social force to a generalized intellectual claim, and this, too, is a kind of relevance—the relevance of life multiplying, diverging, pushing in every direction, even ahead.

The last philosopher in the English-speaking world to have exerted anything like this kind of influence was Wittgenstein. Though they were not often openly expressed, his ambitions were, in their way, as great as those of Descartes or Kant, for he thought that he had changed the direction of philosophy, made

> a 'kink' in the 'development of human thought', comparable to that which occurred when Galileo and his contemporaries invented dynamics; that a 'new method' had been discovered, as had happened when 'chemistry was developed out of alchemy'; and that it was now possible for the first time that there should be 'skilful' philosophers, though of course there had in the past been 'great' philosophers.

His 'new method,' he said, was philosophy in the sense that it was very general, was independent of any special results of science, and 'was fundamental both to ordinary life and to the sciences.'[23]

Such exalted promises are inherent, I think, in the appeal of a great philosopher to his disciples. The magnetism of his person is largely, to be sure, the magnetism of his ideas as he expresses them. He and they promise to change his disciples' lives, and perhaps the lives of everyone.

Subcultural Unity

Wherever they are, philosophers define themselves by their relationship with other professional groups, which they imitate and distinguish themselves from. So, in medieval Paris, they imitated and distinguished themselves from the theologians, and so, in early twentieth-century Oxford, they imitated and distinguished themselves from the scientists and other academic specialists, for they now had to be 'philosophers' philosophers,' which meant, not only that they had to satisfy one another, but that they could neither compete too closely with the members of any other academic speciality, nor, by unacademic laxness, religiosity, or eloquence draw on themselves the suspicion that they did not constitute an academic speciality worthy of the status.[1] And so boundaries are formed and relevancies clarified. Centered on universities and on influential periodicals, on, that is, the authorities that give degrees, jobs, and prestige, the philosophical communities or subcultures develop. There are, of course, other kinds of approximately philosophical subcultures, centered on particular literary, artistic, or political movements. But whatever the community is centered on, those who comprise it

> read and use each other's ideas, discuss each other's work, and sometimes collaborate. They have common friends, acquaintances, intellectual ancestors, and thus locate themselves at roughly the same point in sociometric space. Their interaction is facilitated by shared beliefs and values—goals, myths, terminology, self-concepts—which make their work mutually intelligible and valuable . . . Conversely, the boundary of a community is marked by non-interaction, and more definitely by interminable polemics and unresolved misunderstandings.[2]

As members of their own, now usually academic, communities, philosophers have good reasons for not straying far outside them. Some of the reasons are psychological. Outside of their communities, they feel more isolated, self-doubting, and intellectually listless. Others of the reasons are practical. The professional jobs are all within the community and granted in terms of the criteria it sets. Speaking practically, the advancement of philosophers in universities now depends on their professional publications more than on any other factor. The standards set by philosophical periodicals for the acceptance of articles therefore establish the rules of relevance more effectively than any arguments that do not, for whatever reason, affect these standards. Like the periodicals, the standards differ, of course, from one country or, rather, philosophical area to another. To speak a little facetiously, the only common requirement, apart from an academic tone, is a series of references to articles in the same periodical or similar ones. Although a serious sociology of philosophy would have to go into a good deal of detail, the facts I am describing are too well known, at least to professional philosophers, for me to expand on them here.

I do not think, however, that the pressures for companionship or for jobs are alone in determining the standards of professional relevance philosophers adopt. Every philosopher, in which class I would like, for the present purpose, to include both myself and my readers, has the desire or need for the insight that penetrates deeper , he feels, than he has been able to penetrate before. Furthermore, all of us who have practiced philosophy for any length of time have developed a philosophical competence, and, having developed it, we choose and formulate our philosophical problems so as to be able to exercise our philosophical abilities. In other words, our ability to react with an acquired professional competence rewards us emotionally and becomes emotionally relevant to our philosophizing. Professional competence is, I take it, like the blade of a knife: its ability to penetrate depends on its sharpness, that is to say, its narrowness.

Narrow and Broad Standards of Relevance

If this is so, if I or anyone else undertook to propose an unprofessionally broad standard of relevance, one that would deprive a philosopher of his professional sharpness, it would be natural to him, as I have often experienced, to react with annoyance. And if I proposed, as I will, a psychological standard of relevance in addition to the other, I would be proposing to diminish, not only his professional convictions and abilities, but his psychological comfort as well. Psychological analysis reverses the difficult process of personal integration, and a philosopher is therefore unlikely to agree to identify himself with his own disintegration products. After all, each philosopher has grown away from his mere concern with himself and into the world of other men, who together deal with the objective intellectual problems that concern them in common; and each philosopher hopes for and may arrive at self-transcending ideas valuable to others regardless of the process by which they have been discovered or invented.

The resentment against a broad, and especially against an unprofessionally broad, standard of relevance is therefore justifiable in both a personal and professional sense. Like the other areas of intellectual specialization, philosophy preserves itself by means of its withdrawal into itself. By this withdrawal, it saves itself from dispersion and amateurishness, gains concentration and clarity, and becomes technical and independent. But there is also a possible loss. The withdrawal into itself can also be a collapse into itself, by which I mean a severance of intellectual ties with the rest of the intellectual world and a loss of the vital, uninhibited curiosity that is, in the first place, its cause for existence. Philosophy needs a constant expansive force to oppose its need to withdraw into itself, a force to keep it relevant to the vital concerns of other fields of knowledge and of human beings in general, and, in the long run, to preserve its own vitality.

What does one lose by assuming a narrow standard of relevance? One loses distance, the ability to see the borders of philosophy, and to see how, for professional and historical reasons that keep changing, its borders have been drawn and redrawn. One loses the ability to see the whole human context, which alone lends importance to the narrower, more professional standards of relevance. In stubbornly limiting oneself to professional ability, one loses the ability to judge one's professional judgment; and one forgets the extent to which one's environment completes and justifies the arguments that, in a different environment, are visibly incomplete or unconvincing. I certainly do not advocate that philosophers should give up the professionalism they cherish, but only that they should sometimes take a walk outside their professionalism and outside philosophy as professionally defined. The walk might be good for their professional vitality. Like science and art, philosophy can be particularly vital when it is engaged in the process of decontextualizing and recontextualizing itself.

The possible gain can be put by way of analogy with sciences so broad that they are less sciences than collections of ideas and procedures united by their common aim. Metallurgy can be taken as an example. The object of metallurgy is to understand and further the use of metals. To this end, it makes use of microscope, x-rays, infra-red photographs, polarized light, physical stresses, varied practical experience, and a large, characteristic group of ideas borrowed from physics. One can think of metallurgy as a part of the science of materials, and, as such, *any* instrument,technique, or idea that furthers its general end is acceptable. Medicine can be taken as another example. Its object is to understand and promote human health. To this end, it draws on any science or subscience, including, not only the traditional fields of medicine proper, but pharmacology, biochemistry, physics, psychology, and biology, not to mention all the branches of technology, and, for its social organization, economics and sociology. Under the circumstances, to insist that medicine be narrowly scientific would be to destroy it.

Just as an analogy can be drawn between philosophy and biochemistry, it can also be drawn between philosophy and medicine. Narrow aims and standards of relevance, which are essential for more concentrated investigation, serve broader ones. Even if we abandoned the philosophical problems that have always troubled mankind, the problems would not abandon us; we would discover them again, and again invent philosophy to try and cope with them. When philosophy abstracts itself too persistently from its old problems, it reappears, as, in a sense, it is always present, in other, less intellectual guises—as art, literature, or unclassified wisdom or folly. Humans can't be choosers. Philosophy ought not to abandon its character as a demanding discipline; but it cannot abandon its old general aims that sustain its life and, in the larger sense, make it worth pursuing. How can the narrow and general aims be made compatible? Philosophical practice can try to make them so, and philosophical theory can wrestle with this problem too. Philosophy should conduct forays outside itself, into other territories, borrow strangers' eyes, try to see with the help of whomever or whatever can lend it sight. Such, at least, is my conviction.

3
Truth (and Relevance) Again

Psychologism

Having argued that relevance in philosophy should be broadly conceived, I can particularize and argue that psychology is relevant. I do not pretend to know if it is superior, in explaining philosophy and philosophers, to such other disciplines as history, sociology, social anthropology, or even literary criticism. My personal interests, however, and my desire to share the illumination I have experienced lead me to single out psychology, to which I now turn.

First, however, there is an objection that must be faced. Philosophers have long been cautioned against 'psychologism,' which appears to repel them much as sin repels (and attracts) theologians. I therefore owe myself and my readers some account of psychologism, into which I will no doubt be said to have fallen. Intimations of warnings against it appear as early as Plato. Kant, though he does not use the term, contrasts Locke's impotent 'physiological derivation' of concepts, which explains no more than their empirical origin, with his own stringent proof of their legitimacy. Following Kant's lead, nineteenth-century philosophers such as Lotze, Frege, and the Neo-Kantians, Windelband, Rickert, Cohen, and Natorp, all take psychology to be irrelevant to philosophy. Their view has been quite general in the twentieth century—it is characteristic of Husserl and, as well, of Heidegger and Carnap, whom one might expect not to agree in anything.

The term 'psychologism' is said to have come into use during the first half of the nineteenth century, to characterize the rather empirical Kantianism of philosophers like Fries and Beneke, who argued that philosophy must be based upon self-observation.[1] In England, Hume is the obvious predecessor of psychologism, while its outstanding representative is, obviously, John Stuart Mill. The nuances of Mill's thought on the issue are less important for us than the forthrightness of the words in which he proclaimed psychologism.[2] The axioms on which our thought rests, he said, are neither more nor less than 'generalizations from observation' confirmed 'in almost every instant of our lives.'[3]

According to him, the very law of contradiction is founded on the self-observation that teaches us

> that Belief and Disbelief are two different mental states . . . And if we carry our observation outwards, we also find that light and darkness, sound and silence, motion and quiescence . . . are distinct phenomena, pointedly contrasted, and the one always absent where the other is present. I consider the maxim in question to be a generalization from all these facts.[4]

Mill's conclusion was that logic, to the extent that it was a science at all, was 'a part or branch of psychology,' a kind of dependent practical art. Logic, he said, 'owes all its theoretical foundation to psychology and includes as much of that science as is necessary to establish the rules of the art.'[5]

'Psychologism' has been given a narrow sense, according to which it contends that psychology can explain logic, and a broad sense, according to which it contends that psychology absorbs philosophy, or at least serves it as a foundation.[6] Of the attacks on psychologism, in both senses, I think it worthwhile to quote, first, from that of Frege, and then from that of Husserl. Frege wrote, in 1884:

> Never let us take a description of the origin of an ideal for a definition, or an account of the mental and physical conditions on which we become conscious of a proposition for a proof of it . . . Otherwise, in proving Pythagoras' theorem we should be reduced to allowing for the phosphorus content of the human brain . . . We suppose, it would seem, that concepts sprout in the individual mind like leaves on a tree, and we think to discover their nature by studying their birth: we seek to define them psychologically, in terms of the nature of the human mind. But this account makes everything subjective, and if we follow it through to the end, does away with the truth . . . Often it is only after immense intellectual effort, which may have continued over centuries, that humanity at last succeeds in achieving knowledge of a concept in its pure-form, in stripping off the irrelevant accretions which veil it from the eyes of the mind.[7]

In the twentieth century, the best-known and most sustained attack on psychologism is that of Edmund Husserl. It occupies a full five chapters of his *Logical Investigations,* the first volume of which was published in 1900–1901. Husserl there takes psychologism in its narrow sense, that is, as the contention that psychology can explain logic; but in *Formal and Transcendental Logic,* published in 1929, he extends the attack and directs it against the attempt to convert experiential objects of whatever kind into mere psychological experiences. Later, some ambivalence appears, it seems, for he hopes 'to return to the natural attitude,' and, on the basis of his own philosophy, to reinstate a natural, 'genuine' psychology.[8]

In *Logical Investigations,* Husserl's main point is that psychology, as an empirical science, has inevitably vague, uncertain conclusions, whereas logic is by nature precise and certain. There is, he says, a fundamental, unbridgeable gulf between ideal and real laws, between logical and real grounds. Like Kant, he sees the ideal laws as *a priori,* the 'real' ones as empirical. The former enjoy intuitive certainty, the latter are only probable. He is especially concerned to deny that it is a feeling of a certain kind that makes logic valid, or makes us think it is valid:

> There are certain normal circumstances in which every normal person feels self-evidence in connection with the proposition $1 + 1 = 2$, just as he feels pain when he gets burnt . . . Truth is of course only experienced in the sense in which something ideal can be an experience in the inwardly evident judgment . . . The inwardly evident judgment is . . . an experience of primal givenness.[9]*

I do not think it necessary to follow the attitudes of subsequent philosophers toward psychologism, whether the negative attitude of Heidegger and Carnap, or the more positive one of Sartre. Russell, it is interesting to note, began by saying, 'Logic will never acquire its proper place among the sciences until it is recognized that a truth and the knowledge of it are as distinct as an apple and the eating of it,' but ended, like a believer in psychologism, with the words, 'All the raw material of our knowledge consists of mental events in the lives of separate people. In this region, therefore, psychology is supreme.'[10]

As far as I know, during the last decades the most fruitful work on the problem of psychologism has been that of Jean Piaget, whose compromise seems to me more plausible and intellectually more useful than either psychologism or its opposite, logicism. Piaget is careful to avoid either of the two extremes, the illegitimate passage from psychological facts to logical norms, and the illegitimate passage from norms to facts. He finds that the actual relationship between facts and logic is revealed by study of the development of the norms, from their vagueness in childhood to their definiteness in adolescence. Like James and Dewey, he regards thinking as a series of implicit internal activities directed at the external world. Intelligence, to him, arises out of the interaction of the changing mathematical or logical structures in our minds with the varying, external reality that we learn to assimilate or accommodate; for the world is

---

*It is interesting to note that although mathematics provides Husserl with his best example of origin-immune truth, he, like the mathematics-struck Spinoza, believes that the objective truth he has discovered is notably different from mathematical truth. He says, 'Definition cannot take the same form in philosophy as it does in mathematics; the imitation of mathematical procedure is invariably in this respect not only unfruitful, but perverse and harmful in its consequences.' *Ideas* (London: Allen & Unwin, 1913), p. 47.

the product of our actions upon it, of the relations between these actions, and of the symbolic embodiment of these actions.

This account is no doubt too compressed to be clear—Piaget himself is often unclear—but it points to the conclusion that the long debate between those who stress innate and who stress environmental influences on truth is misconceived. Both sides, he contends, exaggerate. As he sees it, the truth is a complex interaction, for 'while the fecundity of the subject's thought processes depends on the internal resources of the organism, the efficacy of these processes depends on the fact that the organism is not independent of the environment but can only live, act or think in interaction with it.'[11]

To return to Frege and Husserl and their argument against psychollgism, it appears that there is no need to quarrel with it, though Piaget perhaps reduces its scope. Everyone, or almost everyone agrees that there must be something in reasoning that is true and a touchstone for other truths. Everyone accepts the rules of arithmetic as valid in themselves, and (almost) everyone agrees that it is intellectually wrong to contradict oneself, and that an evident contradiction is intellectually disturbing. It is easy to point out, as has already been done, that any reasonable defence of self-contradiction must itself avoid self-contradiction and so imply the truth of what it is denying. The philosophers who have taken pride in their self-contradiction have done so, I think, as an act of bravado, a declaration of disobedience, rather than a serious and intellectually suicidal acceptance of self-contradiction.

Mathematical and Similar Subjective Ideas

So far, the position of Frege and Husserl has proved basically acceptable, for although every individual, as Piaget contends, needs experience in order to develop his understanding of mathematics and logic, this need does not weaken the validity of mathematics and logic as such. I have already pointed out, however, that a pluralistic or pragmatic response can be made to the foundational problems of mathematics, and now I would like to call witnesses to show that quite fateful choices in mathematics may be of psychological origin, and that mathematics and logic, though they remain the exemplars of formally valid reasoning, can no longer be seen as simply decisive and can no longer give the Freges and Husserls the comfort they once derived from them. I ask the indulgence of those of my readers who are familiar with the controversy on the foundations of mathematics. I mean to be brief and repeat only what is necessary for my argument.

I do not know how many mathematicians try to articulate and justify their fundamental attitudes towards their subject. Some of them, I assume, are Platonists, who might agree with G. H. Hardy when he says, 'I believe that mathematical reality lies outside us, that our function is to discover or *observe* it and that the theorems we describe grandiloquently as our "creation" are simply the notes of our observations.'[1] Among the Platonists, there were (and perhaps still are) 'logicists,' who, like Russell at the time he was working on *Principia Mathematica,* contended that mathematics was based on, that is, derived its validity from logic. The mathematicians who loved mathematics more than logic were unlikely to agree. Speaking for them, Weyl said that Russell and Whitehead's logico-mathematical structure taxed their faith 'hardly less than the doctrines of the early Fathers of the Church or of the Scholastic philosophers of the Middle Ages.'[2]

As everyone who followed the controversy knows, logicism was never worked out satisfactorily. In the words of Russell, 'I was continually reminded of the fable about the elephant and the tortoise. Having constructed an elephant upon which the mathematical world could rest, I found the elephant tottering, and proceeded to construct a tortoise to keep the elephant from falling. But the tortoise was no more secure than the elephant, and after some twenty years of very arduous toil, I came to the conclusion that there was nothing more that I could do in the way of making mathematical knowledge indubitable.'[3]

Logicism had a rival, formalism, which took pure mathematics to be a purely formal structure referring only to its own consistency and completeness. Both logicism and formalism were opposed by intuitionism. The romantic-philosophic Weyl may be taken, for example, as a moderate exponent of intuitionism; but its most interesting, obscure, and seductive exponent was the Dutch mathematician, Luitzen Brouwer, whose conception of mathematics should help me to make my point.

To Brouwer, mathematics depended on the experience of time, on, that is, the constant splitting of sensation into past and present. 'By a move of time,' he said, 'a present sensation gives way to another present sensation in such a way that consciousness retains the former one as a past sensation, and moreover, through this distinction between present and past, recedes from both and from stillness, and becomes *mind.*'[4]

To Brouwer, this dualizing quality of consciousness was the foundation of mathematics because, to begin with, we divest the two-oneness of consciousness of all its content except its plurality and order, and then, by repeating the sequence indefinitely, we construct the series of natural numbers and, by extension, the whole of mathematics. According to him, this process, in itself wordless, is accompanied by language and logic; but since it precedes them, it determines whatever measure of exactness they possess. Language, to him, is not naturally very exact; traditional logic consists of nothing but the rules to which language is supposed to conform; and modern logic is no more than a by-product of mathematics. Therefore, because logic depends on mathematics, mathematics need *not* conform to all logical rules.

In saying this, Brouwer had in mind mainly the rule of the excluded third, that every meaningful statement is either true or false—any other, third possibility is excluded. He argued that this rule or 'law' had been unjustifiably applied to the mathematics of the infinite or indefinite, and so he rejected most of the mathematical theory of infinite sets and, with it, the extensive areas of modern mathematics that depend upon this theory. Affirming the primacy of mathematics over logic, he said:

> I hope I have made it clear that intuitionism on the one hand subtitles logic, on the other hand denounces logic as a source of truth. Further, that intuitionistic mathematics is inner architecture, and that research in the foundations of mathematics is inner inquiry with revealing and liberating consequences, also in non-mathematical domains of thought.[5]

To Brouwer, the rule of the excluded third, the fundamental 'law' of mundane logic, was no more than a habit derived from the conformity to it of many everyday phenomena. In this he agreed with Mill; but, unlike him, he felt that human freedom had been too limited by the causal sequences of everyday phenomena. True, freedom was given humans by their temporal, mathematical perception, that is, by their ability to imagine new, repeatable sequences, and, from them, to formulate the natural laws that gave them a new manipulative power. But this freedom, this self-directed mathematical action, was finally, he said, disappointing; for there is no truth in the *contents* of experience or in mathematical acts, but in consciousness itself, in the miracle of the self-revelation of forms, in the beauty of a playful, reverential memory, and, above all, in the introspective beauty of free, unwordly mathematics.

If Brouwer were no more than an eccentric Dutch topologist with mystical longings, there would be no need to discuss him here; but he became the leader of a powerful school of mathematicians. The list of more or less intuitionistic mathematicians must include at least Kronecker, Poincaré, Borel, Lebesque, Weyl, and Skolem, all men of decided independence of thought, able and willing to stand up to the arguments of their non-intuitionistic opponents.[6] It became apparent that strictly mathematical arguments were indecisive. Each side sometimes refused to recognize the mathematical entities of the other, each sometimes refused to recognize theorems embodying even entities recognized by both, each found true what the other found false, senseless, or in a way contradictory. Brouwer himself could only conclude that the sides were irreconcilable. He said:

> There are eminent scholars on both sides and the chance of reaching an agreement within a finite period is practically excluded. To speak with Poincaré: 'Men cannot understand one another, because they do not speak the same language and because there are languages that cannot be learned.'[7]

Although the battle has died down, perhaps because neither side has won the victory, or perhaps because neither really wants to abandon the interesting results of the other, the situation remains such that one may be led to speak, with a mathematician (A. Mostowski), of choice by means of 'a metaphysical act of faith.' Or, with another mathematician (E. W. Beth), one may say that no method can ultimately justify mathematical theories and methods, for 'such a justification can only derive from personal and, therefore, always subjective conviction.'[8] With a third mathematician or mathematical logician (H. B. Curry), one may say that contemporary mathematical Platonism is based on 'a metaphysical assumption which is highly repugnant to certain types of minds.'[9] And with a fourth mathematician (H. Weyl), one may conclude that 'the question of the ultimate foundations and the ultimate meaning of mathematics remains open; we do not know in what direction it will find its final solution or even whether a final objective answer can be expected at all. "Mathematizing" may well be a creative activity of man, like language or music, of primary originality, whose historical decisions defy objective rationalization.'[10] Finally, with a fifth distinguished mathematician (S. M. Ulam), one may conclude that because mathematics is like an art, 'values depend on personal tastes and feelings rather than on objective factual notions.' (In a not quite irrelevant aside, I can supplement this conclusion with the remark, made by Ulam, that 'mathematicians tend to be rather vain—though less so than opera tenors or artists.')[11]

Like mathematicians, physicists are sometimes fundamentally divided by their inability to speak the same language. For a long time, the great physicist, Enrico Fermi, could not understand Heisenberg's matrix mechanics, not because the mathematics was so difficult, but because the physical ideas involved were alien to him.[12] The aged Einstein once tried and failed to argue the nature of quantum mechanics with a physicist he himself called 'very ingenious.' 'He could not understand my adherence to logical simplicity,' said Einstein, 'or my lack of confidence in the value of theoretical criteria, impressive as they might be, when questions of principle were at stake. Like all those who think that quantum theory comes close to the heart of the problem, he found my position strange and detached.'[13]

The evidence is clear. Like anyone in any other field, a mathematician or physicist may reach a fundamental scientific impasse that he can solve only by making his own, subjective choice. The arguments of Frege and Husserl against psychologism are therefore severely restricted. As both emphasized, we have no reasonable choice in reasoning except to reason reasonably; but their models of objective reasoning, mathematics and logic, are built, as we now see, not of objective truths alone, but also of temperamental differences, metaphysical acts of faith, and unfathomable variations in creativity.

We are again close to James's dilemma. Mathematics and logic cannot solve it, nor, *a fortiori,* can psychology. Psychological explanations are, in any case, dependent on others. Beyond observation itself, they depend on physics, mathematics, physiology, philosophy, in its larger sense, and logic, in at least its informal sense. The fact is that no type of explanation, mathematical, logical, physical, philosophical, or psychological is quite self-sufficient. Just as, for example, there is mathematics in psychology, there is psychology in mathematics. Each type of explanation depends on others, and they are all linked and interdependent. We are in a great, vague spiral or sphere of explanations or justifications. To a traditional epistemologist, this situation may appear deplorable. It is certainly in contradiction to the old philosophical and scientific belief in linear reasoning, beginning in something unquestionable or unquestioned, and proceeding straight ahead, by infallible rules of procedure. Old and sometimes fruitful as this belief may have been, it is philosophically a dream and bears little resemblance to the actual human situation.

I am left with a conclusion and a question. The conclusion is this: If mathematics, logic, or physics is the model of objective reasoning, and if, nevertheless, mathematicians, logicians, and physicists depend on fundamental, subjective acts of choice, then, *a fortiori,* philosophers, too, depend on such acts. While radical, truth–denying psychologism is absurd, psychology is apt to provide the best explanations available to us of the subjective choices that philosophers make of their respective fundamental truths or attitudes. Assumptions, of course, are assumptions, axioms, if different from assumptions, are axioms, and logic is logic; yet a question obtrudes itself: Why do we choose the particular assumptions, axioms, and logics we choose? Perhaps psychology can contribute to the answer.

Psychology, Alas!

As a result of the problem of psychologism, we have made a fairly long circuit, and returned, by way of an *a fortiori* argument, to psychology, which we can now allow to assume its share of the burden of explanation. Psychology, however, is no complete, fixed science ready to be used intellectually by anyone who needs it. Before I actually make use of it, therefore, I would like to explain how I see it, and especially how I see psychoanalysis, on which I mean to draw most.

Like the other behavioural sciences, psychology seems to me to have made great progress during the past few decades. But this progress has been of a curiously limited sort. It is most obvious in the area that borders on physiology. I think that no knowledgeable person would deny that progress has been made in understanding perception, for instance, or the workings of the nervous system. Ethology has contributed an interesting, relatively new or renewed type of evidence and at least a few key concepts. Furthermore, the practical and conceptual difficulties of psychology have been so great and its competition of ideas so intense, that the level of its sophistication, that is, of its professionally aware intelligence, has risen greatly. Perhaps this rise in sophistication alone is worth all the effort that has been expended in achieving it; but it has not, as I see it, inspired substantial agreement on fundamentals. Unlike physics, chemistry, or biology, psychology—physiological psychology apart—has not acquired a common fund of more or less established facts and theories. Disagreements in psychology are so numerous and deep that, outside of a given subgroup of psychologists, everything of importance seems to be in dispute.

The causes for this lack of clear progress, except in sophistication, seem, on the whole, plain. Observations and experiments on humans are extremely difficult to control in the scientific sense. Too many subtle human factors intervene, and too many subtle disuniformities disturb the process of generalization. Psychologists have drawn up a formidable list of such difficulties: volunteers for experiments may have volunteer-characteristics that invalidate generalizations drawn from them; the preliminaries to testing may create 'pre-test sensitization'; the 'placebo effect' creates self-generated reactions to inert substances and neutral procedures; and experimenters show intended and unintended bias in their own favour. The difficulties are such that I sometimes feel that none of the more complex non-physiological experiments are ever duplicated. Every experimenter tends to find fault with the conceptions or methods of his predecessor and to conduct what is ostensibly the same experiment in an 'improved' version. Because the experiments are not standardized enough for really close comparison, the statistics they furnish are hard to compare and not genuinely cumulative.*

I have mentioned the subtle disuniformities that disturb our psychological generalizations. I cannot now go into the more philosophical problems involved. Instead, I will dramatize the number and subtlety of the disuniformities by citing an arithmetical calculation taken from genetics. It has been calculated that the number of possible combinations of human genes, including their alternate forms, is ten to the ten thousandth power.[1] But this enormous number, assuming it is correct, is misleadingly small, for a gene is neither indivisible nor inert, but in fact divides and rearranges itself in active relationship with its environment. The individual human being, who comprises this enormous range of genetic possibilities, changes at every moment of his life, and every change makes a new possible difference in the expression of his genetic nature and in the person he is coming to be. Though, I suppose, there are chemical or other constraints limiting these genetic possibilities, it is clear that human beings are genetically and therefore behaviourally so complex that they may remain very different from one another even when they seem very similar, and very similar even when they seem very different (I say 'very' to imply that the degree of difference is of great importance to them).[2] The expert in behavioural genetics is therefore likely to say that until we make a detailed genetic analysis of the basis of our behaviour, we are as ignorant in relation to ourselves as were the physicists in relation to physics before particle physics had been developed.

Even if we do not raise any of the other relevant considerations, it is not surprising that we cannot schematize or predict human behaviour in accurate detail. The human statistics we gather and the curves we draw to represent laws of human behaviour are too simple, sharp, and static. Like the other behavioural sciences, psychology is at once too rigidly simple and too philosophically vague.

It is this philosophical vagueness that especially characterizes psychoanalysis. It is impossible for me, in a book that concentrates on other matters, to go seriously into the debate on psychoanalysis and ask whether psychoanalysis is alive or dead, useful or detrimental, or

---

*Readers who think my reaction unduly pessimistic will disabuse themselves if they read a number of the successive annual reviews of psychology issued in book form in the United States. The 'list of difficulties' I have spoken of is the subject of R. Rosenthal & R. L. Rosnow, *Artifact in Behavioral Research* (New York: Academic Press, 1969). Their research on the difficulties of conducting objective research is of course subject to the same difficulties they point out; that is to say, they may have been biased in favour of discovering bias.

scientific or superstitious. For this debate, all I can do is refer the reader to books that seem to me to provide as good an answer as is now possible.[3]

My view, however, is this: Insofar as psychoanalysis constitutes a system or, rather, a concatenation of related ideas, it is rich, suggestive, and often penetrating. It bears earmarks of the Romantic philosophies of the late nineteenth century, which, in turn, bear those of Neo-Platonism. That is to say, the grand polarity of a life-drive, an Eros, locked in mortal balance with a death-drive, a Thanatos, makes psychoanalysis like at least some of the more speculative philosophical systems. Freud had a strong penchant for philosophizing, though he tried to suppress it and said that he had never or hardly ever felt the need for a purely philosophical, definitive unity of things. His life-drive and death-drive and other such conceptions lend a nice symmetry to the 'system' and a stabilizing framework, within which there shelter more modest and perhaps empirically testable hypotheses. In and by themselves, these hypothesized drives are, I find, dramatic, and they remind me of the dramatic concept-pairs of Chinese and Indian philosophy, not to speak of Presocratic philosophy. Apart, however, from their symmetrizing, stabilizing, and dramatic qualities, I do not find them to be intellectually either helpful or harmful. Even the life-drive or life instinct, in which we all informally tend to believe, will one day, I assume, be analysed into more instructive components.

However this may be, the somewhat mythical, metaphysical temperament of psychoanalysis has been necessary to its existence. It has lent it genuine theoretical force, by which I mean that psychoanalytic concepts are discovered not on, but under the surface of human behaviour, of which they give a concentrated and unobvious explanation. Its metaphysical atmosphere does not in itself distinguish psychoanalytic from other embracing attitudes that have been current in the behavioural sciences. The metaphysics of such a resolutely unmetaphysical position as that, for example, of behaviourism has been too prosaic, too simply implicit to be easily made out.

Psychoanalysis is therefore not alone among psychologies in being metaphysical or doubtful; nor are psychologies generally different in being metaphysical or doubtful from any other systematic attempts to understand human behaviour. If psychologism is taken to mean that psychology is more basic than the other behavioural sciences or than philosophy, I do not advocate it. To the extent that psychology is a science, it is lacunary, doubtful, and based on questionable criteria. Even when it is reduced to somehow competent statistics, they apply only doubtfully to particular cases, to which truism it need only be added that all real cases are particular. I therefore prefer to get down to particular biographical cases, discover the context of a philosopher's life, and appeal to all the evidence, whether or not it fits the interests of a particular psychology. For all my use of psychological or, more narrowly, psychoanalytic generalizations, I see no profit in merely translating one set of abstractions, the philosophical, into another, the psychoanalytic; and I want to study a reasonable number and variety of individuals before I conclude whatever I can.

I should add that, to me, the psychological attitudes that will be used here have become less a matter of theory or science than of the experience that has convinced me of their approximate truth. The common observation that parents have a strong and lasting influence on their children has been dramatized, deepened, and refined by psychoanalysis. Once sensitized by psychoanalysis to such evidence, I, for one, have found it confirmed and reconfirmed in my own experience. I have found similar confirmation in experience of something like the Freudian concepts of narcissism and sado-masochism, and, as well, of paranoid or schizoid types of thought. However, I prefer not to discuss these and allied concepts in the abstract. They will emerge informally as they become useful.

The Relevance of Psychology

As I have argued, and as history makes plain, all intellectual fields have fluid boundaries and criteria of relevance. The relative vagueness of philosophy should be exploited to give it relative freedom, and my suggestion is that the boundary that separates it from psychology should be opened (at least on weekends, on proper application). If it were opened, the questions we ask in philosophy might be given two or more different but equally relevant kinds of answers.

Consider the question, for instance, What is it that this philosopher wants to know? This could be taken in the standard philosophical way; but it could also be interpreted to mean the psychological question, What is it that this philosopher wants when he wants to know? Psychologically, the answer might be that, essentially, he wants to know something in the older, more carnal, Biblical sense of enjoying some state of mind or quality of experience.

Put otherwise, the narrower, more evidently philosophical standard of relevance remains essential for the philosopher's usual purposes; but there is a second-order criterion: that which is relevant to the standards of relevance themselves, to their choice, that is, and to the mode and intensity of their application. Such a criterion might be counted as belonging to the scope of 'metaphilosophy.' It might be useful, however, to coin a new term, 'infraphilosophy,' for critical thinking on the conditions on which philosophy depends for its nature and existence. Such a term would allow psychology, though distinguished from philosophy, to be legitimately related to it, rather as logic, for Aristotle, was excluded from philosophy but related to it as its organon. The adoption of such a term would make it easier to give philosophy a legitimately narrow and legitimately broad interpretation. Conceived broadly, philosophy could be regarded as consisting of infraphilosophy, philosophy in the narrow sense, and metaphilosophy, or, more homogeneously, of infraphilosophy, philosophy, and supraphilosophy.

These terminological possibilities do not, however, please me. They codify too much for my taste. It is certainly necessary to be clear about the objects of our thought and therefore about the levels on which we are thinking. Too many philosophical confusions have depended on the joining in thought of what should have been sundered. However, I prefer to consider the psychological ideas I use, not as part of an infrastructure, but as a kind of sensitivity. Compare the sensitization that history makes possible with that made possible by psychology. History sensitizes the present with an awareness of the past, while psychology sensitizes reasoning with an awareness of its emotional overtones and subjective intentions. Historical consciousness serves as an extended memory, while psychological consciousness serves as an extended or interiorized vision, designed, like an infra-red camera, to see in the dark, or, like an x-ray machine, to see into an otherwise hidden interior.

In the name of this possible sensitivity or extended vision, we can return to the question, What is it that this philosopher wants to know? The simplest psychological test of what he 'really' wants (wants beyond what he appears to want) is to observe what he 'really' does (tries to accomplish psychologically) with his intellect. To observe what he does, in this sense, requires us to observe, not only the ideas he is proposing, but the success or failure of the ideas in his and others' eyes and, in fact, all their immediate personal and social consequences.

What is it that he wants? Is this philosopher, this anonymous object of our first, experimental questions, trying, perhaps, to cure his mortality by embodying himself in immortal thoughts? Is he trying, like the explorers who first came to the Americas, to penetrate to the primal source of life, the truth-in-itself, the presence of which, he feels, would excite, delight, or calm him, all superlatively well? Is he trying to resolve some intellectual dissonance that sounds within himself too disturbingly? Is he vindicating himself in his own eyes, perhaps by vindicating himself in the eyes of someone important or once important in his life?

The questions go on (but not too long). Why is this philosopher trying so hard to understand what seems self-evident or trivial to most other people? Is he, perhaps, adding doubt to doubt, as if obsessively expressing, fending off, and recreating some fear or uncertainty? Do his endless, inconclusive reasonings about reality betray a nagging doubt of his own right to existence or betray a hidden memory of his abandonment as an infant? Are his equally endless, inconclusive reasonings about morality the sign of a serious doubt of his worth or decency? Does he answer his doubts by reaching real or impotent certainties, or answer his ambivalence by insisting that not he, but existence is split by paradox? Is he revolting against some father, standing in some father's protective shadow, or trying to become some father he has had or has imagined? Is he using his intellect to attack or conciliate, wound or heal? And when he asks his questions (or when I ask mine) is it really the answers that are wanted?

The possible questions are too numerous and too interesting to spell out in so nearly random a list. The answers are fewer and are generally, I am afraid, too crude. It is too crude to say that the philosopher is motivated by his desire for prestige, rank, money, or sex. Such desires are, in any case, unselective and unable to explain why he particularly chose philosophy in order to satisfy them. Experience, furthermore, teaches us that as we grow older our needs and modes of self-expression grow increasingly autonomous, until, perhaps, old age, when primary needs or desires may rule again. Yet crude desire continues, I think, to lurk in the background, like an eminence grise, and manipulate the philosopher's philosophizing, partly autonomous though it has become. He would no more have started philosophizing in the absence of crude desires than a car would start in the absence of fuel and a motor; nor, as a car would not go on without a functioning motor, could a philosopher go on without his primary, vitalizing desires. It is true that neither motor nor desire are sufficient to determine a destination. Something or someone has to steer them. But they determine the ability to get to destinations at all, and the ease, difficulty, or impossibility of getting to particular destinations.

Even if we forget the crude answers, psychological motives can be considered basic to philosophy. 'The real discovery,' says Wittgenstein, 'is the one that makes me capable of stopping doing philosophy when I want to.—The one that gives philosophy peace, so that it is no longer tormented by questions which bring *itself* into question.'[1] Analogously, if anything in a philosopher's non-rational life were responsible for the urgency of a philosophical problem, the problem would vanish along with the urgency. The problem could then be held to have been only the illusive simulacrum of the urgency. An echo ends with the sound that produces it, a problem with the impulse that produces it, all philosophy with the impulses or anxieties of philosophers. Thus there are philosophers, I believe, for whom philosophy, in its stringent sense, ends as they age. Hume seems to me to be such a temporary philosopher.

Psychology: Ten Brief Answers

I hope that my position so far is not implausible. I continue with a basic question: What can philosophy gain by the examination of philosophers' motives, temperaments, and lives?

Let me answer by making ten brief, interrelated points. They have been prepared by what I have already said and will be justified, as far as I can justify them, by all that follows.

1. *On the genesis of objectivity:* The process by which subjective problems become involved in or transformed into objective ones is crucial to the understanding of philosophy. As a collection of objective problems, philosophy has both a historical and a psychological genesis. To regard either of these as irrelevant is to sacrifice much of the ability to see philosophy in a reasonable perspective and to practice it reasonably.

2. *On philosophers as philosophical instruments:* In analyzing themselves historically or psychologically, philosophers shift their attention from philosophy, seen impersonally, to their own natures as philosophers. Experience, in and out of the sciences, has taught that we understand a conclusion better if we understand the physical or theoretical instruments by which it has been established. The philosopher, who is the instrument of his own thought, is no ideal thinking-machine. The nature of its human instruments can help to explain philosophy.

3. *On the choice of assumptions and rules:* Formal reasoning is unable to explain its own choice of assumptions and rules, except for the purpose of formal consistency and the like. Yet the choice is fateful. It may be possible to clarify it by explanations drawn from history, psychology, and other fields. If so, there is good reason to relax the now usual criteria of philosophical relevance.

4. *On the likeness between implicit psychological processes and explicit reasoning:* If the depth psychologies are even approximately true, the explicit reasoning of every person bears a structural relation to his emotional and implicit or unconscious processes. The relation is not predictable in detail, and its discovery is largely retrospective. But it can illuminate, not only the conscious choice of assumptions, but also the structural connections and intellectually obscure tendencies of a

philosophy. These tendencies may be only implicit and yet have a powerful effect. The likeness between a person's looks, actions, character, and philosophy may help to explain all four of these.

5. *On the attraction of philosophers to certain philosophies, philosophers, and problems:* The examination of the intellectually obscure or irrelevant features of a philosophy may reveal why it has attracted or repelled certain philosophers. A highly logical, minutely reasoned, or heavily qualified philosophy may attract compulsive persons. An introspective philosophy may act as a refuge for timid persons. A self-centred philosophy may attract narcissistic persons. Perhaps all the philosophers interested in music—they will be singled out—are inwardly joined, as perhaps are those—who will also be singled out—who are conspicuously uninterested in it. Perhaps philosophers who show signs of hypochondria or are concerned with suicide—both types will be pointed out—have unobvious but real philosophical similarities. Summarily, it may be supposed that there are philosophies, philosophers, or philosophic problems that attract persons because they express some dominant emotion or temper, such as doubt, fear, anger, indignation, compassion, self-indulgence, or self-division.

6. *On intellectual lapses:* The obscure or unintellectual features of a philosophy are likely to explain something of its intellectual lapses. Everyone but the author of a philosophy seems ready to concede that it has faults. It is possible to try to remedy these by reasoning, of course; but even if the reasoning is plausible, no one can adequately replace the philosopher himself in the construction of a philosophy. If it is *he* or *his* system that one wants to understand, it may be more enlightening, not to correct him, but to show how the presumed faults were natural to such a philosopher in such circumstances. Psychology is more clearly relevant to the explanation of obscurities, lapses, errors, and exaggerations than to that of appropriate or plausible reasoning.

7. *On understanding by means of identification:* All things considered, the formal grasp of the formal elements in a philosopher's thought is not enough for understanding. One needs some sympathy, some ability to project oneself into his problems, some identification with him. As we have seen, fundamentally alien attitudes may make understanding impossible even in mathematics or physics. There is, to be sure, a necessary distance between any two persons, which it is not the normal business of philosophy to abolish. Nor can philosophy substitute the mechanism of identification for the freedom of critical reasoning. But the inability to imagine oneself in the position of someone else is a serious philosophical restriction. Psychology can help explain the restriction and perhaps weaken it.

8. *On philosophical curiosity and consistency:* Some of the drives, needs, or problems that underlie or constitute philosophy are relatively opaque to philosophical understanding. For example, philosophy as such is unable to explain the tenacious curiosity by which it is generated. It is likewise unable to explain its need for consistency and, beyond this, the need shown by many philosophers to create entire thought-structures ruled by harmony. Curiosity digs, consistency founds, consonance erects. Do we not want to understand why?

9. *On the need for information:* Whatever its pretensions, philosophy draws and must draw on the sciences and the arts. Epistemologists, who have often ignored professional psychology, have often unknowingly trespassed on it. The fairly recent sense-data theory of Russell, Broad, Moore, members of the Vienna Circle, and others is a case in point, for psychologists had long since found that the sense-datum was a more or less theoretical construct, particularly as it related to vision.[1] Learning theory has become far more sophisticated than it was, but philosophers may make assumptions that depend on earlier, now clearly oversimple versions of it. Even the attempt of contemporary philosophers to be modest and competent and confine themselves to the clarification of concepts soon intersects with lexicography, linguistics, psychology, and, I fear, non-verbal matters to which the concepts relate. Recalling his Oxford philosophical training, a psychologist remarks:

> To examine the use of words is to plunge into muddle, innuendo, ambiguity, fantasy and internal contradiction. It is to discover words used for private ends, as counters in personal relations, and defined allusively, in the light of the participants' experience. To examine the use of words is to tackle the whole of psychology, cultural anthropology and semantics combined; areas of endeavour for which the Oxford philosopher was academically and temperamentally unprepared.[2]*

10. *On one's relationship to one's own ideas:* Lastly, the relationship of a philosopher to his own ideas is never neutral. He is not merely their advocate, but their creator, and he feels them to be of his own substance. His opinion of himself rises with their success and falls with their failure. I will later use the phrase 'idea-intimacy' to designate his tie with them.

---

*'A common avenue to philosophy is a reaction to science (as one is taught) and one looks for a neater or less painful way of doing interesting intellectual work. As a result of this phenomenon, philosophy tends to attract impatient innovators who are eager to say new things and believe that a combination of native wits with a command of one's native language, or diligence with a facility in logic-chopping, should be sufficient for doing most interesting intellectual work.' H. Wang, *From Mathematics to Philosophy* (London: Routledge & Kegan Paul, 1974), p. 374.

Non-Verbal Philosophizing

It is hard to imagine how philosophers might dispense with words, or what they would gain if they could. Mystics and authors of science fiction have made suggestions, but they are hard to apply to philosophy as we know it. Sometimes art is considered to realize what philosophy can express only in pale abstractions. Schelling, who took this view, said, 'It is art alone that can succeed in making objective with universal validity what the philosopher can only represent subjectively. . . .'[1] Schopenhauer made the claim that music was, essentially, philosophy, and that, if we could conceptualize it perfectly, it would be 'at once a sufficient repetition and explanation of the world in concepts . . . and hence the only true philosophy.'[2] Looking back at his *Birth of Tragedy*, Nietzsche was sorry he had not dared to communicate its message in poetry. 'Compared with music,' he said, 'all communication by words is shameless; words dilute and brutalize; words depersonalize; words make the uncommon common.'[3]

In spite of such claims and sensitivities, and in spite of my own love for the implicit, I mean only to point out to what a degree non-verbal elements may enter into philosophical discourse. I assume that the connection between the non-verbal and the verbal or logical is often unknown to us, but none the less essential. The scientific ideas that arose in Einstein's mind began, he explained, not in words, but in elements 'of visual and some of muscular type. Conventional or other signs have to be sought for laboriously only at a secondary stage, when the . . . associative play is sufficiently established and can be reproduced at will.'[4] Even when ideas begin in words, they may be nascent and inward, and words spoken aloud may disturb them. Such was the experience of Wittgenstein, who wrote, 'Sometimes the voice of a philosophical thought is so soft that the noise of spoken words is enough to drown it out and prevent it from being heard, if one is questioned and has to speak.' Elsewhere, Wittgenstein wrote, 'There really are cases in which the sense of what a person wants to say is much clearer in his mind than he can express in words. (This happens to me very often.) It is as if one saw a dream-picture distinctly, but could not describe it in such a way that someone else, too, could see it.'[5]

Non-verbal communication between individuals takes place, of course, when they are in intimate contact. Its most apparent effects on the history of philosophy are through the intimate, faithful disciples who propagate a philosopher's ideas and, sometimes, his mannerisms. It takes place by means of bodily stance and motion, changes in the pupils of the eyes, and changes in the quality, pitch, loudness, and rhythm of the voice.[6] As will later be described, Wittgenstein's body participated obtrusively in his teaching. Like him, the philosopher-sociologist, Georg Simmel (1858–1918), who was an extraordinarily effective teacher, intensified his words by his bodily gestures. 'He so-to-speak picked up' an idea he was formulating 'with his hands, his fingers opening and closing; his whole body turned and vibrated under the raised hand . . . His intensity of speech indicated a supreme tension of thought.' Somebody said of him, 'One can see how his brain operates, how he joins ideas like a carpenter joins wood . . . One is led to participate in the construction. One doesn't listen, one participates in the thought process.'[7] G. E. Moore's 'devotion to the truth was . . . palpable. In argument his whole frame,' as I have said, 'was gripped by a passion to confute error and expose confusion.' His frequently-repeated precepts were 'branded into the consciousness of his students by a variety of startling forensic devices (opening wide his eyes, raising his eyebrows, sticking out his tongue, wagging his head in the negative so violently that his hair shook.'[8] When Russell was asked whether Moore's prestige was partly due to his diffidence, he answered, 'No, it was his vehemence,' to demonstrate which Russell reproduced 'Moore's famous "O-o-o," expressing not so much disapproval as astonishment that any friend should be capable of holding so outrageously false an opinion.' Russell, too, used his voice with impressive authority, especially, so an intimate friend reports, to defend important assertions for which he would not or could not produce any grounds.[9]

In a sense, and with no mystical implications, one can agree with Heidegger when he claims, 'What is spoken is never, and in no language, what is said.'[10] In a sense, the recent Oxford philosophers, explicit as their interest in language was, and precise as they tried to be, may have been speaking what they did not explicitly say. Many of them

> were formidable talkers: their words tumbled out with a rapidity that was at times scarcely credible, yet always seemed to fall into syntactically correct patterns. And this emphasis on gramatically correct speech, on speaking 'written' sentences, was at times so extreme as to suggest that the mouth had taken on for these men and women some especial significance. Even their tones of voice were hall-marked—what now seems an implausible combination of the booming, the stacatto, and the slightly nasal.[11]

Philosophers like Wittgenstein and Bergson, both of whom were unusually sensitive to music, commented on the importance of what may broadly be called the musicality of language. Understanding a sentence, said Wittgenstein, is akin to understanding a theme in music, because the sentence has its individual patterns of variation in loudness and tempo;

and, in the sense that musical themes cannot replace one another, neither can sentences.[12] To him, the abstract meaning was not self-sufficient, for 'in philosophy it is significant that such-and-such a sentence makes no sense; but also that it sounds funny . . . One who philosophizes often makes the wrong, inappropriate gesture for a verbal expression.'[13] He said, 'Sometimes a sentence can be understood only when one reads it in the *correct tempo*. My sentences should all be read *slowly*.' It was because he wanted to be read slowly that he used punctuation marks with such frequency.[14]

Bergson's respect for the musicality of language was so great that he insisted that the full understanding of a philosopher was impossible without sensitivity to the philosopher's rhythms. Taking a page or so of Descartes' *Discourse on Method,* he tried to demonstrate that it was by virtue of its punctuation and, above all, by its proper reading aloud that the movement of Descartes' thought was transmitted from Descartes' mind to ours.[15] We cannot make our words say what we want them to, he insisted, 'if the rhythm, the punctuation and all the choreography of discourse do not help, by a series of nascent movements, to lead the reader to describe a curve of thought and feeling analogous to that we ourselves describe.'[16] His own writing was musically cadenced, and when he lectured, his flexible voice lingered and receded with a musicality that expressed his desire for a reticent but profound communion.[17]

The Relevance of Style: Bacon and Locke

Surely, reasoning as such has its styles. Even in so austere a medium as mathematics or logic, it has the sequences and emphases that make it recognizable as the work of a particular person. Here, however, I prefer to consider a philosopher's style in the primarily literary sense of his choice of images, linguistic patterns, and rhetorical strategies. To suggest that a philosopher's style, in this sense, is integral to his reasoning, or, to put it more weakly, to the force of his reasoning, I will make two brief characterizations, followed by a longer one, of philosophers' styles. A philosopher's reasoning, I want to say, is carried by his style and his style by his nature as one wave is carried by a second and the second by a third.[1]

My examples, which I take up in chronological order, are Francis Bacon, John Locke, and Ludwig Wittgenstein.

Anyone who reads Bacon soon becomes aware of his masterly control of rhetoric.[2] The pleasure he takes in his skill and fecundity strengthens the impression he makes of a vigorous, though reflective optimism. To him, rhetoric is not verbal ornamentation, but an intellectual art, part of logic, meant to free the mind of false imagery and seductive words. It rules discourse, collects arguments, defines fields of research, classifies instances, and, in general, establishes order. So understood, it intersects with scientific method.[3]

Bacon is quite capable of applying the rhetorical rules he advocates. The detailed articulation of his writing has prompted its comparison with a branching tree. The articulations of thought must, he says, be definite, for otherwise 'matters touched on are not distinctly apprehended and weighted; and they have not time enough to settle; but one reason drives out another before it has taken firm hold.'[4]

Although Bacon's use of articulation or division is masterly, it follows an old convention. His particular use of aphorisms seems, on the contrary, to have been original with him. He regards an aphorism as a seed of thought, which encapsulates, he says, 'some good quantity of observation.' It is, further, a form of knowledge so 'broken' and attractive that it invites men to enquire further, in contrast to methodical thought, which, 'carrying the shew of a total,' is more limiting.[5] He therefore uses aphorisms to break up the restrictions of systematic thought.

Like his aphorisms, Bacon's examples, analogies, and images are designed to focus attention. He scatters them everywhere profusely, to lend his reasoning colour and make it concrete. Because he is, above all, interested in dramatizing the promise of intellectual inquiry, he multiplies images of travelling and of building. So, by way of image, he takes sea voyages, sails out boldly into the ocean, discovers a clue, cuts a path, wanders fearfully in the dark, and finds that the road of his method ascends and descends. Likewise, by way of image, he builds, sets a cornerstone, sinks the foundations of the sciences firmer and deeper, digs into nature, is an architect, and collects materials to erect and build a true philosophy.[6]

Bacon's rhetorical reasoning proved unusually effective. The historian of the Royal Society, Thomas Sprat, credits Bacon with inspiring its foundation. Leibniz says that Bacon awakened him to philosophy; Descartes shows his strong influence (in the *Regulae* and the last part of the *Discourse*); D'Alembert and Voltaire follow him with eloquence and enthusiasm; and scientists, such as Huygens, Wallis, and Newton see themselves as following his lead. Later, he is often belittled, and Swift mocks his ideas and style; but there is no doubt of his great influence, and none, it seems to me, that his style furthered it.

Locke's writing is altogether less ostentatious than Bacon's. Taken naively and immediately, his *Essay Concerning Human Understanding* may seem no more than a friendly, sometimes pedantic, sometimes careless, sometimes clumsy meandering. Yet, taken in historic context, his style was both purposeful and convincing.[7] As he hoped, it inspired a friendly and even passionate confidence. His 'Epistle to the Reader' sets the tone. He appeals to the Reader modestly. His book has been no more than a diversion, he says, and he hopes it may divert the Reader. He will not commend his work. It is true, nevertheless, that he enjoyed writing it, for he enjoyed the intellectual hawking and hunting. Everyone who sets his thoughts to work enjoys the hunter's satisfaction. Locke addresses the unknown Reader intimately, as 'thou,' and he appeals to him to join him and experience the pleasures of clear thinking. If Locke and if he, the Reader, are candid, Locke will not be harmed or offended by the Reader's censure. The book stands or falls with the Reader's opinion, Everyman's opinion, for it is not meant for masters of the subject. Let me tell you, Locke says, how it all began, in conversation with five or six friends, and how it continued, by fits and starts, until at last, in the leisure of retirement, there was time to put it into its present order.

This confidential, apparently hesitant tone gives way to a brisker, less personal one; but Locke continues to write simply and in the first person, sometimes in a quasi-dialogue. He appears to expect his readers to identify themselves with him, so that he and they will together oppose his more stubborn or professional critics. His invitation to his readers is not merely by means of direct, sympathetic talk. He asks them to introspect, and to observe themselves or their children. He tells them how the paper before him changes as he writes on it, and how his words sound when they are read back to him. As his moods and subjects vary, his style varies. There are few short cuts. The book jogs along at the 'plain' man's pace. When it grows long-winded or arid, moments of near-intimacy give relief. Its anti-rhetorical honesty is relieved by metaphors. Even eloquence may momentarily break in.

The words, 'An Essay,' in the title of Locke's book indicate that he has meant to carry out an informal experiment in thinking. Voltaire contrasts its honest prosiness and anatomizing diligence with the imaginative Romance that Descartes has composed. Think simply, honestly, slowly, carefully, says Locke, and you will learn more by your modest endeavour than your predecessors have learned by their immodest flights of imagination. Locke wants to involve his readers in a common human responsibility. To do so, he has

> to translate philosophy into the vernacular, so that no man need be intimidated either by the difficulty or the remoteness of the subject. Philosophy, then, must be naturalized to the human understanding and, when possible, domesticated to the human understanding. In many different

ways, the *Essay* invites men to partake of its enterprise, appealing now to this mood in a reader, now to that one: its hospitable author makes the process of thinking about thinking so engaging that men naturally took up his book, and took him, so generously recorded in his *Essay*, as a model for self-experiment, for self-assaying.[8]

The Relevance of Style: Wittgenstein

The problem of the style of *Philosophical Investigations* is raised by Wittgenstein himself, in his preface. He belittles himself with, I think, a deeper sincerity than Locke, and says, 'The best that I could write would never be more than philosophical remarks.' To justify himself, he says that his thoughts were crippled when he tried to force them on, against their natural inclination, in a *single* direction. In saying this, he assumes some separation between himself and his thoughts, a separation that contrasts strongly with his attitude in the book proper, but that reflects, I suggest, his real condition. To his negative justification, he adds a positive one, which is that the very nature of his investigation made it necessary to follow his thoughts wherever they were naturally inclined to go, for the investigation, he says, 'compels us to travel over a wide field of thought criss-cross in every direction.' He adds, 'The philosophical remarks in this book are, as it were, a number of sketches of landscapes which were made in the course of these long and involved journeyings.'

To travel criss-cross means, to Wittgenstein, that 'the same or almost the same points were always being approached afresh from different directions, and new sketches made.' Some of these sketches, he tells us, were badly drawn or uncharacteristic. When only the tolerable ones were left, they had to be arranged and sometimes cut down 'so that if you looked at them you would get a picture of the landscape. Thus the book is really only an album.'

Wittgenstein's beginning is, we see, relatively intimate, though much briefer and distinctly more enigmatic than Locke's 'Epistle to the Reader.' It is not clear why it should be so apologetic, why, that is, the book should be considered 'only' an album, when Wittgenstein's goal, which he surely values, requires him to compose his book as a series of detached sketches. Even if they had all been well drawn or characteristic, the effect would still have been of what he calls an album. There is a strong hint, which may ally him with Bacon, that he prefers to be open to experience, to think, in Bacon's sense, 'brokenly,' rather than with smooth consecutiveness; but he does not defend the separateness of his sketches with the optimistic vigour that Bacon shows in defending the

separateness of each of his aphorisms. The air seems less expansive, the
eyes seem directed in rather than out and up.

However it should be characterized, Wittgenstein's initial intimacy and
apology arouse interest. The intimacy is maintained. Wittgenstein first
brings a quotation from Augustine, which he does not follow, as might
be expected of a philosopher, by a statement of his own reaction or an
argument. Instead, he enters a long, meandering meditation, which
changes from monologue to dialogue, the dialogue being perhaps with
himself or perhaps with some other, undesignated person, whom he
addresses, as he would himself or a close friend, with the intimate
pronoun, 'du,' 'you'—'I almost always write dialogues with myself,' he
says elsewhere.[1] This invitation to converse intimately, or to enter into
Wittgenstein's conversation with himself, is, however, limited, does not,
that is, extend to anything emotional or seriously personal. A moment's
comparison with the intimacy solicited by Kierkegaard or Kafka, who do
have some affinity with Wittgenstein, illustrates the distance that
Wittgenstein always maintains. His intimacy seems restricted to his
informal tone and the fairly natural associative path he follows.

In reading *Philosophical Investigations,* we soon become aware that
Wittgenstein makes few if any flat assertions. He makes no attempt to
establish either facts or argument, but, instead, he hypothesizes, asks
questions, and encourages himself, his companion, or us, his readers, to
imagine certain things. Thus, if we follow him, section after section,
from the beginning of the book, we find him saying, 'Now think,' 'Let us
imagine,' 'Augustine, we might say,' 'It is as if someone were to say,'
'Imagine a script,' 'If we look at the example,' and 'We could imagine
that.'[2] Wittgenstein sounds to me as if, as a child, he had often talked to
himself and played with imaginary companions.

Wittgenstein's solicitations to hypothesize, question, and imagine
continue throughout his book. So, for example, in a randomly chosen
later part, he begins successive sections with such phrases as, 'I can look
at the clock,' 'Suppose I wanted to justify,' 'Why can't my right hand?' 'let
us remember,' and 'Let us imagine.'[3]

Given this manner of expressing himself—should it be called the
imaginative child's technique, or the technique of the imaginary
playmate?—it is harder to resist Wittgenstein than if he had been arguing
straightforwardly. If we, like him, are curious and imaginative, why
shouldn't we imagine along with him? There is nothing to do but play
intellectually in this game without apparent winners, though this
impression will disturb those who enter games only if the rules and
winnings are clear to them. The possibilities remain open. Wittgenstein
nowhere forces us; he simply asks our cooperation in thinking. At least
that is the impression that is initially made.

Now to Wittgenstein's images.

As he proceeds from hypothesis to question to imagined situation, Wittgenstein invites us to use images. Some are ordinary, homely ones, while others, as befits an imaginative man interested in engineering, have the air of science fiction. The homely image appears, for example, when he invites us to think of the tools in a tool box, the hammer, pliers, saw, screwdriver, and so on, and their different functions, which he compares with the different functions of words.[4] The fantastic image appears, for example, when he invites us to imagine that 'human beings or creatures of some other kind are used by us as reading machines.'[5]

The purpose of Wittgenstein's criss–cross journey does not become obvious very quickly. The reader may grow uneasy or impatient. This is not, after all, an ordinary game. Why make this unconventional intellectual effort? Wittgenstein's eventual answer is that we should make it in order to alleviate our suffering. He says that we, that is, philosophers, suffer from the misinterpretations of our forms of language. These misinterpretations 'are deep disquietudes; their roots are as deep in us as the forms of our language and their significance is as great as the importance of our language.'[6]

It becomes clear that Wittgenstein proposes to overcome these disquietudes, not by arguing, but by showing us familiar things or ideas in different lights, from different angles, so that we should suddenly see them just as they are, rather than as convention and ingrained linguistic habits have been displaying them to us. In proposing this cure by renewal of vision, Wittgenstein reminds me of the Buddhists who argued that illusion, Samsara, is identical with truth, Nirvana, but to see the truth plain, without its illusory overlays or associations, we needed to change our way of looking at things. Some of these Buddhists proposed systematic exercises in thinking and seeing, while others relied more on sudden insights.

In accord, then, with the style and substance of this thinking, Wittgenstein proposes no clear general hypotheses, with the exception of the hypothesis (or dogma) I have just mentioned. This absence of general hypotheses is strange in a philosopher. In fact, Wittgenstein proposes to do away entirely with explanation, and leave only description. What he wants is to get to know things, and his description is therefore a close pointing at them, he says, to help get our vision into exact focus. He chooses words and images carefully, because it is their function to get us to see into the workings of language and release us from the captivity of misunderstanding, from the pictures we have not been able to get outside of. 'Philosophy simply puts everything before us, and neither explains nor deduces anything.'[7] The reason is that 'the aspects of things that are the most important for us are hidden because of their simplicity and familiarity. (One is unable to notice something—because it is always before one's eyes.)'[8]

In trying to make the familiar visible again, Wittgenstein is trying, in a sense, to make it unfamiliar. He prefers the perceptual freshness of childhood to the unobservant though functional habit of adulthood. His attempt is reminiscent of what psychologists call, 'jamais vue,' the sudden, inexplicable inability to recognize the most familiar things, places, or persons. In this condition, everything becomes totally new. Psychologically, the experience of 'jamais vue' seems to express great anxiety, and its aim seems to be to abolish the world that causes it. If Wittgenstein makes any reader uneasy, it may be just because the slow clarification by criss-crossing, though meant to ease his disquiet, expresses some of it.

There are other, more simply stylistic features of Wittgenstein's philosophy that may, in time, increase the disquiet. First, there are the oscillations between technical issues of logic or philosophical grammar and matters of sensation and perception. The oscillation itself is unusual, and in its course there come up odd images, such as the image of the creatures we might use as reading machines. We are also invited to perform odd acts of imagination, such as looking at a stone and imagining it to have sensations, and even, in an abstract way, to make our perceptions strange. We are asked to make our perceptions strange, I think, because, while Wittgenstein is ostensibly talking only of words, his concern with words is motivated by the desire to suggest something beyond them. Think, for example, what he means and suggests when he says, '*Hearing* a word in a particular sense. How queer that there should be such a thing! Phrased like this . . . .'[9]

Wittgenstein's oscillation of attention and his odd choices and sequences of images remind me of a sentence in Samuel Beckett's *Murphy*. Though the sentence is negative, its sequence of images, except for the end, appears similar:

> He could not get a picture in his mind of any creature he had met, animal or human, scraps of bodies, of landscapes, hands, eyes, lines and colours evoking nothing rose and climbed out of sight before him, as though reeled upward off a spool level with his throat.[10]

The kind of image that most obviously introduces disquiet is the repeated image of pain. In one series of paragraphs, after he has asked if it is possible to imagine a stone having sensations or a corpse having pain. Wittgenstein on occasion asks, on occasion states:

> But isn't it absurd to say of a *body* that it has pain?
> What sort of issue is it: Is it the *body* that feels pain?

How am I filled with pity *for this man*?
I am turned to stone and my pain goes on.
'When I say "I am in pain" I am at any rate justified *before myself*.'[11]

In two later groups of adjacent remarks, Wittgenstein says:

'I believe that he is suffering'.—Do I also *believe* that he isn't an automaton?[12]

A doctor asks: 'How is he feeling?' The nurse says: 'He is groaning'. A report on his behaviour. But need there be any question for them whether the groaning is really genuine, is really the expression of anything? . . .

If you observe your own grief, which senses do you use to observe it? A particular sense; one that *feels* grief? Then do you feel it *differently* when you are observing it? And what is the grief that you are observing—is it one which is there only while it is being observed?[13]*

A touch which was still painful yesterday is no longer so today.

Today I feel the pain only when I think about it (That is: in certain circumstances.)[14]

My grief is no longer the same; a memory which was still unbearable to me a year ago is no longer so.
That is the result of observation.[15]

There is much more of this talk of pain. The conclusion that Wittgenstein used it quite often is confirmed by the index to his book. By casual count, the number of sections in which pain, as indexed, is mentioned, comes to forty-nine. Futhermore, under the word, 'pain,' the index refers to entries under 'feeling,' 'groan,' 'head-ache,' 'sensation,' and 'tooth-ache.' Furthermore, as sub entries under 'pain' one finds 'pain expression,' 'imagine pain,' '*my* pain,' 'naming pain,' 'others' pain,' and 'pain in stone.'

After all these entries, I can't help saying, 'Imagine the person who compiled the index.' Wittgenstein regards his choice of examples and way of displaying them as philosophically important. It should be added that the choice and way are also psychologically important. What is sensed in these images and the talk about them is a great effort of detachment and of the self-observation that accompanies it. As is known,

---

*Compare the questions Wittgenstein is asking, including the question that ends, 'Do I also *believe* that he isn't an automaton,' with the following account:

'The five-year-old daughter of a severely schizo-affective woman was admitted to the hospital in a state of acute panic . . . When the acute disturbance subsided, the child behaved like a robot and appeared to need directions before she could act at all. In the interviews she would reiterate such questions as, "Why do you laugh?" "Do you feel happy when you smile?" "If I pinch you, will you feel sad?" "Do you cry when you feel sad?"' E. J. Anthony, 'A Clinical Evaluation of Children with Psychotic Parents,' in R. Cancro, ed., *The Schizophrenic Syndrome: An Annual Review*, vol. 1 (New York: Brunner/Mazel, 1971), pp. 252–53.

one of the means of neutralizing psychological and even physical pain is to exteriorize it, that is, to look at it as if from the outside. To use a drastic simile, Wittgenstein is like a patient scrutinizing himself detachedly as he is being operated on. He might even be his own surgeon —I've read of such a case. But when he describes what he is experiencing, it is in a tight voice issuing from a mask-face.

I think that Wittgenstein's effort to detach himself is also visible in his frequent use of the idea or image of the picture, for the picture is an impersonal representation or exteriorization. The index to *Philosophical Investigations* lists many references to it. The sub-entries under 'picture' are '(mental) picture, *cf.* image,' 'picture (in the sense of conception, model),' '(ordinary) picture, *cf.*, illustration, landscape, photograph, projection, representation, puzzle-picture,' '(*Tractatus*) picture.' This is not to mention the separate entries for 'picture-object' and 'picture-rabbit.'

Something in all this is style, something goes beyond it. There is a conspicuous discordance between the multiplied images of pain and the careful, wandering, obsessive, and objective talk, not about pain, but about the use of pain-words. I think that much of Wittgenstein's force is the ensuing sense of a troubled searching undertaken out of obscure motives. Though more aggressive and intellectually expressed, it is not unlike the condition attributed by Beckett to his character, Watt, caught as Watt is between words and inexpressibles:

> Not that for a moment Watt supposed that he had penetrated the forces at play, in this particular instance, or even perceived the forms that they upheaved, or obtained the least useful information, concerning himself, or Mr. Knott, for he did not. But he had turned, little by little a disturbance into words, he had made pillow of old words, for his head. Little by little, and not without labor.[16]

The key, stylistic and other, is perhaps given by a remark that I have already quoted in part. Wittgenstein says, 'Philosophy simply puts everything before use, and neither explains nor deduces anything.—Since everything lies open to view there is nothing to explain. For what is hidden, for example, is of no interest to us.'[17]

The last claim, that what is hidden is of no interest to us, sounds strange. Is this a renunciation of Wittgenstein's previous doctrine, that what is of most interest to us is necessarily beyond language and logic? Is the previous renunciation one, essentially, of language, and is this renunciation one of everything unknown, meaning, everything kept secret from it? Different answers are possible, as the literature on Wittgenstein shows. However, his claim should be taken, I think, as a wish. He again and again implies that, rightly observed, everything is what it is, to the degree that there cannot be anything more to see or say about seeing. Rightly observed, the surface either is or is exactly equivalent to the depth. 'The human body is the best picture of the human soul,' he says.[18] He feels that his precision cancels out secrets, or, in the terminology I would prefer, detaches or neutralizes them. Understanding philosophy then turns out to be seeing things precisely and saying what one sees and has somehow always known.

A Conjecture on Philosophical Atomism

The examples I have given of the relevance of style complete my argument on the relevance of psychology to philosophy; but I would like to add a pendant to this chapter, an attempt to show how the history of an important complex of philosophical ideas can be completed by psychological considerations. The conjecture I am about to make is hazardous, I admit. I cannot give anything like proof for it, and yet it seems to me, as I hope it will to you, rather plausible. If plausible, the ends of a fragmentary explanation are joined.

The complex of ideas to which I am referring is that which makes up philosophical atomism. It is shared, interestingly, by two distant, different groups of thinkers, the Buddhists and the Moslem theologians (the Mutakallimun), and by five modern Western philosophers, namely, Hume, Mach, James, Russell, and Wittgenstein (of the *Tractatus*). The list could be lengthened, but these two groups and five individuals are sufficient for my purposes. The Logical Positivists might be added.

The atomism that unites all these can be put positively or negatively. Positively, with certain philosophical or religious qualifications, the universe was taken to be atomic. Even sensation and perception were taken to be so, or, in other words, experience was regarded as an atomic construction. Negatively, again with some qualifications, every group and person I have named was opposed to the idea of a substantial or metaphysical soul, or to such soul-equivalents as a metaphysically coherent self or consciousness. Negatively, too, the Madhyamika Buddhists and all the rest in my list were opposed to the metaphysical idea of causality. It should also be noted, whether as a positive or negative doctrine I do not know, that many, perhaps most, Buddhist philosophers agreed with Hume, James, and Russell in accepting what was later called 'neutral monism,' the view that 'mind' and 'matter' are constructions we make out of something that is neither, but prior to both. Again, there are qualifications to be made, but they do not affect the basic argument.

Such views were held by the Buddhists and Moslems in question as, I would say, dogmas, designed to buttress their respective religions; but these dogmas were elaborated and defended with considerable philosophic acumen. The interest of the Buddhists was to convince everyone that substance in general and self in particular were illusions that kept people in the bonds of suffering, and that should therefore be destroyed. The intellectual instrument used to destroy the illusions was the dissolution of everything into its atomic constituents, the constituents being considered real or relatively real, and the assemblages made of them, quite unreal, which is to say, merely temporary, without independent existence, metaphysically illusory. This dissolution was extended, not only to every object and person, but to time as well, and, in some doctrines, to space. The Buddhist philosophers, it is true, though favouring nominalism and denying substances, including selves, did believe in an inexpressible transcendental reality, altogether beyond words. In this they were not unlike James and at least the earlier Wittgenstein.[1]

The conservative Muslim theologians, the Mutakallimun, were primarily inspired by their opposition to the deterministic philosophers, who were, in the Moslem context, Aristotelians (with a usually Neo-Platonic cast). These philosophers, the theologians held, were endangering belief in the primacy of God's will and, therefore, the faith of Islam. By their atomic dissolution of substances and of causal forces, the theologians left God as the only metaphysical reality. In terms of European philosophy, they were Occasionalists. Their atoms, like the Buddhist ones, had an only infinitesimal persistence in time, perishing 'as soon as' they came into being, having no power of existence in themselves, no 'own-being,' as the Buddhists would say. Except for their very atomicity, these atoms were very different from the Greek ones, for they were, not indestructible, but ephemeral and metaphysically contingent, and they composed, not only matter, but time and space as well.[2]

Clearly, there is a *prima facie* resemblance between all the atomists I have mentioned. The motives for the atomism of the Buddhists and Moslems are easily explained; but what of the others? Each of the other atomists states his philosophical arguments, of course; but something in these arguments sounds arbitrary or unfinished to me.

To explain what I have just said, I would like to go back in time for a moment, to the ancient Greeks. Then, before scientific arguments for atomism could be offered, atomism was only one of a number of metaphysical possibilities. How was a Greek to make a reasonable choice from among the ideas available to him? Within his intellectual reach, he had the Aristotelian conception of matter and form; the Pythagorean conception of numerical-geometrical structure; the Neo-Platonic conception of the many derived from the One; the Aristotelian conception (developed by commentators) of different minima for different materials; and the Stoic conception of world-tension, which bears some resemblance to modern field-theory. From our later standpoint, there were no good theoretical arguments, and, above all, almost no empirical tests. If we look back, it seems that a level-headed philosopher, whatever his instinctive preferences, ought to have sided with the restrainedly sceptical Academics, ought to have argued, with Sextus Empiricus, against all dogmatists, or ought, perhaps, to have joined Lucian in his antiphilosophical ironies.

What can we take to be good arguments on the matter? If we are thinking only of 'material' atoms, we should remember that their actual existence was still being disputed in the early twentieth century, by Mach and other philosophical scientists. It is often said that the first decisive arguments for the physical existence of atoms, as contrasted with their use as convenient fictions, were those given by Jean Perrin, when he and his assistants, peering through ultra-microscopes at tiny particles of gamboge and gum mastic in Brownian motion, were finally able to determine the average density, weight, and size of molecules and atoms. It was only in 1913, when Perrin described his work in a widely-sold book, that even stubborn opponents of atoms admitted them into the light of reality.[3]

Mach, though, held out. To him, microsensations, not atoms, were the source of experience, while all so-called material objects, including atoms, were consciously or unconsciously constructed symbols for relatively stable groups of sensation-elements. 'Whenever in later life, in Vienna, anyone spoke about atoms in his presence he would interrupt them with the question: Have you seen one? (Habn S' eins gsehn?).' Even his belief in elements of sensation remained tentative, because he did not like to grant them any metaphysical finality.[4]

The history of atomism therefore teaches us that in prescientific times there could not have been, by our standards, any decisive arguments for or against either the atomic hypothesis or its rivals. The choice between them could not have been simply rational. This is all the more true with respect to a theory of atomic sensations or perceptions.

I will admit that the idea of micro-sensations summated by us into perceptions has an intuitive plausibility greater, so far as I am concerned, than the competing ideas I can think of. The atomization of the self, however, seems to me contra-intuitive. I have no doubt that the arguments of such philosophers as Shankara, Augustine, and Descartes, which take self-existence to be self-evident, are natural to most people, while the contrary arguments, to the effect that the self is a mere collection of sensations and thoughts, are unnatural to them. To be fair, I will qualify and say that under certain cultural or psychological conditions, the naturalness of the arguments may tend to be reversed. Culturally, the kind of Buddhist or Moslem doctrines I have described may tend to reverse them, and, psychologically, sudden or chronic difficulties may also do so. But when Russell says that there is no central Jonesness in Jones, who is only a certain correlation among appearances, ordinary people without Buddhist training will, I feel sure, be puzzled, and the Joneses of the world will revolt. The genuinely felt absence of self is crippling.[5] Selfhood is, in a sense, even biochemical. The body's immune system 'recognizes' bacteria, viruses, transplants, and other foreign intrusions as 'non-self.' I do not contend that such facts must be philosophically decisive, but only that philosophers must take them seriously.

Therefore, when I think of the atomism of Hume, James, Russell, and Wittgenstein, I conclude that it must have been their inward experiences that made them receptive to the atomic disintegration of the self. To Russell, body and mind were only logical constructions, and the whole person only 'relations of the thoughts to each other and to the body.'[6] The position of Wittgenstein is more complicated, combining Hume and Russell, it seems, with Schopenhauer. Along with Hume and Russell, he argues that he can experience his own fragments, so to speak, but never himself as subject; with Russell, he argues that humans, like anything designated by 'proper names,' are no more than relatively coherent collections of 'simples'; and with Schopenhauer, he argues that the subject is not contained in but is the limit of the world, able, like the eye, to see everything but itself.[7] He thus resembles the Buddhists in disintegrating the self but believing, all the same, in what is beyond seeing or saying. For the present discussion, the fact that he was a philosophical atomist, to whatever final degree, is enough.

To my mind, the whole philosophical debate has been very incompletely rational. Chemistry and physics yielded evidence that made atomism rationally debatable, but not much before Dalton, whose table of atomic weights appeared in the early nineteenth century. Atomic sensation and perception have become, I suppose, rationally debatable in terms of the functioning of our nervous system; but scientific evidence has played no part, as far as I know, in twentieth-century arguments for philosophical atomism. Certainly, Russell's contention that it is logic that shows that human beings are only assemblages is extraordinarily divorced from empirical considerations. The history of philosophy testifies that neutral monism was only one view among others; and, at least until certain ideas of modern physics had taken root, the denial of metaphysical causality had no obvious rational advantages over its affirmation. Finally, there has been no necessary connection between atomism of matter and of self, between atomism of self and neutral monism, or between any one or all of these and denial of metaphysical causality. My stress on inward experience is therefore designed to answer an inclusive question: What joins this atomism with this egolessness with this neutral monism with this causelessness?

Please do not mistake me. When I contend that during most of the long debate over atomism there were no sufficient rational reasons for adopting atomic views, and surely none for uniting the various kinds of atomism, I do not mean that I am clever enough to have refuted the philosophers I have mentioned. The Europeans among them, it is needless to say, were capable, creative thinkers; and I can assure those who are unfamiliar with the Buddhist and Moslem philosophers in question that they were, at their best, distinctly sharp in argument. I mean only that if I disregard all non-philosophical explanations, that is, all historical and psychological ones, and confine myself, as best I can, to 'pure' philosophy, the preferences of these philosophers for their several atomisms become very nearly inexplicable. It is only when we consider the preferences historically, psychologically, and biographically, that they cease to be so nearly arbitrary.

To make my meaning clearer, let me undertake a brief sketch of the historical connections insofar as they are known to me. I begin with Moslem atomism. There are no signs that it was indigenous. We know that the Moslems were acquainted with Greek atomism, the influence of which is early evident in al-Razi, the philosopher-scientist of the ninth and tenth centuries. But the atomism of the Moslem theologians has pronounced Indian traits, a fact which, speaking historically, can easily be explained.[8]

The connection between Islamic and European philosophy was extensive, of course, in the Middle Ages, and Islamic atomism was well known to European philosophers. They had a clear, comprehensive summary of it in Maimonides' *Guide of the Perplexed*, and it also appeared in the Latin translation of Averroes. In the thirteenth century, Thomas Aquinas levelled an attack on Islamic atomism, while in the fourteenth, Nicholas of Autrecourt, the 'medieval Hume,' was, it appears, influenced by it.[9] To complete the historical chain in the most summary way, Aquinas and Nicholas of Autrecourt were known, the latter perhaps only indirectly, to Malebranche, and Malebranche was known to Berkeley and Hume. In his *Treatise*, Hume refers to a chapter in Malebranche to which Malebranche attaches an explanation that says, 'I deny that my

Will is the true cause of the Motion of my Arm, of the Ideas of my Mind, and of other things which accompany my Volitions. For I see no Relation between so different things.'[10]

It is evident that there may have been a historical tie between all the atomists I have been discussing. But the tie was always optional, for there were always, as I have said, other views to choose from; and ordinary people must usually have had an intuitive preference for the unatomized, metaphysical self, the self that, we know, Hindu and European philosophers generally preferred. Like the simply philosophical justification, the historical tie is not enough to explain why a certain complex of atomic ideas attracted philosophers at such different times and places, and why, even if the tie existed, it carried the ideas successfully from culture to culture and philosopher to philosopher. Why, in other words, was the option exercised? Other kinds of explanation having proved insufficient, I find it helpful to complete them with a psychological one. Put, I am afraid, with brutal quickness, the psychological explanation is this: Malebranche, Hume, James, Russell, and Wittgenstein were all undermined by suffering. At least Hume, James, Russell, and Wittgenstein underwent deep depressions, and all were tempted by suicide—Hume on only one known occasion, however. All of these four adopted approximately Buddhist solutions to the pains of life. I forbear adding details and documentation, which will be provided later, in the biographical accounts. I may add that Malebranche, whom I will not treat biographically, underwent both physical and emotional suffering. In his youth, it is said, he had 'all the sicknesses known in his times.'[11]

Of Mach, I know less. I know of no suicidal depression; but he underwent the approximately mystical experience I have reported on a previous page, he had difficulty, from childhood on, with the perspectival recession of three-dimensional objects, and he had difficulty as a child, strange as it may sound, in perceiving causal connections. His father, disappointed with his failure to learn, ridiculed him. The upshot was that he was isolated, lonely, and sensitive. A biographer reports:

> Mach's aversion to the notion of force was both ontological and ethical and was grounded in his childhood upbringing and health. Mach was physically weak, frequently ill, engaged in no contact sports, is not known to have been physically punished, and always disliked military 'heroes' and people who triumphed by 'force'.[12]

Like James, Hume, Russell, and Wittgenstein, Mach adopted a near-Buddhist solution. This was so evident that his writings were soon translated into Burmese. In later life, he was glad to acknowledge his kinship with Buddhism and his hope to attain Nirvana. To him, the sciences were a form of Buddhism, and he praised them for 'making man disappear in the All, in annihilating him, so to speak.'[13]

The conclusion can now be reached. From the standpoint of an ordinary man with the ordinary 'unenlightened' desire to live, Buddhism teaches something akin to suicide, in other words, the painfulness and worthlessness of the desire itself. From the standpoint of an ordinary Westerner with ordinary self-sufficiency, Islam teaches a difficult self-abnegation or 'submission' to the will of God. These are self-abolitions of one or another sort. It does not require much thought to grasp that concern with suicide may be related to the philosophical abolition of the self. Nor does it take much knowledge of psychology to understand that depression, with its accompaniment of depersonalization and derealization, can destroy one's feeling of internal and external unity, continuity, and reality. In such a condition, one feels oneself or the world or both to be unreal, the quality of subjective time may vary, and every ordinarily continuous experience may be subjectively fragmented. Such a condition changes one's attitude towards self, toward substance, and toward causality. It is even possible that metaphysical causality will be denied in order, somehow, to loosen the malign, intractable grip on oneself of whatever is felt to be the cause of one's suffering.

I am not confident that my explanation of the atomic thought-complex is correct. It may well be mistaken historically, psychologically, or biographically. Even if basically right, it is, I am sure, too simple. Besides, as I said in beginning my explanation, it can in no reasonable sense be proved. Yet it has explanatory power. It helps complete the answer to the question why all these so apparently different men became convinced of the same unobvious views.

4

Creation

An Illustrative Myth

Rather many pages ago, at the beginning of this book, I anticipated your question with my own, and asked, for my sake no less than yours, why I was writing it. I gave three answers, which I assumed I might generalize. My first answer, that I wanted to persuade you, therefore led me to consider the importance to philosophers of the desire to persuade.

Hoping that I might have been persuasive, I went on to my second answer, that I had something to say that seemed to me both true and important. To make myself clear (and persuasive), I then explained my attitude towards truth. My obvious purpose was to counter the usual objections that are levelled against any position such as mine. With the same purpose in mind, I related the idea of truth to that of relevance, and I distinguished a more narrow, technical sense of relevance from a broader one. The narrower sense, I argued, helped to maintain the integrity of a field of study, but the broader one helped to understand the whole object of study more completely or deeply. To see better, we may have to violate a border and gain some new vantage ground. I proposed that philosophers gain the vantage ground of psychology. Having enumerated the ways in which insight might profit as a result, I began to illustrate them by means of an analysis of three philosophical styles and a brief, speculative account of philosophical atomism.

Now, having finished two of my answers, I have reached the third: After prolonged thought, I feel the need to express myself on the subject. Generalizing, as before, from myself, I would like to discuss the need to create. I cannot confine this discussion to philosophy, but I will try to make helpful distinctions and give philosophical examples.

Every philosopher worth the name creates a pattern of ideas. This pattern must be, at least in part, the truth he is looking for. Has he discovered this truth or invented it? The answer varies in accord with the philosopher's personality and philosophical stand. In terms of his own efforts, he feels, I suppose, that his philosophy is created by himself; but if he also feels, as do most philosophers, that his philosophy consists of objective truths, it follows that he can only have discovered what was already in existence. I think that most philosophers are, in fact, ambivalent on this point and would emotionally prefer to be regarded as in some sense the proprietors and even creators of the truths they have discovered. My own, verbal solution is to say that a philosopher does not create, but constructs his philosophy, by making his own particular order among the truths he has discovered for his philosophy. That is, a philosopher cannot discover a new truth or a new nuance of an old truth without in a sense, the sense of idiosyncratic formulation, choice, or arrangement, constructing it. Every truth-construction a philosopher makes is therefore also a personal one.

This construction of the truth is not, of course, limited to philosophers. It is also practiced by poets, novelists, artists, and scientists. They all begin with an obscure stirring, an attraction the source of which they probably cannot recognize, and possibly do not want to. They see the world around them in the light of their own natures. The world, like themselves, is obscure or unformed, and it needs, in consequence, to be investigated and shaped; and as the external difficulty is resolved or the external material shaped, the internal world is felt to be more clearly known or more clearly shaped.

As I write this, I am reminded of an Indian creation myth from South America. The hero of the myth, the father of the tribe, was named He-who-is-appearance-only. In the beginning, the myth says, there was nothing but mere appearance, nothing really existed. All that He-who-is-appearance-only could try to grasp was a phantasm, an illusion. But phantasms are by nature like dreams, and so it was a dream that enabled He-who-is-appearance-only to press the phantasm to his breast. There was nothing to support it, and it was only by means of his breath that he could hold it attached to the thread of a dream. Because, as he could see, there was nothing, he said, 'I have attached that which was non-existent.' Then he extended his fingers again. They searched for the empty phantasm and tied the emptiness to the dream-thread and held it, magically, like a fluff of raw cotton. He-who-is-appearance-only seized the bottom of the phantasm and stamped upon it again and again. Then, having dreamed it and stamped it solid, he finally allowed himself to stand upon the dreamed earth. Standing there, he continued and completed the act of creation.[1]

This legend seems insightful to me. I do not think it extravagant to say that every deeply creative writer, artist, scientist, and philosopher at first approximates its hero and is in some way unreal to himself. There is, I think, a confusion in life between the undesired and the unreal, and a constant temptation to think away the reality of whatever is not desired, just as there is a contrary temptation, to think whatever is desired into reality. I will later discuss the effect of death on the sense of reality. I have no doubt that it can be strong. At any rate, the deeply creative person is dissatisfied with what he finds. He looks for something else. The world he sees, because it is not the world he wants, is rejected and, as rejected, felt to be insubstantial. To escape this insubstantiality, he sinks himself into his dreams, though he knows that they are dreams and not yet a world for him. He searches and finds something too amorphous to be real, but projects this into his dreams. By projecting, dreaming, and thinking it, he gives it emotional solidity, makes of it an emotive or intellectual ground on which to stand, and, standing there, he continues to create what he has discovered. To the extent that this process succeeds, he and his world lose their illusory quality. The one stands, the other supports, and each lends the other substance.

A semi-failure, doubt, or insubstantiality can also result. Think of the tension between success and failure in Kafka, who writes in a parable of the

> many who complained that the words of the wise are always mere parables, and of no use in daily life, which is the only life we have . . . One man then said, 'Why do you resist? If you followed the parables, then you would become parables yourselves, and thus free of your daily cares.' Another said: 'I bet that is a parable.' The first said: 'You have won.' The second said: 'But unfortunately only in parable.' The first said: 'No, in reality in parable you have lost.'[2]

Many of the examples to be given in this chapter will echo the truth of the Indian myth and the sub-truth of the Kafkan parable. Søren Kierkegaard illustrates the truth with unusual directness. He himself gives life and existence, he says, to the 'pale, bloodless midnight shapes' he fights against. By his insight and creative ability, he knows how to reduplicate thought dialectically so that it becomes, not simply thought, but life itself. 'It is one thing,' he says, 'to be penetrating in books, and another to redouble that which is thought, dialectically, in existence . . . The dialectic in books is merely that of thought, but the reduplication of that thought is action in life.'[3]

Nietzsche, who knows the myth-truth well, says that man's 'needs as a creator invent the world upon which he works, anticipate it; this anticipation (this "belief" in truth) is his support.' In an image, almost a parable, of his own, Nietzsche says of genuine philosophers, 'With a creative hand they reach for the future, and all that is and has been becomes a means for them, an instrument, a hammer. Their "knowing" is *creating*, their creating is a legislation, their will to truth is—*will to power*.'[4]

Writers, Artists, Scientists, Philosophers

The desire, even the need to create is common to persons of all sorts. Many of them approximate philosophers, at least in some eyes, including their own. Poets and novelists, for instance, often resemble philosophers, and it seems clear to me that the distinction between them and philosophers fluctuates in accord with different personal, professional, and social demands. We continue to think of the poetic Presocratics and of Lucretius as philosophers, although they find their places in the histories of literature; Dante and Shakespeare have what is known, no doubt ambiguously, as a philosophic temperament; and Mallarmé hopes to catch and concentrate the truth into some echoing semblance of itself. Schelling, Schopenhauer, and Nietzsche on art as philosophy have already been cited. To the Germans, as it is unnecessary to say, Goethe can be everything. If I go on to more recent poets I have read, I recall Valéry, who has provided me with apt quotations, and Wallace Stevens and Auden, who are temperamentally philosophical. In praise of poetry, an ancient Greek philosopher said, 'Poetry is a more philosophical and serious business than history; for poetry speaks more of universals, history of particulars.'[1] A more recent, more poetic philosopher said, 'Singing and thinking are the stems neighbour to poetry. They grow out of Being and reach into its truth.'[2]

It is not surprising that writers by no means professional philosophers may regard their ideas, even when quite explicit, as a central and integral part of their writing. There are so many examples that they need hardly be cited. Certainly, among the novelists, Balzac, Zola, Turgenev, Tolstoy, Kafka, Mann, and Musil are also novelists of ideas, sometimes only a step away from the more personal, imaginative, or poetic philosophers, such as Pascal, Kierkegaard, Nietzsche, James, Bergson, Unamuno, Ortega y Gasset, Heidegger, and Sartre. Hume and Berkeley are exceptionally gifted writers; and Rousseau, Voltaire, and Diderot, whatever we think of the stringency of their reasoning, are, each in his own person, thinkers of historic stature, talented storytellers, and men with a great gift for language.

The relationship of these men of words to those who create in non-verbal media is not simple. Some aestheticians favour the analogy between the verbal and non-verbal arts, and others do not. But many painters, sculptors, dancers, musicians, and architects have had a sense of mission and have regarded their art as a demi-ethics, demi-philosophy, or demi-theology. By their own standards, they might be considered non-verbal philosophers. Leonardo, it may be recalled, regarded painting as 'a subtle invention which brings [natural] philosophy and subtle speculation to bear on the nature of all forms.' To him, the painter, like a lesser god, contained the universe, first in his mind, and then in his hands.[3]

To skip, for the sake of illustration, to another century and another, lesser, painter, we may recall the belief of Mondrian, who wrote, 'The evolution of consciousness [in art] causes beauty to evolve *into truth.*'[4] It may also be recalled that the surrealist painter, Magritte, thought of himself as philosophical, because he was concerned to question stereotyped habits of thought. His work is said 'to disclose the intellectual integrity and searching mind of a philosopher rather than the aesthetic and painterly concerns of an artist.'[5]

Having so far stressed possible likenesses, let me try to make some distinctions. Let me try, first, to distinguish between artists in general, including poets and novelists, and scientists in general. The work of artists is emotionally more transparent, that of scientists, correspondingly, emotionally more opaque. In the case of scientists, the desires, emotions, or fantasies go, as it were, through a series of filters that deprive them of their particularity. The artists use colour, texture, shape, weight, sound, and bodily movement, all of which have a close, more or less primitive and organic correspondence with emotions, while the scientists use an often mathematical theory, mechanical and electronic equipment, not to speak of the isolating uniformity of the laboratory, and the stylized empirical test—for the sake of a clear contrast, I have ignored the contemporary artists who, like scientists, express themselves by means of mechanical and electronic equipment.

Now think, not of the media used, but of the individuality of the users. The artist I am imagining wants to be appreciated for himself, is openly egoistic in his art, wants to compel other sensibilities to merge with his. In contrast to him, the scientist I am imagining wants, at least on the surface, to become unindividual, that is, assimilated into science, and so, in the end, unegoistic, or, perhaps I should say, pan-egoistic, for he is willing to merge his sensibilities and intellect with those of the other scientists. The artist is openly ambivalent, takes intellectual abstractions to be illusory, and creates individual concretions of his ambivalence. The scientist, in contrast, tries to avoid self-contradiction, of which ambivalence is the emotional counterpart, tends to take abstractions, in the ordinary sense of the word, to be real, and participates in the joint creation of logically structured theories. He hopes for objectivity and wagers his professional life on his ability to achieve it.

I find these distinctions hard to make and I am unsure of them. I can easily think, as perhaps you can, of objections. I know that artists and scientists are individuals. I am trying, however, to describe them as types, because I believe that philosophers, to the extent that they are distinguishable, fall between the artists and scientists. The philosophers exist, I mean to say, in the always-unresolved tension between art and science. I will therefore now try to distinguish between scientists in general and philosophers in general, though the medium of both is abstract ideas, and though each of them is undoubtedly an individual.

I have already stated the banal and approximate truths by which we characterize scientists. Scientific ideas must be submitted to public, relatively exact, historically established tests. Although it is hardly possible for theoretical scientists to give up philosophizing altogether, they make the attempt to look on it as the subjective accompaniment of objective thinking. They attempt, in other words, to cut thought loose from its more individual characteristics. Ideas for which acceptably rigorous tests cannot be established are excluded and, together with them, questions that thoughtful men necessarily ask themselves and answer. Many of the conclusions that express or rule our acts have not been the subject of an exact science and will never, I think, be scientifically validated or invalidated.

This conclusion leads us to the philosophers. Like other persons working in the medium of ideas, philosophers try to resolve dissonances between the ideas with which they are professionally concerned. Often, as I have said, they have searched for exact laws, for the discovery of which they have tried to invent new, potent methods. There is much, then, in which the philosopher may be taken to resemble the scientist. But while the scientist can use the laws and formulas of others without adaptation, the philosopher, working more personally, creates the bond between himself and other interested men by translating previous philosophy into his own. To do so, he must display the shared ideas he intends to translate or has already translated; but he cannot remain faithful to the intentions of their original authors. To translate, he must mistranslate, must quote selectively, rearrange, distinguish by his own criteria what is and is not important, and always appear to understand a previous philosopher better than the philosopher understood himself. In Husserl's seminar, for example, when texts from classical philosophers, such as Descartes, Hume, Berkeley, or Fichte, were the ostensible subject of discussion, the real subject was always Husserl's own thought.[6] Wittgenstein used to stimulate himself by imagining the historical development of thought to have been different from what it actually had been.[7] As Kant explained to students, 'Every philosophical thinker builds his own work, so to speak, on the ruins of another.'[8] The more creative the thinker, the more intellectually ruthless he is likely to be, the less punctilious in acknowledging his sources, the less just in judging other thinkers. 'I have understood something when it seems to me that I could have invented it; and I know

it completely when I end by believing that it is I who have discovered it.'[9]
Then, with full confidence in my rights as its discoverer, I establish and
modify its interpretation. My piracy has become my property.*

Philosophers Are Vague, Philosophy Is Dense

I have made whatever distinctions I can. I would like to assume their
approximate truth and now try to define the philosopher, the exemplar
or archetype that seems to preside over the actual motley of
philosophers. To be sure, there are difficulties in the way of the
definition, of which two, of quite different kinds, obtrude themselves.
The first difficulty, which I have emphasized and illustrated, is that
history affords us many different exemplars of the philosopher. To make
the definition possible, therefore, I will assume that it might not have
been suitable for any earlier period of history. This assumption allows
me to exploit the sharp contemporary contrast between philosophy and
exact science, and allows me, further, to refer, rather circularly, to an
already existing tradition of philosophy.

Even, however, if I restrict my definition to the present, I am faced
with many fairly different exemplars. I have been speaking of the creative
philosopher, as if it were self-evident that all interesting philosophers
were creative, or as if creativity were a self-evident quality of
philosophizing. Nothing of this is really self-evident. More than a few
philosophers are scholars or critics at heart. Though philosophers by
profession, they identify themselves more with those who read then who
renovate philosophy, and they make philosophies into termini of
thought rather than its points of departure. It has been noted that many
of the famous critics of literature and art—men such as Samuel Johnson,
Sainte-Beuve, Macaulay, Ruskin, and Berenson—had no children. I do
not know if this generalization can be extended very far, or if it applies to
the philosopher-critics. I would like, however, to hazard the guess that
system-makers and poets of abstractions cherish their systems or
philosophic poetry as if they were children, while the philosopher-critics
do not cherish, but discipline such children, and may even attempt to
criticize them to death.[1]*

---

*Much the same has been said of poets (and could be said of others). See H. Bloom, *The
Anxiety of Influence* (New York: Oxford University Press, 1973). The distinguished historian of philosophy, Harry Wolfson, used to contend that philosophy should be studied as
the history of the misunderstanding of the concepts of one philosopher by another.
Philosophical ideas evolve, he said, in a series of transformations by intentional and unin-
tentional misunderstanding.

*A description of the English physicist, Ernst Rutherford (1871–1934), makes the
distinction between creator and critic particularly clear. 'He had no use for critics of any

The relation of the philosopher-critic to the philosopher, text, or system he criticizes may well be that of hostile dependence. But the relation between philosopher and philosophy is something I mean to go into soon, and here I will simply ignore the difference between the creative philosopher and the philosopher-critic, though the dominant figure in my imagination is undoubtedly the creative one.

I now come to my second difficulty in defining, which is the tinge of irony I cannot eradicate from my definition. The truth is that I find it hard, at this point, to distinguish between the ironical and the factual. Perhaps this is because my expectations were misdirected for so long, or perhaps because, as Kierkegaard would insist, the full truth about human beings can be put only indirectly and ironically.

Ironically enough, after all these preliminaries, my definition of the philosopher is bound to appear, not only over-simple, as it is, but anticlimatic. By way, then, of anti-climax: *The philosopher is the person who thinks vaguely, intensively, and, he hopes, fundamentally, in close relation to the traditions of philosophy.*

If this definition appears too non-committal, I am willing to hazard another, the ironical sound of which is stronger. This time, the definition stresses the philosopher's creativity as a form of intellectual radicalism. Philosophers take positions very strange to ordinary people. They have, that is, an inner need to choose between alternatives that to ordinary people are not worth distinguishing, or a need to pursue ideas well beyond the bounds of common sense. From this perspective, then: *The philosopher is the person who tries to persuade people to accept abstract, unscientific ideas that seem, at least at first, absurdly scrupulous, outrageously exaggerated, or, simply, fantastic.* In proposing this definition, I am seemingly ignoring the possibility of a truly common-sense philosopher (who might, if he existed, be particularly outrageous), and ignoring the possible likeness, which I will discuss later, between the philosopher and the psychotic.

Though I am smiling as I write this, I am also serious. The ironical-sounding qualities I have been ascribing to the philosopher are just those that have enabled him to stimulate others intellectually, sometimes, as in the case of Plato, Aristotle, and other great

---

kind. He felt both suspicion and dislike of the people who invested scientific research or any other branch of creation with an aura of difficulty, who used long, methodical words to explain things which he did perfectly by instinct. "Those fellows," he used to call them. "Those fellows" were the logicians, the critics, the metaphysicians. They were clever; they were usually more lucid than he was; in argument against them he often felt at a disadvantage. Yet somehow they never produced a serious piece of work, whereas he was the greatest experimental scientist of the age.' C. P. Snow, *Variety of Men* (Harmondsworth: Penguin Books, 1969), pp. 16–17.

philosophers, over many hundreds of years. These qualities of vagueness, intensiveness, scrupulousness, exaggeration, and fantasticality are those that determine, when embodied in effective philosophical words, that a great philosophy, like a great painting, novel, or poem, cannot be exhaustively analyzed. It has a verbal body like the one a poet constructs, the inexhaustibility of which is described by Valéry in these words:

> The poet's business is to construct a sort of verbal body that has the solidity as well as the ambiguity of an object. Experience shows that an over-simple poem, for example an abstract one, is inadequate, and exhausted at first sight. It is no longer even a poem. The ability to be reread, savored again, depends on the number of meanings compatible with the text, and this number itself results from a clarity that imposes the obligation to interpret, and an indefiniteness that repels interpretation . . . The *meaning* of poems is only a quasi-necessity, not a *goal* . . . A comprehensible but 'beautiful' line of poetry *is beautiful by what is incomprehensible in it . . . The stimulus must therefore be situated in the incomprehensible.*[2]

Valéry's idea that a poem repels essential interpretation is old and widely accepted, of course. Our contemporary paradigm of the great philosopher, Wittgenstein, accepts it without qualification.[3] It is true, he says, that language can manifest something of our ultimate interests, something of the ethical or religious meaning of life; but the expression of this meaning in words has no analysable content, for ultimates are beyond logic, reason, words. Nothing we say about them, he holds, turns on the truth, falsity, or meaninglessness of the words.[4] Whereas I have merely attributed vagueness to philosophy and implied that this vagueness has often been constructive, Wittgenstein must regard philosophy as either inexorably shallow or emptily ambitious. I find his position or positions facile and verging on dogmatism. Unlike the earlier Wittgenstein, I do not believe that there is a clearly fixed limit to our ability to explain, and, unlike the later Wittgenstein, do not believe that philosophy depends on an imprecise use of words, twisted awry, out of their natural contexts. I think that questions on ethics, religion, or the meaning of life can be answered as well as most other general ones. The answers are likely to be inadequate, but not completely so; and the feeling of their adequacy is often, as I have contended, a subjective matter related to a particular notion of relevance.

Despite what I have just said, great philosophy is philosophy that is never fully explained. This fact may be taken to indicate that, like poetry, it has a not fully verbalizable content, which one must also feel. It seems to me, to be a little more explicit, that a philosophy is great, not because it is inexplicable, but because it is hyper-explicable, by which I mean, subject to many, always partial or temporary explanations.

A philosophy that arouses particular interest arouses a particularly thorough and subtle explanation. The more thorough and subtle this explanation, the greater the possibilities for objection to it, and the greater the demand for another or a still more thorough and subtle explanation; and the longer the interest is sustained and the more widely it is spread, the greater the number of interpreters with different points of view that will turn to it. In other words, the more this philosophy is explained, the more it will appear to need explanation, and the more explanations it will in fact receive.

I do not mean to imply that this process of increasing explanation is never interrupted. But if I am right, Valéry's measure of a poem by its incomprehensibility supplies a partial measure of a philosophy as well. When, like the poem he speaks of, a philosophical text unites clarity with indefiniteness, and when, in spite of its interpreters, it remains attractively enigmatic, its interpretation does not come to an end. Its value then resides less in its meaning as fixed by any particular interpretation, even its author's, than in its ability to generate new meanings. Clear, vague, attractive, and dense, it continues to arouse life and so to reveal the life that has been successfully transferred to it.

Creative Autonomy

What kind of person is it who toils to establish such a densely expressive life outside himself? His interest in creating recognizably personal extensions of himself is, among other things, I think, a demand for autonomy, for the right to constitute himself imaginatively or intellectually as he pleases. I would expect a person of this kind to be stubbornly individual in what most concerns him and to resist all encroachments on his self-expression.[1] I am reminded of the intellectual autonomy so often demanded and exhibited by philosophers—of the whole proud independence exhibited by Socrates; of 'the elbowroom in all directions' that Montaigne needed; of the detachment from philosophical tradition willed by Descartes; of the detachment from community and past willed by Spinoza; of the desire of even the young Hobbes 'to prove things after my own sense'; of Locke's hatred for a 'slavish temper'; of Hume's decision, born in illness and depression, to depend on his own reasonings alone; of Kant's intractable freedom and advocacy of freedom; of Schelling's axiom, 'The beginning and end of all philosophy is—freedom'; of Nietzsche's exclamation, 'Independence of soul! . . . No sacrifice is too great for that'; of Wittgenstein's satisfied remark, 'It is good that I did not let myself be influenced.'[2]

Such examples could easily be multiplied; but at least a few of the great philosophers should be allowed to express themselves on the matter more fully. Let us, to begin with, take Leibniz. His autonomy as a thinker, he said, was based on the fact that he had taught himself and that he had looked for something new in every science, even before he had understood its already established content. His reward, he said, was double:

> First, I did not fill my head with empty and cumbersome teachings accepted on the authority of the teacher instead of sound arguments; second, I did not rest until I had traced back to the tissues and roots of every teaching and had penetrated to its principles. By such training I was enabled to discover by my own effort everything with which I was concerned.[3]

Hume, so opposed to Leibniz philosophically, was like him in his need for autonomy. When he was sixteen years old, he was already writing to a friend, 'I hate task reading.'[4] Although his family assumed that he was destined for the law, Hume himself, he says, 'found an unsurmountable Aversion to every thing but the pursuits of Philosophy and general Learning'; and from the Abbé Dubos, who wrote that every man of genius had a particular aptitude, he took the reflection, 'Too careful and elaborate an Education prejudicial; because it learns one to trust to others for one's Judgement.'[5] During his long crisis, which will be described, between the ages of about eighteen and twenty-three, Hume read widely and became convinced that earlier philosophers had been too subjective and imaginative, so that he had no choice but to depend on himself alone. He wrote:

> I believe 'tis a certain Fact that most of the Philosophers who have gone before us, have been overthrown by the Greatness of their Genius, that little more is requir'd to make a man succeed in this Study than to throw off all Prejudices either for his own Opinions or for those of others. At least this is all I have to depend on for the Truth of my Reasoning, which I have multiply'd to such a degree, that within these three years, I find I have scribbled many a Quire of Paper, in which there is nothing contain'd but my own Inventions.[6]

Like the young Hume, the young Berkeley was determined to be his own man. In his philosophical notebooks, he wrote to himself:

> I am young, I am an upstart, I am a pretender, I am vain, very well. I shall Endeavour patiently to bear up under the most lessening, vilifying appelations the pride & rage of man can devise. But one thing, I know, I am not guilty of, I do not pin my faith on the sleeve of any great man. I act not out of prejudice & prepossession. I do not adhere to any opinion because it is an old one, a receiv'd one, a fashionable one, or one that I have spent much time in the study and cultivation of.[7]

Like the other philosophers I have been citing, Kant insisted on his autonomy, which seems to have been painfully infringed on in his childhood. He continued to remember with 'fear and alarm' the 'youthful slavery' of his school days, when he had been forced to pray regularly. Stimulated, it may be supposed, by such memories, he insisted that the will of children should never be broken by discipline and reduced to slavishness. He went so far as to advocate that a child should be taught to endure opposition and privation, in order 'to acquire those things which are necessary to make him independent.'[8]

The autonomy he demanded for children, Kant also demanded, of course, for adults. To him, the subjection of the actions of one man to the will of another was dreadful. Concretely and abstractly, he demanded autonomy. Of himself, still a young philosopher-scientist, he said, 'I have already fixed on the path I mean to keep to. I will set out on my course, and nothing will hinder me from accomplishing it.'[9] Beyond his own, personal autonomy, he proclaimed that of man as such. In his *Anthropology,* he argued that a child, unlike an animal, enters the world with loud cries, 'for he regards his inability to make use of his limbs as *constraint* and so immediately announces his claim to freedom.'*

The 'savage' not yet used to submission, he said, 'knows of no greater misfortune than falling into it.'[10] Very generally, 'Every rational being exists as an end in himself,' and 'The *autonomy* of the will is the sole principle of all moral laws and of the duties conforming to them.'[11]

To guard his autonomy, like the savages he imagined warring in order to keep their distance and freedom, Kant kept a frequently hostile distance from other philosophers. Although he had partial praise for a number of them, especially Hume, who had given him, he thought, useful insights, he had no philosophical heroes. The Scholastics and Spinoza were, in his eyes, only mistaken; Socrates, though a lover of wisdom, was still a barbarian; and Leibniz, though full of learning, was dogmatic. For a moment in his career, he was enthusiastic over Rousseau; but then his usual resistance set in, he tried to examine him rationally, undistracted by his beautiful style, and he found 'strange and absurd opinions,' theatrical eccentricity, and hypochondria.[12] Briefly, in Kant's view, 'The true philosopher, as a self-thinker,' must regard all systems of philosophy as objects for his own critical philosophizing and 'must make free, not slavishly imitative use of his reason.'[13]

---

*Like Kant, Kant's infant demands independence, while, like Hegel, Hegel's demands interdependence. According to Hegel, when the infant makes its wants known by screaming, it shows that it feels certain of its right to demand the satisfaction of its needs from the world. *Hegel's Philosophy of Mind,* trans. W. Wallace & A. V. Miller (London: Oxford University Press, 1971), pp. 58–59 (section 396, *Zusatz*).

My last example of the philosopher's demand for autonomy is that of Husserl. According to him, everything in true philosophy must be established by the philosopher's own thought. 'Amid the chaos of philosophies,' only such an autonomous thinker 'realizes that he has really no choice at all, since no one of these has taken care to free itself from presuppositions, and none has sprung from the radical attitude of autonomous self-responsibility which the meaning of a philosophy demands.'[14]

Incomprehensible Beginnings

The philosopher's search for autonomy, which, I assume, begins early in life, may be taken for granted. Its beginning and even its presence may never, as such, have interested him, for he may never have known its absence; but philosophers have sometimes experienced the search as an endless, incomprehensible passion, and have then been acutely conscious of it. It may have been aroused, as we have seen, by some event, at times nothing more, externally, than the reading of a book, even an incomprehensible one, that exerts a strange attraction.

Because we have been speaking of Husserl, the attraction of incomprehensible reasoning may be illustrated by the way Heidegger was first attracted to this philosopher. Heidegger was then a theological student whose own attempts to penetrate into philosophy led him, he tells us, to Aristotle's distinction of the different meanings of 'being.' To help himself decide which meaning might be basic, he borrowed the two volumes of Husserl's *Logical Investigations* from the library; but though he kept them on his desk for a long time, they were of no help. As Heidegger explains, he could not understand them. 'I was so perplexed by Husserl's work,' he says, 'that in the following years I read it repeatedly, without sufficient insight into that which captivated me. The charm that emanated from the work extended to the externals of the printed surface and the title page.' Heidegger adds that he returned to Husserl's book several years later, but although he started it repeatedly, it became clear to him only in 1913, with the publication of Husserl's *Ideas*.[1]

I cannot guess what Husserl himself would have thought of the attractive power of his book, or whether he would have been puzzled that his passionate search for clarity could attract more by its passion than by whatever clarity it shed. For Husserl believed that philosophers, unlike scientists or artists, could adopt their profession only by means of a deliberate, conscious, rational choice. Compare the philosopher with the scientist and artist, he says. The scientist and the artist may each have a pure love for the fields they enter, but this love can develop unconsciously, by a kind of straying. The philosopher, however, must necessarily make a personal resolution—no one can stray into philosophy by accident.

The contrast Husserl has drawn between artist and scientist, on the one hand, and philosopher, on the other, does not strike me as plausible. But when he describes the philosopher, he is undoubtedly thinking of himself, and he is animated by his own sense of mission. Abstract, repetitive, and turgid as he generally is, he now grows enthusiastically voluble and sweeps the reader, as he may have swept his auditors, along the current of his enthusiasm. No one, he says, can stray into philosophy by accident, because the philosopher's desire to know is so comprehensive and fundamental that he must soon lose his naiveté and impose on himself a new, universal, and absolute radicalism. He must assume the risk, by himself, or in association with others like him, of searching out the ultimate foundation of truth and science; he must search for the transcendental clarity that drives out the chimeras of both scepticism and dogmatic metaphysics; he must, like Descartes, question all his previous convictions, however they were acquired; and then, and only then, he must try to approach the ideal, the knowledge that, in all its breadth, unites rational and irrational, intuitive and non-intuitive, and embraces all judgment and all the acts of the self.[2]

The Husserl who speaks in this way, the inspired Husserl, would disagree with my contention that a philosopher is unlikely to be clearly aware of the motives that lie behind his choice of profession. Yet I wonder if his passionate devotion to the philosophic quest, a kind of knight-errantry in pursuit of the radical, absolute, and universal truth, could have been explained by him except as a self-evident, self-imposed task. However this may be, his last years were spent in the mood of doubt, historical assessment, and even, perhaps, of compromise. 'The dream,' he said, whether in sorrow or irony, 'is over.' He expressed himself with considerable ambivalence and acknowledged that philosophy began as an enigma and remained one, except to 'secondary thinkers, who should not, in truth, be called philosophers.' Emphasizing that the philosopher 'understands the others in whose company, in critical friendship and enmity, he philosophizes,' he said:

> I know, of course, what I am striving for under the title of philosophy, as the goal and domain of my work. And yet I do not know. What autonomous thinker has ever been satisfied with this, his 'knowledge'? For what autonomous thinker has 'philosophy,' in his philosophizing life, ever ceased to be an enigma?[3]

Not long after Husserl's death, the English philosopher and archeologist R. G. Collingwood published his autobiography, which dwells on the enigmatic beginning of his interest in philosophy and on the repeated wellings up, which he could not understand, of his need to work on philosophical problems. The memorable occasion on which Collingwood first felt attracted to philosophy was that on which, out of simple curiosity, he took down a little black book that bore the title, *Kant's Theory of Ethics.* As the eight-year-old began reading this translation of the *Grundlegung zur Metaphysik der Sitten,* he was attacked by a strange succession of emotions. The first emotion was intense excitement, for he felt that things were being said that he must at all costs understand. Then, to his shame, came the discovery that, although the words of the book were English and its sentences grammatical, its meaning baffled him. 'Then, third and last,' says Collingwood,

> came the strangest emotion of all. I felt that the contents of this book, although I did not understand it, were somehow my business; a matter personal to myself, or rather to some future self of my own . . . I did not, in any natural sense of the word, 'want' to master the Kantian ethics when I should be old enough; but I felt as if a veil had been lifted and my destiny revealed.
>
> There came upon me by degrees, after this, a sense of being burdened with a task whose nature I could not define except by saying, 'I must think.' What I was to think about I did not know; and when, in obeying this command, I fell silent and absent-minded in company, or sought solitude in order to think without interruption, I could not have said, and still cannot say, what it was that I actually thought. There were no particular questions that I asked myself; there were no special objects upon which I directed my mind; there was only a formless and aimless intellectual disturbance, as if I were wrestling with a fog.
>
> I know now that this is what always happens when I am in the early stages of work on a problem. Until the problem has gone a long way towards being solved, I do not know what it is; all I am conscious of is the vague perturbation of mind, this sense of being worried about I cannot say what. I know now that the problems of my life's work were taking, deep down inside me, their first embryonic shape.[4]

Idea-Intimacy and Idea-Autonomy

The ideas we conceive belong to our human substance. How should I put our intimacy with them? They are clear, obscure, and both at once. At their clearest, they are unspoken words, alone or linked; at their most obscure, they are fragments of words, perhaps joined, like the head of a dim centaur, to an image-body; and they may even be or begin in elements of a muscular type, Einstein has told us. It is we who summon them up, for they are, so to speak, our internal actions; but they seem also to come unbidden, and then to be summoning us up to act in accord with them. They are not sensations, though they have a near-sensuous immediacy, and they are not emotions, though they express and represent them. Especially when spoken out, they give sensations and emotions the syntactic form and peculiar detachment that our intellect confers upon them, for, in spite of their intimacy, they can be detached from us with little or no obvious damage. It is surely their virtue to be detachable, that is, capable of being abstracted and expressed. When expressed, they are subject to the reactions of others, and we use our ideas' now somewhat impersonal presence to share and further arouse our curiosity, critical intelligence, and emotion—all things told, to speak for us. Speaking, they say very different things, and it can be astonishing to consider how wide a range of experience they open, how widely they extend our individual perspectives with the perspectives of an indefinite number of other persons.

Keeping all this in mind, we can think for a moment of the philosophers' use of ideas to solicit or imagine intimacy. The natural examples are the philosophers whose desire for intimacy is more open. Take Montaigne, who frames his ideas so that, by their frankness and mutability, they seem almost to put us within his mind, as they seemed to him, long ago, almost to lodge his mind within his readers and allow them 'to penetrate the opaque depths of its innermost folds, to pick out and immobilize the innumerable flutterings that agitate it.'[1] Montaigne says, 'I speak to my paper as I speak to the first man I meet,' and he adds, to emphasize his entire presence in his essays, 'I am the first to do so by my entire being.'[2] It is not his deeds he writes down, 'It is myself, it is my essence,' he says.[3] Because his book is himself, ambivalence enters, and because the book is Montaigne, so does irony, and he laughs with fond irony at himself in the shape of his book:

> How often and perhaps how stupidly have I extended my book to make it speak of itself! Stupidly, if only for this reason, that I should have remembered what I say of others who do the same: that these frequent sheep's eyes at their own work testify that their heart thrills with love for it, and that even the rough, disdainful blows with which they beat it are only the love taps and affectations of maternal fondness; in keeping with Aristotle, to whom self-appreciation and self-depreciation often spring from the same sort of arrogance.[4]

If we turn from Montaigne to another openly self-dramatizing philosopher, Kierkegaard, we share, as he wanted, the curse under which he lived, and our attention is seduced by his successful and yet unfulfilled seduction of Regina. If, instead, we turn to Nietzsche, we see him leaving his cave, triumphant and glowing, as Zarathustra, or, as Christ or Christ's rival, waiting for the adoration he has prophesied for himself. Sartre involves us in dramas of sex, authenticity, and failure, and, later, of sad seriality and triumphant totalization. Wittgenstein is sure that no one will understand the ideas of his *Tractatus,* but, turning to an unknown future companion, hopes that 'some day someone will think them out again for himself, and will derive great pleasure from finding in the book their exact expressions.'[5] Later, he comes to use the musing style that has been described, making his invitation to intimacy inherent to his entire message. Yet, whatever the immediate invitation to intimacy, the future beckons to him and to others more appreciatively than does the present. Even the studiously unromantic Kant is unable to keep himself from fantasies of future appreciation, and he says, or is reported as having said, 'I have come with my writings a century too soon; after a hundred years, I will first be rightly understood, and then my books will be studied anew and accepted.'[6] Nietzsche seeks his future appreciators more vehemently. He reckons they will be very few. 'Maybe,' he says, at once reproaching and praising himself, 'they will be the readers who understand my *Zarathustra*: how *could* I mistake myself for one of those for whom there are ears even now? Only the day after tomorrow belongs to me. Some are born posthumously.'[7]

Lonely Nietzsche, alone with his thoughts. He regrets that they are no longer as colourful, young, and malicious as before. He notices that they look too immortal and dull to live much longer. How alive they once were, and how alive he was, he thinks, as he addresses the 'sudden sparks and wonders' of his solitude, 'you my old beloved – *wicked* thoughts!'[8] He was, to be sure, a particularly imaginative and poetic thinker, but love for the ideas one has created is not the sole prerogative of such as he. Exact scientists, too, exhibit it. In telling how he fell in love with his own theory, a physicist says it was like falling in love with a woman, a condition possible only 'if you do not know much about her, so you cannot see her faults. The faults will become apparent later on, but after the love is strong enough to hold you to her.'[9] Without something like love, what could a creative scientist accomplish? Einstein, paying tribute to Max Planck and to the 'inexhaustible patience' he devoted to the general problems of physics, says, 'The emotional condition which fits him for this task is akin to that of a devotee or lover; his daily striving is not the result of a definite progress or programme of action, but of a direct need. . . .'[10]

As implied by the reactions I have cited, the relationship between a person and his ideas takes the various forms of human intimacy. All the emotions, love, pride, possessiveness, jealousy, shame, guilt, anger, hate, can come into play, all the attitudes that humans take toward one another can also be taken toward ideas. However, of the possible attitudes or complex of attitudes, the most usual and revealing is that which governs the relationship between parent and child, especially mother and child. In the common metaphor, the work of art or of thought is born. To continue the metaphor, the umbilical cord attaching it to its creator is then cut, and the work becomes separate, deserving, its creator feels, both autonomy and intimacy with others. In other words, he wants for his creation what he wants for himself.

Think first of the example of the painter and his painting. Matisse says of it:

> The work is the emanation, the projection of self. My drawings and my canvasses are pieces of myself. Their totality constitutes Henri Matisse. The work represents, expresses, perpetuates. I could also say that my drawings and my canvasses are my real children.[11]

Think of the example of the writer and his book. Virginia Woolf was advised by her doctors not to have children. Her husband, Leonard Woolf says:

> Her writing was to her the most serious thing in life, and, as with so many serious writers, her books were to her part of herself and she felt to part of herself somewhat in the same way as a mother often seems to feel that her child remains still part of herself. And just as the mother feels acutely the slightest criticism of her child, so any criticism of her book even by the most negligible nitwit gave Virginia acute pain . . . The mother wants the child to be perfect for its own sake, and Virginia . . . wanted her books to be perfect for their own sake.[12]

Kafka identifies himself with his art much as Matisse and Virginia Woolf do with theirs. He writes in a letter, 'I am my novel, my tales are I.'[13] He feels, unfortunately, that his work cannot grow really independent, because it reflects his own weaknesses.

> If I were ever able to write something large and whole, well shaped from beginning to end, then in the end the story would be able to detach itself from me and it would be possible for me calmly and with open eyes, as a blood relation of a healthy story, to hear it read, but as it is every little piece of the story runs around homeless and drives me from it in the opposite direction.—At the same time I can still be happy if this explanation is correct.[14]

It is, parenthetically, interesting that when Kafka contemplates what he takes to be his failure as a writer, he becomes the psychologist and takes satisfaction in his abstract understanding of his failure. The autonomy of his understanding compensates for the lack of autonomy, in his eyes, of his art.

Montaigne, a more stoical, self-sufficient person than either Virginia Woolf or Franz Kafka, was able to free his book more easily, and to feel more confident, not only that it would make its way in the world, but that it was in some ways better than he:

> To this child, such as it is, what I give I give purely and irrevocably, as one gives to the children of one's body. The little good I have done for it is no longer at my disposal. It may know a good many things that I no longer know and hold from me what I have retained and what, just like a stranger, I should have to borrow from it if I came to need it. If I am wiser than it, it is richer than I.[15]

Nietzsche's confidence in his work may be retrospectively justified, but it had, as he knew, tragic overtones. I hear these in a few words that come just before the end of *Thus Spoke Zarathustra*. There, Nietzsche, destined to remain unmarried and childless, has Zarathustra say, 'My children are near.' The tragic overtones are louder in an already mad letter written to Burckhardt on 5 January, 1889, in which he speaks of 'the children I've brought into the world,' and mentions 'my son.'

Potency, Birth, Renewal, Impotency

It is evident that, in speaking of their work, creative persons have frequently referred to love and birth, and have made sexual analogies of various kinds. A few examples have already been given, and a few may now be added, the first, again, that of Montaigne, the second, that of Kierkegaard.

Montaigne, to bring out his desire to write well, said, 'I do not know whether I would not like much better to have produced one perfectly formed child by intercourse with the muses than by intercourse with my wife.'[1] Kierkegaard, though he found marriage impossible, did not hesitate to use the images of pregnancy and birth for his own experience. He wrote, 'I have sometimes sat for hours enamoured of the sound of words, that is to say when the pregnancy of thought is echoed in them . . . .' Yet the idea of giving birth was difficult for him, and the image of the pregnant writer could give way to that of himself as a man suffering birth pangs, sure that the births would be very difficult, 'among other things because he would not scream.'[2] Kierkegaard's objections to screaming in men who give birth imply, I assume, that he wuld have liked to discover some way to mute the suffering in which his own guilt, sexual difficulty, childlessness, and creativity all played a part.

As the result of such reactions and of the observations of depth psychology, it may be supposed that not only a metaphorical, but an actual connection exists between sexual and otherwise creative life. How often the connection is direct, I cannot guess, but I am sure that it sometimes can be. Let me give Descartes and Hegel as possible, though highly speculative, instances.

Descartes appears to have been shy of sexual intimacy. Yet he did have a liaison, with a servant girl we know only as Helen, and he did have an illegitimate daughter, Francine. He mentions his daughter only once in his letters, and then only as his 'niece.' Only once does he record any date connected with her, and this, on the flyleaf of one of his books, is taken to be the date of her conception, Sunday, 15 October, 1634. Francine was born on 19 July, 1635. Descartes is said to have loved her. She brought great joy into his life, we are told, and when she died, in 1640, he was very grieved.

The period during which Francine was born and still lived were unusually happy and productive ones for Descartes. He had hesitated for years before he finally undertook to publish the results of his thought. His hesitation, though inspired, he said, by the condemnation of Galileo, had a certain parallel with his masculine shyness. Finally, however, as we see in a letter of 1 November, 1635, he set to work correcting his *Dioptric*. The following year he was already planning to have this and three additional French treatises published. In 1637, the four were published together under the comprehensive title: *Discourse on the Method for Conducting One's Reason Well and Seeking the Truth in the Sciences. Further, the Dioptric, the Meteors, the Geometry, which are Essays in this Method.*

Hesitation is thus matched against hesitation, and birth against birth. When Descartes' correspondent, the scientist, Huygens, wrote to Descartes that he had 'devoured' the *Discourse*, which had satisfied him extremely, Descartes revealed his pride in, I should guess, the double evidence of his potency. In a letter of 29 March, 1637, he wrote back to Huygens, expressing his joy and excusing the unbound condition of the *Discourse* and the *Geometry*:

> I must acknowledge my weakness to you; I am more vain than I thought, and what you have done me the honor of writing about the *Discourse on Method* has moved me with more joy than any good fortune I can imagine having . . . These are two infants that I send quite naked, because the publisher persuaded me that it was not proper to bind and cover the book before they were completely finished, as two or three leaves of its table of contents were still lacking, any more than it would be to give clothes to infants from

the first day they came into the world . . . They were born at almost the same time and in consequence have the same horoscope as Mademoiselle your daughter, a fact which makes it impossible to have a poor opinion of their fortune, and I wish a long and happy life to all that are born under that constellation.[3]

Although what I have guessed about Descartes seems to me factually possible and psychologically plausible, the evidence is too slight for any conclusion to be drawn. In the case of Hegel, the evidence, though also insufficient, seems to me internally more convincing. The fact is that Hegel's illegitimate son, Ludwig, and his first book, the *Phenomenology*, were born together; and the birth of the first may have had something to do with that of the second, in which it is reflected, at least by way of an image. Hegel had been undergoing serious difficulties. For a long time he had been piling up drafts and lecture notes for a book that he announced but had not been able to write. Others, Schelling, J. F. Fries, and Krug, had published and got ahead academically. Not only was he in great financial difficulties, but also troubled by philosophical difficulties. Perhaps above all, there was the question whether he had the ability to write a book.

> In the spring of 1806, when he finally began to write, seeking clarification in the process, without any clear idea of what exactly would happen on paper, he made a woman in Jena pregnant, and he knew it as he kept writing away and found that the book was radically changing under his hands . . . Then in January, when the boy's birth was expected any day, Hegel suddenly added his immensely long preface to the introduction of his system, although that introduction already began with an 'introduction' of nineteen pages. Some of those who know Hegel's writings best consider this preface Hegel's most important essay.[4]

I do not know Hegel well enough to go much beyond the coincidence itself, the sudden evidence of potency, philosophical and other. But the *Phenomenology* has a strange, sometimes powerful mixture of the abstruse, concrete, and poetic. As Hegel was later to say, this was his voyage of discovery. It conveys a feeling of intensity and of renewal and growth, a feeling at one point expressed in the prolonged image of the birth of a child:

> It is surely not difficult to see that our time is a time of birth and transition to a new period . . . Just as in the case of a child the first breath it draws after long silent nourishment terminates the gradualness of the merely quantitative progression—a qualitative leap—and now the child is born, so, too, the spirit that educates itself matures slowly and quietly toward the new form . . . Yet

what is new here does not have the perfect actuality any more than the newborn child; and it is essential not to overlook this.[5]

The promise of renewal underlies all creative activity. The activity itself is a renewal which, while it lasts, dominates the imagination. For the sake of renewal itself, every creative philosopher seems to say, 'Begin again, from the beginning!' Plato fixes his erotic-intellectual vision on the fixed, profound beauty of the Ideas; Wittgenstein tries to stare relaxedly at speech, things, and thought, in order to see with a precise freshness, as if for the first time; Husserl, in order to be a true beginner, forbids himself questions about value, being, usefulness, beauty, and goodness, hoping to see what there is as it is, and so to be rejuvenated. 'It is through this abstention,' Husserl says, 'that the gaze of the philosopher in truth first becomes fully free. . . . Given in and through this liberation is the discovery of the universal, absolutely self-enclosed and absolutely self-sufficient correlation between the world itself and world-consciousness.'[6]

Reminiscent of mysticism, such ambitions are so radical that they court failure. Husserl knew this, and in describing himself as a true beginner, implied that he hoped to make discoveries, but that he might lose his way. He alternated sharply between feelings of elation and ecstatic productivity and of inferiority and paralyzing discouragement. The elation accompanied the sense that his vision was sharp, the discouragement, that it was dull. Clarity, he felt, was the whole value of life. In 1906, during a crisis in his career, he wrote in his diary, 'I have been through torments (*Qualen*) from lack of clarity and from doubt that wavers back and forth. . . . Only one need absorbs me: I must win clarity, else I cannot live; I cannot bear life unless I can believe that I shall achieve it.'[7]

Husserl's ambition and fear are expressed in a story he told, in 1929, about the pocket knife he had received as a child. 'Considering that the blade was not sharp enough,' he said in a depressed vein, 'he ground it again and again until it became smaller and smaller and finally disappeared.'[8]*

When depressed, the story tells us, Husserl felt (or recalled, or appeared to recall) that he had lost both vision and potency. This makes it easier to understand why he equated clarity with life and unclarity with death. A scholar says that Husserl composed his writings like a melody, in the sense that they immediately reflected his smallest psychic perturbations. Whole pages of his manuscripts are filled with stereotyped

*My friend, the psychoanalyst, Dr. Mortimer Ostow, tells me that Husserl's story is a common childhood fantasy expressing the fear that potency is destroyed by excessive masturbation.

involutions that seem almost devoid of meaning. But then, like the nugget in a gold-prospector's pan, a glittering thought appears.[9] Seeing it, Husserl must have thought that he had proved himself once again.

Cosmic Potency: Plotinus, Kant, Schopenhauer, Bergson

As I have been contending, love, potency, and birth are not metaphors suggested to philosophers by merely accidental association. The truth is, I take it, that much of the philosophy and theology of the world, both Eastern and Western, is based on such metaphors. For a brief while, let me single out the metaphor of potency. In the West, the most influential example of its use is given by Neo-Platonism, which can be understood as a prolonged fantasy of eternal potency related to eternal, spontaneous love and birth.

Let me explain what I mean. At the top of the Neo-Platonic hierarchy, there is the One, which is the same as the Good, which is the same as Perfection. Perfection is taken to be naturally creative, but, unlike the human artist, in no way exhausted by the process of creating. It neither desires nor thinks anything, for desire shows that something is wanting, while thought is always for the purpose of fulfilling a want. Thought begins only at the stage of the Divine Mind, the Nous, which perpetually tries and fails to become Perfection, and which, in the attempt, gives birth to the multitude of images, the forms. Creativity is therefore the result either of Perfection itself or of the desire for it.

If this is true, what is the case of the philosopher, who, as an imperfect being conscious of his imperfection, engages in philosophic thought? The answer is that the philosopher ought to know that philosophy is consciousness of love that leads to the formless One. But, asks Plotinus, 'is that enough? Can we end the discussion by saying this?' His answer, which at once explains and diminishes philosophy, is put in the following words:

> No, my soul is still in even stronger labor; perhaps she has still something which she must bring forth; she is filled with birth-pangs in her eager longing for the One . . . The soul runs over all truths, and all the same shuns the truths we know if someone tries to express them in words and discursive thought: for discursive thought, in order to express anything, has to consider one thing after another; this is the method of description; but how can one describe the Absolutely Simple? It is enough if the intellect comes into contact with It: but when it has done so, while the contact lasts it is absolutely impossible, nor has it time, to speak; reasoning about It comes afterwards.[1]

All of this Plotinian philosophy, of which I have merely reminded the reader, may strike one as absurd; but it is, as I have said, a fantasy of the potency of the self-sufficient One, and of the fertile love the One arouses in beings that are and are not the One itself. Yet whether an intellectual perversion, a bracing fantasy, or the very truth, Neo-Platonism has had the greatest influence on the history of thought. Augmented by Aristotelianism and merged with Christianity, it dominates the European Middle Ages and the Renaissance. Its influence is strong in such classic philosophers as Descartes, Leibniz, and Spinoza. It remains alive in the German Idealists, and, because it lives in Hegel, lives in Marx and the Marxians as well. Kant, to the extent that he is influenced by Leibniz or Wolff, shares in it, and he has at least some temperamental affinity with it, as I will immediately show. Schopenhauer combines it with Indian metaphysics, Kantianism, and weariness of sex. Nietzsche, though he denies it, retains its emphasis on creativity. His creative hero attempts to be his own God or Perfection, for God, he says, has died. In the twentieth century, Plotinus, though philosophically diminished, lives on in Bergson and Whitehead. Perhaps, too, in Sartre. Perhaps, by the agency of Schopenhauer or otherwise, something of him is left in Wittgenstein, in the conviction that nothing of essential importance is capable of being said in words.

The affinity of Kant for such thought is striking, though he later takes his critical precautions against it. We see the affinity, early in his career, in his *Universal Natural History and Theory of the Heavens*. Playing the speculative cosmogonist, he expresses his delight in the idea of the genesis of the world. Unlike the Neo-Platonists, it must be admitted, he prefers and is excited by the successive creation of the world in time. He takes the destruction of worlds lightly, as no more than 'a necessary shading amid the multiplicity' of suns, because their production costs nature nothing.[2] Phoenix-like, nature revives itself from its ashes through all the infinity of times and spaces. 'All nature, which involves a universal harmonious relation to the self-satisfaction of the Deity, cannot but fill the rational creature with an everlasting satisfaction, when it finds itself united with this Primary Source of all perfection.'[3]

Schopenhauer, more sexually active than Kant, but not sexually happy, prefers the morning of life, before sex exercises its tyranny, when 'the world lies before us so fresh, so magically gleaming, so attractive.'[4] To our sorrow, 'the will wills life absolutely and for all time' and simultaneously 'exhibits itself as the sexual impulse which has an endless series of generations in view.'[5] Cheerfulness and innocence disappear, and unrest, uneasiness, and melancholy enter our consciousness. In this now melancholy world, the act of procreation is

> related to the world as the solution is related to the riddle. Thus the world is wide in space and old in time, and has an inexhaustible multiplicity of forms. Yet all this is only the phenomenon of the

will-to-live; and the concentration, the focus of this act of will, is the act of generation. Hence in this act the inner nature of the world most distinctly expresses itself.[6]

Here, finally, reversed and again made positive, is the metaphor of potency as it appears in the philosophy of Bergson:

> So, from an immense reservoir of life, jets must be gushing out unceasingly, of which each, falling back, is a world. The evolution of living species within this world represents what subsists of the primitive direction of the original jet, and of an impulsion which continues itself in a direction the inverse of materiality.[7]

Self-Creation: Montaigne

The subject and the fantasy of creation yield to those, I think, of self-creation, which may, in fantasy, be their aim. Self-creation of a kind takes place in every human life, in the sense that one's view of oneself influences what one becomes. Here, however, I am concerned with the especially creative person, who, in making something else, makes himself. He begins, I suppose, by simply expressing himself. Having expressed himself, he is surprised at least by the definiteness his externalized self has assumed, and perhaps by the discovery that he is different from or more than the self he has always known. Before long, he sees that what he has so far done is still crude, that is, not shaped, mastered, or differentiated enough. If he is an artist, the artist I have in mind, he is best satisfied when his intervention is most thorough, when he has fingered each fraction of clay or put his brush to each sub-area, or, more generally, when his domination is pervasive enough for him to recognize that what he makes is really his. His desire, which does not end as long as he remains creative, is expressed in increasing differentiation, for his response to his own work influences him to develop it in greater detail, to discover what he has overlooked, to complete what he has left unfinished, and to particularize what he has left general. He increases, so to speak, in detail. Hobbes goes so far as to urge the philosopher to attend consciously to his own differentiation.

> If you will be a philosopher in good earnest, let your reason move upon the deep of your own cogitations and experience; those things that lie in confusion must be set asunder, distinguished and every one stamped with its own name set in order; that is to say, your method must resemble that of creation.[1]

As the process I am describing goes on, the creator's dominance over his creation grows more marked and his mature characteristics more evident in it, as if it were the face, marked by time, of an experienced older person. Whether or not the creator is in fact an integrated person, there is an increasing likelihood that he will reach an optimal integration of his interests, desires, and experiences in the objects or thoughts he creates. I assume that one of the great attractions of creative work is the ability it confers to reach an at least emotional and symbolic integration. When Virginia Woolf said that she hoped that her books, her children, would be perfect for their own sakes, she meant, I take it, that she hoped that they would be better integrated, more perfectly formed, than she was, and that their superiority over her, for which she would be responsible, would be what would give her the utmost satisfaction. Such a hope helps explain the stubbornness with which the creative artist, philosopher, or scientist attempts to create original, which is to say, autonomous works. The feeling of his own autonomy is so dependent on the degree and kind of autonomy achieved by his works, his externalized self-fragments, that he may be said to create himself by their means. The prevalence of such a theme in the Renaissance is one of the reasons why it deserves its name.[2]

It would be interesting to show the process of self-creation as it develops in one of the classic philosophers, Descartes, perhaps, or Leibniz, or Kant; but the demonstration would require painstaking analysis of a kind that has never, so far as I know, been undertaken. The process is far easier to make out in thinkers like Montaigne, Kierkegaard, and Nietzsche, who so often make themselves the chief objects of their own thought. Of this group, I will choose Montaigne to illustrate what I have been saying. His development is relatively clear and has already been analyzed, by himself and others, from the standpoint of self-creation. We know which of his essays he wrote first and when he made the various additions to the essays he had already written. The copy of his *Essays* with marginal additions in his own hand even gives us a visual sense of his growth. All things said, he is an easily available example of a process that I take to be characteristic of creative persons in general.[3]

Montaigne's early life seems to have been very full, and yet, in a sense, not very definite. At once a humanist, estate-owner, magistrate, soldier, mayor, and diplomat, he lived out his father's strenuous ideals, to which his love of freedom and idleness was, however, a form of resistance. He could surely sense that he was more than the embodiment of his father's wishes, but he could not decide what he should make of himself, and he showed both his resistance and his indecision in the Stoical belief of his early essays that it was best to capitulate to the pains one could not avoid. His early essays were tentative, brief, and not very self-assertive, yet their success, not to speak of his travels and his two terms of office as mayor, helped his self-confidence to grow and allowed him increasingly to be himself. The unbound copy of his essays, from which the posthumous edition was prepared, shows him visibly reacting to himself and growing over the margins and onto separate slips of paper, rather like a tree growing ring around ring around its pith. Like the tree, he retained everything he had been, without forgetting or diminishing what he had been; but his present self now saw the doubts, dreams, fears, and obscurities that the printed pages cast back at it, and seeing what he was, and seeing everyone in himself, his reticence vanished. He repeated without shame all the criticisms others had made of him, including that he was cool, refused to take advice, and was self-centered. Like other old men, he revived himself by his sharp, comical, and obscene commentary on life. Having found the plain, subtle truth, he grew more independent of the ever-changing self beyond which he had once been unable to see. He no longer wanted to be so caught in his inclinations that he could not depart from them or twist them about knowingly.[4]

Montaigne had dedicated himself, as he said repeatedly, to the task of self-examination, and this he did not regret. Unsystematic though he was, he studied himself in the same passionate detail as a late medieval philosopher split logical hairs or a contemporary analyst distinguishes variant senses of an identical-seeming word. Finally it was evident to him that he and his book had each made the other. In modelling the book-figure on himself, he said, he had had to fashion himself so often that the model had to some extent grown firm and taken shape. His conclusion was, 'I have no more made my book than my book has made me—a book, consubstantial with its author, an integral part of my life . . . .'[5]

A request

With the subject of self-creation I have finished the answers to the three questions I asked myself at the beginning of this book. I do not know how persuasive I have been, though I must have run into the resistance that I described as inevitable. In any case, now that I have made my basic attitudes and justifications as clear as I can, it is time to make the request that every would-be persuader implies: Whatever objections you have felt or will feel, whatever weaknesses you have discovered or will discover here, give my ideas a fair hearing. The eventual conclusion belongs to each reader for himself; but if this conclusion is not to be foregone, surrender to the argument for the while, think not only of its weaknesses, but of its possible strengths; and when my examples are not persuasive enough, try to think of more persuasive ones; and regard the search, not as that of the writer alone, but of the writer and the reader, yourself, together. Until we have to part, give me your help. In return, I promise to remember that my argument is always tentative. I will try to think of its weaknesses and confess them when it seems to me that I should, and I will try to think, not only of examples by which to make my case, but of counterexamples as well, though I am afraid that the counterexamples will always be harder for me to find.

5
Childhood and Reality

I have said what I could on the issues of persuasion, truth, relevance, and creation. They are all of great importance. Here, however, I see them as preliminary, because, for me, the central issue is the relationship of philosophy to the philosopher's experience of life, life at every age and in every condition, but mostly at its beginning and in the condition of essential dependence.

I begin, then, with the basic couple, of mother and child. Despite what I have heard of fabulously retentive memories, I do not believe that any grown person can recover in his mind the situation of the tiny, still unfinished child, completely dependent for its existence on those who care for it. Noisy and, in its way, active as it is, it has no effective power except that to claim help. It is, at once, very helpless, very self-centered, very responsive, very flexible, very tough, and very fragile.

It is while one is so, during the beginning of life, that one's primordial attitudes begin to form. The substratum is genetic, but it is hard to identify, that is, isolate as the regulator of growth and response, because it is never isolated in life, and reveals itself only in ways that are particular to particular environments. Heredity and environment are not only hard, but, in a real sense, impossible to disentangle from one another. Environment, we know, begins to exert its influence in the womb itself, where everything from nutrition, the permeability and size of the placenta, the mother's moods, and even the rhythm of her heart-beats may affect the child. The first, sometimes pronounced differences between identical twins are explained by the differences in their womb environment, in prenatal circulation, for instance. The size, structure, and function of the brain are affected, it seems, by the quantity and quality of both nutrition and stimulation. Stimulation, for instance, has been shown to affect the sheathing and branching of the nerves. Well-known though now problematic experiments with kittens show that if vision in early life is limited (for example, to stripes in one direction), there is no triggering of brain cells to respond to the absent stimulation, and the kittens

108

remain blind to visual stimulation of a kind they have not already experienced. The general conclusion is that stimulation in early life is necessary to preserve or establish even the abilities we consider innate.[1]

I cannot go on here with these difficult, often controversial matters. Nevertheless, I want to point out how especially difficult it is to distinguish in practice between heredity and environment when one thinks of the close, sensitive interchange of experience that goes on between mother and infant. Each becomes the other's frame of reference, echoes the other, and changes in response to the other. It has been said that this patterned interaction becomes the leitmotif that identifies a child as belonging to its particular mother.

Not only does a child become particularized, but it develops as a more or less stable and separate individual. If the relationship with its mother or mother–equivalent is stable and pleasurable enough, the structures of the self, to use a compressed and perhaps analogical expression, respond by developing stably and pleasurably. For reasons that will soon be discussed, the child becomes relatively well able to distinguish itself, its parts, and its functions, and to distinguish itself from other objects and people. If fortunate in its relationship with the world, it becomes basically trusting, and its trust makes it more likely that everything and everyone will be seen as helpful, dependable, and reassuring than as the opposite. It is such trust, or its opposite, basic distrust, that is later translated, not only into emotional and moral attitudes, but into the intellectual distinction between existent and non–existent, or real and unreal, as found in philosophical systems. This idea, too, will be explained. On the assumption that it is at least part of the truth, I will further assume (but try also to show) that the child's initial learning, especially its initial mode of dependence on others, remains forever embedded in its ideas on the nature of reality. The child, I say, is father to the philosopher.[2]

Let me shift from this abstract description to a concrete instance, which shows how mother and child together succeeded in creating confidence, independence, and an intense striving for mastery.

The child to which I am referring suffered at birth from lack of oxygen, and, perhaps as a result, moved clumsily, ate poorly, and responded slowly. His mother encouraged him endlessly, urging him to reach out and grasp and manipulate the objects around him. He tried hard, but not very successfully. When he tried, for example, to reach a small red cube, on which he fixed his eyes intently, he struggled towards it with his whole body, but his arms and wrists moved too jerkily and without enough control. The observer who described this commented, 'I doubt if I have ever seen a baby in whom there was such a wide discrepancy between his desire to achieve a particular goal, such as securing an object, and his total inability to do so.'

The mother continued to help the child, especially by involving him in games, which were so pleasant to both that it was hard to tell which of them was the more eager for them. This mutual training continued, and the child developed, difficult step by step. In time he became a strikingly attentive, well coordinated pupil, 'very much an achiever, constantly striving for approval and recognition.' In the words of the observing psychologist, 'He attacks things with intensity. There seems to be relatively little competitive element in his motivation and his need for mastery is not based on competition with peers. He is appropriately independent of his teacher. . . .' He had become a well adapted, highly concentrated, very able boy.[3]

Destruction of Being

The instance I have just described is an unusually favorable one. It may serve us when we discuss the intense curiosity and application of philosophers and others who begin to exhibit their great need for accomplishment while they are still children. But the relationship between mother and child may be much less favourable, and it is to this sometimes radically destructive possibility that I now turn.

First, however, a word on the evidence for what I am about to say. I have earlier pointed out how problematic the evidence in psychology is likely to be. However, the quantity and quality of evidence for the point I want to make is overwhelming. If any psychological thesis at all has been established, it is the thesis that help and love or neglect and hate in a child's early years are of great though by no means exclusive importance in establishing its nature, or, in the simplest words, its ability to be stable and happy.[1]

I do not want to exaggerate. The evidence I am referring to is faulty. There are intuitively convincing case histories, but it is hard to generalize from them. There is an abundance of statistics, but much of it is likely to be superficial. Sociological variables may have been neglected. The issue of heredity and environment resists analysis, for things are rarely just what they seem to be. A child's close environment may have simulated the effects of heredity; or perhaps it was the child's heredity that provoked one change, that provoked another change, and so on, the whole chain simulating the effects of environment alone. Even if I am right in supposing that early experience leaves, not only ineffaceable memories, but active predispositions, mental and physical, human resilience is far too great to rule out alternatives and changes in development. One learns that however plausible a generalization on such issues may appear to be, it is subject in time to increasingly many distinctions, and that the distinctions, however proliferated, are never sufficient to explain a particular individual difference.

All the same, it seems to me that there is enough evidence for the great importance of the mother–child relationship. I have reached this quite ordinary conclusion because it seems intuitively right to me and because it has been supported by the observation of animals, both in the wild and in experiments too severe to inflict on human infants. Those who insist on the entire uniqueness of human beings or of philosophers must excuse me the indignity of the animal comparison. Indignity apart, it is apparent that a young bird or mammal reared in isolation from its own kind behaves in an exceedingly bizarre manner. An Indian jungle fowl so reared will, in a manner of speaking, court itself, and will whirl strangely, while a puppy isolated during its critical period will stand paw raised and forced into a wall-angle and will show great fear of the outside world. Surely, for social mammals 'even temporarily breaking contact with individuals and surroundings to which a primary attachment has taken place is a strongly disturbing experience.'[2]

Well-known experiments on monkeys have provided especially striking evidence. Those isolated from birth sat staring into space, clasped their heads in their hands and kept rocking, pinched themselves compulsively, and even chewed or tore at themselves till they bled. When matured, they were unwilling to mate. The few females that bore infants as the result of the seductions or assaults of healthy monkeys proved either indifferent or cruel to the infants. 'As for the infants, the extremes of sexuality and aggressiveness in their behaviour evoke all too vivid parallels in the behaviour of disturbed human children and adolescents in psychiatric clinics and institutions for delinquents.'[3] It should be recalled, however, that later studies have shown that monkeys, though isolated from birth, remain able to solve such problems as experimenters usually pose them, and remain, to the encouragement of their human therapists, though socially damaged, socially redeemable.[4]

Of course, every self-respecting investigator would remain cautious in drawing parallels from animal to human infants. It seems reasonable to assume that human infants, whose attachment to their mother is far more prolonged, have far more prolonged opportunities to develop straight or awry, and have more complex and culture-mediated responses to their difficulties. Yet it is hard simply to deny the parallels, or to forget that early human experience, to whatever degree it may be reversible, is in fact often not reversed. Some children are redeemed, some not, and many remain in an intermediate state.

Social isolation is only one of the harsh experiences a child may undergo. Another, obviously, is parental selfishness, by which I mean the inability or lack of desire of a parent to sense the child's independent needs. A true, psychotic instance is that of the mother who, instead of feeding her hungry child, opened her mouth and said, 'Feed me.' Parents may use their children too much for their own parental gratification; or they may be otherwise demanding, cruel, or cold. There is no need to go through the whole litany, which is familiar from experience and observation. The results are, naturally, bad, though experience shows how they can be turned to sometimes surprisingly good ends. What exactly the bad results will be, or how deep or lasting, cannot be predicted—people and situations differ too much.[5]

At their extreme, in childhood schizophrenia, or in what is called or miscalled 'autism,' the results are terribly dehumanizing. Again, I must add a word of caution. The experts are divided, and they do not always impress one another with their arguments. As an expert has said, 'Errors of generalizing beyond data and excessive pride in one's own observations and conclusions are more easily repeated than avoided.'[6] No one knows very well what part heredity plays in the conditions in question (some highly specific kinds excepted). It is often difficult or impossible to tell if the cause is not some impairment or chemical imbalance of the brain. Subjectively, however, I am led by case histories to conclude that at least some of these dehumanizing conditions are of purely social or psychological origin, and that many of them are partly of this origin.

Distinctions have been drawn between 'hospitalism' or 'infant marasmus' (wasting away, passivity); infantile 'autism' (early and extreme social unresponsiveness); 'symbiotic psychosis' (attachment to but inadequate separation from the mother); and infantile 'schizophrenia' (occurring in later childhood). All these conditions, whether or not really different, can be subsumed under the imprecise but perhaps necessary term, 'psychosis,' meaning a deep disturbance in the grasp of reality. Therefore, instead of trying to maintain distinctions, subject, it seems to me, to great semantic and empirical difficulties, I will concentrate on the generally destructive effects of childhood psychosis, on what I have called 'the destruction of being.' I will rely primarily on one experienced observer, Bruno Bettelheim, whose special interest is autism. His conviction that autistic children must be separated from their families, and his personality, perhaps, have aroused a good deal of professional opposition to him. Furthermore, his view of autism has been attacked as 'virtually obsolete.'[7] I choose him, nevertheless, to maintain some uniformity of outlook, and also, I must confess, out of partiality to his character-izations, which fit my purpose.[8] The accuracy of his use of the term, 'autism,' is of less interest to me than the veracity of his case histories, which no one, to my knowledge, has seriously questioned.

In Bettelheim's opinion, 'Infantile autism . . . stems from the original conviction that there is nothing at all one can do about a world that offers some satisfactions, though not those one desires, and only in frustrating ways.' A child with such a conviction 'withdraws to the autistic position. If this happens, the world which until then seemed only insensitive appears to be utterly destructive. . . . But since the autistic child once had some vague image of a satisfying world, he strives for it—not through action, but only in fantasy. Or if he acts, it is not to better his lot, but only to ward off further harm.'[9]

This kind of child is likely to be insensitive to physical pain. It appears to be as alienated from its own body as from the external world. As an expression of its alienation from its body, to which it is not, so to speak, easily or exactly joined, it moves in an odd, uncoordinated way (in direct contradiction to Bettelheim, some observers report that an autistic child is likely to be very agile and graceful). The child seems to be defend-ing itself against internal and external threats by means of an extreme passivity, all its energy being devoted to the blotting out of the stimuli that threaten pain. Emotion itself is blotted out, even anger. When the child does become angry, it is advancing out of its autism, because it is acknowledging the existence of the anger's object.

This kind of child looks without seeing, listens without hearing, and gazes away vaguely, at nothing in particular. If it does look towards something, it moves only its eyes, because to make a grosser movement would be to acknowledge that the reality it denies does in fact exist. If it speaks, it finds it relatively easy to name things, naming being imper-sonal and noncommittal; but whatever it says, it says tonelessly, with the even, insensitive voice of a deaf person, who does not modulate his voice because he has never heard it.

To such a child, negation comes easier than affirmation. When it uses the word, 'yes,' it is likely to do so in a contextually specific way, to mean, for instance, 'Yes, father, take me on your shoulders.' 'Yes' as a general term of affirmation is extraordinarily hard for the child to learn, as is the possessive pronoun, 'my.' 'I' may be replaced by 'you,' because the existence of the self as really separate is too hard to acknowledge.

Phrases such as, 'I am,' or 'I want,' commit the child to being identifiably separate and subject to attack, and are therefore avoided.[*][10]

Attack becomes impossible only if the child is either absent or omnipresent, and so the autistic child can be regarded as trying to destroy either being or being's distinctions. It would prefer either nothing or only one thing to exist. Such an attitude is reminiscent of mysticism, and also, to a degree, of the destruction of being that is expressed in the ambivalent negations of Nirvana.

Creation of Being

Let me turn from this sad Nirvana, being's destruction, to the state in which, as I see it, being is created. Like the destruction, the creation of being is native to the child. I therefore continue to consider the child's experience, to which I again add something about animal life generally.

To live, the child must learn to act in the world and, in its own terms, to learn to understand it. It is able to learn because it is moved by pleasure and pain, directed by curiosity, educated by playfulness, and given insight by increasing objectivity. Pleasure and pain, then, joined with curiosity, playfulness, and objectivity are the means by which, in educating itself, the child creates being. For the child is always exploring, always attracted to the unstable, the unusual, the slightly unknown or dangerous, always, within the limits set by fear, altering, destabilizing everything, teasing the world to emerge, and always familiarizing itself with its own powers and weaknesses.

This constant exploration, stimulated by curiosity and playfulness and rewarded by pleasure, is opposed to boredom, lethargy, and depression. Of these last, negative states, depression, in particular, deserves some thought here. As we have all experienced, it is the painful lethargy that

---

*Other researchers may attribute the difficulty in using 'yes' and 'I' to echolalia, the tendency to repeat the words just heard, those, for example, in a question just asked, which is likely to contain the pronoun, 'you.' For my purpose, it is enough if there are *some* children whose difficulties with 'yes,' 'I,' and the like can be explained as Bettelheim explains them. A recent summary of research on autistic language suggests how unwise it is to be dogmatic:

'Weiland and Legg (1964) have noticed that *few personal pronouns* are used by autistic children, and that the pronoun "we" is particularly avoided. Cunningham (1968), however, found no differences in the use of first and second person pronouns between autistics and controls. Goldfarb et al. (1972b) mention an avoidance of first person pronouns, whereas Bartak et al. (1972) suggest that when regarded in terms of sentence position, there is *no* difference in the use of various pronouns.' L. Baker, D. P. Cantwell, M. Rutter & L. Bartak, 'Language and Autism,' in E. R. Ritvo, ed., *Autism* (New York: Spectrum Publications, 1976), pp. 124–25.

results from more failure than one is psychologically able to bear. It is the nearly-willed intensification of helplessness, and is often, perhaps most often, caused by the loss of the love that one expects, hopes for, or simply needs. The threat it makes is the loss of interest and vitality. To regain vitality, each of us, child or adult, turns to whatever can excite us pleasurably, for under the threat of depression, pleasure becomes an acute need. I emphasize the need because, as I will try to show, a good deal of philosophy is created in response to depression, which the philosopher attempts to transcend by means of a consuming interest, which uses helplessness and lovelessness as a stimulus to intellectual creation and power, and hence to pleasure.

To return to the subject of exploration, it is interesting to broaden one's perspective and think, not only of the child and the philosopher, but of other curious, exploratory animals, of which I choose for a brief comment, following Konrad Lorenz, the rat, the monkey, and, especially, the raven. The three are all indefatigable explorers, hungry for new perceptions. A raven will spend days observing anything new, until, making a first, daring experiment, it suddenly attacks the unknown something with its beak and, as suddenly, flies away. If the unknown being is revealed to be lifeless, the raven tries to peck or tear it to pieces and to hide the resulting fragments; if it is revealed to be alive but unaggressive, the raven pursues and, if possible, kills it; and if it is revealed to be impenetrable, unshatterable, or dangerous, the raven quickly learns to leave it alone. So the raven, by curiosity, claw, and beak, learns to classify the world in terms of its own needs and powers. It is one of the group of creatures, including rat, monkey, and man, whose curiosity helps make them strikingly intelligent and adaptable.[1]

A word more on exploration and curiosity. To be curious means to get pleasure in trying out as many things as possible. It means pleasure in the playing of games and the transformation of as many experiences as possible into games, which satisfy curiosity at least in part without involving the curious person in any real danger. For human beings, the pleasure in games is both imaginative and, often, intellectual. In trying things out and in transforming our experience into games, we explore our environment, that is, we give our world shape, content, colour, and power, by acting on it and compelling it to react, though as undangerously as possible. We use imagination and intellect as the raven uses beak and claws, making the world come into richer and clearer being and gaining the power that comes with knowledge.

Curiosity, we see, and the playful exploration it initiates, make as much of the world as possible intimate, first to the child, and later, in other, often rarefied forms, to the adult. Expressed perceptually, curiosity creates perceptual familiarity; expressed manipulatively, it creates manipulative familiarity; expressed intellectually, it creates intellectual familiarity. Through this varied familiarity, we perceive, manipulate, and understand more effectively, and the vagueness in and around us is increasingly dispelled. It is surely curiosity that makes a conscious, powerful objectivity flourish as it does.

All I have been saying applies particularly to the child, whose curiosity and playfulness are so easy to perceive and of such clearly biological importance. If I have been describing artists, scientists, and philosophers correctly, the child is their primal kin. This is the more true if the child excels in alertness, sensitivity, imagination, or intelligence. A gifted child is an intensified child. Its pleasures and pains arise more quickly and acutely, its curiosity, if not too heavily checked, reaches out more daringly, and its response to its parents, in need, love, and hatred, is more intense than that of an ordinary child. A child of this intensified kind may soon begin a love affair with the world, which, like other love affairs, intensifies both pleasures and pains.

Let me illustrate with the example of Tolstoy. As a child, he

> seemed to feel everything more intensely than others. His hair-trigger emotions, high spirits, and keen enjoyment of everything set him apart. His sister recalled that he was like a ray of light. He would dash into the room with a happy smile, as if he wished to tell everyone about a new discovery he had just made. If he were petted, tears of joy filled his eyes, and they named him 'cry-baby Leo'. He often expressed his uncommon sensibility in outpourings of love and in eager attempts to win affection. In a sense, this acute sensibility defined the man and the literary artist.[2]

I suppose that each of the creative men we are interested in was once an intensified child of one or another sort. In such a child, whose pleasures and pains are both enhanced, the creation of being is unusually active. Out of its perceptions, movements, manipulations, imaginings, and thoughts, out of its curiosity, investigative love, and intelligent fear, this child creates a more varied, interesting, and quite possibly more objective world than other children.[3]

I may have been speculating too incautiously. If so, the phrase about the creation of being should be taken as a metaphor. Abandoning the metaphor, we might say that we use our biological capacities to elicit just those traits of the world that we particularly need to know. The traits are given their structure in keeping with our biological needs and capacities. The world finally elicited is therefore coordinate with the needs of the human beings who have elicited it, and, within limits, differently coordinate with each particular human being.

Differentiation of Being

In the beginning, if my description is acceptable, being is both destroyed and created. It also undergoes a process of increasing differentiation, which I would like to consider briefly, in terms of three psychological processes: self-love, self-internalization, and self-demarcation. Unlike the processes they are taken to signify, the three terms are of no importance in themselves.

In the beginning, self-love, as I see it, has at least two different aspects. The first is self-love in the sense of self-esteem. It comes basically, as I have said, from the smoothness, unselfishness, and constancy of the mother's care for her child. Through the benign constancy of its mother and other intimates, the child learns to think well of itself and others. The world is then experienced as basically helpful and trustworthy. The opposite experience has, of course, the opposite result.

The second aspect of love is more simply physical. If the mother touches and manipulates her child with pleasure, the child is taught to take pleasure in its own body, in the turning of its joints, the pull of its muscles, and the coordination of its limbs. It is then apt to move not only efficiently but also gracefully, just as, having experienced the right pleasure, it is apt, like a considerable number of philosophers, to think gracefully. But if a child is taught to dislike its body, it is apt, like a considerable number of philosophers, to move clumsily. An unpleasurable, uncoordinated body, I assume, is one that the child prefers to be distant from and even disown, in other words, deprive of being. Some deprivations are subtle. If it is the mother's habit to hold the child awkwardly, her uncomfortable or insecure arms may be generalized, as the child grows up, into an uncomfortable or insecure world. In such a world, the person, like Alice in her hole, may feel himself falling and falling. Or, like Humpty-Dumpty, he may feel himself on the edge of a shattering experience.

Self-love and the whole self-experience in which it is embedded have, it seems, an initial indeterminateness, without clear separation of the internal from the external. Experience becomes clearly internal only when the child begins to differentiate more acutely, that is, to divide everything into itself and the rest, and the rest into persons who are, like the child, internal, and things, which are not.

This process, the child's bifurcation of being, is a decisive accomplishment in everyone's life. Because there are many people in whom it remains relatively incomplete and others who feel endangered by its finality, many philosophies and all the varieties of mysticism resist it. The bifurcation leaves the child the separate, self-aware possessor of its own exclusive internality. The child can now live a hidden, internal, as well as a public, external life. Given the chance of being hidden or public, the child, who is now the person, can live more intensely in either way and, in accord with its balance of intensities, can come to feel that being, reality, belongs fundamentally to either internal or external life. In other words, both kinds of life can be regarded as equally real or unreal, or the one can be singled out as real and the other as unreal, illusory.

I have been describing how a child becomes internal (and perhaps external) to itself. The process is also one of self-demarcation. I use this term to name the child's ability to recognize and govern itself as a hierarchy, into which its original near-anarchy of impulses gradually develops. Relying on its parents as alter egoes, the child is able to overcome much of its fear, including its fear of its own impulses. With parental help, it isolates and imprisons the impulses that may be harmful to itself. Parental tolerance, too, is needed, for unless its impulses are tolerated within reason, its conscience is likely to grow too strong, and the child to become seriously inhibited, rebellious, or both. Overconscientiousness, with its philosophical sequels, obviously characterizes philosophers like Kant, Schopenhauer, Nietzsche, and Kierkegaard. Each of them fails to demarcate himself effectively enough. Each fails, I mean to say, to recognize and tolerate important aspects of himself, or even himself as a whole.

Self-demarcation is also, of course, sexual. To be satisfactory, it requires satisfactory relations with both parents, who should ideally have satisfactory relations with one another. Perhaps the first essential for a son is his mother's pride in his masculinity, and for a daughter, her father's in her femininity. In the absence of such pride, sexual identity is likely to remain undeveloped, as it remained, I think, among many of the famous philosophers. I will try to show that this lack of self-demarcation may be directly or indirectly reflected in a philosopher's thought.

Self-demarcation is furthered by the creation of an area intermediate between what is strictly oneself and strictly other than oneself. Much of the present book is concerned with this intermediate, strongly but not wholly subjective area. For the child or the creative adult, this area is large and rich. Here, in the circle of its imagination's light, the child plays, and here works of art, philosophies, and scientific theories are brought into being.[1]

Absence, Death, Denial, Creation, and Being

I must go on and describe the child's dependence on its parents. Needless to say, it is great, for without their help and intimacy, the child withers.

Their mere absence is hard to bear, their prolonged absence creates anxiety and depression, and their death is so painful that it is impossible to accept. The child's sensitivity to absence and to death, the most prolonged absence of all, is strongest until about the age of five, remains quite strong until the age of fifteen, and as the memory of our own parents should convince us, never disappears completely.[1]

The child, however, is resourceful. When its parent is gone, it will do or imagine what it can to restore the loss. It will pretend that the parent is there. Alternatively, it will be noticeably good, bad, or sulky, the goodness being meant to demand a reward, which is the parent's return, the badness being meant to punish the parent into returning, and the sulking being meant to reproach the parent for not being at home.

Whatever happens, the absent mother or father remains present in the child's imagination; and the child continues to speak and play with them even if they have died. Its very attempt to react to death implies death's denial. The attempt may therefore have a primitive religiosity. The child may, for example, reinstate a parent in the magnified form of God, or it may try to be always good, itself becoming the parent, so to speak, by keeping the parent's protective goodness alive. The psychological ways of reinstating a mother or father, substituting for them, or otherwise overcoming the impact of their death are very numerous. In one case I have read of, the child, associating death with particular ages and dates, developed an interest in numbers, as if mastery of numbers were also mastery of the death they marked. This child, as it turned out, became a mathematician. In another case, the child, unable to cry, felt empty and cut off as by a glass wall from everything that was happening.[2]

When its parents are absent, the child grows sad and anxious. 'Why,' it asks, 'is mother gone so long?' It says, 'When she comes back, I will tell her how angry I am, so she will never go away again.' Such anger is hopeful; but if it is ineffective, it may turn into the anger of despair, meant to punish everyone indiscriminately for the suffering that has been inflicted on the child. And so it happens that the parent who has disappointed the child badly, or who has returned after a long absence, or who, worst of all, has died, is reacted to with sadness, anxiety, anger, hope, and, of course, love. These emotions may be simultaneous or successive. Love, fear, attachment, and reproach may turn into one complex relationship. The predominantly angry child may battle the world angrily, while the frightened child may retreat into its imagination or into its bodily sensations. The angry battle makes the world even more hostile; the retreat into imagination makes the outside world even more frightening and unreal; and the retreat into bodily sensations excludes the frightening world from the only pleasures and pains that remain consciously admissible into experience. Helpless, complaining, and ill, the child may demand endless care; depressed, it may try to vanish (except as anger revives it) even from itself.

These reactions to absence and death, though I have intimated rather than explained them, remain alive in the character of the adult, at least as tendencies. They remain as the tendency to deny anything too painful; to grow angry at the disappointing world; to summon up and multiply all the great fears; to combine anger with love or reproachfulness with dependency; to live in the exclusive reality of one's imagination or one's body; to grow ill and pathologically afraid of illness; and to grow depressed. Every kind of human ingenuity is mobilized to counter absence and death; but every defence is in some way a surrender.[3]

Death poses everyone, not only the child, the most extreme problem. As children, adolescents, or adults, we try and fail to imagine death. We imagine it as weakness, pain, paralysis, suffocation, and loss, all of which we know; but to imagine anything is to be self-evidently alive and so to fail to imagine death. Curiosity, by means of which we explore everything, fails with death, for death, taken directly and prosaically, is impenetrable to any form of consciousness. It seems to be a second presence, parallel to life, a nothing that is emotionally something.

I have been speaking mainly of childhood, but I should at least mention adolescence. Adolescence has an evident closeness to absence and death. In saying this I do not want to take sides in the controversy between those who think that adolescence is typically a period of storm and crisis, and those who think that it may be and most often is a relatively peaceful state of transition.[4] In either case the need to break away from parents and establish one's own independence is the problem. To break away from parents is to cause their absence and hint at the great absence, death. To break away and to build an emotional defence against the feeling of absence, helplessness, or death, the adolescent may attach himself to new ideals or ideal persons or engage in an angry or cynical devaluation of his parents' ideals. Consciously or unconsciously, he strives for independence by means of his fundamental questioning, his devaluation and revaluation. Out of fear and desire, he must arrive at independence.

Fear, and especially the fear of absence and death, stimulates a creative response in some persons. It should therefore not be surprising that among the philosophers there have been many who were sensitized in childhood to absence and death, for they have been of the sort to whom the reality of death, whether acknowledged or not, has spelled the death of the commonsensical reality that is all that most people are able to acknowledge. The death of this reality raises the most general and persistent of philosophical problems, that of being or existence. My opinion is that this problem is not, at bottom, a rational one. I say this knowing that it can be given rational form in certain technical contexts; but then it ceases to be the classical philosophical problem. I say it, too, with genuine respect for the physicists, who turn from particle to cosmos with the same breathtaking audacity; and I say it with genuine respect for the neurophysiologists, who, against great odds, penetrate the folds and interactions of the brain more deeply every year. The historical truth is that the philosophers, who have so often posed the problem, have now and then explained why reason cannot grasp, let alone solve it. When we attempt to understand anything, they have pointed out, we consider its origin, development, and use, we observe how and to what it reacts, and we compare and contrast it with something else of its own or of a different kind. This is true even if what we are trying to understand is purely intellectual. There is at least a variable web of relationships in terms of which we can understand it. But what of existence? Where and how does it begin, what does it react to, and with what can it be compared and contrasted? What is its place in any variable web of relationships? Of course there are answers. Theology and philosophy are filled with them, and contemporary cosmology makes and remakes its conjectures every day. The persisting diversity of the answers is itself a sign that no one of them is generally persuasive. It is a question whether the absence of being or existence as a whole can ever be conceived and whether or not there is anything to compare it with as a whole. It is even a question whether such general questions about existence make any abstract sense.

It is only when we transpose the problem of being or existence as such into the problem of life and death that it begins to make clear sense. For very nearly all of us, living or living well is all our hope and dying or dying badly all our fear, and the vocabulary of 'existence' and 'non-existence' is the abstract counterpart of our hope and fear and the thoughts and imaginings that cluster around these. When we do transpose the problem, being or existence is, of course, equated with life, and non-being or non-existence with death. 'True' existence then becomes equivalent to that in life which demands the most attention or gives the greatest rewards, while 'illusory' being or existence becomes equivalent to that which, in fact or feeling, does not or ought not to demand any attention or give any reward that we value. To say that existence as a whole is 'illusory' is thus to express disappointment in life, to find it not to have fulfilled its promise and therefore to be painful, repulsive, insipid, or thin.

In saying this, I do not want to engage in one of the classical philosophical debates on the meaning of existence. On the contrary, I want to suggest that it is a fact that attitudes towards existence as a whole, whatever it may be and whether or not it is clearly conceivable, are based on or strongly influenced by our experiences. This is particularly true of experiences of success and failure and life and death, and most true of our experiences as small children, when we live, gladly or sadly, in keeping with the life, character, and death of those who have borne us and are responsible for our survival.

After this surfeit of generalities, I think it is time to give some particulars of the evidence for them. I therefore turn to a number of great philosophers, in the attempt to show how the thought of each of them expresses, transposed into his characteristic abstractions, what he senses to be the quality of his life.

6
Descartes to Rousseau

Some Preliminary Words

The biographies that follow have cost me a good deal of effort, not least because they are so brief. Their brevity and approximate similarity in structure should make it easier, when the time comes, to compare them. I may sometimes have documented too little or too much, and my contact with the primary sources has been variable; but I have tried to create a genuine bond with these sources.[1] My own memory, even with respect to philosophers I know well, is so often fallible in detail that I have tried to document even well-known facts or views. The whole point of these miniature biographies is, as it must be, their selective emphasis; but I have tried to leave them individual enough, close enough to the primary data, to allow a reader to impose his own emphasis and arrive at different conclusions. In other words, I have wanted to suggest certain conclusions, yet not to dominate or twist the data beyond redemption by others. The questions I have sometimes asked are not designed to insinuate interpretations by means of rhetoric rather than arguments. They are neither more nor less than questions I have asked myself and been unable to answer.

Despite my emphasis in the biographies, I have never said or wanted to suggest that the psychological factors explain everything of importance. I have not wanted to reduce philosophy to simpler constituents or to explain it away, but to establish more of its personal context and significance. Psychological are to philosophical factors as foundations to superstructures: they establish only their gross limits. Although, as I have earlier said, my interpretations are psychoanalytical in spirit, I have not tried to be psychoanalytically refined or profound, and I may have ended my accounts where a psychoanalyst would begin his. I have used only rather simple general principles to justify my interpretations and have as far as practicable sought out the basic evidence again in each case. Abstract psychological concepts, even such as I have myself named and described, are rarely if ever openly applied. They remain in the background, while the foreground, if I am successful, is dominated by the texture of each philosopher's life and thought.

I have written a total of twenty biographical accounts. I have sometimes been struck with the feeling that, to understand my subjects
thoroughly, I would need twenty lives of my own. Having only one, I
have done what I could with a reasonable fraction of it. Except for
occasional cross-references, each biography is dealt with independently;
but throughout the three chapters into which they are organized, the
biographies are numbered consecutively, from one to twenty, to remind
the reader that they are also links in a chain of evidence, the whole
of which will be discussed when it is completed.

The philosophers considered in the present chapter are Descartes,
Pascal, Spinoza, Locke, Leibniz, Berkeley, Voltaire, Hume, and Rousseau, each appearing in the order of his birth. The choice of these
philosophers is relatively easy to justify in terms of their influence on
philosophy and intellectual life generally. Except for the absence of Hobbes, the choice comes as close as possible, I think, to the established
consensus. Bayle or Gassendi might have been included, but, Hobbes
apart, all of the period's philosophers now conventionally thought to be
the greatest are here. Judged by the standards of the continental Europeans, Berkeley may not belong; but his likeness to Mach and the
Positivists and his importance in the eyes of Husserl might justify his
presence even to the continentals.

Before I go on to Descartes, a word on two omitted biographies. those
of Montaigne and Hobbes. Having written the two biographies, I have
retained their basic data in the table summarizing the biographies I have
dealt with. As a result, the table contains data on twenty-two, not twenty
philosophers. I own that I would be happy to have included Montaigne's
biography, because I like him and because his style of philosophizing
introduces the themes in which I am most interested. If he were included,
I would have dwelt on his loss of deep intimacy with others, except
through his *Essays*, which united his dead father, his dead friend, La
Boétie, and his own relatively motherless self, in the intimacy of his
ruminations, all shared with the anonymous reader, Montaigne's link
with the outside world. But despite my desire to include Montaigne, I
recall that I have written on him in previous pages, and I know that, to be
published, I have to be careful to limit the number of pages I write.

The omission of Hobbes has the same basic practical reason, the need
to keep my book within practicable bounds. This reason is supplemented
by two others. The first, ignoble one is that his birth-date precedes that
of Descartes, with whom it is conventionally natural to begin. The second reason, which should be more acceptable, is that I did not succeed, in
my own estimation, in understanding Hobbes well enough. Though I
would have stressed the flight of his father, his own early 'contemplative

Melancholinesse,' his fear (the source of fear as the basis of his political thought), and his boldness, I found the biographical data thin and my ability to use them persuasively too limited.

As Descartes himself would have thought only right, I therefore begin with Descartes and his conviction that true philosophy originated with him. The first sentences, like those in subsequent biographies, adopt an annalist's factual style.

Descartes

1. René Descartes, born in 1596. He lost his mother very early in life and was separated too soon, it seems, from his father as well. In a rare reference to his mother, he says that she died a few days after his birth.[1] He apparently did not know the truth, which was that she died over thirteen months later, soon after the birth of a girl who herself survived only very briefly. Descartes writes that his mother died 'of a lung disease caused by some disorder' (the words he uses, 'quelques déplaisirs,' may also mean 'some distress' or 'some misfortune'). In the letter in which he makes this confidence, he assumes that he inherited his own dry cough and pale complexion from his mother, and he goes on to say that he coughed and remained pale until after the age of twenty, so that all the doctors who saw him before that age condemned him to die young. But he adds, reassuringly, that his sickliness, 'which was as if natural' to himself, was little by little overcome by his inclination to see things so as to make them as agreeable as possible and to make his chief satisfaction depend on himself alone.

We are told elsewhere that Descartes was 'extremely frail until the age of thirteen.'[2] It is interesting that he identifies his ill, youthful self with his mother, implying that he inherited the threat of his own death from hers. He sees his cheerfulness and independence as a way of countering illness and, no doubt, sadness. As his study of *The Passions of the Soul* shows, he takes sadness, like other emotions, in a mental and a physiological sense. Both may have an obvious cause, he says, but may also result from an unknown association in the brain.[3] According to him, in sadness the pulse is weak and slow, and the heart feels constricted and suffers icy chills that communicate their coldness to the rest of the body.[4] To explain the pallor that often accompanies sadness, Descartes says that sadness contracts the orifices of the heart, and the blood, growing thicker and colder, retreats toward the heart, while the face, in particular, becomes pale and sunken.[5] But pallor, he says, does not come from sadness alone. In children it may be a substitute for tears of anger. 'There are some who grow pale instead of crying when they are angry, which may testify to judgment and extraordinary courage in them, that is, when it is because they consider the greatness of the evil and prepare themselves for a strong resistance, in the same way as do older people.'[6]

I assume that in these explanations Descartes is also drawing on his own experience and making a number of equations. He is, I would say, equating his own coughing with his pallor and his mother's death; his coughing, pallor, and mother's death with the anticipation of his own death; his pallor with his sadness; his pallor with his suppressed tears of anger and with the judgment and courage, which he undoubtedly attributed to himself, to overcome misfortune; and his ability to react with Stoic cheerfulness and emotional independence with his later good health and contentment.*

Descartes connects not only paleness, but also appetite with sadness. In his early notes, he writes, 'I observe that if I am sad, or if I find myself in danger, or if serious matters preoccupy me, I sleep deeply and I eat with very great appetite. If, on the contrary, joy relaxes me, I neither eat nor sleep.'[7] In the *Passions* he adds the explanation that one's first sadness, at least that unconnected with hatred, must have been caused by lack of nourishment.[8] The explanation is extended in a letter in which he writes, 'I quite believe that sadness destroys the appetite of some people, but because I have always experienced in myself that it increases it, I have based myself on that.' His kind of reaction, he says, depends on insufficient or unhealthy nourishment at the beginning of life, in which case 'the movement of the animal spirits which destroys the appetite has thereafter always remained joined with the passion of sadness.'[9] To put it in modern terms, loss of appetite in sadness is the result of an unconscious association made in infancy. Descartes also says, in effect, that an unassuaged infantile appetite survives in him.

What I have been repeating about pallor, sadness, and insufficient nourishment is all related, I think, to the early death of Descartes' mother. Her absence was accentuated by what may be judged to be the emotional absence of his father, caused by circumstance, unconcern, or both. The father, whose father and grandfather had been physicians, was a councillor of the Parlement of Brittany. The Parlement met at Rennes, to which the father had to go for sessions of three or four months each

---

*I do not mean to imply that Descartes draws only on himself for his theory. His attention had been drawn to the phenomena of blushing and pallor by the *De Anima* of J. L. Vives, the seventeenth-century humanist, who, like Descartes, refers openly to his own experience. See the introduction to Rodis-Lewis's edition of *Les passions de l'ame*, p. 28, note 1.

year, leaving the family at home, in La Haye (The Hague). The father
was away when Descartes was born, as well as when his wife and infant
daughter died.[10] When Descartes was four, the sessions of the Parlement
were lengthened to six months each year. It was about then, too, that
Descartes' father remarried. Descartes and, most likely, his elder brother
and sister grew up in La Haye in the home of their grandmother.[11]
Descartes scarcely mentions her in his letters. That he was also cared for
by another woman we know only from the report that on his deathbed
he dictated a letter asking that his nurse, 'who had always taken care of
him during his life,' should be provided for.[12] When Descartes was
fourteen, his grandmother died, but this was, in any case, some three or
four years after he had been sent to boarding school.

An early biographer says that Descartes' father called him '*my
philosopher*, because of the insatiable curiosity with which he asked him
the causes and effects of everything.'[13] The feeling that Descartes and his
father were distant from one another is strengthened by a report, the
authenticity of which there is no reason to doubt. According to the
report, his father

> was very annoyed to see that his son gave himself to the study of philos-
> ophy, to the extent of writing and composing books. He no doubt did
> not foresee the importance that would later be attributed to him and his
> writings, when he said. . ., 'Of all my children, I have been discontented
> only with one. Was it necessary to bring into the world a son ridiculous
> enough to have himself bound in calf!'[14]

Descartes appears to have been distant not only from his father but also
from his brother and sister. But the death of his father, when Descartes
was forty-four, moved him deeply, as we learn from a letter in which he
disagrees with 'those who think that tears and sadness belong only to
women' and recalls, 'I not long ago suffered the loss of two persons who
were very close to me and experienced that those who wanted to prohibit
sadness aroused it, whereas I was relieved by the complaisance of those
whom I saw to be touched by my sorrow.'[15]

One of the two persons Descartes was referring to was certainly his
father, while the other may be either his sister or his illegitimate daughter, Francine, both of whom died during the same year. Francine, who
was five, had been sick only three days. Descartes 'mourned her with a
tenderness that led him to experience that true philosophy does not at all
suppress naturalness. He declared that by her death she had inflicted on
him the greatest sorrow he had experienced in his life.'[16] Because
Descartes had no interest in living with Francine's mother, a servant,
there may no longer have been anyone with whom he could be emotionally very close. I think that he had completed the lesson his mother's

death and his father's distance had first taught him, that he ought to make his satisfaction depend on himself alone.

Having followed Descartes so far, we return to him at the age of ten or so, when he entered the Collège de la Flèche. He was to stay there until the age of eighteen or nineteen—the exact dates are in dispute. His father put him under the especial care of Father Charlet, a distant relative, who was or soon became the rector of the school. Charlet was fatherly toward Descartes.

> He granted him among other priviliges that of remaining a long time in bed during the mornings, as much because of his poor health as because he noticed in him a mind naturally disposed to meditation. Descartes, who on awakening found all the powers of his mind concentrated and all his senses calmed by the night's repose, profited by these favorable circumstances to meditate. This practice became so much his habit that he made it a way of studying for all his life. . . .[17]

As this old description indicates, the musing bridge between sleep and wakefulness remained important to Descartes. In a letter written many years later, from Amsterdam, he says that sleep promenades him in woods, gardens, and enchanted palaces. He wakes, and then, he says,

> I mingle my reveries of the day insensibly with those of the night; and when I notice that I am awake, it is only in order that my contentment should be more perfect and my senses participate, for I am not so severe as to refuse them anything that a philosopher might permit them without offending his conscience.[18]

It appears that, with Charlet's help, Descartes had discovered a fruitful self-indulgence not unlike a self-mothering, by which I mean, a sinking into fantasies and optimistic thoughts in the soft, protected environment of a bed.

At La Flèche, Descartes got not only his classical, but his scientific and philosophical education. The teaching methods were pleasant and stimulating. We are told that Descartes was allowed to study mathematics more or less as he pleased and that he astonished even himself by the ease with which he unravelled problems in geometry and algebra. The account of his education given in the *Discourse on Method* is critical less of the school than of the tradition it represented. He was also always concerned, as will be seen, to emphasize his intellectual independence. Many years later, in answer to a question, he recommended Jesuit teaching, especially that at La Flèche, adding that it was very useful to begin philosophy, the key to the other sciences, with the entire course as taught in the Jesuit schools.[19]

The relationship with the Jesuits remained important to Descartes for the rest of his life. After he became a philosopher, he was particularly eager that the Jesuits take up his ideas. It is true that he sought allies among them to defend him against the sometimes dangerous attacks to which he was subjected; but I think that he also sought emotional closeness for himself and his philosophy among his old, sympathetic teachers. The antagonism to the *Principles of Philosophy*, a book which may be said to have been destined for the Jesuits, caused him to turn to Father Charlet. He was turning to him, he wrote, because he was so obliged to him for his guidance and for the care he had taken of him, and because he, Charlet, could prevent the other Jesuits from misunderstanding his intentions.[20] Descartes closed a later letter with the words, 'I beg you to excuse me for the freedom with which I have exposed my feeling to you; this is not because I ignore the respect I owe you, but because, considering you as my father, I think you will not take it amiss if I behave toward you in the same way as I would toward him if he were still alive.'[21] This was more, I take it, than conventional flattery. Charlet's fatherliness had served Descartes particularly well.

When the years at La Flèche were over, Descartes spent some years, obscure to us in their sequence, during which he earned a law degree, developed a taste for gambling, and spent time with his family, now permanently at Rennes. There is no sign that he was attracted to the profession of his father, which became that of his brother as well. Instead, at the age of twenty-two, like other Frenchmen of his kind, he joined the army of Prince Maurice of Nassau as a gentleman-volunteer. This army, though Protestant, was the enemy of the Spanish–Austrian enemy, and was regarded as a good soldierly training-ground. It is not known if Descartes ever participated in a battle. After about a year, he by chance met a young doctor and scientist, Isaac Beeckman, who, like him, had been looking at a mathematical problem posted on a wall. A friendship between the two flowered quickly, and Descartes' scientific instincts were reawakened. He chose a problem in which Beeckman had long been interested and was hoping to solve mathematically: what are the most agreeable musical consonances and why are they such? In answer, Descartes wrote his first work, the *Compendium on Music*, which he dedicated to his new friend and ended with the hope that Beeckman would keep it hidden from others, who 'do not know that it was composed in haste for you alone, amid the ignorance of soldiers, by an idle and amateurish man submitted to a kind of life entirely at odds with his thoughts.'[22]

Then, in the springtime of friendship, Descartes' enthusiasm for

Beeckman was warm and eloquent. 'Love me and be sure that I could no more forget you,' he wrote to him, 'than the Muses themselves. It is they, in effect, who have attached me to you by a bond of affection that cannot end.' A few months later he wrote thanking Beeckman for having shaken him out of his indifference and saying, 'If, by chance, something not to be despised comes out of me, you will be right to claim it entirely for yourself.'[23]

For Descartes, it was a time not only of enthusiasm but of discovery. As he wrote to Beeckman, with the help of a pair of compasses he had invented, he had discovered 'four remarkable and completely new proofs.' Provided, he wrote, he could overcome his natural laziness and Destiny allowed him freedom, he hoped to set all mathematics in order. He hoped to create a new science that would allow the solution of all problems involving quantity. An infinite, incredibly ambitious task! he exclaimed; but he perceived, he told his friend, 'I know not what light in the obscure chaos of this science.'[24]

The letter went on. He had been travelling. The last voyage had been good. He had been forced back to shore by the wind; but the following day he had sailed into even more violent seas in a small boat, and this more in pleasure than in fear, because he had been testing himself, and now, having crossed the seas, a new experience for him, without suffering any nausea, he felt emboldened to undertake a greater voyage.

Descartes' life was always a travelling, often physical and more often intellectual, and a testing of himself. At the moment we are speaking of, he continued to travel physically, in a roundabout way, it seems, to join the army of Maxmillian of Bavaria, this time, too, as a gentleman-volunteer. The direction of his intellectual travelling is indicated by a number of interesting notes he set down.[25] He begins them tamely enough with, 'The fear of God is the beginning of wisdom.' He then writes that he is going on the world's stage masked, like the comedians who mask their flushed faces. The sense of concealment is clear, though not the reason for it. Perhaps he means that here stands a great mathematician disguised in a uniform, which conceals his nature and emotion. He writes that when young he was stimulated by the discoveries of others to ask himself if he could discover things for himself without the help of books; and he reminds himself that, beginning with this question, he came to see that he could proceed according to fixed rules. He writes that science is like a woman: if modest and always by her husband's side, she is respected; but if she gives herself to everyone, she is vilified. He makes a scornful reference to books with more pages than ideas. He refers ambitiously to the mathematical treatise he is imagining.

The idea of the mask returns to his mind: the sciences are masked; once the masks are removed, they will appear in all their beauty. Whoever sees the chain of the sciences completely will find them no harder to keep in his mind than the series of numbers. A sudden modesty or fear then strikes him. He tells himself sternly that fixed limits are set to all minds—they cannot go beyond them.

How many future Cartesian themes have already made their appearance, and what great ambitions! Such themes and ambitions must have been preoccupying Descartes on the night of November 10, 1619, when he had the three dreams that marked a turning point in his life. He was quite sober, he insists. In the first of the dreams he finds himself walking along the streets, and he turns to the left to counteract a great weakness he feels on his right side. Dreaming, he is ashamed of the way he is walking and tries to straighten himself. The walking, the weakness, and the effort to straighten himself foreshadow, I think, the lines that Descartes will yet write, in the *Discourse on Method*, in which he recalls that he spent much of his youth travelling and proving himself in the encounters that fortune offered him. 'I always had an intense desire,' he will say in the *Discourse*, 'to learn to distinguish the true from the false, so as to act clear-sightedly and to walk with assurance in this life.'[26] In the third part of the *Discourse* he further compares those who search for knowledge with travellers who, 'finding themselves lost in some forest, ought never to wander, turning now to one side and now to the other.'

Descartes' stress in the dream on walking straight and in the *Discourse* on walking with assurance in life suggests that he was aware of some weakness in himself. His childhood could not have promoted much self-assurance. Neither as a child nor later did he have more than intimations of a full, stable family life. He walked on by himself, always consciously finding his way, and always depending primarily, as he had learned, on himself.

To return to the dream, the ashamed Descartes trying to straighten himself feels a violent wind that sweeps him around in a kind of swirl and makes him revolve three or four times on his left foot. This swirling is interesting in itself; but we may be reminded that in Descartes' physics, which is still not yet in existence, there is a pervasive motif of turning, circling, or swirling—the pervasive swirl of his physics is given the same name, *tourbillon*, as his dreamed wind. The ideal traveller walks straight, as the unimpeded particle moves in a straight line. But in the physical space he will imagine, as, it will become evident, in the social space in which he lived, particles were in fact never unimpeded, and they were forced, so to speak, to conform and move in approximately circular paths, which expressed, as Descartes was to express in his everyday life, the exact union of compliance with resistance.*

Now, the dream again. What frightens Descartes in it is the difficulty he has in dragging himself along, which makes him think that at each step he is falling down. He begins to pay attention to the way he is walking and to each separate step. In the second part of the *Discourse* he writes, as if guarding himself against the memory of the dream,

> Like one who walks alone and in the twilight I resolved to go slowly, and to use so much circumspection in all things, that if my advance was but very small, I at least guarded myself well against falling.

In the *Meditations*, caution no longer seems to be enough:

> All the course of my life may be divided into an infinite number of parts, none of which is in any way dependent on the other; and thus from the fact that I was in existence a short while ago it does not follow that I must be in existence now, unless some cause at this instant, produces me, so to speak, anew, that is to say, conserves me.[27]

Small, cautious, and methodical as the steps may be, they do not cohere by themselves, they form no continuous path, they lead nowhere. Descartes must seek, he says, for the author of his existence, who produces him anew and conserves him. To search for the author of one's existence is not altogether different from searching for one's unknown mother or one's distant, not especially familiar father. Their emotional support has never become internal and must always be affirmed and reaffirmed. When Descartes asks, in the same *Meditation*, whether he has a power that can itself keep him in existence, he answers negatively. Descartes the methodologist is motivated by his childhood's lack to become Descartes the believer and near-Occasionalist.

It may appear strange that Descartes felt such weakness and dependence at the same time as he felt and demonstrated his need to be independent. The need for independence can be neatly illustrated by his relationship with Beeckman. The spring of their friendship lapsed in

---

*The analogy does not pretend to be more than a guess, nor does it exclude other reasons for the theory of tourbillons. To Descartes, fine matter is a fluid, and he thinks in terms of hydraulic models, somewhat as do Freud and the ethologists, Lorenz and Tinbergen. He sees the body as a circulatory system in which more or less rarefied fluid flows through pipes of varying degrees of fineness. The image and the theory of circulation dominate much of his thought. Since Descartes' particles rub shoulders densely everywhere while Newton's are the separate, relatively sparse inhabitants of a vacuum, the difference might be related to Descartes' feeling of inescapable social pressure as against Newton's real and perhaps satisfactory social isolation, disturbed, of course, by the pulls of gravity. To those who think that analogies, like crimes, ought not to be compounded, I offer my excuses.

time, and after eleven years, in 1630, it reached its winter. In the winter of friendship Descartes complains that Beeckman has been heard saying that he, Beeckman, taught Descartes the contents of the *Compendium on Music*. I will not go into the question to what extent Descartes' musical theory was original or important.[28] From my standpoint, the interesting thing is how angry Descartes becomes at the imputation cast upon his originality. Descartes regrets that he has so far written Beeckman with the deceptive politeness of the French. Beeckman is no doubt boasting that he was Descartes' teacher. Descartes' answer of 17 October 1630, fills thirteen abusive pages in print. Its style is best conveyed by a few excerpts:

> I could in no way imagine that you had become so stupid and that you understood yourself so badly that you might in effect think that I had ever learned from you, or even that I could ever learn anything from you, if not in the way I usually learned from all the things that existed in nature, even the least ants and the smallest worms. . . . But I see clearly by your last letters that you have not sinned in this by malice but are undoubtedly held in the grip of an illness. . . . Consider, I ask you, and see if in all your life you have found or invented anything that is really worth praising? . . . Do you not try to praise me only to gain the more glory by the comparison? . . . But enough of that, I want to treat your illness gently now, and not to use harsher remedies at all; for if I should treat you as you deserve, you would be so burdened with shame and infamy that I should be afraid of driving you to despair rather than giving you health. . . . I am ashamed to propose myself here as an example, but as you often compare yourself with me, it seems that it is in some way necessary. Have you ever heard me praise myself for having taught anything to anyone?

Descartes ends his letter with the hope that he will not be forced to expose Beeckman in public, but that the sinner's repentance may be followed by a renewed friendship—the friendship, if it should now be given the name, was eventually renewed, without much warmth.[29] As I have said, I do not want to go into the substance of the controversy, though the survival of Beeckman's *Journal* shows him to have been an informed and in some ways original scientist. Although Descartes knew how to dip his pen in acid, his letter to Beeckman was an uncharacteristically prolonged and violent outburst. Why was Descartes so angry? I can only speculate on the answer but think it likely that he sensed an infringement on his autonomy and worth. Descartes was no longer a child, student, or tyro. Beeckman's desire to continue to be a mentor, a psychic father, touched on Descartes' unfulfilled need for parents, a need against which he had erected heavy defences. He would not be compared, led, or taught by anyone but himself. In the words of his most scholarly biographer, 'Above all, Descartes admired almost nothing and no one.'[30]

It was out of the need to be and to be known as original that Descartes refrained from composing his *Geometry* as clearly as his own ideals demanded. In the *Geometry* itself he pointed out that his readers ought to have the pleasure of mastering the problems themselves and the benefit of training their minds without excessive help. But to a correspondent he wrote that he had 'made a book which demands readers not only very learned in all things that have been known up to now in geometry and algebra, but also very industrious, very ingenious, and very attentive persons.'[31] He estimated the number of such persons in the land of his correspondent as two. To another correspondent he stressed that his *Geometry* was difficult in order to thwart his scientific enemies:

'My *Geometry* is as it should be to keep Roberval and his like from vilifying it unless their vilification redound to their own confusion; for they are not able to understand it, and I have composed it so quite on purpose. . . .'[32]

Yet the desire to be autonomous, that is, to philosophize with no debt to others, was no desire to be isolated. On the contrary, the resolve to strip himself 'of all opinions and beliefs formerly received' was designed to create intimacy, as if, disappointed in one group, he was now seeking for closeness with another.[33] He was appealing to the ordinary upright person, the honnête homme, who had not read too many traditional books, who might not have learned rhetoric, who might speak only the language of Lower Brittany, but who had genuinely good sense.[34] Descartes wrote the *Discourse* in French rather than in the language of his teachers, Latin, in the hope that those who used their natural reason rather than ancient books alone should be able to judge him better.[35] He excluded obscure and technical matters so that even women should be able to understand; and when he learned that a woman, a serious princess, it is true, was reading his books, his response was that he took her judgment more seriously than that of the learned Doctors who preferred the opinions of Aristotle to the truth.[36]

Descartes quite early expressed his ambition to create a methodical, rational, universal language that would allow peasants to judge the truth of things better than philosophers had hitherto done.[37] He seems, in fact, to have had a good deal of sympathy with plain, unlettered people. In his later years, when he was living in the countryside, he showed his interest in the welfare of his faithful cook and valet; he initiated many of the country folk into the principles of his philosophy; he educated and made a friend of a beggarly-looking shoemaker who persisted in trying to see him; and he taught one of his servants, who later became the director of the school of engineering at Leiden. He also spent much time and effort trying to free a peasant innkeeper who, under extreme provocation, had committed murder, and whose imprisonment had left his wife and two small children helpless.[38]

There was much, then, in the nature of Descartes and his philosophy meant to detach him from one kind of person, who belonged to the community of the traditionally or wrongly sophisticated, and to attach him to another kind of person, the sensible, simple, natural, and optimistic. For his goals were, essentially, greater human power and health. The power he tried to further with technological devices, optical, hydraulic, and other, and with a call for 'the invention of an infinity of devices.'[39] As for health, 'the primary good and the foundation of all the other goods of life,' it was his intention, he said, to spend his whole life in medical research; and he stated, truly enough, I think, 'The conservation of health was at all times the principal goal of my studies.'[40] He was, after all, the grandson and great-grandson of doctors, and his own health had worried him greatly in his youth. He hoped to arrive at results quickly, for example, to find a medicine, based on infallible demonstrations, to cure the erysipelas of his friend, Mersenne.[41] When the *Discourse* was published, he asked for reactions from doctors.[42] His letters are filled with medical advice, whether psychological or physical. The key seemed to him to be bodily hygiene and, especially, diet, both of which he pursued so successfully, he thought, that he might live to be a hundred.[43] An abbé who stayed in the country with him for several months and reported on his diet, including omelettes made of eight-to-ten–day–old eggs, believed that the philosopher had discovered the secret of living for three or four centuries.[44] Following a certain disappointment in his medical research, Descartes came to say that one should obey nature, for 'with her perfect internal awareness of herself she knows better than the doctor who is on the outside.'[45] I am almost sorry to disturb this picture of Descartes, the still optimistic researcher, and report that, like a true Stoic, he once wrote in a letter, 'In place of finding the means of conserving life, I have found another, much easier and more sure, which is not to fear death.'[46]

The medical secrets Descartes was searching for seemed to him to depend on anatomy, and so he anatomized very pertinaciously. In the winter of 1629, to give an example, he visited a butcher's shop almost every day to find organs for dissection. Although he read the anatomists,

> he taught himself in a much surer way by personally dissecting animals of different species; and he discovered directly many things more detailed than the ones all these authors had reported in their books . . . He declared to Father Mersenne that after ten or eleven years of searching he had found

nothing, however small, whose purpose, and whose formation through natural causes, he felt unable to explain in detail. . . .[47]

The immediate medical results might be modest in Descartes' eyes, but he thought that anatomy had explained to him the mechanisms of digestion, pulse, distribution of nourishment, and sensation, and he said, with what must now seem strange naiveté, 'I am now dissecting the heads of different animals to explain the makeup of imagination, memory, etc.'[48] To discover how the sense organs were joined to a central mechanism and, perhaps, to the soul, he cut open brains to find the pineal gland; and to discover the other secrets of life, he observed the still-beating hearts of calves and the foetuses, 'some as big as mice, others like rats, and others like little dogs,' in the wombs of slaughtered cows.[49]

I do not think that all this anatomizing curiosity is merely and self-evidently medical and 'philosophical.' I will try to explain; but before I do so, I would like to consider two of Descartes' most characteristic traits, his secretiveness and his resoluteness, and, with them, his philosophic view of God as the creator of truth. The traits and the view will converge, I think, on a plausible image of the philosopher.

It was evident to those who knew Descartes that he preferred to live in solitude (though always with servants). He tried to live so, he said, in order to further his search for the truth, his principal interest in life.[50] At times he wanted none of his acquaintances and perhaps even friends to know where he was, and he might ask not to be written to for a while.[51] His need for solitude seemed allied with restlessness, because he often moved from place to place. In Holland, he lived in Amsterdam, Franeker, Deventer, Utrecht, Leyden, Santport, Endegeest, Egmond du Hoef, Egmond, and no doubt elsewhere.[52] It is true that philosophical polemics disturbed his peace and perhaps stimulated his suspicion of messengers and his concealment of what he had written.[53] But he had long ago seen himself as the masked comedian and had rather early in his career adopted the Ovidian motto, 'He has lived well who has lived secretly.'[54] Much of his life was spent, it should be recalled, in the quasi-secrecy of his own morning meditations and waking dreams.

The relationship in Descartes between openness and secrecy is allied, I think, with another, which is central to his thought, between resolution or certainty, on the one hand, and irresolution or uncertainty, on the other. He builds, of course, on the conception of axiomatic truths and infallible method, and he is usually very sure of himself, his philosophy, and his science. Yet he is fairly quickly driven or drives himself to positions with at least an air of paradox. He searches for the sure way to exploit life and live long, but is tempted to the stoic acceptance of whatever happens. He has a positive ideal of science in mind, but maintains, perhaps defensively, that the laws of meteorology are hypothetical.[55] He knows that soul and body cannot, by his standards, affect one another, but in fact do, and when questioned on the problem can only answer, 'This is very difficult to explain; but here our experience is sufficient.'[56] Given such reasons for hesitation, and given his own defensively resolute personality, it is not surprising that he thinks of resolution as a great virtue and irresolution as a great fault. In the *Passions of the Soul* he speaks of the 'abjectness' or vicious humility that 'consists principally in the fact that men are feeble or have a lack of resolution' and cannot, as a result, 'prevent themselves from doing things of which they will afterwards repent.'[57] He also speaks of irresolution as a fear that is both strong and usual in some people, who show 'an excess of irresolution which proceeds from a feebleness of understanding, which, having no clear and distinct conceptions, simply has many confused ones.'[58] It is this fear, irresolution, that he is always combatting with his criterion of clarity and distinctness, his absolute principles, and his step-by-step method. It appears that, to him, resolution and irresolution are simultaneously personal, moral, and metaphysical traits.

These traits lead us to God, who functions in Descartes' system, as in so many others, as an absolute. The great conundrums of every sort are answered in terms of God's nature, which cannot really be interrogated, for here questions stop. Descartes criticizes Galileo for not having made questions stop, that is, for not 'having considered the first causes of nature,' and so for building without a foundation.[59] As for his own physics, he begins with the 'God who, as everyone ought to know, is immutable, acts always in the same way.'[60] To such a God he can safely attach the most general law of physics, the conservation of motion, as well as the laws of inertia and of the passage of motion by impact from body to body, which provide, as a modern historian has said, 'the foundation on which the modern science of dynamics has been constructed.'[61]

Descartes is so set on basing everything on God that he is willing to argue that although the atheist can know that the three angles of a triangle are equal to two right angles, he cannot know this with certainty, for he cannot be sure that he is not deceived.[62] To escape the charge of circular reasoning, he says that he intends this argument to apply when the person in question is not directly attending to what he perceives.[63] Partly to escape the objection that the existence of both God and the eternal truth would mean that there were two immutable, eternal beings, Descartes contends that the truths, such as the equality of the three angles of a triangle to two right angles, are immutable and eternal because God has willed them so.[64] Now Descartes can claim to 'demonstrate the metaphysical truths in a way that is more evident than the demonstrations of geometry.'[65] For God has established his laws in nature and imprinted them on our minds, so 'there is no single one we cannot understand if our mind proceeds to consider it.'[66]

The extraordinarily optimistic conclusion is that all possible science is essentially open to human understanding. But there is an immediate and heavy price to pay, because all truth and, with it, all science is based on God's unintelligible greatness. While the necessity of truth fits the measure of our knowledge, God, who is beyond knowledge, dominates and can change the truth. In other words, the comprehensible is based on the incomprehensible, and Descartes' rationalism has turned into a kind of irrationalism. Descartes is therefore at odds with Thomism, which accepts metaphysical hierarchies and analogies according to which eternal truths belong to the science of God and partake of God's nature.[67]

Useful (and difficult) as God is for Cartesian science and philosophy, he has another major function, which is to sustain the world as a whole and each individual within it. 'From the fact that we are,' says Descartes, 'it does not follow that we will be a moment afterwards' unless the same first cause that produced us continues to produce, that is, conserve us. The very fact that we endure proves the existence of God.[68] Thomism, too, believes that the world requires God's constant support, but between him and embodied beings it interposes a hierarchy of substantial forms and essences. Descartes' doctrine, which makes God the direct, efficient cause of everything, even himself, has a new immediacy and simplicity that parallels the immediacy and simplicity of his physics.[69]*

At this point, having discussed the philosophical usefulness of Descartes' God in his system, I would like to return to the psychological possibilities. I cannot believe that Descartes was compelled by historical or philosophical reasons to conceive just the God he did. His God created philosophical difficulties for him no less than resolved them, and because there were, logically speaking, other conceptions of God he might have chosen, the God he did choose must also have been psychologically useful to him. For one thing, this God was metaphysically intimate and

---

*I know of no positive evidence that the views of Descartes were influenced by Islamic theology, that is, the Kalam, which believed that God could do the impossible even in the logical sense, and that he created everything constantly and directly. Descartes could have found much of Kalam argument in Aquinas or elsewhere. H. A. Wolfson, *The Philosophy of the Kalam* (Cambridge, Mass.: Harvard University Press, 1976), pp. 518–21, 542–4, 584–86, 589–92. M. Fakhry, *Islamic Occasionalism and Its Critique by Averröes and Aquinas* (London: Allen & Unwin, 1958).

unceasingly supportive. In Descartes' later years, the thought of the all-knowing, all-supportive God filled him with extreme joy. To reach the love of God, he said, the incomparably greatest and most perfect of loves, we should 'consider that he is a mind, or a thing that thinks,' and that he resembles our soul's nature enough to persuade us that our soul is an emanation of his sovereign intelligence.[70]

This stress on our closeness to God by means of intelligence is the stress natural to a thinker whose abstractions not alone give him great pleasure but answer some demand of his conscience. It brings us back to Descartes' curiosity, probably characteristic of him as a child and certainly as an adult. Curiosity is a subject that interests him. We see this when he offers the opinion 'that wonder [as the French *admiration* may be translated] is the first of all the passions.' He defines wonder as 'a sudden surprise of the soul which causes it to apply itself with attentive consideration to the objects which seem to it rare and extraordinary.' But wonder, though useful, is also dangerous in Descartes' eyes. This passion, he says, 'may entirely prevent or pervert the use of reason' by interesting us excessively in what deserves little or no attention.[71] In his dialogue, *The Search for Truth*, a participant declares, 'The desire for knowledge, which is common to all men, is an evil which cannot be cured.' He equates the evil with the insatiability of the desire, which sustains itself, 'for curiosity increases with knowledge.' The suggested remedy is to be satisfied with the general principles of things, with the help of which everything particular can be simply explained, so that 'the passion for knowledge . . . will no longer be so violent.'[72]

There is a chance that Descartes' not easily satiable curiosity was accompanied by guilt that influenced him not to pry into frivolous or over-seductive particulars. The supposition that he felt guilty over his curiosity is confirmed by the careful account that his early biographer, Baillet, gives of his death. Having lost and then regained consciousness, 'he concluded that, since God had given him the free use of his reason, he therefore permitted him to follow what it dictated to him, provided that he refrained from desiring to penetrate too curiously into his decrees and from showing uneasiness at the occasion.' The following night Descartes declared that he had resolved to die, in the hope that God 'would accept the voluntary sacrifice he offered him in expiation of all the faults of his life.'[73]

I have no way of interpreting these death-bed reactions exactly, but guilt alone and guilt in curiosity both appear. Guilt and curiosity are not, we know, unnatural companions. Our knowledge of Descartes' life is insufficient to explain why the two appeared together in him; but something may be guessed on general principles. The absence of a mother was not only a misfortune to him, but was somehow his fault. Why, otherwise, should he mistakenly connect her death with his birth? And in searching for the source and nature of life, was he also searching for her, and feeling guilty at the search, the success of which might only confirm his responsibility? Was his study of medicine an attempt to escape the illness she had conferred on him and escape his own misfortune or guilt by association with her? Was his relative isolation and lack of desire to marry, an emptiness, sucpicion, or fear that also allowed him to remain in distant contact with a mother he could not remember at all? Descartes may also have felt guilty because he was rather distant from his father, who appears to have been unhappy with his choice of profession. In any case, Descartes' emotional distance from others and his proud declarations that he was beholden to no one were also defensive.

Descartes' life was characterized by a willing loneliness and an unwilling fear of being lost; but also by the courage and intelligence, those of the pale child who refused to cry, to find a methodical way of going ahead. All his life he searched, not only into thoughts, but into literal bodies and organs of animals. He grew to love the distant God and to submit to his will; but this was an incomprehensible God and will, vaguely reminiscent of Descartes' distant father and of Descartes himself. The philosophical certainties Descartes reached were in near-equilibrium with uncertainties, for they were always threatened with paradox and circularity. Yet, and therefore, he was a great thinker. He was perhaps the most able mathematical thinker of his time.[74] He reduced geometrical to algebraic problems, transferring algebraic to geometrical structures. He gave traditional geometry the idea of constant and variable, projecting onto mathematics, I am tempted to say, the gist of his own problem, and he formulated the ideal of a universal mathematics. His physics was comprehensive, audacious, and simple enough to be put, if only by others and with corrections, into mathematical form, and his physiology, though in large part fantastic, was entirely mechanical and easy to grasp and investigate. As I have said, he even inspired the great Newton, who made good use of the principle of inertia, which Descartes, it seems, was the first to state in unambiguously universal form, though Newton hated him and scribbled 'error, error' on his copy of Descartes' *Geometry*.[75]

But Descartes the scientific philosopher belongs to his own time, for his science, though not the ideal he held of it, is primitive and outmoded. His attractiveness has come to be centered in the way in which he dramatizes his predicament of doubt and certainty and, forgetting precedent, begins from himself. As a beginning, this is permanent, and it remains in the endless present of a lyric or autobiography. It is his need to be original and find his way, for himself, not in the company of parents or traditions, that we feel most keenly. He begins from a beginning that each of us can enact, for it corresponds to feelings shared by everyone to whom philosophy is natural. His problems and responses are renewed in each impressionable reader.

Something of what little we can say of Descartes' relationship with women has already been said. He himself writes in a letter that, when a child, he fell in love with a slightly cross-eyed girl of his own age, after which he tended to love cross-eyed people.[76] When Descartes was twenty-nine and his relatives pressed him to marry, he made the acquaintance of the young and meritorious Madame de Rosay, so we hear; but Descartes told her that while she did not seem ugly to him, there were no feminine beauties comparable to those of the truth. He had seen too many men, he said to her, who had, unlike himself, been duped by women, to which ungallant remark he added that a beautiful woman, a good book, and a perfect preacher were among the most difficult things to find in this world.[77] More gallantly, he disarmed a rival lover and then returned the lover's sword with the words that the lover owed his life, not to him, but to the lady.

Descartes' relations with a servant girl, who bore his daughter, Francine, in 1635, when Descartes was thirty-nine, have already been mentioned. Before Francine's death, he tried to have mother and daughter come and live close to him. Four years after Francine's death, Descartes, alluding to her mother, spoke of 'a dangerous commitment from which he had extricated himself, almost ten years ago,' the time when Francine had been conceived. God, 'by a continuation of the same grace,' he said, 'had preserved him until now from backsliding.'[78] Perhaps there is a muted reference to the mother of his child in the *Passions*, when he says that a not very loving husband may shed genuine tears at his wife's funeral 'even though he meanwhile feels a secret joy in his inmost soul.'[79]

Descartes enjoyed the company of some children. He was interested, for instance, in those of Huygens, one of whom became the famous mathematician.[80] His one significant companionship with a woman was that with the princess Elizabeth, whose father, Frederick, who died of the plague, had been Descartes' own age. The philosopher and the very well-educated princess, who knew five languages and had scientific ability, met more often in letters than in person. Descartes was flattered by her interest in his books. Everything, science, personal problems, and illnesses, got into the correspondence, including a few rare confidences of Descartes, on which I have drawn. Descartes dedicated the

Principles of Philosophy to her, and their discussions on the nature of the emotions led him to compose the *Passions of the Soul*. Descartes and Elizabeth were both intellectually and emotionally useful to one another.

Queen Christina, who invited Descartes to Sweden, was a learned, forceful, interesting woman of a sort. Seduced, I suppose, by the prospect of becoming the Queen's philosopher, he made the trip. This turned out to be a literally fatal mistake, for he died in Sweden, perhaps of pneumonia.

Pascal

2. Blaise Pascal, born in 1623. His childhood is best described in the words of his elder sister, Gilberte:

> From the time my brother was old enough to be talked with, he showed signs of a quite extraordinary mind by the little answers, very much to the point, that he gave, but even more by questions, which surprised everybody, on the nature of things. This beginning, which gave good hopes, was never belied, for to the extent he grew older, his power of reasoning grew, so that he was far ahead of his age.
>
> Meanwhile, my mother having died by 1626, when my brother was only three years old, my father, seeing himself alone, devoted himself more vigorously to the care of his family, and, as he had no other son but this one, the quality of only son and the other qualities he recognized in this child gave him so great an affection for him that he could not decide to commit his education to anyone else and from then resolved to teach him himself, as he had been doing, my brother never having set foot in a *collège* [secondary school] or had any teacher but my father.
>
> In 1632 my father retired to Paris, where he brought us and established his residence. My father's plan to bring up my brother, who was then only eight, was greatly aided by this retirement, for it is sure that my father would have been unable to take the same pains out in the country, where the exercise of his office and his continual visitors would have distracted him considerably. But in Paris he was quite free; he applied himself unreservedly and had all the success that could be won by the care of as intelligent and affectionate a father as could be.[1]

Now began Pascal's extraordinary education. The father did not want to overtax him too soon with Latin. Instead, he discussed the general structure of languages with him, showing him how languages had been reduced to grammatical rules, which had exceptions to be noted, but which made the languages communicable from country to country. Pascal thereupon understood why there were rules of grammar, and when he came to learn them, he applied himself to just what needed the most work.

The father then went on to other matters. He often talked to him about the surprising effects of nature, such as those of gunpowder and the like. The son took great pleasure in these conversations, but he wanted to know the reason for everything, and was dissatisfied when the father was unable to explain or gave only the customary, mistaken explanations.

> For he always had an admirably clear mind for the detection of mistakes, and one can say that the truth, always and in everything, was the sole object of his mind, for nothing but his knowledge was ever able to satisfy him. From his infancy on, he preferred only whatever seemed to him obviously true, so that when not given satisfactory reasons, he never let the matter go till he found someone who could satisfy him.[2]

Pascal's sister, from whom all this account has been taken, goes on to tell the story I have told earlier, how, despite his father, he reconstructed part of Euclidean geometry for himself. As I have described, the feat became known to his father, who was overjoyed, and who relented and allowed Pascal to read Euclid for recreation. Soon after, Pascal began to take part in mathematicians' discussions.[3]

I may, at this point, interpolate what should have become obvious, that Pascal's father was well off and had little to preoccupy him in Paris but the education of his children, especially his son; that he himself loved mathematics; that he stressed analytical understanding; and that he took great pride in the accomplishments of his son. Of Pascal's earliest years we know really nothing of importance except that he was motherless. When the family moved to Paris, a housekeeper was hired to look after him and his two sisters.[4] The account of his childhood and adolescence I have repeated makes it appear as if Pascal's life were dominated by a preceptor-father. Pascal's eager response shows that he soon recognized the pleasure of sheer thinking and solving of problems; but he also wanted, I suppose, to please and emulate his father. His filial response was not unlike Montaigne's, or as we will see, unlike Leibniz's and Mill's. The psychological explanation given for Descartes' curiosity might also fit his. That is, his extreme desire to know the causes of things might have expressed a craving to know more about his earliest life, especially with his mother, whose memory had no doubt become tantalizingly vague.

When Pascal was fifteen, the family peace was shattered by the flight of the father. What had happened was this: The father had taken part in a meeting of investors who protested that the financial policies of the government were ruining them. Their anger verged on the seditious, and Cardinal Richelieu had their leaders imprisoned. Pascal's father disguised himself and fled, leaving his three children in Paris. Scheming to get him

pardoned, his friends decided to use Jacqueline, Pascal's attractive, precocious, and poetic younger sister, as their instrument. Jacqueline thereupon wrote a sonnet to the pregnant queen and verse-compliments to her
ladies, but these failing their purpose, she was given a role in a play that
Richelieu was to attend. When the play was done, she presented
Richelieu with a versified request to recall her father from exile.[5] This
time her plea was successful, and the father was recalled and given the
post of commissioner of taxation of Upper Normandy. The Pascal family established itself, as a result, in Rouen, though father and son would
often return to Paris and its scientists. Pascal, the son, first won his place
among the scientists when, at sixteen, he wrote a brief, pregnant work on
conics, that is, projective geometry.[6]

Soon Pascal was given the opportunity to help his father and show that
he could live up to his father's ambitions. They were both engaged in
long and monotonous tax calculations, and Pascal got the idea of lighten-
ing them by means of a sort of clockwork adding machine. The idea was
not in itself complicated, but the craftsmen and materials at hand made
the execution devilishly hard. Within a period of two years, Pascal
constructed more than fifty models of his machine.[7] According to his
sister, Gilberte, the father took such pleasure in Pascal's scientific
progress that he was unable to see that it was costing him his health. She
wrote that the difficulty of conceiving and implementing the reduction
of an entirely mental science to machine form fatigued Pascal excessively.
'This fatigue and the fragility of his health for the past few years made
him subject to persistent ailments, the result being, he sometimes told us,
that from the age of eighteen not a day had passed without some pain.'[8]
But Pascal took enormous pride in his machine, which he advertised
however he could and saluted with a sonnet of his own devising. His
pride was still evident, years later, when he offered Queen Christina of
Sweden the gift of his machine, 'which performs arithmetical calculations without a pen and without counters.' In the letter accompanying his
gift, Pascal declared that he especially venerated those who had attained
the highest rank in power or knowledge. He wrote, 'The same degrees of
rank may be encountered among geniuses as among nobles, and it seems
to me that the power of kings over their subjects is but an image of the
power of minds over those minds which are their inferiors, over those
whom they have the right to lead by persuasion.'[9] This letter of implicit
but clear praise for himself should be recalled when Pascal attacks his
own pride.

Pascal was changing. From about the age of twenty-two, his religious
tendencies became more evident. He was influenced by two ardently
Christian doctors who treated his father's fractured thigh. Gilberte says

that up to the age of twenty-four he had felt protected by providence from all the vices of youth and had confined his curiosity to natural things. He attributed this self-restriction to his father's teachings. As his sister says:

> He told me several times that he joined this duty to all the others he had got from my father who, himself respecting religion very greatly, had inspired him from childhood and given him the maxim that whatever is the object of faith cannot be that of reason. These maxims, which were often reiterated to him by a father for whom he had very great respect and in whom he saw very great knowledge accompanied by extremely clear and extremely powerful reasoning, made so great an impression on his mind that, whatever the discourse he heard made to the libertines, he was not moved by it at all and, though very young, regarded them as people who approved the false principle that human reason is above all things and who did not understand the nature of faith. Thus this mind, so great, so capacious, and so filled with curiosity, which searched with such care for the cause and reason of everything, was at the same time as submissive in all matters of religion as a child.[10]

According to Gilberte, her brother's desire to please God grew to such an extent that by the age of twenty-four his love of perfection filled the house. The father too, she says, grew increasingly assiduous in the practice of Christianity. As for the younger sister, Jacqueline, 'she was so touched by the discourses of my brother,' says Marguérite, 'that she resolved to renounce all the privileges she had so loved until then and devote herself completely to God.'[11] It was not incidental to this resolution that Jacqueline refused an offer of marriage.[12]

By the time Pascal was twenty-four, his elder sister reports, his ailments had grown severe, to the point that he could no longer drink liquids unless warmed and administered drop by drop. He suffered, as well, from an insupportable headache, a warmth in the intestines, and 'many' other unspecified ailments. The doctors, whose medicine he stoically accepted, advised him to give up all intellectual pursuits and divert himself in more conventional ways. Complying, as usual, with their wishes, he entered what is known as his worldly period.[13] Yet at twenty-five he wrote an emotional letter in which he said that he was becoming increasingly conscious of his lack of ability, and that instead of bringing light to others, he was himself troubled or confused. God alone could give him calm, he wrote, and promised to apply himself and search for Him.[14]

By now Jacqueline was determined to become a nun, but the father, arguing that his health was poor, got her to promise not to become a regular nun during the short time that was all, he was sure, that remained to him.[15] On September 24, 1651, Pascal and Jacqueline were witnesses to his death. Pascal was twenty-eight at the time. Our insight into his reaction comes from a long, emotional, Augustinian kind of letter, really a treatise, to Marguérite and her husband, who had not been present at the father's death. Pascal says in the letter that death is the penalty imposed on man to expiate his crime, and 'death alone can deliver the soul from the lust of its members.' Life is and ought to be, he says, a perpetual sacrifice completed by death, and Jesus Christ, by his coming into the world, gave himself as a living sacrifice to God. His conclusion is, 'Let us then consider life as a sacrifice.' Unless we have recourse to the mediation of Jesus Christ, 'everything in man is abominable.'[16] Death without Jesus is detestable, with him it is holy and joyous.[17] Pascal's mother had died long ago. He himself had long been ill. Now his father, the mainstay of his life, had died. If life could be accepted and understood at all, it could be so only, to Pascal, as the fulfilment of a sacrifice.

In the letter, Pascal goes on to say that his father was lost, not at the moment of death, but of baptism, when he came to belong to God.[18] We should think of him at death as only beginning to live. Then comes the sentence that lingers behind so much of his thought;

'If we are to overcome this horror more fully we must indeed understand its origin.'[19]

Pascal continues that he and the rest of the family should do what is possible to restore their father to life within themselves. Their father still lives in the union of their hearts; they must inherit the affection he bore them. 'If I had lost him six years ago,' Pascal writes, 'I would have been lost.' Now, though he would have been helpful for the whole of life, 'he is not quite so indispensable.' It is to be hoped that God's decree is the best 'for His glory and our salvation.'[20]

Released from her promise by the father's death, Jacqueline, without telling Pascal, entered the convent of her choice. Pascal, an irascible but quickly remorseful man, raged at Jacqueline in an uncharacteristically violent and prolonged fury. She threatened to stop seeing him. He again fell into a rage and got one of his violent headaches; then, looking at her, he was filled with pity and gave his consent. But a difficulty remained. She wanted to make over her share of the estate to the convent, while he and Marguérite objected. Jacqueline grew sick. They met; he raged; she remained silent; he gave in.[21] The final relationship between them is expressed by Gilberte in the following words:

> He could not love anyone more than he loved my sister, and he was right. He saw her often; he spoke to her of everything without reserve; in everything, without exception, he was satisfied with her, for there was so great a correspondence between their feelings that they were compatible in every-

thing; and surely their hearts were only one heart, and they found in one another consolations that can be understood only by those who have tasted something of this same happiness and who know what it is to have and return a love, with confidence and without fear of any division, in which everything satisfies.[22]

I cannot linger and recall more of Pascal's life, except for the night of November 23, 1654, when from about ten-thirty to about twelve-thirty at night he underwent an extraordinarily intense experience, which he records in the form of Biblical quotations interspersed with exclamations of his own. He writes, 'Fire'; he quotes the phrase, 'God of Abraham, God of Isaac, God of Jacob'; and he adds to this phrase, 'Not of philosophers and scholars.' Then he writes, 'Certainty, certainty, heartfelt, joy, peace. God of Jesus Christ. God of Jesus Christ . . . Let me not be cut off from him for ever!'[23] Pascal's health kept growing worse, while his inward drama continued and confirmed his depreciation of science. When the famous mathematician, Fermat, suggested that they meet, Pascal's answer was that Fermat was the most gallant man in the world, but that he sought him out, not because he was a mathematician, but because of his integrity and intellectual penetration. Pascal, once the irrepressible child-lover of mathematics, had become disillusioned with it:

> For to speak to you frankly about geometry, I consider it to be the highest exercise of the mind, but at the same time I know it to be so unprofitable that I make little distinction between a man who is merely a geometrician and a skillful artisan. Therefore I call it the most beautiful trade in all the world, but after all it is only a trade, and I have often said that it is good to test but not to employ our capacities, so that I would not take two steps for geometry.[24]

Pascal also told Fermat that he was so weak that he could not walk without a stick, ride a horse, or ride more than a short distance by carriage. Death was in the offing. Jacqueline died in October of 1661. In spite of his great love for her, his response to the news was only, 'God grant us that we die in so Christian a way!'[25] He himself died, at the age of thirty-nine, less than ten months later.

Pascal's life, epitomized in his last words, 'May God never abandon me!' seems to me to expose with particular clarity the yearning for protection or safety that, I think, animates so much even abstract thinking.[26] It has moved me to see Pascal at the beginning, with his intense need to know, which served his own and his father's pride and his curiosity about origins, and then to see Pascal at the end, when the desire to know had become the desire *not* to know. His curiosity was sacrificed to his feeling of safety. Intellectual knowledge was too qualified, he came to feel, too external and divorced from his real self. His admired powers of thought could not answer his deepest needs. When he asked himself, 'If someone loves me for my judgment or my memory, do they love me? me, myself?' he answered, 'No, for I could lose these qualities without losing my self.'[27] In these words, Pascal reminds me of Wittgenstein, who did not want to be loved for his money or, later, for his philosophy, but for himself. I think that, somewhat like Wittgenstein, Pascal was trading the intellectual for the experiential sense of knowing. He came to feel that Jesus Christ could by his pain, which resembled but went beyond his own, atone for all sins, especially the elementary sins of having been born weak, sensual, and proud. And he came to feel that the God he sought was not simply his father, but an answer to the father, because God clarified the father's will by insisting on virtue and depth of feeling rather than intellectual accomplishment. This God, the fatherhood, so to speak, of his father, loved *him*, not his qualities. To be worthy of such essential love, Pascal would have to be, he felt, exactly sincere, and so his need to know the truth intellectually survived in his inability not to tell the truth and in his horror at even the smallest deception.[28]

In love for truth, Pascal was like Montaigne. There was also a likeness in the relation of both to their fathers, for both were anxious to preserve their fathers' existence in and around themselves. We know that Pascal read and admired Montaigne, whose scepticism he directed against the pretensions of Cartesian metaphysics.[29] But he also condemned Montaigne's lewd words, his scientific credulousness and ignorance, and his indifference to salvation. Pascal's father had taught him that reason must not question faith, and his own life had taught him that reasoning could as such give no protection against suffering; how then could Montaigne be so indifferent to true security and so careless of the pain in which humans paid for their security that he did not care whether or not he died as a Christian? Because we die in order to gain life, dying, Pascal believed, had to be extremely difficult. But Montaigne, he said, 'thinks only of dying a death of cowardly ease.'[30]

Pascal, once devoted to the abstract sciences, discovered, he said, that most people were not interested in them, and that he could not communicate by their means. Perhaps, he thought to himself, he would have more companions if he studied man, for man must be interested in himself; but he discovered that even fewer people study man than geometry. Yet is it not true, he asked, that even the science of man is not that which man ought to have? Is it not true 'that it is better for him not to know himself if he wants to be happy?' In Pascal's French, 'Mais, n'est-ce pas . . . qu'il lui est meilleure de s'ignorer pour être heureux?'[31] In the light of such a contra-Socratic, contra-philosophical view, he could say of Montaigne's great egoistic self-exploration, 'What a foolish idea of painting his own portrait! And at that, not casually or against his principles, as anyone may make a slip, but according to his own principles and as his prime and basic intention.'[32]

Pascal's attitude to sensual love was, of course, negative. A 'Discourse on the Passions of Love' has been attributed to him. If it is his, it must have been written before he became ascetic and self-punishing. He wanted to remain sexually pure. In the words, again, of Gilberte:

> He had so great a respect for that virtue that he was continually on guard to prevent offense against it, whether in himself or in others. It is unbelievable how strict he was in this matter. I was even embarrassed in the beginning, because he had comments to make on almost everything, no matter how innocent-seeming, in the world. If, for example, I happened to say that I had seen a beautiful woman, he would rebuke me for it and tell me that such things ought never to be said in front of servants and young people, because I did not know what thoughts might be aroused in them. I dare not say that he could not even endure the caresses my children gave me. He claimed that they could only harm them, that one could show them affection in a thousand other ways.[33]

It shows the force of sisterly love or Pascalian persuasion that, in spite of initial resistance, Gilberte came to agree with him on this as on all other points. She had known their mother longer and, unlike him, had married and experienced what it was to have children of one's own; and yet he persuaded her.

Spinoza

3. Baruch, Bento, or Benedictus Spinoza, born in 1632. He experienced at least six deaths or separations. His mother, Hanna Deborah, died when he was six; his half-brother, Isaac, when he was seventeen; his sister, Miriam, when he was nineteen; his stepmother, Ester, when he was twenty-one; and his father, Michael, when he was twenty-two. His sixth and last separation, which he must in some sense have willed, was that from the Jewish community of Amsterdam, when he was twenty-four. The break with the Jews must have been relatively sudden, if we may judge from the fact that less than eight months before it, Spinoza had acted as or at least been considered a willing member of the community, for he had been inscribed in its records for a gift of six florins to its fund.[1]

Spinoza's break was most probably catalysed by Juan de Prado, a philosophically-minded physician, who aroused a group of young Talmud students, Spinoza among them, against traditional religion and in favor of what may be called, in the context of the period, deism.[2] De

Prado himself must be understood as one of the Marrano emigrants to Holland. Nominal Christians in Spain and Portugal, the Marranos, unlike most other European Jews, were allowed to study in universities. 'Perhaps the first modern Jews,' when they reverted to Judaism in Holland, they were apt to question the accepted Jewish principles and practices. A contemporary polemicist, himself a Marrano, writes that some of those who reached Holland return to Judaism humble and willing to learn.

> Others come to Judaism who, while in Idolatry, had studied various profane sciences such as logic, physics, metaphysics, and medicine. These arrive no less ignorant of the Law of God than the first, but they are full of vanity, pride, and haughtiness, convinced that they are learned in all matters, and that they know everything. . . . They make a show of great science in order to contradict what they do not understand, even though it be all true, all holy, all divine . . . And the worst of it is that they also spread this opinion among some who, because of either their youth or bad nature, presume themselves wise. . . . Without much effort the ignorant philosopher, as well as those who hold him in affection, falls into the abyss of apostasy and heresy.[3]

Spinoza and de Prado were both excommunicated, though the latter made efforts to have his sentence retracted.[4] Two years or so after the excommunication the pair were still seen together. 'These two persons,' the testimony runs,

> had professed the Law of Moses and the Synagogue had excluded them because they had ended in atheism. And they themselves said to the witness that they had been circumcised and had observed the law of the Jews, and that they had changed their opinion because it had seemed to them that the said Law was not true and that souls died with bodies and that there was no God except philosophically.[5]

Whatever the exact causes of his break with the Jewish community, Spinoza found it easier, it seems to me, because he had experienced so many earlier separations. These separations had somehow made childhood remote to him and allowed him to write, in a remarkable sentence, 'The man of mature years believes the nature of children to be so different from his own, that it would be impossible to persuade him he had ever been a child, if he did not conjecture regarding himself what he sees of others.'[6]

Yet Spinoza remembered his father with affection. This is a reasonable inference from a letter of consolation he wrote to a friend who had lost his young son. 'A father so loves his son,' he said, 'that he and his beloved son are like one and the same being,' so that the father necessarily participates 'in the ideal essence of the son.'[7] It may be significant that the crisis that led to his excommunication occurred after his father's death, as it may also be significant that Spinoza was scornful at the 'empty superstition and womanly tenderness' on which the law against killing animals is based.[8] His scorn prompts me to ask what memories he had of womanly tenderness and why it seemed absurd to him.

Despite Spinoza's correspondents and disciples, he made the impression of a man whose life 'was that of a true solitary.'[9] In the words of an early biographer, he 'seemed to live all to himself, always lonely, and as if buried in his study.'[10] The preface to the posthumous edition of his works says,

> He spent most of his time in investigating the nature of things, in reducing discoveries to order, and in communicating them to his friends. . . . Such ardour for the pursuit of truth was burning within him that, according to the testimony of those with whom he lodged, for three successive months he would not go out into the open.[11]

The discoveries that Spinoza was reducing to order were primarily, from his own standpoint, those that related to love and hate. His hate seems to me to have been more concrete, more particularized, than his love, which was diffuse and impersonal. The evidence is that he exercised a good deal of effort to master his emotions, meaning, of course, his negative emotions. Plausible early testimony says that his anger or displeasure was marked by only slight external clues, and that he sometimes left the company out of fear that he might be overcome by his emotion.[12] He is reported 'never to have said anything in conversation that was not edifying. He never swore; he never spoke irreverently of the divine majesty; he sometimes attended sermons, and he exhorted others to go to church assiduously.'[13] The impression of self-restraint is strengthened when we hear that 'no one ever saw him very sad or happy.'[14] All this carefulness and restraint fit in well with Spinoza's geometrical method and with his admonitory definition of bondage:

> The impotence of man to govern or restrain the affects I call bondage, for a man who is under their control is not his own master, but is mastered by fortune, in whose power he is, so that he is often forced to follow the worse, although he sees the better before him.[15]

Spinoza's emphasis on restraint fits in psychologically well with the evidence he gives of suspiciousness and anger. 'Men's common failing,' he says, 'is to confide their plans to others, though there be need for secrecy. . . .'[16] He satirizes the insulting self-confidence of most people when they are successful and their fatuous prayers for advice when they fall into difficulties.[17] Not even the most experienced man, he says, knows how to keep his silence properly. This failure leads to trouble, for men are 'more prone to take vengeance than to return benefits' and easily excited into a brutish rage.[18] Therefore 'the free man who lives among the ignorant strives as much as possible to avoid their favours.'[19]

Such suspicion shades easily into anger, and anger into the desire to get back at tormentors, real or potential. An early biography says that to pass the time 'he would find some spiders and let them fight with one another; or he would find some flies, throw them into the spider's web and watch this battle with great pleasure, even with laughter.' He would also, magnifying glass in hand, investigate the smallest flies and gnats.[20] The report of his pleasure in the fighting of insects appears basically true, because Spinoza himself writes:

> Everyone observes with admiration and delight in animals the very things which he detests and regards with aversion in men. For example, the wars of bees, the jealousy of doves, etc., things which we detest in men and for which we nevertheless consider animals more perfect.[21]

Spinoza is especially attentive to the possibility of transforming love into hate and the opposite. Hate that displaces love is stronger, he believes, for the displacement:

> If a man has begun to hate a beloved object, so that his love to it is altogether destroyed, he will for this reason hate it more than he would have done if he had never loved it, and his hatred will be in proportion to his previous love.[22]

How much of Spinoza's own experience lies behind this psychologically acute observation? Perhaps it reflects his reactions to Judaism, which he at times describes more unfavourably than the facts make necessary. He, for example, invidiously repeats Matthew's charge that the Jews were given the commandment, 'Love thy neighbour and hate thine enemy.'[23] Perhaps, too, Spinoza's observation reflects his difficulties with the remaining members of his family. They not only broke with him, as his excommunication may have made necessary, but tried to exclude him from his share of the father's inheritance; and after his death they refused to pay his burial expenses or inherit his estate which, as they ascertained, was too 'burdened with debts.'[24]

Even though Spinoza insisted that political authorities should rule spiritual affairs, and even though he defended the kings against the prophets, who, in his opinion, 'rather irritated than reformed mankind by their freedom of warning, rebuke, and censure,' Spinoza appears to have had a natural sympathy for those who act or speak out bravely.[25] He is said to have drawn himself in the costume of the barefooted Neapolitan fisherman who seized power in Naples in 1647–48. We are told, that is, that Spinoza used to draw ink or charcoal portraits of notable visitors. In an album of such portraits, says the witness,

> I found on the fourth page a fisherman drawn in a shirt with a fishnet on his right shoulder, completely in the way the notorious Neapolitan rebel leader Masaniello is depicted in historical pictures. Mr. Henrik van der Spyk, his last landlord, said of it that it resembled Spinoza himself to a hair and that it had undoubtedly been drawn after his own face.[26]

Although there is no way of verifying the anecdote, we find Spinoza holding up to admiration those who give their lives in a good cause:

> Men whose consciences are clear do not fear death or beg for mercy like criminals, since their minds are not tormented by remorse for deeds of shame; they think it a merit, not a punishment, to die for a good cause, and an honour to die for freedom. And since they give their lives for a cause that is beyond the ken of faineants and fools, hateful to the unruly, and dear to the good, what are men taught by their death? Only to emulate them, or at least to hold them in reverence.[27]

Aiming as he did at certainty, Spinoza became the most rationalistic of the rationalistic philosophers of his time, the only one who dared to believe that man and God could be identical in what they understood.[28] 'He who has a true idea,' he said, 'knows at the same time that he has a true idea, nor can he doubt the truth of the thing.' As he explained, 'Truth is its own standard. We must remember, besides, that our mind, in so far as it truly perceives things, is a part of the infinite intellect of God, and therefore it must be that the clear and distinct ideas of the mind are as true as those of God.'[29] The mysterious and occult were thus expelled everywhere, from God, from soul, and from union of body and soul, for they were all in principle as clear as geometry itself.[30]

To a correspondent who questioned his philosophical self-confidence, Spinoza answered:

> I do not presume that I have found the best Philosophy, but I know that I think the true one. If you ask me how I know this, I shall answer, in the same way that you know that the three angles of a triangle are equal to two right angles. That this is enough no one will deny whose brain is sound, and who does not dream of unclean spirits who inspire us with false ideas which are like true ones: for the truth reveals itself and the false.[31]

With Cartesian and other falsifying spirits so disposed of, Spinoza could spare no more than two brief, cavalier paragraphs to dispose of the sceptics. In one he bade them 'to remain silent, lest perchance they might suppose something which has the savor of truth.' In the other he proclaimed that 'if they deny, oppose, or grant, they do not know what they deny, grant, or oppose; and therefore they must be regarded as machines which lack any mind at all.'[32]

Although he disposed of the sceptics so quickly, Spinoza was nevertheless faced with the at least apparent experience of error and doubt. His response was, in Neo-Platonic vein, that error and doubt are by nature absences or lacks, are, that is, essentially unreal. As might be expected, it was hard for him to work out this position coherently.*

Interested as he was in finding certainty, Spinoza disposed of a subtly analogous problem, that of suicide, by means of terminological fiat. The very possibility of suicide ran counter to his proposition that 'the endeavour after self-preservation is the essence itself of a thing,' and counter to his corollary that 'endeavour after self-preservation is the primary and only foundation of virtue.'[33] According, then, to Spinoza,

> No one . . . refuses food or kills himself from a necessity of his own nature, but only when forced by external causes . . . External and hidden causes also may so dispose his imagination and may so affect his body as to cause it to put on another nature contrary to that which it had at first, and one whose idea cannot exist in the mind; but a very little reflection will show that it is impossible that a man, from the necessity of his nature, should endeavour not to exist, or to be changed into some other form, as it is that something should be begotten from nothing.[34]

Doubt and error reduced to nothing, the certainty of his own certainty altogether clear to him, and the very thought of self-destruction discarded as contrary to nature and, appearances notwithstanding, impossible, Spinoza was freed to concentrate on the eternity he wanted to be part of. To be eternal, he knew, he had, in his sense, to be dispassionate, and this dispassionateness could be achieved by the slow transformation of passions into clear thoughts and the slow linking of clear thoughts with one another. For 'an affect which is a passion ceases to be a passion as soon as we form a clear and distinct idea of it'; and an affect detached from the thought of an external cause and connected with other thoughts brings an end to the love or hatred toward the external cause, and an end, as well, to the mind's fluctuations that arise from these affects.[35]

The end was superlative love. Spinoza's confessed need as a younger

---

*Joachim, who goes into the problem carefully, comments:

'My attempt to extract from Spinoza's exposition in the *Treatise* his principal contentions in regard to doubt, and to weave out of them a complete restatement of his theory, has ended in an open admission of failure. The theory, as I predicted, falls hopelessly to pieces . . . It cannot be restated–and the reason is plain. For the theory, when examined in detail, shows itself to be in fact no single, coherent doctrine at all.' H. H. Joachim, *Spinoza's Tractatus de Intellectus Emendatione*, p. 197. See also H. G. Hubbeling, *Spinoza's Methodology*, pp. 35—38; and C. De Deugd, *The Significance of Spinoza's First Kind of Knowledge*, pp. 104–29.

man for something eternal to love has been cited on an earlier page. His *Ethics* concludes in the assurance that he had indeed gained his objective. 'Blessedness,' he there says with all the certainty he had arrived at, 'consists in love towards God.' The wise man 'is scarcely ever moved in his mind, but, being conscious by a certain eternal necessity of himself, of God, and of things, never ceases to be, and always enjoys true peace of mind.'

But this peace was, so to speak, one-sided. If we use the simple human terms that do not appear in the abstract propositions of the *Ethics*, we may say that this God does not have a responsive parent's nature. He is, instead, like a distant, preoccupied mother or father, who receives love but returns none of it—except in the safety that emanates from a stable, enveloping presence as such.

The end of the *Ethics* specifies that the blessed man 'possesses the power of restraining the lusts [libidiness]. . . . The power of restraining the lusts springs from blessedness itself.'[36] What did Spinoza know of them? He is said to have fallen in love with the daughter of his learned, adventurous Latin teacher, Van den Enden. 'Of her Spinoza often said that he had taken a strong liking to her and wanted to marry her, although she was rather frail and had a misshapen body, simply attracted by her acute mind and exceptional learning.'[37] As the story runs, a fellow student, Kerkering, noticed Spinoza's interest, grew jealous, and won the girl's favour with the gift of an expensive pearl necklace.

We know that Kerkering did marry the girl, Clara Maria. There is no independent evidence that the story of Spinoza's attraction to her is true; but he was interested enough in the strategies and perfidies of love to read Ovid's *Amores*, as he shows by a quotation, or rather, misquotation, in the *Ethics*.[38] Ovid's moral, which Spinoza has apparently forgotten or misconstrued, is this: 'If you want me to become a rival for your girl, forbid me to.' Four propositions after citing Ovid, Spinoza reveals a fantasy that demonstrates that he knows what it is to be sexually jealous:

> The man who imagines that the woman he loves prostitutes herself to another is not merely troubled because his appetite is restrained, but he turns away from her because he is obliged to connect the image of a beloved object with the privy parts and with what is excremental in another man: and in addition to this, the jealous person is not received with the same favour which the beloved object formerly bestowed on him,—a new cause of sorrow to the lover, as I shall show.[39]

In the style of Spinoza's philosophy, the woman has immediately been transformed into an 'object,' an object, he says elsewhere, of man's mere lust for his natural inferiors, the females.[40] The woman become an 'object' or 'thing,' the modesty of Spinoza's ethical geometry is resumed.[41] He has returned to his ideal, which is to consider human actions and appetites as if they were lines, planes, or bodies.[42] As he wanted, he has transformed one kind of eternal triangle into another.

Locke

4. John Locke, born in 1632. He was fortunate in retaining both of his parents until adulthood, for his mother died when he was twenty-two and his father when he was twenty-seven. There is a report that his mother was extremely beautiful. He is reticent about her but does say that she was 'a very pious woman and an affectionate mother.'[1] His father, a small landowner and attorney, was clerk to the Justices of the Peace, whose administrative duties ranged from price regulation to punishment of vagabonds, subjects Locke was later interested in. The character of Locke's home is described as 'set by the hard and uncompromising presbyterianism of the men who briefly ruled England in the late 1640's.'[2] Correspondingly, Locke's father is said to have been stern, unbending, and taciturn, and Locke himself testifies that in the beginning he was distant and severe. Yet the mature Locke 'never mentioned him but with great respect and affection.'[3] This respect and affection are evident in Locke's correspondence, from the perhaps only conventional salutation ('Most dear and ever loving father') and conventional close ('Your most obedient son') to his heartfelt request to his father to protect himself by not joining either side in the political struggle.[4] During his father's last illness, Locke beseeches him not to 'endanger the only comfort' his children have left by 'too pressing a care' for them. 'A father is more than all other relations,' he says, and ends that the greatest satisfaction he can imagine in the world is the hope to repay his father for all his care and indulgence.[5]

When Locke was ten, his father fought in a losing battle against the Royalists. 'He was a captain in the Parliamentary Army at the time of the Civil War in England, and by that means a private sufferer in the public calamities: which probably was the sole cause of his fortunes being impaired.'[6] But the war brought at least one advantage to the family, because the father's former commander recommended Locke, then fifteen, to Westminster School, reputed to be the finest boarding school of all.[7] Locke there absorbed the Royalist position.

When Locke was twenty, he was accepted at Oxford, which had just been purged of its many Royalists. He seems to have made a good reputation as a student, but he disliked the 'obscure terms and useless questions' of the prevailing Scholastic philosophy and was repelled by the public disputations, which he thought to be aimed more at wrangling and ostentation than truth.[8] In time he grew discouraged and uncertain if he were really fit for the scholar's career.[9] To his father he wrote that mankind was untrustworthy, that he could rely on no human being, and he complained that passion was everywhere being mistaken for reason.[10] Now nearing thirty, he was beginning to philosophize; and after the philosophic fashion of the times, he wrote out elaborate classifications of the whole of human knowledge, as if mapping out the universe of thought before trying to find his place in it.[11] It remained characteristic of him to make orderly general plans, fulfilled, if at all, in prolix and disorderly ways.[12]

In answer to a pamphlet that argued that religious ceremonial was morally 'indifferent,' Locke wrote an answer, which he did not publish, holding the opposite. In its preface he attacks tyranny and anarchy as the twin scourges of mankind and hopes that the miraculous Restoration will ensure the people's obedience, security, and happiness. 'As for myself,' he goes on, 'there is no man who can have a greater respect and veneration for authority than I. I no sooner perceived myself in the *world* but I found myself in a storm, which hath lasted almost hitherto, and therefore cannot but entertain the approaches of a calm with the greatest joy and satisfaction.'[13] Soon, however, Locke qualifies and says, 'Besides the submission I have for *authority* I have no less a love of *liberty* without which a *man* shall find himself less happy than a *beast*.' He then arrives at a crucial 'but,' which expresses his antagonism to the liberty that allows contention and persecution and his fear that if 'indifferent' things are not limited, social peace will be ended.[14] Locke's answer leans heavily toward authoritarianism, but it reflects Locke's genuine tension between the extremes of authority and liberty.

Just at the time of his father's death, Locke became a tutor at Oxford. His interest in science, medicine, in particular, had already been awakened—some prescriptions in his early medical notebook were apparently taken from his mother.[15] His mentor in science in general was Robert Boyle, and in medicine the great physician Thomas Sydenham, both men who valued 'the consideration of things themselves.'[16]*

He began to read Descartes and found him strikingly different from

---

*'Locke had in his library over sixty titles of Boyle's publications, many of them given to Locke by Boyle . . . Most of the ingredients in Locke's science of nature are found in Boyle, expecially in the *Origine*. The verbal similarities are often striking.' J. W. Yolton, *Locke and the Compass of Human Understanding*, p. 35, note 1. See also p. 41.

Locke and Sydenham became friends in 1667. Locke more than once praised Sydenham's method, which insisted on paying the most careful attention to the facts and accepting only the medical hypotheses that a carefully-observed experience suggested. According to Sydenham, diseases must be described 'with the utmost accuracy; imitating in this the great exactness of the painters, who, in their pictures copy the smallest spots of moles in the originals.' Yolton, op. cit., p. 59, note 1.

the philosophers he had studied as an undergraduate. In the words of a friend, 'The first books (as Mr. Locke himself told me) which gave him a relish of philosophical studies were those of Descartes.'[17]

Now came a decisive shift in Locke's fortunes. He met Lord Ashley, the future Earl of Shaftesbury, and the two immediately charmed one another. Ashley soon invited Locke to live with him as his personal physician.[18] Deeply interested in the commercial prosperity of England, Ashley had come to the conclusion, based largely on the example of Holland, that prosperity depended on religious toleration. The conclusion and the example were both sympathetic to Locke, who had by then travelled in Holland, and he was stimulated to write a number of draft essays on tolerance. These argue, as he was later to argue in public, that the authority of the ruler was meant for the benefit of his subjects. They also deny tolerance, as Locke was always to deny it, to atheists and to Roman Catholics, potentially disloyal he thought, because the subjects of another ruler, the Pope.[19]

Ashley had for years suffered from a suppurating cyst of the liver. When it appeared that it was endangering his life, Locke had Ashley's abdomen opened and the cyst drained. Ashley was convinced that Locke had saved his life and he gratefully encouraged him to develop his talents. It was in Ashley's house that the conversation took place 'about the principles of morality and received religion' that stimulated Locke to begin the *Essay Concerning Human Understanding*.[20] Locke participated regularly in the discussions of Ashley and his political friends, who liked him because, though respectful, 'he had a mixture of pleasantry and becoming boldness of speech.'[21]

Ashley, now Lord Shaftesbury, entrusted Locke 'with his secretest negotiations, and made use of his assistant pen.'[22] When Shaftesbury was imprisoned on a charge of high treason, Locke, then at Oxford, was observed by a spy, who reported that 'John Locke lives a very cunning unintelligible life here.'[23] Shaftesbury fled to Holland, where he soon died. To Locke he represented an ideal. A friend recalled Locke as having praised Shaftesbury as 'the most consummate statesman' in England, 'if not of the age he lived in';

> who had a compass of thought, soundness of judgment and sharpness of penetration that (in some extraordinary instances of his sagacity) has been fancied almost more than human. . . . Everything in him was natural, and had a noble air of freedom, expressive of that character of a mind that abhorred slavery, not because he could not be the master, but because he could not suffer such an indignity to human nature.[24]

Sensing danger, Locke fled to Amsterdam. There he again saw and was impressed by religious tolerance. For months at a time he travelled, making new medical acquaintances, and perhaps engaging in political conspiracy.[25] When the English government issued a warrant for his arrest, he went into hiding, where he remained for about a year. While in Holland he was able to work at his books, including the *Essay*, in which he regretfully recognized 'the ill effects of writing in patches and at distant times.'[26] Finally, after a stay in Holland of some five years and five months, he returned to England. He was fifty-six years old. Toward the end of the same year, 1689, his three most important books, the *Essay*, the *Two Treatises*, and the *Letter on Toleration* were all in press.

In following Locke's career to this point, we have not been able to reveal much of his inner nature. Compared with many other philosophers, he is personally opaque. Even in an age dangerous to philosophers, his tendency to conceal himself was unusual:

> He had an almost Gothic fondness of mystery for the sake of mystery: he used all kinds of little cyphers, he modified a shorthand system for the purpose of concealment, and on at least one occasion he employed invisible ink [in a letter to a woman]. He guarded his anonymity as an author with elaborate care. He kept secrets from people who were supposed to be his closest friends . . . But because Locke was sometimes secretive for a good reason and sometimes neurotically secretive and sometimes perhaps secretive simply for fun, it is difficult to make out exactly what he was doing at certain times of his life.[27]

I must confess that, not understanding Locke's nature, I do not understand his secretiveness. Whatever in it was not a defence against political danger, which was real, or against polemical invective, which could be distinctly unpleasant, might have helped to defend him against the entangling alliance of marriage. But I suppose that Locke's opacity as a person is also related to something else in his nature, his tendency to intellectually unclear but practically effective compromises. Especially in ethics and politics, his thought strikes an unclear compromise between opposed principles, one of which may dominate at one time or point and another at another, but none of which is ever really given up.[28]

Locke's ideal of clarity and order but his unclarity and disorder in fact are apparent in his attitude towards order itself. He wants to order ideas, he is sure that there is a natural order to them, but he shies away from ordering them formally and does not want to go beyond their simple, 'natural' juxtaposition. Furthermore, though he believes in such informal natural order, he gives no extended example of it. More particularly, he thinks that if we had unambiguous symbols for moral concepts, they could be arranged in an assured, so-to-speak Euclidean order; and he claims to derive moral principles from self-evident propositions.[29] But looked at closely, derivation in his sense appears to mean, not a formally logical connection, but only a diagrammatically clear one. Yet he does not, in fact, derive anything in even his diagrammatic sense. Unable to show the systematic, logical connections between moral concepts, he does no more than list moral rules in his usual rather haphazard way. He continues in his unclarity and gives no claim up. Even in the *Reasonableness of Christianity*, in which, becoming sceptical of rational proofs of morality, he falls back on revelation, he continues to believe that, *in principle*, morality can be deduced by reason. He is therefore caught between a practical fideism and a theoretical rationalism, yet shows little sign of discomfort.[30]

Locke's uncompromising insistence on such a logically undemonstrated and probably indemonstrable compromise is not, to my mind, the result of intellectual incoherence, but of the attempt, using theory and experience, to solve the practical problems of society. Locke works like a judge trying to fit together particular problems and particular principles, though some of the principles are at least potentially contradictory. Refusing to ignore a problem in question or give up any of the principles he approves of, he bends his reasoning almost casuistically in favor of a desirable practical end. He wants revelation *and* reason, order *and* liberty, objectivity *and* subjectivity. He believes in the objective world and the objective truth, but knows that they are grasped subjectively. He understands the possibilities of scepticism, he is aware of the difficulty in proving that ideas in fact resemble their objects, and he knows and stresses the limitations of human knowledge and the mere probability of much of it. But though his answers to scepticism are not at all painstaking, he accepts whatever hypothesis or belief he thinks necessary at a given moment, and goes on with his intellectual work.[31]*

Locke simply did not aim at the goal of so many other philosophers, the sharp solution of sharply-defined universal problems. The conclusion he wanted was less spectacular than functional, and the relative balance of his nature and his ability to assimilate experience for his philosophical purposes did make his solutions at least seem viable, as is attested by their widespread popularity. His interest in empirical complexity and his relaxed assimilation into his philosophical schemes of everything that appeared to be either factual or socially desirable, constitute his relative

---

*'Locke's resolution of the philosophical problems discussed in the *Essay* parallels what he believed was God's own resolution of the human dilemma, as stated in the writings of Christianity. If, ultimately, the epistemological views of Locke, the Christian, cannot be satisfactorily reconciled with those of Locke, the philosopher, it is the faith of the former which ensures the salvation of the latter.' R. Ashcraft, 'Faith and Knowledge in Locke's Philosophy,' in J. W. Yolton, ed., *John Locke: Problems and Perspectives* (London: Cambridge University Press, 1969), p. 223.

adequacy to the situation as it in fact was and contribute to his personal opacity. Perhaps he finally tended, in philosophy as in medicine, 'to discard all hypotheses in favour of careful clinical observation from which a diagnosis could be made by analogy.'[32]

Yet something more illuminating can be said of a particular relation between Locke's personality, experience, and philosophy. This depends principally, I think, on his reactions to his father. I find the key in a brief reminiscence:

> His father used a conduct towards him when young that he often spoke of afterward with great approbation. It was that of being severe to him by keeping him in much awe and at a distance while he was a boy, but relaxing still by degrees of that severity as he grew to be a man, till he being become capable of it, he lived perfectly with him as a friend. And I remember on this occasion he has told me that his father after he was a man, solemnly asked his pardon for having struck him once in passion as a boy, his fault not being equal to that correction.[33]

When Locke writes on the subject of education, he describes his father's conduct as the correct way of bringing up a child. The younger the child, says Locke, the greater the care that must be taken not to give in to its whims. By 'humoring and cockering' their little children, parents make it impossible for a sound character to develop.[34]

> Those therefore that intend ever to govern their children should begin it whilst they are very little; and look that they perfectly comply with the will of their parents. Would you have your son obedient to you, when past a child? Be sure then to establish the authority of a father, as soon as he is capable of submission, and can understand in whose power he is. If you would have him stand in awe of you, imprint it in his infancy; and, as he approaches more to a man, admit him nearer to your familiarity: so you shall have him your obedient subject (as is fit) whilst he is a child, and your affectionate friend when he is a man . . . For liberty and indulgence can do no good to children: their want of judgment makes them stand in need of restraint and discipline. And, on the contrary, imperiousness and severity is but an ill way of treating men, who have reason of their own to guide them, unless you have a mind to make your children, when grown up, weary of you; and secretly to say within themselves, 'When will you die, father?'[35]

In another such passage, Locke speaks of the importance to children's education of 'the severity of the father's brow.' Locke's mother was apparently not his disciplinarian. The father's severity, he again says, should be relaxed in time, 'even to that degree, that a father will do well, as his son grows up, and is capable of it, to talk familiarly with him; nay, ask his advice, and consult with him. . . . The sooner you treat him as a man, the sooner he will begin to be one. . . .'[36]

The parallel between Locke's childhood and his educational recommendations is obvious. It is perhaps also from his childhood, or, rather, its conscious austerity, that Locke derived his prosaic responses to art. When he visited the great buildings of France, his response was to measure their dimensions.[37] He depreciated the teaching of music to children.[38] He opposed teaching a child, a boy, that is, to write poetry even if he had a gift for it:

> If he has a poetic vein, it is to me the strangest thing in the world, that the father should desire or suffer it to be cherished or improved . . . I know not what reason a father can have to wish his son a poet, who does not desire to have him bid defiance to all other callings and business. . . .[39]

Locke's educational views have been influential, but they do not constitute his important contribution as a philosopher; and his views on poetry and music are of only marginal interest. But the influence of his father is evident at a crucial point in the argument of his *Second Treatise of Government*. It will be recalled that the *Two Treatises of Government* were written primarily in answer to the argument of Robert Filmer that God had vested a father's authority in Adam, who had transmitted it to the Patriarchs, who had in turn transmitted it to the monarchs of the world. Filmer's purpose was, of course, to drive home that this sacred inheritance could not legitimately be contravened by revolution.

Locke's answer was that Filmer had not made the necessary distinction between the authority of a ruler over his subject and that of a father over his children; whence Filmer's incorrect, pernicious defence of the ruler's absolute and inalienable inheritance of his authority. Like Hobbes, Locke points out that the child has two natural rulers, mother as well as father, and asks how this joint authority can be passed on completely to a single monarch. But unlike Hobbes, who holds that the father (like his own father) may abdicate his authority to the mother, Locke easily accepts the father's dominance and says, 'It being necessary that the last Determination, *i.e.* the Rule, should be placed somewhere, it naturally falls to the man's share, as being the abler and the stronger.'[40]

Locke's basic argument against the principle of the inheritance of authority is fully in keeping with that by which his father had brought him up. It begins with the notion that every man has an equal right to his natural freedom.[41] In Locke's words, this is the argument that follows:

> Children, I confess, are not born into this full sort of *Equality*, though they are born to it. Their Parents have a sort of Rule or Jurisdiction over them when they come into the world, and for some time after, but 'tis but a temporary one. The Bonds of this Subjection are like the Swadling Cloths they are wrapt in, and supported by, in the weakness of their Infancy. Age

and Reason as they grow up, loosen them till at length they drop quite off, and leave a Man at his own free Disposal.[42]

A man is made free, says Locke, by his maturity, that is, by his ability to make reasonable discriminations.

> If such a state of Reason, such an Age of Discretion *made him free*, the same shall make his Son free too . . .[43] Thus we are *born Free* as we are born Rational; not that we have actually the Exercise of either: Age that brings one, brings with it the other too. And thus we see how *natural Freedom and Subjection to Parents* may consist together, and are both founded on the same Principle.[44]

Locke then concedes that it is natural for the father to become a ruler, because his children have grown used to his authority; but his authority extended beyond childhood requires the children's at least tacit consent. 'Thus the natural *Fathers of Families*, by an insensible change, become the *politick Monarchs* of them too. . . .'[45] Locke also points out that when a father stops caring for his children, he loses his power over them, which now belongs to the foster-father.[46]

This whole argument assumes that fathers act out of paternal affection and do generally fulfill their natural obligations. In short, fathers are like the one he knew and, like him, must be prepared to relinquish authority as soon as a son matures.[47]

Locke's defence of toleration is made easier for him, it appears to me, because it stresses the necessary coexistence, which he had experienced to an intense degree, of obedience and freedom. His interest in toleration, fostered, no doubt, by the practical needs of Shaftesbury, led him to collect all the books on the subject he could find, including those of Spinoza.[48]

Locke had experienced the ills of dogmatism often enough to hold that it would 'become all men to maintain *peace*, and the common offices of humanity, *and friendship, in the diversity of opinions*. . . .'[49] In the *Letter on Toleration* he accepts differences in form of worship that had earlier seemed to him too difficult to tolerate.[50] But on one point he remains adamant, that it is impossible to tolerate atheists, 'for the taking away of God, even only in thought, dissolves all.'[51] Whatever the justification for this conclusion, Locke remains true to his father's piety.

Locke's tolerance is quite different in quality from that of Montaigne, Voltaire, or Russell. Montaigne, like a modern anthropologist, comes to recognize the equal validity of all customs that are not inherently cruel or do not offend the simple truth. His tolerance is wide, and within its range is the product of a sincere scepticism and an interest in all the varieties of human behaviour. It is in part the stimulation that his curiosity gives him: he would hate not to be able to travel in body and especially in mind. Voltaire's tolerance, as will be seen, rests on a desire to attack the enemy. The attack is zestful and theatrical, and is animated perhaps by a measure of inverted cruelty, for Voltaire identifies himself with victims. Russell has a similar identification with victims, especially of human stupidity or vindictiveness, for he learned to use his sharp intelligence, as will be seen, to overcome the isolation and sadness of which he himself had been the victim. Locke's tolerance, as far as I understand it, is mainly the product of his good relationship with his father and mother, and of his varied and on the whole satisfactory experience with human beings. He does not identify himself with victims as such. On the contrary, if they violate the ethos he grew up with and accepted, if, that is, they refuse to be industrious, he considers them 'robbers of the poor' and subject to punishment and forced labour.[52] His tolerance is in memory of his father's difficulties in life, of the Royalists who had once persuaded him of their cause, and of the good Dutch tolerance. The father he had assimilated had grown by virtue of the Shaftesbury he had assimilated and by the rich experience of life he had undergone. Besides, the ideal of tolerance helped him to control his anger—his father's training had not left him spiritless. There was a time at Oxford when he was considered 'a man of turbulent spirit, clamorous and never contented.'[53] His French translator, Pierre Coste, who knew him well, said that he was a naturally hot-tempered man who had learned to control his feelings.[54] Locke's reserve of anger also shows in his adamant defence of everyone's natural autonomy. He cautions parents against imposing 'slavish discipline' on their children.[55] In one essential thing he is quite obdurate: he identifies himself with the truth, and the truth with his indifference to attack upon it. To a friend he writes, 'If I have anything to boast of, it is that I sincerely love and seek truth with indifferency whom it pleases or displeases.'[56]

Autonomy, a sense of his own independent worth, meant a great deal to Locke. As the reminiscence I have quoted makes clear, he remembered it to his father's eternal credit that he had once asked his pardon for having struck him unjustly as a boy. This apology at once recognized that Locke had become mature and therefore free; that truth had, as it should, a hold on the conscience; and that a father's moral authority over his child was a just one. On this background, of his father's austerity, care, and honesty, of the suppressed anger I have assumed at his father's early severity, and of his stubborn desire to maintain the equivalence of truth and self-assertion, we can understand his enthusiasm for Shaftesbury as a man who 'abhorred slavery . . . because he could not suffer such an indignity to human nature.'

Locke was in some ways romantic. During his student years at Oxford he wrote many coyly flirtatious letters.[57] Some of this correspondence with women was prolonged; and there are hints of his interest in marriage.[58] Locke's most serious love was for Damaris Cudworth, whom he met when she was twenty-four and he fifty. She was the extremely well-educated daughter of the Cambridge Platonist, Ralph Cudworth. She compromised effectively enough to keep the philosophical faith with both Platonistic father and Empiricistic Locke. Poems exchanged between her and Locke make it seem that the love of the one never coincided in time with the love of the other. Each wanted just friendship exactly when the other wanted just love. After her marriage to a baronet, she gave the ill, ageing Locke refuge in her house, where, with all his belongings and nearly five thousand books, the now famous philosopher worked and received guests. She became closer to him than anyone else, and much of the more personal information on him comes from her.[59]

When Locke was seventy, Anthony Collins, a young admirer of his writings, grew attached to him. Locke was lovingly grateful to the man who 'fastened' him again to the world.[60] Locke also had deep affection for children. He wrote letters to Elizabeth Clarke, the daughter of a good friend, in which he called her 'wife' and 'mistress.' He also 'made himself the guardian and protector of all his friends' children.'[61]

Locke was, then, a warm man who depended emotionally on his friends. He wrote to one of them, 'To live is to be where and with whom one likes.'[62] He seems to have been eager to play the father's role without undergoing the preliminary inconvenience of marrying or having children. As such an unmarried or grandfatherly father, he was more indulgent than his own father had been to him.[63] I cannot guess why he did not marry. His mother may have been too difficult or, more likely, too easy. What 'too easy' might mean in the context of his life, I do not, however, know. There is only the bare fact that he did not marry.

Leibniz

5. Gottfried Wilhelm Leibniz, born in 1646. His mother, who lost her parents at the age of eleven, was brought up first in the family of a professor of theology, and then, before her marriage, in that of a professor of law. She had the reputation of an intelligent, pious, and gentle woman. After the death of her husband, Leibniz's father, she took care to further the education of her children. She herself died when Leibniz was eighteen. According to her eulogy, she was 'badly disposed toward no one' and 'took pains to live with all in peace and harmony . . . Though

disquieted by the many temptations of the malevolent, she nevertheless excelled everyone in patience, in which she had acquired much practice, and easily forgave even those who had offended her.'[1]

Leibniz's father lost both parents before he was of college age. He was supported as a student at the University of Leipzig by his mother's brother. After studying law and philosophy, he became Professor of Morals at the university, of which he was also the actuary. When his son, Gottfried Wilhelm, was just three days old, the father was already evidencing the hopes he cherished for him. The occasion was the ceremony of baptism, during which the infant raised his head, so that his head and eyes were moistened with the water. The father thereupon wrote in his family chronicle:

> I hope and foretell that this is a sign of faith and the best omen that this son, with eyes raised all his life to God, will be all godly, burning with love for God, and in this love will do remarkable deeds, for the honour of the Most High, as well as for the welfare and development of the Christian Church, and for his and our welfare.[2]

The father died 'of a consuming disease that lasted only eight days.'[3] Leibniz particularly remembered how he had taught him to read, and how a second auspicious event, an escape from danger, had aroused his hopes. In Leibniz's words:

> I was born to my father when he had reached his fiftieth year, and I was hardly six years old when I lost my father, so that I have only a weak memory of him; but the rest I have heard from others. Two things only I remember. The one was, when I learned to read early, that my father, partly by various stories and partly by a German booklet, laid particular stress on instilling a love for secular and Biblical history in me. He did this with such success that it gave him extraordinary expectations for the future. The second is a remarkable occurrence and still remains as alive in my memory as if it happened the day before yesterday . . . I was toddling back and forth on a bench, placed against the wall, to which a table was drawn up. At the table stood my aunt, who wanted to dress me. But I climbed mischievously onto the table, and when she tried to catch me, I stepped back and fell on the floor. My father and my aunt screamed, they looked there and saw me unharmed and smiling at them, but almost three steps away from the table, much further than a child could reach with a jump. In this my father recognized a particular favour of God and on the spot sent someone to church with a note so that, in keeping with custom, a thanksgiving prayer to God should be offered after the services. This gave rise to much talk in the city. Partly from this accident and partly from I know not what dreams or omens, my father conceived such great hopes for me that he often drew the ridicule of his friends on himself. Only, I can neither enjoy his assistance nor can he take pleasure in my progress.[4]

Leibniz has left other childhood memories. Once, at about the age of twelve, he came on an illustrated edition of Livy. By repeatedly comparing the illustrations with the text he succeeded in teaching himself a much more difficult Latin than he had been learning in school. A teacher discovered what had happened and demanded that Leibniz's studies not be disturbed by such absurdly premature reading. Luckily, however, a learned, well-travelled nobleman happened to be there and to overhear the teacher. 'Struck,' in Leibniz's words,

> by the schoolmaster's should I say ill-will or simple-mindedness, by which he grasped everyone by one and the same measure, he began to demonstrate to them how unfair and insufferable it would be if the first seed of developing genius should be stifled by the severity or crudity of the teacher. One must do the opposite, favour the uncommonly promising boy and come to his aid with every possible means. So he had me brought, and as he heard nothing absurd from my mouth in answer to his questions, he did not desist until he had extracted the promise from my relatives that access would be allowed me to my own father's library, which had so long been kept under lock and key. I was as jubilant over this announcement as if I had found a treasure. For I was burning with eagerness to lay sight on the Ancients whom I knew only by their names. . . .[5]

In still another account, Leibniz tells of his adventures in his dead father's library. The reading hunger he displayed there foreshadows the same impulse in Nietzsche and Sartre. Speaking of himself in the third person, Leibniz says that when an eight-year-old he often hid himself in the library

> for entire days and, hardly able to stutter Latin, now picked up and now returned every book on which his eyes fell. Opening and closing the books indiscriminately, he nibbled here, skipped there, just as clarity of expression or aptness of content captivated him. It appeared as if he had taken Fortuna as teacher, or as if he thought he had heard the *Take, read!* (of Saint Augustine) from a higher voice. For the boy, deprived by a higher fate of another's advice, needed this characteristically youthful boldness, fostered by God for his welfare.[6]

A number of years later, at about the age of thirteen, Leibniz had a further emotionally-charged intellectual experience—he discovered logic. 'As soon as I began to read logic,' he says,

> I was greatly stirred by the classification and order that I perceived in its principles . . . My greatest pleasure lay in the categories. . . . I soon made the amusing discovery of a method of recalling to mind, by means of the categories, something forgotten when one has a picture of it, but cannot get at it in his brain. . . . Nebuchadnezzar could perhaps have reconstructed his

forgotten dream in this way . . . Whenever I found a list of things belonging together, and especially when I found a genus or universal under which a number of particular species was subsumed, as for example, the number of the emotions or of the virtues and vices, I had to put them into a table to see if the species fell into a successive order.[7]

In a passage I have quoted earlier, Leibniz tells how lucky he was to have been self-taught and to have refused to rest (as Nietzsche was to refuse) until he had 'traced back the tissues and roots of every teaching and had penetrated to its principles.' Acquaintance with logic and philosophy released his creative impulses and 'a multitude of fancies,' he says, 'came to birth in my brain and were scratched down on paper to be laid before my astonished teachers.' With great joy, he arrived at the idea of an alphabet of human thoughts.[8]

Having come so far, we can reflect a moment on Leibniz's early life. We see, above all, the father's great ambition and the son's desire to fulfill it. When Leibniz finally ranged at will in his father's library, how could he not have felt the presence of the man whose legacy he had taken over? The voice he thought he heard in the library was surely his own, which is also to say, his father's, for the boldness that, with God's help, he sensed was his father's love and ambition speaking in him. Yet, lacking sufficient guidance, his reaction was indiscriminate. Logic stirred him because it promised to classify and order everything. It also promised to recover memories (perhaps of his father), to reconstruct dreams, and to classify (and perhaps clarify) emotions, virtues, and vices. The fact that he could already astonish his teachers with his fancies gave substance to his father's prophecies and his own hopes.

There is a sense in which Leibniz never advanced beyond this stage of indiscriminate, almost chaotic reaching out for something that would gratify and astonish, and of the perception that order would have to be imposed on or discovered in the near-chaos. Leibniz's writings, which include over 15,000 manuscript letters, are very often on particular, restricted subjects, which he deals with in many variations. Though he hoped to logicize the whole universe, he failed to index his own papers, which expressed so many logical and other hopes, with the result that, unable to find what he had written on a given subject, he wrote something more and different on it. It seems that it was not really in his nature to write the careful, well-developed synthesis that he, in effect, often demanded.[9]

Much the same problem arose in his diplomatic life. It was complained of him that, as a diplomat, he corresponded endlessly, made endless trips, and displayed endless curiosity, but could not in practice either bring matters together or bring them to an end.[10] It is an amusing and significant footnote that, after a time, Leibniz scanted or distorted his duties as a librarian. He gave excuses to keep people, including the Duke himself, out of the ducal library. He wanted to keep the library to himself, much as, it seems to me, he had kept his father's library.[11] He proliferated plans, but not fulfilments, for he was restless and incapable of prolonged orderliness. His faithful servant, Eckhart, said of him, 'He is much too distracted and in wanting to do everything and be involved in everything, he can bring nothing to an end, even with angels as his adjutants.'[12]

Leibniz slowly fitted his philosophizing to his deeper needs, one of which was an answer to death. When he substituted mechanistic for Scholastic structures, he continued to believe in the mind's immortality. Even so, mechanism was unsatisfactory, because, he discovered, extended atoms were not true metaphysical entities. He multiplied examples of the persistence of life through change. He recalled the burial of a silkworm in its cocoon, 'the resurrection of dead flies . . . the experiments on men frozen to death, drowned or strangled whom one has restored to life,' and he decided that there must be entelechies or souls that 'cannot be engendered or destroyed.'[13] And not only the soul, he decided, but also 'the animal itself and its organic machine' were conserved, though in a form too small for us to sense.[14] Life, he decided, neither begins nor ends, because 'death, like generation, is only the transformation of the same animal, which is sometimes augmented and sometimes diminished.'[15]

All of this appeared to Leibniz to be logically and metaphysically necessary. But even if he had been more persuasive to other philosophers than he in fact was, I could not help suspecting that he reasoned so in order to diminish the dominion of death. Lacking evidence, I can only wonder if his doctrines in any way softened the loss of his father (or mother, or both). There is, however, evidence that he continued to conceive of his life in the pattern his father had set for him. We see this in a letter he wrote at the age of thirty to his prospective employer, the Duke Johann Friedrich of Hannover. The letter recalls earlier correspondence and continues:

> I still retain the same feelings, and in fact believe that a man like myself, who is occupied by no other interest except, by striking discoveries in art and science, to make a name for himself and oblige the public by useful works, must look for only a great prince with insight enough to judge the worth of things, a liberal way of thinking, and rule over his actions in accord with the principles of fame. . . .[16]

In the same year as this letter, Leibniz also wrote a self-characterization that can serve us as a guide. He describes himself according to the then-prevailing theory of humours, explains that his voice is weak but clear and unable to pronounce the letter *k* and the gutturals, and then, speaking of himself in the third person, he adds detail on detail:

> In his boyhood he was already leading a sedentary life and did not undertake much activity [in his old age he sometimes remained in his easy chair reflecting and, no doubt, sleeping, for days at a time].[17] In his adolescent years he had already begun to read a great deal and reflect on different things, so that in most fields of knowledge he was an autodidact. He also burned with desire to penetrate everything more deeply than usually happens and to invent something new.
>
> His inclination to society is weaker than that which impels him to solitary reflection and reading. But if he finds himself in some company he knows how to converse rather pleasantly, but profits more from jocular or cheerful conversation than from the play or amusement that depends on bodily movement.
>
> He does flare up easily, but just as his wrath rises quickly, it also soon passes.
>
> One will never see him either excessively cheerful or sad. Pain and pleasure he senses only moderately. Laughter often alters only his face, without stirring his inward parts.
>
> He is fearful in beginning a task but bold in carrying it through. Because of his weak sight, his faculty of imagination is not lively. Because of the weakness of his memory, a small loss in the present affects him more than the greatest in the past.
>
> He is endowed with excellent inventive power and judgment, and it is not hard for him to think out various things, to read (with understanding), to write, to speak extemporaneously, and, when necessary, to investigate abstract ideas by incessant reflection down to the very basis, from which I conclude that he has a dry and spirituous brain.
>
> His vital spirits are excessively active. I am therefore afraid that he, with his lean body, will one day die of a feverish illness or of exhaustion because of his incessant studying and his too frequent meditations.[18]

To this relatively ample self-characterization, a few further notes may be added. It is himself Leibniz appears to be speaking of when he maintains that persons very sensitive to insults have natural brief compassion for those whose difficulties might have been their own, or when he mentions the persons who recall even the smallest insult but forget it as soon as their honour is restored. 'Ingenious people,' he says, 'are sharply affected by both great and small insults, but like a straw fire, which is soon burned out.'[19] He often stresses that he looks for the good rather than the bad in people and books.[20] And very strikingly and aptly, he says, 'Everything easy is hard for me, everything hard, in contrast, is easy.'[21] To this remark, made in the course of discussion of quick as against slow thinking, we may add the words in which Leibniz's servant, Eckhart, describes his conciliatory nature. 'He spoke well of everyone,' he says, 'turned everything to the best, and was considerate even of his enemies. . . .'[22] These words irresistibly recall Leibniz's mother. Leibniz's conciliatory nature is, of course, reflected in his attempt 'to uncover and unite the truth buried and scattered under the opinions of all the different philosophical sects.'[23] He saw his philosophy as the union of Plato with Democritus, Aristotle with Descartes, the Scholastics with the moderns, and theology and morality with reason.[24]

After all this personal description, I would like to concentrate on two characteristics of Leibniz as a philosopher, his desire to know and his desire for harmony in independence. His desire to know was conceived by him as the way of approaching God. He reasoned in approximately the following way: Happiness requires consciousness, and therefore only a spirit, a conscious being, can be happy. To be happy is to be in a state of harmony, and the greatest harmony or felicity requires the admission into oneself of the universal harmony, which is to say, God. 'All felicity is harmonious.' But this truth is recognized only by those who do not complain at the world, who know that, however painful it may be, it is the best of all possible worlds.

> So in the world no indignation is ever just, no transport of the soul other than tranquillity is free of impiety. To desire in the way that refusal of satisfaction would commit one to suffering is a sin, a hidden anger against God, against the present state of things, against the consecutiveness and universal harmony on which this state depends.[25]

A word of comment on these views of Leibniz. This prohibition of complaint, this equating of indignation with sin, this tranquillity by philosophical force majeure is a philosophical transposition of the Leibniz who was never too cheerful or sad and who did not allow even laughter to move him internally. I think that only a man who wants to complain and feels indignant and troubled can be as unqualified as Leibniz in outlawing such negative reactions. Maybe, in taking negative reactions to be denials of cosmic order, he was resisting some chaos of his own, some feeling of lostness, some hidden anger at the good father who had instilled faith in him and then abandoned him. Perhaps to be dissatisfied with things as they are is to him to rebel against fathers, whether human or divine.

It is notable that, to Leibniz, the tie with God, like the tie with his father, is by way of knowledge. Speaking of God, he says, 'One cannot love him without knowing the perfection of his beauty . . . That is to say, one must know the marvels of reason and the marvels of nature.'[26] In the same vein, 'The more one gives reasons for his love, the more one loves God . . . The highest function of our mind is the knowledge or what is the same thing, the love of the more perfect being. . . .'[27] The knowledge Leibniz is speaking of is literally and simply that of the scholar, scientist, or philosopher. For God favours such beings as 'are capable of knowing great truths with regard to God and the universe . . . God draws from them infinitely more glory than from all other Beings.'[28]

This position of Leibniz, his own variation of Neo-Platonism, does not keep him from stressing the independence and completeness of each person or spirit. He says, 'One spirit alone is worth a whole world since it not merely expresses the world but also knows it and conducts itself after the fashion of God.'[29] But though each member of the world, each of the substances that populate it, is independent, the will of God establishes harmony between them, for God is in the relation of 'a prince to his subjects and even a father to his children.'[30]

Whatever this may mean metaphysically or theologically, on the level we are concerned with here, it strikes me as an odd, distant, and cautious expression of intimacy. Intimacy is a state Leibniz seems on the whole to have resisted. He already contained the piety, intellectual ambition, and flight by death of his father; the piety, resignation, and conciliatoriness of his mother, and his own unrelenting curiosity and autonomy. Perhaps some unknown quantum of emotional detachment was added by parents each of whom had suffered the fairly early death of both parents. Whether so or not, Leibniz mirrored his state of unintimate closeness or of intimate distance in the doctrine of monads. This doctrine allowed the soul and every other real unity to 'arise from its own nature by a perfect *spontaneity* with regard to itself, yet by a perfect *conformity* to things without.'[31] By virtue of such a 'hypothesis of agreement' the extremes of autonomy and unity could be joined. This aim was furthered, Leibniz was sure, by the demonstration that space and time were secondary to order or logic. From boyhood on, as he said, he had sat rather than moved, and his world came to be, like him, active in thought but essentially immobile. I do not even know if it is a joke to call it the world as the seated thinker, thinking ceaselessly and bit by bit to maintain and grasp its own infinity.

As might be expected, Leibniz's spirit of conciliation did not extend to his philosophical rivals, Descartes and Spinoza. Descartes he regarded as a great man gone wrong. He accused him of being ungrateful to the many philosophers and scientists he had pillaged. He accused him of depending on the rhetoric of doubt and the show of novelty in order to create a sect and win applause, and he accused him of substituting a subjective response for an objective, logical proof.[32] As for Spinoza, he both fascinated and repelled him more. I do not think that he ever said or wrote a public word in his favour, and he quite soon broadcast the opinion that Spinoza's *Tractatus* was intolerably licentious. But to Spinoza himself he wrote inviting correspondence and praising his 'very penetrating judgment.' He visited Spinoza, tried, after his death, to buy his manuscripts, and read his posthumous works eagerly.[33] When he went through the *Ethics*, he found its proofs to be faulty and its doctrines pernicious to Christianity. He was no doubt fascinated by Spinoza and perhaps influenced by him, but he ended by regarding him, in a stereotyped way, as the deterministic enemy, whose philosophic resemblance to himself he would like forgotten.[34]

That Leibniz was less bold than Descartes and more simply compassionate than Spinoza is suggested, in each case, by a pair of neatly contrasting anecdotes:

Leibniz's servant, Eckhart, reports that once the philosopher was the only passenger in a small barque. A terrible storm blew up, and the sailors, as Leibniz often told Eckhart, supposing that Leibniz was ignorant of their language, agreed in his presence to throw him overboard and share his effects. He made believe that he had not heard anything, but then took out a cross and pretended to pray. Seeing that he was no heretic, the soldiers relented. When Descartes was in a very similar predicament, he drew his sword and forced the sailors to abandon their plan.[35]

The contrast with Spinoza comes by way of the report that Leibniz was taken with the remarkable structure of the fly. 'That is also reason why Herr von Leibnitz never killed a fly, however much it inconvenienced him, because he thought it would be a misdeed to destroy so ingenious a mechanism.'[36] This reluctance may exhibit the admiration of the scientist more than the compassion of the man, but it contrasts sharply, not only with the anecdote that Spinoza enjoyed watching spiders killing flies, but with Spinoza's own statements, which I have quoted earlier, that we take pleasure in the wars of insects and that pity is womanish.

Leibniz's double-faced attitude toward Spinoza suggests a fault for which Leibniz has often been criticized, a certain lack in everyday truthfulness and political decency. He was willing to propose a joint attack of Europe on Egypt in order to save Germany from a possible French attack; and he was willing to suggest that an English loan be repaid by allowing English buccaneers to plunder the French coast. He justified diplomatic lying clearly enough.[37] It even appears, after careful investigation, that his title of nobility was granted to him by none other than himself.[38] Furthermore, his desire for praise or fame was such that he may have earned Diderot's barbed epigram, that he was 'a sage or a madman, as you please . . . who loves the sound of eulogy as a miser the sound of a coin.'[39] It is only fair to add that Diderot also said that when one compares one's talents with those of Leibniz, 'one is tempted to throw away books and go and die quietly in some obscure corner.'[40]

Leibniz liked children. It is said that he had them brought to him, watched them playing as he sat in his easy chair, and then dismissed them with cake.[41] There was a rumour that in his youth he had had a natural son, none other than his servant, Wilhelm Dinniger, who was greatly favoured by Leibniz for a time, but who grew insolent and was dismissed.[42] When Leibniz was fifty, the idea of marriage crossed his mind, but when the woman in question asked for time to reflect, he lost the inclination. It was too late, he said.[43] When he held that for him everything easy came hard and everything hard came easy, he might well have included marriage among the easy and therefore hard things. But he had lived so long with his own thoughts, had become so much his own synthesis of differences, that he could no longer wish to have his intimacy violated by any other person, and he did not marry.

Berkeley

6. George Berkeley, born in 1685. His parents survived into his fifties. If I were to hold the extreme thesis that a person can become a philosopher only if one or both of his parents die while he is young, Berkeley would be a clear counter-instance. 'They were a happy pair in life, and happy in not being divided in death. It cannot be said that they died an untimely death, both being near ninety. They lived to breed up six sons, gentlemen. They lived to see the eldest [George] a bishop some years before their death. . . .'[1]

We know that Berkeley had a strong dislike for his youngest brother, Thomas. Thomas was condemned for bigamy, and when Berkeley learned that, unknown to him, some of his money had been used in the defence of Thomas, he said that he would not have spent half the sum 'to have saved that villain from the gallows.'[2] Thomas, one assumes, was the brother who eloped with 'a lady of family' and then stubbornly refused to marry her, with the result that Berkeley considered him a scoundrel and refused to see him when he came on a visit.[3] In contrast, he remained close to his brother, Robert, who had a distinguished career in the church.

Berkeley's surviving letters say nothing about his parents. As far as I know, there are only two short sentences in his works that cast light on his early emotional life. The one, put down in a philosophical notebook, to which we will return, says, 'Mem: that I was distrustful at 8 years old and Consequently by nature disposed for these new Doctrines.'[4] The word 'distrustful' in the memorandum replaces 'sceptical,' which has been crossed out. The other, at least somewhat significant sentence says, to the same effect, 'From my childhood I had an unaccountable turn of thought that way.'[5]

At eleven, Berkeley went to boarding school, and at fifteen to Trinity College, Dublin. He got his B.A. degree and then, two years later, was elected a Junior Fellow. It was 1707, and he was twenty-two. Between July or August of that year and August of the next, he wrote out his philosophical doubts and solutions in brief often aphoristic form in two notebooks, now called, in their published form, *Philosophical Commentaries*. The ideas he was to use were all there, though in scattered form, his 'first arguings,' of which we have no direct trace, giving way to 'second thoughts.'[6] The philosophers who influenced him most were Locke, Malebranche, and Bayle. Locke, it has been said, furnished him with his grammar of philosophy, Malebranche with the stimulus, the irritant, while Bayle showed him the weaknesses, or, rather, the dangers of Malebranche.[7] Then, at the respective ages of twenty-four, twenty-five, and twenty-eight, he published the three books that made him the philosopher we know, *An Essay Towards a New Theory of Vision, A Treatise Concerning the Principles of Human Knowledge*, and *Three Dialogues Between Hylas and Philonous*.

Berkeley was still to live an eventful life; but his most creative period as a philosopher was over. Obliged by university statutes to take Holy Orders, he had done so, and quite willingly, his subsequent life appears to show. He remained a fellow a total of seventeen years, becoming a tutor and acting successively as Librarian, Junior Dean, Junior Greek Lecturer, Senior Greek Lecturer, Divinity Lecturer, Senior Proctor, and Hebrew Lecturer.[8] For our purposes, we need not describe his travels in Europe, not even the occasion on which he, with a drawn sword, and a friend, with a drawn pistol, faced down a huge dark Alpine wolf that 'turned about and made a stand with a very fierce and daring look.'[9]

At the age of thirty-seven Berkeley reached the decision that he should spend the rest of his life in Bermuda, where he intended to build a college in which planters' sons and Indians from the American mainland should be educated, each type of student in accord with its needs. In spite of his great powers of persuasion, and in spite of a near-miraculous grant from the House of Commons, the project was never carried out. At forty-nine he was appointed Bishop of Cloyne, in Ireland, where he spent the rest of his days in the energetic honourable fulfilment of his duties.

The failure of the Bermuda project affected Berkeley's previously buoyant spirits. 'With the shattering of that gorgeous and eager dream of his against the rough touch of reality, something of the bloom of being went from him,—something, too, of his old elasticity in hope and joy; and in their place came the sadness of a riper wisdom, and the sweetness of having drunk of a bitter cup.'[10] An illness that had troubled him since his early thirties became chronic, and 'he was often troubled,' we are told, 'with the hypochondria' and with 'nervous cholic.'[11] Something should be said of his illness, not least because it plays the central role in a psychoanalytic interpretation of his life, according to which his philosophy, like his illness, is fundamentally related to the desire to rid himself of something dangerous or, so to speak, poisonous.*

I do not know how Berkeley's illness would be diagnosed today, but it caused him great pain and considerable internal bleeding. He blamed the illness on his sedentary life. He thought that in tar-water he had discovered a cure for himself and even, surprisingly, for all human ills. Both his illness and supposed cure are reflected in the words he wrote in *Siris*, his last and, for a time, most successful book, meant to propagate the use of tar-water for the good of mankind. Of himself, Berkeley said:

> Studious persons . . . pent up in narrow holes, breathing bad air, and stooping over their books, are much to be pitied . . . My own sedentary course of life has long since thrown me into an ill habit, attended with many ailments, particularly a nervous colic, which rendered my life a burden, and the more so because my pains were exasperated by exercise. But since the use of tar-water, I find, though not a perfect recovery from my old and rooted illness, yet such a gradual return of health and ease, that I esteem my having taken this medicine the greatest of all temporal blessings, and am convinced that, under providence, I owe my life to it.[12]

Siris turns out to be a medico-philosophical book, which moves from medicine proper to chemistry at large, to an attack on Newton's physics, to the denial that nature as such can be a true cause, and to a discussion of the cosmic mind. *Siris* does not repudiate any of Berkeley's earlier doctrines and even repeats, in more or less explicit form, the essential early

---

*The interpretation referred to is that in J. O. Wisdom, *The Unconscious Sources of Berkeley's Philosophy*. This is the only book-length study of a philosopher known to me written by an author with professional competence in both philosophy and psychoanalysis. It is a careful, clear book, more technical in its analysis than I have found congenial or useful here, and more dramatically speculative. Its interpretations based on Berkeley's illness and his acceptance of tar-water as a panacea relate to the period well after he had written the books that made him an important philosopher. They are, of course, likely to give insight into earlier tendencies that were echoed in later ones. Though the emphasis in my account is different, and though my interpretation is more restricted, I have certainly profited from Wisdom's analysis.

ones. But the early, often astringent intellectuality is replaced by a pious, Neo-Platonic, tradition-laden enthusiasm.

In judging the connection between Berkeley's life and philosophy, it may at once be pointed out that his philosophy, like his medical panacea, was aimed at the expulsion of an evil, that caused by sceptics, atheists, and fatalists, and marked especially by belief in the existence of matter:

> The existence of matter, or bodies unperceived, has not only been the main support of atheists and fatalists, but on the same principle does idolatry likewise in all its various forms depend . . . Matter being once expelled out of nature drags with it so many sceptical and impious notions, such an incredible number of disputes and puzzling questions, which have been thorns in the sides of divines as well as philosophers and made so much fruitless work for mankind, that if the arguments we have produced against it are not found equal to demonstration (as to me they evidently are), yet I am sure all friends to knowledge, peace, and religion have reason to wish they were.[13]

There is much of the air of panacea in Berkeley's philosophical proposals, and more enmity against his chosen opponents than one might expect from an ordinarily equable, fair-minded man. Like most of his critics, he is apt to set up straw men in place of opposing philosophers. He fulminates against the 'miserable refuges' of the atheists and the 'wild imaginations' of Vanini, Hobbes, and Spinoza[14] Against them he directs an anger like that he directed against his younger brother. He castigates the deists as bullies who join natural rudeness with 'a delicate sense of danger.' The last words may provide a hint of ambivalence, for elsewhere he says of himself that 'I know not what it is to fear, but I have a delicate sense of danger.'[15]

Berkeley's chosen opponents include the mathematicians. There is more than one sign in his *Philosophical Commentaries* that he admires or envies these experts in a science he too practised, and with considerable competence. Weighing pro and con, he sees wit in Newton at least; he thinks the mathematicians possess reason but use it for ignoble purposes; he says that some of them have 'good parts, the more is the pity'; and he admits that, despite their 'trifling subjects . . . their Method and arguing are excellent.'[16] But his attitude is mostly negative, for, in his opinion, the mathematicians need to be chastened. He is opposed to their tendency to believe in an abstract, more-than-empirical reality. He prefers to regard mathematics as a calculative skill rather than a form of speculative knowledge. In the course of time, as *De Motu* and the *Analyst* show, his devaluation of mathematics grows more modulated and just.[17] He deserves praise for his clear-headed antagonism to Newton's attempt to arrive at continuity by means of the method of 'fluxions.' He generally wants to break up every possible extra-mental unity or continuity into separate, incoherent 'ideas' whose being and coherence with one another will then depend on the mind that senses them.[18]

When we look back at the whole of Berkeley's philosophy, we find, I think, certain parts that are defended sharply and clearly, and others that seem, if not arbitrary, at least more nearly assumed than defended. It is not clear to me, for example, why Berkeley is so emotional in opposing belief in the more or less independent existence of matter. It is always self-evident to him that matter is the rival of the sort of God he prefers. In his notes, he says, 'Matter once allowed. I defy any man to prove that God is not matter.'[19] Berkeley is of course against the idea, attributed to Locke, More, Raphson, and others, of considering God himself as extended. To him, 'It seems dangerous to suppose extension which is manifestly inert in God.'[20] The very existence of extension as such appears to him to endanger belief in God. In the elliptical language of his notebooks:

> The great danger of making extension exist without the mind. in yt if it does it must be acknowledg'd infinite immutable eternal etc. wch will be to make either God extended (wch I think dangerous) or an eternal, immutable, infinite, increate being beside God.[21]

Such statements, though clear in themselves, puzzle me because so many sincerely pious philosophers have no great difficulty in allowing matter or extension an at least relative existence. The image of a builder using material that already lies to hand, or endowed with the power of creating basic materials, including, perhaps, space and time, with which he builds, is an image that has often appeared in mythology and subsequently in theology and philosophy. But Berkeley will have none of it. The God he envisages is more exclusive, excluding even the shadow of the possibility of any other substance. Maybe Berkeley's exclusiveness shows fear that God's rival is attractive, or, alternatively, that God is so necessary to him that the mere possibility of a rival dismays him. The latter suggestion is conveyed by another of the notes I have been quoting:

> Strange impotence of men. Man without God. Wretcheder than a stone or tree, he having onely the power to be miserable by his unperformed wills, those having no power at all.[22]

Berkeley may be echoing Malebranche, who stresses man's impotence in the absence of God, because, according to Malebranche, every instance of human willing is a cue to which God responds by providing the appropriate ideas.[23] Even if Berkeley does not hold to this position, he needs the sense of a God who is close, as if in constant conversation with him, every sensation and shift of sensation giving renewed evidence of God's closeness and unending concern. Our visual world, he holds, is an optic language that is necessarily connected with knowledge, wisdom, and goodness.

> The instantaneous production and reproduction of so many signs, combined, dissolved, transposed, diversified, and adapted to such an endless variety of purposes, ever shifting with the occasions and suited to them, being utterly inexplicable and unaccountable by the laws of motion, by chance, by fate, or the like blind principles, doth set forth and testify the immediate operation of a spirit or thinking being; and not merely of a spirit, which every motion or gravitation may possibly infer, but of one wise, good, and provident Spirit, who directs and rules and governs the world.[24]

When I read this passage, I remember others like it, and feel that Berkeley's aesthetic sensitivity is so great that he cannot take the world in a simply matter-of-fact way. He responds too strongly to the nuances of experience; and in everything he senses, as children do, something additional, subtly like a personal emotion and a conscious will. Nature, to him, cannot be uncaring, or purposeless, or dead. If it were any of these, he would be left with his temptations unprohibited and his goodness unnoticed and unrewarded. He would then be like a child that is good in order to earn the praise and love of a parent, but who has no one to be good for when the parent is gone. Berkeley is very sensitive to the possibility that he will be abandoned. He has evidently experienced the fear of the world become alien.

The manner in which Berkeley escapes from the possibility of an alien or deceptive world is philosophically as simple as it is bold. It begins in Descartes and Locke, who had renewed the classic distinction between 'primary' and 'secondary' qualities. Descartes and Locke, that is, had distinguished between qualities such as colour and odour, which, they said, were subjective, and the colourless, odourless, real particles, with real, mathematically expressible qualities, that produced a colour- or odour-response in us when they struck our sensory organs. Descartes in particular had argued that the world must be material, meaning, extended, because if it were not, God, who is utterly truthful, would have created a naturally deceiving world. Pious though Berkeley was, he could not accept Descartes' assurance; and, for what appear to me to be emotional reasons, he could not accept the belief in matter or extension. He therefore accepted the attack on Descartes he had read in Bayle's *Historical and Critical Dictionary*. Bayle there wrote,

> This proof of Descartes is very weak; it proves too much. Ever since the beginning of the world, all mankind, except perhaps one out of two hundred millions, has firmly believed that bodies are coloured, and this is an error. I ask, does God deceive mankind with regard to colours? If he deceived them about this, what prevents him from doing so with regard to extension.[25]

Once we assume that *any* sensation is deceptive, said Bayle, then any other, of whatever kind, may be so; for God does not force us to believe that colours or extension exist outside of our minds, but only to conclude that they *seem* to exist there. Malebranche was right, he said, in holding 'that we are not invincibly led to believe in the existence of anything other than God and our mind.'[26]

Aware of the possibilities of deception, Malebranche could advise nothing better than faith in the existence of an external world, a faith that Berkeley could not easily stomach. Then came the solution. Why not do away with the mysterious, possibly deceptive external world, the matter or extension that endangers God and makes decency pointless? Why not simply accept that 'to be is to be perceived.' This principle soon developed into the more comprehensive one, 'To be is to be perceived or to perceive.' Only perceptions and minds existed, they alone constituted the whole of existence, and it became unnecessary to believe that something other than perceptions, something, so to speak, behind them, caused them. Away with extension and mysterious powers and the whole farrago of pseudo-explanations! Now the world could be taken to be exactly as it appeared and nothing either more or different.

Once discovered, the new principle became obvious to Berkeley, and he said to himself in his notebook, 'I wonder not at my sagacity in discovering the obvious tho' amazing truth, I rather wonder at my stupid inadvertency in not finding it out before. . . .'[27] The amazing truth once grasped, he could extend it with the traditional belief that the orderliness of the world depended on the willed and orderly activity of God. For a moment he was troubled by the problem that Descartes too had faced: when a person's thoughts stop, as in sleep, does that person go out of existence? He answered the question by reasoning that if the being of the soul was to perceive, and if, apart from perceiving, only perceptions exist, then time and existence had no meaning apart from the activity of perceiving. Existence and perceiving were therefore the same and self-intermittency was impossible.[28]

The solution, as I have said, was simple, bold, and retrospectively obvious to Berkeley. It filled him with pleasure and seemed to end the rational possibility of either scepticism or materialism. But the solution was unviable for others. Reasonable doubt was soon cast on it; and the doubt was elaborated by a prominent Scottish philosopher, Andrew Baxter, who cast Berkeley's argument back into his teeth. Berkeley argued, said Baxter, that he perceived only his perception, and not its cause, for which reason the cause could be denied—no need to assume the imperceptible, the I-know-not-what other then the perception itself. But what then of God? asked Baxter. If He was not perceived, He did not, by Berkeley's criterion, exist; or else He was no more than a perception in the mind of man. The argument against material substance was equally fatal to spiritual substance, so the sceptics and atheists that Berkeley had presumed routed had in fact been rearmed by him.[29]

It is interesting to note that Hume, in his few references to Berkeley, does not bring up any objection like Baxter's. In the longest of his references, a footnote, Hume acknowledges drawing an argument from Berkeley and adds:

> Most of the writings of that very ingenious author form the best lessons of scepticism, which are to be found either among the ancient or modern philosophers, Bayle not excepted. He professes, however, in his title-page (and undoubtedly with great truth) to have composed his book against the sceptics as well as against the atheists and free-thinkers. But that all his arguments, though otherwise intended, are, in reality, merely sceptical, appears from this, *that they admit of no answer and produce no conviction.* Their only effect is to cause that momentary amazement and irresolution and confusion, which is the result of scepticism.[30]

Hume, we see, answers not with logic but psychology. By this time, his own scepticism had been tempered. I think, however, that the reason that Berkeley's argument was able to convince Berkeley himself but not Hume may have been connected with a psychological difference between the two. Berkeley was a relatively self-confident man. Though preoccupied for a while with the philosophical problem of an intermittent self, he seems never to have entertained serious doubts of his own existence. He could not be a sceptic because he could not doubt his own or God's substantiality, and because he was devoted to the morality and religion that scepticism undermined. But why did he find it so easy, for the sake of this, his natural, native faith, to transform the external world into no more than perceptions? For all his arguing, the transformation struck others as absurd. I can answer only by reminding the reader of Berkeley's statements that he had been unaccountably sceptical or distrustful by the age of eight and that he was by nature disposed for his new doctrine. I will not pretend that the meaning of Berkeley's 'sceptical' or 'distrustful' is psychologically clear to me; but I think it reasonable to suppose, on general principles, that it refers to an early experience of derealization, in which the world, its reality withdrawn from it, appeared pale and insubstantial. Berkeley's subsequent philosophical derealization of the external world was quite enough to convince Hume that Berkeley, whatever his protestations, was teaching scepticism. For Hume had experienced and philosophically formulated, not only an external world voided of substance, but also a self voided of it (as I will explain psychologically in my account of Hume). In Hume, as in others, a derealized world was the counterpart of a depersonalized self, so he could not appreciate the distinction that to Berkeley, with his different experience, was axiomatic.

I do not know with what degree of seriousness to take the suggestion I have just made, though I find it interesting. There is, however, no real doubt of Berkeley's basic psychological health. Not only was his learning genuine and varied, extending from the classics to science and theology, not only was he aesthetically sensitive, especially to architecture, not only was he helpful and public-spirited, and not only was he handsome, but he was a very loving husband and doting father.[31] He married late, it is true, at the age of forty-three, and his wife was no mere woman, but a paragon of femininity and humanity, unaffected, cheerful, intelligent, well-educated, practically capable, and devoted. But in the light of the relationships we have so often discussed between men and women and parents and children, it is a pleasure to repeat the words in which his wife commended him, after his death, to one of their sons:

> How carefully was your infancy protected by your dear father's skill and mother's care. You were not, for our ease, trusted to mercenary hands; in childhood you were instructed by your father—he though old and sickly, performed the tedious task himself, and would not trust it to another's care. You were his business and his pleasure. . . . . He made home pleasant by a variety of employments, conversation, and company; his instructive conversation was delicate, and when he spoke directly of religion (which was seldom) he did it in so masterly a manner, that it made a deep and lasting impression. You never heard him give his tongue the liberty of speaking evil. Never did he reveal the fault or secret of a friend . . . Humility, tenderness, patience, generosity, charity to men's souls and bodies, were the sole end of all his projects, and the business of his life. In particular I never saw so tender and amiable a father, or so patient and industrious a one. . . .[32]

All this, and philosophy too. I find it hard to believe.

Voltaire

7. François Marie Arouet, or Arouet de Voltaire, as he called himself from the age of twenty-four, born in 1694. His mother, whom he hardly mentions, died when he was seven. Three children died young and three survived. In order of age, the three survivors were Armand, Marie Marguerite, and Voltaire himself.

Voltaire was convinced that he was the bastard of a little-known poet, Rochebrune or Roquebrune. According to a contemporary, Voltaire 'claimed that it was to his mother's honour that she preferred an intelligent man like Roquebrune, musketeer, officer, writer,' to Voltaire's ostensible father, 'who was by nature a very commonplace man, and said that he had always flattered himself that he owed his birth to Roquebrune.'[1]

Voltaire's ostensible father, François Arouet, was a notary who became an advocate and then a high tax-official. On one of the few occasions that Voltaire mentions him, he speaks of him as a grumbler.[2] As for Armand, Voltaire disliked and perhaps even hated him. The Arouet family included some very pious Jansenist members, and Armand became one of the fanatical kind of Jansenists 'whose exclusive belief in salvation by grace led them to condemn every sort of amusement, and to seek greedily for all apparent manifestations of divine favour, not excluding self-mutilation and graveyard epilepsy.'[3] Voltaire said of Armand, 'His savage customs disgust me.'[4] With his sister, however, he had a good relationship. When he was unable to visit her himself, he wrote to a friend, 'My heart has always turned to her. I am sure you will give her a little friendship for me.'[5] When she died—Voltaire was thirty-one at the time—he wrote to the same friend, echoing Hamlet in his own not quite perfect English:

> I have nothing to tell you on that account but that you know my heart and my way of thinking. I have wept for her death, and i would be with her. Life is but a dream full of starts of folly, and of fancied, and true miseries. Death awakens us from this painful dream, and gives us, either a better existence or no existence at all.[6]

To turn to Voltaire's education: when he was ten, he was sent to a Jesuit *collège*, among whose teachers there were classicists and humanists to whom he always felt grateful. 'Nothing,' he said, 'will blot out in my heart the memory of Father Porée, who is equally dear to all who studied under him. No man ever made study and virtue more agreeable.'[7] He later expressed astonishment that such knowledgeable, dedicated men could be wedded to such erroneous religious doctrines.

While at the *collège*, Voltaire already gave evidence of extraordinary poetic gifts; and he already fell in with a group of hedonists, free-lovers and free-thinkers, whose company he continued to frequent after he graduated at the age of sixteen. His father, 'a decent man much angered by his conduct,' tried to remove him from the scene of temptation by sending him to Caen, and from Caen to The Hague, where he became an attaché to the French ambassador. But when, at nineteen, he tried to elope with a charming local girl, the mother complained, and Voltaire was returned to France. Back in Paris, he hid from his furious father, who had obtained an order of imprisonment, until his submission by letter and his agreement to be articled to a lawyer smoothed things over.[8]

Now Voltaire's poetic gift began to determine his fortune. Poetry gained him the love of an actress, the esteem of the Regent, and the mild exile the Regent visited on him in return for the versified hint that the Regent had committed incest. The graceful flattery of a verse epistle won the Regent's pardon, though Voltaire's less forgiving father called him drunk with success and the praises of the great, his 'sheer poisoners.'[9] Voltaire's troubles were not over. A police spy asserted that Voltaire was continuing to defame the Regent. As a result, Voltaire was, rather comfortably, it must be admitted, installed in the Bastille, where he wrote his first play, *Oedipe*, and part of a long epic poem, the *Henriade*. After some eleven months, he was released and again exiled from Paris, he again protested his innocence, was again believed by the Regent, and his exile was remitted by degrees. He had suffered, he wrote, the rigours of an unjust imprisonment, but had learned to harden himself against adversity and had found an unexpected courage in himself.[10]

When Voltaire's play, *Oedipe*, was produced in Paris, it had an unprecedented succss and won him instant fame. The Regent gave him a gold medal and an annuity, and the King of England, George I, a gold medal and watch, the watch being dispatched, on Voltaire's instructions, to his father. The improvement of relations between son and father was demonstrated on the latter's death a few years later, for his will granted Voltaire a third of the residual estate. But the father also demonstrated his doubts by leaving the legacy in trust, causing Voltaire some financial difficulties.[11]

The year of his father's death, the *Henriade* was published, and it, too, was immensely successful. At twenty-seven, Voltaire appeared to have won his place in French letters and society. The next few years only amplified his success, by way of the mistress he shared with the Prime Minister, by way of the tears and laughter of the Queen at his plays, and by way of the friendship of a financier. But one day he exchanged insults with the chevalier de Rohan, who had servants waylay and beat him. Voltaire's evident intention to challenge de Rohan to a duel caused the de Rohans to have Voltaire committed to the Bastille, from which he was released on his promise to go to England.[12]

England was an adventure. Voltaire responded to London in the spring with lyrical enthusiasm; but soon he grew rather disillusioned with English weather, character, and institutions, and rather depressed.[13] He recovered, however, and wrote the *Philosophical Letters*, his first sustained piece of propagandizing for tolerance and reason, two qualities that marked the English far more than the French, he thought. Though banned in France, the *Philosophical Letters* made a great impression there, spreading the reputation of Newton and of Locke, the modest sage and skilled anatomist of the mind, whose philosophy, said Voltaire, contrasted so strongly with the brilliant romancing of Descartes.[14]

When Voltaire returned to France, after about two years in England, he was determined to become financially independent. His daring and luck secured this goal within a year.[15] In following Voltaire to this point, we have gone through a major cycle of his life, from initial bastardy to literary and social fame, from the suffering of tyranny to effective attack on it, and from often humiliating dependence to independence of means and thought as great as any such a man could have in his time and place. Somewhat frivolously and deviously, he had arrived at the open, powerful defence of reason with which his name is associated. The limits of my brief accounts of philosophers do not allow me to follow him in narrative style through the rest of his long, active career. Nothing will be said of his interesting though painful attempt to live with Frederick II, the King of Prussia. Only a little will be said, later on, of the long period he spent with Mme du Chatelet, of the conjuncture of difficulties that plunged him into the state of mind he reveals in *Candide*, or of his courageous defences of Calas and La Barre. Whatever I can say about all these will be oriented toward our major goal, the understanding of a philosopher's thought in the light of his basic human relationships and experiences.

In reading Voltaire, one soon notices that, for all the sheer quantity of his works and the number of his letters, he did not reveal his intimate thoughts. His notebooks do not contain a single intimate word on himself.[16] Once, it is true, he let slip the phrase, 'Where flee far away from myself?'[17] But as a rule, he spoke in a waspishly objective tone, or he acted some role or other. He loved to write, stage, and act in plays; he was a masterly story-teller; he was hungry for magic-lantern and marionette shows; and he wrote under as many as three hundred pseudonyms.[18]

One can get somewhat below Voltaire's glittering, varied surface if one pays attention to his anxieties, most often reported by others. His health, for one thing, always troubled him. He must have supposed it to have been bad from the beginning, for, referring to himself in the third person, he wrote in an autobiography, 'He has several times told me that at his birth it was thought that he could not live and that having been privately sprinkled by the midwife, the ceremony of baptism was put off for several months.'[19] In one letter he attributed his ill health to heredity and said, evidently thinking of Rochebrune as his father, that he 'was born of parents who were unhealthy and died young.'[20] He was, by his own description, 'thin, tall, dried-up and bony,' and though we must, by our own standards, protest against the word 'tall' (in his prime he was some 5 feet 3 inches), his thinness struck everyone, especially when, in his old age, he turned positively cadaverous.[21]

To Voltaire's ill health, which he guarded against by diet and exercise, there must be added the episodes of depression, when his normally supple eloquence would become a stiff taciturnity. By his own account, he would alternate quickly between active optimisim and depressive emptiness.[22] There were episodes, too, of loss of consciousness. In one of them, described by his valet, Longchamps, he left Paris with a fever. His limbs paralyzed and, apparently dying, he was brought into an inn along the way. He begged Longchamps not to abandon him, not to allow him to die there, so Longchamps put him into the carriage, which drove on to their destination. Voltaire, who had lost consciousness, regained it only several hours later. The event, we are told, was not untypical.[23]

Menaced by illness, depression, and episodes of the sort described, Voltaire, to judge by his writings, was also the prey of a number of repetitive fantasies. Beginning with the *Henriade*, which contains a moving description of St. Bartholomew's Night, when the Huguenots were slaughtered, there appears the fanatic priest with the dagger.[24] The approach of the anniversary of that night would give him a fever and leave him prostrated in bed.[25] In the *Philosophical Dictionary* he writes, with unconcealed emotion, 'The most detestable example of fanaticism is that of the bourgeois of Paris who hastened in St. Bartholomew's night to assassinate, butcher, throw out of the windows, cut in pieces the fellow citizens who did not go to mass.'[26]

Although the victims of St. Bartholomew's Night were the Huguenots, Voltaire took his brother's kind of Huguenot as another image of fanaticism. He writes with a contained anger,

> Once fanaticism, has cankered a brain, the disease is almost incurable. I have seen convulsionaries who, talking about the miracles of Saint Pâris, gradually became excited depite themselves: their eyes blazed, their limbs trembled, passion disfigured their faces, and they would have killed anyone who contradicted them . . . How can you answer a man who tells you that he would rather obey god than men, and who is therefore sure to deserve heaven in cutting your throat?[27]

Such a question may havè brought back memories of his brother. Voltaire's secretary, Wagnière, tells us that he kept among his papers a 'collection of convulsions' edited by Armand.[28]

Voltaire felt the suffering of others very keenly. Just to hear of it might make him cry. In dreams he would sometimes relive the experiences of the victims, Sirven, Calas, or La Barre, whose names he was trying to rehabilitate.[29] When he describes the young LaBarre, his words revive the pain of the victim and the cruelty of the judges who 'ordered not only that his tongue be torn out, his hand cut off, and his body burned on a slow fire, but they also put him to the torture, to discover exactly how many songs he had sung, and how many processions he had watched with his hat on.' Voltaire concludes, 'There is no nation more cruel at bottom than the French.'[30]

Voltaire is under a strong inner compulsion to speak so of cruelty. What he says grows complicated when his natural but forced optimism is under the strain of misfortune, when the pain of the death of his long-time mistress, Mme du Chatelet, is followed by his humiliation by Frederick, and by other, less important, but still genuine humiliations. Then, in 1755, the Lisbon earthquake submerges personal pain in impersonal disaster, and, finally, the Seven Years War commits large-scale human cruelty with no rhyme or reason. Voltaire's pessimism grows and, with it, his impulse to act against it, to strike, with every rhetorical and imaginative device at his command, at 'the infamy' that poisons human life.[31]

He writes constantly, feverishly, and obsessively—but never forgets to correct what he writes. The emotion that drives him is always controlled by the style that expresses it. His stories are about himself, though disguised, of course. Much of *Candide*, for example, is disguised, stylized reminiscence. Like Voltaire, Candide is a bastard; like the baronette Voltaire is thinking of, Cunégone is sexually appetizing; but like Mme Denis, Voltaire's love, she becomes fat and ugly. The Turkey of his story is like the Prussia of his experience; and so on.[32]

The very style of *Candide* embodies its shifting activity. Its many verbs form small word-clusters, small centres of action, that join in larger clusters and actions, the movement of physical adventure and psychological reaction corresponding to the movement of the language. Style and story energize one another, and both energize the sado-masochistic wit with which Voltaire reenacts his fantasies and ambitions and their drastic failures.[33] The womanly beauty is balanced against the ugly shrew, and the utopia against its depraved opposite. He loves to create a utopia that degenerates into reality, and in this sense his tales resemble his histories, which demystify traditional fictions, devalue 'enthusiasm,' and cast a cold eye on partisanship. His imagination refuses to be limited to traditional history, which comprises only the Bible, Greece, Rome, and medieval and modern Europe. It reaches out to Eldorado, Paraguay, China, India, and other places. Whatever he recites, in tale or history, the good is always justice and reason and the evil always injustice and unreason, for 'ideas of justice,' he writes, 'are as clear, as universal, as ideas of health and sickness, truth and untruth, fitness and unfitness.'[34] Whatever wrongs have been done to him are universalized to the wrongs done to everyone everywhere, and taken with a sense of personal injustice. He clearly identifies himself with all the victims of oppression, all the bastards, the unprotected, the fatherless. But the intensity of his emotion and the often morbid imagery in which he expresses his hatred of oppression argue that somewhere in his being he is his brother Armand or his 'father,' with whom, as oppressors, he identifies himself. His Bartholomew Night prostrations repulse him from what has attracted him. I believe, too, that his universalism and attacks on localism and patriotism are protests against the narrowness of one of his fathers and the spuriousness of both. To speculate further, he is also perhaps searching for the emotional colour his mother has been supposed to have lent his life in the beginning.

Voltaire's virtues are at least to some extent the obverse of his faults. A word–portrait, drawn, most probably, by Rousseau catches the connection and likeness very well. The portrait says of him, 'Gay by nature, serious on principle, open without frankness, politic without subtlety, sociable without friends . . . He loves grandeur and despises the great . . . He is sensible without principles, and his reason has fits like the madness of others. His mind is just, his heart unjust, he thinks all things and mocks everything.'[35]

It is true that Voltaire can be selfish, vain, and dishonest in his personal dealings. Because he does not trouble to be very consistent, and because his peculiar depth is compounded of his peculiar ambivalence, the deadliest epigram levelled against him is that he is 'a chaos of clear ideas.' Although the image of the eighteenth–century *philosophe*, he is hardly, in the most current sense, a philosopher at all. Unless he is transcribing the ideas of others, his thought is essentially the translation of his own affectivity and is just as mobile and unstable. Yet, as I have said, justice is his passion, and he is deeply, fanatically, compulsively anti-fanatical.

The relation between Voltaire's wit and his own and others' suffering is particularly interesting. When, in May, 1778, he lay dying, he sent a brief letter to his physician, Tronchin, saying, 'The patient of the rue de Beaune has been suffering all night and still suffers from the convulsions of a violent cough. He asks your pardon for giving you so much trouble for a corpse.'[36] Another letter shows his relation to the suffering of others. A tendentious trial had resulted in the execution of general Lally-Tollendal, accused of ineptness or worse in the attempt to re-conquer India. Voltaire had been helping the son to vindicate his father, and when the son wrote to Voltaire, then on his deathbed, that the vindi-cation had succeeded, Voltaire, rousing himself from his lethargy, wrote, 'The dying man revives on learning this great news. He affectionately embraces Monsieur de Lally. He sees that the King is the defender of justice. He dies happy.'[37] After writing the letter, his last, Voltaire lapsed into coma and died four days later, at the age of eighty-four years and some months. His last pleasure was characteristically double: in the triumph of the victim of injustice, and in the brief elegance in which he cast this pleasure into the teeth of death.

Voltaire had many liaisons and was, in effect, married twice, once for a prolonged period to Mme du Chatelet, and later to his niece, the daughter of his sister. Emilie, Marquise du Chatelet, knew English, Italian, Latin, and other languages, and she loved and understood the arts, especially music. But her most particular interests were in philosophy, mathematics, and physics. With great diligence, she gathered and studied the works, in various languages, of contemporary scientists. While not a scientist with innovating power, she wrote a clear summary of Leibnizian ideas and made a creditable translation of the whole of Newton's *Principia* into French. This translation appeared posthumously with a preface in which Voltaire praised her supple intelligence and devotion to science.[38]

Mme du Chatelet did her best to protect Voltaire, not least against himself. For a long while, the two were happy together, and they never lost their mutual devotion. She thought that it was age, illness, or satiety that made his love wane, but it was, instead, as his letters show, his love for his niece, Marie Louise Denis. Mme Denis is described, whether cattily or justly I do not know, as very fat, ugly and kind, an unmalicious liar, and an unintelligent, emotional, domineering, unpretentious person.[39] She was not, on the whole, either agreeable or faithful; but each of her selfish acts was answered by Voltaire, almost unwaveringly, with acts of love.[40] The mere fact that he had such a relationship with his beloved sister's daughter is psychologically interesting, though I do not feel that I can speculate on it profitably.

During the latter part of his life, Voltaire, a quite wealthy man, presided over a large establishment, which had permanent guests, whom he maintained, perhaps sixty servants, and often fifty or so transient guests.[41] When turned to for help, he and Mme Denis adopted a poor girl who was a relative of Corneille and bore the great dramatist's name. Voltaire was delighted, on her arrival, with her naturalness and gaiety. He acted toward her in a concerned, fatherly way. He later issued an edition of Corneille's dramatic works in order to gather a dowry for her. Mme Denis, to her credit, proved to be a responsible fostermother.[42] Although Voltaire's marriage, like his birth, were not recognized by law, he had become a genuine paterfamilias and patriarch.

Hume

8. David Hume, born in 1711. His father died when Hume was two. His mother survived until he was thirty-four. Towards the end of her life,

when she grew ill, he refused for a time to leave her. After learning that she had died, he was found 'in the deepest affliction and in a flood of tears.' Her death, he wrote, made an immense void in the family.[1]

In the brief autobiography that Hume composed in the last year of his life, he said a few words about his family and then went on to his studies and preferences:

> My Father, who passed for a man of Parts, dyed when I was an Infant; leaving me, with an elder Brother and a Sister under the care of our Mother, a woman of singular Merit, who, though young and handsome, devoted herself entirely to the rearing and educating of her Children. I passed through the ordinary Course of Education with Success; and was seized very early with a passion for Literature which has been the ruling Passion of my Life, and the great source of my Enjoyments. My studious Disposition, my Sobriety, and my Industry gave my family a Notion that the Law was a proper Profession for me: But I found an unsurmountable Aversion to everything but the pursuits of Philosophy and general Learning. . . .
>
> My slender Fortune, however, being unsuitable to this plan of Life, and my Health being a little broken by my ardent Application, I was tempted to make a very feeble Trial for entering into a more active Scene of Life . . . I went over to France, with a View of prosecuting my Studies in a Country Retreat; and I there laid that Plan of Life, which I have steddily and successfully pursued: I resolved to make a very rigid Frugality supply my Deficiency of Fortune, to maintain unimpaired the Improvement of my Talents in Literature.
>
> During my Retreat in France, first at Reims, but chiefly at La fleche in Anjou, I composed my Treatise of Human Nature.[2]

The explanation, 'My health being a little broken,' is too slighting a reference to a long though variable period of depression, which extended from the age of nineteen to that of twenty-three. Within the last three years of this period, he scribbled, he said, 'many a Quire of Paper, in which there is nothing contained but my own Inventions.'[3] The *Treatise* was already in the making.*

Hume's depression is described in a long letter, written in March or April of 1734, to an anonymous doctor, who may have been Dr. John Arbuthnot.[4] It is not known whether or not it was actually sent. This letter seems to me to give such significant clues to the relationship between Hume's state of mind and the philosophy he was in the process of

---

*Hume made three statements about the composition of the *Treatise of Human Nature*, from which it may be concluded that he projected it before he was fourteen or fifteen, planned it before he was twenty-one, and wrote it before he was twenty-five. E. C. Mossner. *The Life of David Hume*, p. 73.

creating that I would like to follow it in some detail, quoting from it, paraphrasing, and interpolating my own comments.[5]

Hume begins by saying that he had a strong inclination to 'Books and Letters' from his earliest infancy. His extensive reading showed him that philosophers and critics disputed endlessly on even the most fundamental matters. Seeing this, Hume, so he writes, 'found a certain Boldness of Temper' growing in him and leading him 'to seek out some new Medium, by which Truth might be establisht.' After much thought, he decided, at the age of eighteen, to give up the study of law and become a scholar and philosopher. This decision made him, he said, infinitely happy. However, he recalled, citing a date he could not easily forget, 'about the beginning of September 1729, all my Ardor seem'd in a moment to be extinguisht, & I cou'd no longer raise my Mind to that pitch, which formerly gave me such excessive Pleasure.'

This condition, which naturally made Hume uneasy, lasted for nine months. In his opinion, the 'Distemper,' as he called it, had largely been brought on by books, such as those of Cicero, Seneca, and Plutarch, which were full of moral exhortations. Struck by these exhortations, Hume undertook to improve his understanding, and, with it, his temper and will. He wrote:

> I was continually fortifying myself with Reflections against Death, & Poverty, & Shame, & Pain, & all the other Calamities of Life. These are no doubt exceeding useful, when join'd with an active Life . . . but in Solitude they serve to little other Purpose, than to waste the Spirits. . . .

Something of Hume's state of mind must have been reflected in a manuscript, written at about this time, that he later burned. As he recalled in 1751:

> Tis not long ago that I burn'd an old Manuscript Book, wrote before I was twenty; which contain'd, Page after Page, the gradual Progress of Thoughts on that Head [the subject of religion]. It begun with an anxious Search after Arguments, to confirm the common Opinion: Doubts stole in, dissipated, return'd were again dissipated, return'd again; and it was a perpetual Struggle of a restless Imagination against Inclination, perhaps against Reason.'[6]

For all our ignorance of the details, there is no difficulty in seeing that Hume was undergoing an attack, or a series of attacks of depression. While we cannot know its exact causes, we do know that he had defied the family decision to study law, that his financial future was insecure, and that a growing independence or rebelliousness of mind was asserting itself in the form of particularly religious doubts. In any case, the absence of a father must have made him feel insecure. He apparently needed the philosophy books he read, and they apparently activated and focused his latent insecurity, to which a sense of guilt easily attached itself.

To proceed with Hume's letter on his depression, he tells that he got some scurvy spots on his fingers, and then, in April, 1730, when he was nineteen, he noticed more clearly that his mouth was watery. The doctor he consulted laughed at him and told him that he had caught 'the Disease of the Learned.' The doctor, says Hume, 'found great Difficulty to per-swade me, finding in myself nothing of that lowness of Spirit, which those, who labor under that Distemper so much complain of.' But Hume took his advice, in the form of bitters, anti-hysteric pills, a English pint of claret every day, and a daily ride of eight or ten Scotch miles. This he continued for about seven months. He now became somewhat indulgent to himself and studied only in moderation and when in a good mood. On his return to town, he was very careful to walk, ride, and maintain a regular diet and way of life, and he found that he could, within limits, resume his ambitious studies. He expected that when he returned to the country, he would be completely recovered. But he was mistaken, for the next summer, about May, 1731, his appetite suddenly became so ravenous, he wrote, 'that in 6 weeks time I past from the one extreme to the other, & being before tall, lean, & raw-bon'd became on a sudden, the most sturdy, robust, healthful-like Fellow you have seen, with a ruddy Complexion & a chearful Countenance.' Hume's heart also palpitated more obviously than before; but the appetite wore off by degrees.

Hume's ravenousness calls for comment. I assume that all of us have experienced that eating is a natural, primitive way of dealing with dis-comfort, frustration, or sadness. Depression may therefore be countered by excessive eating. Adolescents sometimes 'withdraw from social con-tacts, become increasingly inactive, seek comfort in food, and thus grow progressively fatter.'[7] The authority whose words I have quoted considers that such people may be

> defective in their awareness of being self-directed, separate individuals with the ability of identifying and controlling their bodily urges, and of defining their needs and presenting them in a way that they can find appropriate and satisfying responses. They suffer from a basic disturbance in the area of self-awareness. . . . Patients often complain about feeling 'empty', and behave as if their center of gravity were not within themselves but some-where in the outside world, controlled by someone else. This disturbance in bodily awareness is associated with what has been called 'weak ego bound-aries', 'disturbed body image', or 'identity confusion'. . . . They fail to achieve a sense of ownership of their own body.[8]

Perhaps no individual fits such generalizations perfectly. I do not think that Hume does; but that they are not, in his case, wide of the mark is shown by the sequel of his letter, in which he writes:

> I have given you a full account of the Condition of my Body, & without staying to ask Pardon, as I ought to do, for so tedious a Story, shall explain how my Mind stood all this time, which on every Occasion, especially in this Distemper, have a very near Connexion together . . . I have notic'd in the Writings of the French Mystiks, & in those of our Fanatics here, that, when they give a History of the Situation of the Souls, they mention a Coldness & Desertion of the Spirit, which frequently returns, & some of them, at the beginning, have been tormented with it many Years. As this kind of Devotion depends entirely on the Force of Passion, & consequently of the Animal Spirits, I have often thought that their Case & mine were pretty parralel, & that their rapturous Admirations might discompose the Fabric of the Nerves & Brain, as much as profound Reflections, & that warmth or Enthusiasm which is inseparable from them.
>
> However this may be, I have not come out of the Cloud so well as they commonly tell us they have done, or rather began to despair of ever recovering. To keep myself from being Melancholy on so dismal a Prospect, my only Security was in peevish Reflections on the Vanity of the World & of all humane Glory. . . .

He thinks that all his philosophy will not help him in his present situation, and that he should for a time, but only for a time, 'seek out a more active Life.'[9]

Hume's comparison of himself with the mystics seems well taken to me. Both he and they, in the states he refers to, were suffering from severe depression, which is a state of coldness, apathy, withdrawal, and bitter reflection. It is also likely to be a state of derealization or depersonalization, one, that is, in which the external world, the person himself, or both lose their sense of substantiality—their emotional solidity and coherence, one might say.

Hume's letter contains a passage to which I would like to return, because it gives a strong, almost direct clue to the nature of his philosophy. In this passage, Hume writes:

> My Disease was a crule Incumbrance on me. I found that I was not able to follow out any Train of Thought, by one continued Stretch of View, but by repeated Interruptions, & by refreshing my Eye from Time to Time upon other Objects. Yet with this Inconvenience I have collected the rude Materials for many Volumes; but in reducing these to Words, when one must bring the Idea he comprehended in gross, nearer to him, so as to contemplate its minutest Parts, & keep it steddily in his Eye, so as to copy these Parts in Order, this I found impracticable for me, nor were my Spirits equal to so severe an Employment.[10]

The common and accurate diagnosis of this difficulty of Hume would be, I think, that he was trying to suppress disturbing thoughts, which kept breaking into his philosophizing and fragmenting it. It is surely striking, though not psychologically surprising, that Hume's broken, ambivalent process of thought was paralleled by a doctrine of the non-coherence of events and of egos. That is, his psychological incohesiveness was reflected in the doctrine that there is no necessary, metaphysical connection between cause and effect or between one and another moment of consciousness.

Hume's letter comes to the general conclusion, to which he always remained faithful, that science and morality must be based on an experientially validated psychology. He held that the moral philosophy transmitted to us from antiquity was, like natural philosophy, too exclusively hypothetical, depending more on invention than experience. 'Every one,' he said, 'consulted his Fancy in erecting Schemes of Virtue & of Happiness, without regarding human Nature, upon which every moral Conclusion must depend. This therefore I resolved to make my principal Study, & the Source from which I wou'd derive every Truth in Criticism as well as Morality.'[11] In other words, Hume's self-observation during the period of his illness determined for him the basis of his philosophizing, for he had experienced, as he said, the very close connection between the functioning of his mind and his 'distemper.'

Hume's letter allows us to understand the emotional passages of the *Treatise* in which he reflects his disturbance during at least part of its composition and, perhaps, the loneliness and fear aroused in him by its more radical doctrines. These passages are by no means mere rhetoric. In one of them, Hume writes:

> The wretched condition, weakness, and disorder of the faculties, I must employ in my enquiries, encrease my apprehensions. And the impossibility of amending or correcting these faculties, reduces me almost to despair . . . This sudden view of danger strikes me as melancholy . . . I cannot forbear feeding my despair, with all those desponding reflections, which the present subject furnishes me with in such abundance.

Hume continues:

> I am first affrighted and confounded with that forelorn solitude, in which I am plac'd in my philosophy, and fancy myself some strange uncouth monster, who not able to mingle and unite in society, had been expell'd all human commerce, and left utterly abandon'd and disconsolate.[12]

Fears and guilts are crowding, in, and Hume begins to raise the obsessive questions in which a person may express his insecurities and his doubts about himself and about his relations with others and with all the dark world.

Where am I, or what? From what causes do I derive my existence, and to what condition shall I return? Whose favour shall I court, and whose anger must I dread? What beings surround me? and on whom have I any influence, or who has any influence on me? I am confounded with all these questions, and begin to fancy myself in the most deplorable condition imaginable, inviron'd with the deepest darkness, and utterly depriv'd of every member and faculty.[13]*

Hume's melancholy does not, however, continue. Nature, he says, cures what reason cannot, his 'philosophical melancholy and delirium' pass, and he resolves to live, talk, and act 'like other people in the common affairs of life.'

Though not commonly recognized as such, the *Treatise*, it is evident, reflects a dramatic struggle within Hume himself. The *Treatise* declares even more incisively than his letter:

> There is no question of importance, whose decision is not compriz'd in the science of man; and there is none, which can be decided with any certainty, before we become acquainted with that science . . . And as the science of man is the only solid foundation for the other sciences, so the only solid foundation we can give to this science must be laid on experience and observation.[14]

In his *Treatise*, Hume detaches cause from effect, appearance from substance, and idea from self, and so creates a partial analogue to philosophical Buddhism, which is an instrument of purposeful detachment from life and pain, the two of which it takes to be synonymous. He also detaches morality from natural law. Only a vital natural faith is left to him, namely, that succession will continue to be regular and that he himself is somehow one. Philosophically, to him, substance and ego depend on the gentle force of association, as faith accepts it, while society depends on the contagion, gentle or not, of human sympathy.

Hume had thus arrived at a bare minimum, but a sane one, and he could proceed with cautious confidence, his obsessive need for doubt transformed, with the help of his authorial and philosophical pride, into a reasonably cheerful, not unreasonable detachment.

Hume saw himself in the end much as others did. Looking back at his

---

*Speaking of the predilection of obsessional neurotics for uncertainty, Freud says that they turn their thoughts to necessarily doubtful subjects. 'The chief subjects of this kind are paternity, length of life, life after death, and memory—in the last of which we are all in the habit of believing without having the slightest guarantee of its trustworthiness.' S. Freud, 'Notes upon a Case of Obsessional Neurosis,' *Standard Edition*, vol. 10, pp. 232—33.

life and speaking in the past tense of eulogy, he said:

> I was, I say, a man of mild Dispositions, of Command of Temper, of an
> open, social, and cheerful Humour, capable of Attachment, but little suscep-
> tible of Enmity, and of great Moderation in all my Passions. Even my Love
> of Literary Fame, my ruling Passion, never soured my humour, notwith-
> standing my frequent Disappointments.[15]

No doubt with the aid of his mother's devotion, he had won the kind
of victory over himself that he appreciated. But this victory was, so to
speak, imposed. At the age of thirty-seven, the frame of mind in which
he had suffered his depression could still recur. Ill at the time with a
violent fever,

> in the Paroxysms of his Disorder He often talked, with much seeming
> Perturbation, of the Devil, of Hell, and of Damnation, and one night, while
> his Nursetender happened to be asleep, He rose from his Bed, and made
> towards a deep Well, which was in the Court-yard, with a Design, as was
> supposed, to drown himself, but, finding the Back Door locked, He rushed
> into a Room where, upon a Couch, the Gentlemen of the Family were, He
> well knew, used to deposite their Swords. . . .[16]

At the very end of the *Natural History of Religion*, Hume concluded that
'the whole is a riddle,' but that human reason was so frail that we could
hardly suspend our judgment as we should unless we set one kind of
superstition quarrelling with another, 'while we ourselves, during their
fury and contension, happily make our escape into the calm, though
obscure, regions of philosophy.' Hume was glad to stand above the
quarrelling of others and, even more, above that which had taken place in
himself. But quarrelling remained latent in his great need to escape it.

In the words of a woman acquaintance, Hume 'was one of the sweetest
tempered Men & the most Benevolent that ever was born . . . There was
a simplicity & pleasantness of Manners about him that were delightful in
Society. He was a Charm in domestic life!'[17] He was attracted to women
and attractive to them, in spite of his physical grossness and vacant
stare.[18] When he was twenty-three, a young woman, making her third
confession of fornication, accused him, with what truth we cannot tell, of
being the father of her child.[19] At thirty-seven, when in Turin, he fell in
love with 'a Lady of great Beauty, Sense, and Spriteliness,' the young,
married Countess of Duvernan. A witness who, at her suggestion, hid
himself behind a curtain saw the 'old fat Philosopher' sink down and try
to embrace her knees, and then saw him repulsed with 'Tears trickling
down his flabby Cheeks.'[20] Later, in France, Hume grew devoted to the
salon hostesses, Mme Geoffrin, Julie de l'Espinasse, and, above all, Mme
de Boufflers. In the case of the last, a time came when 'their friendship
mellowed into something more intimate than friendship.'[21]

Hume seems at one time to have proposed marriage, though without success. At the age of sixty he once again thought of 'the taking a Wife,' namely, the young, charming, humorous Nancy Orde, but the idea came to nothing. He was, as he knew, a cautious man, and it may well have been he, describing his own character, who said, 'Licentious in his pen, cautious in his words, still more so in his actions.'[22]

Perhaps something in Hume's imagination related stoical philosophy with women as equal instruments of an unruffled, pleasurable life. So it at least appears from a letter written to a friend in 1776, when he was sure he would soon die. 'Death,' he said, 'appears to me so little horrible in his Approaches, that I scorn to quote Heroes and Philosophers as Examples of Fortitude: a Woman of Pleasure, who, however, was also a Philosopher, is sufficient. I embrace you, Dear Sir, and probably for the last time.'[23]

Rousseau

9. Jean-Jacques Rousseau, born in 1712. Ten days after his birth, his mother died. Though he never knew her, Rousseau was proud of her beauty, her education, and her ability to draw, sing, play the lute, and write verse; but he felt that his birth had been too costly.

> I was born weakly and sick. I cost my mother her life, and my birth was the first of my misfortunes . . . I was born almost dying; they had little hope of saving me. I carried the seed of a disorder that the years have reinforced. . . . A sister of my father, an amiable and sensible woman, took such good care of me that she saved me . . . Dear aunt, I forgive you for causing me to live, and I am grieved not to be able to repay at the end of your days the tender care you lavished on me at the beginning of mine. My nurse Jacqueline, too, is still alive, healthy and strong. The fingers that opened my eyes when I was born may well close them at my death.[1]

Rousseau's father was apparently an adventurous man and certainly an imaginative one. A watchmaker, he had spent some years in Constantinople, from which he had returned to Geneva. He was fond of music and had for a time taught dancing. He and his wife, Rousseau's mother, had been childhood sweethearts, and he was devastated, Rousseau tells us, by her death.

> I never knew how my father stood this loss; but I do know that he was never consoled for it. He thought he saw her again in me, but could not forget that I had robbed him of her. He never kissed me that I did not feel by his sighs, by his convulsive hugs, that a bitter grief was mingled with his caresses; but they were all the more tender for it. When he said to me, 'Jean-Jacques, let's talk about your mother,' I said to him, 'All right, father, but we're going to cry,' and this word alone drew tears from him. 'Ah,' he said, with a groan,

'Give her back to me, console me for her, fill the void she has left in my soul.
Would I love you so if you were no more than my son?'[2]

Rousseau had a brother seven years older than himself, who was learning the father's trade. The affection lavished on Rousseau, he says, left the
brother rather neglected and apt to grow disobedient and indulge in
escapades, first at home, and then, when he was apprenticed to another
watchmaker, there as well. 'I almost never saw him,' says Rousseau.

> I can hardly say that I ever got to know him; but I did not cease to love him
> tenderly, and he loved me, as much as a rascal is able to love. I remember
> that once when my father punished him severely and in anger, I threw
> myself impetuously between the two, hugging him tightly. Covering him
> so with my body, I got the blows directed at him, and I remained in this
> position with such stubbornness that finally my father forgave him, either
> disarmed by my cries or unwilling to hurt me more than him. Finally my
> brother turned so bad that he ran away and disappeared completely.[3]

Rousseau describes himself as unusually sensitive as a child and as
fascinated by reading. He says:

> I do not know how I learned to read. I only remember the first reading I did
> and its effect on me: this is the time from which I date my unbroken con-
> sciousness of myself. My mother had left some novels. My father and I set to
> reading them after supper. In the beginning, it was only in order to give me
> practice by the reading of amusing books; but soon my interest grew so
> strong that we read by turns without respite, and spent the night in this
> occupation. We could never stop before the end of the book. Sometimes my
> father, hearing the larks in the morning, would say, ashamed, 'Let's go to
> bed. I'm more of a child than you.'[4]

Rousseau, who was about seven at the time, soon went on to another
kind of book. His favourite was Plutarch, and the discussions around it
with his father, he says, influenced him to become permanently proud,
intractable, spirited, and impatient with servitude. He was happy then,
for everywhere around him, as he remembers, there was only gentleness
and there were only the best persons in the world.

> My father, my aunt, my nurse, my relatives, our friends, our neighbours, all
> those around me, may not always have done my bidding, but did love me;
> and I loved them in return. My desires were so rarely excited and so rarely
> crossed that it did not enter my mind to have any. I could swear that until
> my subjection to a master, I did not know what it was to have a longing.
> When I was not reading or writing with my father, or when I was not taking
> a walk with my nurse, I was always with my aunt, watching her embroider,
> hearing her sing, sitting or standing near her, and I was happy.[5]

Rousseau adds that, although his own passion for music did not develop until long afterward, he is sure that he owed it to his aunt,

> who knew an enormous number of tunes and songs, which she sang in a
> thin, very sweet voice. The serenity of soul of this excellent woman kept
> musing and sadness away from her and all that surrounded her. The allure of
> her singing was such that not only have many of her songs always remained
> in my memory, but even now that I have lost her, some totally forgotten
> since my childhood come back to me as I grow older, with a charm I cannot
> express.[6]*

Summarizing the development of his character until then, Rousseau
writes:

> So there began to form or display itself in me that heart at once so proud
> and so tender, that effeminate yet indomitable character which, vacillating
> always between weakness and courage, self-indulgence and virtue, has all
> my life set me into contradiction with myself, to the effect that abstinence
> and enjoyment, pleasure and wisdom, have all equally escaped me.[7]

This vacillation may serve to introduce a fear that otherwise would
hardly fit into the idyllic reminiscences we have just repeated. In a letter
Rousseau recalls that 'the most hideous thing never frightened me in
childhood, but a figure hidden under a white veil gave me convulsions.
On this point as on so many others I will remain a child until death.'[8]
What could have been the source of this image of horror? Perhaps something connected with his mother's death, or to the disaster that struck
Rousseau at the age of ten, when his father fled from Geneva. The reason
for the flight was a quarrel. The father had trespassed on a field while
hunting, and had exchanged angry words with its owner, even aiming
his gun at him. On meeting the man four months later, the father proposed a duel, which the man refused with an aspersion on his challenger's
low birth. Rousseau's father then drew his sword and wounded the man
in the cheek. Now afraid of arrest, the father fled, preferring, in Rousseau's words, 'to expatriate himself for the rest of his life rather than cede
a point on which honour and liberty appeared to him compromised.'[9]
Put in the charge of his uncle, Rousseau was sent for two years to
board and study with a village pastor, a kind and intelligent man. Rousseau became the close friend of the pastor's sweet, slender son, who was

---

*Writing of himself in the third person, Rousseau elsewhere says of himself, 'I have
never seen any man as passionate as he for music, but for such as speaks to his heart . . . He
sings it with a weak and broken, yet animated and sweet voice. He accompanies it not
without trouble, with fingers that tremble less because of his years than because of invincible timidity . . . When painful feelings afflict his heart, he looks to the clavier for the
consolations that men have refused him.' 'Second Dialogue,' *Rousseau juge de Jean Jacques*, p.
873.

his own age. Life in this household was affectionate and peaceable. One day, the pastor's sister, who acted with a mother's love and authority, beat Rousseau in punishment, and, in doing so, gave him sexual pleasure. This beating revealed and fixed his masochism. 'Who could have believed,' he asks, 'that this punishment received at the age of eight from the hand of a woman of thirty, determined my tastes, my desires, my passions, my very self for the rest of my life, and this in a sense exactly contrary to that which should have naturally developed?'[10]

A no less small but momentous event resulted from the discovery of a comb with its teeth broken off on one side. Rousseau was accused, but though he was innocent, appearances were against him, and for the first time he was convicted of lying. Beaten and beaten again, he remained inflexible, and emerged, he says, shattered but triumphant. But his triumph was a terrible one for him. Here he was, as he recalls, ordinarily timid and docile, although when aroused, spirited, proud, and indomitable, a child always governed by the voice of reason, always treated mildly and justly, without even the idea of injustice, and now suddenly put to such a terrible proof, and by just those whom he most cherished and respected. 'What an overturning of ideas! What a disruption of feelings! What an upheaval in his heart, in his brain, in all his little intelligent and moral being!'[11] The result, Rousseau emphasizes, was profound and lasting:

> That first feeling of violence and injustice has remained so deeply engraved in my heart that all thoughts that recall it summon the first emotion back; and that feeling, in origin relating only to myself, has taken on such consistency in itself, and has so detached itself from any personal interest, that my blood boils at the spectacle or the recital of any unjust act, regardless of who suffers from it or where it is committed, as if its effect rebounded back on me. When I read of the cruelties of a fierce tyrant, of the foul, subtle machinations of a priest, I would gladly go and stab the wretches, though I die a thousand deaths for it. I've often got into a sweat chasing or throwing stones at a rooster, cow, or dog, any animal I saw tormenting another solely because it thought itself the stronger. This reaction may be natural to me, and I think it is; but the deep memory of the first injustice I suffered was so long and so powerfully bound up with it, that it must have reinforced it powerfully.
>
> There ended the serenity of my childish life. From that moment I stopped enjoying pure happiness, and even today I feel that the memory of the charms of my childhood stops there.[12]

This is a convenient point at which to stop the narrative of Rousseau's life, for its major themes, as he saw them, have emerged clearly. He saw his life as beginning in an innocent peopled solitude, a premoral paradise, broken into by untruth and violence. He still had many lessons to learn, particularly in evil. The worst of them came with his apprenticeship to a boorish, violent young engraver, who, he says, quenched all the fire of his youth and coarsened his nature, teaching him 'to covet in silence, to lie, and finally to steal—an idea that had until then not entered my mind, and that I have not been able to cure myself completely of since then.'[13] Rousseau also had lessons in sexuality to learn, in human relations, and in art; yet his character had become, as he often repeats, what it was always to remain.

Although we have already discussed one confessional philosopher, Montaigne, and will discuss another, Kierkegaard, it is Rousseau who, of all the philosophers I deal with, most willingly and consciously fits himself into the pattern repeatedly exhibited in these pages, according to which basic inclinations of character and thought are more or less set in childhood. It should not, of course, be forgotten that Rousseau finished his *Confessions*, from which the account here has necessarily been taken, in 1770, when he was fifty-nine, and everything is therefore seen in the hindsight of the writer who is discovering himself in his unforgettable childhood.

The contrast between Rousseau and Spinoza, who found it hard to believe that he had ever been a child, is very striking. Not without pride, Rousseau, sitting, in judgment on himself, says:

> Of all the men I have seen, the one whose character derives most completely from his temperament alone is J.J. He is what nature has made him—nature has modified him only little . . . Now, in the ripeness of his age, after sixty years of griefs and troubles, time, adversity, and men have nevertheless changed him very little. While his body has grown old, his heart remains still young. He still retains the same tastes, the same passions of his youth, and until the end of his life he will not cease being an old child.[14]

Like a child, who wants its parents' love to answer its own person and needs exactly, Rousseau insists that everyone appreciate the full measure of his uniqueness. Yes, Montaigne praised himself for his sincerity, but it was only outward, for he drew attention to only such of his faults as were innocuous. But there is no one 'who does not have odious ones. Montaigne paints a likeness of himself, but in profile.'[15]

In contrast to Montaigne, says Rousseau, he is totally sincere. 'Here is the harsh but sure proof of my sincerity. I will be true; I will be so without reserve; I will say everything; the good, the bad, finally everything.'[16]

Such sincerity needs a new, unique style in which to be conveyed:

> For what I had to say, it was necessary to invent a language as new as my project; for what tone, what style could disentangle this immense chaos of

such different and contradictory feelings, often so ignoble and sometimes so sublime, by which I was endlessly agitated.[17]

The Confessions begins with the note, 'Here is the only portrait that exists or will probably ever exist of a man painted exactly after nature and in all its truth,' and it ends in almost a threat against anyone who will not believe that this is so:

> I have told the truth. If anyone knows something contrary to what I have just disclosed, though it be proved a thousand times, his knowledge is lies and impostures, and if he refuse to go deeply into the matter and clarify it with me while I am still alive, he loves neither justice nor truth. As for me, I declare publicly and without fear: Whoever, even if he has not read my writings, will examine my nature, my character, my morals, my likings, my pleasures, and my habits with his own eyes and will be able to believe me a dishonorable man, is himself a man to be stifled.[18]

Rousseau often speaks like the child wanting to protest its essential goodness to its parents, or to anyone. He wants every reader or acquaintance to forgive him, mother-like, for every transgression because, at heart, he is innocent. The confession of faults, however real, is openness and therefore innocence. He wants to be, he knows he is, transparent. He says, 'I would like to be somehow able to make my heart transparent to the reader. . . .' Again, he says, 'My heart, as transparent as crystal, has never been able to hide even a weak emotion.' And again, he says, this time in the third person, 'His heart, as transparent as crystal, cannot hide anything that happens; each movement he experiences transmits itself to his eyes and face.' And still again, he contrasts those 'the obscure labyrinth of whose hearts' he finds impenetrable, with himself, 'whose heart as transparent as crystal cannot hide any of its movements.'[19]

Yet strangely, to Rousseau, all this transparent innocence goes unrecognized; and yet perhaps not strangely, as he had begun so painfully to learn from the episode of the broken comb, which complemented his obscure complicity in his mother's death. The very explanation he discovers is only a sharpening of the paradox:

> God is just; he wants me to suffer; and he knows that I am innocent. That is the cause of my trust, my heart and my reason cry out to me that my trust will not deceive me . . . My turn will come sooner or later.[20]

Rousseau, who is harsh enough against his contemporaries, is harshly treated by them, especially by the *philosophes*, once his friends, but now his sworn enemies, whom he suspects of plotting against himself and his works. He is afraid that his papers will be disfigured or destroyed.[21] He used to write, he says, in unending anxiety to keep his papers 'from the rapacious hands of my persecutors,' but he now knows that his disquiet is useless, and that he will refrain from erecting new monuments of his innocence, as he calls his writings.[22] Paradoxically, at least if the world is just, as it must be, Rousseau finds himself abandoned, more drastically than when his father had abandoned him, and he proposes what is for him a counsel of despair, impassibility:

> Here I am alone on the earth, no longer having any brother, any fellow being, any friend, any society other than myself. The most sociable and most loving of humans has been proscribed by unanimous accord . . . All is finished for me on earth. No one can any longer do me either good or evil. Nothing remains for me to hope or fear in this world, and I find myself tranquil at the bottom of the abyss, a poor unfortunate mortal, but as impassible as God himself.[23]

Rousseau's persecution, often cruel, though not uncaused by himself, sometimes pushed him over the border of sanity into paranoia. Hume, who helped him to find asylum in England after he had been expelled from Berne, found him at first to be 'mild, and gentle and modest and good humourd.' He found, too, that he wrote, spoke, and acted 'from the Impulse of Genius, more than from the Use of his ordinary Faculties,' and he compared him favourably to Socrates. But less than three months later, Hume, disabused, was writing that Rousseau was desperately resolved to rush into a solitude that would make him unhappy, as all situations made him, and that he was poorly read and lacked curiosity. Hume wrote impatiently:

> He had only felt, during the whole Course of his Life; and in this Respect, his Sensibility rises to a Pitch beyond what I have seen any Example of: But it still gives him a more acute Feeling of Pain than of Pleasure. He is like a Man who were stript not only of his Cloaths but of his Skin, and turn'd out in that Situation to combat with the rude and boisterous Elements, such as perpetually disturb this lower World.[24]

Rousseau's isolation, suffering, and paranoid tendency were all obviously connected with 'the seed of a disorder' he thought he had been born with. The disorder was a constriction of his urethra, which caused his urine to be retained and to dribble, and a hernia, which required him to press on his abdomen in order to empty his bladder. He was terribly afraid of the embarrassment his condition might bring on him, and the very thought of the embarrassment could provoke an attack that caused him to faint or make a scene. He had a fantasy of waiting in pain in a circle of women until he could get away, and then, in full sight of other beautiful women, of descending a brightly illuminated staircase, of crossing a courtyard, observed by many people, and of finally having to piss on some noble white-stockinged leg. His attacks seem to have often coincided with the beginning of real or fancied servitude, as when he worked for a tyranical ambassador, or when he was to have presented himself before the King in order to get a pension. In his own eyes, his malady shared in the uniqueness characteristic of everything he was or did. He declared, 'The strange malady that has been consuming me for thirty years and that, to all appearances, will terminate my days is so different from all the other maladies of the same type, with which the doctors and surgeons have always confounded it, that I think it will be to the public good if it should be examined in its very seat after my death.'[25]*

Yet there were times and conditions in which Rousseau felt at peace. In the country, he could give himself up to his lazy nonchalance, follow his impulse, and row out into the lake. The leaving of the shore, he writes, gave him an unintelligible access of joy, perhaps a secret congratulation of himself in now being out of reach of the wicked.

> Often leaving my boat to the mercy of wind and water, I abandoned myself to reveries which, for all their foolishness, were none the less sweet. Sometimes I cried out with emotion, 'O nature, O my mother, here I am under your sole protection! Here there is no adroit, villainous man who thrusts himself between you and me.'[26]

If nature, at such times, was his mother, was the villainous interferer his father, generalized into all those who came between himself and the dreamy peace he longed for? I cannot do more than ask the question and recall that he had experienced his mother only through the eyes of his father, who at once idealized her, identified him, their son, with her, and accused the son of being responsible for her death. At any rate, the state of maternal peace, which he had really known in the presence of his aunt, was also reflected in the experience he considers to be that of existence as such, in which 'time is nothing, in which the present always endures, but without marking its duration or having any trace of succession, without any feeling, of deprivation or indulgence, of pleasure or pain, of desire or fear, except for that of our existence.' As long as the state persists, says Rousseau, whoever enjoys it enjoys full, perfect happiness, 'which leaves no void in the soul.'[27] In this state, which Rousseau often entered, he says, in solitary reveries on the island of St. Pierre, he had filled the kind

---

*Rousseau's wish was observed, and an autopsy was performed the day after his death. The surgeons, whose technique must, by our standards, have been primitive, reported that there was no observable urological abnormality, so that Rousseau's difficulties must have resulted from spasm or from enlargement of the prostate, though even the latter condition could no longer be observed. J. Starobinsky, 'Sur la maladie de Rousseau,' J.-J. Rousseau: La transparence et l'obstacle, p. 444.

of void his mother's death had left in his father and himself, a void no doubt enlarged in himself by his father's flight.

Rousseau's basic intellectual problems and solutions all came from his life, as he knew. His own origin had not been obscure, but had been truncated, and his own early peace had been shattered, so he was always searching for the causes of the difficult transition from at least emotional equality to inequality, from security to insecurity, from innocence to guilt, and, most generally, from good to evil. Good was the time when everything around him had been gentleness and amiability, when everyone, father, aunt, nurse, relatives, friends, and neighbours had loved him and he them, and when he had been unconscious of having any particular desires. But that was a state of innocence, and he had learned that evil, which was largely servitude, arose from the practical needs people had for one another. The independent intercourse of the free is sweet, but the need for help and the discovery that wealth could be accumulated create servitude, which he had first experienced in his apprenticeship to the young, brutal engraver.[28] Hence the dramatic first sentence of the *Social Contract*: 'Man was born free, and he is everywhere in chains.' It is not, he says, that he wishes to destroy learning and art and plunge the world back into its first barbarism, but that he hopes to retard human decadence and regain some of the happiness that is still possible.[29]

Rousseau suffered a particularly keen conflict between the desire for dependence and the desire for independence. He remained dependent because he had had only a totally ideal mother, a too quickly removed mother-substitute, and a runaway father, all of whom had strengthened his need by serving it well for a time. He had known real emotional reciprocity and had enjoyed real protection; but the transition to the world had been too quick and, at crucial moments, too brutal. He could not stand the dependence the world forced on him. He remembered the discussions with his father that had made him impatient with servitude, and also the fact that his father had fled from a man who refused to duel with him because of his lower class origin. Rousseau's very body revolted against servitude by creating urinary crises whenever it threatened. Servitude, in his eyes, not only made one an instrument, but by subjecting one's will and forcing one into deception and lies, deprived one of the innocence, love, and power of decision without which morality was impossible. He therefore says in the *Social Contract*:

> To renounce freedom is to renounce one's human quality, one's human rights, and even one's duties. There is no possible recompense for anyone who renounces everything. Such a renunciation is incompatible with the nature of man, and in depriving his will of all freedom one deprives his actions of all morality.[30]

The social pact that is formed must therefore be between persons who retain their freedom. But a difficult consequence follows, not unlike that which follows when a good parent punishes a child in order to make it conform to its own better self. For in order that the pact not remain a merely empty formula, says Rousseau, commitment to it tacitly implies 'that whoever refuses to obey the general will should be constrained to do so by the whole body, which signifies nothing other than that he should be forced to be free. . . .'[31]

This consequence is surely an invitation to tyranny but it reflects something important, not only in the reality of Rousseau's experience, but in that of most people. A commentator cogently explains that Rousseau, perhaps more than any writer before him, draws our attention to the fact that our sense of duty makes us feel both thwarted and liberated. The sense of duty does not allow one to submit to the will of anyone else, even that of God, yet, in the absence of any external compulsion, it binds one to abide by itself. Rousseau argues that men

> would not submit to rules unless they had appetites and passions needing to be controlled for their better satisfaction, but insists that they feel about the rules as they do not feel about the appetites and passions. That is why, though men speak of the rules as *restraining* them, they speak of the appetites as *enslaving* them. As creatures of appetite they feel thwarted by the rules, but as moral beings they wish to keep them . . . They wish they were law-abiding even when in fact they are not. This is what Rousseau calls their *constant will*. But it is strong in them only when they feel that the law is not the will of others imposed on them.[32]

In these ideas, Rousseau was expressing a basic human ambivalence, which he felt intensely in himself, described with care, and tried to resolve philosophically. The natural goodness he had experienced as a child was enough, he knew, only for childhood, while the older, passion-ridden person needed something more: virtue. Virtue he saw as the union of feeling with reason, each of which is necessary to the other. Without feeling, he believed, we cannot be morally sensitive, but without reason we cannot make moral judgments. Put otherwise, reason compares and teaches; but lacking the rule of conscience, which issues from a pure heart, it falls into error, sophistry, or plain selfishness.[33]

Rousseau knew that he himself fell quite short of the desirable union of feeling with reason. He continued to long for effortless symbiosis with a mother and for full autonomy, and he grew and remained angry at the world that had, he thought, robbed him of both. Because fame alone could not give him what he wanted, he was sure that it was not in recognition of his real self. Once he said, almost as Nietzsche and Wittgenstein were to say, 'I do not hope for much, but I still have one desire.

If I learn one day that this writing has been read by a man with an honest heart and sane judgment, I will not ask for more, and I will die content.'[34] Finally always innocent in his own eyes, he imagined his will both autonomous and identical with a larger one, such as ideally joins mother with child. His thought combined guilty self-exposure, narcissistic self-righteousness, and sometimes even philosophical perceptiveness.

Rousseau's relationships with women are best followed in the *Confessions*, where he speaks with his customary desire to redeem by revealing himself. The self-revelation of his masochism has already been described. The oncoming of his adolescence is reflected in *Emile*, where he says that adolescence is an age foretold by 'the murmuring of nascent passions' and by a revolt against guidance.[35] When nearing the age of sixteen, he first came to know Mme de Warens, who, herself childless, became his 'Maman' and, for a time, his mistress. He appears to have divided women into the blond, with whom his sexual communion was spiritual, and brunettes, with whom it was passionately erotic.[36] He fell in particularly desperate love with the brunette Mme d'Houdetot, who entered his life dressed like a man, in riding breeches and carrying a riding crop, he particularly recalled. As he was writing his novel, *La Nouvelle Héloïse*, at the time, he turned the correspondence between its hero and heroine into an imaginary correspondence between himself and Mme d'Houdetot—in addition to a quite real correspondence he carried on with her. But Rousseau's most lasting relationship was with an illiterate washerwoman, Thérèse Levasseur, with whom he first took up at the age of thirty-two, at a moment when he was feeling sorry for the insults she had to bear. Though a good housekeeper, she is described as 'jealous, stupid, gossipy, and a liar.' But she did patiently care for a very difficult man, to whom she bore five children that neither of them, it appears, wanted, and who did not take her in marriage until, at fifty-seven, he conducted a strange ceremony at which everyone burst into tears.[37]

The matter of Rousseau's abandoned children has particularly intrigued scholars. Some of them, refusing to believe that he ever bore any, claim that either he invented them, perhaps to create interest in his *Confessions* by implicating him in acts of genuine callousness, or that Thérèse invented them. Thérèse, that is, might have invented children whole cloth in order to attach him to her, or might have invented only his paternity in order to conceal the real cause of their birth. The details of the debate are wearying, and I accept the verdict that in the present state of research 'one may accept the veracity of Rousseau with respect to the account of the abandonment of his children.'[38] Thérèse never offered to show him the children, nor did he ever ask to see them; but he undoubtedly believed in their existence.

Rousseau's rationalizations of the abandonment of his children make interesting but sad reading. He was too poor, he says, to support them; and if, to support them, he had tried to earn more by his writing, the domestic worries and disturbances would have been too much for him. He then would have had to ask for the favour of some low employment. He was, further, painfully and mortally ill. And how could the children carry the double misfortune of poverty and illegitimate birth? Furthermore, the foundling home brought them up without spoiling them. Lastly, Plato had recommended that fathers not know their children, who should be handed over to the care of the state.[39] In another set of rationalizations, Rousseau adds that his facility of speech and thought were too poor for him to bring up children. He was sad, he says, not to have a few moments again of sincere, pure caresses, but he had lost his old ease and familiarity with children. 'Children do not like old age, the aspect of sinking nature is hideous in their eyes; and I would prefer to abstain from caressing them than to annoy or disgust them.'[40]

7
Kant, Hegel, Schopenhauer

Preface to a Trio

The philosophers I am discussing continue to be numbered consecutively, for they are links, as I have said, in a chain of evidence, from which Kant, Hegel, and Schopenhauer are not removed by their separate grouping. In describing Kant, I have been able to give a good many personal details, which fit into a total image that helps to clarify his philosophy. As presented here, he may seem pathetic, but it is hard to feel protective towards him, not only because he grew a thick enough carapace, and not only because he was a controversialist well able to defend himself, but also because he was a tenacious, productive, and finally very impressive thinker. There is more in him than I have ventured to understand, and in what I have ventured, I have not always convinced even myself.

The companion section, on Hegel, is briefer, in large part because I have discovered less that would reveal him as a person. Because he is so encompassing, I have confined my explanation to the general character of his philosophy, and, in particular, to what I take to be its origin in his own kind of constructive ambivalence.

I do not mind saying that if I had to choose between Kant and Hegel as philosophers, I would choose Kant; but both have had such enormous influence on modern thought, far beyond the confines of philosophy itself, that I have thought it reasonable to separate them, together with Schopenhauer, from the other philosophers. I have not especially tried to contrast Kant and Hegel, yet they are a very different pair, and the influence of their philosophies has necessarily carried with it some shadow of their different persons. They still live among us. So, in a different way, does Schopenhauer. Emotionally, he is related to Kant by a strong though qualified reverence, and to Hegel by a strong, unqualified contempt. Otherwise, he is related to Kant by way, as he says, of Kant's distinction between the empirical and intelligible, which he, Schopenhauer, brings, he thinks, to a consistent conclusion. To Hegel he is related positively by his strong, detailed interest in both art and science, and by his metaphysical boldness. The three make a genuine, if disharmonious trio.

Kant

10. Immanuel Kant, born in 1724. He was the fourth of nine children, of whom one died at birth, and two during their first year.[1] The parents were exceptionally decent and peace-loving.[2] When asked about them, Kant answered:

> I can take pride only in that both my parents, in exemplary uprightness, ethical propriety, and order, without leaving a fortune (but also no debts), gave me an education which, looked at from the moral standpoint, could not be any better, and for which, every time I remember it, I find myself stirred with the most grateful feelings.[3]

On another occasion, emphasizing the same qualities, Kant said, 'Never, not even a single time was I allowed to hear anything improper from my parents, never did I see anything unworthy.'[4] Kant particularly remembered the forbearance with which his parents had reacted during a difficult period of their lives. His father was a craftsman, a harness maker (Kant's great clumsiness with his hands is therefore noteworthy).[5] In Kant's words:

> a quarrel, from which my father too suffered considerably, broke out between the saddlers' and the harness makers' guilds over their respective rights. But even in the talk at home this dispute was treated by my parents with such forbearance and love towards their opponents, and with such firm faith in providence that the thought of it, though I was only a boy then, will never leave me.[6]

The father, who was to Kant the less impressive of his parents, required him to be industrious, upright, and, above all, to avoid lies.[7] On his death, when Kant was twenty-one, Kant wrote in the family record book:

> Anno 1746, on March 24, in the afternoon at four-thirty, my beloved father was called away by a holy death. God, who in this life did not grant him the enjoyment of happiness, allow him, therefore, to partake of eternal happiness.[8]

Kant's mother had died earlier, when he was only thirteen. He remembered the pious, fervent woman with particular emotion.[9] Whenever he spoke of her, 'his eye glistened, and each of his words,' it is testified, 'was the expression of a heartfelt and childlike reverence.'[10] It was she who had shaped his character, he said, and who had laid something of the foundation of what he was to become. She would take her son, her 'Manelchen,' out into the open and teach him to identify plants and tell him what she knew of the structure of the heavens. After he entered school, and especially after he entered the Collegium Fredericianum, at the age of eight, the character of the walks changed. She had already been astonished at the sharpness of his mind, but now, beginning to dominate, he would explain to her what she herself could not understand. Her own great curiosity, the early biographer tells us, was satisfied, 'and her hopes for the future were extraordinarily brightened.'

The biographer goes on to say that 'Kant regretted her death with the affectionate, tender sadness of a kindly disposed and thankful son, and in the last years of his life was still emotionally stirred each time he told the circumstances of the loss that had been so early for him.'[12] The story was that a woman, a beloved friend of Kant's mother, had been abandoned by her fiancé and had grown seriously ill. To persuade her to take her medicine, Kant's mother had tasted it first, using a spoon that had been in the woman's mouth. 'This occasion was her death. She lay down on the same day and died soon thereafter as a sacrifice to friendship.'[13]

Recalling his childhood walks with his mother, Kant said:

> She often took me outside the city, drew my attention to the works of God, spoke with a pious delight of His omnipotence, wisdom, and goodness, and impressed upon my heart a deep reverence for the creator of all things. I will never forget my mother, for she planted and nourished in me the first seed of goodness, she opened my heart to the impressions of nature, she aroused and enlarged my thoughts, and her teaching has had a lastingly wholesome influence on my life.[14]

Kant's memories of his mother, who appears to have been much the most influential person in his life, make an interesting comparison with a well-known passage in the *Critique of Practical Reason*:

> Two things fill the mind with ever new and increasing admiration and awe, the oftener and more steadily they are reflected on: the starry heavens above me and the moral law within me . . . I see them before me, and I associate them directly with the consciousness of my own existence . . . The former begins from the place I occupy in the external world of sense . . . annihilates, as it were, my importance as an animal creature. . . . The latter, on the contrary, infinitely raises my worth as that of an intelligence by my personality, in which the moral law reveals a life independent of all animality and even of the whole world of sense. . . .[15]

This passage obviously reveals Kant's tendency toward dualism; but its most interesting words for us are, 'I associate them directly with the consciousness of my own existence.' These words seem to me to echo the closeness he had enjoyed with his mother, the infusion of life that, by virtue of her curiosity and moral sense, had become her existence in himself: the sensitivity to the starry heavens, which spoke to him of a fascinating but enormous and indifferent natural world, and the sensitivity to the moral person he was within, beyond sensuality and the senses, who drew her approval and, with it, her love.

In spite of Kant's gratitude to his parents, childhood did not impress him as a happy stage of life. He was mainly impressed with its difficulties. To those who saw it as happy, he objected:

> Many people imagine that the years of their youth are the pleasantest and best of their lives; but it is not really so. They are the most troublesome; for we are then under strict discipline, can seldom choose our own friends, and still more seldom can we have our freedom.[16]

Although he emphasized how troublesome strict discipline is to children, Kant approved of it, so long as it was not 'slavish.' He thought that working-class people, especially, spoil their children by playing with them 'like monkeys, singing to them, caressing, kissing, and dancing with them. They think indeed that they are doing a kindness to their child in always running to him when he cries, and playing with him, etc.; but he only cries the more.'[17]

Either Kant's experience of childhood, his ideal of it, or, most likely, both, led him to insist that caressing and playing with a child not only harmed the child but shamed the parents. It must have been the sensuality he objected to, and the feeling that the child, in wanting more of it, would become 'self-willed and deceitful.' If it were not the sensuality he objected to, why should he have said that caressing and playing with a child betrayed its parents' weakness to it and lost their necessary respect in its eyes?[18]

Drawing, it may be, on his own experience, Kant said that 'the thirteenth or fourteenth year is usually the time in which the feeling of sex develops itself in the youth.'[19] A psychoanalytic commentator has used this statement to make a far-reaching conjecture:

> Kant's mother, it should be remembered, died in 1737, when Kant was in his thirteenth year. Toward her, he felt a warmth which he did not feel toward his father who lived on until 1746. What would be the effect of the death of his mother on a Pietist boy of thirteen? His first sexual stirrings were concomitant with the death of his mother. Thus, we may surmise, a deep guilt was placed upon Kant's sexuality. In his unconscious, he would associate his own sexual lust with the death it brought his beloved mother. Herein, we may surmise, was the source of that hypochondria which afflicted Kant in his youth so that he hated life itself. And here as well was

the basis of his attitudes toward marriage and women. He atoned for his guilt by remaining faithful to his mother's memory, and ridiculed the learned and polite women he met.[20]

It seems, at any rate, that Kant had deeply troubling associations with childhood. Such may well be the explanation of the fact that in his old age melodies of the folk songs he had heard in his earliest youth kept sounding unpleasantly in his ears, and no matter what effort of abstraction he made to banish them, they continued.[21]

Consistently, Kant advised that all novels be taken away from children. Novel reading, he said, weakened the memory, 'for it would be ridiculous to remember the novels in order to relate them to others.' Children who read novels imprison their imaginations in the 'inner romance' awakened by them, and sit about mooning and empty, without any serious thoughts.[22] In Kant's eyes, novels were harmful to adults as well, because they permit our minds to interpolate happenings we invent into the novelist's story, so 'the course of our thought becomes *fragmentary*, in such a way that we let ideas of one and the same object play in our mind in a scattered way instead of as combined in accordance with the unity of the understanding.'[23]

Kant evidently favors intellectuality and order; distractions have some danger for him. The art he prefers is therefore disciplined. He agrees that art must allow some free sensory play. Unrhymed poetry, however, he considers to be prose gone mad; and he does not want a talented poet to give himself up to such poetry, love poetry, for example, as it is a 'mere play of sensations' of the sort everyone already has. But if the poet, like Pope in the *Essay on Man*, uses his intellect to create a harmonious play of virtue with these sensations, he is doing something really meritorious.[24] Although he enjoyed reading poetry, Kant did not hesitate to say that poets and musicians have no character, because they reduce everything to feeling.[25] The complete absence of references in his works to Goethe is, for a German of his time, most unusual, and doubtless significant.[26]

Kant's opinion of music was that it might well be the most pleasurable of the fine arts, but because it was bound up with mere sensations, it was the lowest of the arts from the standpoint of judgment. It was also too apt to be enslaving, or, in his words, not urbane. 'For owing chiefly to the character of its instruments, it scatters its influence abroad to an uncalled-for extent (through the neighbourhood), and thus, as it were, becomes obtrusive and deprives others, outside the musical circle, of their freedom.'[27]

Kant advised his students not to allow a serious interest in music to distract them from science. He was also afraid that it would make them effeminate.[28] He went to concerts, however, and listened with pleasure to

the military bands that marched past his house; and once he heard and
uncommonly liked the sound of a spinet played at full volume. He preferred music happy and combined with words.[29] Unfortunately, a concert he attended in memory of Moses Mendelssohn struck him as no
more than an endless moaning. He had hoped, he said, that other sentiments, such as that of triumph over death, might have been expressed;
and out of the fear that other concerts might be similarly disagreeable to
him, he stopped attending them altogether.[30]

If we turn back from the arts to people again, we find an essentially
similar distancing. For one thing, Kant kept his distance from his sisters
and his one surviving brother. He helped his sisters with money, but
although they lived in the same city, Königsberg, he did not exchange a
word with them, it seems, for twenty-five years.[31] When, in his old age, a
sister came to his home to help him, he had difficulty recognizing her. As
soon as he learned who she was, he apologized for her lack of culture.[32]
The reason he gave for not meeting his sisters was their difference from
him in cultural level; yet he remained almost as distant from his cultured
brother, to whose warm, even entreating letters, Kant returned cold
ones. 'I can no longer bear that such a separation should continue, we are
brothers,' he wrote to Kant.[33] To another warm letter, Kant answered
after a delay of two and a half years, saying that he had been too busy to
answer earlier, but that his unconcern was only apparent. During the
brief remnant of life that was still his (he was then sixty-eight), he would
continue to think brotherly thoughts, he added.[34] Some years later he
informed his brother that one of their sisters had died the previous summer. He had doubled the pension he used to give her, he said, and had
transferred it to her children. Not a word of regret escaped his pen.[35] But
maybe this was because he disliked mentioning the recently dead.[36]

Kant's relations with friends were far more cordial. Though he was
not effusive with compliments, his friendship was as solid, a friend said,
as good, substantial prose.[37] He was faithful to friends and particularly
active in furthering the interests of the younger ones among them, whose
successes he shared emotionally.[38] 'He really had not a single enemy;
and he surely had more friends than any man in a similar position before
him.'[39] Perhaps his most trusted and intimate friend was the English
merchant, Green, in whom Kant had such confidence that he wrote not a
single sentence of the *Critique of Pure Reason* before submitting it to his
judgment, as Kant himself told a disciple-biographer.[40] The book,
Observations on the Sentiment of the Beautiful and the Sublime, was composed at the house of another friend, a head forester.

Yet Kant also often kept his distance, and increasingly so as he aged.
His letters were for the most part austerely dedicated to advancing his

philosophy or his career. Reread today, they are strikingly bare of references to his own or his correspondents' personal experience or condition,
except for his frequent references to his health. Except for one mention of
a possible frost, he does not refer even to the weather, and not, in any
concrete way, to current events, or to anything in the literary or learned
world apart from the fortunes of Kantianism.[41] The letters are flattering
and sometimes obsequious. Although the style of florid compliment was
then usual, Kant's flattery is worth noting because he himself spends
some effort considering the 'casuistical question' of whether or not the
words, 'Your most obedient servant,' at the close of a letter should be
taken as a lie. In the *Metaphysics of Morals* he allows the formula because
no one is taken in by it; but in a letter he appears to declare against
harmless lies of any sort.[42] Whatever Kant's attitude to formulas of greet-
ing and farewell, it is difficult to believe that his moral theory would
allow him to flatter a friend in a letter addressed to him and discuss him
acidly in a letter addressed to someone else. He swears eternally worthy
friendship to his follower, Reinhold, but six days later writes to another
follower, Beck, on Reinhold's philosophical shortcomings.[43] When Kant
is worried that a rival, Eberhard, is recruiting mathematicians against
him, he writes to the mathematician, Kästner, who had seemed to be on
Eberhard's side, 'assuring the Nestor of all German mathematicians' of
his 'unlimited respect,' after which he puts his case.[44] But in his notes
now collected under the title of *Opus posthumum*, he attacks Kästner as
'invidious, envious, and hostile,' even 'immoral.'[45] I am not saying this to
convict Kant of any great moral failure, but only to point out that the
struggle in support of his philosophy could persuade him to relax his
moral rigour somewhat. When his ambition was seriously engaged, he
was not up to the standard his parents had set him.

In spite of everything I have repeated about Kant's friendships, he was
reluctant to become intimate and was capable of declaring against friendship altogether. There were only two or three friends, who had been his
fellow students, whom he addressed with the intimate 'du,' and in time
he grew reluctant to use it in addressing even them. Maybe he was
influenced by the belief that his mother had died as a sacrifice to friendship. In any case, he was wary of obligations. He took a present most
unwillingly, and when his protests were unavailing, gave the present
away, on the spot, if possible.[46] The friend and support of Kant's last
years, Wasianski, writes:

> Kant had adopted the delusive paradix of Aristotle, 'My dear friends, there
> are no friends.' He seemed not to grant the expression *friend* the usual mean-
> ing, but to take it somewhat as the word *servant* in the closing formula of a
> letter or in the usual complimentary greeting . . . Until now Kant had been

sufficient unto himself, and as he had known suffering only by name, had needed no friend.

But his weakness had grown oppressive, Wasianski says, and 'he was open enough to avow that he now agreed with my opinion and did not regard friendship as a mere chimera.'[47]

The most radical and Kantian expression of Kant's opposition to friendship, that is, to the very ideal of friendship, occurs in a posthumous note to the *Anthropology*:

> Friendship is a restriction of favourable sentiments to a single subject and is very pleasant to him towards whom they are directed, but also a proof that generality and good will are lacking. The latter is much better, and to have no friends, but to be equally well disposed toward everyone is the most noble. By means of the former one absolves oneself of the general duty. All brotherhoods are cabals. Whoever has friends and power is very harmful. A prince must have no attachments, but also not be indifferent.[48]

Kant's distance from people, which is his reluctance to become really intimate, is related to his unhappiness. When I say this I do not mean that Kant in his prime appeared unhappy. One of the friends and biographers I have been citing says, to the contrary:

> Kant's disposition was by nature meant for cheerfulness. He saw the world with a glad look, apprehended its enjoyable external side and transferred his cheerfulness to external things. Therefore he was usually disposed to be happy . . . His disposition always remained even and only seldom was his equilibrium upset by an emotion . . . The ruling propensities of his heart were humane and benevolent, and the profoundness of the metaphysical speculations of his mind were not able to dry out his heart and rob it of its constituent feelings.[49]

There is no hesitation in these words at all. But though their writer was Kant's intimate friend and we are so distant from Kant, I am sure that a consideration of the philosopher's anxieties, his interest in his health, not to say his hypochondria, will convince the reader that the above description of Kant's cheerfulness is quite misleading if taken at face value.

It is clear that Kant sees himself as naturally disposed to hypochondria, which he ascribes, at least in himself, to purely physical causes. He also makes it clear that he was for a time depressed almost to the point of suicide. In his own words:

> On account of my flat and narrow chest, which leaves little room for the movement of my heart and lungs, I have a natural predisposition to hypochondria, which in earlier years bordered on weariness of life. But the

reflection that the cause of this oppression of the heart was perhaps only mechanical and could not be removed soon brought it about that I paid no attention to it, and while I felt an oppression in the chest, in my head there reigned peace and good humour, which did not fail to communicate themselves in society, not (as usual with hypochondriacs) by fluctuating moods, but intentionally and naturally.*

And because one takes more pleasure in life by what one does in the free use of it than by what one simply enjoys [i.e. experiences passively], intellectual exertion, by means of a different kind of favoured vital consciousness (Lebensgefühl), can counter the hindrances concerning only the body. The oppression has remained; for its cause lies in the structure of my body. But I have become master over its influence on my thoughts and actions by turning my attention away from this feeling, as if it did not concern me at all.[50]

Because Kant saw himself as a natural hypochondriac, it is particularly significant that he took hypochondria to be a mental illness. In one place he calls it 'a kind of insanity,' while in another he says, 'Between insanity and healthy understanding there is no considerable division, for hypochondria fills the gap,' or, in his own German, 'Zwischen dem Wahninn und gesunden [Verstande] Sinnen ist kein deutlicher Abschnitt, denn die Hypochondrie fuellet das Mittel aus.'[51]

Relatively early in his career, in an essay on the subject of headaches, Kant writes:

> The fantastic mental disposition is nowhere commoner than in hypochondria. The chimeras which the illness hatches do not deceive the outer sense, but only give the hypochondriac a delusion of the perception of his own state, either of body or soul, which for the most part is only an empty quirk . . . so that the patient feels in himself almost all illnesses of which he only hears. He therefore speaks of nothing more gladly than of his indisposition, willingly reads medical books. . . . Because of the occurrence of such internal fantasies the images in his brain often develop a strength and duration which are burdensome to him . . . whereupon his state much resembles that of a psychotic, except that it exercises no compulsion. The evil is not deeply rooted.[52]

*I apologize for the clumsiness of my translation of Kant. But here, as elsewhere in passages even the tone of which serves as evidence, I have translated rather literally. Whoever thinks that a close translation of Kant can be put into simple, straightforward English is invited to turn to the original.

The word that I have translated 'oppression of the heart' is *Herzbeklemmung*. I do not know with what degree of precision Kant meant to use the word, though he was, as will be seen, quite versed in the medical terminology of his time. In modern German the word is the technical equivalent of *angina pectoris*, which is defined in the unabridged Webster's as follows:

'A disease characterized by paroxysmal attacks of substernal pain of short duration that is usually associated with a sense of apprehension or fear of impending death, precipitated by effort or emotion, and relieved quickly by rest or administration of nitroglycerin.'

Relatively late in his career, in the *Anthropology*, Kant gives a similar description. Speaking of the hypochondriac, he says, 'And when this patient—who for all his everlasting sickliness can never be sick—consults medical books, he becomes completely unbearable because he thinks he feels in his body all the diseases he reads about.'[53]

It is worth noting that in his letters Kant writes that he is sickly without ever being sick.[54] In the passage I have been quoting, he goes on to speak of the deceptive gaiety of the hypochondriac and so may recall the description already cited of his cheerfulness. He writes:

> A characteristic sign of this sort of diseased imagination is the excessive gaiety, lively wit, and joyous laughter which the patient sometimes feels himself to give way to—hence the ever-changing plays of his moods. Childish, anxious fear at the thought of *death* nourishes this disease. But unless we turn away from these thoughts with virile courage, we shall never be really happy in life.[55]*

At this point I am (really) afraid that we should get down to detail. The excuse that we are by nature attracted to such detail must, I am afraid, remain formally subservient to the relevance of the detail to Kant's philosophy. The fact is that Kant had an extraordinarily intense interest in his health. Before we go into this interest, some words may be spared to describe him physically. Contemporary descriptions make him something that I imagine the wind might blow over. He was barely five feet tall, his head was very large in relation to his body, and his chest was very flat, verging on concavity. He was so thin he had to use special springs, which I refrain from describing, to keep his stockings up. Only Kant, an intimate says, could have supported and maintained such a body for so many years. His face, however, was very pleasant, and his eyes were fascinating.[56]

---

*As far as I know, hypochondria is now more usually felt to be a symptom rather than a disorder in itself, and it is not much dealt with as a separate category in recent psychiatric literature. Freud related it to narcissism and paranoia. Sullivan, who believed it to be a defence against paranoia, said of it, 'Constantly talking about one's body and symptoms effectively rules out any other topics, averts intimacy, and bypasses hedonism.' A. M. Freedman, H. I. Kaplan & B. J. Sadock, *Modern Synopsis of* Comprehensive Textbook of Psychiatry (Baltimore: The Williams & Wilkens Co., 1972), pp. 365–67.

A recent book on psychosomatic problems states that hypochondriacs are narcissistic and withdraw almost completely from emotional contact with those who mean most to them. Withdrawal from persons is compensated for by increased interest in one's bodily condition. The hypochondriac feels that he is different from his body, which he merely possesses. He suffers the world and, in turn, troubles it, using his suffering body as a means of emotional communication. D. Eicke, *Der Körper als Partner als Partner*, pp. 19, 25.

As I have pointed out, the only extensive non-philosophical comments in Kant's letters were those on his health. To exaggerate, one might say that he communicated by means of philosophical abstractions and medical complaints. As will be seen, he thought philosophy both diverted the mind from disagreeable feelings and aroused it to life.

Except for an attack of the ague, which he thought he cured by a vigorous walk, Kant could remember no illness during his early life. But although he did not often need or take medical advice, he was often indisposed, for, to repeat his already quoted words, though never really sick, he never felt well. He talked of nothing with greater natural interest than hygiene, diet, and the prolongation of life. 'Perhaps no man ever lived,' says an intimate, 'who paid a more exact attention to his body and everything that affected it.'[57] He shared every bodily sensation and every change of condition with his friends.[58] After making what seemed to him a sufficient trial of medicines, he came to the conclusion that they were all, without exception, poisonous to him.[59] His various indispositions plagued him constantly, as he wrote to a medical friend, and heartburn and constipation in particular, he thought, clouded his brain and made him interrupt his intellectual effort.[60]

To remain healthy, Kant ordered his life very rigorously. By the time he had grown old, he took the condition of his health to be a work of art created by himself.[61] His interest in new medical discoveries and theories, which he hoped to apply to himself, was intense. He sometimes went too far, and his friends saw it as a sign of old age that the pressure he felt on his brain was attributed by him to a special kind of electricity in the air, the same electricity, he was convinced, that had caused a cat epidemic in Vienna, Copenhagen, and elsewhere, and that he tried to detect by the changing configurations of the clouds.[62] His friends learned that it was useless to contradict this theory, for Kant had become quite certain that the condition of his health depended on the weather.[63] To make out the direction of the wind, he would often take a look at the weathervane, and to guard his health the better, he would often check his thermometer, barometer, and hygrometer. He would also calculate the phases of the moon exactly and open a window for brief moments in order to test the exact quality of the air.[64]

For the sake of his health, Kant took great pains never to sweat. During the heat of the summer, he dressed lightly, and when, despite his precautions, it seemed to him that he might be on the verge of sweating, he would stand still in a shadow, as if waiting for someone, until the danger had passed. If on some sweltering summer night he felt even a trace of sweat, he emphasized this fact as if he had undergone a distinctly troubling experience.[65] I will not try to interpret this particular fear except to say that his sweating must have been a reminder of the animality from which he preferred to dissociate himself.

The technique of breathing was of particular interest to Kant. He took the trouble to train himself to breathe through the nose alone, even when asleep, because he was convinced that only so could he get rid of the sniffing and coughing that threatened to disturb his sleep. To avoid getting up at night when thirsty, he learned to take several deep breaths, at the same time expanding his chest and, as it were, drinking in the air. This process quenched his dangerous nighttime thirst quickly.[66]

A different kind of sign of Kant's anxiety was given on the occasion when a servant broke a wineglass. The pieces of glass were all painstakingly gathered on a plate and exhibited to him. He felt that he could not allow his servant to dispose of the fragments, and he remained worried that they might harm someone until they were buried near an old wall in his garden.[67]

All Kant's anxiety for his health was concentrated in his interest in reaching a great old age. For many years he would get the monthly mortality statistics from the chief of the Königsberg police, and from these he would each time calculate his own life-expectancy. To encourage himself, he memorized and would on the right occasions recite a whole list of men who had enjoyed long life.[68]

Suffering as he did from so many anxieties and so concerned with precautions against them, Kant also reflected on the relationship between abstract thinking and the state of his health. He came to regard thinking as literally essential to his life. 'To a scholar,' he said, 'thinking is a means of nourishment, without which, when he is *awake* and *alone*, he cannot live.' But thinking did not go well, he was sure, with other absorbing activities. Thus if one tried to occupy oneself intensively with a definite problem while eating, the result was, he said, hypochondria; and if one tried to think intensively while walking, the result was dizziness. One must therefore be careful not to accompany but to alternate strenuous thinking with eating or walking. The problem appeared difficult to him, because, as he said, 'It is hard for the studious to abstain from reflection when taking a walk by themselves.' The force of life could sustain only physical or intellectual effort, but not both at once. However, he regarded the imagination's free play as, unlike abstract thought, compatible with eating, walking, or the like.[69]

I cannot interpret these dicta of Kant, which he took very seriously, except in the general sense of a distinction between his sensuous animal self and his unsensuous thinking self, between which, he had learned, there was a distinct incompatibility. But he came to regard philosophy itself as a means of stimulating and even prolonging life. In making this contention, he distinguished between superficial philosophizing, which was somewhat helpful, and philosophy proper, which had a more profound effect:

> Philosophizing that does not make one a philosopher as a result is also a
> means of defence against many disagreeable feelings and, at the same time,

an *arousal* of the mind, which in its preoccupation provides an interest that is independent of external incidents and is for precisely that reason, though as play alone, nevertheless strong and sincere and does not allow the vital force to cease. *Philosophy*, in contrast, which has its whole interest in the ultimate goal of reason (which is an absolute unity) bears with it a feeling of power, which may well compensate in a certain measure for the bodily weakness of old age by means of the rational appreciation of the value of life—But the novel prospects that appear for the widening of knowledge, even when they do not exactly belong to philosophy, gain the same end, or something similar; and insofar as the mathematician takes an *immediate* interest in it (not as a tool for a different purpose) he is to that extent also a philosopher and enjoys the benefit of such a kind of stimulation of his powers in a life that is rejuvenated and prolonged without exhaustion.[70]

It should not be surprising that Kant was or in time became compulsively rigid.[71] He led the conversations of his dinner guests according to a fixed sequence.[72] The moving of a pair of scissors or a chair from their accustomed places gave him acute discomfort.[73] Going to sleep became a fixed, elaborate ritual, as part of which his watch was hung on a nail between his barometer and thermometer.[74] It is not at all incidental that he so loved his watch that he would sometimes say that if he were in need, it would be the last of his possessions he would sell.[75] When the old servant was changed and Kant's friend and helper came to have tea with him, Kant was unable to accept his friend's presence at this unusual time and courteously asked him to sit behind him, where he could not be seen, for, as he explained, he had had no living soul with him at tea for more than half a century.[76]

In the latter part of his life, Kant's unhappiness became open. He declared, 'Life is a burden to me, I am tired of bearing it. And if the angel of death were to come this night and call me from here, I would raise my hand and say, "God be praised!" ' He then added, 'I am no poltroon. I still have strength enough to take my life, but I hold this to be immoral. Whoever deprives himself of life is a beast. . . .'[77] The undertone of misanthropy that had always, I think, been there, was now voiced unambiguously. There was not much good in mankind, he said, explaining, 'Everyone almost hates the other, tries to raise himself above his fellow-men, is full of envy, jealousy, and other devilish vices. *Homo homini* not *deus* but *diabolus*.'[78] With equal misanthropic asperity he remarked, 'If a man were to say and write all he thinks, there would be nothing more horrible on God's earth than man.'[79] His dreams grew murderous:

> Out of individual scenes of his dreams his imagination composed entire frightful tragedies, which made so strong an impression that their effect persisted in him long after he awoke. Almost every night he imagined

himself surrounded by thieves and murderers. In terrible progression this nightly disturbance by dreams was such that in the first few moments after awakening he would take his servant, who was hurrying to calm and help him, for a murderer.[80]

Kant's rigidity and suffering lead me to recall that he had a great love for birds, which, I imagine, represented freedom to him. In the springtime he awaited their return with rising expectation. Towards the end,

> the one joy that nature still allowed him . . . was the return of a warbler [I hope that this is the right translation of *Grasmücke*] that sang before his window and in his garden. Even in his joyless old age, this one joy remained to him. If his friend remained away too long, he said, 'It must still be very cold on the Apennines.'[81]

He was still sometimes capable of happiness. The memory of his birthday always cheered him up. A few weeks before his death, at the age of seventy-nine years and almost ten months, his friend Wasianski, on whose memoir I have often drawn, was still trying to encourage him by counting the days that remained until his eightieth birthday.[82] But Kant weakened and then grew unconscious. Unconscious, he uttered his last words—what did they mean?—'It is good.'[83]

I admit having been seduced by the description of this austere and in its own way heroic life. But now I have to try to show some connection between Kant's life and thought.

One of the general characteristics of Kant's thought is his refusal to take the easy way out. He often seeks and even tenaciously maintains a difficulty that other philosophers, the German Idealists, for example, simply extirpate intellectually. Such other philosophers unify the world by dazzling or blinding intellectual prestidigitation, while rigid, honest Kant not only divides everything into the realm of appearances and the realm of reality as such, but also stubbornly resists the unification of the two by means of the old antithesis between illusion and reality, or by means of the old Neo-Platonic theory of gradation of being. The world for him is both two *and* one. On the one side, we have sense objects and the faculty of understanding, which prescribes a priori laws for nature; and on the other side, we have freedom, which is above nature and essentially exempt from it, and the faculty of reason, which prescribes *a priori* laws for freedom. Nature and understanding on the one side, and freedom and reason on the other apparently coexist, but neither side determines anything in the other. 'To that extent, then, it is not possible to throw a bridge from one realm to the other.'[84]

Kant needs and wants to create an almost dual world, of fact and obligation, and it is divided rather as Kant himself was. That is, he was its plan and precursor, in the very beginning, as we have seen him, a child who was shown the heavens above and taught the moral law within, and who felt both the connection (in part his closeness to his mother) and the difference. Later, as a philosophical physicist, he undertook to reveal the *a priori* laws, quite unconnected with morality and religion, of the external world. From the standpoint of logic alone, there was perhaps nothing to stop him from declaring that appearances and reality need not be distinguished, and that the set of necessary relationships he had revealed was exhaustive in every respect; or that there was at least a consistent structural likeness between 'appearances' and 'reality.' Or he might perhaps have been like one of the Neo-Kantians who held that reality was the asymptote of appearances, which could be more and more closely but never completely identified with it. But Kant needed and wanted to keep appearances quite distinct from reality. His reason, put briefly and decisively, was this:

'If appearances are things in themselves, then freedom cannot be saved,' or, in German, 'Denn sind Erscheinungen Dinge an sich selbst, so ist Freiheit nicht zu retten.'[85]

If there was no freedom, the world in which his mother died of helping a friend and his father died without reward would be the ultimately real world, and the punishment of the one, the unrewarded decency of the other, and his own endless thought and endless self-rule would be no more than brute, intolerable facts. This possibility was made the more intolerable by his knowledge that his parents' dignity, which he cherished as his inheritance from them, had depended on their freedom to act as they thought morally right. Therefore, although the bridge between realms was so tenuous for him, he was forced to assume the unknowable thing-in-itself that gave the rewards unclaimable in the world of the senses.

But the unknowable, though not in a sense philosophically acceptable to Kant, was also ominous. For Kant was a difficult enigma to himself. 'I do not ever understand myself sufficiently,' 'Ich mich nicht einmal selbst hinreichend verstehe,' he wrote in a letter.[86] The remark sounds innocent; but it is psychologically expressive in a man with such unrelenting curiosity. Its significance becomes apparent when we see how opposed he was to unregulated introspection.

> To eavesdrop on ourselves when our thoughts occur in our mind *unbidden* and spontaneously . . . is to overturn the natural order of the cognitive powers, for then the principles of thinking do not come first (as they should), but instead follow after. If this is not already a form of mental illness (hypochondria), it leads to it and to the lunatic asylum.[87]

Kant wanted to know more of himself than he did, but he was afraid to. *This* thing-in-itself was not simply unknown, it was forbidden; for it was Kant's suppressed emotional life, I take it, and he was afraid that if it was revealed, he would be devastated.

Kant therefore had much to control and hide. The spontaneity he feared was in part controlled by the spatial, temporal, and logical order he set for the world, in a compulsive intensification of its *a priori* laws he had, he believed, discovered. Order of every kind, as we have seen, relieved his anxiety. At the age of forty-four he had proudly written that he was unconcerned enough about his or other views to often overturn whole structures in his search for truth; but at the age of fifty-five, speaking, it is true, of his health, he wrote, 'All change makes me anxious.'[88] To reduce the possibility of change, it was important for him to believe that order was all-encompassing, and that it was *his* order, and he therefore insisted that the completeness of the pure philosophy he had taught was the best indication of its truth; yet he was troubled by the gap between pure philosophy and physics, so he worked on, though old and 'as it were mentally paralyzed,' to pay the 'unpaid bill' of his uncompleted though surely completable philosophy.[89]

Kant's first *Critique* was meant to reform the dogmatic or fanatical metaphysics of his time. Were his arguments meant only to secure his freedom from others, or were they also aimed, however obscurely, against inner, emotional demands such as perhaps threatened his sanity? Despite his insistence on the principle of fairness, and despite his dislike of dogmatism and his arguments against it, he was himself dogmatic in practice. 'He cannot bear to hear others talk much,' an otherwise admiring visitor noted, 'becomes impatient, at least for the moment, if anyone professes to know anything better than he does, monopolizes the conversation, and professes to know everything about all countries, places, divisions of the earth, and the like.' He could not really suffer opposition. 'Direct contradiction insulted and—when it was persisted in—embittered him. He surely did not force his opinion on anyone, but reciprocal obstinacy caused him real grief.' His dogmatism was not merely the response of a man made inflexible by age and fame. Even

> in earlier years Kant was not used to contradiction. His penetrating understanding; his always ready and, in accord with circumstances, often caustic wit; his extensive learning, by virtue of which he could enter every conversation, and which would not allow any alien opinion or untruth to be imposed on him; his universally recognized noble sentiments; his strictly moral mode of life, had all created such a superiority over others that he was secure against impetuous contradiction. But if someone ventured in company to contradict him too loudly or in an attemptedly witty way, he knew how to lead the conversation by giving it an unexpected turn that won everyone for his opinion and so made the most audacious wag timid and silent.[90]

Kant's theoretical insistence on universality, fairness, and undogmatic reason and his frequent dogmatism in practice show, as is otherwise evident, that he was ambivalent. His ambivalence, which made him both social and unsocial, made it easy for him to conclude that unsociable sociableness was a basic characteristic of mankind.[91] He held that the egotism of each individual clashes with the same individual's need to live in association with others. Everywhere in his person and thought there reappear the fact of antagonism and the ideal of unity. His hypochondria, the sign of a war he waged against at least himself, was his literally embodied antagonism and unity. His physics and his politics exhibited the same antagonism and unity, a kind of polar opposition that becomes explicit in his contrast of antinomical arguments.[92] Once he said,

> All evils come from the lack of unity in the world as a whole. This is the source of antagonisms. When there is perfect unity, not only regarding substance but regarding forces as well, everything must agree with the natural essence and must therefore be good.[93]

This statement regarding everything should of course apply to Kant himself.

Kant himself. Like other extremely moral persons, he could not be happy with himself, and his slight misdemeanours could trouble him for a long time. Though he regarded human beings as by nature good, he became sure that they were also by nature radically and inexplicably evil. I think this was largely because his parents had been very good to him and simultaneously, from a psychological standpoint, very harsh. He could admit this harshness, as he could admit the temptations and deviations the harshness defined inwardly for him, only in the sense of an unintelligible evil rooted in human beings as such. This evil meant, he said, that despite man's consciousness of the moral law, man qualified the law by ruling that he could deviate from it.

> He is evil by *nature*, means but this, that evil can be predicated of man as a species . . . That such a corrupt propensity must indeed be rooted in man need not be formally proved in view of the multitude of crying examples which the experience *of the actions* of men put before our eyes . . . This evil is *radical*, because it corrupts the ground of all maxims; it is, moreover, as a natural propensity, *inextirpable* by human powers.

As far as human beings go, said Kant, there is 'no conceivable ground from which the moral evil in us could have originally come from.'[94]*

Because his parents had been rigidly moral, because he believed that

---

*Goethe and Schiller objected to the view that man was radically evil. It is this kind of objection that stands behind Goethe's letter to Schiller, in which he says:
'I am very eager to read Kant's *Anthropology*. The pathological side of man that he always stresses, and that may perhaps have its place in an Anthropology, pursues us through almost everything he writes, and this is what gives his practical philosophy such a peevish appearance. It is surprising and lamentable that this cheerful and jovial spirit has not been able to clear his wings completely from the filth of life and actually has not quite overcome certain gloomy impressions of his youth, etc.' Letter of 22 Sept., 1797, in W. Kaufmann, *Hegel: A Reinterpretation* (Garden City: Doubleday (Anchor Books), 1965), note pp. 29–30.

man was radically evil, because he believed in absolute justice based upon universal principles, and because he was both morally unbending and psychologically rigid, Kant was a moral rigourist. A tyrant over himself, against whom he never allowed himself to rebel, he could never agree to the right of rebellion. 'It is the people's duty,' he laid down, 'to endure even the most intolerable abuse of supreme authority.'[95] In his view, the formal condemnation to death of a monarch, such as Louis XVI, over-turned all concepts of right. 'It is regarded as a crime that remains eternal and cannot be expiated, and appears to resemble the crimes the theologians consider as sins that cannot be forgiven in either this or the next world.'[96]

Continuing with the same rigour, Kant said, 'The law of punishment is a categorical imperative.'[97] This conclusion requires that punishments must be equal to crimes. Therefore a person who insults another must be shamed in punishment—punishment by fine would mean that a rich man could insult with impunity.[98] Someone who steals makes all property insecure, so he must be condemned to convict labour, meaning, to tem-porary or permanent slavery. And if someone has murdered, 'he must *die*. In this case there is no substitute for the satisfaction of justice,' because a life in the greatest possible pain is not equal to any death.[99]

Kant, who had in effect learned to punish himself severely, could not agree to lighten or suspend the punishments of others. He criticized Beccaria's proposal to do away with capital punishment as 'sentimental-ity' and 'affected humanity.'[100] To illustrate the fixed rationality of punishment Kant imagined the case of an island people who decided to break up their society and scatter over all the world. It would be their obligation, he said, to execute the last of the murderers left in prison, to ensure that everyone get his just deserts and the blood guilt not be attached to those who had delayed justice by not insisting on the execution.[101] Kant's attitude toward sexual crimes may have been characteristic of his period, but looked at from our perspective, it is strikingly harsh. He thought masturbation to be 'a violation of one's duty to oneself and . . . certainly in the highest degree opposed to morality.' The reluctance to name it, he said (without himself naming it), shows that it is fundamentally more degrading than suicide. Yet despite the severity of the crime, he said, 'It is not easy to produce a rational demonstration of the inadmissibility of that unnatural use' of a man's body merely to gratify the man's own animal drive.[102] Kant was right, of course. It was not rational demonstration, but his early training and his sexual attitudes that led him to believe that sexual crimes irrevocably destroy a man's humanity.

Beyond his attempt to contain impulse and chastise crime, Kant attempted to minimize the importance of pleasure and pain. But after depriving pleasure and pain of their usual functions, he was left with the problem of integrating them with the *a priori* rational elements his analysis favoured. It seems to me that he deals with the problem as honestly as usual, but that he approaches it with care verging on anxiety, and that his success is questionable. I take it that one reason for his difficulty is that his abstract, philosophical integration of the sensual and intellectual is influenced by their lack of integration in himself.

Kant is firmly opposed to the usual notion that pleasure has something to do with the determination of good and evil. He writes, 'If with Epicurus we let virtue determine the will only because of the pleasure it promises, we cannot later blame him for holding that this pleasure is of the same sort as those of the coarsest senses.'[103] No principle based on personal happiness can be morally decisive, he writes, because such happiness is determined by desire.[104] He believes that pure reason 'must be able to determine the will by the mere form of the practical rule without presupposing any feeling or consequently any idea of the pleasant or unpleasant.'[105] And he finds it 'astonishing how intelligent men have thought of proclaiming as a universal practical law the desire for happiness. . . .'[106]

Happiness, then, and morality have nothing essential to do with one another. But having said this, Kant is puzzled. He cannot escape the idea that feeling or something like it, or at least a gratifying consciousness, does in fact accompany the doing of virtuous deeds. He cannot understand 'how a mere thought containing nothing sensuous is to produce a sensation of pleasure or displeasure.'[107] Finally he hits on what he takes to be a solution. He substitutes the term *respect (Achtung)* for that of *pleasure* and says, with, it seems to me, some hesitation, 'Respect as the consciousness of the direct restraint of the will through law is hardly analogous to the feeling of pleasure, though in relation to the faculty of desire it produces exactly the same effect, but from different sources.' He then looks for 'a word to denote a satisfaction with existence, an analogue of happiness which necessarily accompanies the consciousness of virtue, and which does not indicate a gratification, as "happiness" does.' He hits on the word, 'self-contentment,' which he says may also be called 'intellectual contentment.'[108]

I think I understand why Kant's philosophical principles force him to these verbal manoeuvres. I call the manoeuvres verbal because the something that 'produces exactly the same effect, but from different causes' is a something that gives a philosopher or scientist too easy a way out. I do not know if Kant had a better way out, and I see no reason to invent a new Kantianism now in order to try to find it; but it seems clear that his difficulty stems from his childhood Pietism and his fear of sensuality. He is too honest not to recognize the importance of pleasure in fact, but he insists on removing it from honourable natural functions, and where this proves too difficult, he rebaptizes it and, with its new name, grants it a new immunity to the 'pathological,' as he calls whatever has to do with the 'passions.'[109]

In the introduction to the *Critique of Judgment*, Kant makes a renewed attempt to solve the problem and, at the same time, to unify his system, that is, to bridge the gap between natural law and freedom. The gap troubles him because it intimates a dualism he does not and cannot mean. He had earlier thought that it was fruitless to try 'to bring the treatment of the beautiful under rational principles,' but now the once impossible idea of a generally valid pleasure seems to him to give the solution.[110] Now he adds the faculty of judgment to the faculties of understanding and reason, and judgment, using the concept of purpose, bridges the gap between nature, which is necessity, and freedom. He discovers the clue in art, in which, he points out, we are able to actualize our purposes.[111] For the actualizing of purpose in art gives rise to the pleasure of the spontaneous and harmonious accord of the faculties, a pleasure that is universally valid; and the same pleasure in response to nature, accompanying the same accord of the faculties, allows us to think of purpose as actualized in nature, and so to find freedom in necessity itself.[112] This much understood, nature and freedom, though forever different, can be seen to intersect in man; and man can be understood as able to fulfill himself by either finding himself in nature or imposing himself on it.[113]

I think that the man who says this is a bolder, more self-confident, and more philosophically united Kant. He has grown to this boldness and unity by his own enormous efforts. The split he has inherited and perhaps widened stops growing. In spite of his potential psychosis, which he grasps as such, he remains sane. He has undergone great trials, and in the weakness of old age, loneliness joins physical weakness, self-control gives way somewhat, and weariness and misanthropy are permitted to emerge. Yet Kant, as shown by the *Critique of Judgment*, reaches a kind of completeness, and comes to an end that seems to me to return him to his beginning. I see him and his mother walking together and the pleasure of their mutuality joining them with one another and their surroundings. The possible harmony of appearances, their tie with the thing-in-itself, appears more openly. In the terminology I have used, being has been both destroyed and created. Granted Kant's problems, the creation, differentiation, and union of being have prevailed as well, perhaps, as possible, and he has won a great, though still rather sad triumph.[114]

There remains something to be said on Kant's relationships with children and women. With respect to children, there are two opposite-sounding reports. The one is that Kant was lovable in old age with children, like a grandfather among his grandchildren.[115] The other is that when some children once threw stones into his garden, raising the possibility that he would be hit, he sent for the police and from that time on went into his garden only rarely. He was afraid, the account goes, that the children might have to be punished if they hit him.[116] He was again exhibiting the fear of his own emotions that kept him from intimacy, and again clothing the fear in a moral explanation.

As a younger man, Kant was a welcome salon guest, erudite, instructive, eloquent maybe, and suitably adroit with compliments. His interest in women is visible in *Observations on the Feeling of the Beautiful and the Sublime*, which he wrote at the age of forty. In this book he distinguishes between agreeable and charming women, he speaks of the laughing looks that can disturb a man, and he makes eloquent remarks on the nature of a truly companionable marriage.[117] He even repeats and slightly develops an idea that becomes important in Freud, namely, that the image of the mother 'remains the pattern all feminine figures in the future must more or less follow so as to be able to stir the fanciful ardour, whereby a rather coarse inclination is compelled to choose among the different objects of a sex.'[118]

Influenced, it is said, by Winckelmann, but also, no doubt, by his own nature, Kant writes in his notes, 'Female beauty is only relative, the male absolute. That is why all male animals are beautiful in our eyes, because they have relatively little charm for our senses.'[119] It has been contended that at about the age of forty, Kant's view of life grew narrower and his judgment of women more negative.[120] His posthumous notes are frankly hostile. I run a number of them together without comment:

> It is laughable that a man wants to make himself loved by a young woman by means of understanding and great merits . . . Woman does not betray herself easily and therefore does not get drunk. Because she is weak she is sly. . . Woman is vengeful . . . They say that the desire for honour is the last weakness of the wise. I think that unless the wisdom is of the kind that presupposes old age, the love of women is the last weakness . . . Woman makes of man what she wishes. Formerly she made heroes and now she makes apes . . .[121] The weakness of the man as against the woman is no shame . . . Everything depends primarily on the satisfaction of the woman, but the man fixes the means for that . . . The female sex has more feeling and heart than character . . . Men love the soul greatly, women the body. They believe that the soul is good enough if only they can get it into their power.[122]

One final Kantian and perhaps Freudian reflection:

> 'A reason why parents want their children to marry advantageously is that they should not wish their death.'[123]

Kant's judgments on women are surprising if compared with the unfailingly favourable ones he made on his mother. A psychoanalyst might say that he was resisting the women who might try to usurp her place. But perhaps he was making an unconscious attack on her. In favour of this possibility it may be recalled that Kant believed his predisposition to hypochondria to be caused by a constricted chest. It happens that he attributed his 'really concave chest,' along with his general appearance, to his mother, and he may have obscurely felt that she was to blame for this heritage, as she was to be obscurely blamed, though publicly praised, for his painful morality.

Kant once thought of marrying a gentle, pretty widow; but he began to calculate income and expenses and delayed his decision from day to day until she left and married someone else. Then there was a handsome Westphalian girl whose company he obviously liked; but she was a woman's travelling companion, and by the time he undertook to pay her a call, she was already far away. He is also said to have considered and then lost his enthusiasm for a Königsberg lady, very likely the Luise Rebekka Fritz who in her later years used to boast that Kant had once loved her.[124]*

As an old man, Kant is reported to have said, 'When I could have used a wife, I could not support one; and when I could support one, I no longer needed any.'[125] But he retained his feeling for womanly beauty and charm. When he was already seventy years old, the fiancée of the son of his friend, Motherby, pleased him so much that he would always ask her to sit at the table where he could see her, away from his blind eye.[126]

Hegel

11. Georg Wilhelm Friedrich Hegel, born in 1770. An attack of smallpox at the age of six blinded him for several days and nearly caused his death. At the age of eleven (the age usually given, thirteen, appears wrong), he barely survived the disease that attacked his family and proved fatal to his mother.[1] 'During his student years he had tertian fever and on that account spent a few months at home where on his good days he read Greek tragedies, which were his favourite reading, and botany . . . .'[2] In adolescence and later, as will be emphasized, he suffered periods of depression. So did his sister, Christiane, three years younger than he, to

---

*Kant researchers will one day have a twenty-volume computer-generated index to his works to help them. In the meanwhile, it can be revealed that 'Kant's correspondence with women constitutes only 1/46 or 0.0217 of his total correspondence,' a fact I set down as precise numerical evidence of his degree of communication with members of the sex that in his time was still called 'fair' and the like. A. Lange, 'Kant's Correspondence with Women, A Contribution to a Statistical Evaluation of Kant's Correspondence,' in *Proceedings of the Third International Kant Congress*, ed. L. W. Beck (Dordrecht: Reidel, 1972), p. 684.

whom he was quite close. It is this closeness, I assume, that is translated into Hegel's dictum that the brother-sister relationship is ethically higher than any other, because brother and sister are both truly individual and truly unselfish in relation to one another. But he construed the relationship one-sidedly when he said, 'The loss of a brother is . . . irreparable to the sister, and her duty to him is the highest.'[3] Generalizing, I assume, from himself, he defined a brother's nature with what may easily appear to be comical solemnity. His opinion was that

> the brother is the member of the family in whom its spirit becomes individualized, and enabled thereby to turn towards another sphere, towards what is other than and external to itself, and pass over into consciousness of universality. The brother leaves this immediate, rudimentary, and, therefore, strictly speaking, negative ethical life of the family, in order to acquire and produce the concrete ethical order which is conscious of itself.[4]

In a perhaps unfair but simple translation, this means that Hegel was glad to have become independent of his family and to have become a philosopher, conscious of his embracing, objective consciousness.

Hegel's father had a minor financial post in the government. We are told that he was on good terms with his son; but when the latter was attracted to Rousseauism and the French Revolution, violent arguments broke out between them.[5] It seems that the father was also opposed when Hegel wanted to abandon the theological career on which he had set out. It was only after his father's death that Hegel decided to devote himself to philosophy alone.[6] This suggests that the death of the father released him to do as he pleased.

I do not know of any particularly revealing remarks by Hegel on his parents, though on the anniversary of his mother's death he wrote that he always continued to remember her.[7] This memory must be reflected in his statement that 'in the early years it is education by the mother especially which is important, since ethical principles must be implanted in the child in the form of feeling.'[8] As far as I know, Hegel never refers to his parents with much emotion, and it may easily be his own relative coolness that finds expression in his statement, 'It is noteworthy that on the whole children love their parents less than their parents love them.'[9]

Christiane describes Hegel's early education in a few economical sentences:

> As a boy of 3 he was sent to the German school, and in his 5th year to the Latin school. At that age he already knew the first declension and the Latin words that go with it; for our blessed mother had taught him. She was, for those days, a woman of education and thus had considerable influence on his first studies. In all classes he received a prize every year because he was always among the top five; and from his 10th to his 18th year he was the first in his division in the Gymnasium.[10]

It is apparent that Hegel became an intellectual very early. A biographer who knew him personally says that his desire for knowledge caused him to attach himself to adults, such as his teachers.[11] His attention turned to books, he remained friendly, but neglected to develop any physical skills. His sister notes of him, 'Lacked all bodily agility. Must have been easy to get along with, for he always had many friends; loved to jump, but was utterly awkward in dancing lessons.'[12] As a disciplined, studious fifteen-year-old, he earned the nickname 'The Old Man' from his fellow-students. He soon began and throughout his life continued to keep a systematic record of everything he studied, and he accumulated notes and indexed excerpts from books. 'In all his wanderings he always kept these incunabula of his formation.'[14] Everything was grist for his excerpt mill—philology and literary history, aesthetics, aphorisms and witticisms, 'experiences and physiognomics,' mathematics, physics, psychology, pedagogy, and philosophy.[15]

At the age of fifteen, Hegel also began to keep a diary, which is very nearly the antithesis of what one might take an adolescent's diary to be.[16] Instead of personal problems and emotions, he writes down facts he comes across, critical comments on the textbooks he is reading, reflections on the nature of a 'pragmatic history,' lists of books he has bought, rather abstract reflections on women, superstitions, and so on. When a day passes with nothing serious to record, he takes this fact seriously enough to explain why. Personal matters win their place in his diary only if they appear to him to illustrate some general principle.[17] Perusing the diary, we find the record of a public concert, of a fire, and of a hard winter, followed by some words on the evils of loving money and an appreciative remark on the gift of a Latin lexicon he received. He composes a Latin oration in the diary, he argues against dictating a theme in German for transcription into Latin, he puts down his school timetable in the margin, he says that he and his friends watched pretty girls, he makes notes on Vergil and Demosthenes, he is curious about a musical clock and a star atlas, and, on Sunday, he works on trigonometry.[18]

If we consider his notes, excerpts, and diary, and to them add his school essays, which I have not described, we see Hegel to be serious, to have a wide variety of miscellaneous interests, and to be correspondingly omnivorous. He is, in the term I have used, differentiating himself intellectually, and he seems to want to assimilate and reflect on all possible knowledge. But what he gathers and reflects bears only indirect witness to the state of his emotions. Some further insight into his development can be gained, I think, from his later philosophical interpretation of childhood and its transition into youth and adulthood. He of course means to speak of human beings in general, but he can hardly avoid drawing on his own experience. In his philosophy, he takes childhood to be the time of natural harmony, when the individual is at peace with himself and the world, and he says, 'The oppositions which may occur in childhood remain devoid of any serious interest. The child lives in innocence, without any lasting pain, in the love it has for its parents and in the feeling of being loved by them.'[19] Yet all this innocence and mutual love do not, in Hegel's mind, contradict the need to impose discipline.

> To allow children to do as they please, to be so foolish as to provide them into the bargain with reasons for their whims, is to fall into the worst of all educational practices; such children develop the deplorable habit of fixing their attention on their own inclinations, their own peculiar cleverness, their own selfish interests, and this is the root of all evil.[20]

In contrast to childhood, adolescence, as he describes it philosophically, appears distressing to Hegel. He gives an odd or at least oddly-phrased reason, which is that adolescence requires preoccupation with details. This reason inevitably recalls his preoccupation with details of all kinds in his diary and suggests that it conceals a more vital interest, which is being thwarted. He in fact connects adolescent interest in details with 'hypochondria,' with 'repugnance to the actual world,' and even with the possibility of death:

> The occupation with details can at first be very distressing to the man, and the impossibility of an immediate realization of his ideals can turn him into a hypochondriac [by which Hegel means, I think, a depressed person]. This hypochondria, however difficult it may be to discern in many cases, is not easily escaped by anyone. The later the age at which it attacks a man, the more serious are its symptoms. In weak natures it can persist throughout the entire lifetime. In this diseased frame of mind the man will not give up his subjectivity, is unable to overcome his repugnance to the actual world, and by this very fact finds himself in a state of relative incapacity which easily becomes actual incapacity. If, therefore, the man does not want to perish, he must recognize the world as a self-dependent world which in its nature is already complete, must accept the conditions set for him by the world and wrest from it what he wants for himself.[21]

In Hegel's opinion, as a child becomes a man, it undergoes the strain of what, in his language, is 'the antithesis,' that is, of a potential but still subjectively limited universality. But having undergone the strain and made the transition, a man recognizes the objective necessity and reasonableness of the world as he finds it.[22] At the time the man first enters practical life, he may still be 'vexed and morose, but in spite of this he finds his place in the world of objective relationships and becomes habituated to it and his work . . . And the longer the man is active in his work, the more does the universal rise into prominence out of the welter of particulars.'[23]

It stands to reason that Hegel's description of the passage from childhood into adolescence and adulthood reflects his personal life, and there is in fact a good deal of evidence, direct and indirect, that Hegel went through periods of severe anxiety and depression.[24] One significant piece of evidence comes from an essay he wrote at the age of twenty-three. In this essay he explains the difficult condition of the youth who because of circumstances has withdrawn into himself, who has decided to make a virtuous man of himself, but who is not experienced enough to know that he cannot become virtuous by means of books. Suppose, asks Hegel, that such a youth picks up a moralizing book, reads it morning and evening, and reflects on it all day. What will the result be?

> Gloomy and anxious he goes out into society, where no one is welcome save he who knows how to be amusing, hesitantly he tastes of some pleasure that satisfies only one who brings a cheerful heart to it. Pierced right through by the sense of his own imperfection, he abases himself before everyone, the company of the other sex does not amuse him, because he is afraid that the light touch of some girl may set a blazing fire coursing through his veins, and this makes him stiff and gauche—but he will not put up with it for long, he will shake off the control of this surly tutor, and will be the better off for it.[25]

Soon after writing this essay, which he never finished, Hegel left for Switzerland, the 'land of divine freedom,' where he had a position as a tutor. He claimed in a letter that his isolation there was good for the development of his spirit and heart.[26] Yet when he returned after three years he was, his sister testifies, 'very withdrawn, and only happy in the circle of close friends.'[27] From his correspondence with the poet, Hölderlin, it appears that his faith in his ability had weakened.[28] But in Switzerland he had learned to comfort himself by communing with nature. 'As there,' he wrote, 'I sought to be reconciled with myself and with other men in the arms of Nature, so here I often fly to this true mother, to separate myself again from other men in her company, and to protect myself from their influence under her aegis, and to prevent any covenant with them.'[29] We have seen such communion with nature in place of men, in the life of Rousseau, and will see it again in the lives of Nietzsche and Russell. It is interesting that Hegel reacted to bleak mountains, not as sublime, but as monotonous, 'eternally dead' masses, while a waterfall impressed him as the image of free play, of eternal motion onward. The still, bleak mountains suggested the painful immobility of depression to him, I think, and the waterfall, the pleasure of release from it.[30]

It is not known how long Hegel's emotional withdrawal persisted. But he later revealed something of his emotional past in a letter to a follower who had become deeply depressed. Hegel wrote reassuringly that he himself had survived such a condition. He knew, he said,

> this descent into dark regions where nothing shows itself to be firm, deter-minate, and secure, where splendours flash everywhere, but next to abys-ses. . .—where the beginning of every path breaks off again and runs into the indefinite, loses itself, and tears us out of our destiny and direction.

He went on:

> From my own experience I know this mood of the mind, or rather of reason, once it has entered with interest and its intimations into a chaos of appearances and, though inwardly sure of the goal, it has not yet come through, not yet into the clarity and detailed grasp of the whole. I have suffered a few years of this hypochondria, to the point of enervation. Indeed, every human being may well have such a turning point in life, the nocturnal point of the contraction of his nature through whose narrows he is pressed, fortified and assured to feel secure with himself and secure in the usual daily life; and if he has already rendered himself incapable of being satisfied with that, secure in an inner, nobler existence. —Continue with confidence; only science, which has led you into this labyrinth of the mind, is capable of leading you out and healing you.[31]*

Later, Hegel declared in his lectures that a man changes from a youth to an adult during the years from twenty-seven to thirty-six, and that at about twenty-seven in particular a man has 'to conquer a certain hypochondria.'[32] The decade Hegel mentions was just that, in his own life, between his return from Switzerland and the writing of the *Phenomenology*. The writing of this book was preceded by the crisis I have described on an earlier page. I should suppose that this and earlier crises were echoed in the words of the *Phenomenology* in which Hegel speaks of the 'unhappy consciousness,' which is the alienated soul conscious of its self as a divided nature, as 'a doubled and merely contradictory nature,' all 'pain and sorrow' over its existence and action.[33]

The threat of depression never lifted completely. When Hegel wrote to his intended bride, whom he married when he was forty-one, he found it necessary to excuse his 'perhaps only hypochondriac pedantry.' Ten years later, we find him writing to a friend, 'You know I am an anxious man,'

---

*It has been claimed that the 'hypochondria' spoken of in this letter 'is a peculiarly intellectual experience, rather than a psychological condition in any ordinary sense. It is the feeling—which has certainly afflicted every author if not every man—that although one knows where one wants to go, one does not quite know how to get there.' H. S. Harris, *Hegel's Development: Toward the Sunlight: 1770—1801*, p. 265. This is a distinction that I find impossible to make. In sharp contrast, a biographer of Hegel raises the possibility that Hegel's depression was psychotic, while a psychopathographer concludes that Hegel was clearly schizoid. G. E. Müller, *Hegel: Denkgeschichte eines Lebendigen*, pp. 169 – 70. A. Künzli, 'Prolegomena zu einser Psychographie Hegels.'

and to his sister that his profession was such that he could not always be without 'apprehension and anxiety,' whether well-founded or not.[34] During his last years, when he was at the height of his fame, the constantly growing number of his friends and adherents gave him, as his wife later recalled, inward happiness. Physically healthy, and as if rejuvenated, she said, he worked with greater freedom and satisfaction, and she no longer heard him repeat in annoyance that to be a philosopher was to be condemned by God. During his last year or so, however, a long spell of 'cold fever' left him with a sense of growing weakness, which led to frequent moments when he felt 'inexpressibly unhappy and discontented.'[35] His quite unexpected death, at the age of sixty-one, was attributed to cholera.

No doubt as the result of his own and his sister's psychological difficulties, not to speak of the prolonged insanity of his friend, Hölderlin, Hegel became interested in the subject of insanity. Espousing the humane ideas of Philippe Pinel, he criticized the 'harsh, arrogant, contemptuous treatment' of the insane. He argued that their treatment should usually be both physical and psychological, and he insisted that the psychiatrist should continue to appeal to the rationality and moral sense of the insane. 'The insane deserve considerate treatment,' he said, 'because their rational nature is not yet entirely destroyed. Lunatics still have a feeling of what is right and good.'[36]

Hegel characterized insanity rather as he had adolescence, that is, as the self-division of the soul and the soul's imprisonment 'in an isolated particularity.'[37] It does not seem wrong to say that, from his standpoint, his own system was a particular demonstration of sanity, for it established a conscious appreciation of the hierarchical independence of things quite opposite to that of the insane self, 'engrossed with a single phase of feeling' it is unable to subordinate within 'the individual system of the world which a conscious subject is.'[38] The insane person, he said, no longer knows himself 'as a self-accordant, inwardly undivided subject, but as a subject disrupted into two different personalities.' He is unable to resolve the contradiction between his consciousness that he is one particular person living among others, all of whom share his inward experience of an immediate 'I,' and a 'particular, isolated idea severed from the total actual world.'[39]

'Madness proper,' said Hegel, usually results from the dissatisfaction with the actual world that drives a person to shut himself up within his own subjectivity. 'The passion of vanity and pride is the chief cause of this psychical self-imprisonment.' One effect may be disgust with life, possibly a brooding melancholy that develops into an uncontrollable impulse to commit suicide.[40] I particularly cite these words because they applied to Hegel's sister. Tragically, after many years of essential loneliness, she suffered an attack of insanity. She and Hegel had much in common. Not only did she resemble him in appearance, but, like him, she developed the habit of making extracts from books. She also wrote sermons and composed verses, some of which are said to be moving. Up to the time of her 'nervous illness' she had worked as a governess. Although Hegel offered her a refuge in his home, she went to live with a relative, a postal official, and then, after some years, with the relative's brother, a pastor.[41] Her condition has been described as a kind of 'hypochondriacal melancholy with occasional outbursts of hysteria' intensified at times to the point of insanity. She was particularly afraid of a lonely, dependent old age.[42] It had been her own rejection of a suitor, it seemed, that had put her into the frame of mind that had led in time to a decisive attack of 'nervousness' and bizarre behaviour.[43] Her open and violent jealousy of Hegel's wife became evident. There is an undated note in which her guardian responds angrily to her reproaches and reminds her that when she had been brought to him sick, years before, she had lain all day on the sofa wailing and screaming, full of 'deep hatred' for her sister-in-law and 'deep dissatisfaction' with her brother, as well as with all the others who had become the objects of her anger.[44]

The breakdown of Hegel's sister, related, as it is, to her jealousy of his wife, makes a sadly ironic commentary on his philosophical assurance that brother and sister are, as such, ideally related to one another, for the reason that 'they do not desire one another' and have neither given nor taken independence from one another, but are to one another in the stable equilibrium of both freedom and good will. Thinking, perhaps, of his sister's troubles or of the inferiority he assigned to women in general, Hegel had qualified and written that, although the sister foreshadows the nature of ethical life, 'she does not become conscious of it, and does not actualize it.'[45]

As time went on, the condition of Hegel's sister deteriorated. Shortly before she learned of Hegel's death, she became convinced that all the doctors had turned their magnets and electrical devices against her, and she tried to dress to protect herself against these assaults. She attempted suicide a number of times. The news of her brother's death left her apparently indifferent, but several hours later she broke into loud crying. For a few weeks she became rational and outwardly calm; but then she took a walk and drowned herself.[46]

Hegel's nature, like his philosophy, was complex. He remained always the orderly man, noting all his household expenses and trying to foresee the smallest details. He wrote relatively few letters, it has been said, because he was so concerned to polish and rewrite them before they were sent. He was not, however, pedantic in human relations. On the contrary, he was a natural, open, and quite welcome guest, who knew how to talk to each person in accord with his interest, even to a woman about her jewelry—he noted every new ornament a woman acquaintance would wear. He himself was a natural, concerned host. Many people, of course, wanted favours from him. Some appeared to think their demands on him were justified by their interest in his philosophy; but he responded with good humour and did what he could to help.[47]

That was one side of Hegel. But he was also determined, obstinate, and severe. In his life as in his philosophy, a warm relationship was one that was likely to have progressed from a good but external one, through anger or contradiction, to closeness. To those who simply contradicted him, he was pitiless. 'The philosopher of contradiction could bear no contradiction.'[48] Nor could he usually bear even to remain in the company of those who had contradicted him. His rages were massive, his rebukes formidable, and his hate, once he thought it justified, was notably thorough.[49] His criticism, furthermore, easily lapsed into sneering and invective.[50]

Hegel's very manner of speech was an index of something difficult and complicated in his nature. Briefly, 'His speech-organ was not favourable to speaking.'[51] This became evident when he was a student of theology.[52] Before he was called to his post at the University of Berlin, the Prussian Minister of Interior, who was apparently responsible for the appointment, inquired anxiously if his lecturing was still 'obscure, muddled, nervous, and confused.'[53] A contemporary trying to explain what was so troublesome in Hegel's speech said that he must in a sense have thought in nouns, that is to say, that when he considered a subject, the relationships appeared to him as if they were figures engaged in mutual activity, which he then had to translate into words.[54] Although Hegel gesticulated a good deal, his gesticulations and the changes in his voice did not seem in harmony with what he was saying. He seemed to be trying to express too much at once; and this effort increased as he grew older and his thought more complex. Late in his life, even the draft of a letter would assume a complex, crossed-out, fragmented, written-around appearance.[55] Heine complains:

> To be honest, I rarely understood him, and it was only through subsequent reflection that I attained an understanding of his words. I believe he really did not want to be understood: hence his delivery so full of clauses . . . Altogether, Hegel's conversation was always a kind of monologue, sighed forth by fits and starts in a toneless voice. The baroqueness of his expressions often startled me, and I remember many of them.[56]

The most insightful and eloquent description of Hegel lecturing is given by his follower, H. G. Hotho. I am sorry I can quote only part of it.

Hotho says:

> Exhausted, morose, he sat there as if collapsed into himself, his head bent down, and while speaking kept turning pages and searching in his long folio notebooks, forward and back, high and low. His constant clearing of his throat and coughing interrupted any flow of speech. Every word, every syllable detached itself only reluctantly to receive a strangely thorough emphasis from the metallic-empty voice with its broad Swabian dialect, as if each were the most important . . . Slowly and deliberately, making use of seemingly insignificant links, some full thought had limited itself to the point of one-sidedness, had split itself into distinctions and involved itself in contradictions whose victorious solution eventually found strength to compel the reunification of the most recalcitrant elements.[57]

When we turn from the manner to the matter of Hegel's speech, we find, as Hotho has in effect been saying, its parallel or twin. We find, that is, a marvellously intricate intersection of conflicting impulses, a conflict that rises above itself in, so to speak, employing, governing, and criticizing itself. The idea of destruction arises in it everywhere, but it is everywhere constructive, for it always culminates in construction; this construction, it is true, yields again to destruction; but the whole process, which is constructive, contains destruction as no more than one of its necessary elements. Negative is positive. Even the self-consciousness 'torn to distraction in its inmost being,' which is no more than the 'inner perversion of itself,' and no more than 'consciousness gone crazy,' has, in *being* unreal, a kind of reality, that is, a constructive outcome.[58] I will not try to say what this constructive outcome is, but confine myself to repeating what Hegel declared toward the beginning of his philosophical career, namely, that '*Entzweiung*,' meaning both 'bifurcation' (or 'dichotomy') and 'discord,' 'is *the source of the need for philosophy*,' because life 'forms itself through eternal opposing.'[59]

The idea that negative is positive, or, rather, that the negative is essentially contained in the positive is essential to Hegel's characterization of philosophy. Philosophy, he says,

> is the process that generates and runs through its moments, and the whole movement constitutes the positive and its truth. This truth . . . includes the negative as well—that which might be called the false if it could be considered as something from which one should abstract. The evanescent must, however, be considered essential. . . . The appearance is the coming to be and passing away that itself does not come to be or pass away; it is in itself and constitutes the actuality and movement of the life of truth. The true is thus the bacchanalian whirl in which no member is not drunken; and because each, as soon as it detaches itself, dissolves immediately—the whirl is just as much transparent and simple repose.[60]

To this characterization, which stresses the dynamic union of the negative and the positive, the evanescent and the permanent, I would like to add a nuance from a different text, in which Hegel asserts that there is 'a philosophy which is neither scepticism nor dogmatism . . . that is, therefore, both at once.'[61]

Negative and positive, evanescent and permanent, sceptical and dogmatic, each alone and both and all together. If I try to reword Hegel's meaning in a psychological vocabulary, my translation runs, 'Philosophy is a formalized, hungry, and omnivorous ambivalence.' It is formalized because Hegel had assimilated the cautions of discipline so thoroughly. He had needed or accepted discipline quickly and completely enough to have become old, as the other students saw, by the age of fifteen. In the process of this premature ageing, Hegel set out to placate himself and the world by self-mastery, and, as well, to ward off emotional threats by grasping and arranging every detail of every kind in the world. This grasping and arranging can never be completed, and so Hegel's philosophy, always needing more details and more generalizations within which to order them, is always hungry. Why so hungry, I do not know; but he, like his sister, was a devourer of knowledge. All his appetites seem to have turned into a single intellectual omnivorousness. To become single, however, this omnivorousness had to contain, not only details and generalizations, but all of Hegel's ambivalence, for it was 'neither scepticism nor dogmatism,' but 'both at once.' And it was both because he was thwarting vital impulses, and because the task he had set himself was depressingly difficult. Especially during adolescence, he felt the threat of the unintegrated detail, which is to say, the temptation that might distract him from his attempt to master and unify the world and himself. He also felt threatened by the indefinite or unformed, which I take to be the depressive mood that might at once engulf discipline, ambition, and self-approval.

It should be understood that Hegel took the indefinite or unformed to be something very powerful, of the nature of substance, and, as such, abstract, undifferentiated, and possibly destructive. Why destructive? Because substance, according to Hegel, was closely related to night, and night was a whole array of darkly primal possibilities. As the dark chaos in which possibilities took on body, night was the mother womb, where the creative mystery of birth took place. As the dark, fearful abyss, it was the disarray and disintegration of things. And it was also isolation in the Hegelian sense of natural innerness, of Self as pure, that is, as absolute self-centredness. This night-isolation, he thought, was related to and quite as evil as discreteness, the desire or ability to see or care for only the single thing and so to exist in isolation.

In using this metaphor of night along with its attendant metaphors of dark chaos, mother womb, and fearful abyss, which of course echoed the Romantic literature of his times, Hegel was exhibiting both his repulsion and attraction by what *he* took to be the matrix of existence and *we* may take to be, as well, his unclearly perceived, still unregulated desires. I think that there is a passage in which Hegel lets the cat out of his night metaphor. In this passage, using his customary abstractions, he speaks of night as the 'empty nothing' that includes in its simplicity an endless realm of representations, and he speaks of it as the innerness of nature and as pure self. Then he says, 'One catches sight of this night when one looks people into the eye—into a night that becomes *fearful*. . . .'[62] There is something in the night that Hegel perceives to be his loneliness, shyness, and distance from unknown persons and dangerous passions. He mates this fear and depth, which he considers feminine, with the brightness of day, which is, to him, clear but powerless exteriorization. Truth or reality is then the union of both, the light penetrated by the darkness and so made substantial, given materiality. The potent, chaotic, creative, dark mother is contrasted and paired with the impotent, clear, external day.[63] One wonders if this contrasted pair is only a Romantic metaphor, or if it says anything about Hegel himself in relation to his mother and father. As will be seen, Schopenhauer, whose relationship with his parents was different, contrasted the mother-principle, intelligence, which he took to be superficial, with the father-principle, character, which he took to be deep. It is amusing to speculate that Hegel, by inventing a philosophy in which thesis and antithesis were always included in and superseded by synthesis, was in effect giving himself and other children the victory over their parents. Philosophy has more than one use.

Hegel coveted everything at once. He refused to surrender to distracting temptations, but he refused, as well, to surrender the temptations. As best he could, he joined detail and generalization, the ephemeral and permanent, the moving and still, the dark and bright, the angry and conciliatory. They all, and in all times, past, present, and future, had to become a single, essentially timeless structure, the interpenetrating clarity of which at once marked its truth and allowed him to be its master. Was this the end one could attribute to an infinitely romantic, infinitely bureaucratic god who created the world in compulsive detail in order to feel at once identical with his creation and superior to it? Or was it the end one could attribute to a god of hyphenation who was sceptical-believing, bound-free, and everything else opposite and joined?

I am not myself god enough to know, nor do I want to substitute my metaphors for the reality of Hegel and his thought. I therefore turn, as usual at this stage of my accounts, to women, marriage, and children. I have already told of Hegel's illegitimate son, who was born in 1807. As time passed, Hegel seemed destined, like so many preceding philosophers, to bachelorhood—by a German reckoning I have read, Fichte was the first of the 'world-historical philosophers' to marry. But in 1811, a little after his forty-first birthday, Hegel married Marie von Tucher, who was about twenty years younger than he. Christiane, whose later jealousy I have described, was overjoyed.[64] The marriage turned out to be eminently satisfactory to both husband and wife, for she revered him, and he presided over both her and the household with meticulous devotion. Unfortunately, Hegel's illegitimate son, who is described as alert and attractive, had no great share in the familial happiness. There is a story that his mother appeared at Hegel's wedding bearing Hegel's written promise to marry her, and that she behaved there in the most vulgar way, so that she had to be appeased and indemnified. When Ludwig, at the age of ten, joined the Hegel family, it included two other boys, one of four and the other of three. In a letter written much later, at the age of eighteen, Ludwig complained that his hopes had been badly disappointed, and that his stepmother had favoured her own sons. He said, 'I always lived in fear, without loving my parents—a relationship that had to produce a constant tension.' Although he had set his heart on medicine, Hegel insisted that he work for a businessman, and when he refused, Hegel stopped supporting him. 'I will no longer call him father,' wrote Ludwig, complaining that Hegel had not even troubled to take his leave of him by means of a direct letter. Before Ludwig went off as a soldier to Batavia, where he soon died of a fever, he wrote to his sister's foster-father asking for 'information about the final circumstances of my dear mother, about the final circumstances of her death, and her relation to Herr Hegel . . . I am in such uncertainty about all this,' he added, 'yet these are things that are very close to me.'[65] He was the kind of detail that could not be reasoned or coerced into integration.

Schopenhauer

12. Arthur Schopenhauer, born in 1788. Much of his early life was spent on his parents' country estate, with its flowers, fruit trees, horses, dogs, and (his mother tells us) eight snow-white lambs, each wearing an English bell.[1] The whole picturesque surroundings of Danzig, including the harbour, the two lighthouses, and the open sea were visible from the estate. We have no way of knowing just how Schopenhauer experienced his early childhood, but his mother gives the assurance that, day and night, she hardly had any thought other than for Arthur. Like all young

mothers, she says, she was 'firmly convinced that no more handsome, pious, and intelligent child lived on God's earth.'[2] But paradise though the country estate may have been, an imminent Prussian invasion frightened Schopenhauer's parents, who fled to Hamburg, where they settled.[3] Reflecting unhappily on this event, Schopenhauer once wrote, 'So, in tender childhood—I was then in my fifth year—I already became homeless; and since then I have never acquired a home.'[4]

Many years afterward, Schopenhauer, then a doctoral candidate, described his parents in the following words:

> My father was Heinrich Floris Schopenhauer; my still living mother, known for the series of her writings, was born Johanna Henrietta Trosiener . . . My excellent father was a well-to-do merchant and a royal Polish *Hofrat*, though he never allowed himself to be called by the title. He was a severe, hot-tempered man, but of faultless integrity, rectitude, and inviolable fidelity, and gifted, as well, with outstanding insight into business. How much I owe him, I can hardly express in words, for even if the career he decided to open to me as, in his eyes, the best, was not suited to my nature, I can give thanks to that man alone for an early introduction to useful knowledge, and then for the freedom, the leisure, and all the resources for the pursuit of the goal for which alone I was born, a scholar's education. . . .

Out of thankfulness, said Schopenhauer, he would always cherish and hallow 'the memory of these inexpressible merits and kindnesses of the best of fathers.'[5]

Schopenhauer particularly valued the financial and therefore intellectual independence that his father's inheritance gave him. He could philosophize, he said, without being forced to beg or demean or betray himself, only thanks to his father. 'That I could live the truth,' he wrote in tribute to him, 'without becoming its martyr, I owe to you. . . . Everyone afforded pleasure and instruction by my enterprise should know that it could as little have been accomplished without you as without me, and your name must become known as far as mine is able to carry it; for this is all I can do to repay you for your great benefactions.'[6]

Schopenhauer's reference to the career wrongly chosen for him recalls the father's ambition that his only son inherit his business, while the reference to an early introduction to useful knowledge recalls the father's ambition that his son become a man of the world. For the sake of the latter ambition, it seemed important to the father that Schopenhauer learn French. He therefore took Schopenhauer, who was nine years old at the time, on a trip to France and England, at the end of which, to make him as French as possible, he left him in Le Havre with a business acquaintance. This acquaintance, as Schopenhauer remembered him, was 'a dear, good, gentle man,' who had him brought up with his own son of the same age.[7] The time spent in this man's home, Schopenhauer said, was 'by far the happiest' of his childhood.[8] Such a remark makes it appear that Schopenhauer had not been particularly happy with his own parents. A possible reason is that his parents may not have been very happy with one another, for his mother, who was almost twenty years younger than his father, is said to have respected rather than loved him. Or maybe it was the stability of a good home from which one did not move too much that appealed to Schopenhauer.

When Schopenhauer, then twelve, returned home, his father was delighted by his ability to speak French. For the next few years, Schopenhauer studied in a private school, run by a Dr. Runge, which had strong Pietistic leanings. Happy in this school, Schopenhauer developed a strong desire to become a scholar. This desire conflicted, of course, with his father's ambition; but his own stubbornness and Dr. Runge's urgings finally swayed the father to suggest a choice: either Schopenhauer enter the Gymnasium immediately and continue with his formal studies, especially Latin, or he go with his parents on a long pleasure tour of Europe. If he chose the tour and, with it, learning from 'the book of the world,' he would have to promise to make his career in business. Schopenhauer chose the latter alternative, and for two years, during the ages of sixteen and seventeen, travelled in England, Scotland, Holland, Belgium, and France. He thought that these travels taught him a good deal.[9] Sensitized, it may be, by his Pietistic education, he was particularly struck by the wretchedness of the poor.

On his return to Hamburg, Schopenhauer fulfilled his promise and became a clerk in the firm of a respected merchant. But his whole nature protested this unwelcome occupation. He neglected his duties and thought only how to gain time to read at home or, at the least, to devote to his thoughts and fantasies. With no way out of his predicament, he hid books under the counter and read them when no one was watching. He was seventeen and miserable. Then, suddenly, in April, his father was found lying dead in a canal. The members of the family assumed that he had committed suicide. The blow to Schopenhauer was terrible. As he remembered it:

> In the midst of this unhappiness, there soon came the terrible blow of fate: my best beloved father was torn away from me by the sudden chance occurrence of a cruel death. As a result of this tragic event, my mind grew increasingly gloomy, to a point not far from true melancholia.[10]

Long after the event, the father's death, a great turning point in Schopenhauer's life, was reflected in the *World as Will and Representation*, where Schopenhauer, generalizing from himself to mankind, wrote that a mourner weeps over the fate of the deceased, but weeps all the same over the lot of mankind, in which his own is contained. This is the more true, he wrote,

> the more closely he was related to the deceased, and most of all therefore when the deceased was his father. Although to this father life was a misery through age and sickness, and though this helplessness is a heavy burden to the son, the son nevertheless weeps bitterly over the death of his father for the reason stated.[11]

Remembering the sequel to his father's death, Schopenhauer said:

> Although I was already, so to speak, my own master, and my mother in no way stood in my path, I continued to attend to my post with the merchant, in part because the excessive pain had shattered my resolution, in part because, immediately after my father's death, I made it a matter of conscience to carry out my father's decisions, finally because I believed I was already too advanced in age to be able to learn the ancient languages.[12]

Schopenhauer spent almost two years in miserable spirits. His mother had moved to Weimar, where she presided over a fashionable salon that Goethe himself favoured. Hearing from her son how unhappy he was, she consulted a learned young friend, who wrote to Schopenhauer to give up his job and turn immediately to the study of Latin and Greek. When Schopenhauer received the letter of advice, he broke into loud, happy crying. Given his mother's blessing, he felt released from the promise to his father and filled with pleasurable anticipation.[13] He was just nineteen, and in a rush to get ahead.

While Schopenhauer was making up the secondary school studies he had missed, he began to try his hand at verse composition. Unluckily for him, a teacher at whom he had directed some satirical verses was outraged, with the result that another teacher, on whose private lessons Schopenhauer depended, refused to go on coaching him. Hearing of the difficulty, Schopenhauer's mother wrote him a long adminishing letter, which could not have added to his happiness. He had to change, she said. Not that he was evil, spiritless, or uncultured. On the contrary, he had everything that might make him an ornament of human society. However, he was unbearable to live with.

> All your good qualities are obscured and made useless to the world by your over-cleverness, solely because you cannot control the rage to know every-thing better, to find fault everywhere but in yourself, to improve and rule in everything. This exasperates the people around you, no one wants to be improved and enlightened by force in this way, least of all by so unimportant an individual as you still are. No one can bear being reproached by you, who yourself have so many weaknesses, and least of all in the overbearing

manner that, suspecting no objections, announces in oracular tones: this is
the way things are.[14]

On the advice of friends, Schopenhauer's mother suggested that he
either transfer to a Gymnasium elsewhere or return to Weimar and take
private lessons with a Greek scholar there. After he had decided to return
to Weimar, she wrote to him in another long admonishing letter:

> Do not doubt that I truly love you. I have proved it to you all my life. It is
> necessary to my happiness to know that you are happy, but not to be a
> witness to that happiness. I have always told you that it would be very hard
> to live with you, and the more closely I watch you, the more this difficulty
> seems to me to grow, at least for myself. I do not conceal from you that so
> long as you are as you are, I would make any sacrifice rather than agree to
> live with you . . . Your ill humour oppresses me and is out of tune with my
> cheerful disposition, which is anyway of no use to you. Look, dear Arthur,
> you came to visit me for only days and each time there were violent scenes
> over nothing and nothing again, and each time I first breathed freely when
> you were away, because your presence, your complaints over unavoidable
> matters, your somber face, your bizarre opinions, which you pronounce like
> the judgments of an oracle, with no objections allowed, oppress me . . .
> When you will be older, dear Arthur, and see things more clearly, we will
> agree better with one another, and perhaps I will then spend my best days in
> your house with your children, as befits an old grandmother. Until then let
> us try to see that the thousand little teasing remarks should not embitter our
> minds and drive love out of them . . . You may eat with me on my social
> evenings if you will refrain from disagreeable disputation, which annoys me,
> as well as from all lamentation over the stupid world and human misery
> because this always gives me a bad night and bad dreams and I like to sleep
> well.[15]

When Schopenhauer turned twenty-one, his mother gave him his
share of the father's inheritance, and this fortune, to which a sum inherited from an uncle was later added, made it possible for him to live on
his income in comfort. He decided to go to the University of Göttingen,
where he studied medicine for a year, after which he switched to
philosophy. When told that philosophy was not a practical subject, he
answered, 'Life is a difficult business. I have continued to try to reflect on
it.'[16] He had long ago learned to play the flute (against his mother's but
not father's will), and now he added guitar playing to fluting.[17] On the
advice of his philosophy teacher, he studied Kant and Plato with particular attention. In them he found the mainstays of his thought; and when he
later added the Upanishads and Buddha, the obviously great influences
on his thought were complete. As was then the custom, he changed
universities, and he took up philosophy and the sciences at the University

of Berlin. Fichte, whom he heard there, displeased him. The physics, physiology, anatomy and the like that he studied fitted in well with an old passion to understand the nature of life.[18] By 1813, when he was twenty-five, he had written his doctoral thesis, *The Fourfold Root of the Principle of Sufficient Reason*, and received his doctorate. The name of the thesis inspired the mother to ask if it was something for druggists. To this he answered that it would still be read when her works had disappeared, to which answer she quipped that the whole edition of his book would still be available then.[19]

A word is in place here on Schopenhauer's mother. Some of her acquaintances regarded her as self-centred and as making a particular affectation of her learning. Her father, like her husband, had been an intelligent, enterprising businessman and, like him, subject to fits of violent anger. It seems that she may have been attracted to violent emotion, especially anger, and, attracted or not, to have shielded herself against it by means of cheerfulness and intellectuality. The letter to her son cited above therefore emphasizes how important it is to her not to have her good humour disturbed. The intellectual or at least literary rivalry that sprang up between Schopenhauer and herself was in effect an attempt by him to excel her on her own grounds. She was correspondingly annoyed by his intellectual arrogance and belittled his thesis (to which Goethe later gave conspicuous praise). Schopenhauer's intellectual response to the whole situation was to consider women to be both intellectual and shallow, and to spurn the intellect, at least in philosophical theory, in favour of the will.[20]

Schopenhauer's philosophy was still, however, to be developed. To return to the relations between mother and son, which made them now unconcealed rivals, Schopenhauer went back to Weimar and his mother's home. Their antagonism became only the stronger. He was sure that she was wasting the money his father had earned. He had already accused her of not having loved the father and of not honouring his memory.[21] The latter accusation was greatly intensified by the evidence that she had become the mistress of her tenant, a poet and minor government official (who, on the mother's urging, later proposed to her daughter, Schopenhauer's sister). Schopenhauer is also said to have accused her of responsibility for the father's suicide.[22] It is to her that he must be referring in an essay when he writes that it is foolish to let a mother administer her children's share of the father's inheritance.

> In most cases, such a woman will squander on her paramour all that the father of the children has earned out of consideration for them by the labour and industry of his whole life. It will be all the same whether or not she

marries the man . . . After the death of her husband, the actual mother often
becomes a stepmother . . . But generally a wife who has not been fond of her
husband will not have any affection for the children she has had by him, that
is to say, after the maternal love has passed which is merely instinctive and is
therefore not to be credited to her moral qualities.[23]

Whatever the exact accusations, Schopenhauer left Weimar in May of
1814 and appears never to have seen his mother thereafter, although she
was to remain alive for twenty-four more years.[24] Only in 1831, when he
was in a state of particular loneliness, did he resume correspondence with
his family, first with his sister, who was overjoyed, and then with his
mother.[25]*

The brief account I have given of Schopenhauer's early life, with its
ominous over- and undertones, should prepare one to learn that he was
inwardly lonely and pathologically anxious. His friend, disciple, and
biographer, Wilhelm von Gwinner, from whom I have taken almost all
the biographical facts I have recounted, summed up Schopenhauer's life
in the rhetorical question, 'Did he not go through his whole life hurt like
a child that has been angered at play—lonely and misunderstood, true
only to himself?'[26] Like Kant, to whom he felt such philosophic closeness,
Schopenhauer could repeat and accept the misanthropic words, 'Homo
homini lupus.'[27] We are told that 'in his maturity he held almost any
contact with people to be a contamination, a defilement.'[28] In a posthumous note he explained that as soon as he had begun to think, he had found
himself at variance with life. In youth, this variance had troubled him, he
wrote, because he had thought that the majority would prove to be right;
but by the age of fourteen, he had come to see that it was perhaps he who
was in the right. However, the world had become empty and desolate for
him.

Throughout my whole life I felt myself terribly lonely and always sighed
deeply, 'Now give me a human being!' In vain. I remained lonely. But I can
honestly say that it was not my fault. I turned no one away, fled no one who
was human in mind and heart. I found nothing but miserable wretches,
narrow minds, base hearts, and dull wits; except for Goethe, Fernow,
perhaps F. A. Wolf and a few others, who were all twenty-five to forty years
older than I was. Therefore my indignation at individuals gradually gave

*In her will, dated 1823, Johanna Schopenhauer disinherits her son. She writes in the will,
'This disinheritance is justified on my part by the conduct of my son since 1881, which has
been too terrible for me to repeat here in writing. Letters still kept among my papers verify
this conduct, which is the cause of the silent grief that has gnawed at my life since that time.'
H. H. Houben Damals in Wwimar! Errinerungen und Briefe von und an Johanna Schopenhauer, p.
253.

way to a quiet contempt for the whole of mankind. I early became conscious of the difference between myself and others; but I thought: first get to know a hundred, and you will find your man; then—you will find him among a thousand; at length—he must come, if only among many thousands. Finally I came to realize that nature is infinitely parsimonious, and that I had to bear (Byron) the 'solitude of kings' with dignity and patience.[29]

Schopenhauer's loneliness divided him even from his sister, Adele, even during the years, preceding his break with his mother, when they were corresponding. Adele Schopenhauer is represented as talented and intelligent, though not attractive. We hear that she suffered greatly from unpleasant family scenes. Schopenhauer regarded her (rather as Hegel regarded *his* sister) as the only woman he had loved without sensuality. In her diaries she wrote, 'A glimpse of what love could have given him, of what it could have made him, a look into the past and the future destroyed my cheerfulness; longing and grief raged violently in my soul.'[30] In letters to her brother she complained that he did not understand her. 'It hurts me,' she said, 'when I perceive how you still lack all the master keys to my being, how you always, so to speak, let them fall from the hand in which I lay them.'[31]

Schopenhauer's life was pervaded, not simply by loneliness, but also by anxiety. Assuming that his temperament was inherited, his mother reminded him of his father's 'strong inclination to melancholic brooding.'[32] At every age, anxiety was likely to assail him. We find it, for example, in a poem, written at the age of twenty, in which he says, 'In the midst of a stormy night/ I awoke in great anxiety,/ Heard it raging and heard it storming/ Through yards, halls, and by the towers/ . . . Great fear seized me,/ Felt so lost, so alone and forsaken;/ How distant was yesterday/ With its air and its splendour.'[33]

Some idea of the variety and persistence of Schopenhauer's fear is given by an account that his biographer, Gwinner, may well have copied down verbatim, merely changing Schopenhauer's 'I' to the third person and perhaps adding a word here and there:[34]

From his father he inherited the dread, verging on mania, that he himself cursed and against which he expended all the force of his will. It sometimes attacked him on the most insignificant occasions with such power that he could see before him only the possibility of a hardly imaginable misfortune. A fruitful imagination sometimes heightened this disposition unbelievably. Already as a six-year-old, he was found by his parents, when they returned home one evening, in the greatest despair, because he fancied himself abandoned by them forever. As a youngster, he was troubled by imaginary illnesses and quarrels. While studying in Berlin, he for a while thought himself consumptive. At the outbreak of the war, he became convinced that he would be impressed into war service. The dread of smallpox drove him from Naples, of cholera, from Berlin. In Verona he was seized by the idée fixe that he had taken poisoned snuff. When, in 1833, he was about to leave Mannheim, an inexpressible feeling of dread overcame him without any external cause. For years he was persecuted by fear of criminal proceedings, fear of the loss of his property, and fear that his own mother would contest his share of the inheritance. If any noise was heard at night, he got out of bed and reached for sword and pistol, which he kept permanently loaded. Even without any especial provocation, he was preoccupied with continual anxiety, which led him to search for and see dangers where there were none. The anxiety intensified the slightest annoyance endlessly and made intercourse with people altogether difficult.[35]

Impressive as this catalogue may be, it is far from exhaustive, for Schopenhauer took precaution after precaution to allay his anxiety. He hid his valuables so thoroughly that the Latin instructions in his will hardly sufficed to reveal some of them. He took to keeping his account book in English, a language he must have thought foreign to the unduly inquisitive or simply thievish, while, in a crescendo of caution, he wrote his important business notes in Latin or Greek. To further mislead thieves, Schopenhauer labelled his possessions misleadingly, his securities, for example, *Arcana medica*. To avoid drinking infected water, he always carried a leather water-flask with him. As an additional precaution, he would lock away the stem and bowl of his pipe after each time he had smoked it. He would never entrust himself to a barber's razor. Troubled by the danger of premature burial, he gave instructions that if he appeared to die, his presumed corpse should be kept in an open coffin until his death was beyond all doubt.[36]

It should be added that Schopenhauer, like Kant, was not only extraordinarily careful of his health, but, like him, proud of his success in maintaining it. I will add no details, except that he took particular care of his eyes, which he accounted the most valuable of the sense organs, bathing them while open so as to strengthen their nerves.[37]

Schopenhauer's deep interest in both suicide and insanity was provoked, I suppose, by the manner of his father's death. The metaphysical position Schopenhauer took made suicide a crucial issue, for he in effect advocated it, though he took care to distinguish the benign type he favoured from the violent one.[38] Finding life, at least theoretically, too onerous to bear, he was ready to praise any man who refused to have anything to do with the conception of children; and he was even ready, strangely, to praise the intelligence of a child that decided, so to speak, to be born dead. He himself, he explained, had avoided marriage out of pity for the son he might have had.[39]

As I have intimated, insanity may have particularly interested Schopenhauer because he supposed his father to have been its victim. It appears that in the period before his presumed suicide, his father had been growing increasingly deaf and increasingly sensitive and violent. His conduct already grown eccentric, it became more obviously so when affected by strange lapses of memory.[40] Schopenhauer, who came to make frequent visits, he reports, to insane asylums, theorized that insanity was a kind of lapsing of memory.[41] According to his explanation, violent mental suffering

> becomes insufferably great only in so far as it is a lasting pain, but as such it is only a thought, and therefore resides in the *memory*. Now if such a sorrow, such painful knowledge or reflection, is so harrowing that it becomes positively unbearable, and the individual is in danger of succumbing to it, then nature, alarmed in this way, seizes on *madness* as the last means of saving life. The mind, tormented so greatly, destroys, as it were, the thread of its memory, fills up the gap with fictions, and thus seeks refuge in madness from the mental suffering that exceeds its strength, just as a limb affected by mortification is cut off and replaced by a wooden one.[42]*

It is on the whole easy to see the basic influences of Schopenhauer's life on his philosophy. These include, first, his distinction between intellect or intelligence and will; second, his stress on sexuality as the ultimate human drive; third, his metaphysics of music; fourth, his doctrine of genius; and fifth, his appreciation of death. Let me take up these influences briefly one by one.

First, then, intellect and will. To Schopenhauer, the intellect, considered as a metaphysical element, is adventitious or secondary, although of obvious practical importance. According to him, the son inherits his intellect from the mother. This holds true even though women, because generally weaker, do not exhibit intellect to the degree to which favourable circumstances allow it to develop in the son. Instances in which men seem to inherit their father's mental gifts are merely accidental.[43]

In contrast to the intellect, the will, says Schopenhauer, is 'the true inner being, the kernel, the radical element in man.' It should therefore be assumed, as experience in fact confirms, that 'man inherits his moral nature, his character, his inclinations, his heart, from the father.'[44] The

---

*Though incomplete as a theory, Schopenhauer's analysis of the cause of insanity seems to me really insightful. He has in fact been called the father of depth psychology, whether of Freud or of Jung. His distinction between will and intellect resembles that between id and ego. Like Freud, he postulates a life-drive and a death-drive, the latter of which, again like Freud, he considers to be 'the true end of life.' See A. Hübscher, *Denker gegen den Strom*, pp. 271–72.

relation between father and son, Schopenhauer believes, is closer than
that between son and mother.

> Between father and son there exists actual identity of being, which is the
> will, but between mother and son there exists mere identity of the intelli-
> gence, and even this subject to certain conditions. Between mother and son
> there can exist the greatest moral contrast, between father and son only an
> intellectual.[45]

Schopenhauer finds additional confirmation that the moral inheritance is
from the father in examples such as those of Orestes and Hamlet. Therefore, he says, 'the son appears as the moral representative and avenger of
the father,' while it would be revolting and absurd for him to appear as
the opposite, the moral representative and avenger of the mother. To the
objection that some children show no sign of having inherited their
father's character, Schopenhauer answers briefly that paternity is uncertain. It is also possible, he says, that an apparently unpaternal character is
created because, not the will, but the motives that set the will in motion
are inherited from the mother's intellect.[46]

Schopenhauer's text demonstrates that he tries to support his view by
means of empirical examples; but these are clearly selected to support
what he in any case believes in. It is hardly necessary to add that his view
is an almost comically exact projection of his attitude toward his own
mother and father, whom he used as living proof that he was right.[47] Of
course, it has not been unusual for mothers to be concerned with a son's
education and fathers with his profession, in some rough correspondence
with Schopenhauer's doctrine; but it seems particularly false to contend,
as he does, that the character is unaffected, except superficially, by the
mother. There is surely no law, metaphysical or genetic, that even suggests that intellect is inherited from the mother and will from the father.
Nothing, I am afraid, stands behind it but Schopenhauer's personal
experience abetted, perhaps, by certain Romantic commonplaces that he
was under no philosophical compulsion to adopt.

Schopenhauer's stress on sexuality has a more plausible biological
basis. Speaking biologically, it is not hard to maintain that sexuality is
'the ultimate goal of almost all human effort.' But Schopenhauer is
interested in displaying sexuality in an unfavourable light, and he therefore continues, 'It has an unfavourable influence on the most important
affairs, interrupts every hour the most serious occupations, and sometimes perplexes even the greatest minds . . . Every day it brews and
hatches the most perplexing quarrels and disputes, destroys the most
valuable relationships, and breaks the strongest bonds.'[48] Schopenhauer
says in his determinedly biological way, 'The genitals are the real *focus* of

the will, and are therefore at the opposite pole to the brain, the representative of knowledge, i.e. to the other side of the world, the world of representation. The genitals are the life-saving principle assuring to time endless life.'[49]

To put this stress on sexuality into the context of Schopenhauer's personal life, it must be recalled that his sexual drive was strong, he says, even in childhood. His sexuality caused him endless suffering. He experienced it as an immediate misfortune, the effect of which he tried to lighten by occupying himself with business, reading, the theatre, flute-playing, long walks, and sailing. All the same, he would fall prey to temptation and react with disgust and depression. He was therefore happy when his sexual drive began to weaken.[50] His philosophy concentrates on recommending what he himself found so difficult, a life of abstinence.

Schopenhauer's metaphysics of music undoubtedly reflects his own experience. As he admitted, his theoretical knowledge of music was confined to a single handbook. His musical ideal was Rossini. He said, 'I admire and love Mozart and go to all concerts in which Beethoven's symphonies are played, but—when one has heard much Rossini, everything else is ponderous in contrast.' He railed against Wagner's music and called him 'a poet and no musician,' but his attitude to Wagner was more complex than appears on the surface, and in the end he may not have been so distant from him.[51] But whoever his favourites, music was essential to him all through his life. He would sit motionless and with eyes closed during the whole of a Beethoven symphony, then leave it the moment it ended, to avoid the dilution of the effect by the lesser music that followed.[52] It appears safe to assume that he would never have regarded music as exalting unless he had himself experienced it as such, experienced it as, in his description, a paradise familiar and yet remote, easy to grasp and yet inexplicable, with the ability to reproduce 'all the emotions of our inmost being, but entirely without reality and remote from all pain.'[53]

Schopenhauer's doctrine of genius is an expression of a doctrine that was and is still perhaps current. But his particular reading of the doctrine is influenced by the personal view that geniuses, whom he takes to possess knowledge freed from the demands of will, are animated to the point of disquiet. The reason is that the present 'does not fill their consciousness. This gives them that restless, zealous nature, that constant search for new objects of contemplation, and also that longing, hardly ever satisfied, for men of like nature and stature to whom they may open their hearts.'[54] Here Schopenhauer's essential loneliness again makes its appearance, as does his hot temper when he says, 'It is well known that we seldom find great genius united with preeminent reasonableness; on the contrary, men of genius are often subject to violent emotions and irrational passions,' not because the faculty of reason is weak, but because the will is vehement.[55] Schopenhauer himself is said to have held frequent loud monologues when he was out walking in the street, a habit that may explain why he insists that geniuses 'are inclined to soliloquies, and in general may exhibit several weaknesses that actually are closely akin to madness.'[56] To put this conception within the perspective of Schopenhauer's personal life, it should be recalled that he was certain, as will be seen, that he was a genius, the kind of man able to discard his personality and 'become *pure knowing subject*, the clear eye of the world.'[57]

How and to what extent Schopenhauer's attention became fixed on death we already know. It is death, he says, that 'is the real inspiring genius of philosophy. . . . Indeed without death there would hardly have been any philosophizing.'[58] I do not take exception to this statement, though it is hardly susceptible to proof, but think it true of Schopenhauer particularly in relation to his individual experience. His attraction to death as the cure of life and, in particular, of sexuality drew him to the solution he found in the Upanishads, in which death is seen, he says, as 'the painful untying of the knot that generation with sensual pleasure had tied.'[59] Man imagines that he lives in his own person alone. 'Death teaches him something better.'[60]

There is left, finally, the doctrine of the extinction or Nirvana that Schopenhauer advocated, especially for men such as himself, whose higher intellectual powers made them susceptible to much greater suffering, he thought, than ordinary men.[61] In men such as he, the will must learn something resembling its own self-extinction, which leads to the nothingness that our real world surely is.[62]

With the doctrine of Nirvana, I end my direct presentation of Schopenhauer's philosophical principles as his life influenced them. But I feel that I must say more on the subject of his ambivalence. Somewhere in his non-Nirvanic heart, I feel, Schopenhauer hated his father and loved his mother, or at least loved the childhood he had spent with her on the country estate while his father, busy in the city, was mostly away.[63] There is evidence of deep feeling against his father in an answer he gave to the question why he was so pessimistic. Schopenhauer said:

As a youth I was always very melancholic, and once—I may have been some eighteen years old—I thought to myself, though still so young: 'A god is supposed to have made this world? No, a devil, rather.' I had certainly by then had much to suffer in my upbringing, as a result of my father's severity.[64]

In this one remark, we suddenly perceive the devil, or one of the devils, to which Schopenhauer had been trying to become indifferent by detaching himself. His misanthropic detachment protected him much as his mother's determined cheerfulness had protected her from anger or depression.

It is significant that Schopenhauer speaks of early childhood as an ideal time, when the genital system is not yet active. He says:

> Just because the terrible activity of this system still slumbers, while that of the brain already has its briskness, childhood is the time of innocence and happiness, the paradise of life, the lost Eden, on which we look back longingly through the whole remaining course of our life. But the basis of that happiness is that in childhood our whole existence lies much more in knowing than in willing. This state or condition is also supported from the outside by the novelty of all objects. Thus in the morning sunshine of life, the world lies before us fresh, so magically gleaming, so attractive . . . Every child is to a certain extent a genius, and every genius to a certain extent a child. The relationship between the two shows itself primarily in the naivety and sublime ingenuousness that are a fundamental characteristic of true genius.[65]

The mother, then, if only the purely instinctive one that Schopenhauer has spoken of, must have her due place: without her there is no paradise or childish approximation of genius. I can suggest another possible clue to Schopenhauer's early relationship with his mother. In describing the country estate in which he spent his childhood, his mother mentions two tiny Spanish dogs.[66] It is just possible that Schopenhauer loved dogs because they recalled his early paradise to him, a paradise that was such because it had a presiding mother. The mature Schopenhauer's affection for dogs was remarkable. He kept portraits of them on his walls, and when his poodle, Atma, died in 1849, he mourned him profoundly. He said that the sight of every animal gave him direct gratification, 'dogs most of all, and then all free animals—birds, insects, and whatever they are.' The sight of people, on the contrary, he said, almost always aroused his 'decided repugnance.'[67] He is credited with the almost incredible sentence, 'If there were no dogs, I would not want to live.' The sentence is no less strange in its German form, 'Wenn es keine Hünde gäbe . . . möchte ich nicht leben.'[68] To him, animals hinted at paradise in their lack of both anxiety and hope, in their untroubled enjoyment of the present, and in their composure, which, in his words, can put 'our own frequently restless and discontented condition' to shame.[69]

There remains something to be said of Schopenhauer's attitute towards himself as a philosopher, toward other philosophers, and toward women. He believed that he had a particular biological fitness to be a philosopher. He believed, that is, that his short stature made it much easier for his heart to supply his brain with blood (which he took to be

extraordinarily hot in himself). In addition, as his very respectable
shoemaker reported, he believed that his big and therefore intelligent
head was matched with his small feet, and vice versa. He consequently
preferred his boots as short as possible, even if they pinched somewhat.[70]
He is said to have taken unalloyed pleasure in the growth of his fame, and
to have hoped to live quite long, to see with his own eyes the complete
downfall of professional philosophy, which he hated.[71] He wanted death
to bring him victory. 'That soon the worms will gnaw my bones,' he
wrote, 'is a thought that I can bear—but the philosophy professors my
philosophy!'[72] He was convinced that the future would show that all
previous philosophers had handled philosophical problems superficially
in comparison with himself. 'Thus mankind,' he said, 'has learned much
from me that will never be forgotten and my works will never sink into
oblivion.'[73]

In another statement that must be read to be believed, he showed how
impressed he had become by his own philosophical merits:

> Within the limits of human knowledge in general, my *philosophy* is the
> real solution of the riddle of the world. In this sense it can be called a
> *revelation*. As such, it is inspired by the spirit of *truth*—in the fourth book
> there are even some paragraphs that one might consider inspired by the
> Holy Ghost.

(For doubters, I repeat the last sentence in the language of the Writ
itself: 'Inspirirt ist solche vom Geiste der *Wahrheit*: sogar sind im vierten
Buche einige Paragraphen, die man als vom *heiligen* Geiste eingeben
könte.')[74]

Philosophers other than himself generally displeased Schopenhauer.
There were only three, he once said, who really merited the title:
Buddha, Plato, and Kant.[75] The other philosophers he had occasion to
speak of, he often subjected to abuse. Fichte, he called a charlatan, and his
philosophy, nonsensical.[76] Schelling, in whom he found some small
redeeming merit, reasoned extravagantly and absurdly, he said.[77] Rosenkranz (whom I have used extensively in my account of Hegel) was no
more than a miserable scoundrel ('ein erbärmlicher Lump') to him. But
he saved his choicest denigration for Hegel, whom he saw, to use
Hegelian terminology, as his antithesis. Hegelry, he said, mincing no
words, was 'devoid of truth, clearness, intelligence, and even of common
sense,' and lacked all the qualities that his own philosophy so brilliantly
exhibited.[78] He denied Hegel the title of thinker, philosopher, or even
sophist, though he was willing to concede to the German university-
pedants that he was a kind of artist, though of so low a grade that only his
disciple, Rosenkranz, could sink below it.[79] Summarizing the condition
of German philosophy in his time, he wrote, in his own English:

I will not mention the numberless monstrous and mad compositions which were called forth by Kant's works as 'the sun, being a god, breeds maggots kissing carrion'—but so much did by and by degenerate our German philosophy that we now see a mere swaggerer and charlatan, I mean Hegel, with a compound of bombastical nonsense and positions bordering on madness, humbug about a part of the German public, though but the more silly and untaught part, to be sure. . . . The more enlightened part of the learned public certainly take him for what he is, while this also holds no other philosopher in esteem but Kant, who alone therefore is universally read. . . .[80]

Although Schopenhauer's published denunciations do not appear inhibited, he kept a secret notebook in which he recorded subjective, meaning, especially complimentary and derogatory remarks (the latter made by him) about himself, as well as remarks on others 'too sharp and bitter' to be published during his lifetime. He seems to have told a few of his more intimate partisans that he wanted the notebook published after his death. It was destroyed, however, by his biographer and executor, Gwinner, on Schopenhauer's express wish, he insisted.[81]

Women fared no better than philosophers in Schopenhauer's opinion. He regarded them as childish, silly, and shortsighted, as 'a kind of intermediate stage between the child and the man, who is a human being in the real sense.'[82] Women, he maintained, were mentally myopic and able to see clearly only what was very close to them. He did not grant them even the virtue, if it is that, of beauty, for he saw them as the *'unaesthetic'* sex. 'Only the male intellect, clouded by the sexual impulse,' he charged, 'could call the undersized, narrow-shouldered, broad-hipped, and short-legged sex the fair sex.' Considering women's natural weapons to be dissimulation and lying, he accused them of influencing men to conceal natural reactions, to sham beliefs, to disavow ideas, to 'blush not to be vile enough,' and to express the paternal tenderness that assured the birth of still another child destined to be taught to lie. He stated that women had never created a single really great work of art, or any work of permanent value. To this he added that they had no genuine feeling, even in the sense of appreciation, for music, poetry, or the plastic arts.[83]

I do not know how Schopenhauer reconciled his sentiments on women with his early attraction to the actress, Karoline Jagemann, a woman, he told his mother, he would take home even if he found her breaking stones on the highway. Karoline Jagemann was the only woman, Schopenhauer's biographer tells us, who inspired the philosopher-to-be to write a love-poem that year.[84] In later life, when he was already a confirmed misogynist, he struck up a friendship with the young sculptress, Elisabeth Ney, whom he called 'very pretty' and 'indescribably charming.'[85] Her very presence made him cheerful, he said. He appreciated the bust she made of him, and was the more grateful when she modelled his faithful poodle as well. He explained to her that his vehemence against women was the result of his having had so detestable a mother.[86]

Schopenhauer was, to be sure, a willing or unwilling slave of women in some sense, for he did have affairs with them. In Italy, he relished 'not only beauty, but also beauties.'[87] Some of his affairs were serious, and, on his own admission, he several times considered marriage seriously.[88] For a while he agonized over a Venetian woman. Not long thereafter he acquired a mistress in Frankfurt, but when she became pregnant, he fled, leaving instructions with his sister to give the woman money. The little girl that was born died after a few months. Years later, in Berlin, the demi-mondaine, Caroline Medon or Meudon, became his mistress. He alternately quarrelled and made up with her, but he supported her for ten years, for, as he later admitted, he loved her very much. It is likely that she had a child by him. At any rate, she kept writing him for money, and he provided for her in his will. Despite the report that, to his satisfaction, his sexual impulse weakened in time, women remained sexually indispensable to him, and when one Frankfurt girl repulsed him as too old, he found himself a 'necessary' replacement. Once he did weaken enough to declare that if he had lived for the sake of his earthly life, he would have done well to marry; but as his life was ideal and intellectual, marriage had to be sacrificed. He assumed, that is, that 'the yoke of marriage' would have made it too difficult for him to have created his philosophy.[90] Urged in old age to marry for the sake of his comfort, he answered that his mother had failed to take care of his father. 'When my own father,' he recalled, 'was confined, ill and miserable, to his invalid's chair, he would have been abandoned had not an old servant performed so-called charitable duties for his sake. The lady, my mother, entertained company while he lay lonely, and amused herself while he suffered bitter pains. That is womanly love!'[91]

Schopenhauer argued that almost all the true philosophers, among whom he counted, for the purpose, Descartes, Leibniz, Spinoza, and Kant had not married. It may be assumed that Leibniz, whom he did not elsewhere rank so high, was allowed to enter this list in order to make Schopenhauer a better case.[92] The truth is that here, as elsewhere, Schopenhauer had a case to make, a loneliness to still, a fear to conquer, an appetite to slake, a father and mother to love and hate, a world to conquer, and a hard, bright ego to nullify or mollify in at least his philosophical ruminations.

8
Mill to Sartre

On Choosing These Philosophers

The present chapter, like the two previous ones, has no explicit argument. It is an exploration, this time of the lives and thought of Mill, Kierkegaard, James, Nietzsche, Santayana, Russell, Wittgenstein, and Sartre, eight philosophers in all. The choice of philosophers is distinctly more arbitrary than before. One reason is that convention is no longer as clear a guide to the great or 'great' philosophers. Not only is my choice rather personal, but it fits none of the national traditions. A German will immediately miss Fichte and Schelling at the end of the preceding or beginning of the present chapter, and, later on, Husserl, Heidegger, and perhaps Jaspers, not to speak of the plausible candidates between Schelling and Husserl. I am less sure who will be missed by a Frenchman, but perhaps Ravaisson and surely Comte and Bergson. The Englishman may miss Spencer or Bradley, or, closer to our own time, Moore. The American will miss Peirce, Dewey, and possibly Whitehead, who may be counted an English mathematician and philosopher of science, but an American metaphysician. Carnap, too, will be missed, primarily, I think, by the American. The Italian will no doubt miss Croce, and the Spaniard Unamuno and Ortega y Gasset. The Pole, to limit ourselves to the twentieth century, will miss Twardowski and the members of the Warsaw school. I begin to quail when I think of all these and of all the others whose names I have not even mentioned.

What should I have done? I might have tried to amalgamate the current standards of philosophical greatness, unclear as they are, of at least the Germans, French, and English and Americans, and composed a long and in the end, I am afraid, not very satisfactory list. But I have made it a rule to include philosophers only when the biographical evidence seems to me sufficient for my purpose, and only when I think I have a sufficient general grasp of their thought. Even apart from my own preferences, which must have made some difference, my rule has set severe limits on the philosophers I have been able to deal with in the present chapter. The group chosen therefore does not pretend to include all the great philosophers of the period, whatever the criteria for them, but simply important or interesting ones who can reasonably be subjected to the kind of analysis we are engaged in. Although some of them are conspicuously suitable for such analysis, I have not consciously chosen them to fit any position I hold; and I have been careful to include philosphers from different countries and of distinctly different philosophical types.

I have one final excuse. It is not this time that books must be limited to a practicable, publishable number of pages. This time, I must admit that accounts of twenty different philosophers, though they do not satiate my curiosity, begin to burden me with the sheer effort involved in writing them. I may not have worked long enough for the sake of the accounts themselves, but I have worked quite long enough for my own sake.

I postpone to the following chapter any attempt to generalize about the philosophers.

Mill

13. John Stuart Mill, born in 1806. His mother, Harriet, was then twenty-three.

> She was an exceedingly pretty woman; had a small fine figure, an aquiline nose (seen in her eldest son), and a pink and dun complexion. One letter of Mill's to her she preserved, as perhaps the fullest and strongest of all his affectionate outpourings. The depth and tenderness of the feeling could not well be exceeded; but, in the light of after years, we can see that he too readily took for granted that she would be an intellectual companion to himself. . . . As an admired beauty, she seems to have been chagrined at the discovery of her position after marriage.[1]

Although her good looks were accompanied by a good nature, James Mill soon fell out of love with her and did not trouble to conceal that he regarded her as stupid. As one of the children said, they lived 'as far apart, under the same roof, as the north pole from the south,' for while the husband was preoccupied with his intellectual concerns, she was preoccupied with housework.[2] A friend said that the son, John, appeared very devoted to her, though only deferential to his father.[3] A visitor described her in later years as 'a tall, handsome lady, sweet-tempered, with pleasant manners, fond of her children; but I think not much interested in what the elder ones and their father talked about.'[4]

James Mill, the father, was the son of a devout, prosperous village shoemaker and a servant girl. Despite the nature of the work she had done, she was a proud woman, determined that her son should rise in life. 'It was the fancy of those that knew her, that she was the source of her son's intellectual energy.' Her influence on him is apparent in his ambition to establish for himself 'that name in the world for wisdom and knowledge which was the darling object even of my infant years to think I should one day attain.'[5] Occupying himself with study, he neither helped his father nor worked in the fields.[6] With the help of a local patron, a baronet, he went to the University of Edinburgh, where he studied theology. But he was eking out a living as a journalist and newspaper editor when he made his fateful acquaintance with the philospher, Jeremy Bentham, whose Utilitarianism he accepted. He was a very diligent man, able to work twenty hours a day at his *History of India*, and he spent a good deal of effort in educating his children; but he was irritable at home.

> In his advancing years, as often happens, he courted the affection of the younger children, but their love for him was never wholly unmingled with fear, for, even in his most amiable moods, he was not to be trifled with. His entering the room where the family was assembled was observed by strangers to operate as an immediate damper. This was not the worst. The one really disagreeable trait in Mill's character, and the thing that has left the most painful memories, was the way he allowed himself to speak and behave to his wife and children before visitors.[7]

Generally considered an unfeeling man, he was convinced that he demonstrated love for his children by detecting and prohibiting rather than applauding their 'vices.'[8]

As Bentham's aide, amanuensis, and disciple, James Mill accepted the doctrine that all minds were much the same to begin with. Education, he thought, was a matter of controlling associations rightly. That is, if a child, especially in its critical earlier years, were exposed to the right sequence of pleasures and pains, and if it were taught to reason accurately, it would learn how to act unerringly for the sake of its own ultimate happiness.[9]

With the blessings of Bentham, who was hoping both for a demonstration of Utilitarian principles and for the assistant he so needed, James Mill set out to give his son a model education. At the age of three, therefore, John learned Greek and Arithmetic, at eight, Latin, algebra, and geometry, and, at twelve, logic and philosphy. Not everything went easily. When, at seven, he tried to read Plato's *Theaetetus* in Greek, he failed to understand anything of it; but he soon outstripped his father in mathematics and had to continue with the help of books alone.[10] To force him to exert his mind, his father insisted that he try to find out everything for himself before any explanations were offered. His education, says John, was one of strenuous, progressive understanding, not of mere cramming of the memory.[11] Yet John was convinced that, despite his phenomenal accomplishments, which gave him, he said, an advantage of a quarter of a century over his contemporaries, any average, healthy boy or girl could, given the same training, accomplish the same end.[12]

In his *Autobiography*, which he first drafted at the age of forty-seven, he expressed considerable resentment, toned down in the published version, against his mother and father.

> That rarity in England, a really warm hearted mother, would in the first place have made my father a totally different being, and in the second would have made the children grow up loving and being loved. But my mother with the very best intentions, only knew how to pass her life in drudging for them. Whatever she could do for them she did, and they liked her, because she was kind to them, but to make herself loved, looked up to, or even obeyed, required qualities which she unfortunately did not possess.[13]

As for his father, said Mill,

> He resembled most Englishmen in being ashamed of the signs of feeling, and, by the absence of demonstration, starving the feelings themselves. If we consider further that his temper was constitutionally irritable, it is impossible not to feel true pity for a father who did, and strove to do, so much for his children, yet who must have been constantly feeling that fear of him was drying it up at its source. This was no longer the case, later in life and with his younger children. They loved him tenderly: and if I cannot say so myself, I was always loyally devoted to him

In a suppressed passage, Mill said, more severely, 'Mine was not an education of love but of fear . . . My father's children neither loved him, nor, with any warmth of affection, any one else.'[14]

The results, Mill said, were unhappy. He was too afraid of his father to express himself frankly or spontaneously to him. He was also deprived of a will of his own. As he said, 'I was so much accustomed to expect to be told what to do, either in the form of direct command or of rebuke for not doing it, that I acquired a habit of leaving my responsibility as a moral agent to rest on my father, my conscience never speaking to me except by his voice.'[15]

Deprived of his own will, Mill was also physically slow and clumsy. 'I never could, nor can I now,' he said, 'do anything requiring even the smallest manual dexterity . . . I was continually acquiring odd or disagreeable tricks which I very slowly and imperfectly got rid of. I was, besides, utterly inobservant. . . .'[16] It does not take much psychological perspicuity to recognize that Mill was resisting his alert, decisive father. The acquisition of 'odd or disagreeable tricks' makes this conclusion practically unavoidable. Mill was also deficient in social abilities. For the sake of his education, he had been preserved from contact with children outside of the family; but when he was about fourteen, his father decided that he had to learn how to get along with other human beings, outside of the family circle, and he was therefore sent to live for a year with the Samuel Benthams in France. The visit was difficult for him, but for a whole year, as he wrote, he breathed a free and companionable atmosphere.[17] He was, however, eighteen, before he made his first intimate friend, John Roebuck, a student of law. Roebuck saw how learned and informed in politics he was, but also how ignorant of society and, above all, of women. 'He had never played with boys; in his life he had never known any. . . .'[18]

There was, of course, an emotional price to pay. At the age of twenty, Mill, the model product of a model education, suddenly entered a state of what he called 'dry heavy dejection.' He blamed the habit of analysis, which has a tendency, he said, to wear away the feelings. Vanity, ambition, benevolence, all seemed to have dried up within him. In his words, 'I was . . . left stranded at the commencement of my voyage, with a well equipped ship and rudder, but no sail; without any real desire for the ends which I had been so carefully fitted out to work for; no delight in virtue or the general good, but also just as little in anything else.'[19]

Mill's cure began with the reading of a passage in the memoirs of the French writer, Marmontel. In this passage, Marmontel, whose father had just died, told how he had felt and made his family feel that he, the son, could now be everything to them. Mill responded very emotionally.

> A vivid conception of the scene and its feelings came over me, and I was moved to tears. From this moment my burthen grew lighter. The oppression of the thought that all feeling was dead within me, was gone. I was no longer hopeless: I was not a stock or stone . . . I gradually found that the ordinary incidents of life could again give me pleasure. . . .[20]

His reaction surely depended on a fantasy of the death of his father; but the explicit lesson he learned from his depression was that the feelings must be cultivated no less than the intellect. He had loved music since childhood, though this love had repeatedly failed him during his depression. Now he discovered poetry, especially that of Wordsworth. He wrote:

> What made Wordsworth's poems a medicine for my state of mind was that they expressed, not mere outward beauty, but states of feeling, and of thought coloured by feeling, under the excitement of beauty . . . From them I seemed to learn what would be the perennial sources of happiness, when all the greater evils of life shall have been removed. And I felt myself at once better and happier as I came under their influence.[21]

The subject of his health continued to preoccupy Mill. His father's mother and brother had both died of tuberculosis, and his father, too, eventually died of it, at the age of fifty-four. It was also fatal to one of his brothers, Henry, while another, George, committed suicide to avoid suffering its final stages. Not unnaturally, Mill was convinced that it would kill him as well. His companion, later his wife, Harriet Taylor, whose relationship with him will immediately be described, was still another of its victims.

Mill's depression at the age of twenty, which helped to liberate him from his father and Bentham, was only one of a number. It was to such attacks he wrote to Carlyle, that he was indebted for his most valuable insights. A physical and apparently psychological breakdown kept him from visiting his dying father. In his letters, he complained a good deal about his health.[22]

When Mill was twenty-four, he fell in love with the beautiful, graceful, dark-eyed, low-voiced, emotional, and intellectual Harriet Taylor, a merchant's wife. Yet, of all her qualities, it was the poetry in her that excited him most, he said. She was ambitious to be a writer, and he advised and confided in her. After ups and downs in their relationship, an arrangement was worked out according to which he would stay with her when her husband was away and she with him during summer weekends. This arrangement, which defied public opinion, remained in force for almost twenty years, until her husband died. During this whole period, she and Mill remained on Platonic terms, it seems, committing 'no impropriety.' Some two years after the husband's death, they were married. They were very sensitive to criticism, open or implied, of their relationship, and Mill became an instant enemy of anyone who said an untoward word about it. This sensitivity caused him in time to break even with the members of his immediate family, except his mother, who pleaded helplessly for reconciliation.[23] His youngest sister complained in a letter to him of his 'evident dread lest any of your family should show the least affection for you.'[24]

After seven years of marriage to Mill, Harriet died. He had hardly reacted to the deaths of his father and mother, but now he suffered dreadfully.[25] 'The spring of my life is broken,' he wrote; and he struggled repeatedly to express the height of her virtues and the commensurate depth of his grief. He decided to dedicate the remainder of his life to spreading her ideas and carrying out her ideals. With her daughter, Helen, who now devoted herself to his care, he set up a marble monument surrounded by flowers and trees, a shrine to her memory.[26] Ironically, however, the complaining, suspicious, and seclusive temper of his married years was replaced by affability, the renewal of old friendships, and a good deal of public activity.[27]

Although Mill's writing is ordinarily moderate and qualified, his praise of Harriet is neither. To him, she was 'a living type of the most admirable kind of human being,' whom he could admire 'without reservation & restriction.'[28] Everything he could possibly want was in her, he thought: great reverence, outstanding intellectual gifts, boundless generosity, genuine modesty, simplicity, and sincerity, and a passion for justice that was also burning indignation at anything brutal, tyrranical, or dishonorable.

> Alike in the highest regions of speculation and in the smallest practical concerns of daily life, her mind was the same perfect instrument, piercing to the very heart and marrow of the matter; always seizing the essential idea or principle. The same exactness and rapidity of operation, pervading as it did her sensitive as well as her mental faculties, would with her gifts of feeling and imagination have fitted her to be a consummate artist, as her fiery and tender soul and her vigorous eloquence would certainly have made her a great orator, and her profound knowledge of human nature and discernment and sagacity in practical life, would in the times when such a *carrière* was open to women, have made her eminent among the rulers of mankind.[29]

Of course, no one else could see Harriet with the same eyes. Others sometimes saw her as vain and almost ordinary; but to him she was muse, guide, protector, and much more. His love, reverence, and dependence are pitched strangely high—unless one considers the degree to which she was an idealized combination of his father and mother. I do not know how seriously to take the fact that she bore his mother's name, Harriet, but it is without doubt significant that he depended on her in domestic matters as childishly as he had depended on his mother. No less significantly, he depended on her for guidance and criticism, for an energizing alternation of praise and blame, as much as he had on his father. Like the father, too, she was an idealistic social reformer. However, quite unlike both parents, she was emotionally open and poetically sensitive, and so she shared in the Wordsworthian response that had been medicine to him in his depression. In Mill's eyes she was an ideal man-woman, one, that is, who combined the highest feminine and masculine qualities. I say this in part because soon after he had come to know her, he wrote, 'The women, of all I have known, who possessed the highest measure of what are considered feminine qualities, have combined with them more of the highest *masculine* qualities than I have ever seen in but one or two men, and those one or two men were also in many respects almost women.'[30]

Mill was unequivocal in stressing Harriet's influence on his thought. He has been suspected of exaggerating, but she did obviously suggest, prescribe, veto, interpolate, and help him to plan. She for example insisted that the later editions of *Principles of Political Economy*, which he described as their 'joint production,' give a more favourable account of socialism than the first edition. 'We know that Harriet had,' at the least, 'a place in two important chapters, and can assume that she helped with perhaps four more.'[31] Mill declared that Harriet was particularly valuable in steadying him and giving him a juster sense of what was more and less important. The main theme of *On Liberty*, that society ought not impose its values and standards on individuals so implacably, was a theme she herself had written on earlier, with a similar plea that eccentricity should be allowed.[32] The same thoughts occurred both to him and Harriet, Mill said, so it was difficult to identify which of them was responsible for exactly what. But *On Liberty* was to him a true marriage of minds. In his words:

> The 'Liberty' was more directly and literally our joint production than anything else which bears my name, for there was not a sentence of it that was not several times gone through by us together, turned over in many ways, and carefully weeded of any faults, either in thought or expression, that we detected in it.[33]

Yet whatever Harriet's influence, the fundamental philosophical influence remained that of his father and of Bentham. It is therefore particularly interesting to see Mill's uncritical acceptance of them followed by harsh criticism of their insufficiencies, and then by a partial retraction of the criticism. The lesson his depression had taught him was one that his teacher, Bentham, had never learned. Bentham's experience of life had been too incomplete:

> He never knew prosperity and adversity, passion nor satiety: he never had even the experiences which sickness gives; he lived from childhood to the age of eighty-five in boyish health. He knew no dejection, no heaviness of heart. He never felt life a sore and weary burthen. He was a boy to the last. Self-consciousness, that daemon of the men of genius of our time, from Wordsworth to Byron, from Goethe to Chateaubriand, and to which this age owes so much both of its cheerful and its mournful wisdom, never was awakened in him. How much of human nature slumbered in him he knew not, neither can we know. . . . His own lot was cast in a generation of the leanest and barrenest men whom England had ever produced; and he was an old man when a better race came in with the present century. He saw accordingly in man little but what the vulgarest eye can see . . . Knowing so little of human feelings, he knew still less of the influences by which those feelings are formed: all the more subtle workings both of the mind upon itself, and of external things upon the mind, escaped him . . . Man is never recognized by him as a being capable of pursuing perfection as an end; of desiring, for its own sake, the conformity of his own character to his

standard of excellence, without hope of good, or fear of evil, from other source than his own inward consciousness.[34]

Mill's father was no Bentham in ignorance of life, yet much of this criticism must be recognized to be directed against the father. Mill criticized his father explicitly for 'impatience of detail' and said, 'A defect running through his otherwise admirable modes of instruction, as it did through all his odes of thought, was that of trusting too much to the intelligibleness of the abstract, when not embodied in the concrete.' By narrowness of view and excessive abstraction, he implied, his father, along with the other Utilitarians, too often became the slaves of their own hypotheses.[35]

Yet Mill remained convinced that Bentham was 'a great benefactor of mankind,' who had, with unprecedented ability, hunted 'half-truths to their consequences and practical applications.' For although Bentham neglected far too much, 'there is hardly any thing positive in Bentham's philosphy which is not true.'[36] Mill remained his and his father's disciple in remaining an associationist, in continuing to believe in the principle of the greatest happiness of the greatest number, and in retaining 'a deeply rooted trust in the general progress of the human race.'[37] Although such deep yet partial faithfulness to a parent's ideals is usual, I find Mill's case interesting because I know of no other in which one recognized philosopher inherited his philosophy, or much of it, from another who was his literal father. Would it make any sense, in a case like this, to think of the inheritance as depending on nothing more than the philosophical arguments the father taught his son? The question is, of course, rhetorical.

The relationship between Mill's life and philosophy is at once plain and complex. Any assessment of it must reckon with the effects of his struggle against depression. He discovered, as did William James after him, that depression was allied with fatalism. He said, 'During the later returns of my dejection, the doctrine of what is called Philosophical Necessity weighed on my existence like an incubus. I felt as if I was scientifically proved to be the helpless slave of antecedent circumstances. . . .'[38] Mill pondered on the issue till he saw the light. 'The train of thought which had extricated me from this dilemma,' he wrote in the *Autobiography*, 'seemed to me, in after years, fitted to render a similar service to others; and it now forms the chapter on Liberty and Necessity in the concluding Book of my "System of Logic."'[39]

The *System of Logic*, then, contains the generalized solution of Mill's personal problem. The solution is that the feeling we have of

> being unable to modify our character *if we wish*, is itself the feeling of moral
> freedom we are conscious of . . . The application of so improper a term as

Necessity to the doctrine of cause and effect in the matter of human character seems to me one of the most signal instances in philosophy of the abuse of terms, and its practical consequences one of the most striking examples of the power of language over associations. The subject will never be generally understood until that objectionable term is dropped.[40]*

Mill's depression also taught him that the simple doctrine he had learned of the association of pleasures and pains could not fit the complexity of human experience, for 'human beings are not governed in all their action by their worldly interests.'[41] In view, perhaps, of his own suffering, and later that of his wife, he adopted the not uncommon doctrine, which we have already found in Rousseau and Schopenhauer and will find again in Kierkegaard and Nietzsche, that superior persons undergo greater than ordinary suffering. That is, in his own words, 'A being of higher faculties requires more to make him happy, is capable probably of more acute suffering, and certainly accessible to it at more points, that one of an inferior type; but in spite of these liabilities, he can never really wish to sink into what he feels to be a lower grade of existence.'[42] The justification of his suffering was the complexity and refinement of his experience, as was his accomplishment in politics and philosophy. Both he and his wife had learned not only that superior beings suffer more, but they needed more freedom, because 'genius can only breathe freely in an *atmosphere* of freedom.' Interference with the freedom of geniuses, he thought, would only cause them to lose their necessary boldness, or make them harmfully wild or erratic.[43] In any case, it was unproductive and cruel for the public to interfere with anyone's purely personal conduct.[44] In saying this Mill was indirectly referring, it may be assumed, to the public opinion that censured his relationship with Harriet before their marriage.

Mill's philosophical doctrines were thus clearly influenced by his emotional response to his education, that is, by his depression, and by the social disapproval he experienced as the result of his relationship with Harriet. His response, as we have seen, was a belief in human freedom, in motivation beyond the merely worldly, in the necessity and utility of the suffering of superior persons, and in the importance of personal freedom. His whole response was linked to two perhaps more general influences

---

*Mill resembled James not only in his solution of the problem of fatalism, but in his conclusion that God, assuming he exists, is not omnipotent, but limited. The limitations of the Creator's power, Mill says, probably result from the qualities of the substances and forces of which the universe is composed, or by the Creator's insufficient skill. Mill's God is not particularly moral but at least half-heartedly kind and utilitarian, paying 'some regard' to 'the happiness of his creatures.' Mill is distinctly more prosaic and less mystical than James. See 'Theism,' the third essay in *Three Essays on Religion*, in *Essays on Ethics, Religion and Society*, ed. J.M. Robson, especially pp. 455, 457, 459, 466.

of his life: a great and constant sensitivity to the issue of dependence and independence, and a finely balanced ambivalence, which required him to give serious consideration to all sides of an issue.

Mill's sensitivity to dependence and independence comes up everywhere in his works. It is of course the major subject of *On Liberty*. His own early and continued struggle over it is transposed into such impersonal words as, 'The struggle between Liberty and Authority is the most conspicuous feature in the portions of history with which we are earliest familar, particularly in that of Greece, Rome, and England.'[45] It is his own and Harriet's struggle that is transposed into the words, 'Protection . . . against the tyranny of the magistrate is not enough; there needs protection also against the tyranny of the prevailing opinion and feelings. . . .'[46] It is, finally, his own and everyone's struggle that is transposed into the words, 'Over himself, over his own body and mind, the individual is sovereign.'[47]

It appears that liberty shows itself unobtainable to Mill except as a mean between extremes, which is most easily maintained, at least in his case, by a complexity of reference to arguments, theoretical possibilities, and real practices. The result, as I have said, is a finely balanced ambivalence, an equal attentiveness to individual and to group, to the pressure of custom and to the need for liberty. The words that best bring out the ambivalence of his thought are those attributed to him (by Kate Amberly, Bertrand Russell's mother), that the great thing is 'to consider one's opponents as one's allies: as people climbing the hill on the other side.'[48] I interpret these words in the light of the love I assume for his mother and the later contempt he expressed for her, and the great admiration and near-hatred he expressed for his father. He needed, above all, to be free; but in the critical years of his mature life he found his freedom only in dependence on another's judgment and conscience. To put it paradoxically, to be free he had to be rather bound, to be at peace he had to be rather at war with himself. But whether or not this interpretation of his character is just, it is worth recalling that Mill had an extreme interest in the American Civil War. In his words, 'My strongest feelings were engaged in this struggle, which, I felt from the beginning, was destined to be a turning point, for good or evil, of the course of human affairs, for an indefinite duration.'[49] The issue of slavery, I assume, was intensified in Mill's mind by its involvement in a civil war, which brought the issue so much closer home, to this own life and character.

I think that Mill's ambivalence granted him substantial freedom to judge the issues. They were (and are) such that a clear taking of sides was (and is) apt to falsify their genuine human complexity. It is therefore characteristic of Mill to say, quite rightly, that everywhere but in mathematics, truth 'is not a single but a double question; not what can be said for an opinion, but whether more can be said for it than against it.'[50] The analytic care with which he faced individual and social problems comes out in the words:

> The field of man's nature and life cannot be too much worked, or in too many directions; until every clod is turned up, the work is imperfect; no whole truth is possible but by combining the points of view of all the fractional truths, nor, therefore until it has been fully seen what each fractional truth can do by itself.[51]

It therefore also stands to reason that it is best not to suppress even opinions that seem clearly wrong, even if only because they may quicken the true, opposing opinions into life and effectiveness. As in Mill's own nature, every ruling impulse must have its counter-impulse, for the good and the true, insofar as within our reach, lie complexly between the extremes.[52]

Mill's ambivalence is also visible in his attitude toward women. He is forthright enough in wanting to free them from subjection. His interest in women's rights antedated his acquaintance with Harriet Taylor, making it plausible to believe that it was his mother's drudgery, which he seemed more to scorn than pity, that first suggested to him that women needed to be freed. If I am right, the ambivalence lies in the fact that his strong concern for his mother could appear only implicitly. There may well be both a defence of his mother and an attack on his father in his opposition to sexual intercourse as an 'animal function' inflicted on women against their inclinations. There may also have been dislike of sex itself, which comes out in a diary entry that says, 'I am anxious to leave on record at least in this place my deliberate opinion that any great improvement in human life is not to be looked for as long as the animal instinct of sex occupies the absurdly disproportionate place it does. . . .'[53]

Harriet's view was similar. Soon after she met Mill, she wrote, 'No institution that could possibly be devised seems to me so entirely tending to encourage and create mere sensualism as that of marriage. In the first place, it makes some mere animal inclination respectable and recognized in itself.' Likewise, when Mill had written the first draft of his *Autobiography*, she wrote to him that it would provide 'an edifying picture for those poor wretches who cannot conceive friendship but in sex—nor believe that expediency and the consideration for the feelings of others can conquer sensuality.'[54] The fact is that she was approximately an invalid during the years of her marrige with Mill, and therefore perhaps estranged, or further estranged from sex. For several years of the marriage she suffered difficulties in walking, which may have been of hysterical origin. Thereafter, she suffered from tubercular hemorrhages. All things considered, it is not unlikely that she and Mill refrained from sexual intercourse.[55] There is nothing in their extant correspondence about the possibility of having children. But Mill had children of a more intellectual sort, the works he called his 'mental offspring.'[56]

Kierkegaard

14. Søren Aabye Kierkegaard, born in 1813. His mother was protective and unintellectual. Her granddaughter describes her as 'a nice little woman of an even and cheerful disposition. The intellectual development of her children was rather over her head . . . She was especially content' when a transitory illness forced them into bed, 'for then she wielded her scepter with joy and kept them as snug as a hen does her chickens.'[1] It is strange that Kierkegaard, so voluble about himself and his father, is so silent about her. A plausible reason may be his absorption of the attitude of his father, who continued to regard his first, deceased wife as his true one. But though Kierkegaard nowhere mentions his mother, it is possible that his good-natured impudence as a youth, and his childlike whimsicality and tenderness are related to his mother's cheerfulness and protective care.[2]

Cheerfulness was certainly no inheritance from the father, whom Kierkegaard calls, 'the most melancholy man I have ever known.'[3]* The father had become wealthy enough to have retired from his wholesale grocery business. Already fifty-six at the time of Søren's birth, he was severe, brooding, and oppressively religious. To the son's delight, however, he retained a lively, even exuberant imagination. Thus when the son asked permission to go out, the father would usually refuse, but on some happy occasions, he would take the son's hand and, walking back and forth in the room, talk with great vividness and detail as if they were walking wherever it was that the son wanted to be, whether a castle in Spain, the seashore, or the streets of his own city, Copenhagen.[4]

The father also displayed a dialectical gift that astonished and delighted the son. This gift was most conspicuous in the philosophical or theological arguments that the father loved to conduct with his visitors. He would encourage a visitor to put his case as fully as possible, but then

---

*Søren's elder brother, Peter, suffered, like the father, from melancholy. Peter's son, who was confined to an insane asylum, made a logical epitome of his life in the words, 'My uncle was Either/Or, my father is Both/And, and I am Neither/Nor.' W. Lowrie, *A Short Life of Kierkegaard*, p. 27.

turn the tables on him with dramatic suddenness. The father was furthermore able, as if by some mysterious intuition, to divine and in a word confute what the son was about to say. 'What other children get through the fascination of poetry and the surprise of fairy tales, he got through the calmness of intuition and the alternations of dialectic. This was the child's joy; it became the youth's delight.'[5]

Although he was the favourite son, Kirkegaard remembered his childhood as terribly painful. He had been sickly, perhaps because of spinal trouble, and he would at times fall down helplessly, unable to move.[6] His upbringing, he said, had submerged him in a dismal Christianity.[7] He over and again spoke of 'a thorn in the flesh' that kept him from entering into the usual relations of life and that subjected him to the consciousness of sin and guilt.[8] 'I am in the profoundest sense,' he observed, 'an unhappy individuality which from its earliest years has been nailed fast to some suffering or other, bordering on madness, and which must have its deeper roots in a disproportion between soul and body; for (and that is what is extraordinary) it had no relation to my mind.'[9]

No one knows precisely what this 'thorn' or 'disproportion' may have been. Kirkegaard more than once hinted or said outright that his suffering was his share of his father's secret guilt. The fact that he consulted a doctor to discover whether he could resolve 'the discord between the psychical and the physical' and, by acting through his will, realize 'the universal' of marriage, raises the likelihood that his difficulty was sexual.[10] The father, it has been guessed on the basis of Kirkegaard's writing, revealed that he had visited a brothel, and that he feared, not only that he had contracted a venereal disease, but that he might have passed it on to his children.[11] If this guess is true, the pious old man must have suffered torments of guilt and fear. These would not conflict with another possibility, that the son was wholly or partially impotent. When, within the space of two years, the mother and three of the children all died, the familial sense of guilt and gloom deepened. Peter and Søren were persuaded that they, too, would die before long, leaving the old father to be punished by his very survival.[12]

After the father's shattering confession, whatever it was, Kierkegaard turned away from him. He felt as if he were Faust and Mephistopheles was guiding him into the world of sin. He wanted, he wrote, 'to feel all the sluice gates of sin open within his own breast.' He wanted 'to surrender to Satan so that he could show me every abomination, every sin in its most dreadful form. . . .'[13]

Now that Christianity was diminished in his eyes, Kierkegaard turned to politics, aesthetics, and philosophy, especially the philosophy of

Hegel.[14] He first learned Hegel by means of Danish intermediaries, but in time studied Hegel himself, emerging with substantial respect, but also with an ironically expressed repugnance. In Hegel's philosophy, he wrote,

> the passionate question of truth does not even arise, since philosophy has begun by tricking the individuals into becoming objective. The positive Hegelian truth is as illusory as happiness was in paganism. The individual could not know whether he was happy until all was at an end [a saying attributed to Solon], and so here: only the next following generation can know what the truth was in the preceding generation. . . .Everything is relative; except that here, everything is relative in the continuing world-process. But this cannot help any living individual . . . Outside the *Logic*, and partly also within the same . . . Hegel and Hegelianism constitute an essay in the comical. Blessed Hegel has presumably by this time found his master Socrates; and the latter has doubtless found something to laugh at, if Hegel otherwise remains the same.[15]

Hegel, wrote Kierkegaard, was perfectly right in claiming that the human dilemma of either-or did not exist in pure abstract thought; but pure abstract thought was not existence.

> One must therefore be very careful in dealing with a philosopher of the Hegelian school, and, above all, to make certain of the identity of the being with whom one has the honor to discourse. Is he a human being, an existing human being? Is he himself *sub specie aeterni*, even when he sleeps, eats, blows his nose, or whatever else a human being does?

And if, continued Kierkegaard, this philosopher in fact exists, and if he is then in the process of becoming and faces the future, and if, facing the future, he must act, 'does he not in that case face the future with infinite passion? Is there not then for him an either-or?'[16]

After becoming discontented with the abstractions of Hegel, Kirkegaard turned to Hamann, who conceptualized for him the limitations of philosophy.[17] He drifted back towards his father's position, that is, to a universally human, ethical philosophy; and his return was reinforced by an emotional reconciliation with himself, with his father, and with God.[18] Soon thereafter, the eighty-two year old father died. Kierkegaard, who was twenty-six at the time wrote:

> I had so heartily wished that he might live a few years longer, and I regard his death as the last sacrifice his love for me occasioned; for not only has he died from me but *died* for me, in order that if possible something may be made of me still . . . He was a faithful friend.[19]

For a time it now appeared to Kierkegaard that he could live the normal life of a human being. He finished his studies, making a normal career possible, and became engaged. But he could not bring himself to continue the engagement, and so he failed, in his own terms, to realize what was universally human and ethical. The first spontaneity of life was over for him. Either–or now faced him. Only guilt and penitence, he taught himself, could prepare him for the qualitative leap to a new spontaneity.[20]

It was obvious to Kierkegaard, as it should be obvious to us, that his whole difficult life nourished his thought. He soon assimilated his father's love for dialectic in both the sense of logical explication and the sense of reversal by diametric opposition. This was the art, he wrote, that was to be 'the serious business' of his life.[21] The painful but fascinating relationship between himself and his father transformed him into a psychologist spying into the recesses of human nature, especially the secret causes of gloom, guilt, anger, and the refusal of life. In order to 'exist in himself' and yet 'peer into life and other men,' he became a 'double-thinker,' dissociated from himself and suffering from the thought that he could not quite live his own life.[22] He wrote pseudonymously, his characters, split off from himself, thinking the thoughts of still other characters and refusing to implicate Kierkegard openly in anything they professed. Even when he took on his own name, he remained the ironist looking at himself, too, from a distance.[23]

In 1848, the thiry-five year old Kierkegaard, who had by then lived longer than he thought either possible or just, felt the stirrings of a metamorphosis. He felt he had to try to come to himself and consider his melancholy 'with God on the spot.' The anticipated metamorphosis took place on the 19th of April. 'My whole nature is changed,' he wrote with emotion. 'My close reserve, my introversion, is broken—I must speak. Great God, give me grace!'[24] From then on, he no longer hid behind pseudonyms, but communicated directly, though, as I have said, not always without irony.

Kierkegaard's metamorphosis clarified his love and his hate. His love, he wrote, freed him from his excessive self-concern:

> There is something painful in being obliged to talk so much about myself. . . But now, thank God, now I breathe freely, now I actually feel an urge to speak, now I have come to the theme which I find inconceivably pleasant to think about and to talk about. This God–relationship of mine is the 'Happy love' in a life which has been in many ways troubled and unhappy. And although the story of this love affair (if I dare call it such) has the essential marks of a true love story, in the fact that only one can completely understand it, and there is no absolute joy but in relating it to one only, namely, the beloved, who in this instance is the Person by whom one is loved, yet there is a joy also in talking about it to others.[25]

The hate clarified by the metamorphosis was for official Christianity. Its symbol in his eyes was Bishop Mynster, whom he is said to have admired and loved, not least because he had been his dead father's pastor. He had often been on the verge of attacking this pastor he loved, but had managed to restrain himself. However, when the Bishop died, and still another official Christian Professor Martensen, eulogized him as 'a genuine witness for the truth,' he began a harsh polemic against him, or rather against the lie he took him to represent. 'Quite simply—I want honesty,' Kierkegaard said.[26] It would have been best, he said, if Bishop Mynster could have been persuaded to confess that he had taught no more than a mild version of the true, uncompromising Christianity. But now that he had died without confessing this truth, it had become an irrevocable fact that his preaching had 'hardened Christianity into a deception.'[27] Kierkegaard now understood, he said, that the extraordinary men who had preceded him had all aimed at spreading Christianity, while his task, in contrast, was 'to put a halt to a lying diffusion of Christianity, and to help it to shake off a mass of nominal Christians.' He would therefore be more alone than anyone before him. He had long been convinced that a genius was alone in the sense of being close to madness; and now he, Kierkegaard, was the more alone in having been given an isolating religious mission.[28]

Yet though Kierkegaard's love and hate reached this kind of clarification, they remained, it seems to me, inextricably mingled. This is apparent if we consider his final opinion that 'true religious ideality. . .is readily described as morbidity.' and that this morbidity is nothing other than 'a higher health.' By this he means, very explicitly, that the love of God requires the greatest possible disgust with life. In his own words, 'Only the men who are brought to this point of disgust with life and are able to hold fast by the help of grace to the faith that God does this from love, so that not even in the inmost recesses of their soul is there any doubt concealed that God is love—only these men are ripe for eternity.'

This conclusion becomes painfully transparent when Kierkegaard goes on to say that God is pleased most by the man who believes that it is out of love alone that God 'with the cruellest imaginable cruelty does everything to deprive him of all joy in life . . . And every time he hears praise from a man whom he brings to the uttermost point of disgust with life, God says to himself, This is the right note.' In the end, Kierkegaard's rationale is this:

> Through a crime I came into existence against God's will. The fault, which in one sense, is not mine, even if it makes me a criminal in God's eyes, is to give life. The punishment fits the fault: it is to be deprived of all joy of life, to be brought to the supreme degree of disgust with life.[29]

I cannot discuss the possible theological importance of such words; but their psychological meaning is so plain that it scarcely needs to be stated. Kierkegaard, who was in the end too self-centered, self-righteous, and polemically fierce to be pitied, was still dominated by his need to justify and become reconciled with his gloomy, guilty old father, the Person by whom he had been loved, the only person with whom he had had established emotional communion, the person who constituted so much of his inner being.

Kierkegaard's successful but barren wooing of Regina Olsen should be read in the eloquent but compulsively prolix repetitions of Kiergaard himself. He came in the end to regard women with a suspicious, ironical distance. What caused a woman most fear, he said, was that the 'opponent' she tried her utmost to seduce would only laugh. Women seemed instinctively to suspect that he would react to their greatest efforts by bursting out with laughter. 'Alas,' he added, 'there is some truth in this that it could end with my bursting out laughing. But the reason is neither my great virtue nor my great spirituality but—my melancholy.'[30]

As in the instance of Nietzsche, it is hard to believe that such insight and such blindness could coexist so intimately in the same man.

James

15. William James, born in 1842. His father's father, with whom I think I should begin, made a fortune in business and became a well-known leader in civic and religious affairs. As Henry, the philosopher's father, remembered him, he was easy to get along with but incurious about his son's life. When the son suffered a gunshot wound, the father's great, even excessive solicitude was therefore memorable.[1] But the mother, 'nothing but' a good mother, 'was maternity itself in every form, and the most democratic person by temperament' that the son, Henry, ever knew.

Thinking back to his childhood, Henry attributed his unhappiness at the time to the family's emphasis on self-preservation and its lack of 'a *spontaneous* religious culture.'[2] Its orthodox Protestantism was too oppressive. On Sundays, for instance, the children were not allowed to play, dance, sing, read stories, whistle, ride a pony, walk in the country, or swim in the river.[3] Not unnaturally, the lively, sensitive boy was 'never so happy at home as away from it.'[4] His conscience troubled him, not so much when he stole loose silver from a 'magical' drawer in his father's dressing table as when he wounded anyone's self-respect or caused needless suffering. When his conscience was aroused, he would feel 'the terrors of hell' and 'a dread of being estranged from all good men.'[5] Generalizing in later years about the 'veritable secret source' of his intellectual restlessness, he wrote, 'During all my early intellectual existence, I was haunted by so keen a sense of God's *natural* incongruity with me—of his *natural* and therefore invincible alienation, otherness, externality, distance, remoteness to me—as to breed in my bosom oftentimes a wholly unspeakable heartsickness or homesickness.'[6]

When Henry was thirteen, he suffered a terrible accident. While trying to stamp out a fire he and some other boys had set, he burned his right leg so badly that it had to be amputated above the knee. Because of infection, the stump had to be amputated again—all this at a time when anesthetics were not yet in use. During his long convalescence he became introspective, while his father proved unexpectedly tender. However, when he got to college, which bored him, his frivolity and extravagance alienated his father. His emotions were obviously in conflict, for he abandoned college, returned after a while, and then tried to placate his father by studying law and bookkeeping.[7] After his father's death, he entered Princeton to study theology, but found the Presbyterianism taught there as strict as his father's had been. He came to prefer the belief that people could be saved, even if only collectively.[8] The money he had inherited was enough to live on, with the result that he did not have to exercise any profession; but he became a prolific author. Although he married, he remained always restless, always happier somewhere else, and he travelled incessantly with his growing family.

Two years after the birth of his first son, William, he underwent a terrifying experience. As he described it,

> Suddenly—in a lightning flash—'fear came upon me, and trembling, which made all my bones to shake.' To all appearances it was a perfectly insane and abject terror, without ostensible cause, and only to be accounted for, to my perplexed imagination, by some damnèd shape squatting invisibly to me within the precincts of the room, and raying out from his fetid personality influences fatal to my life. The thing had not lasted ten seconds before I felt myself to be a wreck; that is, reduced from a state of firm, vigorous, joyful manhood to one of almost helpless infancy.[9]

The doctors he consulted told him he had overworked his brain; but someone directed him to the writings of Swedenborg, in whom he discovered the cure. Under Swedenborg's influence, he grew to believe that God was infinite love and wisdom, that the soul after death was pure spirit, and that God's real creation was the aggregate of all humanity, 'Divine-Natural Humanity,' as he called it, in which selfhood or selfishness was abolished.[10] His peace of mind was sustained by his unaffected, steady, practical wife.[11] He loved her, as he loved his children, tenderly, yet, strangely enough, 'he wished sometimes that the lightning would strike his wife and children out of existence, and he should suffer no more from loving them.'[12]

Recalling the premature discipline his father had enforced, he decided to allow his children to remain in their natural childish innocence, and to bring them up in freedom, spontaneity, and love. He was sure that the atmosphere of freedom would lead them to be good not out of fear but out of delight in their goodness.[13] In practice, this attitude resulted in an interesting but intermittent and rather chaotic eduction, in which plans, tutors, and schools were often changed.[14] As his second son, named after him, Henry, said, 'The literal played in our education as small a part as it perhaps ever played in any, and we wholesomely breathed inconsistency and ate and drank contradictions.'[15] This education was, so to speak, intended, but it paralleled what Henry James called 'our poor father's impulsive journeying to and fro.'[16]

William James had shown an early talent for drawing and, though interested in science, he thought of becoming a painter. Excited by Delacroix's colours and, no doubt, his vitality, he copied and recopied 'Dante and Vergil in Hell.'[17] His father, however, distrusted painting as a profession, so William and Henry were enrolled in a scientific preparatory school in Geneva. William liked it, especially the anatomy course; but the restless father, who believed in giving his children new experiences, decided to move William and his two younger brothers to Bonn, where, among other things, they would learn German.[18] But William soon argued his father into allowing him to study painting, and the whole family returned to the United States.[19]

William James was now eighteen. He began to study painting with William Hunt, an old acquaintance, but gave it up after a time for unexplained reasons. perhaps because Hunt told him that America did not value painters. In view of his later history, it should be noted that he developed eye trouble and 'nervous indigestion' at about this time.[20] Having abandoned painting, he entered Harvard, where he studied chemistry to begin with, and then comparative anatomy, 'in a vast museum, at a table all alone, surrounded by skeletons of mastodons, crocodiles, and the like, with the walls hung about with monsters and horrors enough to freeze the blood.'[21] When the course was over, he hesitated over the next step, but finally decided on the natural sequel, medical school.[22]

Something, however, was seriously amiss. Both he and his sister, Alice, showed symptoms of grave mental disturbance. He was, in his own words, 'on the continual verge of suicide,' while she, who for years had suffered violent, unpredictable attacks of hysteria, began to fall unpredictably into dead faints, especially in the midst of interesting conversation.[23] This period of disturbance was also that during which William 'enjoyed the sensation' of a lecture by Charles Pierce, and during which he began to wrangle on philosophical problems.[24] He found it difficult to go on working in the hospital, because he was having severe back pains, so he asked his parents if he could spend a year in Germany, where the mineral baths might help his back, where he might learn German really well, and where he might attend university lectures.[25]

William wrote amusing letters home, and for a time all seemed well. Finally, however, he wrote to his father, asking him not to tell the others that his back symptoms had got worse, and that, though he was not exactly low-spirited, 'thoughts of the pistol, the dagger and the bowl' had usurped too much of his attention.[26] Soon thereafter he wrote to his father complaining of their alienation from one another. 'You live in such mental isolation,' he said, 'that I cannot help often feeling bitterly at the thought that you must see in your children strangers to what you consider the best part of yourself.' To this personal complaint he added a philosophical one: he was baffled by the undefined terms and lack of logic in his father's articles.[27]

In the spring of the following year, William, who was then twenty-six, felt physically apathetic and mentally restless. His curiosity about the relationship between body and mind, a relationship his life had so often brought to his attention, was becoming stronger.[28] It seemed to him that his life was a dead drifting.[29] When he felt better again, he decided to travel. Finding that it was too expensive to stay in Europe, he returned to the United States and his medical examinations.[30] Although it was very difficult for him to study, he passed his medical examinations, which were oral.

Later that same year, he entered into a new crisis, the most severe he had yet suffered. It culminated in the terrifying, apparently causeless depression that has been briefly mentioned in an earlier chapter. In his diary he wrote, 'Nature & life have unfitted me for any affectionate relations with other individuals . . .'[31] He became engrossed in his father's works and in brain pathology and body–mind relationships. His diary records a prolonged 'great dorsal collapse.' He was touching bottom, he wrote, and thinking whether or not to 'throw the moral business overboard.'[32] Living in dread, terrified to be alone, he felt astonished at his mother's 'cheerful unawareness of the danger'; but he was careful not to disturb her by revealing his state of mind.[33] Meditating painfully, he recalled that the French philosopher, Renouvier, had defined free will as the ability to choose to sustain one of a number of possible thoughts, and, in agreement with Renouvier, he chose to gain his salvation 'in accumulated acts of thought' and in 'the self-governing resistance of the ego to the world.'[34] His suicidal mood came to an end. He was now free to begin the career that was to lead him successfully from the subject of physiology to that of psychology, and from psychology to philosophy.

When James was forty, his mother died. In reaction, his brother, Henry, who was then in America, wrote to a friend, 'You know my mother and you know what she was to us—the sweetest, gentlest, most natural embodiment of maternity—and our protecting spirit, our household genius.'[35] In his notebook he recorded, 'It is impossible for me to say—to begin to say—all that has gone down into the grave with her. She was our life, she was the house, she was the keystone of the arch. She held us all together, and without her we are scattered reeds.'[36] The father, who said of her after her death, 'She really did arouse my heart, early in our married life, from its selfish torpor, and so enabled me to become a man,' was unwilling to survive her in the body. Within a year of her death, longing to rejoin her and enter 'into the spiritual life,' he committed an unusual form of suicide—he gradually refused to eat. After finally becoming inarticulate, he died.[37] Henry visited the cemetery he was buried in and wrote to William, 'He lies extraordinarily close to Mother, and as I stood there and looked at this last expression of so many years of mortal union, it was difficult not to believe that they were not united again in some consciousness of my belief.'[38]

Just before his father died, William, knowing how ill he was, wrote him a parting letter, which the father was unfortunately never to receive. Though, as I have written, he had been troubled by his father's illogic and mysticism, now, after saying, 'Dear, dear old mother is waiting for you to join her,' he acknowledged his debt to him:

> In that mysterious gulf of the past into which the present will fall and go back, yours is still for me the central figure. All my intellectual life I derive from you; and though we have often seemed at odds in the expression thereof, I'm sure there's a harmony somewhere, and that our strivings will combine. What my debt is to you goes beyond all my power of estimation,—so early, so penetrating and so constant has been the influence.'[39]

This tribute to a dying father was at least close to the truth. Father and son were alike in many ways.[40] They were both vivacious, wayward, and affirmative. Both were impatient of established ideas, and both believed in belief. Their intimates, who recognized the likeness, tried to express the difference. Alice James said:

> Though the results are the same, they seem to come from such a different

nature in the two; in William, an entire inability or indifference to 'stick to a thing for the sake of sticking,' as someone said of him once; whilst Father, the delicious infant! couldn't submit even to the thralldom of his own whim; and then the dear being was such a prey to the demon homesickness.

Another opinion was that 'there was more of sheer aboriginal force in the father,' while the son 'was more mundane, more highly socialized . . . more securely restrained.'[41]

James himself pointed out that while his father's style was vivacious, his ideas were monotonously few.[42] Yet the vivacity of both James's style and ideas, the constant openness he demanded of himself and the world, seem to me to constitute a reality in which, like his father's, it was possible to travel impulsively and endlessly. The friend speaking of William might also have been speaking of his father when he said:

> 'Active tension,' uncertainty, unpredictability, extemporized adaptation, risk, change, anarchy, unpretentiousness, naturalness—these are the qualities of life which James finds most palatable, and which gives him the deepest sense of well-being. They are at the same time the qualities which he deems most authentic, the accents in which the existent world speaks to him most directly. . .There is something of his restlessness in it, something of his preference of the unusual to the orderly; it is to some extent his way of escape from a tendency to morbid self-preoccupation. On the other hand, it is a direct expression of his creative and richly imaginal fancy; a projection of his variety; and the cosmic sympathy by which he rejoiced in strange and varied otherness.[43]

The father's love for variety was of course limited philosophically by his monism, to which James objected, for all monism oppressed him—just as his father had sometimes oppressed him by the mere force of his personality. But James's pluralism was designed to allow different individuals, such as those in his own family, to coexist in natural peace, for James said that his radical empiricism proposed the social analogy, with

> plurality of individuals, with relations partly external, partly intimate, like and unlike, different in origin, in aim, yet keeping house together, interfering, coalescing, compromising, finding new purposes to arise, getting gradually into more stable habits, winning order, weeding out.[44]

The words, of course that go back to his family life are 'keeping house together.'

James's major books can be related to his father's interests. *Varieties of Religious Experience*, James said, was designed to do some justice to his father's kind of experience, by interpreting to the 'philistine much that he would otherwise despise and reject.'[45] His *Pragmatism* was a bridge over the family gaps, for it required scientific loyalty to the facts he had learned along with the confidence he and his father had acquired in human and cosmic values.[46] 'Pragmatism,' he said, 'may be a happy harmonizer of empiricist ways of thinking with the more religious demands of human beings.'[47] In *A Pluralistic Universe* he even accepted the view that minds or fields of consciousness might overlap and interpenetrate, and much in effect like his father, he now said, 'The believer is continuous, to his own consciousness, at any rate, with a wider self from which saving experiences flow.'[48] In *Essays in Radical Empiricism* he wrote, in a similar vein, 'In that perceptual part of *my* universe which I call *your* body, your mind and my mind meet and may be called coterminous.'[49] And in 'Final Impressions of a Psychical Researcher,' he concluded that

> there is a continuum of cosmic consciousness, against which our individuality builds but accidental fences, and into which our several minds plunge as into a mother-sea or reservoir. Our 'normal' consciousness is circumscribed for adaptation to our external earthly environment, but the fence is weak in spots, and fitful influences from beyond leak in, showing the otherwise unverifiable common connection. Not only psychic research, but metaphysical philosophy, and speculative biology are led in their own ways to look with favor on some such 'panpsychic' view of the universe as this.[50]

Seen coldly, James's personal qualities and philosophical beliefs could be judged to be persistent weaknesses. Santayana, who saw them coldly, said, 'He was really far from free, held back by old instincts, subject to old delusions, restless, spasmodic, self-interrupted. . . .'[51] This could of course be a judgment of James's father, or of James's dependence on his father.

Before I end my account of James, I should like to dwell a little on the relationship between him and his brother, Henry, even though it is much easier to see what Henry owned to William than the reverse. The two brothers were close, affectionate, and appreciative of one another. William said to Henry, 'I feel as if you were one of the two or three sole intellectual and moral companions I have,' while Henry called William, 'My protector, my backer, my authority, and my pride.'[52]

It is well known that William did not particularly care for Henry's later style. He called it 'supremely great' in its 'peculiar way,' but added, 'The bare perfume of things will not support existence, and the effect of solidity you reach is but perfume and simulacrum.'[53] I suspect that this criticism of style of writing contained an implicit criticism of style of life. But Henry seems to have been unreservedly appreciative of William's philosophy. On reading *Pragmatism*, he wrote to William:

> I simply sank down, under it, into such depths of submission and assimilation that *any* reaction, very nearly, even that of acknowledgement, would have had almost the taint of dissent or escape. Then I was lost in the wonder

of the extent to which all my life I have (like M. Jourdain) unconsciously pragmatised. You are immensely and universally *right*. . . .[54]

Henry's reaction to *A Pluralistic Universe* was equally unreserved. He wrote to his brother:

> It may sustain and inspire you a little to know that I'm *with* you, all along the line—and can conceive of no sense in any philosophy that is not yours! As an artist and a 'creator' I can catch on, hold on, to pragmatism and can work in the light of it and apply it; finding, in comparison, everything else (so far as I know the same!) utterly irrelevant and useless—vainly and coldly parallel![55]

Henry's reaction to *The Meaning of Truth* was, if possible, even stronger:

> I find it of thrilling interest, triumphant and brilliant, and am lost in admiration of all your wealth and power. I palpitate as you make out your case (since it seems to me you so utterly do,) as under no romantic spell ever palpitate now; and into that case I enter intensely, unreservedly, and I think you would allow almost intelligently.[56]

The love and identification are very evident, and we can understand why Henry said after William's death:

> I sit heavily stricken and in darkness—for from far back in dimmest childhood he had been my ideal Elder Brother, and I still, through all the years, saw in him, even as a small timorous boy yet, my protector, my backer, my authority and my pride.[57]

After such ardent compliments on both sides, it comes as a shock to read that when William refused to become a member of the Academy of Arts and Letters, he gave as a reason the fact that his brother had been chosen before him. 'My younger and shallower and vainer brother is already in the Academy,' he wrote to that august body.[58] These words have been excused with the explanation that they are no more than an ironical joke of the sort then understood by the Boston Brahmins.[59] In part they only repeated what the younger brother had always believed, that William was the more profound of the two. But even if a joke, the words echo some hidden animus. The easiest guess is that there was an old jealousy between them, more marked on the part of William, who, in the normal course of events, would have had to yield to his mother's attention in favor of Henry. If this is true, the enthusiastic adoption of his ideas by Henry may have seemed, not simply a tribute, but an appropriation of what was rightfully his own. In any case, it has been noted that, despite their mutual praise, they found it hard to live together, and 'both relapsed into petty illnesses when they had to be together for too long a time.'[60]

A persuasive case has been made that Henry's later style, though disliked by William, was a way of expressing William's 'Pragmatism' and 'Radical Empiricism.' Henry, that is, was trying to express by means of style what William was trying to express by means of philosophy; for Henry wanted to capture the everlasting renewal and novelty of conscious life, and the fluxlike nature of 'pure experience' on which we superimpose artificial though necessary beginnings and endings.[61]

Not only did Henry, like William, affirm and try to exhibit in words the fluidity, indeterminacy, and novelty of life, but, like him, he more and more succumbed as he aged to their dead father. Like his brother, he refused to become an outright mystic, while all the same tending to believe in processes rather than entities, to deny the split between subject and object, and to make the problem of immortality and the supernatural central to his thought.[62] It is apparent that the father had transferred to both sons much of his intellectual curiosity, intellectual and physical restlessness, poetic apprehension, and, at the end, his dematerialization of the world and mystical assurance of survival after death.[63]

I end, as usual, with women, or rather with a woman, because in this case there is only one that need be spoken of. She came into the picture on a night of 1876, when his father announced to William, then thirty-two years old, that he had met William's future wife. Eager to meet her himself, William discovered her vitality, her luminous complexion, her resonantly musical voice, and, perhaps above all, her startling candour. They fell in love; but he believed himself unfit to marry her and sent her agonized, delaying letters. To remove temptation from his path, so she said, she travelled to Quebec. But the distance between them lent courage, he courted her more whole-heartedly, and they were married.[64] Everyone in the two families involved strongly approved of the match, except for Alice James, who became violently antagonistic to Alice, William's new wife. It is said that about the time the engagement was announced, she grew close to insanity. For obscure reasons, she remained an invalid all the rest of her life; but she displayed great courage. Even at the end, when she was dying of cancer, she took no comfort in thinking of immortality, and she resented the attempt of William to get the Boston medium, Mrs. Piper, to relay messages to her from their dead father and mother.[65]

William James now had a faithful ally in his struggle for health. She had long ago learned the stresses of life—her father had committed suicide.[66] James's humour, his understanding, and the particular tactics experience had taught him were all enlisted in his struggle, but he was sure that it was she, with her cheerful, somewhat stoical temper and her devotion, who saved him. The letters they exchanged should become available to the public in the year 2023. Until then, it may be difficult to verify the truth of what, following James's biographer, I have claimed on her behalf.

Nietzsche

16. Friedrich Willhelm Nietzsche, born in 1844. His mother, the daughter of a pastor, is said to have been adaptable, obedient, modest, and immovably pious, but also full of temperament, and to have liked to recite poetry and attend theatricals.[1] His father, as Nietzsche, remembers him in the superlatives of love, was 'The perfect image of a country parson! Endowed with mind and temperament, he lived a quiet, simple, but happy life, and was honoured by all who knew him.'[2] Nietzsche's sister adds, I think significantly, that the father was a great advocate of physical exercise, and himself skated and took long walking tours.[3] He occupied himself a good deal with his son, 'his little friend,' as he called him, who used to sit quietly and watch his father work.[4]

The father was a gifted musician. Friends would drop in on a Sunday to hear him play the piano. His improvisations, says Nietzsche's sister, made a great impression. He not only played, but also, apparently, composed music, none of which has remained. His playing fascinated little Fritz, as the son was called. When Fritz cried for some unknown reason, the sister tells us, 'our father was asked to play the piano. Then Fritz became still as a mouse, sat up straight in his little carriage, and did not take his eyes off the performer.'[5]

The father, we learn, was very sensitive. That is, he could not bear any quarreling. A quarrel in his congregation or family might cause him to retreat to his study and refuse to eat, drink, or talk. Any little dispute between his spirited wife and her sister-in-law would lead him to shut his eyes and sink himself in faraway thoughts.[6] Perhaps there was some disparity between husband and wife, as we may gather from the Nietzschean aphorism that speaks of 'the unresolved dissonances' between parents as echoing in the child's being and 'constituting its inner tale of woe.'[7]

When Nietzsche was four, his father died. An autopsy confirmed the cause to have been 'softening of the brain.'[8] A few months later, his younger brother, Joseph, died, and he was left in a family composed of himself and five women, his mother, his younger sister, Elizabeth, a grandmother, and two maiden aunts, one of them especially good-hearted, and the other, who was interested in charities and church affairs, especially nervous. At this difficult turning-point in the life of the family, Nietzsche's mother proved her maternal devotion, her determination, and her resourcefulness.[9]

When Nietzsche was about eleven, the grandmother and the kind aunt died. The mother disembarrassed herself of the surviving, nervous aunt, and she and the two children became a family all to themselves. The mother was only thirty at the time, and her cheerfulness and vivacity could now come to the fore. Elisabeth later wrote, 'We saw our dear mother more and more as a beloved though also stern elder sister, who could share our childish perceptions and remain close to all our undertakings.'[10]

At six, when Nietzsche entered school, he was already able to read and write, was already, like his father and sister, near-sighted, and already, we are told, a pious, reflective lover of solitude. His manners were unchildishly polite, and he could bring tears with his expressive recitation of Bible passages, a talent that no doubt inspired the name, 'The Little Pastor', by which the children called him.[11] Those who knew him in secondary school describe him in much the same way, as mannerly, seclusive, and intellectual. His love for music had developed, and his talent for improvisation at the piano was such that a friend said of him, 'I do not believe that Beethoven himself could have improvised in a more poignant way.'[12] In the words of another, highly musical friend, 'Surely, all his being was steeped in music, music was the soul of durable and profound satisfaction.'[13] Once when he was ill, Nietzsche wrote to his mother, 'Where I don't hear music, everything seems dead to me.'[14] It is hard to avoid the impression that music remained his emotional tie to his dead father.

To judge from Nietzsche's autobiographical writings, the death of his father was a catastrophe that cast its shadow over the whole of his subsequent life. Between the ages of fourteen and twenty he wrote at least six different accounts of his early life and the great hiatus caused by his father's death. One of these accounts, an elaborate one, was written at the age of fourteen, one at fifteen, two at seventeen, one at nineteen, and one at twenty; and to these may be added the curriculum vitae he wrote and rewrote at the age of twenty-four.[15]

The account written by Nietzsche at fourteen reads as if the events it describes, by then years in the past, were still quite fresh in his memory. It includes the words on his father that I have already quoted, and it praised him for his fine behaviour, his cheerfulness, his interest in literature and music, and for his particular talent for improvising variations on the piano. Nietzsche also remembers his father's study, on the top floor, and the rows of books that made it his favourite place. Then came the catastrophe.

Until that time prosperity and joy had always shone on us, our life had flowed smoothly, undisturbed, like a bright summer's day; but then black clouds towered up, lightning flashed, and the blows of heaven came down ruinously. In September 1848 my beloved father suddenly became mentally ill . . . My beloved father had to suffer atrocious pains, His illness continued until July 1849; then the day of deliverance approached. On the 26th of July he sank into deep slumber and he awoke only occasionally. His last words were: Fränzchen—Fränzchen [so he called his wife]—come —mother—hear—hear—oh God!—Then he sank to holy rest. †††† on the 27th of July 1849. When I woke up in the morning, I heard loud crying and sobbing all around me. My dear mother entered in tears and wailed aloud: 'Oh God! My good Ludwig is dead!' Although I was still very young and inexperienced, I nevertheless had an idea of death; the thought of being forever separated from by beloved father struck me and I cried bitterly.[16]

The following days went by in tears and in preparation for the funeral. Oh God! I had become a fatherless orphan, my mother had become a widow.—— On the 2nd of August the earthly remains of my dear father were entrusted to the bosom of the earth. The congregation had the grave dug. At one o'clock in the afternoon the ceremony began to the tolling of all the bells. Oh, their dull clanging will never leave my ears, I will never forget the gloomy-sounding melody of the hymn, 'Jesus My Trust.'[17]

Nietzsche continues that hardly were the wounds a little healed when he had a dream in which he heard organ-notes in the church like those at the funeral. 'Then I saw,' he says, 'what the cause was, a grave suddenly rose and my father in his shroud descended from it. He hurried into the church and returned shortly with a little child in his arms. The grave-mound opened, he stepped in and the cover dropped back on the opening.' The next day, his little brother, Joseph, suddenly became ill and died within the course of a few hours. 'Our pain was enormous,' Nietzsche writes. 'My dream was completely fulfilled. The little corpse was also placed in the arms of the father.—In this double misfortune God in heaven was our only consolation and protection. This happened at the end of January 1850.'[18]

A little further on, after Nietzsche has told how the remaining family moves to the town of Naumberg, and after he has written, with a double exclamation point, 'Ade, ade, dear paternal house!!' he reflects:

In my young life I had already seen much sorrow and affliction and was therefore not quite as gay and wild as children usually are. My schoolmates used to tease me because of this seriousness. This happened not alone in the Bürgerschule [the higher-grade elementary school], no, but also later in the Institute and even in the Gymnasium. From childhood on I looked for solitude and found myself happiest where, undisturbed, I could be alone with myself.[19]

Nietzsche found this solitude and was happiest, he explains, in 'the free Temple of Nature.' He also, he says, enjoyed thunderstorms, the crash of the thunder and bright flashes of lightning increasing his reverence for God.[20]

It is not possible to repeat much of Neitzsche's other autobiographical accounts here. His preoccupation with the past made it clear to him that to understand himself he would have to consider the conditions under which he had been brought up, 'especially the years of childhood.' The kind of clarity he won is evident in the account, written at the age of twenty, in which Nietzsche estimates the effect on him of his father's death:

> I am convinced that the death of so outstanding a father as he, deprived me, on the one hand, of fatherly help and guidance for later life, and, on the other, laid the seed of seriousness and reflectiveness in my soul.
>
> Perhaps it was a drawback that from then on my whole development was not supervised by a manly eye, but that curiosity and perhaps also craving for knowledge led me to the most varied educational materials in the greatest disorder . . . So this whole time from my ninth to my fifteenth year was characterized by a true search for a 'universal knowledge,' as I was accustomed to call it . . . Awakened by a particular accident, I began music passionately in my ninth year . . .[21]

Nietzsche goes on to say that this planless wandering in different fields of learning eventually aroused a contrary desire to study in a more circumscribed but penetrating way. Now that he is about to go on to university, he says, he wants 'to trace the particular back to its deepest and broadest grounds.'[22]

The last autobiographical account I would like to recall now is a trial *vita* composed at the age of twenty-four. Nietzsche writes in it of his father's death, of his subsequent overexcited search for universal knowledge and satisfaction, of his great attraction to music, and of the decision he had reached to study something unemotional and precise.[23] Nietzsche is apparently under stress. The stress is all too clear in the sudden, ominous note he writes down for himself at about the same period. He says in the note, 'What I am afraid of is not the frightful figure behind my chair, but its voice: also not the words, but the horrifying unarticulated and inhuman tone of the figure. Yes, if it only talked as humans talk!'[24] Composure was already something to be consciously striven for. In the trial *vita* Nietzsche goes on to explain:

> I wanted a counterweight to the earlier varied and restless inclinations, a science that might be cultivated with cool deliberation, with logical

coldness, with steady application, whose results would not affect my emotions very directly. All of this I then believed I could find in philosophy.[25]

At this point we may return to our account of the progress of Nietzsche's life. It had been assumed that he would continue the tradition of both sides of the family and, like his father, become a pastor. But he had been becoming disenchanted with theology and had been undergoing a general change of mind and character. I think that he was about seventeen when the strain between official Christianity and his own views began to become apparent to him. As he explained in a letter to friends, 'Christianity is really a matter of the heart. . . .The chief teachings of Christianity express only the basic truths of the human heart; they are symbols. . . .'[26] By the time he was twenty or so, he was no longer able to contain his disagreement. When he returned home from the university on an Easter holiday, he was bronzed and sturdy, and his sister noticed how much more openly self-sufficient he had become. In the course of a stormy quarrel with his mother, during which she burst into tears, he announced his decision to quit the study of theology. The pious aunt Rosalie brought the quarrel to an end by declaring that every great theologian suffered periods of doubt. Nietzsche's mother then expressed the hope that nothing more should be said of all these inner difficulties, and she promised not to try to coerce Nietzsche into anything that offended his conscience.

Caught between the different members of the family, Nietzsche's sister, Elisabeth, was in a difficult position. What her brother had said had begun to disturb her. In the hope of having her faith fortified, she decided to visit her very pious uncle, a pastor. Nietzsche did not grasp, she says, how boundlessly difficult it was for her to entertain an opinion different from that of the brother she adored above everything.[27] He was, after all, her beloved teacher, whose words she treasured, whose writings she collected, whose practical problems she dealt with, and whose pact in 'one law: the truth' she abided by.[28] His long, persuasive letter proved far more clear and serious than anything her uncle could tell her, and she ended by siding with her brother. But Nietzsche, who was anxious to remain his normal, polite self, was happy not to give open expression to the deep changes he was undergoing, and she kept urging him to be as kind as possible to their mother, whom she calls beloved and revered.[29] In fact, Nietzsche seems to have remained gentle in discussing Christianity. I assume this because Nietzsche still expresses himself in a conciliatory way some six years later. Writing to a friend before whom there was no need to be reticent, he says:

Every discussion of philosophy and religion . . . certainly belongs among the saddest necessities of life—if one is driven to it, one must arm oneself with wisdom and mildness. It is so extremely difficult, in such contestations, to keep oneself free of all bitterness . . . Always stress by deeds your innermost agreement with the dogma of love and compassion—that is the permanent bridge that can be thrown over such chasms.

It is, furthermore, a noble art to keep *silent* at the right time in such matters. The word is a fearful thing and seldom the right one on such occasions. How much must one not express! And it is precisely basic conceptions of religion and philosophy that belong to the pudenda. They are the roots of our thought and will. Therefore they should not be exposed to the glaring light.[30]

Nietzsche's intellectual interests had begun to broaden. He had become interested in Schopenhauer, and his reading, particularly of Lange's *History of Materialism*, had awakened his interest in Democritus, in the English philosophers, in Kant, and in Darwin.[31] To Schopenhauer he reacted, his sister wrote, as to a friend or father, because he had been 'so bitterly deprived by the premature death of our father.' Schopenhauer, she noted disapprovingly, had inspired him to hold 'frightful discourses' against women.[32]

Although his mature musical compositions were far from Wagnerian in spirit, Nietzsche became deeply infatuated with Wagner's music, and then with both Wagner and his wife, the formidable but to him mysteriously charming Cosima.[33]* He wrote that when close to Wagner, he felt close to the divine.[34] In time, the Wagners became very nearly father and mother to him, though Wagner was more difficult than the father he remembered from early childhood. 'To satisfy him,' he told a friend, 'arouses me more and to a higher pitch than any other force. For it is *difficult*—and he says all, what he likes and does not, and is for me like a good conscience, punishing and rewarding.'[35] As it turned out, Nietzsche was unable to accept either Wagner's doctrines or conduct without limit, and a ten-year friendship came to a painful end.[36]

Nietzsche's health, which had always troubled him, grew increasingly

---

*Years after his friendship with the Wagners had ended, he recalled in a letter that his earliest music had been similar to music that Wagner was to write only later:

'On Sunday I was in Naumberg to prepare my sister a little for *Parsifal*. It felt strange enough. Finally I said, "My dear sister, *precisely this kind of music* is what I was writing when I was a boy, at the time I was writing my oratorio"; and then I took out the old manuscript and, after all these years, played it—the *identity*, of *mood* and *expression* was fabulous! Yes, a few parts, for example, "The Death of the Kings," seemed to me more moving than anything we had played from *Parsifal*, and yet they were wholly *Parsifalesque*! I confess that it gave me a real fright to realize *how* closely I am *akin* to Wagner . . . What sudden *décadence*!! And what Cagliostroism!'

From a letter to Peter Gast, July 25, 1882, as translated by C. Middleton, in *Selected Letters of Friedrich Nietzsche*, p. 190.

bad. Violent headaches had kept him out of primary and secondary school for long periods of time. His later history has led to the supposition that he contracted syphilis as a student. But he might also have suffered from neurosis or incipient psychosis and, in later years of his sane life, from intoxication by pain-relieving drugs.[37] Nietzsche's illness has inspired so much controversy that the reader may be interested in a summary of the evidence, which I put in three brief, admittedly inexpert paragraphs:

The evidence for syphilis is largely hearsay: the psychiatrist Lange-Eichbaum reported that a reputable neurologist had told him that two Leipzig doctors had treated Nietzsche for syphilis. These doctors are said to have written letters, subsequently destroyed, to this effect. The reputable psychiatrists who observed Nietzsche after his breakdown were sure that it had been caused by syphilis. Furthermore, while raving at the Basel clinic, he said that he had 'specifically infected himself twice.' Because his father had died of a brain disease, and because his own eye-trouble and headaches antedated his presumed infection as a student, it has been supposed that he suffered from congenital syphilis. Such syphilis may manifest itself in children of five to fifteen in 'photophobia, pain, lacrimation, gradual loss of vision,' and an 'old man' look.[38]

Against these hypotheses, it must be said that even if Nietzsche's doctors believed that he had contracted syphilis, and even if the raving Nietzsche voiced a suspicion that had lodged in his mind, there was then no test for syphilis, and its external sign, a sore or rash, is hardly specific to it.

When Paul Duessen visited Nietzsche in the fall of 1887, he saw that Nietzsche seemed to drag himself along, leaning a little to one side, and that his speech was hesitant. It is true that neurosyphilis may cause 'a peculiar halting gait,' but there are other possible causes, including arterial disease, which may or may not be related to syphilis.[39]

Whatever the cause of Nietzsche's bodily pains, he suffered from them often and acutely. He had been 'swallowing them' as if born for the purpose, he once wrote to Wagner.[40] To a doctor he wrote, a few years later, 'I am on the whole happier than ever before in my life: and yet!—constant pains, several hours a day feeling very like seasickness, a semi-paralysis, which makes talking hard for me, and, for variety, furious attacks (the last one forced me to vomit for three days and nights, I thirsted for death).'[41]

Much as Nietzsche suffered physically, he suffered no less from human isolation. 'If only I could give you an idea,' he wrote to a friend, 'of my feeling of *loneliness*! No more among the living than among the *dead* do I have anyone I've felt related to.'[42] The whole of *Zarathustra* was therefore 'a dithyramb on loneliness' in which Zarathustra taught '*redemption* from nausea.'[43]

As his thought shows, Nietzsche's loneliness expresses his need for his long-dead father and, though he came at times to hate them, for his still living mother and sister. It also shows his constant struggle to gain independence of all of them and of all that they represented. When young he had written, 'In everything God has led me Securely, as a father his weak little child . . . I have firmly decided to dedicate myself forever to his service.'[44] His extended and violent attack on this decision shows that he never got emotionally free of it, and his contrary aims were, as he sometimes recognized, analogous and, it seems to me, compensatory.[45] As he once explained, in 1881, to a friend, he had never despised Christianity in his heart.[46] When Zarathustra said of Christ, 'He died too early; he himself would have recanted his teaching, had he reached my age,' Nietzsche, I think, was expressing a fantasy in which his father was Christ who, as such, had come to learn that his son, Nietzsche, was right.[47] But such a fantasy was not an easy one to sustain because it required an identification with suffering and ostracism, and, even beyond this, with the suffering that was caused, not only to the Christians but by them. It was in an access, I think, of such masochism that Nietzsche said, 'I do not read but *love* Pascal.' The reason he gave was that Pascal had been murdered, body and mind, by Christianity.[48] This means, I take it, that Nietzsche felt that his father, the representative of Christianity that he had been closest to, might somehow have been responsible for his, Nietzsche's, sufferings. In the face of the death, the pain, and the emotional bondage Nietzsche had endured, he could retain the security of his childhood ideas only as they continued to exist in their opposites. He therefore blamed his troubles on 'that damned "idealism" ' that reminded him, it appears to me, of his father and his father's death, for Nietzsche identified instinctive pity and self-sacrifice with 'the *turning against* life, the tender and sorrowful signs of the ultimate illness.'[49]

I have made many assertions in the last paragraph. Let me attempt to cite more of the evidence in their favour, especially in favour of the assertion that the relationship with the father was decisive for Nietzsche's philosophy no less than for his life.

First, let me recall some of Nietzsche's aphorisms on fathers in his early books. These show an ambivalence toward the father, that is, *his* father, not even hinted at in his early autobiographical accounts. The aphorism, 'If one had no good father, one should then invent one,' means that Nietzsche may have understood that he had idealized his dead father, that is, invented him better than he had really been.[50] But the aphorism, 'Fathers have to do a great deal to make up for having sons,' says that simply to be a son is painful, and that a father, that is, *his* father, is for that reason guilty.[51] 'In the ripeness of life and understanding a man is overcome by the feeling that his father was wrong to beget him,' is surely the same attack on the same father (and on himself, the son who ought not have been born).[52] Two further, later aphorisms have a perhaps more complex meaning. The first of these is, 'Often the son already betrays his father, and the father understands himself better after he has a son.'[53] In context, this aphorism means no more than that later generations reveal the potentialities of the earlier ones. Perhaps, however, the words, 'betrays his father,' or rather, 'his father's betrayer,' 'der Verräter seines Vaters,' carry the associations of actual betrayal. If such is the case, the aphorism implies the father's self-discovery in the antagonism of the son, who, despite this antagonism, fulfills the father.

The second aphorism says, similarly, 'What was silent in the father speaks in the son; and often I have found the son the unveiled secret of the father,' meaning that the father, in spite of appearances, could know and come to effective expression only in the son. Here the context is unambiguously negative, for the immediately preceding sentence in Nietzsche's text is, 'Aggrieved conceit, repressed envy—perhaps the conceit and envy of the fathers—erupt from you as a flame and as the frenzy of revenge.'[54]

Still another aphorism claims that 'fathers and sons have much more consideration for each other than mothers and daughters.'[55] This aphorism, unlike the preceding ones, seems merely arbitrary to me, and can hardly have any other source than Nietzsche's own view of his family life.

In *Zarathustra* and the *Genealogy of Morals*, Nietzsche insists on the blood relationship between himself, or the person or persons in whose name he is speaking, and the priests. Zarathustra, for example, proclaims that the priests are evil enemies. 'Yet' he proclaims, 'my book is related to theirs, and I want to know that my blood is honoured even in theirs.'[56] Then, significantly for Nietzsche, Zarathustra adds that the priests are meant to live as corpses, that their speech smells of death chambers, and that 'whoever lives near them lives near black ponds out of which an ominous frog sings its song with sweet melancholy.'[57] Does this passage reflect the scene of the burial of Nietzsche's father, and the clanging of the bells and 'gloomy-sounding melody' that accompanied it? The *Genealogy of Morals* lays down that priests are ill and neurasthenic, and that the ascetic priest opposes the healthy person because 'the priest is the first form of the *delicate* animal. . . .'[58] Then, in the *Antichrist*, Nietzsche complains that 'philosophy has been corrupted by theologian's blood. The Protestant parson is the grandfather of German philosophy,' as Protestant parsons had of course been the father and grandfathers to his own philosophy.[59] In the *Will to Power* he again insists on the closeness of philosopher and priest and states that the philosopher aspires to take authority into his own hands. In the abrupt words of his probably unrevised text:

> The *philosopher* is a further development of the priestly type:—has the heritage of the priest in his blood; is compelled, even as a rival, to struggle for the same ends with the same means as the priest of his time; he aspires to supreme authority.[60]

Ecce Homo records Nietzsche's claim to be defined and set apart from all the rest of humanity by the fact that he has exposed Christian morality. He says, 'Blindess to Christianity is the crime *par excellence*—the crime against life.'[61] What is most terrible of all, he says, is that 'the concept of the *good* man signifies that one sides with all that is weak, sick, failure—suffering of itself,' and he immediately exclaims, 'Ecrasez l'infâme!'[62]

It is in *Ecce Homo*, I believe, that Nietzsche reveals what he has against the father he is never tired of praising, and what he has, therefore, against Christianity and 'goodness.' Here, in *Ecce Homo,* Nietzsche makes the last of the reviews of his life, still referring with great feeling to the death of his father. In almost the same words he used to characterize the ascetic priest in the *Genealogy of Morals*, he calls him 'delicate, kind, and morbid.' He then adds, 'In the same year in which his life went downward, mine, too, went downward: at thirty-six I reached the lowest point of my vitality. . . .'[63] He himself, he tells the reader, is a decadent, but also the opposite, for he has turned his will 'to health, to *life*, into a philosophy.'[64] He states, 'I consider it a great privilege to have had such a father,' and concedes that any other privileges he may enjoy stem from this one. But he adds the fatal qualification, '*not* including life, the great Yes to life.' He recalls, on the one hand, that his father was responsible for his involuntary entrance 'into a world of lofty and delicate things,' and, on the other, that there had been a heavy though fair price to pay. He says, 'That I have almost paid with my life for this privilege is certainly no unfair trade.'[65] He praises the 'incomparable father' who passed on the inability to predispose people against him, to such effect that he, Nietzsche, is not predisposed against even himself.[66] Soon thereafter, he says, most revealingly, 'At another point as well, I am merely my father once more and, as it were, his continued life after an all-too-early death.'[67] The open identification with his father is here joined with the sense of recurrence that plays so crucial a role in his thought. Then, further on in the text, there is an astonishing sentence, as if he had suddenly forgotten the paradise of his early childhood and youth, 'Altogether, I have no welcome memories whatever from my whole childhood and youth.'[68]

Finally, in the last passage I will cite in this connection, Nietzsche speaks of his admiration for the fact that 'precisely at the right time, my father's *wicked* heritage came to my aid—at bottom, predestination to an early death.'[69]

The evidence seems to me to be strong. Nietzsche was, in effect, accusing his father of passing on to him his weakness and the possibility of an early similar death, for which reason he, Nietzsche, would denounce and surpass nationalism, Christianity, and conventional truth and goodness, everything connected with the father he felt so close to. For all these signified the death whose threat to him he had painfully learned to oppose with life and life's values. His father, he had come to feel, had been drawing him, as he had drawn Joseph, his brother, down to the grave. This feeling, I think, is the nerve of the emotion that animates Nietzsche's philosophy—the simultaneous longing for the father and rejection of him.

It is possible that even the relativity or murkiness of the truth that Nietzsche stresses reflects the complexity of his love in antagonism. 'The criterion of truth resides in the enhancement of the feeling of power.'[70] Given his loneliness, his illness, and his fears, Nietzsche was ready to accept as truth whatever restored his pleasure, creative accomplishment, self-esteem, and feeling of power. Truth in this sense often meant the feeling of power given him by his ability to see sharply and state sharply what he had seen. This power to see and state sharply, this surgical mind and tongue, was largely the gift of his painful conscious or near-conscious ambivalence. As person and thinker, he loved, moved, and has his being in intelligently and painfully formulated ambivalence. To say this is of course not to give a magic key to his individuality.

Women were a special problem to Nietzsche. It appears to me that he was too bound to them and too resentful of his bondage to, more specifically, his mother and sister. When he proposed marriage to a mere acquaintance, he was rejected. For a brief while, he wanted Lou Salomé to be his disciple and, if he soon died, his inheritor. He may have wanted to marry her; but his attempt to live with her and his philosopher-friend, Paul Rée, in a physically Platonic, philosophically effervescent, and emotionally intense relationship, alienated both of them and made it increasingly hard for him to get along with his conservative mother and jealous sister, both of whom thought the liaison with Lou was evil. Elisabeth grew to be Lou's deadly enemy, he said.[71]* Elisabeth wrote of

---

*In his painstakingly documented book, *Frau Lou*, Binion has come to the conclusion that Lou Salomé simply made up the story of Nietzsche's proposal to her. However, Nietzsche's friend, Mrs. Overbeck, reported that he told her that he had said to Lou, 'To shelter you from gossips, I see myself obliged to ask for your hand,' but that he found Mlle Salomé did not take these words for a marriage proposal. C.A. Bernouilli, *Franz Overbeck und Friedrich Nietzsche: Eine Freundschaft*, 2 vols. (Jena: Diedrichs, 1908), vol. 1, p. 336.

'Mama's terrible scenes with Fritz' over Lou, the relationship between him and Lou being such that 'poor Mama saw only three possibilities: either he should marry her, or shoot himself, or go mad!'[72] On almost the same day, February 10, 1883, that Elisabeth wrote these words, Nietzsche wrote to a friend that he had had to bear tormenting, ghastly memories. 'So for example it has not left my memory for a single hour,' he said, 'that my mother called me a disgrace to my father's grave. Of other examples I will remain silent—but a pistol-barrel is now a source of relatively pleasant thoughts to me.'[73] About a year later, when he had become reconciled with his mother, he wrote to her complaining that his sister had meddled with most sacred emotions and pursued and tormented him, for the sixth time, he specified, in two years.[74]

Nietzsche's misery was completed when Lou and Rée went off together. He tried to overcome his feeling of vengefulness, which he despised, but their conduct had strengthened it, he discovered, aroused a suicidal urge, and brought him 'step by step,' he said, 'closer to madness.'[75] *Zarathrusta* bears the signs of this tension, not least in its comments on 'the bitch sensuality.'[76] When Nietzsche wanted to dramatize the difficulty of winning the truth, he asked, too well taught by experience, 'Supposing truth is a woman—what then?'[77]

In his last period as a sane man, Nietzsche made the impression, a witness said, of a lonely man, sunk in himself, who frequented a certain bookstore. His landlord remembered that he had often improvised for hours on the piano, mostly, as his musical daughter informed him, on Wagnerian music.[78] Nietzsche himself, who sometimes felt how ominous his condition was, nevertheless claimed elatedly that he might be 'the foremost philosopher of this age,' standing fatefully between two millenia.[80] Yet he remained obsessed, as always, by his father, mother, and sister. There is evidence for the constancy of this obsession in a passage he rewrote for *Ecce Homo,* but which his publisher apparently refused to print. The passsage, rediscovered and published in its place in the book in 1969, is at least on the verge of madness.[81] In it Nietzsche once again recalls his wonderful father, but for his mother and sister he has only invective. Their instincts, he says with hate, are incalculably coarse, their treatment of him fills him with inexpressible horror, they have directed their 'infernal machine' against him, they are 'poisonous reptiles.' He expresses his hate with two philosopher's insults, the first, that their physiological contiguity to him makes it possible to believe in preestablished *dis*harmony, and the second, that the deepest objection to his doctrine of eternal recurrence is the recurrence of his mother and sister. He is grateful to have known Cosima Wagner and recognizes that Richard Wagner is much the most closely related to him of all men. One is *least* related, he writes, to one's own parents. Julius Caesar or Alexander, that Dionysos in the flesh, could each be his father.

This passage, which is psychologically so tragic, is not as easily deciphered as it may seem at first glance. Although Nietzsche praises his father and violently repudiates his mother and sister, he wants to be least related, it seems, to both his parents, and he is preoccupied with replacing his father with someone far grander. As Freud would say, 'He is turning away from the father he knows today to the father in whom he believed in the earlier years of his childhood; and his phantasy is no more than the expression of a regret that those happy days have gone.' By the time Nietzsche wrote the above passage, even the father he explicitly remembered, his childhood father, was too ambivalent, small, and deadly a figure to be an ideal.

When Nietzsche's sanity first gave way, his raving and singing were interpolated with remarks 'about himself as the successor of the dead God, the whole punctuated, as it were, on the piano.'[82] He was put under the care of his mother, who was happy to have 'this child of my heart,' as she called him, back again, and he was happy to follow her about.[83] Even in insanity, it gave him great pleasure to improvise for hours at the piano.[84] 'Without music,' he had once written, 'life would be a mistake.'[85]

Santayana

17. Jorge Augustín Nicholás de Santayana, later known as George Santayana, born in 1863. His mother was the daughter of a Spanish official who was sent to the Philippines to govern a small island. He died after a short while there, leaving his daughter, who was to be Santayana's mother, without family, friends, or resources. She proved able to meet the situation, however. When the man who was to replace her father arrived, she left for Manila, where she met and married a young American merchant, George Sturgis. In less than a year she gave birth to a beautiful, blue-eyed boy, and then, fifteen months later, to a girl, Susana. At the age of two years and seven months, the boy died.[1] The mother did not mourn violently, her health was not affected, she continued to bear children, and she continued to care for her appearance, do her embroidery, and tend her flowers; but the death of her perfect boy made her resistant to pleasure and ordinary pain, and established in her 'a reign of silent despair, permanent, devastating, ruffled perhaps by fresh events on the surface, but always dark and heavy beneath. . . .'[2] Verbally, says Santayana, she was positivistic and superficial; morally, she remained attached to principles that meant little to her; and psychically, she was determined, cold, and 'passionately dispassionate.'[3]

Unexpectedly, George Sturgis died; but again Santayana's mother-to-be showed courage and resourcefulness, as if the need aroused by her loss had revived her energies. With her children, she undertook the long voyage to Boston, where her husband had left relations and a little property, and where she had promised to bring them up in the event of his death.[4] Some years later she went on a visit to Madrid, where she again met the official and friend who had replaced her dead father as governor of the island, and she married him.[5] He was Augustín Ruiz de Santayana. In his boyhood he had worked in the studio of a painter of Goya's school. Later, he had studied painting and law, while for his pleasure he translated the tragedies of Seneca into Castilian blank verse.[6] To his son, the philosopher, Santayana, he transmitted, not only his interest in painting and in handiwork, but also in poetry in general and Latin literature (such as Lucretius) in particular, and, beyond these, an interest, shared by his wife, in the ocean spaces and exotic scenes of the East.[7] Jorge, who heard his parents' stories, loved the world they had traversed by ship. 'From childhood on,' he says, 'I have lived in the imaginative presence of interminable ocean spaces, coconut islands, blameless Malays, and immense continents swarming with Chinamen, polished and industrious, obscene and philosophical.'[8] This inheritance of the open world was also one, he says, of 'belonging elsewhere, or rather of not belonging where I live . . . This is rather consonant with my philosophy and may have helped form it.'[9]

Santayana's father was a well-travelled man with 'a seasoned and incredulous mind,' and he 'hated shams, among which he placed religion, and hated complicated purposes or ambitions, with all the havoc they made.'[10] He was also 'a hypochondriac, always watching his symptoms and fearing that death was at hand.' Santayana says that he does not know the source of his father's hypochondria. He guesses that it may have been the effect of insidious tropical ailments, but, whatever the cause, 'the sense of impediment, of insecurity, was constant' in his father. 'It defeated any clear pleasure in any project, and mixed a certain bitterness with such real pleasures as he enjoyed. They were snatched, as it were, from the fire with a curious uneasiness, as if they were forbidden and likely to be punished.'[11] This was true in spite of the father's theoretical rationalism, materialism, and freedom from superstition.

His wife, Santayana's mother, resembled her husband in opposing superstitition and regarding all religion as the work of human imagination.[12] She was not, however, really attached to her husband, nor to men as such. Apart from her dead father, she was attached only, Santayana says, to her few woman friends. 'To men, even to her two husbands, she seems to have been cold, critical and sad, as if conscious of yielding to some inevitable but disappointing fatality.' Not suprisingly, therefore, her second marriage was unhappy. Both his father and his mother, says Santayana, were rational persons, yet their marriage was irrational. 'It was so ill-advised a union that only passion would seem to justify it; yet passion was not the cause. I say so with assurance . . . It still remains obscure what the irrational force was that carried the day.'[13]

It was in keeping with the mother's nature and loveless marriage that she decided to keep her pledge to her first husband and take her children by him and live in Boston with the Sturgises. She undertook the voyage, which was then a difficult one, when Jorge was five years old. The parents separated, Jorge remaining behind with his father and with the passionate, rhetorical, almost illiterate aunt who cared for him.[14] A new and distinct phase of life began for him. He did not clearly feel or understand what was going on, he says,

> but somehow the force of it impressed my young mind and established there a sort of criterion or standard of reality. That crowded, strained, disunited, and tragic family life remains for me the type of what life really is: something confused, hideous, and useless. I do not hate it or rebel against it, as people do who think they have been wronged. It caused me no suffering; I was a child carried along as in a baby-carriage through the crowd of strangers; I was neither much bothered nor seriously neglected; and my eyes and ears became accustomed to the unvarnished truth of the world, neither selected for my instruction nor hidden from me for my benefit.[15]

When Santayana was eight, his father took him to live with his mother and the Sturgises. He assumed that his son's education and prospects would be better in the United States. 'I prefer his good to my pleasure,' he wrote to his wife. But Santayana, musing later on his father's decision, asked,

> How much of this was clearness of vision, how much was modesty, how much was love of quietness and independence?. . . There was a terrible moral disinheritance involved, an emotional and intellectual chill, a pettiness and practicality of outlook and ambition, which I should not have encountered amid the complex passions and intrigues of a Spanish environment . . . But then I should have become a different man; so that my father's decision was all for my good, if I was to be the person that I am now.[16]

Santayana, who was then eight years old, arrived with his father in Boston, not knowing a word of English. His father remained for about a year, after which he returned to Spain. Santayana was not to see him again until 1883, when, at twenty, he returned to Spain to visit his father, thereafter renewing his visits during the summers.

To return to the eight-year-old just arrived in Boston, he was taken under the wing of his sister, Susana. 'By virtue of her remarkable Sturgis warmth and initiative,' she was, Santayana says, 'the greatest power, and certainly the strongest affection in my life.' In his words, she was a 'second mother or godmother.'[17] She had always taken the lead among the children, and now she immediately helped to acclimate Santayana, to begin with, by teaching him English. She also interested him in architecture, so that he would spend his afternoons drawing plans of palaces and cathedral fronts. She had always warmed, he says, to everything interesting and vivid, including religious doctrines and practices, and she taught Santayana his advanced catechism. As a result, their mother who was hostile to her, blamed her for arousing Santayana's love for images, church functions, and theological mysteries, which were in her eyes, 'dangerous and morbid.'[18]

In time, Susana began to lose her previous interest in society. 'There was sullen disunion and hostility' at home. She read the works of Saint Teresa and planned ways in which she might offer up her life to save the rest of the family. When, to foster her religious life, she entered a convent, she kept protesting in her letters that she loved her mother very much. These protestations struck Santayana as strange. His reaction was, 'She couldn't love our mother very much; only enough to suffer, as I did not, from her hostility.' She left the convent before the period of novitiate had ended. Finally she returned to Spain, where, at the age of forty-one, she married an old admirer, a Catholic widower with six children.[19] Though, as it appeared to Santayana, she was at bottom a sensibly humane person, she had no talent for speculation and instead of finding peace in religion, she turned it 'into a problem and a torment,' becoming fanatical against her natural good sense. Her marriage displeased and disheartened Santayana, for he regarded it as one of convenience; and his disillusion with her, the person to whom he was most closely attached, was also in part a disillusion with Catholicism. Her fanaticism only accentuated the disillusion.[20] He had hoped that they 'could have joined forces and lived very happily together' in Spain, but she, his second mother, had imitated his first, and his father as well, and had abandoned him.[21] Besides, her religiousness was an attack on the rationalism of his father and their mother, and so also an attack, to whatever degree, on Santayana's reason and emotion.

The year following Susana's marriage, Santayana was shaken by two deaths. The first was that of his father, an impressive, sobering experience for Santayana had never before seen anyone die. The father had become a poor, deaf, half-blind man of seventy-nine, who had tried to hasten his own end. Santayana writes:

> The fact that he was my father whose character and destiny were strikingly repeated, with variation, in my own, called up a lurid image of what life in the world was likely to be: solitary, obscure, trivial, and wasted. I must not look

ahead. Ahead, after youth was gone, everything would grow sadder and sadder. I must look within or above.[21]

The second death was that of his pupil and friend, Warwick Potter, his last real friend, he felt. He had insensibly come to think of him as a younger brother and as part of himself.[22] Now, after the two deaths, Santayana was unwillingly and irreparably separated from almost everything he had been attached to, from Spain, England, and Europe, and from his youth and his religion.[23] He responded with depressed, stoical reflections: it was not his world but the world of others; the truth of life could be seen only in the shadow of death; possession of things or persons could be good only if it were in the imagination; perfect love, to be really such, must be founded on its own frustration, that is, on despair, that is, on the despair of possessing it in fact.[24]

The outcome, says Santayana, is that he became a sort of hermit, out of sheer preference for peace and obscurity.[25] Though requested twice, he never went back to Harvard, where he had both studied and taught, nor even to the United States. With the help of a small inheritance, he lived in England for a few years, where he knew Russell, in Paris with C. A. Strong, a philosopher-friend from his student days at Harvard, and finally in Rome. His few possessions were all distributed, and his society was reduced to that of sincere friends and persons who were intellectually sympathetic in his eyes.[26] At the age of seventy-seven, he became a paying guest in a nursing home run by nuns. There he died, in 1952.

From my standpoint, Santayana's life is unambiguously instructive. As he himself repeatedly said, though in his own vocabulary, his life was an object lesson in the effect of too many separations. From the beginning, his parents taught him 'a sense of belonging elsewhere, or rather of not belonging where I live,' he said.[27] Susana taught him Catholicism, but then, by her marriage and fanaticism, disburdened him of it, so he was caught, an unbelieving believer, between her fanatical approval and his parents' flat rejection of its claims. He had lived, as he expressed it, in 'an ugly town, a stinted family, a common school; and the most troublesome and inescapable of its denizens was the particular body in which my body found itself rooted.' He was spiritually free, but biologically captive, for 'this compulsive and self-tormented creature called "Me" was more odious and cruel to the "I" within than were the sea and sky. . . .'[28]

Who, after all, was Santayana, to begin with, but a 'small utterly insecure waif' who wrecked himself upon his world?[29] There had undoubtedly been a time of exaltation in his youth, of which he could say:

'I knew Leopardi and Musset largely by heart, Schopenhauer was soon to become, for a brief period, one of my favourite authors. I carried

Lucretius in my pocket. . . .Spinoza, too, whom I was reading under Royce himself, filled me with joy and enthusiasm. . . .'[30]

But youth ended for Santayana in disappointments. As his sister had grown impatient with society, he had grown impatient with teaching. Whatever roots and ties he may have had he renounced in favor of the detachment he had always known and now wished to practice more fully, as if to avoid any future disappointments and to agree that Spinoza and Schopenhauer were basically right in the withdrawal, partial or whole, that they had preached. His parents had long ago taught him how much was illusion, his mother by her reaction to the loss of her perfect boy, his father by his doctrines, hypochondria, and bitterness, his sister by her irrational cruelty, especially to herself.

Having learned relatively young that 'the only knowable reality is unreal because specious' while 'all other reality is unreal because unknowable,' he had concluded that it was best 'to entertain the illusion without succumbing to it, accepting it openly as an illusion, and forbidding it to claim any sort of being but that which it obviously has. . . .'[31] Death renewed the lesson for him and emphasized that nothing could be truly possessed. The only good to be got out of persons or things, his life taught him, was to possess them in idea.[32] Like an Indian philosopher, like, perhaps, Plato, or like, as I have said, Spinoza, he felt that finite being in itself never existed, but only that the One or the Absolute existed within it, which is to say, within himself, Santayana.[33] What remained to him after this lesson in the finite and infinite was his own moral of detachment: be a spirit in contemplation of essence.[34] To understand this moral, one must recall that he defined an essence as 'an idea lifted out of its immersion in existing objects and in existing feelings,' so that 'recognized as a pure essence its very clarity seems to strip both objects and feelings of their familiar lights: reality becomes mysterious and appearance becomes unreal. . . .'[35]

Santayana's philosophy was thus a protective derealization meant to help him to escape the pain and treachery of men and things by depriving them of their biological coerciveness. His shield and his freedom were a peculiarly naturalistic, peculiarly Platonic kind of metaphysics. He believed, as he said, in a desperate but also joyless solipsism which takes metaphysical revenge 'on fate, nature, and circumstance.'[36] Thereupon he became the withdrawn, vengefully sybaritic spectator. But these last, severe-sounding words need not be taken with full seriousness, because all he in fact wanted was 'to spend drowsy hours drawing, cleaning, or making something, or even mending clothes.' 'Pleasant is solitude,' he said in the end, 'among manageable things.' As a writer proud of his facility, he added, 'And among manageable things, the most manageable for me are words.'[37]

After all that has been said, it is not surprising that Santayana did not want to marry or get very close, biologically or emotionally, to other people. A critic of his own lax philosophizing, he hoped that someone might some day express what he had meant more effectively than he himself had been able to do. 'Yet for my own happiness,' he said in a posthumous essay, 'I was philosophical enough.'[37]

Russell

18. Bertrand Arthur William Russell, born in 1872. His mother and sister died when he was two, and his father, 'after a long period of gradually increasing debility,' about a year and a half later. He says that he remembered nothing of his mother, and of his father only that he had seen him in his bath and that he had got a page of delightfully red print from him.[1] Apparently he forgot his dying father's kiss and the words, directed at him and his brother, Frank, 'Goodby my little dears for ever.'[2]

Russell was brought up by his grandparents on his father's side. The grandfather, who had twice been Prime Minister, was an old man, and he died when Russell was six. The grandmother, far younger than her husband, was the person who brought Russell up. He recalls that at the age of four or five he would lie awake thinking how dreadful it would be when *she* would die.[3]

Luckily for Russell, his grandparents' garden was large and wild. Until he was eighteen, he tells us, it played a very large part in his life; and gardens remained necessary to his happiness, as did the kind of unimpeded sunsets he saw from his grandparents' garden. The garden seemed to remember its past splendour, and he lived in the past with it.

> I wove fantasies about my parents and sister. I imagined the days of my grandfather's vigour . . . My father and mother were dead, and I used to wonder what sort of people they had been . . . Throughout the greater part of my childhood, the most important hours of my day were those I spent alone in the garden, and the most vivid part of my existence was solitary . . . Throughout my childhood I had an increasing sense of loneliness, and of despair of meeting anyone with whom I could talk. Nature and books and (later) mathematics saved me from complete despondency.[4]

Russell remembers wishing that his parents had stayed alive. He said this to his grandmother when he was six, and her answer, that he was lucky they had died, made him suppose she was jealous of them.[5] He 'vaguely sensed a dark mystery,' for he was told almost nothing about them. The main outline of their lives did not become known to him until he was twenty-one.[6] They had been, he then discovered, ardent social reformers, ready to practice what they believed in. In someone else's description we read,

> They were really a kind of fairy-tale couple. They were handsome, young, and gifted; liberal nobly born, 'a mixture of fun and earnestness,' and very much in love . . . The whole texture of their thought was steeped in Mill's opinions, dangerously advanced; and their contempt for society together with their determination to act up to their beliefs made them rash.[7]

Their advocacy of birth-control caused a particular uproar.

Russell, whose mother had got Mill to be his god-father, learned to think of her as having been 'vigorous, lively, witty, serious, original, and fearless,' and not least of all, 'beautiful.' His father he characterized, less favourably, as having been 'philosophical, studious, unworldly, morose, and priggish.'[8] The two adjectives, 'morose' and 'priggish' do not necessarily imply that Russell felt any great distance from his father, because Russell, as will be evident, was a very sad adolescent, and, looking back at his youth, was sure that he himself had been 'priggish.' In any event, he was proud of his father's integrity and willingness to see the weak points in his position and the strong ones in his opponents'.[9] Yet it was bewildering to him to find that he had gone through very nearly the same mental and emotional development as his free-thinking father.[10] When Russell got into social and legal difficulties as a result of the cause he advocated, he must have remembered that his father had lost his seat in Parliament because of his advocacy of birth-control, and this his mother, too, had sometimes got into hot water because of her radical opinions.[11]

The memory of Russell's grandfather, as reflected in the words of his widow, also influenced Russell considerably. The grandfather had believed in orderly human progress, a gradual end to war, and the worldwide extension of parliamentary government. Such views 'made it imperative and natural,' says Russell, 'to do something for the good of mankind.'[12] Besides, his grandmother, as he could see in retrospect, was fearless, public-spirited, and indifferent to the opinion of the majority.[13] At least among the living, he says, she was the most important person to him throughout all his childhood.[14] Her great affection and care for his welfare made him love her as a child and gave him 'that feeling of safety that children need.'[15] When he was twelve, she gave him a Bible, which he kept, and on its flyleaf she inscribed her favourite texts, among them, 'Thou shalt not follow a multitude to do evil,' and 'Be strong and of good courage; be not afraid, neither be Thou dismayed, for the Lord Thy God is with thee whithersoever thou goest.' These texts, says Russell, influenced his life profoundly and retained some meaning for him even after he had ceased to believe in God.[16]

But Russell's grandmother had traits that made things difficult for him, for she lived an austere life, particularly strict in anything that touched on morality. He says she did not realize that she was responsible 'for a morbidness which produced tragic results in her own children,' among them, of course, Russell's own father. 'I was, in fact, unusually prone to a sense of sin,' he recalls. 'Many of my most vivid early memories are of humiliations.'[17] An attempt was made to keep away his elder brother, who was regarded as a bad influence, and Russell, who both feared and admired his brother, naturally resented this enforced separation.[18]

Though his grandmother was a well-educated, politically aware woman, she was, by Russell's account, averse to logic. 'Everything that involved reasoning had been totally omitted from her education, and was absent from her mental life.' Nor did she serve all the emotions well. So far as he could make out, she did not understand what it was like to be in love, and sex was a forbidden subject to her.[19]

Russell considered his childhood, especially in its earlier years, to have been on the whole happy.[20] But as adolescence approached, his loneliness became oppressive. His grandmother's intellectual limitations and Puritan morality became quite trying. Her prohibitions caused him to be deceitful and to keep silent about anything that really interested him. He began to meditate endlessly and systematically on the arguments in favor of Christian beliefs, and though he anticipated great unhappiness if he ceased believing in God, freedom, and immortality, his faith in all three finally succumbed to the reasoning he brought to bear against them.[21] All this reasoning was of course kept from his grandmother, who ridiculed philosophizing and 'practiced a form of humour, which, though nominally amusing, was really full of animus.'[22]

Adolescence, Russell testifies, was a very lonely, very unhappy period. In his words, 'I am obliged to preserve an impenetrable secrecy towards my people. My interests were divided between sex, religion, and mathematics. I find the recollection of my sexual preoccupation in adolescence unpleasant.' Later he recognized, he says, that his idealistic feelings at the time were sexual in origin. He became intensely interested in the beauty of sunsets, clouds, and the trees that changed with the season. He read a good deal of poetry and reflected 'how wonderful it would have been to know Shelley.'[23]

As has already been said, Russell was in part sustained by his interest in mathematics. I have told on an earlier page how his brother introduced him at the age of eleven to Euclid, and how this introduction proved to be one of the great events of his life, 'as dazzling as first love,' but one which left him with lasting questions on the foundations of mathematics. His grandmother wanted him to become a Unitarian minister, but he preferred a career in mathematics. At sixteen, therefore, he was sent to a 'crammer' to prepare for the scholarship examination at Trinity College, Cambridge. 'I was profoundly unhappy,' he says in his autobiography. 'There was a footpath leading across the fields to New Southgate, and I used to go there alone to watch the sunset and contemplate suicide. I did not, however, commit suicide, because I wished to know more mathematics.'[24]

Russell won a scholarship and got to Cambridge, where 'a world of infinite delight' was opened to him. At last, he could say what he thought and find his words accepted as worth consideration, and he could at last pursue his greatest desire, 'to find some reasons for supposing mathematics true.'[25]

The search for these reasons did not exclude love. The time came when Russell fell in love with a Quaker girl, Alys Smith. When he told his family that he had proposed to her, they protested that she must be a cheap fortune-hunter. Strangely, he discovered a diary of his father's, partly written, for the sake of concealment, in shorthand, and he saw the parallel between his and his father's life: his father had proposed to his mother at the same age as he to Alys, his grandmother had said to his father almost what she had said to him, and his father had written down the same reflections in his diary as Russell in his. 'This gave me,' says Russell, 'an uncanny feeling that I was not living my own life but my father's once again, and tended to produce a superstitious belief in heredity.'[26]

Feeling that something drastic had to be done to prevent the marriage, Russell's family informed him explicitly of what he had already dimly suspected, that an uncle and aunt had been insane, and that his father had suffered from epilepsy—a doubtful diagnosis on later reflection, says Russell. It was also pointed out that Alys had a rather queer uncle. Russell got 'the best medical opinion,' which was that, under the circumstances, a couple ought not to have children; but when he proposed a childless marriage, he was told that contraception was gravely injurious to the health, and it was hinted that it was the use of contraceptives that had made his father epileptic.

A thick atmosphere of sighs, tears, groans, and morbid horror was produced, in which it was scarcely possible to breathe. The discovery that my father had been epileptic, my aunt subject to delusions, and my uncle insane, caused me terror, for in those days everybody viewed the inheritance of mental disorders superstitiously . . . On 21 July, 1893 (which I subsequently learnt to be Alys's birthday), I dreamed that I discovered my mother to be mad, not dead, and that, on this ground, I felt it my duty not to marry.[27]

Russell's fear persisted for the rest of his life. He writes:

> Ever since, but not before, I have been subject to violent nightmares in which I dream that I am being murdered, usually by a lunatic. I scream out loud, and on one occasion, before waking, I nearly strangled my wife, thinking that I was defending myself against a murderous assault.

I merely pause to remind the reader of the aged Kant's analogous dreams and continue with Russell's words:

> The same kind of fear caused me, for many, years, to avoid all deep emotions, and live, as nearly as I could, a life of intellect tempered by flippancy. Happy marriage gradually gave me mental stability . . . but the unconscious fear has persisted.[28]

In spite of his fear and the opposition of his family, Russell married Alys. He was then twenty-two. His emotional troubles vanished and he entered what he later considered to have been the intellectually most fruitful period of his life. He read widely in mathematics, philosophy, and history; and he reached the decision that, if he proved able enough, he would devote his life to philosophy.[29] After studying Peano's logic, he turned to the logical analysis he had long wanted to do. He would discuss his ideas with his friend and teacher, Whitehead, end the discussion with some problem in the evening, and then discover in the morning that the problem had solved itself while he slept. It was a time of intellectual intoxication for him. Within a matter of weeks, his intellectual bafflement of years cleared up. Russell says, 'Intellectually, the month of September 1900 was the highest point of my life.'[30] He set to work to write the *Principles of Mathematics*. It was October of 1900.

In February of the following year, when Russell was twenty-nine, he underwent the dramatic moral 'conversion' that has been described in an earlier chapter p. 13. Russell was apparently in silent love with Mrs. Whitehead, whose pain triggered the conversion.[31] Suddenly overwhelmed by what he felt to be the unendurable loneliness of the human soul, his prolonged and for years exclusive interest in exact analysis gave way, as I have reported, to 'semi-mystical feelings about beauty, with an intense interest in children, and with a desire almost as profound as that of Buddha to find some philosophy which should make human life endurable.' He felt pain, but along with it a sense of the ability to dominate pain and make of it 'a gateway to wisdom.'[32]

What had happened, it seems to me, is that Russell's childhood emotions had broken through his adult defenses. There again were his old loneliness, his feeling of semi-mystical beauty, and his desire to

dominate pain, and, accompanying them, 'an intense interest in children.'
The reference to Buddha, whether it goes back to the conversion itself or
to Russell's immediate reaction to it, may also go back to childhood, to
the Buddha whose name he had first discovered in his grandfather's
library—his brother, it should be added, had turned to Buddhism when
at Balliol.[33] In effect, Russell had suddenly projected his own childhood
loneliness on mankind and come to pity himself, so to speak, in the guise
of mankind.

There are two further critical periods I would like to mention. The
first, during the course of which he quite suddenly perceived that he was
out of love with his wife, was that of his most intense work on *Principia
Mathematica*. He says that he discovered the Theory of Types in 1906, and
then had only to write the book out. But writing it out was a prolonged
matter, and for ten to twelve hours a day, for eight months a year, for
three years, he worked at the manuscript, which became more and more
vast. The strain of personal unhappiness combined with that of
prolonged intellectual effort drove him again to thoughts of suicide. He
watched the trains go by and asked himself under which he would place
himself; but the hope of finishing *Principia Mathematica* kept him alive.
Once again, by Russell's own account, mathematics had wrestled
successfully with death. 'So I persisted, and in the end the work was
finished,' he says, 'but my intellect never quite recovered from the
strain.'[34]

The second critical period was that of a year-long friendship with D. H.
Lawrence, who wanted to join forces with him against the war. Russell
admired Lawrence's passion, supposed that his insight into human nature
might surpass his own, and hoped for 'a vivifying dose of unreason.' But
when Russell said that he objected to war because of the suffering it
caused, Lawrence indignantly accused him of hypocrisy and wrote to
him, 'It isn't in the least true that you, your basic self, want ultimate peace.
You are satisfying in an indirect, false way your lust to jab and strike.'
The effect of this letter was devastating. It made Russell believe that his
pacifism was rooted in blood-lust, and for twenty-four hours, thinking
he was not fit to live, he contemplated suicide.[35]

Lawrence's view of his relationship with Russell was quite directly
expressed in his story, 'The Blind Man,' in which the quick, ironical,
intellectual Bertie Reid, who, of course, stood for Russell, was pitted
against the blind, slow, passionate, sensitive Maurice Pervin. Russell was
described as a chivalrous adorer of women, but only as long as they did
not attempt to encroach on his inner life. Obviously impotent,
Lawrence's Russell was 'afraid to approach women physically. He
wanted to do so. But he could not. At the centre of him he was afraid,
helplessly and even brutally . . . At the centre he felt himself neuter,

nothing.' The story ended with the blind man's fingers exploring Bertie Reid's face, arm, and hand, and Reid, required in return to touch the blind man's scarred eyes, about to flee. 'He could not bear it that he had been touched by the blind man, his insane reserve broken in. He was like a mollusc whose shell is broken.'[36]

Lawrence had succeeded in reviving Russell's feeling of sin and unworthiness. By attacking his motives, he had stripped him of his philosopher's pride and reduced him to the sinful child in the presence of the caustic, anti-logical grandmother jibing at philosophy. But the effect of Lawrence's criticism was so devastating because, I think, there was at least some troubling fraction of truth in it. Russell's humour, like his grandmother's could be 'really full of animus.' Beatrice Webb once wrote of him, 'He is a good hater . . . almost cruel in his desire to see cruelty revenged.'[37] Another woman, who loved him, spoke of him as 'often torn between reason and emotion' and often displaying a 'scintillating (and corrosive)' wit.[38] His biographer and friend, Alan Wood, said, 'Russell was often an unkind and merciless critic, particularly in his earliest reviews . . . It is hard to reconcile such strictures with Russell's tremendous capacity for human kindness, which he would even extend to foolish philosophers; and the immense help he was always ready to give generously to students.'[39] Wood also spoke of Russell's 'polemic overstatements and sweeping epigrams.'[40] Analogously, Santayana described Russell 'as benevolence itself to the most humble and hopeless intellectual waifs,' but as also mercilessly satirical and prone to judgments that were 'really inspired by passionate prejudice.'[41] True, Santayana was a rather hostile witness, but Crayshaw-Williams, Russell's good friend in later life, said something not dissimilar. Russell, it seems, was willing to acknowledge that the wit or force of his arguments often depended on over-simplification.[42] Yet he was impenitent and said, quite rightly, I think, 'I *like* being unfair,' and would tend to assume that only fools or knaves could possibly disagree with him.[43] When serious, he would often abandon an initially extreme position, and, like his father, he could accept evidence that contradicted what he believed.[44] But as he grew older his tendency to regard those whose opinions he disapproved of as simply wicked grew on him, and his denunciation of them went to extremes.[45] Russell's heritage and life made him sympathetic with the weak and unfortunate, yet heritage and life also stimulated him to peremptory argument and cruel wit (always in a cause that seemed good to him). He had a share in what may be called the reformer's cruelty, as well as in the reforming philosopher's illusion that he can be quite free of cruelty and irrationality. Russell's own daughter, Katherine, speaks of his 'false and fantastic' teaching that 'people were reasonable and would respond to reasonable argument.' She says, 'He was such a kind man, yet his method of education seems full of brutal assaults on the childish mind. Had he quite forgotten how a child feels?' She adds that her parents' moral perfectionism loaded her and her brother with 'inescapable and, to us, inexplicable guilt.' It seems that his natural sympathy with children was not enough to make him kind to them in a more prolonged, intimate way, or to prevent him from passing on his heritage of guilt to his own children.[46]

Russell often reflected on his general objectives. He had believed since puberty, he says, in kindness and in clear thinking.[47] In *Portraits from Memory*, he describes his objectives as the discovery of knowledge that could be accepted as certainly true and the satisfaction of religious impulses. In 'Reflections on My Eightieth Birthday,' he says, in much the same vein, that his basic objectives are 'to find out whether anything could be known' and 'to do whatever might be possible toward creating a happier world.'[48] In the prologue to the first volume of his autobiography, published when he was eighty-seven, he speaks of the three simple but overwhelmingly strong passions that governed his life as 'the longing for love, the search for knowledge, and unbearable pity for the suffering of mankind.' He says that his search for life is meant to bring ecstasy, to relieve loneliness, and to prefigure in its union the vision that saints and poets have had of heaven. His search for knowledge is meant to reveal the hearts of men, explain the light of the stars, and apprehend how number 'holds sway above the flux.' As for the pity, it always arises, he says, because 'echoes of pain reverberate in my being. Children in famine, victims tortured . . . I long to alleviate the evil, but I cannot, and I too suffer.'[49]

Russell's two objectives or three passions are all clearly related to his early loneliness and self-doubt and to his early sense of 'a dark mystery,' to his childhood garden with its unimpeded sunsets, and to his grandmother, who suppressed both the memory of his parents and his own natural emotions and questions. The two objectives or three passions are therefore also related to the early death of his parents, for Russell says frequently, explicitly, and expressively that he was bound to mathematics because it was an antidote to self-doubt and death. For him, he says, the purpose of mathematics is to overcome 'the terrible sense of impotence, of weakness, of exile amid hostile powers, which is too apt to result from acknowledging the all-but omnipotence of alien forces . . . Mathematics . . . builds a habitation, or rather finds a habitation eternally standing, where our ideas are fully satisfied and our best hopes are not thwarted.'[50] As Russell, speaking for the mathematician, said elsewhere, 'So long as any perfection, however rare and however difficult, can enter into human life, he feels that the world does not exist in vain.'[51]

Given such an objective, it was of great importance to justify or grasp more deeply even the axioms or assumptions of mathematics, in order, once and for all, to establish a firmer basis for existence. The enormous effort Russell expended in trying to establish the unity of mathematics and logic was also motivated by the hope that the certainty of mathematics would become available for the solution of human problems. 'I hoped sooner or later,' he says, 'to arrive at a perfection of mathematics which should leave no room for doubts and bit by bit extend the sphere of certainty from mathematics to the other sciences.'[52] This hope made splits in the life of reason just as troubling to him as the split between reason in general and emotion in general. 'I thought of mathematics with reverence,' he writes, 'and suffered when Wittgenstein led me to regard it as nothing but tautologies.'[53] On the one side, he was faced with paradoxes, on the other, with tautologies: the ideal could not really be maintained.

Despite Russell's particular attachment to mathematics and logic, his curiosity, from childhood on, was always general. He defines the passion to know as encompassing hearts, stars, and numbers. To this list he might have added history, in which he was interested from the time when the history books in his grandfather's library served to help him imagine his grandfather's past.[54] His liking for history, already evident at the age of six or seven, appears to have been lasting.[55] 'I liked mathematics best,' he writes, 'and next to mathematics I liked history.' The fact that he connected history in general with the history of his family makes it seem reasonable that his interest began in his search for a personal past, for a father and mother.[56]

In a sense, Russell's curiosity and hope that it would lead to firm knowledge (the equivalent of the firm recovery of his parents) held his loneliness in check. This seems to be the psychological meaning of his refusal to commit suicide, first during adolescence and then at the time of his disenchantment with his wife, because he hoped to develop his mathematical understanding, that is, arrive at certainty. 'Moreover,' he writes, 'The difficulties appeared to me in the nature of a challenge, which it would be pusillanimous not to meet and overcome.'[57] He also writes that he felt the solution of the paradoxes 'as almost a personal challenge, and I would, if necessary, have spent the whole of the rest of my life in an attempt to meet it.'[58] This means, I take it, that the paradoxes had become emotional equivalents of the difficult problems his life had posed for him. Their solutions were then equivalent to a victory over the problems, while a failure to arrive at their solutions threatened to turn mathematics, his refuge, into nothing better than the rest of his life. I find some at least metaphorical support for this view in the words of a logician who, speaking appreciatively of Russell's logical accomplishments, says, 'The theory of types eliminated the paradoxes by cautery; it burned the morbid combinations of symbols out of the language. It counted them as meaningless.'[59]

Russell records four instances in which he thought of suicide as a distinct possibility, the two I have recalled just above, the instance that resulted from Lawrence's attack on his sincerity, and, lastly, a threat to his wife Alys (who had threatened suicide if he left her) to kill himself if she publicized the name of Lady Ottoline Morrell, with whom he was having an affair at the time.[60]

Whatever Russell tried, he found it impossible to assuage the emotional emptiness or yearning he felt. He was in his forties when he wrote to Constance Malleson, whom he loved:

> I am strangely unhappy because the pattern of my life is complicated, because my nature is hopelessly complicated; a mass of contradictory impulses; and out of this, to my intense sorrow, pain to you must grow. The centre of me is always and eternally a terrible pain—a curious wild pain—a searching for something beyond what the world contains, something transfigured and infinite—the beatific vision—God—I do not find it, I do not think it is to be found—but the love of it is my life—it's like a passionate love for a ghost. At times it fills me with rage, at times with wild despair, it is the source of gentleness and cruelty and work, it fills every passion that I have—it is the actual spring of life within me.[61]

Similarly, in an autobiographical story not published during Russell's lifetime, one of the characters, a Russian novelist, speaks of 'the infinite pain that lies at the heart of life' and is the condition of great achievement. Speaking, it seems obvious, in Russell's voice, he goes on, 'The attempt to escape leads only through terror to madness; but acceptance of the pain leads, through a moment of unimaginable anguish, to a new life, free, boundless, and so filled with mystic glory that the pain, though it still lives and gives life, no longer dominates. . . .'[62]

I think it likely that the suffering of Russell's elder son, which Russell himself attributes to the First World War, was derived from Russell's own unhappiness. He says of his son, 'Beneath the surface John lives in suspicious solitude, unable to believe that anyone can be trusted.' Nowhere does he connect his son's distrust either with his own emotional problems or with the fact that he, Russell, had separated from his son's mother, Dora Black, whom he had left for a young girl. He and Dora both believed in free love, and when he grew impotent with her, he encouraged her to have a child by someone else, while he pursued affairs of his own. To show how free they were from jealousy and competitiveness, they arranged a holiday meeting at which they were joined by their lovers and by the children of both fathers.[63]

Katherine, the daughter of Russell and Dora, talks of 'poor John, trapped between his parents' high expectations and his sister's bitter rivalry.' Eventually he detached himself from all of them. She remembers her parents' Beacon Hill school as 'an emotional disaster' that turned John and herself 'adrift in a hostile world,' and says, 'Sometimes I felt that we were never ourselves to them, but embodiments of a cause: first in their fight against convention, and then in their fight against each other.'[64]

Just as Russell's suffering was often given mystical expression, so, too, was his solace. His early and never quite vanished religiosity took a form approaching nature mysticism, which, I suppose, encompasses his childhood garden and the parents he searched it for. Like Spinoza and Sartre, he longed to be taken into the impersonal whole and to say 'a thing that is not love or hate or pity or scorn, but the very breath of life, fierce and coming from far away, bringing into human life the fearful passionless force of non-human things. . . .'[65]

This kind of desire was no passing. In 'My Mental Development,' written when he was seventy-one, he says:

> I have always ardently desired to find some justification for the emotions inspired by certain things that seemed to stand outside human life and to deserve feelings of awe. I am thinking in part of very obvious things, such as the starry heavens and a stormy sea on a rocky coast; in part of the vastness of the scientific universe, both in space and time, as compared to the life of mankind; in part of the edifice of impersonal truth which, like that of mathematics, does not merely describe the world that happens to exist.[66]

We see that, at least in desire, Russell's garden joins his mathematics. There is also a curious resemblance to Kant, whose philosophy Russell disliked throughout most of his career. In *Portraits from Memory*, Russell advises that the best way to overcome the fear of death 'is to make your interests gradually wider and more impersonal, until bit by bit the walls of the ego recede and your life becomes increasingly merged in the universal life.'[67] Again, Spinoza, though not only he, comes to mind.

Earlier in this book, (p. 78) I have speculated that Russell's philosophical atomism, particularly his denial of the existence of the self as such, was related to his suicidal impulse or, in other words, his feeling of sin, unworthiness, or self-negation. It has also been speculated that his atomism is related to his individualism in ethics and politics—the similarity has been said to lie in the emphasis in both on the externality of relations, that is, on the fundamental independence of things and, equally, of persons from one another.[68] This speculation may seem opposed to mine; but the feeling of one's unworthiness and the desire for one's independence seem to be empirically compatible, and if my accounts of philosophers have not been misleading, may even be characteristic of many philosophers. If so, Russell's neutral monism may represent his desire to become assimilated into the 'passionless force of non-human things.'[69] Yet he persistently contends that 'the whole of what we perceive without inference belongs to our private world,' and he agrees with Berkeley that 'the starry heaven that we know in visual sensation is within us.'[70] His garden had become private to his imagination, could not belong to anyone else, and was not to be completely identified with any inferred external one.

The last of Russell's philosophical views I should like to bring up is his characteristic conviction that logic and science, on the one hand, and ethics, on the other, have no logical connection. He is always, I think, troubled by the split that he asserts. Certainly, knowledge and kindness are two constant and parallel aims in him. In 'Mysticism and Logic,' he contends, not only that the two are different, but that 'the greatest men who have been philosophers have felt the need of both science and mysticism: the attempt to harmonize the two was what made their life, and what always must, for all its arduous uncertainty, make philosophy, to some minds, a greater thing than either science or religion.'[71] Russell finds a link between the two, which is submission to necessity, and concludes, 'The submission which religion inculcates in action is essentially the same in spirit as that which science teaches in thought.'[72]

It is perhaps Russell's unstable equilibrium between different basic impulses that explains his characteristically instantaneous transitions or revelations. I say this with hesitation because I do not think that it accounts for his first immediate bedazzlement by Euclid or his falling in love at first sight with Alys. But it may have something to do with his falling out of love with her during a bicycle ride, or, more accurately, his instantaneous realization that he had fallen out of love with her. About the precise moment, one day in 1894, when he 'saw in a flash' that the ontological argument was valid, I am not sure; but the five dramatic minutes that changed his view of life and the world may fit the hypothesis of the unstable equilibrium, or the incessant desire to escape, by way of a decisive intellectual judgment, from an obsessively troubling ambivalence.[73]*

---

*'What distinguishes obsessional people in the face of a decision is not their mixed feelings, but rather the fact that those feelings are always so marvelously and perfectly balanced . . . It is often noticeable that, despite all the hesitation and weighing of pros and cons that precedes the obsessive-compulsive's decision, the actual decision or the actual change will be made exceedingly abruptly. Despite the total length of time consumed, the decision itself will be quite attenuated as compared with the normal person's; it will be very much like a leap.' D. Shapiro, *Neurotic Styles* (New York: Basic Books, 1965).

I do not suppose that Russell should be classified as an obsessive-compulsive. But his prolonged intellectual struggles or attempts to give intellectual solutions to the problems of his life have a strong obsessional quality.

Irrespective of Russell's impetuous swings from position to position, the basic split between reason and ethics persisted in him. Towards the end of his life, however, he made partial, hesitant attempts to overcome it. He began to hope more openly that values might not be as subjective as he had always proclaimed. He said, for example, that it was the clear duty of all who value scientific knowledge to protest against the new forms of persecution, he found it hard to deny the feeling that it is true to say, 'Murder is wicked,' and he approved of the normal reluctance to agree that all ethical judgments are wholly subjective.[74] Though uncertain of the sense in which ethics might be regarded as 'knowledge,' he urged that ethics be given a broader base in psychology and reason, for to his mind ethics was 'an attempt to give universal, and not merely personal importance to certain of our desires.'[75] Finally, at the age of eighty, he wrote without explanation that 'the two different objectives which for a long time remained separate . . . have only in recent years been united into a single whole.'[76]

Russell's central problem and a hint at its solution can perhaps be discovered in a passage in the second volume of his autobiography. He there says:

> Underlying all occupations and all pleasures I have felt since early youth the pain of solitude. I have escaped it most nearly in moments of love, yet even there, on reflection, I have found that the escape depended partly upon illusion. I have known no woman to whom the claims of intellect were as absolute as they are to me, and wherever intellect intervened, I have found that the sympathy I have sought in love was apt to fail.

Russell then explains that Spinoza's 'intellectual love of God' had seemed to him the best principle by which to love, but that even Spinoza's rather abstract God had proved impossible for him to believe in. He has loved a ghost, he says, and in loving a ghost his inmost self has become almost spectral. He has therefore buried the ghost deeper and deeper, but has not found companionship in human things. The sea, the stars, and the night wind in waste places are more to him than even the human beings he loves best. 'I am conscious,' he ends, 'that human affection is to me at bottom an attempt to escape from the vain search for God.'[77]

We have heard similar words from Russell before, and I think it neither a human nor philosophical indignity to apply the usual interpretation and say that the ghost he loves is the ghost of his absent parents, and that he has turned spectral in loving it because it signifies their absence. His parents' absence has diminished his being, so that he tends to vanish along with them, and wherever he turns, the human affection he gets is no more than an unsatisfactory attempt to assuage the hunger for the missing God, for him or for them who alone can sustain his being fully. Lacking this God, he finds himself within the great, cold, distant, or pervasive things, which are both everywhere and nowhere, emotionally, in particular.

But at the beginning of the passage I have been speaking of, Russell appends a note, dated 1967, which says, 'This and what follows is no longer true.' Before I make the necessary but obvious comment on Russell's note, I must summarize his relations with women. His sexual life was long, varied, and, until the end, unsatisfactory. Complications arose again and again. Thus when he had fallen out of love with Alys and was terrified by the fear that she would commit suicide, he decided to impregnate her and so to make 'the last sacrifice.' According to his journal, the sacrifice 'was not adequately carried out and failed totally.' Alys explained 'why she hated it, and didn't want a repetition at present.'[78]*

The fact that Russell had four marriages, at least two prolonged, serious love affairs (with Lady Ottoline Morrell and Constance Malleson), and many briefer affairs and momentary sexual encounters argues that he was engaged in a search doomed by his nature to failure. Ottoline Morrell said, 'However much I was thrilled by the beauty and transcendence of his thoughts, I could hardly bear the lack of physical attraction, the lack of charm and gentleness and sympathy, that are so essential to me and yet so rare.'[79] Constance Malleson wrote to him, 'I see now that your inability to care for anybody with the whole of you, for longer than a rather short time, may be more painful to you than it is to those who are able to continue caring in spite of everything.'[80] His daughter, Katherine, said:

> He did not expect to keep a woman's love and did not feel, in his heart, that she would lose much if he left her . . . His friendships were like warm and steady fires, and they gave great pleasure; his loves were as spectacular as fireworks and often as brief, and their souvenir was a burnt black shell. Unfortunately, this burnt shell was sometimes a woman who could not stop loving him just because he had ceased to find his ideal in her.[81]

In a discarded sentence of his *Autobiography*, Russell himself maintained that it was not in his nature 'to remain physically fond of any woman for more than seven or eight years.'[82] A woman friend emphasized how

---

*This may be the place to recall that Russell was told by Sir Sidney Waterlow, who was in charge of Foreign Office relations with the Far East, that he had never consummated his marriage with his beautiful wife because, 'under the influence of G. E. Moore, he had become convinced that there was something base about sexual intercourse.' When at the end of three years, he changed his mind, he discovered that he was impotent in relation to his wife. *The Collected Stories of Bertrand Russell*, p. 273 (from Russell's taped memoirs).

impossible an ideal he sought—Cleopatra and Aspasia, Hypatia and St. Theresa, Boadicea and Joan of Arc, not to mention 'Quakers and other Puritan types,' while a judge, in granting Dora her divorce, spoke more prosaically of 'infidelity . . . with persons in the household or engaged in the business in which they were mutually engaged.'[83]

Russell's difficulties in marriage appear, not surprisingly, to be related to his fantasies of his mother. Soon before his first marriage, he had reflected that he would be happy to sacrifice his career, his efforts to achieve virtue, his intellect and everything he had and hoped for, as gifts to his future wife. 'Thank God,' he wrote at the time, 'lust has absolutely no share in my passion. But just when I am happiest, when joy is purest, it seems to transcend itself and fall suddenly to haunting terrors of loss.' The idea of an absolute, lustless devotion is that of a son to a mother, and in Russell's case was naturally accompanied by a fear of loss. That Russell in fact identified mother and wife is verified by his dream, on Alys's birthday, that he could not marry her because his mother was not dead but mad. Significantly, when Russell fell out of love with Alys, he recalled how much she resembled her own mother, who had cruelly humiliated her husband and beaten her son. Once identified with the good mother, Alys was now identified with the bad, perhaps somewhat on the model of his grandmother.[84]

Significantly, too, when Russell's marriage with Alys became unhappy, he wrote in his journal that he bitterly regretted that she had damaged a miniature of his mother which he loved, in his words, 'with the more intensity because I had not permitted the same sort of love to grow up towards any other possession.'[85]

Russell's shortcomings as a lover and husband were related, I assume to those of his thrice-married brother, of whom Russell says, 'He passionately longed to be loved but was such a bully that he could never keep the love of anyone.'[86] Santayana, the brother's close friend, writes of him, 'He had never known a mother's love,' and, 'Russell as a husband, Russell in the domestic sphere, was simply impossible: excessively virtuous and incredibly tyrannical.'[87]

Russell's life was such that although he was always helping his children and showing that, in his way, he loved them, he was usually estranged from them. Katherine writes that he was cut off from all three of us children, 'from John by his breakdown, from Conrad by his (temporary) hostility, from me by religion. He continued to love us all, and I continued to love him; he and I exchanged affectionate letters, but without real communication.'[88]

The troubles were never few and the relationships were never smooth. But a long life can help, and a happy ending is sometimes possible. This is shown by Russell's note of 1967 and by the prosaic but touching poem with which he dedicates his *Autobiography* to the wife of his old age, Edith. In this poem he says that he sought peace and found everything else, ecstasy, anguish, madness, loneliness, and solitary pain; but now, so he writes to the wife he married at eighty, he has, knowing her, found ecstasy and peace, he knows rest; and he ends:

I know what life & love may be.
Now, if I sleep,
I shall sleep fulfilled.

It had taken Russell a long time, eighty full years, to find the sustaining intimacy that his childhood had denied him and that his philosophy had never striven for effectively enough. But his last year, when he was too weak to walk more than a few yards from his front door, was perhaps the happiest of his long life.[89]

Wittgenstein

19. Ludwig Josef Wittgenstein, born in 1889. His grandfather must be mentioned, if only for one positive and one negative trait, both of which formed part of the heritage he transmitted to his son, Karl, Ludwig's father. The positive trait was a deep interest in music. The negative was a strong desire to impose his will on his son, who had been expelled for bad behaviour from the famous *Gymnasium* in which he had studied, and who wanted to go to technical school. When the father objected to Karl's plan, Karl ran away from home and, with the aid, it is said, of a forged passport, reached the United States. Arriving penniless in New York City, he took a succession of jobs, as a waiter, restaurant or music-hall violinist, barge-hand, violin and mathematics teacher, and nightwatchman and then teacher at an asylum for children. After two years he reached a sort of reconciliation with his father and returned to Vienna, with new clothes, some money, and, above all, a distinctly changed personality, at first apathetic and obedient.

Karl Wittgenstein began his new life with a few engineering courses and some odd jobs, and he then became a draftsman and worked on plans for a steel-rolling mill. Although he had had little prior training, his capacity for work and his quickness to learn earned him rapid advancement. Before long, as such things go, he established himself as the most prominent developer of the Austrian iron and steel industry. His success was the result of his introduction of technological changes, his organizational ability, and his audacious entrepreneurial spirit. In keeping with such traits, he was full of criticism for Austria and its government and full of admiration for the United States, whose inhabitants seemed to him ideal in thier industriousness, reckless egoism, and love of freedom. It is not surprising that he himself was criticized for egoism. Descriptions of his personality show him to have been complex and formidable. He had a stormy, though unvindictive temperament, we are told, an inborn lack of respect of authorities and conventions, an extraordinarily quick apprehension, a brilliant gift for repartee, and even an amiable humor. In 1898, at the age of fifty-one, he retired from active business, his decision to retire fortified, perhaps, by attacks on him as a profiteer and stock-market manipulator. Much of his later life must have been occupied with art, for he was the Maecenas of the generation of Austrian artists who took part in the Secession movement.[1]

I can say much less, almost nothing, I am afraid, about Wittgenstein's mother, the daughter of a Viennese banker. She was gentle and musical. 'It was largely due to her that the Wittgenstein home in Vienna became a centre of musical life where Johannes Brahms was a frequent guest.'[2] Because she was a pianist, it may be she who was involved in a repeated hallucinatory experience that her son, Ludwig, reports. He says, 'I have such anxiety over anyone's playing piano in the house, that when it has occurred and the tinkling has stopped, I have a kind of hallucination, as if it were continuing. I can hear it quite clearly, although I know that it is only in my imagination.'[3] I should guess that it may be primarily his own mother to whom Ludwig is referring when he says, 'Look at people,' and continues:

> One is poison for the other. The mother for the son and the opposite, etc. etc. But the mother is blind and the son is too. Perhaps they have a guilty conscience, but how does that help them? The child is bad, but no one teaches it to be the opposite, and the parents spoil it through their stupid affection; and how should they understand it, and how should the child understand it? They are so to speak *all* bad and *all* innocent.[4]

Both father and mother created a family with strong musical and artistic interests. The father continued to play the violin, the eldest son, Hans, excelled on a number of instruments, the second son, Kurt, played the cello, the fourth, Paul, was to become a well-known piano soloist, while Ludwig, the fifth son and the youngest of the children, was deeply imbued with music, though it was only in later life that he learned to play a musical instrument, the clarinet. The remaining, third son, Rudi, was interested in the theatre. Of the daughters, one, Hermine, was an able painter, while another, Margarete, the family rebel, was an Ibsenite whose favourite thinkers were Schopenhauer, Kierkegaard, and Weininger. Ludwig is said to have loved and fought Margarete all his life.

She befriended Freud, of whom Ludwig at one time considered himself a disciple, though a distinctly critical one.[5] There is little information on Ludwig's childhood and youth. His sister, Hermine, does, however, tell us that he showed great interest in technical things.

> The construction of a sewing machine, for example, was already so clear to Ludwig at the age of ten that he was able my means of little wooden sticks, wire, etc., to produce a small model which actually sewed a few stitches. In order to do that, of course, he had to make a detailed study of the big sewing machine in all its parts and stitching phases, something which the old family seamstress looked upon with suspicious displeasure.[6]

Ludwig did not care to talk about his youth, 'which to him was a most painful recollection.'[7] He said to a friend, 'I had an unhappy childhood and a most miserable youth.'[8] At the age of twenty-three he confided

> that for nine years, till last Xmas, he suffered from terrible loneliness (mental, not physical); that he continually thought of suicide then, and felt ashamed of never daring to kill himself; he put it that he had had 'a hint that he was *de trop* in the world' but that he had meanly disregarded it. He had been brought up to engineering for which he had neither taste nor talent.[9]

It is all too easy to associate Ludwig's loneliness and suicidal thoughts with the death of Hans, who committed suicide when Ludwig was thirteen, and with that of Rudi, who committed suicide when Ludwig was fifteen. Hans, who had begun to compose at the age of four, had insisted on becoming a musician while his father had insisted that he become a businessman. Finding life at home impossible, Hans escaped to America, where, at the age of twenty-four, he killed himself. Rudi 'committed suicide in similar circumstances.'[10] These few bare words are all I have found on Rudi's death; but the words, 'in similar circumstances,' have a terribly ominous sound. They give no clue to the inward life of the wealthy, cultured, highly social family, except, that is, that it was tragic.

In keeping with the father's educational ideas, Ludwig, like the other children, was educated at home. He showed little ability for the school subjects he was taught, though he was interested in mechanics, as we have seen. When his father discovered how little progress he had made, he decided to send him to a technical secondary school. Ludwig's preparation had not fitted him for entrance into the more demanding Viennese schools, so, after being given some coaching, he was sent to study in Upper Austria, in Linz. There he lived, between the ages of about fourteen to seventeen, in the home of a teacher.[11] A schoolmate of his later told Hermine Wittgenstein that

> Ludwig had appeared to all of them as if blown in from an alien world. He had a completely different life-style from theirs, addressing his school-fellows, for

example, with the formal pronoun 'Sie', which created a barrier, apart from the fact that his interests and the books he read were totally different from theirs.

Hermine then adds, 'But above all he was uncommonly sensitive. . . .'[12] I can guess that he took the decision to send him to Linz as a sentence of exile. Whether so or not, his stay there coincided with the beginning of his nine years of terrible loneliness.

Ludwig's hope to study with the physicist, Ludwig Boltzmann, was frustrated by Boltzmann's suicide. He entered the Technische Hochschule in Berlin, where he occupied himself in the study of aerodynamics, a subject in which he had previously become interested. His disappointment with Berlin sent him, after three semesters, to England, where he registered as an engineering research student at the University of Manchester. Experiments in kite-flying were followed by attempts to design a jet engine and then a jet reaction propeller. Propeller design led him to concentrate on mathematics, and mathematics to concentrate on its own foundations.[13]

Now Ludwig took his first steps toward the profession of philosophy. In the words of his sister, Hermine:

> He was suddenly seized so strongly and so completely against his will by philosophy, i.e., by reflections about philosophical problems, that he suffered severely under his double and conflicting calling, and felt inwardly divided. One of several transformations that he was to undergo in his life had come over him and shaken his whole being. At that time he was concerned with writing a philosophical work and finally decided to show the plan of this to a Professor Frege at Jena, who was involved with similar questions. Ludwig found himself in those days to be in a constant, indescribable and almost morbid state of excitement, and I very much feared that Frege, whom I knew to be an old man, would not be able to muster up the patience and understanding to deal with the matter with the required seriousness. I therefore was greatly worried and afraid during Ludwig's trip to Frege, but it went far better than I had anticipated. Frege strengthened Ludwig in his philosophical quest and advised him to go to Cambridge to study with a Professor Russell, which Ludwig then did.[14]

Russell reacted to his new student with interest, with bewilderment, and then with enthusiasm. He found him to be perverse, stubborn, and somtimes to be stammering out merely dull things. But this intenseness overwhelmed Russell, who wrote:

> He had pure intellectual passion in the highest degree; it makes me love him. His disposition is that of an artist, intuitive & moody. He says every morning he begins his work with hope & every evening he ends in despair—he has just the sort of rage when he can't understand things that I have.[15]

Russell even went so far as to say that he could now relax and leave all sorts of difficult technical work to Wittgenstein. He was now less anxious to live, he said, because he felt that Wittgenstein would do the same work he, Russell, should do, and do it better.[16] But he soon observed Wittgenstein's instability, and on 31 October, 1912, noted that Wittgenstein was on the verge of a nervous breakdown, not far from suicide, and dominated by a feeling of sinfulness. 'Whatever he says,' wrote Russell, 'he apologizes for saying. He has fits of dizziness & can't work—the Dr. says it is all nerves . . . He makes me terribly anxious—it is all so real, & I know it so well.'[17]

Wittgenstein's life was to get no easier. In January, 1913, his father died. Wittgenstein found this death not too difficult to suffer because it was, he felt, of a 'beautiful,' encouraging kind.[18] Not long afterward, his brother Paul lost his right arm in the early stages of the First World War. Ludwig, whose hernia exempted him from army service, was both eager to defend the fatherland and to take on a demanding task. He was successful in enlisting in an artillery regiment, where his engineering skill won him the unofficial status of an officer. On his own repeated plea, he was sent to the front.[19] The reason for his plea, he was later to say, was that he had volunteered for the army as a form of suicide, to find death.[20] Both before and after his appointment as a regular artillery officer, he won decorations for bravery. He is said to have been companionable with his men and able to calm them in battle, mainly by going on with his artillery observation even under heavy fire.[21]

Trouble now followed trouble. In August of 1918, his favourite uncle died. In October he learned that the manuscript of the *Tractatus*, which he regarded as his life's work and longed to see in print, had been rejected.[22] Two days after he learned of the rejection, his brother, Kurt, an officer on the Russian front, shot himself because his soldiers had abandoned the field, or, according to another version, in order to avoid capture.[23] In November, Ludwig was taken prisoner on the Italian front. News then reached him that his beloved Cambridge friend, David Pinsent, to whom he was to dedicate the *Tractatus*, had died in action.

In the summer of 1919, when he was released from prison camp, Wittgenstein returned to Vienna. There he talked of suicide and insisted fiercely on giving away all his father had left him to his brothers and sisters, except to Margarete, whose wealth had not been seriously curtailed by the war. 'A hundred times he wished to assure himself that it was completely out of the question that any sum belonged to him in any form whatsoever, and he constantly came back to this point, to the despair of the notary who was carrying out the transfer.'[24] The reason for this act of renunciation, Wittgenstein later said, was that he did not want to have any friends on account of his wealth.[25]

Wittgenstein also decided to take up a quite humble occupation and become a village schoolteacher, in the spirit of the school reform movement then active in Austria. When his sister, Hermine, tried the family tactic of communicating by means of comparisons and said that to use his philosophically trained mind for elementary school teaching was like using a precision instrument to open crates, his answer was, 'You remind me of someone who is looking through a closed window and cannot explain to himself the strange movements of a passerby. He doesn't know what kind of storm is raging outside and that this person is perhaps only with great effort keeping himself on his feet.'[26]

Wittgenstein proved in some ways an excellent teacher, leading the children on with questions and stimulating them with demonstrations. But he did not have patience to deal with untalented or lazy boys, or with girls, whose minds were preoccupied with nonintellectual matters. We are told that 'the giggling of the girls in the mixed classes would try his patience beyond endurance.'[27] He could burst into anger and become rough, and his six arduous, abstemious years as a village teacher ended when villagers brought him to trial on charges of cruelty to their children. Although acquitted, he abandoned his village teaching, in 1926.[28] About six weeks later, when he was thirty-seven, his mother died. For a while he worked in a monastery garden and contemplated becoming a monk.[29]

It is no wonder that 'Wittgenstein had the conviction, he sometimes said, that he was doomed . . . His idea of the helplessness of human beings was not unlike certain doctrines of predestination.'[30] The study of philosophy with Russell was his 'salvation,' he said, but the thought of logic did not drive the thought of suicide out of his mind.[31] The two could coalesce into a single torment, and when he at one point announced to Russell that logic was driving him to insanity, Russell thought that he might be right and advised him to abandon logic for a while.[32]

After his father's death, Wittgenstein had left Vienna, and the thought of returning home, as his mother urged, appalled him. The letter in which he said this to Russell ended with the sudden sentence, 'I often think I am going mad.'[33] Soon thereafter, in January of 1914, he wrote to Russell, this time from Norway, where he was working in his solitary log cabin, of torment, depression, and exhaustion. 'It's terrifying beyond all description the kinds of mental torment there can be! It wasn't until two days ago that I could hear the voice of reason over the howls of the damned and I began work again . . . I *never* knew what it meant to feel only *one* step from madness.'[34]

The inner pain did not end. It is repeatedly evident in the correspondence he held from 1919 to 1925 with his friend, the architect, Paul Engelmann, with whom he had served in the army. In this

correspondence, Wittgenstein speaks of normal human beings as both a
balm and a torment to him; of being in a state terrifying to himself; of the
dirtiness of suicide; of death as moral for him and life as meaningless; and
of his continuing stupidity and rottenness.[35]

Wittgenstein's pain and disturbance made him receptive to the rather
mystical faith expressed by William James and to Tolstoy's rationalized
Christianity. He said that the *Varieties of Religious Experience*, which he
came on before the First World War, had done him a lot of good, and
he thought James 'a real human being' and therefore a good
philosopher. Tolstoy influenced him most through *The Gospel in Brief*,
which he discovered in a bookstore one day during the war. Russell
reported that Wittgenstein 'read and re-read it, and thenceforth had it
always with him, under fire and at all times'; Hermine reported that its
constant presence made the soldiers call Wittgenstein 'The one with the
Bible'; and Wittgenstein himself said, 'This book simply kept me
alive.'[36]

Wittgenstein's *Notebooks* of 1914 to 1916 naturally refer to his chief
preoccupations, the philosophical problems of logic, the meaning of life,
and the morality of suicide. The influence of Schopenhauer is often
evident. Wittgenstein writes, 'Even if all *possible* scientific questions are
answered, *our problem is still not touched at all.*'[37] He reflects that his will,
which is good or evil, penetrates the world, and that good and evil are
connected with the meaning of the world, which may be called God.
Then he reflects, in a sentence which he may already have seen in the
light of Freudian analysis, 'And connect this with the comparison of God
to a father.' He preaches renunciation to make himself independent of the
world.[38] He feels himself dependent on an alien will, which may, he says,
be called God.[39] He reflects that being happy is living in agreement with
the world, and that '*a happy world*' is factually identical with its opposite,
an unhappy world.[40] As logic, he says, is the prior condition of thought,
ethics is the prior condition of the world.[41] Then he adds, as he may
somehow have learned from his family life, 'Ethics and aesthetics are the
same.'[42] In his family, that is, life and death had conspired to show the
identity of music, conscience, conduct, and the meaning of life. This
reflection made, Wittgenstein then reflects that only the willing subject
exists, and he says, 'The I, the I is what is deeply mysterious.'[43] He ends
his surviving *Notebooks* with the reflection, which he also doubts, that
'suicide is, so to speak, the elementary sin,' for 'if suicide is allowed
then everything is allowed,' a point that Kant had made with great
emphasis.[44]

As has already been more than intimated, Wittgenstein was scathingly
self-critical. He wanted to seclude himself in Norway in 1913, a friend
reports, not only to work at logic without distraction, but also because

' "he had not right to live in a world" where he constantly felt
contempt for other people and irritated them by his nervous
temperament.'[45] Years later, on his return from another stay in his
Norwegian hut, he made a double or triple confession to a number of
people. He confessed that he had allowed it to be believed that he was
three-quarters Aryan and one quarter Jewish, when the reverse
proportion was the case; and he confessed, with great emotion, that in
Austria he had struck and hurt a little girl in his class, but had denied
the act to the principal, to whom she had complained.[46]

Wittgenstein was certainly difficult to get along with. 'His opinions on
most matters were absolute, allowing for no argument . . . He had a great
capacity to wound . . . A less inhibited man, one more given to wrath and
quick anger, it is hard to imagine.'[47] Although human kindness was
much more important to him than intellect or taste, he could rebuke a
friend with extreme harshness, and he tended to be suspicious of motives
and character. Once afraid that people might be drawn to him by his
wealth, he was now afraid that they would be drawn to him, not for
himself, but for his philosophy. He complained that he had a great need
for affection but was unable to give it. He insisted on complete honesty.[48]

As a teacher, Wittgenstein was formidably irascible and impatient,
though less impatient, it would seem, with beginners.[49] Fear of him
helped to keep his students' attention at a high pitch.[50] 'He drove himself
fiercely. His whole being was under a tension.'[51] As he sat in the middle
of the room on a plain wooden chair and struggled with his thoughts,
sweat poured down his face. There were long, tense silences during
which he sat in painful concentration, his hands making arresting
movements.[52] 'I cannot possibly do justice,' recalled Moore, 'to the
intensity of conviction with which he said everything which he did
say nor to the extreme interest which he excited in his hearers.'[53]

After lecturing, Wittgenstein 'felt disgusted with what he had said and
with himself' and would immediately go off with a disciple to a film,
where he would 'sit in the very first row of seats, so that the screen
would occupy his entire field of vision, and his mind would be turned
away from the thoughts of the lecture and his feelings of revulsion.'[54]

In spite of the strenuous efforts he made to teach philosophy
Wittgenstein was always 'very dubious as to whether his influence on
others (and on contemporary philosophy) was not more harmful than
beneficial.'[55] He was tormented by what he took to be his failure as a
teacher and commented with bitterness that the only seed he was likely
to sow was jargon.[56] Too many of his students, he said, merely imitated
his voice and manner, and too many misunderstood and distorted his
ideas.[57] He once exclaimed that 'he would gladly see all his writings
destroyed if along with them would vanish the publications of his

students and disciples.'[58] In the preface to *Philosophical Investigations* he said explicitly that he was willing to have this book published in his lifetime only because his vanity had been stung by misleading versions of his work. 'He felt as if he were writing for people who would think in a quite different way, breathe a different air.'[59] In the preface to his *Tractatus* he hoped to give pleasure to someone who had thought similar thoughts. He surely did not suppose the book to be intelligible on conventional reading. When the mathematician and philosopher, Frank Ramsey, went to Austria to study the book with Wittgenstein, he wrote in a letter:

> He often forgot the meaning of what he wrote within 5 minutes, and then remembered it later. Some of his sentences are intentionally ambiguous having an ordinary and a more difficult meaning which he also believes.[60]

The feeling of a very sensitive transmission to a chosen 'brain or another' is again reflected in the preface to *Philosophical Investigations*, in a few brief but expressive sentences, which I need not repeat here. But Ramsey's letter draws attention to the interrupted, spasmodic, and almost wilfully obscure characteristics of Wittgenstein's teaching and writing. 'During the first term,' one of his students recalled, 'I felt that I was hearing a lecture in which there were gaps, such as intermittant deafness might produce.'[61] Another student wrote, 'The considerable difficulty in following the lectures arose from the fact that it was hard to see where all this often repetitive concrete detailed talk was leading to,' and a third student, recalling Wittgenstein's pauses or mental blocks, said simply, 'It did seem that he had difficulty in producing a connected lecture.'[62]

I have said that there was something almost wilfully obscure in Wittgenstein. For his writing, his justification was that he *had* to write in his disjointed, aphoristic style. As has been emphasized in the earlier discussion of his style, the preface to *Philosophical Investigations* explains that he found his thoughts were soon crippled if forced against their natural inclination. Therefore, he said, he made remarks sometimes in a fairly long chain devoted to the same subject, but sometimes the remarks jumped suddenly from subject to subject. This insistance on at least surface disconnectedness applies as well to the *Tractatus*, which would have been only 'an unintelligible waste' if not for its numbering.[63] And though, as he insisted, the point of the *Tractatus* was an ethical one, he volunteered that he had omitted a sentence in its preface that might have been a key to the whole work, a sentence that would have made clear that the part of the *Tractatus* he had *not* written was precisely the important one.[64]

Even the style of Wittgenstein's walking and talking was spasmodic.

'He would walk in spurts, sometimes coming to a stop while he made some emphatic remark and looking into my eyes with his piercing gaze,' said his disciple, Malcolm. 'Then he would walk rapidly for a few yards, then slow down, then speed up or come to a halt, and so on.'[65] His very life, said Wittgenstein, was a process of 'stumbling and falling, stumbling and falling.'[66]

It is possible that this spasmodic quality was a family trait. It seems to have characterized the piano playing of his brother, Paul. I say this because of what I heard on June 13, 1974, when I came with my questions on Paul to the scholar and pianist, Professor A. Vardi, of the Music Academy of Tel-Aviv University, who is a specialist in the music of Debussy and Ravel. He told me that Paul's story had long fascinated him, but that he had heard derogatory remarks about his ability as a pianist and the suspicion that it was only his wealth that had allowed him to buy music from such composers as Richard Strauss and Ravel. Only recently, and with great anticipation, he said, he had heard a recording of Wittgenstein's performance of the concerto that Ravel had written for him. Even though a record, which allows corrections, is ordinarily better than any single performance, Vardi was severely disappointed. He said, to my surprise, that the performance was 'beneath criticism.' Wittgenstein proved incapable of playing all the notes, and at one point unashamedly replaced them with a glissando. The playing, Vardi said, was particularly spasmodic because, though there were moments when Paul played with great intensity, he soon lost his concentration. I suggested the word, 'stammering,' which I will soon use to characterize Ludwig's writing, speaking, and thinking, and Vardi accepted the word as a possible characterization of Paul's playing.

Wittgenstein's 'approach to philosophical problems was essentially aesthetic in the widest sense.'[67] To him, 'philosophy should really be expressed as poetry.'[68] While working on *Philosophical Investigations*, he commented, 'It is impossible for me to say one word in my book about all that music has meant in my life; how then can I possibly make myself understood?'[69] The friend to whom Wittgenstein made this comment said, 'To watch Wittgenstein listening to music was to realize that this was something very central and deep in his life . . . I will never forget the emphasis with which he quoted Schopenhauer's dictum, "Music is a world in itself".'[70]

Wittgenstein held that beauty, like religion, was beyond explanation.[71] He also opposed the 'shallow rationalism' that tried to give explanations for the good.[72] We express the beautiful and the good, he held, with literally nonsensical and yet impressive language.[73] Perhaps this was a reason that he preoccupied himself with the nature and limits of language and with, as he saw it, the related problem of solipsism (and Idealism).

His attraction to solipsism is clearest in the *Notebooks* and clear enough in the *Tractatus*; but he never gave in to it fully.[74] He argued that the genuinely private language that solipsism requires is impossible. No external reference can be made in such a language, nor can real questions be asked in it, and so solipsism, like empiristic scepticism, makes no sense.[75]

On Certainty, which Wittgenstein wrote during the last year and a half of his life, remains preoccupied with the solipsistic and sceptical doctrines that Wittgenstein tended to reject. The preoccupation was more than theoretical. Wittgenstein's position was that the concepts of knowledge and certainty could not be applied to one's own sensations. When Moore tried, in 1939, to prove the opposite, namely, that a person could know that he had a sensation like that of pain, Wittgenstein, his disciple, Malcolm, reports,

> reacted like a war-horse . . . Moore re-read his paper and Wittgenstein immediately attacked it. He was more excited than I ever knew him to be in a discussion. He was full of fire and spoke rapidly and forcefully. He put questions to Moore but frequently did not give Moore a chance to answer. This went on for at least two hours, with Wittgenstein talking almost continuously, and scarcely a word was said by anyone else. Wittgenstein's brilliance and power were impressive and even frightening.[76]

The whole of the later Wittgenstein conveys a feeling of insatiable, anxious, repetitive questioning and answering. 'I ask innumerable irrelevant questions,' he himself once wrote. 'I hope I'll be able to make my way through this forest!'[77] On another occasion he wrote perceptively that we ought not to forget that 'also our finer, more philosophical doubts have an instinctive basis.'[78] It was as if he found the general questions that had once troubled him, those of life and death and good and bad, impossible to answer or too threatening, and therefore broke them up into smaller questions, each of which could be examined in its own rights. He said, 'I keep entangling myself in details, without knowing whether I should talk about these things at all; and it seems to me that I perhaps inspect a wide area only in order to exclude it for once from consideration.'[79] When he was thinking naturally, not, that is, for the purpose of writing a book, he would 'skip about' the theme. To think in forced sequence was 'a torment' to him. 'Should I try it at all?' he asked himself, adding, 'I *squander* inexpressible effort on the arrangement of the thoughts, which perhaps has no value.'[80] This dissociation of his thinking, this hesitancy, this breaking up of and painful attempt to restore its general pattern is in the style, I believe, of stammering. Language itself, it seems to me, was so full of both promise and danger to him that he could not use it as if it were a simply neutral medium.

The promise and danger had physiological correlates. 'He suffered from a minor defect of speech which, however, disappeared later on. He used to struggle for words, especially when trying hard to formulate a proposition.'[81] A disciple reports that when he first heard him 'he had extreme difficulty in expressing himself and his words were unintelligible to me.'[82] Yet 'once he started talking,' as another witness testifies, 'he could hold you in thrall.'[83] On the whole, it was better for him when he, not others talked. 'When he stopped you from saying anything he looked as though by speaking you would inflect a wound,' and he was 'driven to distraction by the manner in which people spoke.'[84]

Wittgenstein's stammer, traces of which, I think he always retained, was paralleled by his idea-stammer, by which I mean, a fierce but blocked searching, a series of hesitancies, and then, sometimes, a sudden resolution. Stammering, in the meaning of which I would like to include the stammering, not only of speech-sounds, but of ideas, may be the response to something the stammerer both wants and does not want to say, or the equally ambivalent response to the activity itself of speaking. Wittgenstein's stammering is likely to have been related to his sadistic tendencies and guilt over them; to his peculiar interest in speech and deprecation of its powers and, often, of its use; to his ambition and self-doubt; and to his at least mild exhibitionism, which was his need for an audience and his revulsion from an audience.[85] He said, 'We fight with language. We are fighting with language.'[86] And he said, 'Words are deeds.'[87] His stammering expressed his whole intense, difficult situation.

Feeling that he was '*de trop*,' that he 'had no right to live in a world,' Wittgenstein first tried to split off and banish the world of hard facts and to continue to exist in the transcendent world in which alone his innocence might be clear and his right to exist retained. Afterward, he tried to apprehend a set of interrelated frames with a complex but hardly understood coherence, or at least a coherence that could not be expressed in generalizations. To express this interrelationship, he used the notion of 'family resemblance,' which he took to apply to a group in which every two members had at least one trait in common, but not, or not necessarily, any trait common at all. If, as might be assumed, he was thinking, even unconsciously, of human families when he first used the term, it might have appealed to him as appropriate to his own difficult family experience, in which genuine closeness was likely to have been hard to maintain and quite differently qualified with each person. His stammered world of kind–cruel, real–false, and I–other, and of games discovered obscurely within other games was his answer to the death with which he had so often threatened himself. Philosophically, it was a more complex version of the attractive and repelling fantasy he had entertained that his own nervous system might be connected with that of another person so that their pains and consciousness, their 'I's might be connected.[88]

If we continue with the attempt to grasp the relations between Wittgenstein's human problems and his philosophy, many possibilities suggest themselves. Perhaps the first is that he was engaged, as he stressed in various ways, in an intense search for clarity. The search is peculiar in that he conducted it in so at least apparently unclear a way. He himself said that he had given hidden senses to his words and had omitted or barely hinted at what mattered most. And yet he complained that he was always misunderstood; and he anticipated further misunderstanding. It will be recalled that he felt he could really communicate the truth he had found only to some possible future individuals. Rejecting almost everyone, he anticipated rejection and usually spoke in rejecting, depressed, or guarded words.[89]

This characterization, like the previous one, implies the ambivalence everywhere evident in both his person and thought. It was his pleasure and need to teach with fierce intensity, yet he was immediately disgusted with what he had taught and with himself as a teacher. It appears to me that he used his teaching to establish some connection with persons interested in his philosophically-expressed problems and therefore in himself; but to establish the connection he had to risk revealing himself; and he was sure in advance that, whatever he said, the others would not really understand him; and if they did understand him, they would value him for his ideas, and not for himself. In effect, he was frightened, repelled, and disgusted by the closeness that his intellectual and emotional intensity did succeed in establishing, and he immediately tried to wipe out the consciousness of this trying experience with the help of the impersonal excitements of a film.

Wittgenstein's ambivalence extended to his profession. To his disciples, he was the model philosopher; but he tried to deflect them from becoming what he was at the time, a professional teacher of philosophy, and to deflect them even from philosophy as such. Often expressing contempt for other philosophers, he might insist that his students stay away from philosophy books altogether.*

---

*Comparing American detective stories with *Mind*, he said, 'How people can read Mind if they could read Street and Smith beats me.' These words make an ironical parallel with those of Sartre, who said in 1963, 'Even now I read the 'série Noire' of detective stories and thrillers more willingly than I do Wittgenstein.' The difference may be that Sartre does not intend his taste for detective stories to imply contempt for Wittgenstein, while Wittgenstein was certainly expressing contempt for *Mind*. See N. Malcolm, *Ludwig Wittgenstein*, p. 36; and J.-P. Sartre, *Les mots*, p. 61. In B. Frechtman's translation, *The Words* (Greenwich, Conn.: Fawcett Publications), the quotation occurs on p. 48.

When his students published anything in which his influence was apparent, he felt misunderstood, angry, and perhaps jealous, and he tried to protect the priority of his ideas.[90] Long before he had experienced his own particular talent, he had felt he was an extraordinary man.[91] But he was at least sometimes unsure of the depth of his originality. He supposed that he might not be able to plant any true seeds of thought of his own, but that he (like Freud) was good soil in which to plant the seeds of others.[92] Estimating himself, he wrote:

> The Jewish 'genius' is only a religious one. The greatest Jewish thinker is only a talent. (I, e.g.)
> There is some truth in it when I think that I am really only reproductive in my thinking. I believe that I have never *invented* an idea-movement, but it has, instead, always been given to me by someone else. I have only picked it up immediately and passionately for my work of clarification. So Boltzmann, Hertz, Schopenhauer, Frege, Russell, Kraus, Loos, Weininger, Spengler, Sraffa have influenced me. Is it possible to draw in Breuer and Freud as examples of Jewish reproductivity?—What I invent are new *comparisons* [or *images, Gleichnisse*].[93]

Wittgenstein demanded sincerity but was not always sure that he himself was capable of it. His sympathies were often with intellectual young men who were, in one way or another, cripples, or at least sufferers, for example, the shy, brilliant, lame Francis Skinner, or the lame friend with whom he toured Brittany.[94] He would see himself in them and entertain ideas of healing them. Because he saw himself in his disciples, he tried, by dominating them, to act out his fatherhood, that is to say, his superiority to himself and his ability to guide and improve himself. So, too, he took up medicine, thought of becoming a doctor, volunteered as a medical assistant, and proposed to devote himself to the care of the insane.[95] Thinking also of himself, he asked whether it was an unfulfilled longing that made a man insane. 'As in life we are surrounded by death,' he said, 'so also in health of understanding by insanity.' In relation to insanity, he defined the philosopher as 'he who must heal many sicknesses of the understanding in himself before he can arrive at the notions of a healthy human understanding.'[96]

Wittgenstein's identification with sufferers made it easy for him to see them as superior, as on the occasion when he found a chronically insane patient to be much more intelligent than all his doctors.[97] But though he did succeed in dominating his disciple-friends 'of childlike innocence and innocent brain,' and though he did attempt to cure philosophers' problems, those manifested, as he supposed, in their problems with language, his mind always retained some sense of his own ambivalence, some paranoid-like suspicion, expressed in his typical cry, 'Intolerable!' and his typical question, 'But is it genuine?'[98]

Wittgenstein's interest in argument and language is, among other things, an identification and competition with his father, who could speak, argue, domineer, and convince so well. In order to remain close to this distant, often irascible, and domineering businessman-father, Wittgenstein internalized his irascibility, his domineering quality, and his businesslike concern with action and results. He said, 'My father was a businessman and I am a businessman too; I want my philosophy to be businesslike, to get something done, to get something settled.'[99] Like his father, he studied and abandoned the study of engineering. At least in his beginnings as a logician and logical atomist, he adopted an engineering approach in philosophy, too, though he whispered in the *Tractatus* that the philosophical engineering that took up so many of its pages was really futile, for what was really important lay absolutely beyond its reach.

I wonder how much of Wittgenstein's dependence on Tolstoy's *The Gospel in Brief*, of which he said, 'This book simply kept me alive,' is the result of Tolstoy's repeated reference to the Father, whose worship makes one independent of time. Tolstoy's words, 'The true life is independent of time: it is in the present,' are like enough to Wittgenstein's in the *Notebooks*, repeated in the *Tractatus*, 'If by eternity is understood not infinite temporal duration but non-temporality, then it can be said that a man lives eternally if he lives in the present.'[100] Tolstoy's 'he who lives by love in the present, through the common life of all men, unites with the Father, the source and foundation of life,' is not unlike Wittgenstein's, 'The meaning of life, i.e. the meaning of the world, we can call God. And connect with this the comparison of God to a father.'[101] Could Wittgenstein not have thought of his father when he read and reread such sentences in Tolstoy's version of the Gospels as,

> The satisfaction of the personal will leads to death; the satisfaction of the Father's will gives true life . . . The true food of everlasting life is the fulfilment of the Father's will . . . Not to fall into temptation, we must at every moment of our life be at one with the Father . . . For a man who lives not the personal life but the common life in the will of the Father, there is no death. Physical death is union with the Father.[102]

Wittgenstein's deep interest in the arts is surely a form of participation in his parents' life. His father loved music but was opposed to a musical career for his sons, if the fate of Wittgenstein's brother, Hans, is any indication; and so Wittgenstein loved music, but refrained from becoming a musician. The musicality of the family was such that music could represent for him the inexpressible depth of life, while his philosophy, which was to him merely logical or verbal, could not resonate with the sustaining familial closeness.

I think that it was Wittgenstein's need for his family that led him, after his difficult experience as a village teacher, to sink himself in the design and construction of a house for his third sister, Gretl. The original plans for the house had been drawn up by his friend, Engelmann. Though Engelmann's basic design seems to have been preserved, Hermine tells us,

> Engelmann had to give way to the much stronger personality, and the house was then built, down to the smallest detail, according to Ludwig's plans and under his supervision. Ludwig designed every window, door, window-bar and radiator in the noblest proportions and with such exactitude that they might have been precision instruments.[103]

Ludwig, in fact, demanded a precision that sometimes appeared unattainable and drove the engineer of the company making the doors into a state of hysteria. Hermine says, 'The strongest proof of Ludwig's relentlessness with regard to precise measurements is perhaps the fact that he decided to have the ceiling of a hall-like room raised by three centimetres just as the cleaning of the completed house was to commence.' She adds, whether out of conviction or loyalty I do not know, 'His instinct was absolutely right and his instinct had to be followed.'[104] Needless to say, the completed houses did not satisfy him in every detail—a troublesome rear staircase window was never altered. In at least this instance, his perfectionism expressed his solidarity with his family and his desire that its life be perfected through his exacting intervention.

Wittgenstein discovered that philosophy might save him; but his condition remained painful and led him to the verge of suicide and perhaps madness. His self-denigration, the feeling that he had no worth and no existence in a world, raised the problem of existence in general. Put in his own words, 'No one can truly say of himself that he is dirt. For when I say it, it can in a sense be true, but I cannot myself be pervaded by this truth: otherwise I should have to be insane, or to change myself.'[105] But though, he concluded, he must ascribe some worth to himself, it was also natural to him to conclude that his writing should be undertaken only under conditions of terrible suffering, so that the truth would not be what it seemed at first sight, for it would be less a theory than a sigh or shout.[106] 'Only when one thinks even much more madly than the philosophers can one solve their problems.'[107]

Wittgenstein decided that the unique fact of existence and the sense of wonder it aroused could not be expressed or justified logically or scientifically.[108] Like the will and values of his father, those of the world, though they determined life and death, could not be understood. To understand or react to them relevantly he had no choice, he believed, but to turn to art, ethics, and religion, all equally indescribable, and to the sincerity that might penetrate them by its moral vision.

In his later philosophy, Wittgenstein dealt implicitly, as his examples show, with loneliness, animosity, pain, and doubt.[109] He did this too by his rather chaotic way of writing about the different senses of the 'same' words. His interest in the peculiarities of language resembled that of a sculptor who organizes his sculpture around the knots and projections of the wood he is using. He hoped to escape from illusion by focusing his vision clearly on details. His aim was not to change but to become adapted to reality by means of clear vision almost alone. As in Freud, the ability to see was itself, he believed, therapeutic.

Judging by his more explicit statements, the events that caused his depression or disgust with himself might have been his lapses in truth or the cruelties he committed. But his whole situation would be more intelligible, as would his frequent attacks on his own decency, if he suffered, as has been claimed, from his attachment to rough homosexual men whom he despised.[110] He certainly was reputed to be a homosexual—recalling their old friendship, Russell said with a cutting non-sequitur, 'Wittgenstein was witty but a homosexual.'[111] And Wittgenstein himself once let fall, 'If you think I'm an old spinster—think again!'[112] I have heard talk of a diary in which Wittgenstein reveals that he is homosexual. There is also a report that he lived with a woman in Norway, and another that he once seemed almost resigned to marriage.[113]

It has been said that Wittgenstein disliked intellectual women.[114] But he did have some women as students and disciples and was friendly with others. His admiration for the misogynistic Otto Weininger, who thought sexual abstinence essential for genius, and his dependence for advice on Dr. Ludwig Hänsel, who was concerned with the sexual purity of boys and polemicized against masturbation and against Freud, are easily compatible with his distance from women and his sense of guilt. So also are Schopenhauer and the later Tolstoy.[115]

It is moving to recall that Wittgenstein's last conscious words were, 'Tell them that I've had a wonderful life!'[116] But it is more characteristic and perhaps no less moving that once, when accused by his disciple, Malcolm, of having argued unfairly, his eyes blazed with anger and he answered, 'If you knew anything at all you would know that I am never unfair to anyone. This proves that you can have understood absolutely nothing of my lectures.'[117] If we take him at his word, it was this, his fairness, his essential human worth, that he had meant all along to make clear.

Sartre

20. Jean-Paul-Charles-Aymard Sartre, born in 1905. His father, a naval officer, died when the child was about one. His mother, Ann-Marie, then about twenty, returned to live with her parents. The result was, as Sartre comments, that until the age of ten he remained alone between an old man and two women.[1]

My description of Sartre's childhood necessarily draws on his own account in *The Words*. This account was conceived in 1953, when Sartre was forty-nine years old, when, 'thrown into the atmosphere of action,' he suddenly concluded that all his previous work had been dominated by a neurosis that had begun in his childhood.[2] He worked at *The Words* intermittently, and though it is a short book, finished it only in 1963.[3] It is compounded in about equal measure of anger and nostalgia, the anger summarized in the sentence, 'I detest my childhood and everything of it that survives,' and in the verdict, 'I was an impostor.'[4] Simone de Beauvoir says of the book, 'Dealing with himself in the past and the present, both alternately and simultaneously, his linguistic invention created the relationship between the adult and the child which forms the book's originality and which gives it its value.'[5] But Sartre's old mother, as I will later repeat, could not recognize her son in his self-portrait as a little boy, while to Sartre at the age of seventy it was 'a kind of novel, a novel in which I believe, but still a novel.'[6] At any rate, it is a vehement, highly stylized, interesting little book, and we have little more than our own common sense with which to redress its possible one-sidedness.

During the last illness of his father, Sartre was put out to nurse and almost died of enteritis and perhaps, he adds resentfully, of resentment. When he regained consciousness, it was, he conjectures, on the lap of a mother who had become a stranger.[7] About two pages further on in the French text of *The Words* he breaks into a short diatribe against all fathers and says, 'There is no good father, that's the rule. Don't lay the blame on men but on the bond of paternity which is rotten. To beget children, no-thing better; to *have* them, what iniquity! Had my father lived, he would have lain on me at full length and would have crushed me. As luck would have it, he died young.'[8] Once again, as an African proverb has it, he who is absent is always wrong—whoever has died too soon is somehow blamed for the fact. Later in his autobiography, however, Sartre regrets the absence of a father, who would, he imagines, have given him the stability and self-respect that would have helped him to determine his future. Lacking the direction a father might have given him, he says, 'Nobody, beginning with me, knew why the hell I had been born . . . I was not substantial or permanent, I *was not* the future continuer of my father's work, I *was not* necessary to the production of steel. In short, I had no soul.'[9] In the terminology I have used, something of his being had been destroyed.

Sartre's nostalgia was centred on his mother. By his description, she was girlish and sisterly, and he and she made a couple lovingly engrossed in one another. 'My mother was mine; no one challenged my peaceful possession of her,' he recalls. 'I knew nothing of violence and hatred. I was spared the hard apprenticeship of jealousy.'[10] One result of this closeness to his mother, he says, is that the image of the mother-sister always attracted him and was reflected in his writings. It was also reflected, I think, in his attachment to Simone de Beauvoir. The family bond attracted him, he maintains, not so much by its amorous temptation as by its taboo against making love. Briefly, in his words, 'I liked incest if it remained Platonic.'[11]

When Sartre's mother read stories to him, he had eyes only for her, and ears only for that voice of hers 'which wavered with servitude.' He took pleasure in her sentences that stopped without ending, in her assurance that weakened and petered out melodiously, struck a silence, and then resumed. For her story or soliloquy isolated her and him like 'two does in a wood.'[12] In his later childhood, when she played Chopin, Schumann, or other romantic music, he would slip into the dark study and act out some marvellous fairytale-like adventure. The rhythm of the piano forced itself on him, the music inhabited his being and, as he acted out stirring romantic victories, furnished him with a past and future.[13]*

Sartre's mother would have preferred him, he tells us, to be a girl. Finding biology an obstacle, she tried to teach him gentleness and impress a kind of sexual indeterminacy on him. His own isolation did the rest and kept him away from violent games (which he was later to support, at least in the form of student revolt). But one day, when he was seven, his grandfather could no longer stand his 'lovely ringlets' and had a barber cut them off. When Sartre returned home shorn of his girlhood, his mother shrieked and locked herself in her room to cry; and his ugliness, which he soon came to suspect, became obvious, especially because he squinted with his right eye, the sight of which he was losing.[14]

Sartre's happiest years as a child began when he was about nine. He

---

*Everybody in his family, says Sartre, was a musician. He himself studied the piano at about the age of eight or nine, then relearned it by himself at the age of twelve. He got as far as Chopin and all but the most difficult sonatas of Beethoven, though without real rhythmic precision, he recalls. He sang airs from operas and operettas, and he even composed a perhaps Debussy-like sonata. He learned to appreciate music from the Baroque to the atonal. Until hindered by the infirmities of age, he would play for hours at a time. J.-P. Sarte, *Situations, X* (Paris: Gallimard, 1976), pp. 167–72.

had no friends, but he and his mother were the 'same age' and inseparable. 'She called me her knight attendant, her little man. I told her everything.' He would even, he says, assume feelings for the pleasure of telling her about them. They communicated in public with collusive winks. Through her he learned to scent, to fear, and to hate the male. Walking with her, he felt that he was giving her his protection.[15] But he talked to himself a great deal and felt that he had two voices, one of which, hardly belonging to him, dictated to the other what to say. He decided he was double and was annoyed and frightened, though his mother was not alarmed when he said to her, 'It talks in my head.'[16]

Sartre's grandfather, though an unsatisfactory replacement for a father, he says was a strong influence in his life. As it turned out, the grandfather's family role was to support Sartre, to find wisdom in his jumbled talk, Sartre's role was to make his grandfather happy, and his mother's role was to devote herself to the welfare of everyone in the family.[17] The grandfather's study was filled with books, among which Sartre found a sanctuary, though he did not yet know what to do with them.[18] He demanded books for himself. In answer to his demand, he got a book that contained the very stories, his mother said, that she had so often told him.[19] He then tried to read by himself, his eyes following the black signs of a book while he told himself a story. Soon, therefore, taught the alphabet, he took a book he knew by heart, and, half reading, half deciphering, he went through every page. 'When the last page was turned, I knew how to read,' he reports. Sartre was wild with joy. The old, dried voices were now his. Books, he writes, were his birds, nests, pets, barn, and countryside. 'The library was the world caught in a mirror,' the world's infinite thickness and variety were now his, he could launch out into incredible adventures, he could read, he had found his religion, he says.[20] Tactfully, his grandfather taught him the names of the illustrious authors, and he would recite the list to himself, from Hesiod to Hugo, without any mistake. He saw them metamorphosed into books, each with its individual physical characteristics. He would take them into his arms, 'carry them, put them on the floor, open them, shut them, draw them from nothingness, and thrust them back into it.'[21] In proud, somewhat apprehensive astonishment, the grown-ups would say that he was devouring the encyclopedia. This alarmed praise satisfied him, and he revelled in the Larousse summaries he had discovered of plays and novels. His mother complained that the grandfather was pushing him too hard and might cause him to waste away, so he was supplied with more childish literature, such as adventure stories, which he cannily concealed from his grandfather.[22]

All this time, his mother kept telling Sartre that he was the happiest of little boys; and yet he was preoccupied with secret fears. 'I saw death,' he writes. 'When I was five, it lay in wait for me . . . I saw it, but I dared not say anything.'[23] A belief in God might have helped, Sartre believes, but the grandfather, who was a Protestant, ridiculed Catholicism and tales of religious miracles, while the grandmother, though nominally a Catholic, believed in nothing.[24] He had a need for God, Sartre felt in retrospect, and God vegetated in his heart for a while, but died.[25] God died the more easily, he conjectured, because he, Sartre, had not come to know his own father.[26]

Sartre soon began to write out adventures of which he was the hero. Words were all-powerful to him, the veritable 'quintessences of things,' and he assumed a moonstruck expression, his later, ironical self says, to match his assumed writer's vocation. To his mother's intense satisfaction, he wrote one and then another novel, the latter of which she herself recopied on glossy paper. In his novels, he was sometimes the hero fighting tyranny, and sometimes the equally powerful opposite, namely, the demiurgic tyrant; and his daydreams revealed to him the monstrous universe that was the underside of his imagined omnipotence. He wrote, he says, to escape from the grown-ups, yet he existed only in order to write.[27]

The underside, the monstrous universe, was of course, his fear, to which his guilt easily attached itself. He developed the lasting ambition to write, his later, Existentialistic self claims, in order to be forgiven for his existence. His later self apparently thinks that he needed to be forgiven for being an impostor-child, withdrawn from real childhood and living in books and imagination; his lack of a father contributed heavily, he thinks, to his withdrawal. As he explicitly prefers, he says rather contradictory things, for he was utilizing his fear to try to rise above it. Death filled him with terror, but it attracted him because he identified it with glory. In his imagination he became embodied in his own posthumous works, which projected their powers through space and time, blasting the wicked, protecting the good and speaking a posthumous 'universal and individual language' that filled every mouth and consciousness.[28]

All this life ended abruptly in 1916, when Sartre was eleven. The cause was his mother's remarriage, to a marine engineer. The couple moved to an apartment of their own, leaving Sartre for the while with his grandparents. He describes the years from 1916 to 1920 as 'the three or four worst years of my life.' He tried to remain in his old relationship with his mother, but she now represented his stepfather, and he lived in a kind of 'internal quarrel' with her. He was, it appears, not only disappointed with the new life, but himself disappointing, antagonistic, and contentious. In school he was no more than mediocre and on bad terms with the other students. He stole books from the family and sold them, and, to be able to entertain his friends, he kept stealing money from his mother.[29] Perhaps he was trying to steal back his mother's love, as a common psychological explanation suggests. He made efforts to love the stepfather but could find no attractive qualities in him; yet, despite his coldness toward him, he tried to use him to get the experience of the paternity he had never known. The stepfather was upset that Sartre had no taste and little ability for mathematics and physics, and was irritated by his negativism in discussion and his desire to reform bourgeois society.[30]

We can hardly follow Sartre through the subsequent details of his career. But it is fully and, it seems, faithfully represented in the several volumes of Simone de Beauvoir's autobiography. Sartre comments on the accuracy of her portrayal,

> I am wholly in accord with what she says about me and with what she says about our relations. I have read her books several successive times and made suggestions to her, but never on what she has said about me. That should be considered an absolute proof. Not only is she the person who knows me best, but I think that all she says on the reciprocal importance of our relations is completely accurate . . . We get angry at one another, as you may suspect, but it is because of problems of a philosophic order, and usually badly posed problems.[31]

In *The Prime of Life*, the second volume of her autobiography, de Beauvoir pictures Sartre as an intensely curious and intensely subjective young man, unwilling to distinguish between his own vision and the actual world that he saw, always wanting the kind of synthetic totality he found in Stoicism or the philosophy of Spinoza, but always attentive to the concrete and individual.[32] When he was told about Phenomenology, which could make philosophy out of anything, he turned pale with emotion. 'Here was just the thing he had been longing for for years—to describe objects just as he saw and touched them, and to extract philosophy from the process.'[33]

Sartre's ideas of psychology were influenced by Jaspers, Freud, and, perhaps above all, by Adler. It appears to have been under Adler's influence that he took to describing people in terms of the parts they played and that he replaced the notion of the unconscious by that of 'bad faith,' all the manifestations of which he was determined to expose.[34] Together with de Beauvoir, he was attracted by dreams, dream-imagery, anomalies of perception, and psychological abnormality—he no doubt remembered the two voices that had talked in his head when he was a child.[35] Given an experimental dose of mescaline, in 1935, he began to hallucinate and fell into a depression. He felt surrounded by ominous creatures, of whom, among the nameless grimacing things, he could single out crabs and octopuses. He was afraid he had become psychotic, but the symptoms ended after about six months.[36] Later, he observed the inmates of a mental hospital with great interest.[37]

The hero of Sartre's *Nausea*, Roquentin, reflects Sartre's psychological crisis.[38] The novel begins with Roquentin's assurance to himself that he is not insane, a conclusion he soon doubts. He likes to pick up and close his hand on objects, especially pieces of paper. He feels very intensely that they are and yet are not part of his.[39] His hand on the table looks like a crab, not like part of himself. Things seem contingent and therefore absurd. The thought arises in his mind that he is nothing but his thought, that he exists by what he thinks, that if he exists, it is because he hates to exist. 'It is I, it is I,' he thinks, 'who pull myself from the nothingness to which I aspire: hatred and disgust for existence are just so many ways of *making me* exist, of thrusting me into existence.'[40] He feels double, mad, faint, superfluous, and he sees and feels strangely identical with the knotty root of a chestnut tree. The huge absurd world, which has no reason for existence but cannot not exist, is revealing itself in the root.[41] 'And I too have wanted to *be*,' he thinks. 'Indeed I have never wanted anything else; that's what lay at the bottom of my life.'[42] As the novel closes, the idea comes to him that by writing a novel he may make a past for himself, be able to recall his life without repugnance, and accept himself.[43]

Being and Nothingness, published in 1943, when Sartre was thirty-eight, often sounds like a metaphysical explication of *Nausea*. It can also be taken to be an explication of his stories, plays, and other novels, in which he stresses the obligation of entering into the suffering of other human beings and the impossibility of doing so. Human beings, but especially the intellectuals among them, must suffer shame and guilt, he believes.[44]

In *Being and Nothingness*, Sartre wrestles with the dualism that threatens to separate the human being, the for-itself, as he calls him, from the non-human world, the in-itself.[45] In this philosophy, a human consciousness is a striving to become as self-sufficient as the non-human world, to attain 'to the dignity of the in-itself-for-itself or in-itself-as-self-cause.'[46] But the goal is hopeless and the striving never successful.

> Everything happens as if the world, man, and man-in-the-world succeeded in realizing only a missing God. Everything happens therefore as if the in-itself and for-itself were presented in a state of disintegration in relation to an ideal synthesis. Not that the integration has ever *taken place* but on the contrary because it is always indicated and always impossible.[47]

This perpetual effort and perpetual failure explain why world and man, that is to say, conscious yearning and non-conscious fulfilment, are indissolubly united and yet relatively independent. There is a transition here that has not been completed, 'a short circuit,' an abortive unity, a 'detotalized totality,' so to speak.[48]

Caught in this situation, what is the human being, what does his consciousness engage in, how can he be fundamentally characterized? Sartre's answer to this triple question is, 'I apprehend being, I *am* the apprehension of being, I am *only* the apprehension of being.' To continue by paraphrasing Sartre: in a sense, which does not, however, suffice for ontological purposes, I am an exhaustive consciousness, because I am simultaneously the consciousness *of* the being, the completeness I emulate, and the consciousness of myself. 'Man himself makes man in order to be God . . . man loses himself in order that the self-cause may exist. We will consider then that all human existence is a passion ...'[49] Sartre hopes that existential psychoanalysis will reveal to man the real goal he is pursuing, a synthetic fusion of world or being, the in-itself, with man, the for-itself. 'Existential psychoanalysis is going to acquaint man with his passion.'[50]

To interpolate a comment to which Sartre, I think, would not object, he appears in *Being and Nothingness* as a sort of lame Spinoza. That is, he wants but feels he lacks the fulfilment that Spinoza wants and believes, in the end, that he has got. My further, I am afraid, obtrusive comment is that Spinoza, for all his losses or separations, had a father up to his young manhood. The difference between Sartre's metaphysics of lack and Spinoza's of fulfilment is also a difference in their respective experiences of fatherhood.

Sartre's *Critique of Dialectical Reason* parts philosophical company with *Being and Nothingness* in several ways. It declares a qualified allegiance to Marxism, it restricts the possibility of freedom, and it is melioristic and even optimistic. But it retains Sartre's old love for the concrete and old desire to fuse with life in every sense. 'To understand itself, to understand the other, to exist, to act, are one and the same movement,' he writes, 'which found direct, conceptual knowledge upon indirect, comprehensive knowledge.' Then he adds what to him is the essential qualification, 'But without ever leaving the concrete.' He sees a dialectical interplay between what he calls 'intellection' and 'comprehension' as part of 'the ambiguity of a discipline in which the questioner, the question, and the questioned are one.'[51]

Though the vocabulary has been renewed and the view become perhaps more practical and hopeful, the central problem of the *Critique* is not unlike that of *Being and Nothingness*. Man grasps everything in terms of its possibilities and so makes the plurality that surrounds him into a unity or, as Sartre expresses the act, totalizes the plurality. In so doing, man constitutes everything as an inert obstacle and simultaneously as an effort to overcome this obstacle. The reason is still what it used to be in Sartre: man is compelled by his nature to try to overcome the lack he feels.[52] Mankind has too long remained a mere plurality of solitudes. Wounded psychically in childhood, a person develops a concealed, complex strategy to help himself survive. But he can be understood by means of an integration of sociology with psychoanalysis and taught to see himself. By this means, and by means of a unity first imposed by terror, man may learn to destroy the prison he has always built for himself.[53]

In the preface to his stubbornly prolix, unfinished examination of Flaubert, Sartre writes, 'For man is never an individual; it would be better to call him a *singular universal*; totalized and, by the same token, universalized by his epoch, he retotalizes it in reproducing himself in it as a singularity.'[54] The impossible yet approachable ideal is, as Sartre would like it, to interiorize the external and externalize the internal or, in other words, to become the one who is the many and the many who are the one.

Regardless of Sartre's denunciation in *The Words* of his earlier self, I cannot doubt that he has remained much of the child he depicted. His emptiness, which is to say, by his own analysis, his humanity in the especial light of his fatherlessness, continued to oppress him. His anger at the absence of a father, his protest against the grandfather who exploited his mother and secluded and appropriated him, making him a pseudo-child, and his jealousy and discomfort in the presence of his stepfather, the narrow-minded engineer, have become his denunciation of bourgeois society, to end which he has been quite willing to use the violence that was part of his childhood fantasies of rule over the world. He still yearns, as he did when a child, to be the hero of a glorious, redemptive adventure that will unite those who, like him, have lived in solitude. He still needs to exert effects on the real world in order to feel himself real, and to purge himself of the guilt and falsity of the unreal, not well-enough-loved child.

How much of Sartre has remained the same under the guise of dramatic change! His emptiness in childhood has remained his emptiness later, his fantasies of violence then have remained his fantasies later, and his fear of death and fascination by it have remained his fear and fascination. As before, death and writing have remained associated in his mind. In 1965, he said, 'Death, you know—on the one hand I never think of it, and on the other it exists continually for me, in the form of a certain blundering urgency in writing . . . I've had the impression that it was necessary to write quickly. With a certain repugnance, I wrote books that were a little too massive, and I am convinced that there is death in that. And this hurry is not unaccompanied by a certain anxiety: "In five or ten years you will no longer be able to write." '55

Sartre's fear has, unfortunately, been justified. In a series of interviews held just ten years later, when he had reached the age of seventy, he revealed that he had lost almost all the sight of his good, left eye, and could no longer read nor, in the sense he valued, write. Because he had lived, he said, to write, his blindness deprived him in a sense of his raison d'être. 'I was and I am no longer,' he stated, adding, however, 'I should be very dejected, but, for some reason I'm unaware of, I feel well enough. When I think of what I have lost, I am never sad nor do I have any melancholy moments.'56 These added words show, I take it, that the sources of his earlier estimate of himself may not have been what he had supposed and proclaimed.

Sartre's stepfather died in 1945, when Sartre was forty, and Sartre then agreed to live with his mother, as she wanted. 'This is my third marriage,' she said in satisfaction. She watched over his comfort, as she had over husband's, but she wanted him to follow her advice, and she was worried by his disregard for convention and public opinion. Yet she ended by adopting his opinions and came to say, toward 1962, 'It is only now, when I am eighty-four, that I have really broken free from my mother.' Publication of *The Words* pleased her greatly, though Sartre's description of his grandfather, her father, shocked her. In talking to a friend, she said of Sartre, 'He understood nothing about his own childhood'; but she was moved by his account of their early mutual devotion to one another. Stimulated by *The Words*, she began to compose her own memoirs.57 She died in 1969, when Sartre was fifty-nine years old.

It appears that Sartre's closeness to his mother in childhood has led him to prefer the company of women to men, though the women must be at least pleasant looking. Ugly women, he says, make him feel ill. He feels attuned to women because their situation, as he sees it, has made them slaves and accomplices at once.58 Giving his preference for feminine companionship a more obviously erotic explanation, he says that one has a richer relationship with a woman than a man even if one does not go to bed with her. The objective and subjective are given together, and one speaks the profound language of hands and faces. 'With a woman, the whole of what one is is there.'59 Sartre's desire to be a singular universal, inner and outer and one and many at the same time, seems to be erotic desire, of the sort that revives the happy years when he and his mother were one, and together repelled the world of men.

Of all women after his mother, Simone de Beauvoir has been of the greatest importance to him. He insists that she has given him total security as a writer. Though he begins by being angry at her criticisms, he ends by always, or almost always, accepting them, because 'they are always made in just the necessary spirit, not from without, but in the absolute knowledge of what I wish to do, and at the same time in the name of an objectivity that I cannot completely arrive at.' Her 'imprimatur,' as he calls it, immunizes him against the criticisms made by others. 'In a certain measure,' he confides, 'one may say that I create for her.'[60] He is certainly lucky to have such a critical and yet sympathetic critic, whose role in relation to his writing is not unlike that played in his boyhood by his mother.

De Beauvoir's memoirs tell us of Sartre's attraction to Olga Koskiewicz, who cared for him during his spell of depression and hallucination. They also tell of the 'ancillary loves' de Beauvoir and he agreed they could allow themselves, such as his affair with the M. to whom he dedicated *What is Literature?* and *Red Hands*. Later, he was close to the gay, 'slightly mysterious' Michelle.[61] Sartre himself has no particular desire to tell us of his sexual and erotic relationships, and much of his life has therefore remained unrevealed, he says.[62] His formal adoption of Arlette el Kaïm as his daughter must have been of importance to him, but what she has meant to him, I do not know. But though there must be much about Sartre that we do not know, he has made for us a persuasive public Sartre or Sartre-simulacrum. He has never wanted disciples, he says, for they do not really enrich or develop their master's thought.[63] At the age of seventy, he sees his life as having been good. It has given him, what he wanted, though it has taught him that what he wanted is of no great importance. 'But what can you do about it?' he asks, and then, hearing the disenchanted tone in which he has spoken, he breaks into uncontrollable laughter.[64]

9
Philosophers in general

A Tabular Summary, with Tentative Generalizations

Each of the philosophers I have written of deserves to be considered in his own right, and I have tried to do him justice as an individual. But I have also hoped and assumed that generalizations could be drawn from the group as a whole. The table I have drawn up to help in the process of generalizing obviously singles out only such characteristics as fit the emphases of this book. A certain circularity has therefore resulted. That is, I have got out of the biographies what I have put into them—parental deaths, depressive inclinations, reluctance to marry, and so on. But I have put such facts in and am now extracting them as openly and fairly as I can, by which I mean that I have done my best not to conceal or exaggerate evidence or choose only philosophers who would yield evidence favourable to my standpoint. If, for example, Berkeley stands out among those listed as a reasonably happy, well-balanced person, in the simple, conventional sense of these words, I do not feel that I have manipulated the list so as to make such happiness or balance conspicuous by its rarity. I must, however, repeat that only the first part of the list can be taken to represent a consensus on the choice of the great philosophers. The second part therefore allows, not statistical conclusions, but tentative impressions, which a more comprehensive list might cast doubt on or even falsify. In any case, I have no ambition to present the facts with genuine empirical comprehensiveness.

In commenting on the table, I have mentioned a number of philosophers whose example seems to me illuminating for the condition or trait in question, even though, for one reason or another, whether my own ignorance or the limitations of space I have imposed on myself, I have not allotted them biographical sketches. These added examples are the random gifts of my memory, and not the result of a search of the literature.

One additional and, I hope, unnecessary caution. The definiteness of a table such as the one I have constructed can easily be misleading. For instance, unless one knows the quality of a philosopher's marriage, the

345

Philosopher	Age at death of or separation from mother or father		Other influential persons	Inclination: scientific, literary, musical, or political				Inclination: hypochondriac, fearful of inherited illness, depressive, suicidal				Age at marriage
	m	f		s	l	m	p	h	f	d	s	
Montaigne	0	35	friend		l		p					32
Hobbes		childhood		s	l	m	p	h				
Descartes	1	4	nurse, teacher	s	l	?		f				
Pascal	3	28	sister	s	l					d		
Spinoza	6	22		s		?	p					
Locke	22	27		s		vs.	p					
Leibniz	18	6		s	l	?	p					
Berkeley	50+	50+		s	l		p					43
Voltaire	7	not old (true father)	mistress	s	l		p	h		d		
Hume	34	2		?	l		p			d	s	
Rousseau	0	10	aunt	?	l	m	p	h	f	d		(36), 56
Kant	13	21		s		vs.	p	h	f	d	s	
Hegel	11	28		s	l	m	p	?		d		41
Schopenhauer	(25), 50	17		s	l	m		h		d		
Mill	48	30	mistress-wife	s	l	m	p	?	f	d		(28), 45
Kierkegaard	21	25			l		p		f	d		
James	39	40	wife	s	l		p	h		d	s	35
Nietzsche	52	4	sister, Wagners	s	l	m	p		f	d	s	
Santayana	(5), 19	(9), 30	sister, friend		l		p			d		
Russell	2	3	grandmother	s	l		p		f	d	s	22, 49, 64, 80
Wittgenstein	23	37	sister	s	l	m				d	s	
Sartre	63	1	grandfather, mistress		l	m	p					(25)

mere fact that he is married is not in itself very illuminating. Further, the inclusion or exclusion of a philosopher from the category marked, 'scientific inclination,' 'literary inclination,' 'depressive or suicidal inclination,' and the like, is sometimes subjective and may depend on insufficient or insufficiently understood evidence.

These preliminary cautions delivered, we may turn to the table itself, which I will scan and comment on column by column.

I begin with an unimportant but possibly necessary comment relating to chronology. Because I did not always know the exact date of some death or separation, I could not always compare it with the philosopher's exact date of birth, so I may sometimes have made an error of a year in giving his age at the time of death or separation. I may add, incidentally, that I was unable to find the dates on which Hobbes's parents died.

The table shows what must appear to be a high frequency of early separations from parents, whether by death or other causes. I do not contend that such separations have been more characteristic of philosophers than others, for I do not know the contextual facts well enough and cannot make any accurate demographic comparisons.[1] Nor do I make the absurd contention that such experiences of separation are sufficient to create philosophers. I think, however, that they have been frequent among them and can often be judged to have been essential to their formation. This judgment is of course subjective, but what I have earlier said about the effect of parental death on children's sense of reality seems to me to make the judgment plausible.

The fact of separation is impressively documented by the table. Of the twenty-two philosophers listed, two had lost both parents and eleven at least one by the age of six. In only six cases did both parents survive until the philosopher was fifteen. But the mere survival of parents may not shield children from the severe experience of separation. Schopenhauer's father made the experience worse by, it was believed, committing suicide, and Schopenhauer's hatred for his mother made it worse, too; Mill was given an unbearable education by a domineering, apparently cold father, and he came almost to despise his mother; James's father had been tragically mutilated and ended his life in a strange form of suicide; and Wittgenstein's father could be very harsh to his sons. If these are the facts, only the families of Locke and Berkeley are left to qualify as good in the usual psychological sense; and Berkeley, we may recall, was suspicious as a child, for unknown reasons, while Locke was at first rigidly disciplined by his father. Painful separations are no doubt common in early life, but it seems nevertheless notable that at least twenty of the twenty-two philosophers may be supposed to have undergone them. They certainly fit the generalization, proposed by psychologists, that persons of exceptional accomplishment have suffered exceptionally heavy parental loss in childhood.[2]

To redress the balance slightly, I may note that Diderot adored his father and appreciated his mother highly.[3] Jaspers, too, praised both his parents, who survived late into their fifties; but he was cut off from much of life, as will later be explained, by his illness. I may also add that separation from 'reality' has many possible causes, among them, sensory defects. The once famous philosopher, Hans Vaihinger, 'wanted to be a man of action, but his extreme nearsightedness forced him into scholarly pursuits. He regarded the contrast between his physical constitution and the way he would like to live as irrational and his defective vision made him sensitive to other frustrating aspects of existence.'[4] It seems likely to me that his desire to modify the Kantian categories into something more empirical may have depended on his experience of near-blindness, as may his whole 'as-if' theory of life-serving fictions.

A few summary comments can be made on the philosophers' relations with their parents. The first is that a parent's death might leave the philosopher in fear that he had inherited some vulnerability or even death from the parent. Descartes feared he had inherited pallor, weak lungs, and a probably early death from his mother; Kant assumed he had inherited a narrow chest and consequent weakness and hypochondria from his mother; Schopenhauer was preoccupied with the problems of insanity and suicide as the result of his father's strange behaviour and presumed suicide; Kierkegaard was convinced that he would die young because of punishment visited on his father; James may have felt his breakdown to be a repetition of his father's; Nietzsche believed that he had inherited madness, perhaps, and an early death from his father; and Russell was haunted by the fear of hereditary madness. The least result of such usually concealed fear or resentment was a powerful ambivalence, for the parent, the source and support of life, was also felt to be the direct source of weakness and death.

The second comment on philosophers in relation to their parents is on the philosopher's frequent loss, in a sense, of childhood, and occasional fixation on it. For the loss one need only recall the forced education given Pascal, Leibniz, Mill, Kierkegaard, and perhaps Wittgenstein, and their lack of normal contact with other children; Spinoza's inability to believe he had ever been a child; the premature elderliness of Hegel and Nietzsche, respectively the young 'Old Man' and 'The Little Pastor'; and Sartre's childhood spent in the almost exclusive company of books and adults. With the unchildish children we can contrast Rousseau, by his own persuasive admission the perpetual child, and possibly James, with his restless, childlike ebullience.

The third comment on philosophers and their parents is on the significant number of the former whose pursuit of philosophy was in manner or substance the pursuit of a parental ideal. In this respect, the effect of the mothers is harder to make out. Leibniz's mother gave him conciliatoriness and strengthened his piety and ambition to study; Kant's mother gave him piety, conscience, scholarly ambition, and confidence; and Nietzsche's mother gave him much of his need to rebel against her, against convention, and against women. But the influence of the fathers is far more apparent. Some of it enters the sons' philosophies only peripherally. Montaigne's father wanted him to excel in literature; Schopenhauer's father wanted him to understand the world and find his way in it in a businesslike way; and Wittgenstein's father gave him philosophical engineering devices and analogies, businesslike demands on philosophy itself, and perhaps a touchy independence, not to speak of a socialistic or communistic bias in reaction against the father's capitalistic bias. The fathers of both Kierkegaard and Wittgenstein were powerfully persuasive, domineering men whose sons were powerfully persuasive philosophers with a love-hate relationship with language that paralleled, I suppose, their hate and love for their domineering, eloquent fathers. But apart from such influences, which may be considered peripheral to the content of the philosophies in question, the philosophical influence of the fathers was to some degree genuinely constitutive in the cases of Pascal, Mill, Kierkegaard, and James. The fathers of Mill and James were themselves explicit philosophers. The case of the elder and the younger Mill is one, as I have said, of the unmistakable though partial inheritance of a philosophy, as clear as inheritance of the shape of a nose—though Mill's nose, as it happens, was not his father's but his mother's. The elder James gave the younger much of his general tendency, rather as Wilhelm Dilthey's father gave him his basic pantheistic feeling of a universal unity.[5] Research, into which I cannot go, suggests that a close, restrictive mother–son relationship fosters the son's verbal ability (might Leibniz, Kant, Hegel, James Mill, or Nietzsche be examples?); that a close father–son relationship fosters independent, analytical thinking; and that deprivation of a father weakens control of impulses and acceptance of authority (might Kierkegaard, in a sense, and Nietzsche be examples?).[6]

The fourth and last comment I have to make on philosophers and parents concerns the philosophers' acceptance or rejection of the idea of God. In my accounts of individual philosophers I have adopted the psychoanalytic view that a child's idea of God is likely to be modelled on its father. That is, it may combine elements taken in any proportion from both parents, but the predominant image in our culture of God as mas-

culine and the formal and often practical dominance of the man in family
life has made the association of God with father more natural than with
mother. However that may be, it strikes me as significant that the four
philosophers, Hume, Nietzsche, Russell, and Sartre, who lost their
fathers earliest in life are all atheistic or close to it. Hume, to be accurate,
seems to have believed in some very remote creator, but his discussion of
God is more marked by carefully expressed scepticism than by faith,
while Nietzsche, Russell, and Sartre are all explicit atheists, but such as
miss God badly and say so. The remaining atheists among the
philosophers are Mill and Santayana. However, Mill, who considers the
possibility of God's existence calmly, and who takes Jesus to be the ideal
guide for humanity, is an atheist, as he says, out of identification with his
atheistic father. The instance of Santayana is more complex, for he was
attracted, with his sister, to Catholicism; but both his parents were disbe-
lievers, so that even if they were gods in his childish imagination, they
taught him the atheism to which he remained faithful in the end.

About mothers and gods I have only a brief word to say. If we except
Russell, because he lost his father, too, quite early, the three who lost
their mothers earliest are Descartes, Pascal, and Rousseau. Granted
Descartes' strong rationalistic learnings, his choice of what we have understood as an irrationalistic God is surprising and may have something to
do with the early death of his mother. Pascal's belief in God is so basically
irrationalistic that it for the most part excludes itself from the realm of
philosophical discussion. Rousseau does argue metaphysically for the
existence of a God. But his 'Profession of Faith of the Vicar of Savoy,'
which contains his major attempt to argue so, is not really typical of him,
and may have been prompted by a temporary desire to argue like a
philosophe. What seems more natural to Rousseau is more obviously
related to his lack of a mother: an ecstatic identification with the whole of
nature, a belief in immortality that allows him the hope to be completely
himself, without contradiction, division, or need, and a faith that he is
fundamentally a spiritual and moral being.[7] It is possible, then, that the
early loss of a mother biases philosophers in the direction of an
irrationalistic or more emotionally apprehended God. I raise this possibility hesitantly, but I do not think that the instance of Kierkegaard contradicts it, for reasons that my account of him should make apparent.

I now turn to the subject of persons other than parents who played
influential roles in the lives of the philosophers we have been discussing. I
mean to refer only to the persons who may be said to have helped
establish a philosopher's character. Some of these, like Rousseau's aunt,
Santayana's sister, and Sartre's grandfather, were substitute parents.
Others, such as Montaigne's friend, La Boétie; Voltaire's mistress, Mme
du Châtelet; Mill's companion and then wife, Harriet; Nietzsche's tem-

porary idols, the Wagners; and Sartre's mistress, Simone de Beauvoir, seem to have been, as the philosophers themselves tell us, important to the development of their philosophical self-confidence, ability, and even doctrines. But though I have mentioned such persons and said something about their influence, I have been remiss in neglecting the subject of the philosophers' identifications with one another. An interesting chapter might certainly be written on the depth of feeling that Kant and Fichte showed for Rousseau; on that of Fichte, at least briefly, for Kant; on that of Nietzsche for Schopenhauer; on that of the Young Mach, the young Dilthey, the young Weyl, and the young Einstein for Kant; and on that of Diderot, Kierkegaard, and Nietzsche for Socrates. Diderot not only mentioned Socrates often in his writings, but wore a ring with an inscribed picture of Socrates, with which he used to seal letters. Perhaps someone will some day make a comprehensive study of such identifications and of the cross-identifications that follow from them.[8]

The categories, 'Scientific Inclination,' 'Literary Inclination,' 'Musical Inclination,' and 'Political Inclination,' are more difficult to apply than they may seem at first glance. The science meant is any science, though I have thought primarily of the more exact sciences. Hume earns his question mark under this category by virtue of his interest in developing a science of man. The influence on him of Newton is often assumed but hard to demonstrate; but whatever his interest in natural science at first, it does not dominate him in later life.[9] Rousseau, a quite different sort of philosopher, earns at least a question mark for his botanizing and interest in anthropology, psychology, and the like. James earns his place here by his interest in medicine and psychology, later displaced by philosophy. As for Schopenhauer and Nietzsche, their rebellious vitality and their emotionality were such that it is easy to forget that both had a strong inclination towards the more exact sciences.

I take literary inclination to go beyond the mere interest in writing that each of the philosophers must have had. Spinoza, Locke, and Kant were all capable of effective writing, but, despite the remarkable rightness for its purpose of Locke's style, none of them seems to me to have paid much attention to their style as such or to literature as such. I have attributed literary inclinations to Leibniz, Hegel, and Mill in virtue of their effective writing at times, but perhaps more in virtue of their enthusiasm for literature. It will be recalled that Mill's conversion to poetry, which his mentor, Bentham, had asserted was no more than rhyming falsehoods, marked a turning point in his life. The rest of the philosophers in the list are distinctly good or great writers, some of whom, like Montaigne, Pascal, Voltaire, Rousseau, Kierkegaard, and Sartre belong at least as much to the history of literature as to that of philosophy.

I have been equally liberal in interpreting 'Political Inclination.' I take it to include direct participation in politics, as by Montaigne, Locke, Leibniz, Voltaire, Mill, and Russell, or indirect participation, by means of writing, as by Rousseau, Hegel, and even James. In a different sense, each of the philosophers who wrote on political philosophy might be included, so that at least Hobbes, Berkeley, Hume, Kant, Nietzsche, and Santayana would have to be added. It is fair, therefore, to conclude that most of the philosophers were interested in influencing political life.

The table thus shows that most of the philosophers in the present group of twenty-two were strongly interested in science, literature, and politics. The extensiveness of their interest bears out my contention that philosophy tends by nature to lie between and sometimes even embrace the poles of science and art. In the context of the present discussion, which has dwelt on the separation of philosophers from persons and, often, the material world, this broad interest may be interpreted as the attempt to use reason to overcome the separation and transform the world into one in which they can feel at home.

Musical inclination seems to me almost a thing apart, well worth investigating in relation to philosophy. Question marks under this heading are meant to note that Descartes, Spinoza, and Leibniz wrote on music, but that I know of no evidence that they themselves were deeply musical. The abbreviation 'vs.' indicates that Locke and Kant belittled music and, along with Aristotle, advised people against learning it too well. But Kant was the only philosopher of the group, I take it, to show a genuine dislike or fear of music.

With no pretensions to completeness, I may add to the already listed names of musically inclined philosophers those of Diderot, Bentham, Dilthey, Bergson, Moore, Cassirer, Adorno, and Popper, the last of whom has declared, 'Music has been a dominant theme in my life.'[10] Schopenhauer played the flute, Mill and Nietzsche the piano, and Wittgenstein the clarinet, but, judging by what I have read, the best performer among the philosophers is likely to have been Bentham, who played the violin, the harpsichord, and the organ. I do not know Bentham's felicific calculus well enough to see what connection there is, if any, between his thought and his music. In the case of most of the philosophers, however, the interest in music makes a difference to their philosophic expression and message. Hobbes's mastery of organization and tone may be related to his musicality. Diderot's thought and language often have the flow and controlled emotionality of music. Rousseau and Nietzsche were themselves musical composers, and I sense that the resonances of their language are musical. It seems to me, too, that Nietzsche and Wittgenstein wrote and arranged their aphorisms with more care to make a series of subtle variations on a theme, the repetitions being arranged in a musical succession, than to achieve a simply logical consistency. Wittgenstein's *Tractatus* is the less literary of his two major books, yet he wrote of it, 'The work is strictly philosophical and, at the same time, literary.'[11] Dilthey's hermeneutics has an emotional innerness like that of music, while his attempt to grasp all the world-views simultaneously has something of the impact of orchestration. As has been explained earlier, Bergson was extremely sensitive to the music of language and contended that unless it were, so to speak, rightly performed, the philosophical message it carried could not be rightly understood.

None of this interest in musicality is external, in the sense of a mere embellishment to personality or thought. It often implies a particular human tie, of Rousseau with his aunt, Nietzsche with his father, Bergson with his father, Wittgenstein with his mother, father, and brothers, Sartre with his mother, and Popper with his mother. In at least three instances, those of Schopenhauer, Nietzsche, and Bergson, music enters into and in a sense becomes epistemology or metaphysics. While I am not sure just what music has to do with philosophy, in Schopenhauer and Nietzsche it serves, I believe, to express and unite a highly ambivalent, that is, discordant personality. Logical abstractions hold such personalities together with too great difficulty or at too great a cost, whereas music can compose emotions with a logic more adequate to their discordancies. Its ability to compose emotions may explain why Hegel, by my account both highly ambivalent and highly logical, that is, ordered in this thinking, was passionately fond of music. His early biographer, Rosenkranz, mentions his preference for the vocal music of Gluck and Mozart. Hegel's praise of instrumental virtuosity as an astonishing inward and outward mastery that achieves freedom by overcoming complex, impracticable-seeming difficulties sounds not unlike his philosophical ideal, and not unlike his lectures considered as a vocal performance.[12]

It is self-evident that the rhythms of language can entice the reader to enter into the thought rhythms of the writer and so help to persuade him; but the connection between musical and verbal logic is obscure. It has been stated that in great music one is dealing 'with events whose distinctive characteristic is precisely this, that they follow at once logically *and* unpredictably from what has gone before: together with what precedes and follows them they form a tightly knit whole.'[13] While I am not sure how persuasive this idea is, as language, too, is both logical and unpredictable, it leads to a further interesting idea: if, unlike Kant, a person allows himself access to his emotions, the unpredictability of music may be easier to experience and enjoy than the unpredictability of words, which are too heavily freighted with moral sanctions or the threat of verbally induced pain or anxiety. In music, the sense of repletion and rest after emotional release comes with less compunction, less dividedness, and less ambivalence.

To return to the table I have drawn up, in the next to last major column, I have noted the philosophers who were hypochondriac or afraid of inherited illness. To explain this, I must again emphasize a statistical point, which is that I do not claim that philosophers are more often hypochondriac or afraid of inherited illness than any other selected group or than the population at large. I contend only that it is more difficult to understand the thought of many philosophers without understanding their fears, depressiveness, and so on, because their philosophies incorporate the fears, depressiveness, and the like, and also defend against them.

It will be seen that I have distinguished between depression and a suicidal tendency. I have assumed, perhaps not quite rightly, that a suicidal tendency is always accompanied by depression, but that the opposite does not hold true. I may have exaggerated in listing Hume as suicidal, for while he suffered the long depression I have described, his one known attempt at suicide was made when he was ill. Apart from Hume, I do not know if any of the twenty-two philosophers ever made an actual attempt at suicide, but at least seven of them were often preoccupied with it. Of more recent philosophers, Husserl may be added to those who suffered from depression, and Camus to those preoccupied with suicide. While I have made no separate category of it, madness, too, makes its appearance among philosophers. Rousseau and Comte underwent spells of it, and Nietzsche, of course, ended his life in madness.

The last column shows that only eight of the twenty-two philosophers married. This preference for bachelorhood is very striking, but I take it seriously only for that part of the list from Hobbes to Kant, because, as I have said, the latter part of the list represents no consensus, and when I have replaced it experimentally with a more inclusive set of names, the proportion of the unmarried has grown much lower. Yet it seems just to remark that the philosophers' experience of separation has often made it undesirable or difficult for them to marry, or, in other words, that they have suffered from psychosexual problems. I may add, more in humour than in earnest, that a recent study has distinguished between and tried to explain the different divorce rates of the British Positivists and the British Neo-Hegelians.[13]

This concludes my observations on the twenty-two tabulated philosophers and my rather hesitant effort to be numerically definite about traits many of which do not easily suffer the application of numbers.

The Challenge of Death: Nietzsche, Camus, and Jaspers

Although I could not anticipate what the biographical accounts of the philosophers would show, or what generalizations they would lead to as a group, the results do not surprise me, for I have often thought of the connection between philosophers' lives and thought. The negative in their lives, their separations, depressions, and sexual limitations, stands out all too clearly. For us and for them, however, the main importance of this negative is that it acts as the challenge to which their philosophies are the response. The starkest form of the challenge is constituted by death, and I should therefore like to dramatize challenge and response by recalling three philosophers, Nietzsche, Camus, and Jaspers, who philosophize in open response to the threat of death.

A word first on the taking of risks in general. The taking of minor risks, which are an inherent part of play, is invigorating and pursued with pleasure. The deliberate taking of major risks is rare in contrast; yet there are persons whose need to experience great stress dominates their lives. The explanation of their need may be that the mastery of external stress wards off old anxieties, perhaps because in returning from danger to safety one's feeling of safety is renewed. Alternatively, the explanation may be that, to overcome fear, one coordinates one's powers and arrives at an experience so intense that one becomes addicted to it, for it creates a self that at moments measures up to one's fantasies.[1] A mountain climber speaks of 'this inclination to inquire, this drive to go higher than need be, this innate ability to carry it off, this radiance in the heart when you carry it off,' and of the exhilarating, addictive, ballet-like skill the climber acquires in the face of danger.[2] The climber is engaged in exploring his reaction to new, at times exacting, experience. 'Climbing,' he may say, 'as I suppose life itself, is a constant process of discovery, of stretching out to find new limits.'[3] A climber explains that he has used his sport, as, I think, philosophers have used philosophy, in order to understand himself.[4]

Philosophers are like mountaineers. I might introduce this theme by recalling that at least one daring philosopher, Berkeley, had been a 'daring mountaineer, of fine physique, as tough and hard as nails, who twice made the perilous crossing of the Alps in winter', and that both Wittgenstein and Popper were mountaineers.[5] It is true that literal mountaineers are rare among the abstraction-prone men we are concerned with; but more than one of them would agree with Husserl when he said that the philosopher's radical search for truth requires him to risk his life in its behalf.[6] For philosophers and other intellectuals, especially the great ones, take deliberate intellectual risks and endanger themselves sometimes even physically in order to arrive at intellectual power and self-mastery that is also, as in the mountain climber, a mastery of the world; and, like the climber, they are often impelled by the fantasy that they will climb a Himalayan peak and survey all existence. The risks they undergo and the price they pay add to their satisfaction when, they feel, they accomplish something intellectual. Wittgenstein therefore respected Russell for having exclaimed, 'Logic is hell!' He himself 'thought that the measure of a man's greatness would be in terms of what his work *cost* him'.[7]

At the extreme, philosophers court death or, rather, exploit their fear of it so as to increase their effort, satisfaction, and self-esteem. For example, Nietzsche exploits his pain and fear constantly, masochistically, and creativity, as I will repeat in a different context. He writes to a doctor:

> My existence is a *terrible* burden. I would have cast it off long ago if I had not been making the most instructive tests and experiments in the intellectual-moral realm precisely in this condition of suffering and nearly absolute renunciation—this knowledge-thirsty joyousness brings me to heights where I conquer all torments and all hopelessness.[8]

A few years later, a friend of Nietzsche writes that Nietzsche would long ago have committed suicide if not for his goal of turning the dross of his sad lot into gold.[9] Towards the end of his sane life, Nietzsche writes to Georg Brandes, in whom he is delighted to find an admirer, 'Recently my sickness has been of the greatest use to me; it has liberated me, it has given me back the courage to be myself.'[10]

Camus cites and to some extent follows Nietzsche. But his concern with death stems from himself, from, I assume, the loss of his father when he was only nine months old, from his illness, and from his stubborn temptation to commit suicide.[11] The statement with which he begins *The Myth of Sisyphus*, that 'there is but one truly serious philosophical problem and that is suicide,' expresses a genuine and personal problem, which he intellectualizes and, perhaps by philosophizing over it, escapes. He says, 'By the mere activity of consciousness I transform into a rule of life what was an invitation to death—and I refuse suicide.' To him, as to Nietzsche, 'That revolt gave life its value.'[12]

Like Camus, Jaspers was influenced by Nietzsche, but, like him, only because his experience was such as to invite Nietzsche's influence. From infancy, Jaspers had some impediment in breathing. At the age of eighteen, it was concluded that he was suffering from bronchiectasis, which Webster's defines as 'a chronic inflammatory or degenerative condition of one or more bronchi or bronchioles marked by dilation and loss of elasticity of the walls.' That same year, at eighteen, Jaspers got an attack, frequently repeated, of bronchial bleeding. His trouble was not alone with his lungs, because his heart had always been quite weak, and in his determination to grow healthy he had overstrained it, to the degree that he had to pause while lecturing in order to gather strength.[13] No wonder he says, 'For me, sickness was a destiny.'[14] Very luckily, he had a protective father and loving mother. He says that the love of his mother and then of his wife gave him the will to live and the courage and desire to be active.[15] Yet his illness kept him from many normal activities. He had to learn even to study in a relaxed way and depend on grasping essentials and on sudden inspiration. Perhaps out of his weakness, the protection afforded him, and his contemplative nature, he began to study the great dead, and, at the same time, to cultivate his very early ambition to become great himself. The relation between his illness and his philosophy is open and considered. What is fundamental to it is put by Jaspers in the following brief words:

> The essence of man becomes conscious of itself only in extreme situations. For this reason, I tried not to veil the most extreme from myself. This was one of the motives which caused me to choose medicine and psychiatry: to come to know the limits of human potentiality, to grasp the significance of what in public is readily veiled and unnoticed. In spite of beloved parents and sister and friends, I was consumed by a yearning for a kind of communication that would be beyond every kind of misunderstanding, beyond anything temporary, beyond every boundary of the all too self-evident.[16]

The Response of Polarization

The challenge of separation, which is that of helplessness, loneliness, and the fear of death, has many possible responses, some of which are exceedingly subtle; but in the present, generalizing chapter, I would like to be usefully schematic and express the philosophers' responses in the vocabulary of polar opposites. My justification is that each philosopher tends to express, on the one hand, his fears and disappointments and, on the other, his defences against them. The idea of separation-experiences and responses to them may be too restrictive to express this polarity fully. Polarization suggests the concept of ambivalence, meaning simultaneous and inseparable affirmation and negation, and of sado-masochism, meaning simultaneous identification with the inflictor of pain and his victim. I have used these concepts without attempting to state or analyze them precisely, in the same almost intuitive way in which I have used other psychological concepts. Of course, sado-masochism is a form of

ambivalence, and, of our group of philosophers, most evidently characterizes Pascal, Rousseau, Schopenhauer, Kierkegaard, Nietzsche, Wittgenstein, and Sartre. In each of these, with the exception of Wittgenstein,
the personal sado-masochism is immediately perceived in his philosophy
as well. It sometimes takes the form I have called 'stuttering.' That is,
philosophers such as Pascal, Kierkegaard, Nietzsche, and Wittgenstein
tend to write in aphorisms, notes, or fragments, as if the effort to express
themselves coherently cannot withstand their powerful contrary
impulses, but comes to more natural expression in spasmodic writing
that resembles a dialogue of perpetually warring selves.

Despite the affinity between ambivalence or sado-masochism and
polarization, at this particular moment I do not want to enter into any
conceptual or psychological subtleties, but only to state, as pointedly and
briefly as I can, what each of the philosophers in the list of twenty-two
was for and against. I will try, in other words, to state the distinction
between good and evil, or the parallel distinction between real and
unreal, that underlies the polarity of each philosopher. It goes without
saying that other, perhaps more convincing formulations of each polarity
can be made.

Montaigne's world, which is the first to be characterized, is the world
of the I, or of anything assimilated or justified by belonging to it,
because, in the end, only the I can be identified with. Montaigne's
counter- or non-world is that of the other. To him, the I is finally good,
while the other is, not evil, but indifferent.

Hobbes has a world of security and logic as against fear and chaos. He
has nothing to fear but fear and human beings; but both, he feels, can be
devastating.

Descartes' world is that of methodical security and the health achieved
by its means, as against methodlessness, lostness, and illness.

Pascal's world is that of protective faith and subjectivity, as against
incredulity and objectivity.

Spinoza's world is that of eternal, impersonal love, as against insecurity,
emotionality, and pain.

Locke's is the world of the exploratory physician, who anatomizes the
process of knowing and forestalls excess and fanaticism.

Leibniz makes a world of self-sufficient, logically and harmoniously
related units, as against mere dependency and against illogic, neither
of which allows reason to protect or harmony to justify whatever
exists.

Berkeley sees or makes a world in which God, ideas, and the good all
rule, in opposition to atheism, matter, and evil.

Voltaire lives the distinction between good, which is tolerant, and evil, which is fanatical.

Hume sees a world of discontinuous unit-experiences associated by a doubtfully or mysteriously single self, and to be understood, therefore, by the laws of association and by the nature of the self.

Rousseau's is a world of naturalness, openness, and innocence, as against artificiality, concealment, and guilt.

Kant divides his world into almost two—the one almost-world being logical and scientific but unreal, and the other, non-logical, non-scientific, but real.

Hegel makes his world into the intelligible, which is dialectically structured and real, and the unintelligible, which is chaotic and unreal.

Schopenhauer finds or makes a world in which the sexless, primordially maternal, and nirvanic is distinguished from the sexually anguished, cruelly maternal, and painfully striving.

Mill wants a world in which the calculable, to be paid in coins of pleasure and pain, is spent in liberty and is victoriously opposed to all that is incalculable, arbitrary, or enslaving.

Kierkegaard divides the world into all that is good, suffers rightly, and is rightly paradoxical, and all that is bad, mercenary, self-satisfied, and merely reasonable.

James fixes an area in the world for the tender-minded, who cannot live without maternal protectiveness, while the other area, in which the tough-minded live, is cold, uncaring, and for him and his likes, uninhabitable.

Nietzsche's world is made bearable to him by the joy of creating values and the aphorisms in which they are fixed, but is made difficult by sadistic small-mindedness, self-delusion, and opposition to greatness of any kind.

In Santayana's world, the passive perception of essences is opposed to crude or dogmatic literality and unrefined pain.

Russell's world, at least in its moral aspect, is inhabited by good and reasonable men, mystical logicians able to go beyond themselves, and striving to overcome whatever or whoever is unreasonable, hidebound, or cruel.

Wittgenstein, in his world, contrasts clearly perceived particulars, intuited values, and philosophic clarity and health, with conventional misperception, attemptedly reasoned values, and philosophic unclarity and illness.

Sartre creates a world of being, which is full, and of nothing or of unfulfilled desire, which is empty; and in the world of nothing, he distinguishes between authenticity, which is self-knowing and painful, and inauthenticity, which is neither, at least not simply.

In the case of each of the above philosophers, I think, the good and substantial are in conflict with the evil and insubstantial or illusory. With the exception of Pascal, Kierkegaard, and in a partial, ambivalent way, Nietzsche, each of the philosophers enlists reason on the side of the good and substantial. Reason is the usual philosopher's saviour, for by making things intelligible he has assimilated them and rendered them harmless. But the philosopher is not always right and surely not always victorious even in his own eyes, for reality is hard to grasp and conceptualize, let alone change and master, and the same experience of separation that prompted him to become a philosopher in order to save himself lingers on to trouble him. The victor and the vanquished cannot quite separate from one another.

The approximately empirical generalizations with which I began the present chapter have led to a broad discussion of the emotional and therefore also intellectual challenges faced by the philosopher. The most notable of these challenges is that posed by death. Like the theologian's, the philosopher's response to the challenge tends to be polarized into the good and bad, real and unreal, and, less theologically, the reasonable and unreasonable. I have made an almost unbearable reduction of each philosopher's polarity to a sentence or two. In the coming chapter I will discuss the challenge, the response, and the polarity in a rather closer, more psychological way.

10

Paradoxical Consciousness

On Words, Especially 'Yes' and 'No'

Some children, I think, are natural-born philosophers, and all philosophers, I am sure, are born children, though often remarkably unchildish ones. I am continuing to consider childhood, because I hope to discover something more of the philosopher's nature in its most primitive stages. I particularly want to ask how and why abstractions come to play so great a role, beginning in early childhood, in the lives of so many of the persons who become scientists and philosophers.

I begin with the subject of language in childhood. By learning to understand and speak in words, the child quickens and deepens its humanization, for they help it to isolate, categorize, and relate the various aspects of its experience. Words help the child to concentrate, remember, imagine, reason, and act, all in a more human way; and repeated aloud and then internalized, they are transformed from directions given it by adults to directions the child gives itself. Arriving, with the help of words, at a necessary analysis of experience and at a human regulation of itself, the child is better able both to escape and to capture, internally and externally, whatever it needs to, and it becomes at once more intelligent, intelligible, and social.[1]

Among the words the child must learn, 'yes' and 'no' are especially prominent, their polarity heightening and socializing its ability to act in its own interests. In other words, in order to survive, the child must learn to organize every thing and person in its world into the sort best to approach, get, hold on to, and, if agreeable to being eaten, to eat, and the sort to keep far from, escape, throw away, and, even if unprotesting, to spit out; and it expresses such psychophysical attractions and repulsions in primitive sounds and motions of pleasure and pain, acceptance and rejection, and, after a time, affirmation and denial. As observed empirically, this process of learning, on the one hand, to accept or affirm, and, on the other, to reject or deny, is complicated and not fully understood. In order to accept and reject effectively, the child must learn that things endure and are of different more or less enduring kinds, that persons are different from other things, and that persons, including itself, have particular identities. Even before it can speak, the child communicates its reactions, positive and negative, with surprising sensitivity, and it learns to smile or direct its fear or anger *at* particular things or persons. It also learns, as it must, to gesture and then say 'yes' and 'no.'

'No,' it seems, comes first. According to a hypothesis broached by Darwin and recently confirmed by the intensive observation of infants, the gesture most often associated with 'no,' the side-to-side shaking of the head, is derived from the movement by which the satiated infant draws its head away from its mother's breast, while the gesture for 'yes,' the up-and-down nodding of the head, is derived from the movement by which the infant draws its head towards the breast.[2] The most obvious objection to this hypothesis is that the gestures for 'yes' and 'no' are not universal—Eskimos are said to reverse them,[3] while, closer to home, Greeks, southern Italians, and Turks indicate an emphatic 'no' by jerking their heads back (and perhaps clicking their tongues).[4] There are also counter-hypotheses. An ethologist may find it natural to suggest that the 'yes'-gesture originates in the animal-movements of ritualized submission, and the 'no'-gesture in those by which an animal shakes something off.[5] One need not choose between hypotheses to decide that it is reasonable to suppose that the two antithetical gestures have an emotive and instinctive basis.

Regardless of their origin, the two gestures and their two equivalent words help establish the separate identity of the child, which uses them to reject or deny and accept or confirm according to its own purposes and in its own, individual style. It seems to me that these purposes and this style remain embedded in the child's future affirmations and negations, abstract as they may become. I am willing to venture that a person is definable by the pattern of his 'yesses' and 'noes', which I assume to be as distinctive as that of his handwriting and perhaps more evocative.

Affirmation and denial, then, exhibit a distinctive, personal pattern; but they serve especially to bring out the pattern's coherence, which is to say, the degree of its consistency and, in this sense, the degree of its reasonableness. I say this because reason appears by nature designed to avoid immediate inconsistency, and, on the appearance of such inconsistency, to correct, minimize, or explain it away, the explanation often being made in the name of a higher, overriding consistency. The charge of inconsistency is therefore disturbing, and one is often prepared to pay a psychological price to remain at least overtly consistent.[6] There is, of course, more than one kind of inconsistency of which one may grow aware. The inconsistency may be between statements alone, between statements and actions, or between statements and facts. In whichever of these relationships the inconsistency is revealed, it is, as I have been saying, disturbing in itself; but if it is strong or persistent, it suggests a considerable ambivalence or, in other words, internal conflict. Intellectual inconsistency may therefore betray and, when open, accentuate anxiety. Reasoning is driven, I should say, by the desire to escape anxiety, and driven hardest when anxieties are extreme.

The point I have been making has often interested psychologists, but seems to have been neglected by philosophers. Let me explain it somewhat further. Intelligence can give pleasure by the very sharpness of its functioning, and it is possible that some sharp persons raise intellectual problems simply because solving them gives them pleasure and a sense of well-being. As I have maintained, however, in discussing persuasion, an intense desire to solve intellectual problems may be an attempt to overcome inward, emotional problems, and be, in fact, a sign of insecurity or anxiety. There is a direct enough tie between intellect and anxiety. We think as much as we do in order to control our lives as well as we can; but the same knowledge that lessens ignorance exposes how much ignorance remains and uncovers threats of which we have not yet been aware. Knowledge, as it turns out, increases awareness of ignorance and is no less capable of promoting than of overcoming anxiety. The connection of knowledge with anxiety is shown in the endless questioning and intellectual stubbornness that express the feeling that to understand and control the world is the same, as if the mastery of abstractions gave us mastery over our fates. This feeling is the main reason, I am convinced, why abstractions are of such great concern to the persons, intellectually stubborn and ambitious, who become scientists and philosophers. There is something like addiction to intellectual accomplishment. The practice of a highly abstract profession, mathematics, for instance, may be like the taking of a drug, which gives euphoria, but, with it, gives evidence of suffering from which the drug repeatedly releases its taker.[7] It is someone with a somehow addictive nature, suspended between playfulness and obsession, elated by his power but requiring the repeated evidence that he still retains it, who creates the densely aligned abstractions to which we give the name 'science' or 'philosophy.'

Precocious Intellectuality

The relationship I have been speaking of, between intellect and anxiety, is most easily observed in the children who make themselves conspicuous by the quantity of information they accumulate, the adult words or attitudes they display, or the intellectual problems they are concerned with. Their intellectuality is likely to be a response to the sometimes crude, sometimes refined pressure of intellectually ambitious parents, whom each child submits to, resists, or both, in its own characteristic way. The child may submit by becoming precociously fluent, informed, or logical, but it may resist by using fluency, logic, or information to manipulate its parents, by making little real sense, by growing passive or depressed, or by remaining physically clumsy.[1] When, as not infrequently happens, the child is precociously introspective, this trait, too, indicates something amiss, the uneasiness or guilt, I assume, of self-criticism.[2]

Let me give a few examples of intellectual precocity that have come to the attention of psychoanalysts. The first is that of a little boy, retarded in practical matters, but with a retentive memory and a tenacious curiosity.[3] He was especially troubled by the problem of birth and by the menace, as he thought it, of an invisible, omnipotent god. His curiosity about birth, which began at the age of four and three-quarters, was expressed in a flood of questions, beginning with, 'Where was I before I was born?' and 'How is a person made?' going on to questions on how trees and flowers grow and how a spring or river is made, and becoming physiologically detailed in questions such as, 'How does a person's skin come on him?' and 'How does anything grow at all?' Other, related questions were on the inner mechanisms of a closet, a revolver, and so on.[4]

This little boy's fear of an invisible God was expressed, it seems, in observations and questions on the nature of reality. After being told that an object used for cooking was called a 'range,' he responded, in a Platonic mood, 'It's called a range because it is a range. I am called Fritz because I am Fritz.' The God he feared had certainly affected his sense of reality, for after he was 'relieved of the compulsion to believe' in this invisible, omnipotent, to him troublingly incomprehensible being, he asked, 'I see what is don't I . . . and what one sees is real. I see the sun and the garden, etc.'[5]

The second example of precocious intellectuality is that of a 'passively hostile,' friendless, unhappy, very intelligent little girl of four, who was intensely afraid that adults would be disappointed in her, and who tried to overcome her feeling that she was never grown up or good enough by trying desperately to be as grown up as possible. She once told her analyst 'that we could be ourselves only when we read books.' In the words of the analyst, her intellect and her sense of reality 'were used to preserve a rigid distinction between approved adult behaviour, allowed to be "real," and despised infantile wishes and feelings, all relegated to the realm of fantasy and "pretend." '[6]

The third example is that of a four-and-a-half-year-old-boy, whom the analyst calls Abel. Abel's parents 'equated the mental and physical with, respectively, the good and the bad.'[7] When he first learned to crawl, his mother was enthusiastic, but she became afraid that he would hurt himself, and when he started to walk, she 'would suddenly become angry and scold or slap him if "he go away from her." ' His babbling, however, pleased her. Until he was three and a half, she would always read to him at mealtimes, while he would look at a picture-book.

> When he dawdled or refused food, she scolded and removed food, story, book. So when his mother was angry, Abel babbled a string of words which always made her laugh and she couldn't stay angry. Speech allowed him to scream, argue, or reassure the mother, and as he matured he achieved greater sophistication and refinement of his technique to calm, excite, or control his mother's mood: he became a 'charmer' . . . His encyclopedic knowledge was acquired effortlessly by looking and listening.[7]

When he entered nursery school, he tried to charm his teacher, too, by his bright talk, his fund of information, and his intense desire to know everything. But he mocked the 'stupid kids' in the school and they, to his consternation, counterattacked.[8]

In conversation with the analyst, this little boy blurted out, 'If you know lots of things you don't have to be scared.' When it was suggested to the boy that he really wanted to play with the toys he kept describing, he answered by explaining how angry his mother got when he made things messy, and said, 'I'd rather talk, I don't want to get dirty.' He said that he would like to make the analyst read to him, like his mother, so they really would be like friends. The analyst adds, 'His seeking or giving of information, his being pupil or teacher, indirectly expressed feelings and wishes of an affectionate quality, which also stimulated anxiety.'[9]

Finally, by deciding to be a doctor, 'a doctor children like,' the boy strengthened his necessary identification with his father and expressed his desire to become immune to illness by learning all that his father and his analyst knew. 'He was now consciously motivated to learn in order to master his environment. The safety of learning was enhanced by the father's pleasure in his intellectuality.' While ignorance threatened him with isolation, that is, the absence of anyone to protect and love him, his father's knowledge could, he felt, give him his father's strength.[10] Knowledge could now both loosen his excessive, symbiotic tie to his mother and allow him to become close to other persons.

The Bodily Clumsiness of Philosophers

I must confedd that as I gave my three examples of precociously intellectual children, I now and then thought of some of the philosophers I have described. I agree that it makes little sense to identify any one of the philosophers with any one of the children, but I am sure that there are instructive analogies. Let me begin to point out the analogies by means of a crude but useful sign, physical clumsiness, of the sort that may be assumed to be a payment for precocious intellectuality. Among philosophers, such clumsiness is well attested for Montaigne, Kant, Hegel, Mill, Russell, and Broad.

Montaigne tells us that his father had been hard to equal in physical agility, but that he himself was surpassed by almost everyone, except in running, in which he was just fair. Continuing to enumerate his short-comings, he says:

> Of music, either vocal, for which my voice is very inept, or instrumental, they never succeeded in teaching me anything. At dancing, tennis, wrestling, I have never been able to acquire any but very slight and ordinary ability; at swimming, fencing, vaulting, and jumping, none at all. My hands are so clumsy that I cannot even write so that I can read it; so that I would rather do over what I have scribbled than give myself the trouble of unscrambling it. And I hardly read any better. I feel that I weigh upon my listeners. Other-wise, a good scholar. I cannot close a letter the right way, nor could I ever cut a pen, or carve at table worth a rap, or saddle a horse, or properly carry a bird and release it, or talk to dogs, birds, or horses.[1]

Kant was the son of a craftsman, but his friend and disciple, Wasiansky, says of him, 'As skillful as Kant was in brainwork, he was clumsy in handiwork. He could govern only the pen, but not the pen-knife. I therefore usually had to cut the quill to fit his hand.'[2] Hegel, who was so sure that his philosophy surpassed Kant's, resembled Kant in his clumsiness. His sister's notes characterize him, as I have said before, with the words, 'Lacked all bodily agility . . . Loved to jump, but was utterly awkward in dancing lessons.'[3] He seems to have learned at least to enjoy dancing, however.

John Stuart Mill's spectacular education was spectacularly unsuccessful from a physical standpoint. In a cancelled passage, partly quoted before, of his *Autobiography*, he writes:

> I grew up with great inaptness in the common affairs of every day life. I was far longer than children generally are before I could put on my clothes. I know not how many years passed before I could tie a knot. My articulation was long imperfect; one letter, r, I could not pronounce until I was nearly sixteen. I never could, nor can I now, do anything requiring the smallest

manual dexterity, but I never put even a common share of the exercise of understanding into practical things. I was continually acquiring odd or disagreeable tricks which I very slowly and imperfectly got rid of. I was, besides, utterly inobservant: I was, as my father continually told me, like a person who had not the organs of sense: my eyes and ears seemed of no use to me, so little did I see or hear what was before me . . . .[4]

Russell, it appears, may have been equally inept with his hands. 'Bertie was, in fact,' a friend writes, 'almost a caricature of the unpractical philosopher, and the idea that he should actually know what to do in a domestic/mechanical emergency was laughable.' The friend illustrates by recalling that he and his wife once had to be out at four o'clock, just when Russell had to have the tea without which he was miserable. The wife therefore prepared everything, 'the tea in the teapot, cup and saucer ready, the kettle filled. Then she wrote out the instructions in chalk on the slate table in the kitchen . . . . When we came back at five o'clock Bertie was miserable and the tea was still unmade.'[5]

The English philosopher, C. D. Broad, who lived, as he describes, under the domination of his mother, and who 'intensely disliked other children, with their noise and their quarrels and their silly games,' makes an almost unbelievable list of his incapacities. His sense of time, he says, is naturally defective, so that he has never been able to keep step with music, or, for that matter, to keep step visually with anyone else. 'I have always hated and feared any kind of drill,' he tells us, 'and have always approached the learning from others of any kind of bodily skill with an expectation of making a fool of myself and a feeling that I shall never be any good at it . . .' He has a passion for model trains, but is utterly incapable, he confesses, of any games or sports. In his words, 'I cannot dance, or skate, or ski, or swim properly, or row, or play tennis or cricket or golf, or ride a horse, or sail a boat, or drive a car . . . In each instance I have been frightened at the outset . . .'[6]

Of physically clumsy scientists, I remember Poincaré, Norbert Wiener, and Hideki Yukawa. Wiener's poor muscular coordination was made the worse by his poor eyesight, which he attributes to immoderate reading at an early age. 'My appearance of clumsiness was accentuated,' he says, 'by the learned vocabulary which I had acquired from my reading.'[7] Yukawa is sure that he chose to become a theoretical physicist in part because he was so poor with his hands. Mathematics and the like were attractive because they allowed him to solve a problem without handiwork or apparatus, and without relation to other people. He adds, 'The process of solving it was also extremely enjoyable in itself.'[8]

In spite of the examples I have given, I do not want to be understood as making the indefensible claim that philosophers or other lovers of abstractions *cannot* be good with their hands. During the Middle Ages, Moslem philosophers were typically physicians, and though they may have left actual surgery to others, they must have had some manipulative skills. Descartes was in effect a physician and, as I have emphasized, spent much of his time in anatomical experiments. Locke, an expert physician by the standards of his time, may have taken part in anatomical experiments and certainly did take part in 'dirty, hot, and complicated' ones in the preparation of medicines.[9] Mill, despite his clumsiness, improvised effectively on the piano.[10] Santayana soothed himself by drawing and other handiwork.[11] Wittgenstein's early skill in building models of machines has been noted. Popper attempted to become a manual worker. When he proved too weak for the role, he learned and practiced cabinet-making.[12]

Precociously Intellectual Philosophers

If we turn from the group of physically clumsy philosophers and scientists, which I have not assembled out of any real investigative passion, and turn to a group of precociously intellectual philosophers, assembled with equal casualness, we may supplement the names of the clumsy ones, all of whom were precociously intellectual, with those of Pascal, Leibniz, Hume, Peirce, Collingwood, and Sartre, all of whom, for all I know, may also have been clumsy.

I need not repeat what Montaigne wrote about his remarkable early education, nor what I have told about the education of the precocious Pascal and the precocious Leibniz. Hume, Kant, and Hegel surely fit the image of the precociously intellectual child. Peirce was the son of an erudite scientist, who encouraged his early profound interest in puzzles, card tricks, codes and whatever else encouraged mental agility.

> They played double-dummy, sometimes from late evening until sunrise, the father severely criticizing every mistake in his son's play. Once given a table of logarithms with an example of logarithmic multiplication, Charles was told to master the use of the table . . . At eight Charles was studying chemistry, and at twelve had a small laboratory in which he conducted experiments in quantitative analysis. At thirteen he read Whateley's *Logic* and later began reading philosophy under the critical guidance of his father.[1]

Russell assumes, it can be recalled, that he was saved in childhood by nature, books, and mathematics. Sartre had the childhood passion, already described, for words and books. Collingwood, the beginning of whose philosophical vocation has been described, attributes his passion for learning to his father and to himself. It was his father's doing, he writes, that he began Latin at the age of four and Greek at six, but his own that he began,

> about the same time, to read everything that I could find about the natural sciences, especially geology, astronomy, and physics; to recognize rocks, to know the stars, and to understand the working of pumps and locks and other mechanical appliances up and down the house. It was my father who gave me lessons in ancient and modern history . . . . But my first lesson in what I now regard as my own subject, the history of thought, was the discovery, in a friend's house a few miles away, of a battered seventeenth-century book, wanting cover and title-page . . . . I was about nine when I found it . . . .[2]

I have no further examples of precociously intellectual philosophers, except that of Kierkegaard, whom I have kept for the last because of the great, ambivalent love for words that began in his childhood. A frail, small boy dressed in peculiar clothing, he was jeered at when he was first sent to school. He was unable to defend himself physically, but his ability to argue had been stimulated by his father's dialectical skill, and he used his sharpened wits to good effect. Latin and especially Greek grammar appealed to him strongly, and he fell in love with classical grammar, implausible as it may seem to other students of the subject. He reports that when he learned the rules for the indicative and conjunctive, an extraordinary change took place in his consciousness—he sensed that everything depended upon how a thing is thought.[3] Grammatical form, he saw, was the invisible soul by which a thought was given life and reality given form. He imagined the different parts of speech as different sorts of men.[4] He spoke to the thoughts he felt imprisoned in his head and asked them to associate with one another; and he tried to reduplicate his words in his life and his life in his words, both taking on substance, sincerity, and reality from one another.[5] Yet although he loved language so and focused his ambitions on it, he came to see that language was also dangerous, because its false sublimities seduced man into appearing more noble than he was.[6] To arrive at the truth, or even to aspire to it, he wrote - to himself, it was necessary to get rid of thoughts, ideas, and egoism; for language was the gift by which we are judged or judge ourselves.[7]

Kierkegaard's anxiety and suffering, his love for his father, his own skill with words, which he flicked to and fro like a rapier, had tempted him into ontological extravagance. I mean that he had tried to make words themselves carry too much of the burden of existence, until he was forced by his own insight and emotion to attack words for being, in philosophical or theological use, no more than they are, abstractions and systematic thought experiments. Yet he never abandoned his ambition to turn them into existences and deeds. In this ambition, he was surely a philosopher.

Paradoxical Philosophers

I think that the preceding examples make it plausible to say that philosophy often begins as a response to anxiety. I would like to continue for the while, however, not with anxiety as such, but with the inner conflict of philosophers, the powerful ambivalence I have often mentioned, which shows itself in their need to deal with philosophical problems by means of ambiguities and antinomies. This need is likely to have arisen in childhood, it can be argued, when the philosophers-to-be were required to respond in contradictory ways. Recent psychological literature has dwelt on the predicament of the child required to love but blamed for not loving naturally and spontaneously. What can a child do when it is coerced to be spontaneous, or faced with some other severely antinomical demand? The response must be as complex as the demand is ambiguous. The child responds, perhaps, by acting or thinking as though the meaning of life were concealed and discoverable only by prolonged searching, or as though life were only the metaphor of a greater, underlying reality. There are also various forms of indirect resistance, as when the child pretends to or achieves a probably resentful indifference. Life, in other words, becomes enigmatic, metaphorical, indirect, or indifferent. The philosophical response to it may therefore be an exacerbated concern with paradoxical problems, which are the abstract counterparts of lives under paradoxical stress.[1]

Such considerations may help us to understand why philosophers may take to paradoxes and why they may keep trying, perhaps not even willingly, to solve or rise above them. To recall only modern philosophers, Kant balances antinomies in order to allow the doubling or quasi-doubling of the world and to suggest that the other, the unknown but free world, is the real one. Yet it turns out that Kant believes that the unknown, free, real world is not so unlike the world it is completely different from. Kant says that man's 'experience of his state on earth and the ordering of nature in general give him clear proofs that his moral deterioration, with its inevitable punishments, as well as his moral improvement and the well-being resulting therefrom, will continue endlessly, *i.e.*, eternally.'[2]

Unlike Kant, but like Neo-Platonists and some Buddhist philosophers, Hegel formalizes the clash of opposites as a hierarchically self-transcending process. Kierkegaard and Nietzsche, having a different nature, glorify and exploit the paradox, as if, unable to beat it, they had decided to join it. In physics, Bohr, influenced by Kierkegaard, Høffding, and William James, finds an analogous resolution in the context of physics, trying to crystallize something useful out of a deep contradiction. The fact that he admires Kierkegaard for turning misfortune and suffering into something good implies, it seems to me, what the background of his own paradox-love may be.

Let me add a few words on the philosophers I have just named, to explain their attitudes toward paradoxicality. To the image I have drawn of Kant, I need add only that, as he testifies, it was the investigation of the antinomy of pure reason that first aroused him from his dogmatic slumber and drove him to the critique of reason itself, 'in order to resolve the scandal of ostensible contradiction of reason with itself'. Kant believed, it has been said, that man was basically an antinomical being, whose antinomical quality came to expression in the antithetical resolution of basic metaphysical problems.[3]

Hegel praises Kant for the importance he assigns the antinomies, but criticizes him, not quite correctly, for confining them to four sets of cosmological arguments. He insists that 'profounder insight into the dialectical nature of reason demonstrates *any* Notion [Begriff] whatever to be a unity of opposed moments to which, therefore, the form of antinomical assertion can be given.'[4] In speaking of contradiction, he insists that it should be grasped and expressed as the law which says, ' *Everything is inherently contradictory.*' Unlike other laws, Hegel adds, this law, of contradiction, expresses 'the truth and the essential nature of things.'[5]

Kierkegaard is a model of the lived contradiction, as he not infrequently says. 'From a child,' he writes,

> I was under the sway of a prodigious melancholy, the depth of which finds its only adequate measure in the equally prodigious dexterity I possessed in hiding it under an apparent gaiety and *joie de vivre* . . . As a child I was sternly and seriously brought up in Christianity. Humanly speaking, it was a crazy upbringing. Already in my earliest childhood I broke down under the grave impression which the melancholy old man who laid it upon me himself sank under. A child—what a crazy thing!—travestied as an old man! What wonder then that there were times when Christianity appeared to me the most inhuman cruelty—although never, even when I was furthest from it, did I cease to revere it . . . .

Explaining, he says that Christianity had, 'to be sure, humanly speaking, rendered me exceedingly unhappy. This corresponds to my relationship with my father, the person whom I loved most deeply. And what is the meaning of this! The point precisely is that he made me unhappy—but out of love.'[6]

This paradox of love is a particular instance, in Kierkegaard's eyes, of the general paradox that abstraction is by nature unable to express the particular and accidental being that is, we know, a reality.

> The difficulty lies in bringing this definite something and the ideality of thought together, by penetrating the concrete particularity with thought. Abstract thought cannot even take cognizance of this contradiction, since the very process of abstraction prevents the contradiction from arising.

Therefore, the abstract thinker himself, who is undoubtedly an existing individual, 'must in one way or another be suffering from absent-mindedness.'[7]

The upshot, for Kierkegaard, is his love of the paradoxical. Speaking of Socrates and thinking of the 'unknown something,' as he calls God, he says:

> One should not think slightingly of the paradoxical for the paradox is the source of the thinker's passion, and the thinker without a paradox is like a lover without feeling: a paltry mediocrity. But the highest pitch of every passion is always to will its own downfall; and so it is also the supreme passion of Reason to seek a collision, though this collision must in one way or another prove its undoing. The supreme paradox of all thought is the attempt to discover something that thought cannot think.[8]

Nietzsche, though he denies the God that Kierkegaard affirms, is equally sure of the inadequacy of abstraction and the logic it gives rise to. He prefers, as we have seen, not abstract truths, but life-enhancing values. His position, in both life and logic, is instructive enough for us to consider it, if not analytically, at least at relative length.

Nietzsche's suffering has already been described and his fear of insanity and his temptation or threat to commit suicide have been mentioned. The fear and temptation became prominent when his relationship with Lou Salomé and Paul Rée (and his mother and sister) became so difficult to bear. Thoughts of suicide became frequent.[9] As for insanity, even before the crisis he had 'wondered in all innocence and malice' if he had any tendency to it.[10] Nietzsche being who he was, it was natural for him to react to the crisis ambivalently, or, to be more exact, sado-masochistically. In drafts of letters to Lou Salomé, he writes, 'Say nothing, dear Lou, in your favour: I have already adduced more in your favour than you could—before myself and before others . . . In me you have the best advocate but also the most inexorable judge.' In two separate drafts he repeats the words, 'It seems to me that no one can think better of you, but no one worse either'—'Ich glaube, es kann Niemand besser von Ihnen denken, aber auch Niemand schlimmer.'[11] (I cannot resist remarking, parenthetically, that the equally ambivalent Kafka wrote to his fiancée, Felice Bauer, 'How can I . . . accomplish what I want to accomplish: Persuade you simultaneously of the seriousness of two pleas: "Hold me dear" and "Hate me!" '[12])*

It may be excessive to suppose that Nietzsche preferred to remain in this state of painful ambivalence, yet a friend writes that Nietzsche was 'screaming like a Philoctetes, and himself doing everything to sharpen the pain of his suffering beyond endurance.'[13] In the evident belief that his pain is to his advantage and credit, Nietzsche says,

> What I think about sacrifice, disappointment, pain, and the like is this: What matters is only that one endures them—for they are the mightiest supports and sources of life . . . Such a pain (it was as if *all* vulnerable places were pierced at once by a knife!) is a high distinction.[14]

It is Nietzsche's often reiterated opinion that nothing great can be accomplished unless under the goad of suffering, more or less willingly applied to oneself. Speaking of Schopenhauer but surely referring to himself as well, he says that the philosopher 'destroys his earthly happiness by means of his courage; he must be hostile even to the persons he loves, to the institutions that begot him . . .'[15] Genuine accomplishments, he is sure, are the product of 'the tension of the soul in unhappiness which cultivates its strength,' just as the true victors and seducers are those with 'powerful and irreconcilable drives' and 'a real mastery and subtlety in waging war against oneself.'[16] Every truly creative man is riven by ambivalence, or, in Nietzsche's epigram, 'One is fruitful only at the cost of being rich in contradictions.'[17]

There is nothing in what I have just repeated that logically requires Nietzsche to question the truthfulness of logic. Yet his praise of inward or emotional self-contradiction is paralleled by his attempt to justify logical self-contradiction. This is perfectly clear in the *Will to Power*, where he explains his view of logic, maybe only to himself, with a degree of elaboration unusual to him. He there observes or complains, like Kierkegaard, that logic brings in fundamental falsification, because it is based on the fictitious assumption that there are in fact identical cases.[18] What underlies logic is not, according to him, the need to know, but the

---

*I relegate to a footnote the extraordinarily sado-masochistic confession of C. D. Broad, who writes that he shares 'most of the likes and dislikes of our late dear Führer,' that is, Hitler, but that if he, Broad, came to rule, he would not put those likes and dislikes 'into practice with the insensate folly and the fiendish cruelty of that lunatic.' *The Philosophy of C. D. Broad*, ed. P. A. Schlipp (New York: Tudor/Library of Living Philosophers, 1959), p. 38.

need to survive, which requires us to abbreviate, subsume, and schematize, and to invent such obviously useful categories as 'substance,' 'subject,' 'object,' and 'becoming.'[19] In the vein of a Kant (or a Buddhist philosopher), he asks, 'Are the axioms of logic adequate to reality or are they a means and measure for us to create reality, the concept "reality," for ourselves?—To affirm the former one would . . . have to have a previous knowledge of being—which is certainly not the case.' Logic 'contains no *criterion of truth*, but an *imperative* concerning what should count as true.'[20]

For such reasons, Nietzsche is constrained to question the law of contradiction itself and to ask what presuppositions already lie at the bottom of it. After we have proposed the self-identical 'A' of logic and mathematics, he says, experience then appears to confirm its presence endlessly.[21] The truth is that 'the subjective compulsion not to contradict here is a biological compulsion . . . But what naiveté to extract from this a proof that we are therewith in possession of a "truth in itself"!—Not being able to contradict is proof of an incapacity, not of "truth".'[22]

Echoing, I think, Plato, Hegel, and Schopenhauer (though speaking, no doubt, for himself), Nietzsche sees the nature of the world in a state of becoming, as impossible to formulate, 'as "false," as "self-contradictory." Knowledge and becoming exclude one another. Consequently, "knowledge" must be something else: there must first of all be a will to make knowable, a kind of becoming must itself create the deception of beings.'[23]

It appears to me clear that Nietzsche's praise of self-conflict and self-conquest, his objection to the laws of identity and contradiction, and his belief in a deceptive prior will are all projections of his own great ambivalence and his own thwarted and creative will. I must immediately add that they are not only or simply such projections. Perhaps I should say that it is the force of the projection that causes Nietzsche to make just his own choices out of a number of open possibilities. It does appear to me that he has got hold of a genuine, difficult problem, of the kind that Piaget deals with when he asks about the relation between logic and mathematics, on the one hand, and uncategorized experience, on the other. I have considerable sympathy for Nietzsche's desire to understand philosophy in the context of human biology and for his near-Pragmatism. As my earlier discussion of truth makes plain, however, I think his objections to logic are impossible to defend, at least in the little-qualified form in which he makes them. His own difficulties, of which he is usually aware, I am sure, are indicated by his use of quotation marks around such words as 'false' and 'self-contradictory.' He does not and cannot answer the question why logic, mathematics, and the categories of thought are in fact biologically useful if they are false to what he calls 'becoming'—itself, he has said, an artificial category. Why quarrel as he does with the assumption, which is so natural, that ideas are practically successful only when they are in some sense adapted to reality and successful in interpreting it truthfully?

Even more to the point, Nietzsche does not and cannot explain how his own arguments are to be taken if, in abandoning the laws of identity and contradiction, he abandons the intelligibility they make possible. Maybe he played with the notion of intellectual as he did with that of physical suicide, the threat of which is often an act of defiance and vengeance, but also a plea for human understanding. Maybe the conventions of logic and language suggested to him the human conventions that had proved so difficult for him. It is noteworthy that he did not commit the intellectual suicide that can be attributed to Pascal and Kierkegaard. Whatever the loss in power of defiance and suggestion, his ideas can be explored in a rational spirit.[24] I feel this with particular keenness because there is something decidedly Nietzschean, not only in my last few pages, but in my whole contention that philosophers may be living ambivalent, so-to-speak paradoxical lives, which they may translate into intellectual ambivalencies and paradoxes, or into the conclusion, shared by Kierkegaard, Nietzsche, and others, that life itself, when judged by the simplistic standards of ordinary logic, is paradoxical—and so much the worse for the logic.

Philosophy and Pathology

Granted what has been said about anxiety and about paradox, it should not be surprising that the attempt to think deeply or carefully can, when extreme, betray a pathological condition. The questions, 'What price do we pay for living—for dying?' and 'Is there a future?' can be counted philosophical, but when asked by a little schizophrenic girl, they were symptoms of her illness.[1] There was certainly something unhealthy about the curiosity, which might be counted scientific, of the 'strangely detached, brilliant' six-year-old who, with great purposefulness, 'attempted to apply a drill to the temple of one of his classmates in order to look into his head to see if the little boy had brains.'[2] Likewise, there was certainly something unhealthy in the condition of the very intelligent, obsessively doubtful student of philosophy who 'suffered the most intense anxiety and appeared to think that he was in danger of complete annihilation' when his intellectual position, which he defended with tenacity and skill, was under attack.[3]

As psychologists have come to recognize, logic itself, either in its general meaning of orderly, reasoned thought, or in its meaning of formal logic, can act as a defence, because it can rule out the threat of unbearable disorder, which is the usual equivalent of the threat of unbearable feelings. The logicality of Spinoza's *Ethics* is psychologically parallel to his emotional restraint in company, as the presumed completeness and correctness of Kant's table of categories is related to his extreme self-control, and as Russell and Whitehead's *Principia Mathematica* is related to their need to counter their inner instability (Russell says of Whitehead, 'Like many people possessed of great self-control, he suffered from impulses which were scarcely sane.'[4])

The possible connection between the logical and pathological has been illuminated by a careful piece of research into the lives of families each of which numbered a schizophrenic among their children. Some of these families constituted an exceptionally logical type. They enforced a 'rigid, ordered, almost ritualistic form of communication' in set subjects and sequences and in 'fully completed sentences and correct constructions.' The psychological object was to outlaw the spontaneity that would reveal the great tensions under which the families laboured.[5]

Such observations raise the question of the possible connection of philosophy with psychosis. It is clear, I assume, that I have accepted the idea that any creative effort or, in the psychoanalytic sense, any sublimation can help to maintain a person's psychological equilibrium. One psychoanalyst has gone so far as to propose the category of 'healthy psychotics,' who, by an intensity of their work or of their human relations, continue to function surprisingly well, even though there are good reasons to diagnose them as psychotic.[6]

This conception, of the healthy psychotic, may seem excessively paradoxical, but there have been many creative persons whose main bridge to reality seems to have been their creative effort itself.[7] Well-known examples among writers or artists might be August Strindberg, Vincent van Gogh, and Edvard Munch, and, among philosophers, Kierkegaard and Nietzsche.[8] Nietzsche might fit the category even if his psychosis had a physical cause. Causes may, after all, interact and supplement one another, and his open psychosis began not far from the point at which his sane philosophy ended, when his 'anxious grandiosity,' having become the conviction that he was the fateful philosopher standing between two millennia, lapsed into psychotic elation.[9]

Even if we set aside Hume's depression and psychotic episode, and even if we discount Hegel's depression, which some have thought psychotic, there is every reason to respect the declarations of Kierkegaard and Wittgenstein that they felt themselves on the verge of madness, and to remember that Rousseau's suspicions rose to a paranoid climax. I think, as I have said, that Kant hinted, indirectly but clearly, that he was not far from insanity, and I think that he kept himself sane by the rigidity of his personal life and by the creativity of his philosophizing.

To my own estimate of philosophers, I add that of Karl Jung, who is capable of drastic reactions and elemental insults. After writing in a letter that Heidegger 'bristles' with 'unconscious subjective prejudices . . . trying in vain to die behind a blown-up language,' he adds:

> Heidegger's *modus philosophandi* is neurotic through and through and is ultimately rooted in his psychic crankiness. His kindred spirits, close or distant, are sitting in lunatic asylums, some as patients and some as psychiatrists on a philosophical rampage . . . For all its critical analysis philosophy has not yet managed to root out its psychopaths. What do we have psychiatric diagnosis for! That grizzler Kierkegaard also belongs in this galère. Philosophy still has to learn that it is *made by human beings* and depends to an alarming degree on their psychic constitution. In the critical philosophy of the future there will be a chapter on 'The Psychopathology of Philosophy.' Hegel is fit to bust with presumption and vanity. Nietzsche drips with outraged sexuality, and so on. There is no thinking *qua* thinking, at times it is a pisspot of unconscious devils, just like any other function that lays claim to hegemony. Often what is thought is less important than *who* thinks it. But this is assiduously overlooked. Neurosis addles the brain of every philosopher because he is at odds with himself. His philosophy is then nothing but a systematized struggle with his own uncertainty.[10]

Philosophical Psychotics

I will say nothing on Jung's reaction to Heidegger, with whom I am not very familiar, and in relation to whom my feelings are much weaker than Jung's. But the possible likeness between philosophy and psychosis, which he, too, accepts, is heightened by the philosophical temperament of some psychotics, especially the paranoids, whose tendency to systematize ideas may result in a tragic parody of a philosophical system.

Let me begin the comparison with the words of a psychotic young woman of nineteen. She addresses her self-portrayal to 'that one alone who may understand it,' or to some who are themselves left alone, or to the three who once gave her a stone instead of bread. In apparent innocence of Nietzsche and his like, she writes elatedly:

> I am distinctly original innately and in development.
> I have in me a quite unusual intensity of life.
> I can feel.
> I have a marvelous capacity for misery and happiness.
> I am broad-minded.
> I am a genius.
> I am a philosopher of my own good peripatetic school.

378 PARADOXICAL CONSCIOUSNESS

I care neither for right nor for wrong—my conscience is nil.
My brain is a conglomeration of aggressive versatility.
I have reached a truly wonderful state of miserable morbid unhappiness.[1]

The parodic temperamental likeness between philosophy and
psychosis may be demonstrated by an experiment in which three confirmed paranoids, each of whom believed he was Jesus Christ, were
confronted with one another.[2] When one of the three Christs insisted that
he was God, for otherwise he would not make the claim, a second
claimant asked him not to generalize and assume that his rivals were
insane, as he had done, just because they were present in an insane
asylum.[3]

A brief conversation between two of the Christs should convey their
simple but earnest philosophical attitude. When one of them said, 'I love the
truth even though it hurts,' the other answered, 'If it hurts too much, man is
wise to turn away from it.' To this the first replied scornfully, 'That's your
belief, sir.'[4]

On another occasion, the lover of the painful truth, who understood
that no one believed him, said, 'Truth is truth, no matter if only one
person speaks it.' Expressing the hope to live alone, he explained, 'My
love is for infinity and where the human element comes in it's distaste-
ful . . . I want positive-idealed love without attachment. That's what my
femaleity wants. Nobody offered it to me so my maleity offered it and I
married myself.' When asked why he was so angry, he answered, 'I'm
always angry. You cannot have sanity without hatred of the evil ideal. I
have love of hatred towards negativism.' To the question, 'Isn't it
uncomfortable to be angry all the time?' he gave the not un-Nietzschean
answer, 'No, it isn't, on the grounds that it's an incentive to go on.' His
goal, he insisted, was to live with the truth, and if society did not want
the truth, it could go to hell. To my mind, his most moving words,
spoken when he was tense and refused to see his nurse, whom he felt had
abandoned him, were, 'Truth is my friend. I have no other friends.'
When asked to reconcile contradictory descriptions he had given, he
would answer that the object he had described had changed from a white
to a black phase.[5]

Such reasoning is the self-expression of rather ordinary persons
under psychotic stress. Under the same stress, more learned or talented
persons, like the judge, Daniel-Henry Schreber, on whom Freud wrote,
and who himself wrote a book in answer to his psychiatrist, or like the
scientist and mystic, Emanuel Swedenborg, or (if I am right in so assess-
ing him) William Blake, are able to elaborate ideas or create poetry
impressive to quite sane persons.[6] Their systems, when they create them,
are no obviously less true or sane than those of the Neo-Pythagoreans or
the Gnostics, or sometimes of the Neo-Platonists. There is nothing that

contradicts experience in the idea of a paranoid leader, whether in politics, religion, philosophy, or, if we qualify carefully, science. Psychotics can resemble philosophers in exhibiting endless curiosity and endless desire to solve abstract problems. They can also resemble philosophers in their ability to fuse disparate kinds of knowledge and create consistent worlds of thought, and they can even, as we have seen, pay the scientist's and philosopher's tribute to the autonomy of the truth and of those who seek it. Sometimes, as I have suggested, they can even *be* philosophers; at least the line between them and philosophers can be very thin.

Philosophers

Despite what I have just said, and difficult as their lives may be, philosophers, along with scientists, use abstractions not only to express, but also to transcend their difficulties. They learn to use their isolation to discover and, each in his own way, to solve problems as no one has discovered and solved them before. Their isolation may then both exhilirate and frighten them, because it may repeat and draw on early experiences of loneliness, abandonment, and weakness. 'I must confess that at the very beginning,' said Einstein, 'when the special theory of relativity began to germinate in me, I was visited by all sorts of nervous conflicts.'[1] 'In philosophizing,' said Wittgenstein 'one must descend into the old chaos, and feel well there.'[2] When difficult experiences are being drawn on, a strong, exaggerated, and even paranoid self-confidence may be helpful. To create at high tension may be in a sense to enter a state between or beyond sanity or insanity. The state may be too radical and strange to be considered sane at the time and place the philosopher is living, and the philosopher himself may show signs of even psychotic stress; but the state may not be simply insane, if only because, as later acknowledged, it has precipitated a valuable insight.[3]

My conclusion is only that philosophy is a far more complex enterprise than philosophers have generally been willing to recognize; and that unless they recognize the degree and nature of its complexities, of its involvements in psychology, not to speak of history and sociology, their efforts to understand the truth are seriously impeded. Their frequent belief that one can by direct unempirical means capture the whole truth is an error. It is an error to think that people, even philosophers, can be simply objective, or, in the Existentialists' sense, truly subjective or authentic. Like other works of verbal art, philosophies are marvellously complex, their intellectuality adding a decisive but often deceptive element to the whole amalgam. What, then, is the truth? At least that there is no short or even very straight road to it.

11
Questions and conclusions

Trivialization?

I must end soon, and I want to use this, my final chapter to ask and answer a number of questions that have become inescapable. The first, on trivialization, may be put in the following way: If philosophy is qualified at every point, as I have been insisting, by personal needs and idiosyncratic emotions, can it be more than an epiphenomenon of philosophers' lives or retain any value of its own?

The question, it seems to me, has a number of answers. The most obvious is the formal answer that nothing in the truth or value of an idea is affected by the circumstances of its origin. These circumstances help to explain just how the idea was arrived at and what its contemporary nuances were, but in themselves they have no bearing on its truth or falsity.

I have no qualms in accepting this formal answer. I find it misleading, however. Even philosophers, who generally seem to accept it, have difficulty in abiding by it. The reason, as I have emphasized, is that philosophical ideas are too vague or unempirical to be judged with the same etiquette of 'true' and 'false' that we follow in mathematics, logic, and the exact sciences. It is therefore natural to be swayed by what we know of the ideas' non-rational causes and effects. Why, in the absence of other considerations, should we be serious about the thought of a man who shows himself to have been ignorant, mentally unbalanced, or merely self-aggrandizing? If we take Schopenhauer's metaphysics to have been mainly a projection of his sexual attitudes, there is little impulse to ask if it is, nevertheless, true or useful. The metaphysics by which he constitutes the world is not, after all, a scientific response to a problem as held by a community of like-minded investigators, and it suffers from the very outset, except romantically, by comparison with modern scientific cosmologies.

The mention of these cosmologies raises an obvious but essential point. Because the distinction between philosophy and science was blurred in the past, and is still often blurred, I think, the philosopher's contentions may be directly contradicted by the presumably scientific ones by means of which he is being explained. Such a contradiction would make it difficult for a contemporary psychologist to accept Schopenhauer's doctrine on women, though it is essential to Schopenhauer's philosophy. Likewise, a mathematician would probably reject much of Kant on mathematics, and a physicist, much of Kant on physics. A physicist might also well object to Nietzsche's theory of eternal recurrence, to which Nietzsche himself attributed great philosophical importance.

Yet the result of non-philosophical explanation is not necessarily the negation or trivialization of philosophy. I do not think its effects can be predicted in advance, and it can certainly be put to many uses; yet it should more often subtilize than trivialize. If I am allowed to speak in terms of my personal reactions, I will use the examples of Kant and Nietzsche to put my meaning.

Long before I had thought of analyzing Kant psychologically, it was evident to me that his faith in Newton, in the exclusive, though metaphysically limited truth of Euclidean geometry, and in the completeness and finality of his table of categories was misplaced. Following the commentators I read, I accepted the historical explanation of his faith, which now seems so dogmatic, in Newton and Euclid, and removed that aspect of Kant from philosophical consideration. I also learned the incomplete environmental explanation for the way he had compiled his categories. The later, psychological explanation for his desire that the table of categories be complete and final did nothing to change an already existing refusal to accept it as such, but it allowed me to feel that I knew why Kant had been so blind.

It was well before I had thought of the psychological explanations, furthermore, that I had rejected Kant's thing-in-itself, at least in the form in which he proposed it. I soon accepted the argument, at which, as I had not yet learned, his opponents and later his Neo-Kantian partisans had arrived, that to know that the thing-in-itself was the cause or ground of the world was to know more than could be known by Kant's own principles. Kant was sure that the subject-in-itself was the substratum that underlay the 'I' we are familiar with, and he was sure that it was proper of reason to speak of the relation between what lay inside the boundary of the knowable to that which lay outside it.[1] He seemed to be walking on the boundary, leaning this way or that, cautious or careless, as served him best at the moment. This impression of a self-serving bias became stronger when I discovered that he argued, as I have said in my biographical account, that phenomena and noumena could not be alike because, if they were, freedom would have to be given up. The psychological explanation for his belief in the thing-in-itself clarified his need and his ambivalence. He might have been more consistent, if less Kantian, had he refused to make his many characterizations of the unknowable. 'Kant's view of ethics ends,' it has been said, 'in a tangle of contradictions and antinomies, in which Kant is constantly saying what is on his own terms unsayable, and saying it in contradictory ways.'[2]

Yet if it was a weakness, even a formal error, for Kant to have known the unknowable as the cause or ground of phenomena, it was a helpful, realistic error. For reasons his biography makes clear, he had too strong an experience of otherness, accident, disorder, and pain, of non-rationality and irrationality, to smooth things over, as did the Idealists who followed him. He respected the systematic neatness of physical theory, but he also respected brute fact. He believed implicitly in his categories, and he believed in his moral absolutes more than in Holy Writ, but he also believed, on not unpersuasive evidence, in the radical evil of human beings. I think that his honesty combined with his personal difficulties to prevent him from supposing the world to be metaphysically ego-like, as Fichte would have it, or the progressive revelation of the cosmic Spirit, as Hegel would have it. His tendency towards Idealism, if it is that, in the *Opus Postumum* is a weakening of the resolute quasi-dualism I have been praising, but the Kant who appears there is no longer himself.

Kant's weakness in ethics was, to my mind, the antithesis he created between absolute good and evil. His moral theory, though intellectually clear-cut at first sight, is inadequate to human beings and human moral situations as they in fact are. This inadequacy is bound up with his personality, as is particularly clear when we recall the harshness of some of the punishments he advocates. Although his notion of the correct standards of punishment must have been influenced by current thought and practice, some of his contemporaries were both more insightful and merciful. Ironically, the half-crazed de Sade, in spite of his pathologically exaggerated libertarianism, was among them.

Yet, despite its implausible antitheses and harsh application, Kant's moral theory was a heroic attempt to discover the universal moral law that so many of us appear to sense but find difficult to state and elaborate. I do not think that Kant's moral principles are simply and provably true; but I do think that we need something not unlike them if we hope to become more nearly human, that is, if our morality is to be more than merely local or adventitious. Despite their radical evil, human beings are respectable, he believes, by nature—their humanity is their holiness. They are essentially free and genuinely responsible, he believes, and they should become more so. He is right in the sense that the quality of our lives depends on our self-appraisal, self-direction, and self-respect, the ideals to which Kant returns like a moth to the flame.

I do not suppose that anyone else sees Kant exactly as I do; but my reaction to him may serve to show that the results of a biographical or psychological approach cannot be fixed in advance. Such an approach may help us to account for an otherwise unaccountable stubbornness, error, or shortcoming, but also for a particular insight, even the unconscious cunning that strengthens the surface logic we approve of. Briefly, although psychological considerations modify one's response to him, they do not necessarily make his philosophy trivial or irrelevant, and they certainly cannot, if reasonably employed, replace all philosophical by non-philosophical arguments.

The example of Nietzsche is different. I have represented him as particularly influenced by his father, or, more exactly, by his father's death, and have interpreted his attitude toward Christianity as revulsion from the adored father who had abandoned him and threatened him with the heritage of death. The attack on his father's values, I have claimed, was an irrational attempt to revenge himself and, simultaneously, to overcome his suffering and presentiment of death.

Does such an interpretation trivialize Nietzsche's attitude toward Christianity? It certainly emphasizes how problematic it is. In the *Birth of Tragedy*, Nietzsche already says that

Christianity was always, essentially and fundamentally, life's nausea and disgust with life, merely concealed behind, masked by, dressed up as faith in 'another' or 'better' life . . . Morality itself—how now? might not morality be 'a will to negate life,' a secret instinct of annihilation, a principle of decay, diminution, and slander—the beginning of the end? Hence, the danger of dangers?[3]

Toward the end of his sane life, Nietzsche says with what must be taken to be hatred:

The Christian church has left nothing untouched by its corruption; it has turned every value into an un-value, every truth into a lie, every integrity into a vileness of the soul. Let anyone dare to speak to me of its 'humanitarian' blessings! To *abolish* any distress ran counter to its deepest advantages: it lived on distress, it *created* distress to externalize *itself*.[4]

The effectiveness of these words and their implausibility strike me as both related to the same source: the refusal to make qualifications. I do not know to what extent Nietzsche studied Christianity. He read at least the New Testament carefully, with a philological eye, and he read Luther, Tolstoy, and Dostoevsky.[5] But regardless of what he read, there is no consciousness in his attacks of the enormous cultural complexity of Christianity, of the variety of its sources and the diversity of its forms, institutions, and practices. I do not understand how he could say what he does if he were at all conscious of the range of Byzantine, Romanesque,

Gothic, Renaissance, and Baroque art, not to speak of the literature of Christianity. His lack of interest in Christianity as a complex historical manifestation makes his attack jejune in this respect. No psychological analysis is needed in order to trivialize his attack. The analysis merely exposes the attack's otherwise mysterious reasons, as well as the reasons for his suspicion that Christianity is a nefarious plot against healthy men and ideals.

There is more, however, to Nietzsche's attack on Christianity. He is, after all, the Nietzsche whom Freud could not read because he excited him too much and threatened his intellectual independence—Freud is reported to have thought that 'the degree of introspection achieved by Nietzsche has never been achieved by anyone, nor is it likely ever to be reached again.'[6] Nietzsche's discussion of guilt, of the inhibition that 'internalizes' man, of the 'bad conscience,' and of the ascetic ideal, are all sharply perceptive. It seems to me exceedingly difficult to generalize, as he generalizes, from individual psychology to complex historical phenomena like Christianity. But if considered only in relation to individuals, there is substantial truth in Nietzsche's belief that the conscience is inhibited cruelty. As usual, he exaggerates and says, 'nothing but.' Yet he is, as he knows, a pioneering philosopher-psychologist.[7]

The psychological analysis of Nietzsche explains his one-sidedness, but also the attentiveness and penetration with which he transformed his personal suffering into hyperbolically stated but very useful truths. His difficulties and failures come clearer, but so do his accomplishments, arrived at, we come to understand, under extremely difficult physical and psychological conditions. He is enhanced rather than diminished when we see him living, half blind, in the lonely, littered room where, prostrated by headaches, afraid, hating, hopeful, elated, he continues to think and creates the truly insightful philosopher we have been discussing.

Fruitfulness?

Even if the question on trivialization has been answered, and it is agreed, as I have just argued, that philosophy is not necessarily diminished by non-philosophical explanations of itself, my approach raises an allied, no less insistent question: If philosophy, unlike science, is unable to reach satisfactorily objective conclusions, of what general use can it be? Its personal and social usefulness to the philosophers who invent it is clear enough, and what their disciples gain is not hard to guess. But what of educated people at large? Do they gain nothing more than a seat at the tournaments at which the monotony of intellectual life is relieved by the mortal cut and thrust and the immortal theatricality of the assembled philosophers? Is philosophy, in other words, only an abstract, self-deluding form of rhetoric?

My answer, both open and implied, has been that philosophical ideas have been fruitful in very many fields. It is hardly possible to imagine the development of civilization in their absence, for the inventive power that animates literature, technology, and science manifests and renews itself in the abstractions of philosophy.

Put so, without expansion, this argument may not be persuasive. Although I have already described the great immediate influence of Descartes, Kant, and Hegel, I will try to make the argument more persuasive by describing the extra-philosophical influence of one of these philosophers, Kant, in sufficient detail. I choose Kant, not only because he is often considered the greatest of modern philosophers, but because I have made a relatively close biographical analysis of him and have gone so far as to consider him a near-psychotic. I limit my account of his influence primarily to the twentieth century and to a number of scientists I happen to have read; yet I think it will prove impressive and will hint at the great fructifying power of philosophical ideas. I begin with mathematicians and physicists, go on to linguists, ethologists, and sociologists, and end with psychologists.

Among mathematicians, Kant's influence was apt to be exerted on those who concerned themselves with foundational problems. Reactions were sometimes amusingly opposite. Poincaré, for example, disagreed with Kant on geometry, but agreed with him on the synthetic a priori character of arithmetic, while Frege disagreed with him on arithmetic, but agreed on the synthetic a priori character of geometry.[1] To my (here quite limited) knowledge, the leader of recent mathematical thought most influenced by Kant was the intuitionist, Brouwer. According to Brouwer, the original Kantian intuitionism had been weakened during the nineteenth century by an increasing emphasis on the logical structure of mathematics, and, even more, by the discovery of non-Euclidean geometry. But intuitionism had been able to recover, he said, by abandoning Kant's belief in the apriority of space while, at the same time, adhering the more resolutely to Kant's belief in the apriority of time, the same 'intuition of basic two-oneness' Brouwer regarded as the basic intuition of mathematics.[2]

If we turn to nineteenth-century physics, we find that Kant influenced, to a varying but considerable extent, such physicists as Oersted, Faraday, and Helmholtz.[3] In the twentieth century, Bohr's principle of complementarity created at least a parallel, it has been argued, to the Kantian thing-in-itself, for Bohr's quantum object, such as an electron, could not be taken to be more than an abstract term arising in the description of phenomena.[4] Planck is said to have been well versed in Kantianism and considerably influenced by it. Einstein, though no Kantian in his physics, was stimulated by Kant. We know on reliable evidence that Einstein read Kant at the age of thirteen and considered him, I do not know for how long, his favourite philosopher.[5] Many years later, when nearing the age of forty, Einstein wrote to his fellow-physicist, Born, that he had just been reading Kant's *Prolegomena* and begun to feel the enormous suggestive power that had emanated and still emanated from the philosopher. Hume, said Einstein, had a much healthier philosophical instinct, but if one conceded Kant his synthetic a priori judgment, one was captured by him.[6]

I am not sure how well Born knew Kant, but he did use him as a kind of thought-coordinate. I gather this from a book in which Born declared:

> Mathematics . . . is made up of structures of pure thinking. The transition to reality is made by theoretical physics, which correlates symbols to observed phenomena. Where this can be done hidden structures are coordinated to phenomena. . . . Sound coordination leads to structures which are communicable, controllable, hence objective. It is justified to call these by the old term 'thing in itself.' They are pure form, void of all sensual qualities. This is all we can wish and expect.[7]

Perhaps as the effect of a typical German education, Heisenberg, too, related his thought to Kant's. To his mind, physicists, in a sense, retained the a priori, because they used the old concepts of space, time, causality, and so on, as a condition, encompassing their very equipment, for observing atomic events. He wrote:

> Kant's synthetic judgments a priori have become practical judgments (we must assume a causal chain of events through the apparatus to the eye of the observer) . . . The 'thing-in-itself' is for the atomic physicist, if he uses this concept at all, finally a mathematical structure; but this structure is—contrary to Kant—indirectly deduced from experience.[8]

Kant's influence on linguistics was exerted largely through Wilhelm von Humboldt.[9] Humboldt, who wrote what has been authoritatively called 'the first great book on general linguistics,' conceived language according to a distinctly Kantian pattern.[10] Just as, to Kant, experience depended on the prior existence of the forms of intuition and understanding, all joined in the unity of consciousness, so, to Humboldt, thought depended on the prior existence of the forms of language, which objectified and joined sensory impressions, in accord with the pre-existing unity of the mind. 'Language could not be invented or come upon,' Humboldt said, 'if its archetypes were not already present in the human mind. For man to understand but a single word truly . . . all language, in all its connections, must already lie prepared within him.'[11]

Humboldt's Kantianism, it must be conceded, was to a degree relativistic, because he believed that the 'inner form' of each language ordered and categorized in its own particular way, so that thought itself was partly specific to the language in which it was expressed. His Kantian, organic, and yet relative conception of language makes him the obvious source of contemporary European linguists such as L. Weisgerber and, through the historical succession of D. G. Brinton, F. Boas, and E. Sapir, of the American linguist, Whorf.[12] Certainly, Whorf's view that we organize the sensory flux by means of the pre-established concepts of the particular languages is Humboldtian and therefore dependent on a Kantian analysis.

From such linguistics, we may turn to ethology, which has an interesting intellectual relationship with it. One of the more recent ancestors of ethology, J. von Uexküll, was an explicit Kantian, His slogan may be taken to be, 'All reality is subjective appearance.' Applied to the study of animal species, this meant that each animal carried its perceived environing world, its *Umwelt*, like an impenetrable shell. The animal was the midpoint, as von Uexküll put it, of its own and its species' appearance-world *(Erscheinungswelt)*, sign-world *(Merkwelt)*, and, if it had a central nervous system, of its own and its species' inner world *(Innenwelt)* and outer world *(Aussenwelt)*. The 'objective world' of human beings was only, he said, the junction of all their superficial, because merely perceived, worlds, and devoid of any reality of its own.[13]

The contemporary ethologist, Konrad Lorenz, who has been influenced by von Uexküll, has recognized and even stressed the kinship between his ideas and Kant's. Elected to Kant's chair at the University of Königsberg, he wrote an essay, 'in the shadow of Immanuel Kant himself,' stating that what he had done was to apply to animals Kant's discovery that thought and perception had functional structures that preceded all experience. He wanted to modify Kant, however, by assuming that space and time were not two independent functions, but were abstracted from a single functional system that gave us the ability to move and perceive movement in both time and space. He came to believe that the evidence of the different senses and different kinds of perceptual mechanisms must be understood as different testimonies to one and the same universe, and he said:

> Kant's postulate of the absolute unknowability of the *Ding an sich* has not prevented anybody from reflecting on the relationship between the phenomenal and the real world. Indeed, I even have a heretical suspicion that Kant himself, less logical but far wiser in this respect than the Neo-Kantians, was

in his heart of hearts not so completely convinced that the two worlds were unconnected. How otherwise could the heavens—which, by the terms of his postulate, only belonged to the world of appearances, which is indifferent to value—have repeatedly aroused the same sense of wonder in him as the moral law?[14]

Lorenz's question is justified, though Kant answers it, from his own point of view, in the *Critique of Judgment.*

Like ethology, sociology shows the influence of Kant. The casual perusal of an account of great sociologists shows that he had at least some influence on Comte, Durkheim, Simmel, Weber, Veblen, and Mannheim.[15] I will concentrate on the case of Durkheim, who may be reckoned, along with Weber, as one of the two principal fathers of modern sociological theory.

Durkheim held that Kant's moral theory could not explain sacrificial love or disinterested benevolence, but he acknowledged that he saw morality with rather Kantian eyes. Like Kant, he insisted that moral duties were not based on their usefulness or pleasure, and, like Kant, he believed in the dignity and autonomy of the individual. But while Kant made morality intelligible by postulating a God, Durkeim postulated, not a God, but a particular society made up of particular individuals sharing their society's collective conscience.[16]

Preoccupied with the nature and importance of the a priori, Durkheim made a similar transposition of Kant's doctrine of the categories, replacing the mind of the individual or mind as such with the mind of a particular society. Our judgments, he said in rough agreement with Kant, are based on categories of the understanding, such as time, space, genus, number, cause, substance, personality, and so on. These categories correspond, he held, to the most universal properties of things. We cannot, for example, think of objects outside of time and space, which constitute abstract, impersonal frames of experience for each individual and for all humanity. But while the empiricists are wrong, Durkheim said, because the categories are universal and necessary, the rationalists are wrong, because they cannot explain how the mind can add to experience or how the categories can be different from time to time or place to place. The true explanation is that the categories originate in society, for reason, like morality, cannot be reduced to individual experience. We think and reflect our thought in the vocabulary of a particular mother tongue. The world exists only to the extent it is thought, and it is totally thought only by society, of whose internal life it becomes an element. Speaking, he supposed, literally, Durkheim said that the world is in society.[17]

If we turn from sociology to psychology, the evidence of Kantian influence remains strong. In Germany, Kant served to maintain the dualism that empiricistic attitudes weakened in France, England, Russia, and the United States. He also stimulated apriorism or nativism, and so led to Mach's 'space form' and 'time form,' to Ehrenfels' 'form quality,' and, through these, to Gestalt psychology.[18]

Among contemporary psychologists, Jean Piaget is the most notable of those I know who acknowledges a debt to Kant. He says that he feels very close to the spirit of Kantianism, though he prefers to dissociate the *a priori* from any notion of priority, whether of time or level. 'More precisely,' he says,

> the construction characteristic of the epistemological subject, however rich it is in the Kantian perspective, is still too poor, since it is completely given at the start. On the other hand, a dialectical construction, as seen in the history of science and in the experimental facts brought to light by studies on mental development, seems to show the living reality. It enables us to attribute to the epistemological subject a much richer constructivity, although ending with the same characteristics of rational necessity and the structuring of experience, as those which Kant called for to guarantee his concept of the *a priori*.[19]

I will end my remarks on Kant's influence with some words on Freud and Jung—others who might have been considered include the psychiatrist, Ludwig Binswanger, and the neurologist, Kurt Goldstein, whose studies of aphasia are still influential.[20] In spite of his express distaste for philosophy, Freud does have some interest in Kant's general principles. This is evident in an article in which he writes that when he assumed the existence of unconscious mental activities, he was, it seemed, extending the corrections that Kant made in the understanding of external perception. In Freud's words:

> Just as Kant warned us not to overlook the fact that our perception is subjectively conditioned and must not be regarded as identical with the phenomena perceived but never really discerned, so psychoanalysis bids us not to set conscious perception in place of the unconscious mental process which is its object. The mental, like the physical, is not necessarily in reality just what it appears to be. It is, however, satisfactory to find that the correction of inner perception does not present difficulties so great as that of outer perception—that the inner object is less hard to discern truly than is the outside world.[21]

I will not ask the complicated question how Kant might respond to this comparison, but content myself with pointing out the obvious, that Freud is comparing the unconscious, cut off from consciousness by repression, with the Kantian unknown source, cut off from consciousness by the organization itself that constitutes the conscious mind. By the terms of the same analogy, the contents of the Freudian conscious are equivalent to Kant's phenomena. Freud's preconscious, furthermore, which binds unconscious contents to 'word-presentation' and so mediates between unconscious and conscious, is somewhat analogous to Kant's schematism, which mediates between intuitions and categories, which are in themselves pure forms.

In my biographical account of Kant, I observed that his idea of the unknowable source might have been inspired or supported by the emotional life he so severely repressed. Now I can give Kant his own back by observing that Freud's idea of the unconscious might have been supported by his encounter with Kant's of the unknowable source.

Freud's doctrine becomes structurally closer to Kant's when, later in life, he divides the psychic apparatus into id, ego, and superego. It is perhaps worth interpolating that Freud's 'ego' is, in German, simply 'das Ich,' 'the I,' the same term that Kant uses, but that is usually translated into English as 'the self.' Freud considers the ego to be largely unconscious, but consciousness, he says, is its nucleus. Freud's idea of the ego is like Kant's in that the ego, as both see it, orders and unifies experience. The ego, Freud says, controls movement and perception, tests reality, thinks rationally, and, among other unifying acts, gives mental processes their temporal order.[22] It is such a conception, I take it, that leads Freud to write:

> There is an area whose frontiers belong both to the outer world and to the ego: our perceptual superficies. So it might be that the idea of time is connected with the work of the system W.-Bw. [perceptual consciousness]. Kant would then be in the right if we replaced his old-fashioned 'a priori' by our modern introspection of the psychical apparatus. It should be the same with space, causality, etc.[23]

The structural analogy between Freudian and Kantian doctrine is completed, well or not, by that between the Freudian superego (and ego ideal) and the Kantian conscience (and ideal of pure reason).

I am not well enough acquainted with Freud's life to know what influence Kant might, in fact, have had on him. The influence of Kant on Jung, however, is acknowledged with enthusiasm. Jung tells us that in his later adolescence he became highly impressed with Schopenhauer, but then puzzled by the inadequacies of his metaphysics; but that the reading of Kant, especially of the *Critique of Pure Reason,* taught him that Schopenhauer had 'committed the deadly sin of hypostatizing a metaphysical assertion.' Jung says that the illumination cast by Kant's philosophy profoundly altered his attitude to the world and to life. 'Whereas formerly I had been shy, timid, mistrustful, pallid, thin, and apparently unstable in health, I now began to display a tremendous appetite on all fronts. I knew what I wanted and went after it. I also became noticeably more accessible and more communicative.' [24]

I must admit that this liberation through Kant is surprising to me, and I do not understand what it means psychologically. Jung notes that there was a period when, as a young man, his scientific materialism was held in check only by what he knew of history and by the *Critique of Pure Reason*. [25] Later, during his second semester at his university, his tendency to believe in spiritualistic phenomena was given philosophical backing, 'just at the right time,' by Kant's *Dreams of a Spirit Seer*, which rejected unverified or merely superstitious accounts of such phenomena, but held, nevertheless, that there was something generically true in them. [26]

Jung compares his archetypes to Plato's Ideas, Schopenhauer's 'ideas,' and Kant's categories. He says that

> what Kant demonstrated in respect of logical thinking is true of the whole range of the psyche. The psyche is no more a *tabula rasa* to begin with than is the mind proper (the thinking area) . . . Just as concrete thinking is dominated by sensuously conditioned representations, abstract thinking is dominated by 'irrepresentable' primordial images lacking specific content . . . They are irrepresentable because they lack content, being nothing but activated functional possibilities, and accordingly they seek something to fill them out. They draw the stuff of experience into their empty forms, representing themselves *in* facts rather than representing facts. They clothe themselves with facts, as it were. [27]

The Kantianism of these last words is especially clear. However, beyond the influence of particular conceptions, such as that of the categories, there is a profound temperamental likeness between Kant and Jung, which belies the striking difference between the two. I am referring to the subtle balance in both of them between metaphysical restraint and belief. With Kantian restraint, Jung declares:

> The psyche cannot leap beyond itself . . . Whenever the psyche does announce absolute truths—as, for example, 'God is motion,' or 'God is One'—it necessarily falls into one or the other of its own antitheses . . . So far as perception and cognition are concerned, we cannot see beyond the psyche . . . We are helplessly cooped up in an exclusively psychic world.

Having said this, Jung declares, with Kantian faith:

> Nevertheless, we have good reason to suppose that behind this there exists the uncomprehended absolute object which affects and influences it . . . . Prohibited though it may be from an objective point of view to make statements out of the blue—that is, without sufficient reason—there are

nevertheless some statements which apparently have to be made without objective reasons.[28]

Philosophicality?

To the two questions I have asked and tried to answer, on trivialization and on fruitfulness, I want to add a third, which interests me very much, although I know that I can say nothing conclusive about it. The question is: If philosophy is what I have been describing it to be, is this description (my book) itself philosophy? I have no hesitation in answering, 'Of course,' but I must qualify what I myself think with what I know of the attitude of others. Let me explain my answer, then, for the last time, and the reasons for their possible disagreement with it.

I have been attempting something that is, to my mind, philosophically difficult but more modest than it may at times have appeared. Although, as I have said, my sympathies lie more or less with the Pragmatists, I have not had the ambition of persuading other kinds of philosophers that they are in principle wrong. I have only made more systematic use of the common observation that all of us, philosophers included, make mistakes, change our minds, show personal and peculiar traits, and grow out of step with the times, not to say, old. That is, I have tried to draw such human characteristics, which are often taken to be peripheral or accidental to philosophy, into the space of philosophy itself and to see them as an interesting, even essential ingredient of its being. Instead of encouraging the bent of so many philosophers to do nothing but create and analyze abstractions, I have insisted that it is important for them to pay attention to their immediate environments and their own personal, apparently trivial characteristics.

There is more than one reason why my attempt may be unpersuasive and even uninteresting to philosophers. It is true that I have used abstract, philosophical arguments and clarifications, but, because it was not to my purpose, I have not made them intensive. Instead, in distinction from most contemporary philosophers, I have tried to establish an empirical case. A case of this kind might be made, in a professional sense, within the bounds of intellectual history or the history of ideas, or within the bounds of social anthropology, sociology, or social or clinical psychology. But I have in fact observed none of these professional bounds and have therefore reasoned in a way, as I foresaw, that does not fit any clear professional definition. This has not been intellectual history, history of ideas, anthropology, sociology, psychology, nor, in the most usual contemporary sense, philosophy. As I have been saying all along, my justification has been that, useful as professional bounds may be, they can also get in our way and finally obscure our vision. They too often tempt us to see things partially, in terms of our professional interests, and not to strive for an adequate total vision.

In our own times, when a philosopher deals with a problem, he usually begins with the abstract arguments of his immediate philosophical predecessors. These he analyses and attempts to modify, extend, cast doubt on, or destroy. When he thinks professionally of science, it may be to use some known conclusion or procedure for his own argument, or to criticize scientific reasoning for its lack of sufficient clarity. He often tends to think of men in other intellectual professions as working, in an intellectual sense, rather blindly. He would like to clear up their confusions and sharpen their logic. He wants a world as free as possible of intellectual ambiguities.

I hope that I have not simply multiplied ambiguities, yet, in introducing so much empirical material and in using, however informally, the ideas of sociologists and psychologists, I have been introducing a non-philosophical indeterminacy into philosophy, as if philosophy could not free itself of its non-philosophical matrix, as if it were a chick with bits of its shell still clinging to it. The philosopher I am imagining wants to get on with his argument, while I have been providing him, not with a single, paradigmatic example to make clear the kind of thing I mean to say, but with many examples suggesting what may be called, if the words are not philosophically offensive, an inductive case. Many of these examples, most notably the biographical accounts of philosophers, are complex and ambiguous and do not easily yield the sharp-etched arguments that give the philosopher his professional substance and often, I feel sure, his personal pleasure. Even, therefore, if what I have been doing has been philosophical in its general intent and temper, it is easy to maintain that it has not been philosophy, but something more garrulous and indefinite, to which the philosopher as such cannot or ought not to respond because it distracts him from his basic purpose and the deployment of his professional skills.

At this point I would like to stress that I, too, agree that there is no reason why someone interested in a philosophical argument or position must also be interested in its author. If he is interested in its author in the sense of wanting to know how the author might defend or develop his position, there is no reason why he must be interested in that author's personal characteristics. This is the more obviously true if the problem is a clearly-defined technical one, such as the solution of a logical paradox. Yet a quite general lack of interest in the subjectivity of philosophers is also a lack of interest in their motives and in their natures as a whole. Such a lack may be penalized much more heavily in philosophy, I contend, than in mathematics, physics, or biochemistry.

My meaning can be put in terms of the philosopher's interest in his

professional language, his code. Much philosophical language is technical
and open only to initiates; but it conveys more than they may see. There
are two basic reasons, it seems to me, for its deceptive quality:

1.   The philosophical code is contained within an encompassing set of
codes by which we live from birth on, and to which we are so used that
we do not ordinarily perceive them. It requires a great conscious effort or
an immersion in a quite different cultural context to make apparent the
nature of the codes by which we have lived and thought. In this rather
Durkheimian sense, philosophical codes may be far better instruments to
express a particular manner of life and thought than to analyze it
critically.

2.   The codes and the messages they carry are designed, consciously
or not, to translate one set of concerns, which are emotional and personal, into another set, of social and intellectual ones. This translation
socializes people and is, luckily for us, largely irreversible; but it remains
effective only as long as it continues to communicate that which it is the
translation of. To be effective, it must convey a great deal that is not on
the intellectual surface.

It is the philosopher's code that allows philosophy to be professional
and relatively autonomous and that lends philosophy the appearance of
an exact science dealing objectively with objective problems. But
although, as I have been insisting, its objectivity is more apparent than
real, philosophy is not simply an epiphenomenon of curiosity, any more
than of emotions or social pressures. Although it grows from and expresses all of these, it also forms, utilizes, and changes them. When the
philosopher demonstrates that he has learned how to use his professional
code, he demonstrates a personal and social accomplishment that is its
own reward, and, if he is able or lucky enough, not that alone. His
cleverness, intelligence, or professional mastery arouse others to emulate
him, and, in this way, support a certain professional way of life. Professional philosophizing is less often a struggle with oneself than a struggle
for status in the philosophical community. Professional or not, however,
it leads at times to a creative intensification of insight as deep as any that a
person can suffer or enjoy.

?

Because the earlier sections of this chapter have been headed, respectively, 'Trivialization?' 'Fruitfulness?' and 'Philosophicality?' I have been
tempted to head this section, too, with a question, such as 'Conclusions?'
or 'Last Thoughts?' Neither of these titles seems right to me, and I have
settled for the question mark alone, to show how fallible I am, for I have
fallen willing victim to the temptations of symmetry, and to show that,

whatever I say or have said, I too know that there are no final answers for us. The question mark says that though many philosophers have tried to limit philosophy, their successes have not been conclusive enough to stifle the old philosophical impulse to understand everything without any conscious limit at all. The question mark therefore stands alone, unqualified. In my own fairly imperial and yet, I hope, not too immodest way, I have been expressing the old, natural, immodest philosophical impulse. Taken at its basic, immodest level, philosophy, I have argued, lies within a continuum of which art and exact science are the two opposite poles. Neither art, philosophy, nor science alone is adequate to understand or express human experience. Life would be more intellectually rewarding, I think, if artists and scientists were more effectively interested in philosophy, and philosophers more effectively in art and science.

In saying this I am obviously expressing my subjective preference. If my understanding of philosophy is just, I have little other choice. I therefore cannot end except by submitting myself to the judgment of my readers. Who are my readers, and what do they want? Are they more impressed by what they may consider to be my attack on philosophy and philosophers or by my attempt to arrive at a more comprehensive understanding, by my threats or my promises? If they are philosophers, they at least love to argue and, as I have argued, are reluctant to yield seriously to the arguments of others. But perhaps I, you (if you are not among them), and they can agree that Aristotle made a mistake when he wrote, I should hope in his youth, that since great progress had been made in a few years, philosophy would be brought to completion in a short time.[1] Perhaps we can agree that Aristotle was wiser, as he was, I presume, older, when he wrote, 'Not only he who is in luck but also he who offers a proof should remember that he is but a man.'[2]

Aristotle's wiser remark remains pertinent. If we were more doggedly serious than it may intend, we might add that it is not so easy to remember just what it is to be human, and just how being human limits us intellectually, for though we cannot jump over our own shadows, we have often been able to jump over our presumed limits. Proud and humble—I suppose that each of us should be both of these in some not too absurd or painful proportion, and that philosophy should help us to arrive at the proportion. But I see that I am preaching, and I know how hard it is to listen to someone else's preaching, or even to one's own, especially at the end, when everybody is preparing to go off again. I therefore end only by saying that I am sorry to be leaving this book, and sorry to be leaving you, its reader, and the dialogue I have imagined between us.

Acknowledgments

Professor Joseph Agassi read early drafts of this book, encouraged me, and gave me useful criticism, general and particular. Dr. Shlomo Biderman, whose training is in both philosophy and clinical psychology, read most of the chapters on individual philosophers and reacted with sympathetic insight, while Dr. Dan Daor (like Dr. Biderman, my colleague at Tel-Aviv University) read and commented on large sections of a still inchoate manuscript. My friend, Professor Rulon Wells, commented in helpful detail on my accounts of Leibniz, James, Russell, and Wittgenstein, while another friend, Professor Walter Kaufmann, did me the same service with respect to my accounts of Kant, Hegel, and Nietzsche, not to speak of parts of the concluding chapters. I have made use of Professor Kaufmann's exemplary translations of Hegel and, especially, of Nietzsche. Professor Wells allowed me to read his copy of Hayek's partial, unpublished biography of Wittgenstein; Professor W. W. Bartley III sent me unpublished material on Wittgenstein's father; and Mr. Avner Cohen, my former student, sent me a memoir by Wittgenstein's sister. Dr. A. Janik made illuminating comments on my pages on Wittgenstein, but this book was already set up at the time, so I could hardly take advantage of his knowledge. Aviva Even-Zohar and Pnina Rodan, the secretaries of the philosophy department of Tel-Aviv University, gave me help that was cheerful, willing, and obviously beyond any formal obligation they might have felt. I also got help from the Faculty of Liberal Arts, in the form of grants for reproduction of the manuscript.

To all those who have helped me in any way I give my heartfelt thanks.

Bibliographic Notes

NOTES TO CHAPTER ONE

Persuasion as Mutuality and Disagreement: pp. 1 – 3

1. L, Wittgenstein, *On Certainty* (Oxford: Blackwell, 1969), Section 612.

Creative Resistance to Persuasion

1. J. G. Crowther, *Scientific Types* (London: Barrie & Rockliff, 1968), p. 85.
2. P. Valéry, *Cahiers*, vol. 1 (Paris: Gallimard (Pléiade), 1973), p. 593, no. 1927.
3. G. W. Leibniz, *Philosophical Papers and Letters*, trans. L. E. Loemker, 2nd ed. (Dordrecht: Reidel, 1969), pp. 152 – 53.
4. To Reinhold, March 28, 1794, in I. Kant, *Briefwechsel*, ed. O. Schöndörffer (Hamburg: Felix Meiner, 1972), p. 662. See Kant, *Philosophical Correspondence*, trans. A. Zweig (Chicago: University of Chicago Press, 1967), pp. 211, 212.
5. J. H. W. Stuckenburg, *The Life of Immanuel Kant* (London: Macmillan, 1882), p. 127. Hamann to Jacobi, Dec. 3, 1786, in K. Vorländer, *Immanuel Kant, Der Mann und das Werk*, vol. 1 (Leipzig: Meiner, 1924), p. 331.
6. R. B. Jachmann, 'Immanuel Kant geschildert in Briefen an einen Freund,' 'Third Letter,' in L. E. Borowski, R. B. Jachmann & A. C. Wasianski, *Immanuel Kant: Sein Leben in Darstellungen von Zeitgenossen*, ed. F. Gross (Berlin: Deutsche Bibliothek, 1912), p. 138.
7. H. Spiegelberg, *The Phenomenological Movement*, 2nd ed., vol. 1 (The Hague: Martinus Nijhoff, 1965), p. 90.

Persuasion of Others as Self-Persuasion: pp. 3 – 5

1. Q. Bell, *Virginia Woolf: A Biography*, 2 vols. in 1, vol. 2 (New York: Harcourt Brace Jovanovich, 1972), pp. 28 – 29. See also G. Spater & I. Parsons, *A Marriage of True Minds* (London: Cape/Hogarth Press, 1977), pp. 67 – 68, 70.
2. W. Kaufmann, *Hegel: A Reinterpretation* (Garden City: Doubleday (Anchor Books), 1966), p. 233.
3. 'Preface,' *Phenomenology*, I.4, in *Hegel: Texts and Commentary*, trans. W. Kaufmann (Garden City: Doubleday (Anchor Books), 1966), p. 108.
4. H. Spiegelberg, *The Phenomenological Movement*, 2nd ed., vol. 1 (The Hague: Martinus Nijhoff, 1965), p. 96. R. Ingarden, in E. Husserl, *Briefe an*

Roman Ingarden (The Hague: Martinus Nijhoff, 1968), pp. 181 (footnote), 153. D. Cairns, *Conversations with Husserl and Fink* (The Hague: Martinus Nijhoff, 1976), p. 39. The conversation is dated 12/11/31.

5. L Wittgenstein, *The Blue and Brown Books*, 2nd ed. (Oxford: Blackwell, 1969), p. v.

6. R. Crayshaw-Williams, *Russell Remembered* (London: Oxford University Press, 1970), pp. 45 – 46.

7. Ibid., pp. 46, 47, 49.

Persuasive Presence: Philosophical Mentors and Saints: pp. 7 – 9

1. *Plotinus*, trans. A. H. Armstrong, vol. 1 (London: Heinemann, 1966), p. 9.

2. Ibid., pp. 25, 31.

3. Proclus, *A Commentary on the First Book of Euclid's Elements*, trans. G. R. Morrow (Princeton: Princeton University Press, 1970), p. xvii. See also Proclus, *Théologie platonicienne*, trans. H. D. Saffrey & L. G. Westerinck (Paris: Les Belles Lettres, 1968), pp. ix – xxvi; and E. Zeller, *Die Philosophie der Griechen*, vol. 3-2 (Leipzig: O. R. Reisland, 1923), pp. 843 – 47.

4. R. B. Jachmann, as trans. in W. Klimke, *Kant for Everyone* (London: Routledge & Kegan Paul, 1951), pp. 34, 35, 36, 38.

5. To Gersdorff, Aug 4, 1869, in F. Nietzsche, *Werke in Drei Bänden*, ed. K. Schlechta, vol. 3 (Munich: Hanser, 6th ed., 1969), pp. 1012 – 13. See also R. J. Hollingdale, *Nietzsche: The Man and His Philosophy* (London: Routledge & Kegan Paul, 1965), p. 70. On the debt to Wagner, see K. Jaspers, *Nietzsche* (Chicago: Henry Regnery, 1965), p. 67.

6. *Ecce Homo*, 'Warum ich so klug bin,' section 1.

7. Q. Bell, *Virginia Woolf: A Biography*, 2 vols. in 1, vol. 1 (New York: Harcourt Brace Jovanovich, 1972), p. 100.

8. H. Holroyd, *Lytton Strachey: A Biography* (Harmondsworth: Penguin Books, 1971), pp. 199, 102.

9. R. F. Harrod, *John Maynard Keynes* (Harmondsworth: Penguin Books, 1972), p. 88.

10. *The Autobiography of Bertrand Russell, 1872 — 1914* (London: Allen & Unwin, 1967), p. 64.

11. R. Schoenman, ed., *Bertrand Russell: Philosopher of the Century* (London: Allen & Unwin, 1967), p. 2.

12. N. Malcolm, *Ludwig Wittgenstein, a Memoir* (London: Oxford University Press, 1958), p. 23.

13. A. Ambrose, 'Ludwig Wittgenstein: A Portrait,' in A. Ambrose & M. Lazerowitz, eds., *Ludwig Wittgenstein: Philosophy and Language* (London: Allen–Unwin, 1972), pp. 13, 24 – 25.

Love's Persuasions: p. 10

1. T. Gould, *Platonic Love* (London: Routledge & Kegan Paul, 1963).

2. Diogenes Laertius, *Lives of the Eminent Philosophers*, trans. R. D. Hicks, 2 vols. (London: Heinemann, 1925), vol. 1, p. 399, vol. 2, pp. 99 – 100.

3. H. Weyl, 'Insight and Reflection,' in T. L. Saaty & F. J. Weyl, eds., *The Spirit and Use of the Mathematical Sciences* (New York: McGraw-Hill, 1969), pp. 282, 283, 287, 298 – 99 (including highly emotional encounters with Kant, Positivism, Husserl, Fichte, and Meister Eckhart).

Axiomatic Experiences: pp. 10 – 13

1. For an English translation of the text of the dreams, or, rather, of a paraphrase of them, see N. K. Smith, *New Studies in the Philosophy of Descartes* (New York: St Martin's Press, 1952).
2. *Treatise on the Correction of the Understanding*, in *Spinoza's Ethics and On the Correction of the Understanding*, trans. A. Boyle (London: Dent (Everyman's Library), rev. ed., 1959), pp. 228, 229.
3. J.-J. Rousseau, *Oeuvres complètes*, ed. B. Gagnebin & M. Raymond, vol. 1 (Paris: Gallimard (Pléiade), 1959), p. 1135. I have used, but completed, the translation in R. D. Masters, *The Political Philosophy of Rousseau* (Princeton: Princeton University Press, 1968), pp. xii – xiii.
4. H. Heimsoeth, *Fichte* (Munich: Ernst Reinhardt, 1923), pp. 27 – 32; H. Saner, *Kant's Political Thought* (Chicago: University of Chicago Press, 1973), pp. 124 – 25.
5. F. Nietzsche, *Werke in drei Bänden*, ed. K. Schlechta, vol. 3 (Munich: Hanser, 6th ed., 1969), p. 133. Also in R. J. Hollingdale, *Nietzsche* (London: Routledge & Kegan Paul, 1973), p. 51.
6. G. A. Wilson, *William James* (New York: Viking Press, 1967), pp. 167 – 69.
7. J. T. Blackmore, *Ernst Mach, His Work, Life, and Influence* (Berkeley: University of California Press, 1972), p. 11. On Mach as the precursor of the Vienna Circle, see R. von Mises, 'Mach and the Empiricist Conception of Science,' and on his 'mysticism' in relation to his theory of elements, see R. S. Cohen, 'Physics, Perception and Philosophy of Science,' both in R. S. Cohen & R. J. Seeger, eds., *Ernst Mach, Physicist and Philosopher* (Dordrecht: Reidel, 1970).
8. *The Autobiography of Bertrand Russell, 1972 — 1912* (London: Allen & Unwin, 1967), p. 146.

Euclidean Emotions: pp. 14 – 16

1. *Aubrey's Brief Lives*, ed. O. L. Dick (Harmondsworth: Penguin Books, 1972), p. 309.
2. 'La vie de Monsieur Pascal, écrite par Madame Périer, sa soeur,' in Pascal, *Oeuvres complétes*, ed. L. Lafuma (Paris: Seuil, 1963), pp. 18 – 19.
3. 'Autobiographical Notes,' in *Albert Einstein, Philosopher-Scientist*, ed. P. A. Schilpp (Evanston: Library of Living Philosophers, 1949, 1951), p. 9.
4. *The Autobiography of Bertrand Russell, 1872 — 1914* (London: Allen & Unwin, 1967), p. 36.

Persuasion for Mutuality: p. 16

1. *Treatise on the Correction of the Understanding*, in *Spinoza's Ethics and On the Correction of the Understanding*, trans. A. Boyle (London: Dent (Everyman's Library) rev. ed., 1959), section 14, pp. 230 – 31.

NOTES TO CHAPTER TWO

Truth Plain, Plural, Pragmatic: pp. 17 – 21

1. J. Buchler, ed., *The Philosophy of Charles Peirce: Selected Writings* (New York: Harcourt Brace, 1948), p. 4. The term 'fallibilism' is also used by Popper. For a comparison of him with Peirce, see E. Freeman & H. Skolimowski, 'The Search for Objectivity in Peirce and Popper,' in P. A. Schilipp, ed., *The Philosophy of Karl Popper* (La Salle, Ill.: Open Court, 1974), pp. 508 – 15.
2. W. James, *Pragmatism* (New York: Longmans, Green & Co., 1907), p. 222 – 23.
3. See *The Meaning of Truth*, ed. F. Bowers (Cambridge, Mass.: Harvard University Press, 1975), pp. 8, 88, 106, 117, together with H. S. Thayer's helpful introduction.
4. J. Bogen, *Wittgenstein's Philosophy of Language* (London: Routledge & Kegan Paul, 1972), p. 137, from Wittgenstein's unpublished notebooks of 1929. Bogen suggests *Philosophical Investigations* Section 90 as a parallel. Wittgenstein's friend, the mathematician, F. P. Ramsey, was influenced by Peirce. In any case, Wittgenstein often referred to James in his lectures. See H. S. Thayer, *Meaning and Action: A Critical History of Pragmatism* (New York: Bobbs-Merrill, 1968), pp. 309 – 13.

Truth and Pragmatism in Mathematics: pp. 21–22

1. A. A. Frankel, Y. Bar-Hillel, A. Levy, with the collaboration of D. van Dalen, *Foundations of Set Theory*, 2nd rev. ed. (Amsterdam: North-Holland Publishing Co., 1973), p. 279.
2. Ibid., pp. 344 – 45
3. L. Kalmár, 'Foundations of Mathematics – Whither Now?,' in I. Lakatos, ed., *Problems in the Philosophy of Mathematics* (Amsterdam: North-Holland Publishing Co., 1967), p. 193.   4. H. Wang, *From Mathematics to Philosophy* (London: Routledge & Kegan Paul, 1974), p. 202.

The Truth Is Certain but Vague: pp. 22 – 24

1. For the development of a similar position on the nature of truth, see A. Ness, *The Pluralist and Possibilist Aspect of the Scientific Enterprise* (Oslo: Universitesforlaget, 1972), esp. pp. 127 – 31. See also, N. Rescher, 'Philosophical Disagreement,' *The Review of Metaphysics* 32 (1978), pp. 217 – 51.

The Ideal of Comprehensive Understanding: pp. 28–29

1. For discussion of the social nature of 'facts,' see J. R. Ravetz, *Scientific Knowledge and Its Social Problems* (London: Oxford University Press, 1971), chap. 6.

Conditions of Relevance: Time, Place, and Function: pp. 33 – 34

1. For Hellenistic education, see H. I. Marrou, *A History of Education in Antiquity* (London: Sheed & Ward, 1956), 'The Second Sophistic movement,' from G. W. Bowersock, *Greek Sophists in the Roman Empire* (London: Oxford University Press, 1969), p. 69.

2. G. Leff, *Paris and Oxford in the Thirteenth and Fourteenth Centuries* (New York: Wiley, 1963), pp. 3ff. For equipment and method, see J. le Goff, *Les intellectuels au moyen âge* (Paris: Seuil, 1957), pp. 93ff.

3. E. Reike, *Der Gelehrte in der deutschen Vergangenheit* (Leipzig, 1900). A. Busch, *Die Geschichte des Privatdozenten* (Stuttgart: Ferdinand Enke Verlag, 1959).

4. H. Schelsky, *Einsamkeit, Freiheit, Idee und Gestalt der deutschen Universität und ihre Reforme* (Munich: Rowohlt, 1963), pp. 27 – 31. H.-J. de Vleeschauwer, *The Development of Kantian Thought* (London/Edinburgh: Nelson, 1962). J. Schmucker, *Die Ursprünge der Ethik Kants* (Meisenheim am Glan: Verlag Anton Heim, 1961), p. 278. F. Delekat, *Immanel Kant: Historische-kritische Interpretation der Hauptschriften* (Heidelberg: Quelle & Meyer, 1963) tries to restore the eighteenth-century context and makes use of the marginal notes Kant wrote on the textbooks he lectured on. The marginal comments are reprinted in the Akademie edition of Kant's works. G. Lehmann, 'Kants Entwicklung im Spiegel der Vorlesungen,' in M. Gueroult et al., *Studien zu Kant's Entwicklung* (Hildesheim: Olms, 1967), p. 148.

Conditions of Relevance: Professional Rivalry: pp. 34 – 35

1. The reference is to book 4 of Locke's *Essays Concerning Human Understanding*.

2. H. Herivel, *The Background to Newton's* Principia: *A Study of Newton's Dynamical Researches in the Years 1664 — 84* (London: Oxford University Press, 1965), p. 42.

Conditions of Relevance: Leadership and Discipleship: pp. 35 – 40

1. See S. Feuer, *Einstein and the Generations of Science* (New York: Basic Books, 1974).

2. For Descartes, see the bibliography of the later section devoted to Descartes (pp. 417 – 19). C. L. Thijssen-Schoute, Le Cartésianisme au Pays-Bas,' in E. J. Dijksterhuis et al., *Descartes et le cartésianisme hollandais* (Amsterdam: Editions françaises d'Amsterdam, 1950). For a summary of

monographic studies of Regius, see P. Dibon, 'Notes bibliographies sur les Cartésiens hollandais,' in Dijksterhuis, op. cit., pp. 280 – 88.

3. To Mersenne, Nov. 11, 1740: *Descartes: Philosophical Letters*, trans. A. Kenny (London: Oxford University Press, 1970) p. 81.

4. Regius to Descartes, Feb. 9/19, 1644. See later bibliography on Descartes. (pp. 417 – 19.)

5. Regius to Descartes, June 4, 1644.

6. To Mersenne, Nov. 23, 1646: C. Adam, *Vie et oeuvres de Descartes* (Paris: Vrin, 1957), p. 493, note.

7. Regius to Descartes, July 23, 1645.

8. To Mersenne, Oct. 5, 1646. To Elisabeth, March, 1647. Thijssen-Schoute, op. cit.

9. Conrad Stang to Kant, Oct. 2, 1796: Kant, *Philosophical Correspondence 1759 — 99*, trans. A. Zweig (Chicago: Chicago University Press, 1967), pp. 224 – 25.

10. H. Saner, *Kant's Political Thought* (Chicago: Chicago University Press, 1973), pp. 133ff., 118ff., 137, 153ff.

11. To Kiesewetter, Oct. 19, 1798.

12. Saner, op. cit., p. 112.

13. 'Open Letter on Fichte's *Wissenschaftslehre*,' Aug. 7, 1799: Kant, *Philosophical Correspondence 1759 — 99*, op. cit., pp. 253 – 54. For Kant's polemics see Saner, op. cit., chaps. 6, 7. For the example of a single controversy, see H. E. Allison, *The Kant-Eberhard Controversy* (Baltimore: Johns Hopkins University Press, 1973). For further quotations from Kant, claiming that he and he alone was right, see Saner, pp. 203 – 204.

14. K. Rosenkranz, *G. W. F. Hegels Leben* (Darmstadt: Wissenschaftliche Buchgesellschaft, 1971; photo-reprint of ed. of 1844), pp. 383 – 83. I have been helped by the translation in W. Kaufmann, *Hegel: A Reinterpretation* (Garden City: Doubleday (Anchor Books), 1966), p. 232. For a view of Hegel's early disciples and some of their more rhapsodic reactions, see F. Heer, 'Hegel und die Jugend,' in G.-K. Kaltenbrunner, ed, *Hegel und die Folgen* (Freiburg: Verlag Rombach, 1970). For the movement, see S. D. Crites, 'Hegelianism,' in P. Edwards, ed., *The Encyclopedia of Philosphy*.

15. H. Spiegelberg, *The Phenomenological Movement*, 2nd ed., 2 vols. (The Hague: Martinus Nijhoff, 1965), vol. 1, pp. 88 – 89.

16. Spiegelberg, op. cit., vol. 2, p. 740, note to p. 125.

17. The quotation on Fink is from D. Cairns, *Conversations with Husserl and Fink* (The Hague: Martinus Nijhoff, 1976), p. 32. Spiegelberg, op. cit., vol. 2, pp. 598 – 99. On Landgrebe's philosophy, see W. Cerf, 'A Metaphysical Phenomenology,' in *Review of Metaphysics* (Sept., 1951). For Fink's position, see his article in Thevanez et al., *Problèmes actuels de la Phénoménologie* (Paris: Desclée Brouwer, 1952).

18. C. L. Thijssen-Schoute, op. cit., p. 219.

19. R. Colie, 'Spinoza and the Early English Deists,' in *Journal of the History of Ideas* (Jan. 1959), pp. 23 – 46; and Colie, *Light and Enlightenment* (Cambridge: Cambridge University Press, 1957). P. Vernière, *Spinoza et la pensée française avant la Révolution*, 2 vols. (Paris: Presses Universitaires, 1954).

20. G. Friedmann, *Leibniz et Spinoza*, 3rd ed. (Idées) (Paris: Gallimard, 1974).

21. Saner, op. cit., p. 113.

22. A. Adam, *Grandeur and Illusion: French Literature and Society 1600 — 1715* (Harmondsworth: Penguin Books, 1974), pp. 127 – 34.

23. G. E. Moore, *Philosophical Papers* (London: Allen & Unwin, 1959), pp. 322, 323.

Subcultural Unity: pp. 40 – 42

1. See the brief but just description by Gilbert Ryle in his introduction to A. J. Ayer *et al.*, *The Revolution in Philosophy* (London: Macmillan, 1956).

2. F. Diesing, *Patterns of Discovery in the Social Sciences*, (London: Routledge & Kegan Paul, 1971), pp. 17 – 18.

Attempts have, of course, been made to understand philosophy by means of the sociology of knowledge. The work of Max Weber on religion is highly suggestive. M. Scheler, ed., *Versuche zu einer Soziologie des Wissens* (Munich/Leipzig: Duncker & Humboldt, 1924) contains, among others, essays on the sociology of knowledge of the Aristotelian school, on the sociology of scholasticism, on the sociology of Realistic and Nominalistic thought, and on the sociology of mysticism. See M. Jay, *The Dialectical Imagination: A History of the Frankfurt School and the Institute of Social Research 1923 — 50* (London: Heinemann, 1973).

NOTES TO CHAPTER THREE

Psychologism: pp. 45 – 48

1. See 'Psychologism,' 'Fries,' and 'Beneke,' in P. Edwards, ed., *The Encyclopedia of Philosophy*. On Fries and Beneke, see also T. K. Oesterreich, *Die deutsche Philosophie des XIX Jahrhunderts und der Gegenwart* (Berlin, 1923, reprinted Basel: Benno Schwabe, 1951).

2. W. Kneale & M. Kneale, *The Development of Logic* (London: Oxford University Press, 1962), p. 377. A. Ryan, *J. S. Mill* (London: Routledge & Kegan Paul, 1974), p. 67.

3. J. S. Mill, *A System of Logic*, 10th ed., vol. 1 (London: Longmans, Green & Co., 1897), pp. 266, 267.

4. Ibid., p. 321

5. J. S. Mill, *An Examination of Sir William Hamilton's Philosophy* (London, 1865), p. 461, as quoted in E. Husserl, *Logical Investigations*, vol. 1 (London: Routledge & Kegan Paul, 1970), pp. 90 – 91.

6. 'Psychologisme,' in A. Lalande, *Vocabulaire technique et critique de la philosophie*, 7th ed. (Paris: Presses Universitaires, 1956), pp. 856 – 57.

7. G. Frege, *The Foundations of Arithmetic*, 2nd rev. ed. (Oxford: Blackwell, 1959), p. vi.

8. E. Husserl, *The Crisis of European Sciences and Transcendental Phenomenology* (Evanston: Northwestern University Press, 1970), pp. 260, 263. H. Spiegelberg, *Phenomenology in Psychology and Psychiatry: A Historical Introduction* (Evanston:

Northwestern University Press, 1972), pp. 7 – 9. There is a detailed account of Husserl's attitude toward psychology and psychologism in H. Drüe, *Edmund Husserls System der Phänomenologische Psychologie* (Berlin: De Gruyter, 1963), pp. 30 – 33, 64 – 114.

9. Husserl, *Logical Investigations*, op. cit., pp. 194 – 95.

10. B. Russell, 'The Axiom of Infinity' (*Hibbert Journal*, July, 1904), in D. Lackey, ed., B. Russell, *Essays in Analysis* (London: Allen & Unwin, 1973), p. 259. *Human Knowledge* (New York: Simon & Schuster, 1948), p. 53. On Russell's changing views of mathematics see *My Philosophical Development* (London: Allen & Unwin, 1959), chap. 17.

11. J. Piaget, *Biology and Knowledge* (Edinburgh: Edinburgh University Press, 1971), p. 345. For Piaget's intellectual autobiography and attitudes toward philosophy see his *Insights and Illusions of Philosophy* (London: Routledge & Kegan Paul, 1972). There are critical essays on Piaget's possible contribution to epistemology in T. Mischel, *Cognitive Development and Epistemology* (New York: Academic Press, 1971).

Mathematical and Similar Subjective Ideas: pp. 48 – 52

1. G. H. Hardy, *A Mathematician's Apology* (Cambridge: Cambridge University Press, 1940), pp. 123 – 24.

2. M. Kline, *Mathematical Thought from Ancient to Modern Times* (New York: Oxford University Press, 1972), p. 1197.

3. *The Autobiography of Bertrand Russell, 1944 — 1967* (London: Allen & Unwin, 1969), p. 222.

4. L. E. J. Brouwer, *Consciousness, Philosophy and Mathematics*, in A. Hill, ed., *Data: Directions in Art, Theory and Aesthetics* (London: Faber & Faber, 1968), p. 12. The more mathematical part of the essay is reprinted in P. Benacerraf & H. Putnam, *Philosophy of Mathematics* (Oxford: Blackwell, 1964). The essay as a whole now appears, along with other relevant ones, in L. E. J. Brouwer, *Collected Works*, vol. 1, *Philosophy and Foundations of Mathematics* (Amsterdam: North-Holland Publishing Co., 1975). See 'Brouwer,' in P. Edwards, ed., *The Encyclopedia of Philosophy*. On intuitionism in general and Brouwer in particular, see Fraenkel, Bar-Hillel & Levy, *Foundations of Set Theory* (Amsterdam: North-Holland Publishing Co., 1973), chap. 4.

5. *Consciousness, Philosophy and Mathematics*, p. 21.

6. Fraenkel, Bar-Hillel & Levy, op. cit., p. 251.

7. Benacerraf & Putnam, op. cit., p. 77.

8. E. W. Beth, *The Foundations of Mathematics* (Amsterdam: North-Holland, 1959), p. 77.

9. H. B. Curry, *Foundations of Mathematical Logic* (New York, 1963), pp. 13 – 14.

10. M. Kline, op. cit., p. 1210.

11. S. M. Ulam, *Adventures of a Mathematician* (New York: Scribners, 1976), p. 90.

12 M. Jammer, *The Conceptual Development of Quantum Mechanics* (New York: McGraw-Hill, 1961), pp. 208 – 209.

13. B. Kouznetzov, *Einstein, sa vie, sa pensée, ses théories* (Verviers, Belgium: Marabout Université (Gerard & Co.), 1967), p. 263.

Psychology, Alas!: pp. 53 – 56

1.   J. Hirsch, 'Behaviour Genetics and Individuality Understood,' *Science* 142 (13 Dec. 1963), reprinted in T. E. McGill, ed., *Readings in Animal Behavior* (New York: Rinehart & Winston, 1965), p. 108.
2.   J. Hirsch, 'Behavior-Genetic Analysis,' in J. Hirsch, ed., *Behavior-Genetic Analysis* (New York: McGraw-Hill, 1967).
3.   The general impression left by the debate in S. Hook, ed., *Psychoanalysis, Scientific Method, and Philosophy* (New York: New York University Press, 1959) is of the sharp attacks of the philosophers and generally weak defences of the psychoanalysts. R. Wollheim, ed., *Freud: A Collection of Critical Essays* (Garden City: Doubleday (Anchor Books), 1974) is more friendly to Freud and more genuinely exploratory though to what effect is not always clear. C. Hanly & M. Lazerowitz, *Psychoanalysis and Philosophy* (New York: International Universities Press, 1970) is dedicated to the memory of Ernest Jones and contains only articles inspired by or friendly to psychoanalysis.

The battle pro and con is often fought over the issue of the therapeutic effectiveness of psychoanalysis. The best general review of which I know is A. E. Bergin, 'Evaluation of Therapeutic Outcomes,' in A. E. Bergin & S. L. Garfield, *Handbook of Psychotherapy and Behavior Change* (New York: John Wiley, 1971). Bergin's verdict is that we hardly know enough to evaluate, either positively or negatively. The attack on the 'traditional forms of therapy,' he says, has been too imprecise and subjective to carry conviction. He believes (p. 263) that psychotherapy 'has had an average effect that is modestly positive.'

Bergin, who attacks H. J. Eysenck's attack on the efficacy of psychoanalysis, is himself (politely) attacked by S. Rachman, in *The Effects of Psychotherapy* (Oxford: Pergamon Press, 1971). It is certain that Rachman's attack has been attacked, and that the matter will not end there, if ever. R. B. Sloane et al., *Psychotherapy Versus Behavior Therapy* (Cambridge, Mass: Harvard University Press, 1975) is a particularly careful study and finds, among the rest, that both rival therapies are effective (p. 225).

The more general attack on psychoanalysis contends that it is not amenable, in whole or part, to scientific testing. But it has inspired many studies in psychology and the other behavioural sciences. The editors of a standard and relatively objective anthology of personality theories say that 'no other theory, apart from behaviorism, has stirred up so many first-rate investigations; no other current theory apart from behaviorism has generated so many hypotheses that have been confirmed.' See G. Lindzey, C. S. Hall, M. Manosevitz, eds., *Theories of Personality: Primary Sources and Research*, 2nd ed. (New York: Wiley, 1973), p. 1.

P. Kline, *Fact and Fantasy in Freudian Theory* (London: Methuen, 1972) is an extensive survey of experiments bearing on Freudian psychology. Kline concludes (pp. 350 – 59) that Freudian *meta*psychology is unscientific, i.e., not subject to empirical test, that much of the theory, nevertheless, consists of testable empirical propositions, and that 'a huge task of research remains.' H. J. Eysenck & G. D. Wilson, eds., *The Experimental Study of Freudian Theories* (London: Methuen, 1973) is an anthology with much the aims of Kline's, but with negative conclusions. Repeating (p. 385) Eysenck's earlier attack on Kline's book, the authors say that if this is the best evidence that can be offered for Freudian theories, 'there is no evidence at all' for them. But although Eysenck and Wilson are invariably critical of experiments favourable to Freud, they make no criticisms, methodological or other, of the unfavourable studies they themselves reprint. S. Fisher & R. P. Greenberg, *The Scientific Reliability of Freud's Theories and Therapy* (New York: Basic Books, 1977) is an attempt 'to appreciate the real complexity' of Freud's 'formulations and to subject them to tests neither softer nor more severe than those customarily applied to evaluating psychological theories.' The authors say (pp. 393, 396), 'Rich findings have emerged, running the gamut from confirmation to contradiction, and at times revealing the totally unexpected . . . Scanning the spectrum of tests we have applied to Freud's theories, we are generally impressed with how often the results have borne out his expectations . . . We have discovered that it is feasible to reduce his ideas to testable hypotheses.' I am impressed by the fact that Eysenck has reviewed Fisher and Greenberg's book half-favourably.

M. Sherwood, *The Logic of Explanation in Psychoanalysis* (New York: Academic Press, 1969) is a conscientious study that opposes 'monolithic' judgments of the whole of psychoanalysis and ends in the statement (p. 259) that 'psychoanalytic explanations are in many essential respects scientific.'

R. Berger & F. Cioffi, eds., *Explanation in the Behavioural Sciences* (Cambridge: Cambridge University Press, 1970) is a collection of critical essays, including one, with comment and reply, on psychoanalysis, that examine explanation in the behavioural sciences and often contrast it with current Anglo–American philosophical explanation.

P. Diesing, *Patterns of Discovery in the Social Sciences* (London: Routledge & Kegan Paul, 1972) considers methods not only in their programmatic, ideal descriptions, but in their actual use. All the methods, Diesing contends, have their strengths and weaknesses. He thinks that the demands made on psychoanalysis to become scientific are misguided (p. 12); and to Hook's attack on psychoanalysis as devoid of scientific, testable meaning, he answers (p. 233), 'Now this is nonsense. Holist theories are not composed of universal empirical generalizations.'

Much as I would like to continue this bibliographical excursus, I must end it here.

The Relevance of Psychology: pp. 56 – 59

1. L. Wittgenstein, *Philosophical Investigations*, section 133.

Psychology: Ten Brief Answers: pp. 59 – 61

1. C. F. Wallraff, 'Sense-Datum Theory and Observational Fact: Some Contributions of Psychology to Epistemology,' *Journal of Philosophy* (1, 1858). C. W. K. Mundle, *Perception: Facts and Theories* (London: Oxford University Press, 1971) tries to bring epistemology into consonance with the current psychology of perception. J. Piaget, *Insights and Illusions of Philosophy* (London: Routledge & Kegan Paul, 1972) complains that the reasoning of philosophers is vitiated by their factual ignorance.

2. L. Hudson, *The Cult of the Fact*, (London: Cape, 1972), p. 38.

Non-Verbal Philosophizing: pp. 62 – 64

1. Schelling, 'Introduction' to *System of Transcendental Idealism* in A. Hofstadter & R. Kuhns, eds., *Philosophies of Beauty* (New York: Random House (Modern Library), 1964), pp. 373, 374.

2. A. Schopenhauer, *The World as Will and Representation*, trans, E. F. J. Payne, vol. 1 (Indian Hills, Col.: Falcon's Wing Press, 1958; reprinted New York: Dover, 1966), section 52, p. 264.

3. F. Nietzsche, 'Attempt at a Self-Criticism,' *The Birth of Tragedy*, in *Basic Writings of Nietzsche*, trans. W. Kaufmann (New York: Random House (Modern Library), 1968), p. 20. *The Will to Power*, trans. W. Kaufmann (London: Weidenfeld & Nicolson, 1968), aphorism 810, p. 428. In Colli & Montinari (see bibliography on Nietzsche, pp. 451 – 52), vol. 8/2, aphorism 10[60] (188), p. 159.

4. A. Einstein, *Ideas and Opinions* (New York: Crown, 1954), pp. 25 – 26.

5. L. Wittgenstein, *Zettel* (Oxford: Blackwell, 1967), section 453. *Vermischte Bemerkungen* (Frankfurt am Main/Oxford: Suhrkamp/Blackwell, 1977/1978), p. 149 (1949).

6. R. A. Hinde, ed., *Non-Verbal Communication* (Cambridge: Cambridge University Press, 1972). E. H. Hess, 'Attitude and Pupil Size,' *Scientific American* (April, 1965).

7. L. A. Coser, *Masters of Sociological Thought* (New York: Harcourt Brace, 1971), p. 211.

8. G. Spater & I. Parsons, *A Marriage of True Minds* (London: Cape/Hogarth Press, 1977), p. 32.

9. R. Crawshay-Williams, *Russell Remembered* (London: Oxford University Press, 1970), p. 155.

10. M. Heidegger, *Poetry, Language, Thought*, trans. A. Hofstadter (New York: Harper & Row, 1971), p. 11.

11. L. Hudson, *The Cult of the Fact*, (London: Cape, 1972) p. 35.

12. L. Wittgenstein, *Philosophical Investigations* (Oxford: Blackwell, 1967), sections 527, 531.

13. L. Wittgenstein, *Zettel* (Oxford: Blackwell, 1967), sections 328, 450.

14. L. Wittgenstein, *Vermischte Bemerkungen* pp. 107 (1946), 129 (1948).

15. H. Bergson, *La pensée et le mouvant*, in Bergson, *Oeuvres* (Paris: Presses Universitaires, 1970), p. 1327. H. Bergson, *The Creative Mind* (New York: Philosophical Library, 1946), p. 102 & note 14, p. 304.

16. H. Bergson, *L'Energie spirituelle*, in Bergson, *Oeuvres*, p. 849. H. Bergson, *Mind-Energy* (New York: Holt, 1920), pp. 56 – 57.

17. R. Mossé-Bastide, *Bergson éducateur* (Paris: Presses Universitaires, 1955), pp. 25 (note 3), 36 – 37.

The Relevance of Style: Bacon and Locke: pp. 64 – 67

1. Studies of philosophical style in general are, to my knowledge, rare. An interesting recent exception is B. Lang, 'Space, Time, and Philosophical Style,' *Critical Inquiry* (Winter, 1975). Lang classifies styles in terms of the presence or absence of the shaping authorial 'I'. See: A. Donagan, 'Victorian Philosophical Prose: J. S. Mill and F. H. Bradley,' in S. P. Rosenbaum, ed., *English Literature and British Philosophy* (Chicago: Chicago University Press, 1971); E. W. F. Tomlin,

'The Prose of Thought,' in B. Ford, ed., *The Pelican Guide to English Literature*, vol. 7, 3rd ed. (Harmondsworth: Penguin Books, 1973).

2. My ideas of Bacon's style are mostly derived from B. Vickers, *Francis Bacon and Renaissance Style* (Cambridge: Cambridge University Press, 1968). See also L. Jardine, *Francis Bacon: Discovery and the Art of Discourse* (Cambridge: Cambridge University Press, 1974); and S. Fish, 'Georgics of the Mind: Bacon's Philosophy and the Experience of His Essays,' in Rosenbaum, op. cit.

3. P. Rossi, *Francis Bacon: From Magic to Science* (London: Routledge & Kegan Paul, 1968), chaps. 5, 6.

4. Vickers, op. cit., p. 46.

5. *The Advancement of Learning*, as quoted in Vickers, op. cit., p. 73. See also Jardine, op. cit., pp. 176 – 78.

6. Vickers, op. cit., pp. 176ff., 179ff., 182ff. On Bacon's collecting of images, Jardine, op. cit., p. 207, note 1.

7. R. Colie, 'The essayist [!] in his *Essay*,' in J. W. Yolton, ed., *John Locke: Problems and Perspectives* (London: Cambridge University Press, 1969). What I say on Locke's style is no more than a partial paraphrase of Colie's sensitive analysis.

8. Colie, op. cit., pp. 260 – 61.

The Relevance of Style: Wittgenstein: pp. 67 – 73

1. L. Wittgenstein, *Philosophical Investigations*, 2nd ed., (Oxford: Blackwell, 1958), sections 1, 4, 14, 18, 174 (uses of 'du'). On dialogues with himself, L. Wittgenstein, *Vermischte Bemerkungen* (Frankfurt am Main/Oxford: Suhr-kamp/Blackwell, 1977/1978), p. 147 (1948).

2. *Philosophical Investigations*, sections 1 – 6.

3. Ibid., sections 266 – 70.

4. Ibid., section 11.

5. Ibid., section 157.

6. Ibid., section 111.

7. Ibid, section 126.

8. Ibid., section 129.

9. Ibid., section 534.

10. S. Beckett, *Murphy* (London: Calder, 1963), p. 172.

11. Wittgenstein, op. cit., sections 286 – 89.

12. Ibid., p. 178.

13. Ibid., p. 179.

14. Ibid., p. 187.

15. Ibid.

16. S. Beckett, *Watt*, in F. Doherty, *Samuel Beckett* (London: Hutchinson, 1971), p. 44.

17. Wittgenstein, op. cit., section 126.

18. Ibid., section 178.

A Conjecture on Philosophical Atomism: pp. 73 – 79

1. Indian atomism: S. Bhaduri, Studies in *Nyaya-Vaisheshika Metaphysics* (Poona: Bhandarkar Oriental Research Institute, 1947). T. Stcherbatsky, *Buddhist*

Logic, vol. 1 ('S-Gravenhage: Mouton & Co., 1958). W. M. McGovern, *A Manual of Buddhist Philosophy*, vol. 1 (London: Kegan Paul, 1923), pp. 85, 96 – 98. Moslem atomism: 'Atomic Theory (Mohammedan),' in J. Hastings, ed., *Encyclopaedia of Religion and Ethics* (Edinburgh, 1908 – 1926). M. Fakhry, *Islamic Occasionalism and Its Critique by Averroës and Aquinas* (London: Allen & Unwin, 1958). Maimonides, *The Guide of the Perplexed* (Chicago: Chicago University Press, 1963). H. A. Wolfson, *The Philosophy of the Kalam* (Cambridge, Mass.: Harvard University Press, 1976), chap. 6.

European Atomism: A. G. M. van Melsen, 'Atomism: Antiquity to the Seventeenth Century,' and R. H. Kargon, 'Atomism in the Seventeenth Century,' both in P. H. Wiener, ed., *Dictionary of the History of Ideas* (New York: Scribners, 1973).

2. See 'Moslem atomism,' note 1 above. In Later Neo-Platonism, physical time was quantized. See S. Sambursky & S. Pines, *The Concept of Time in Late Neoplatonism* (Jerusalem: The Israel Academy of Sciences and Humanities, 1971), pp. 18ff., 79.

3. B. Schönland, *The Atomists (1805 — 1933)* (London: Oxford University Press, 1968).

4. E. N. Hiebert, 'The Genesis of Mach's Early Views on Atomism,' in R. S. Cohen & R. J. Seeger, eds., *Ernst Mach, Physicist and Philosopher* (Dordrecht: Reidel, 1970). J. T. Blackmore, *Ernst Mach* (Berkeley/Los Angeles: University of California Press, 1972), pp. 319 – 23.

5. B. Russell, 'The Philosophy of Logical Atomism,' in *Russell's Logic Atomism*, ed. D. Pears (London: Fontana/Collins, 1972), p. 135. On the absence of a sense of selfhood see G. A. Talland, *Deranged Memory* (New York: Academic Press, 1965), or the same author's brief *Disorders of Memory and Learning* (Harmondsworth: Penguin Books, 1968).

6. B. Russell, *The Analysis of Mind* (London: Allen & Unwin, 1921), chap. 1.

7. L. Wittgenstein, *Tractatus Logico-Philosophicus*, trans. D. F. Pears & B. F. McGuiness (London: Routledge & Kegan Paul, 2nd corrected impression, 1963), propositions 5.542, 5.5421, 5.632, 5.633, 5.641. P. M. S. Hacker, *Insight and Illusion: Wittgenstein on Philosophy and the Metaphysics of Experience* (London: Oxford University Press, 1972), chap. 3. B. Williams, 'Wittgenstein and Idealism,' in *Understanding Wittgenstein*, Royal Institute of Philosophy Lectures, vol. 7, 1972 – 1973 (London: Macmillan, 1974).

8. For some account of the historical connection, see M. Fakhry, *A History of Islamic Philosophy* (New York: Columbia University Press, 1970), pp. 46 – 48. See also, A. Mieli, *La science arabe* (Leiden: E. J. Brill, 1939), pp. 138 – 41. The fundamental essay on the possible relation between Indian and Islamic atomism is S. Pines, *Beiträge zur islamischen Atomlehre* (Berlin, 1936).

9. J. R. Weinberg, *Nicolaus of Autrecourt: A Study in 14th Century Thought* (Princeton: Princeton University Press, 1944), pp. 84 – 85. H. A. Wolfson, (*The Philosophy of the Kalam*, op. cit., note 1, above) argues (pp. 594 – 95) that Nicholas's refutation of the argument for causality is based on Al-Ghazali. For Al-Ghazali's 'theory of custom,' i.e., the Humean notion of causality, see Wolfson, pp. 544 – 55.

10. On Malebranche generally, G. Rodis-Lewis, *Malebranche* (Paris: Presses Universitaires, 1963). Weinberg (see note 9 above) gives no reference but says (p. 229) that Malebranche mentions Nicholas 'in connection with his theory of first and second causes.' In any event, Malebranche quotes Pierre d'Ailly, who quotes some of Nicholas's sceptical arguments. Malebranche may have got his reference from Suarez. See Weinberg's 'The Novelty of Hume's Philosophy,' in

his book, *Ockham, Descartes, and Hume* (Madison: University of Wisconsin Press (1977), p. 122. The strong influence of Malebranche's Occasionalism on Berkeley is described in A. A. Luce, *The Dialectic of Immaterialism* (London: Hodder & Stoughton, 1963). For Hume's mention of Malebranche see N. K. Smith, *The Philosophy of David Hume* (London: Macmillan, 1941), p. 89 and note pp. 89 – 90.

11. For an account of his 'abnormal constitution' and childhood illnesses, one is referred to H. Gouhier, *La vocation de Malebranche* (Paris: Vrin, 1926), which unfortunately, I have not read.

12. Blackmore, op. cit. (note 4, above), pp. 7 – 8.

13. Ibid., pp. 286 – 99. Feuer, op. cit., p. 32.

NOTES TO CHAPTER FOUR

An Illustrative Myth: pp. 80 – 82

1. P. Radin, *Primitive Man as Philosopher* (New York: D. Appleton & Co., 1927), pp. 355 – 56.

2. F. Kafka, 'On Parables,' in *Shorter Works*, trans. M. Pasley, vol. 1 (London: Secker & Warburg, 1973), p. 191.

3. *The Journals of Søren Kierkegaard*, trans. A. Dru (London: Oxford University Press, 1938), sections 345 (Nov. 16, 1840), 651 (1847).

4. F. Nietzsche, *The Will to Power*, trans. W. Kaufmann, aphorism 552, p. 299; F. Nietzsche, *Beyond Good and Evil*, aphorism 211, in *Basic Writings of Nietzsche*, trans. W. Kaufmann, p. 326.

Writers, Artists, Scientists, Philosophers: pp. 82 – 86

1. Aristotle, *Poetics*, trans. G. F. Else (Anne Arbor: University of Michigan Press, 1967), p. 33.

2. M. Heidegger, 'Aus der Erfahrung des Denkens,' in his *Poetry, Language, Thought*, trans. A. Hofstadter (New York: Harper & Row, 1971), p. 13. For the whole subject see P. Wheelright, 'Philosophy and Poetry,' in A. Preminger, ed., *Princeton Encyclopedia of Poetry and Poetics*, enlarged ed. (Princeton: Princeton University Press, 1974).

3. *Paragone: A Comparison of the Arts by Leonardo da Vinci*, trans. I. A. Richter (London: Oxford University Press, 1949), p. 32.

4. H. L. C. Jaffe, ed., *De Styl* (London: Thames & Hudson, 1970), p. 71.

5. S. Gabelik, *Magritte* (London: Thames & Hudson, 1970), pp. 10 – 11.

6. R. Ingarden, 'Meine Errinerungen an Edmund Husserl,' in E. Husserl, *Briefe an Roman Ingarden* (The Hague: Martinus Nijhoff, 1968), p. 111.

7. L. Wittgenstein, *Vermischte Bemerkungen* (Frankfurt am Main/Oxford: Suhrkamp/Blackwell, 1977/1978), p. 77 (1940).

8. I. Kant, *Logic*, trans. R. Hartman & W. Schwarz (Indianapolis/New York: Bobbs-Merrill, 1974), p. 29 ('Introduction,' part 3).

9. P. Valéry, *Cahiers*, vol. 1 (Paris: Gallimard (Pléiade), 1973), p. 19.

Philosophers Are Vague, Philosophy Is Dense: pp. 86 – 89

1. The present atmosphere of philosophy favors criticism. Liam Hudson claims that the Oxford philosophers of the mid-fifties 'lived in fear of committing a solecism—especially one in cold print . . . Looking back, the context they created seems one concerned, almost to the point of obsession, with the question of intellectual control.' L. Hudson, *The Cult of the Fact*, p. 35.

2. P. Valéry, *Cahiers* (Paris: C. N. R. S., 1957 – 1961), 6:118, 25:727, 25:840, 26:525; as translated by J. R. Lawler in P. Valéry, *Poems* (Princeton: Princeton University Press, 1971), pp. 416 – 17, 429.

3. P. Engelmann, *Letters from Ludwig Wittgenstein* (Oxford: Blackwell, 1967), p. 7.

4. 'Wittgenstein's Lecture on Ethics,' *The Philosophical Review* (January, 1965); reprinted in *Philosophy Today*, No. 1, ed. J. H. Gill (New York: Macmillan, 1968), pp. 4 – 30.

Creative Autonomy: pp. 89 – 92

1. On the 'stubborn intellectual autonomy of creative people' in general, see H. J. Butcher, *Human Intelligence* (London: Methuen, 1968), p. 113. On the stubborn autonomy of inventors, see J. Jewkes, D. Sawyers & R. Stillerman, *The Sources of Invention*, 2nd ed. (London: Macmillan, 1969).

2. Most of this group of philosophers will be discussed biographically later on. Sources of direct quotations are: Montaigne, 'Of Vanity,' *The Complete Works of Montaigne*, trans. D. Frame (Stanford: Stanford University Press, 1958), p. 740. S. I. Mintz, *The Hunting of Leviathan* (Cambridge: Cambridge University Press, 1962), p. 2. A. Margoshes, 'Schelling,' in *The Encyclopedia of Philosophy*, ed. P. Edwards. Nietzsche, *The Gay Science*, trans. W. Kaufmann (New York: Random House (Vintage Books), 1974), aphorism 98, p. 150. L. Wittgenstein, *Vermischte Bemerkungen* (Oxford: Blackwell, 1978), p. 11 (1929); see p. 13 (1929).

3. 'On the General Characteristic,' in G. W. Leibniz, *Philosophical Papers and Letters*, trans. L. E. Loemker (Dordrecht: Reidel, 1969), p. 222.

4. *The Letters of David Hume*, ed. J. Y. T. Grieg, vol. 1 (London: Oxford University Press, 1932), p. 10 (to Michael Ramsey, 4 July, 1727).

5. Ibid., p. 1 ('My Own Life'). E. C. Mossner, *The Life of David Hume* (Austin: University of Texas Press, 1954), p. 71.

6. Letters, op. cit., p. 16 (To Dr. George Cheyne, March or April, 1734).

7. G. Berkeley, *Philosophical Commentaries*, ed. A. A. Luce (Edinburgh: Edinburgh University Press, 1944; corresponds to *Works*, ed. A. A. Luce & T. E. Jessop, vol. 1), entry 465.

8. 'Fear and alarm,' K. Vorländer, *Immanuel Kant: Der Mann und das Werk*, vol. 1 (Leipzig: Felix Meiner, 1924), p. 41. I. Kant *Immanuel Kant über Pedagogie, Kants gesammelte Schriften*, vol. 9 (Berlin: Akademie der Wissenschaften, 1923), p. 465; as translated in A. Churton, *Kant on Education* (Boston: Heath, 1906), pp. 27 – 28.

9. I. Kant, 'Vorrede,' section 7, *Gedanken von der wahren Schatzung der Lebendigen Kräfte, Kants gesammelte Schriften*, vol. 1 (Berlin: Akademie, 1902/10), p. 10.

10. I. Kant, *Anthropology from a Pragmatic Point of View*, trans. M. J. Gregor, (The Hague: Martinus Nijhoff, 1974), pp. 135 – 36 (Akademie ed., vol. 7, p. 268).

11. I. Kant, *Critique of Practical Reason and Other Writings on Moral Philosophy*,

trans. L. W. Beck (Chicago: Chicago University Press, 1949), p. 86 *(Foundations of the Metaphysics of Morals*, Akademie ed., vol. 4, p. 129); p. 144 *(Critique of Practical Reason*, Akademie ed., vol. 5, p. 33).

12. H. Saner, *Kant's Political Thought* (Chicago: Chicago University Press, 1973), pp. 202 – 209.

13. I. Kant, *Logic*, trans. R. Hartman & W. Schwarz (Indianapolis/New York: Bobbs-Merrill, 1974), p. 16 ('Introduction,' part 1).

14. E. Husserl, 'Author's Preface to the English Edition,' *Ideas* (London: Allen & Unwin, 1931), p. 29.

Incomprehensible Beginnings: pp. 92 – 94

1. M. Heidegger, *Zur Sache des Denkens* (Tübingen: Niemeyer, 1969), pp. 81 – 84, esp. p. 82 (quoted).

2. E. Husserl, *Erste Philosophie (1923 — 1924)*, Part 1 (The Hague: Martinus Nijhoff, 1959, pp. 18 – 23). My near-translation was made, not from this original, but from the French translation, *Philosophie première*, trans. A. L. Kelkel (Paris: Presses Universitaires, 1972), vol. 2, pp. 24 – 31.

3. E. Husserl, *The Crisis of European Sciences and Transcendental Phenomenology* (Evanston: Northwestern University Press, 1970), pp. 389, 394 – 95.

4. R. G. Collingwood, *An Autobiography* (London: Oxford University Press, 1931), pp. 3 – 5.

Idea-Intimacy and Idea-Autonomy: pp. 94 – 98

1. Montaigne, 'On Practice,' in *The Complete Works of Montaigne*, trans. D. Frame (Stanford: Stanford University Press, 1957), p. 273.

2. Montaigne, 'Of the Useful and Honorable,' and 'Of Repentence,' in op. cit., pp. 599, 611.

3. Montaigne, 'Of Repentence,' ibid.

4. Montaigne, 'Of Experience,' in op. cit., p. 818.

5. L. Wittgenstein, *Tractatus Logico-Philosophicus*, trans. by D. F. Pears & B. F. McGuiness (London: Routledge & Kegan Paul, 1963), p. 3, where the idea occurs in the first lines. The quotation is from a letter by F. P. Ramsey, of Sept. 20, 1923, in L. Wittgenstein, *Letters to C. K. Ogden* (Oxford/London: Blackwell/Routledge & Kegan Paul, 1973), p. 77.

6. In a conversation in 1797 with F. A. Stägemann, as in T. K. Oesterreich, *Die deutsche Philosophie des XIX. Jahrhunderts und der Gegenwart* (Uberweg, *Grundriss*, vol. 4) (reprinted Basel: Benno Schwabe, 1951), p. 509.

7. *The Portable Nietzsche*, trans. W. Kaufmann (New York: Viking, 1954), p. 568.

8. F. Nietzsche, *Beyond Good and Evil*, conclusion, in *Basic Writings of Nietzsche*, trans. W. Kaufmann, (New York: Randon House (Modern Library), 1968).

9. R. P. Feynman, 'The Development of the Space-Time View of Quantum Electro-dynamics,' Nobel Lecture, Dec. 11, 1965, in *Nobel Lectures: Physics, 1963 — 1970* (Amsterdam: Elsevier, 1972).

10. A. Einstein, 'Homage to Planck,' in A. Moszkowski, *Conversations with Einstein* (London: Sidgwick & Jackson, 1972), p. 59. There is a somewhat differ-

ent translation in A. Einstein, *Ideas and Opinions* (New York: Crown, 1954), p. 227.

11. J. D. Flam, *Matisse on Art* (London: Phaidon, 1973), p. 144.

12. L. Woolf, *Downhill All the Way* (London: The Hogarth Press, 1968), pp. 56 – 57, 58.

13. F. Kafka, *Briefe an Felice* (Frankfort: Fischer, 1973), letter of Jan., 1913.

14. *The Diaries of Franz Kafka* (Harmondsworth: Penguin Books, 1964), p. 105. Kafka's desire for independence and sense of failure are particularly open in *Letter to His Father* (New York: Schoken, 1953).

15. Montaigne, 'Affection of Fathers,' *The Complete Works*, (op. cit., note 1, above) p. 293.

Potency, Birth, Renewal, Impotency: pp. 98 – 102

1. Montaigne, 'Affection of Fathers,' *The Complete Works*, op. cit., p. 293.

2. *The Journals of Søoren Kierkegaard*, trans. A. Dru (London: Oxford University Press, 1938), sections 1328 (11 – 1, A 214), 1329 (11 – 1, A 231).

3. C. Adam, *Vie et Oeuvres de Descartes* (Paris: Vrin, 1910; reprinted 1957). Descartes, *Oeuvres philosophiques*, ed. F. Alquié, (Paris: Garnier, 1963), vol. 1, pp. 526, 527.

4. W. Kaufmann, *Hegel: A Reinterpretation* (Garden City: Doubleday (Anchor Books), 1966), pp. 92 – 93.

5. Hegel, *Texts and Commentary*, trans. W. Kaufmann (Garden City: Doubleday (Anchor Books), 1966), p. 20 (*Phenomenology*, 'Preface,' 1/3).

6. E. Husserl, *The Crisis of European Sciences and Transcendental Phenomenology* (Evanston: Northwestern University Press, 1970), pp. 151 – 52 (3/a/42).

7. H. Spiegelberg, *The Phenomenological Movement*, vol. 1, (The Hague: Martinus Nijhoff, 1965), p. 82.

8. Ibid., p. 76, note 1. The story is as told by Emmanuel Levinas (*Husserliana* 1, p. xxix).

9. A. Diemer, *Edmund Husserl* (Meisenheim am Glan: Anton Hain, 1956), pp. 13 – 14.

Cosmic Potency: Plotinus, Kant, Schopenhauer, Bergson: pp. 102 – 04

1. A. H. Armstrong, *Plotinus* (London: Allen & Unwin, 1953), pp. 153 – 54 (*Enneads* 5/3/17).

2. I. Kant, *Universal Natural History and Theory of the Heavens*, trans. W. Hastie (Ann Arbor: University of Michigan Press, 1969), chap. 7, p. 150. See H. L. Tuzet. 'Cosmic Images,' in P. P. Wiener, ed., *Dictionary of the History of Ideas* (New York: Scribners, 1973).

3. Kant, op. cit., p. 155.

4. A. Schopenhauer, *The World as Will and Representation*, trans. E. F. J. Payne, vol. 2 (New York: Dover, 1966), p. 568.

5. Ibid., p. 568.

6. Ibid., p. 570

7. H. Bergson, *Creative Evolution* (New York: Holt, 1911), p. 247.

Self-Creation: Montaigne: pp. 104 – 06

1. Hobbes, *Works*, vol. 1, 13. Quoted in S. I. Mintz, *The Hunting of the Leviathan* (Cambridge: Cambridge University Press, 1962), p. 18.
2. E. F. Rice, *The Renaissance Idea of Wisdom* (Cambridge, Mass.: Harvard University Press, 1958), chap. 4, esp. pp. 107, 119, 121.
3. I often follow F. Rider, *The Dialectic of Selfhood in Montaigne* (Stanford: Stanford University Press, 1973). See the following as well: I. Buffum, *Studies in the Baroque from Montaigne to Rotrou* (New Haven: Yale University Press, 1957), pp. 53 – 60. M. Butor, *Essais sur les Essais* (Paris: Gallimard, 1968). H. Friedrich, *Montaigne* (Berne: Francke, 1949), chap. 5 ('Das Ich'). D. Frame, *Montaigne* (New York: Harcourt Brace & World, 1965). A. Glauser, *Montaigne paradoxal* (Paris: Nizet, 1972). A. Thibaudet, *Montaigne* (Paris: Gallimard, 1963), pp. 89 – 247 ('Création de la vie intérieure').
4. 'Of Three Kinds of Association,' in *The Complete Works of Montaigne*, trans. D. Frame (Stanford: Stanford University Press, 1957), p. 621.
5. 'Of Giving the Lie,' in op. cit., p. 504.
6. Ibid.

NOTES TO CHAPTER FIVE

Primordial Reality: pp. 108 – 110

1. On the mother's heartbeat, see L. Salk, 'The Role of the Heartbeat in the Relations between Mother and Infant,' *Scientific American* (May, 1973). On identical twins, see P. Mittler, *The Study of Twins* (Harmondsworth: Penguin Books, 1974). On heredity and environment, see J. M. Thoday & A. S. Parkes, *Genetic and Environmental Influences on Behaviour* (Edinburgh: Oliver & Boyd, 1968). On nutrition and brain development see J. Dobbing, 'Malnutrition et dévelopment du cerveau,' in *La recherche* (Feb., 1976) which refers to J. A. David & J. Dobbing, eds., *Scientific Foundations of Paediatrics* (London/Philadelphia: Heinemann/Saunders, 1974). On stimulation see the following: H. Nagera, 'Social Deprivation in Infancy: Implications for Personality Development,' in B. B. Wolman, ed., *Handbook of Child Psychoanalysis* (New York: Van Nostrand Reinhold, 1972). M. R. Rosenzweig, E. L. Bennett & M. C. Diamond, 'Brain Changes in Response to Experience,' *Scientific American* (Feb., 1972).
The experiments with kittens I refer to are the well-known ones performed by Hubel & Wiesel, by Chow, and by Hirsch and Spinelli. I have also referred to two reports by R. Lewin in the *New Scientist* of 13 June, 1974 and 20 Nov. 1975.
2. J. Bowlby, *Attachment and Loss*, vol. 1, *Attachment*; vol. 2, *Separation* (New York: Basic Books, 1969, 1973). M. Mahler, *On Human Symbiosis and the Vicissitudes of Individuation* (London: Hogarth Press/The Institute of Psycho-Analysis, 1969), pp. 14 – 32. E. H. Erikson, *Identity* (New York: Norton, 1968), pp. 82, 96 – 7, 103 – 4, 106.
3. L. W. Sander, 'The Longitudinal Course of Early Mother-Child Interaction — Cross-Case Comparison in a Sample of Mother-Child Pairs,' in B.

M. Foss, ed., *Determinants of Infant Behaviour* (London: Methuen, 1969), pp. 210ff. See also R. Schaffer, 'Behavioural Synchrony in Infancy,' *New Scientist* (4, April, 1974). For general account, with full bibliography, see S. M. Bell & D. J. Stayton, 'Infant-Mother Attachment and Social Development . . . ,' in M. P. Richards, ed., *The Integration of a Child into a Social World* (Cambridge: Cambridge University Press, 1974).

Destruction of Being: pp. 110 – 14

1. The first well-known general assessment, combined with later critical reactions, is J. Bowlby, *Maternal Care and Mental Health*, first published in 1951, and M. D. Ainsworth et al., *Deprivation of Maternal Care: A Reassessment of Its Effects*, published together as one volume (New York: Schocken, 1966).

The most comprehensive summaries of the evidence are in the two volumes of J. Bowlby, *Attachment and Loss* (New York: Basic Books, 1969, 1973). The second volume contains a review of the basic psychoanalytic literature, as well as a summary of the relevant information on non-human primates. W. Sluckin, ed., *Early Conditioning and Early Experience* (Harmondsworth: Penguin Books, 1971) is a small but comprehensive anthology bearing on the subject. H. R. Schaffer, *The Growth of Sociability* (Harmondsworth: Penguin Books, 1971), reports on studies of crying and smiling, fear of strangers, the effects of familiarity, etc. For qualifications and objections see M. Rutter, *Maternal Deprivation* (Harmondsworth: Penguin Books, 1972); and A. M. Clarke & A. D. B. Clarke, ed., *Early Experience: Myth and Evidence* (London: Open Books, 1976).

2. J. P. Scott, *Early Experience and the Organization of Behavior* (Belmont, Calif.: Brooks/Cole Publishing Co., 1968), pp. 70 – 71, 75.

3. H. F. Harlow & M. K. Harlow, 'Social Deprivation in Monkeys,' *Scientific American* (Nov., 1962). A Jolly, *The Evolution of Primate Behavior* (New York: Macmillan, 1972), chap. 12, gives a reliable, up-to-date summary of what is known about the relation of primate mothers and infants, including (pp. 232 – 35) observations on the deficiencies, fears, and aggressions of 'early isolate monkeys.' 'Depression' and 'self-directed behavior' are also reported (p. 235).

4. D. G. Prugh & R. G. Harlow, 'Masked Deprivation in Infants and Young Children,' in J. Bowlby, *Maternal Care* . . . and *Deprivation of Maternal Care* . . . , op. cit., pp. 208 – 211. R. Hinde, *Biological Bases of Human Social Behaviour* (New York: McGraw-Hill, 1974), pp. 208 – 11, 234 – 45.

5. A. M. Clarke & A. D. B. Clarke, op. cit., pp. 15, 117 – 19.

6. Schopler, in A. Davids, ed., *Child Personality and Psychopathology*, vol. 1 (New York: Wiley, 1974), p. 233.

7. Ibid.

8. B. Bettelheim, *The Empty Fortress* (New York: The Free Press, 1967).

9. Ibid., p. 46.

10. Ibid., pp. 58 – 59, 62 – 63, 67, 426 – 28.

Creation of Being: pp. 114 – 16

1. K. Lorenz, 'Psychology and Phylogeny,' in his *Studies in Animal and Human Behaviour*, vol. 2 (London: Methuen, 1972).

2. E. J. Simmons, *Tolstoy* (London: Routledge & Kegan Paul, 1973), p. 17. In

view of my general emphasis, I should add that Tolstoy's mother died when he was two years old.

3. The idea of the gifted child's love affair with the world is borrowed from the psychoanalyst, Phyllis Greenacre. Three of her relevant articles, 'The Childhood of the Artist,' 'The Family Romance of the Artist,' and 'Play in Relation to Creative Imagination' are re-printed in her book, *Emotional Growth*, vol. 2 (New York: International Universities Press, 1971). These articles are abstract, that is, bare of examples.

On the psychology of creative men, see the articles of Anne Roe, of which she gives an untechnical summary in *The Making of a Scientist* (New York: Dodd, Mead & Co., 1953); and B. T. Eiduson, *Scientists: Their Psychological World* (New York: Basic Books, 1962).

J. Shotter, 'The Development of Personal Powers,' in M. P. Richards, ed., *The Integration of a Child into a Social World* (Cambridge: Cambridge University Press, 1974), attempts to see early childhood development in the light of contemporary philosophical analysis, that is, as a development that is partly directed by the child's intentions and meanings.

Differentiation of Being: pp. 117 – 18

1. The ideas, though not the terms, in this section stem from Anna Freud and D. W. Winnicott. A. Freud, 'Indications and Contraindications for Child Analysis,' in *The Psychoanalytic Study of the Child*, vol. 23 (New York: International Universities Press, 1968), esp. pp. 41 – 42. For Anna Freud's systematic views see her *Normality and Pathology in Childhood* (London: Hogarth Press, 1966). D. W. Winnicott, *The Family and Individual Development* (London: Tavistock, 1965), esp. pp. 7 – 8, 18 – 19. See also D. W. Winnicott, *Playing and Reality* (London: Tavistock, 1971).

Absence, Death, Denial, Creation, and Being: pp. 118 – 22

1. The estimate of the ages during which one is most sensitive to the absence of parents (or 'attachment figures') is from J. Bowlby, *Separation* (New York: Basic Books, 1973), pp. 202 – 204.

2. S. Anthony, *The Discovery of Death in Childhood and After* (London: Allen Lane, 1971), pp. 154, 203. N. Nagera, 'Children's Reactions to the Death of Important Objects,' in *The Psychoanalytic Study of the Child*, vol. 25 (New York: International Universities Press, 1970), pp. 391, 383.

3. My implication that childhood experiences of absence and death become adult tendencies toward depression, hypochondria, and the like, is based on empirical evidence. As usual, the evidence is ambiguous, though it seems to me on balance to support the implication. See A. T. Beck, *Depression* (Philadelphia: University of Pennsylvania Press, 1967), pp. 226 – 27; and J. Becker, *Depression: Theory and Research* (Washington/New York: Winston/Wiley, 1974), pp. 122, 148, 91.

4. On the normality of many adolescents see D. Ofer, *The Psychological World of the Teen-Ager* (New York: Basic Books, 1969). On adolescence as a difficult, even traumatic, age, see H. Deutsch, *Selected Problems of Adolescence* (London: The Hogarth Press/The Institute of Psycho-analysis, 1968).

NOTES TO CHAPTER SIX

Some Preliminary Words: pp. 123 – 25

My pretensions as a biographer are quite simple. For a survey of psychological studies of biography and an idea of the many formal possibilities, see C. Bühler & R. Eckstein, 'Anthropologische Resultate als biographischer Forschung,' in H.-G. Gadamer & P. Vogeler, eds., *Neue Anthropologie*, vol. 5 of *Psychologische Anthropologie* (Stuttgart: DTV/Georg Thieme Verlag, 1973). S. Friedländer, *Histoire et psychanalyse* (Paris: Seuil, 1975), chap. 2, gives a well-informed, candid, and sensible answer to the question, 'Is psychoanalytic biography possible?'

The notes to each philosopher will be preceded by a bibliography. The more elaborate bibliographies will be arranged, with variations, according to the following plan:

1. *Works*: a. originals; b. translations.
2. *Letters*.
3. *Biography*: a. general; b. studies.
4. *General Studies*.
5. *Special Studies*.

The less elaborate bibliographies will be arranged, with omissions, according to the same plan.

A word more on these bibliographies. The scale and nature of my book rule out any thought of completeness. I am familiar with many good books that I have not included. The bibliographies contain only books and articles that I have actually consulted in writing my accounts. The exception, the occasional book in square brackets, is a source I have not myself consulted but that may be used to check references that I supply.

Apart from the intentional restriction I have mentioned, my bibliographies show some glaring omissions, of which I am quite conscious. For example, I have not had the chance to make use of the recently published volumes of Locke's letters. I have used the standard multi-volume works of the philosophers only on occasion and even then perhaps inconsistently; and there is more, I am afraid, that can be complained of. Apart from human weakness, the only excuse I have is that I have had to depend so much on my personal library. I hope, however, that my contact with the sources is sufficient to allow others to judge my interpretations.

I have sometimes used the translations of others and sometimes my own. I may have modified others' translations without noting the fact.

Descartes: pp. 125 – 42

WORKS

[*Oeuvres de Descartes*, ed. C. Adam & P. Tannery, 13 vols. (Paris: Cerf, 1897 – 1913; reprinted Paris: Vrin/C.N.R.S., 1944 et seq.)]
Oeuvres et lettres, ed. A. Bridoux (Paris: Gallimard (Pléiade), 1953).
Oeuvres philosophiques, ed. F. Alquié, 3 vols. (Paris: Garnier, 1963, 1967, 1973).
Discours de la méthode, ed. E. Gilson (Paris: Vrin, 1947).
Les passions de l'âme, ed. G. Rodis-Lewis (Paris: Vrin, 1955)
The Philosophical Works of Descartes, trans. E. S. Haldane & G. R. T. Ross (Cambridge: Cambridge University Press, 1931).

Treatise of Man, trans. T. S. Hall (Cambridge, Mass.: Harvard University Press, 1972).
Descartes' Conversation with Burman, trans. J. Cottingham (London: Oxford, 1976).

LETTERS

Correspondance, ed. C. Adam & G. Milhaud, 8 vols. (Paris: Alcan (vols. 1 – 2)/ Presses Universitaires (vols. 3 – 8), 1936 – 63).
Descartes: Philosophical Letters, trans. A. Kenny (London: Oxford University Press, 1970).

BIOGRAPHY

C. Adam, *Vie et Oeuvres de Descartes* (Paris: Vrin, 1910; reprinted 1957; vol. 12 of Adam & Tannery, *Oeuvres*).
[A. Baillet, *La Vie de Monsieur Des-Cartes*, 2 vols. (Paris: D. Horthemels, 1691; abrégé, 1693).]
S. S. de Sacy, *Descartes par lui-même* (Paris: Seuil, 1957).
E. S. Haldane, *Descartes: His Life and Times* (London: J. Murray, 1905).
J. R. Vrooman, *René Descartes: A Biography* (New York: Putnams, 1970).

GENERAL STUDIES

H. Caton, *The Origin of Subjectivity: An Essay on Descartes* (New Haven: Yale University Press, 1973).
H. Gouhier, *La pensée métaphysique de Descartes* (Paris: Vrin, 1962).
R. Lefèvre, *Pour connaître la pensée de Descartes* (Paris: Boardas, 1965).
G. Rodis-Lewis: *L'oeuvre de Descartes*, 2 vols. (Paris: Vrin, 1971).
N. K. Smith, *New Studies in the Philosophy of Descartes* (New York: St. Martin's Press, 1952).

HISTORY OF SCIENCE

C. B. Boyer, *A History of Mathematics* (New York: Wiley, 1968).
J. Herivel, *The Background to Newton's* Principia (London: Oxford University Press, 1962).
M. Kline, *Mathematical Thought from Ancient to Modern Times* (New York: Oxford University Press, 1972).
A. Koyré, *Newtonian Studies* (Cambridge, Mass.: Harvard University Press, 1965).
A. I. Sabra, *Theories of Light from Descartes to Newton* (London: Oldbourne, 1967).
R. S. Westfall, *Force in Newton's Physics* (London/New York: Macdonald/American Elsevier).

SPECIAL STUDIES

E. Aziza-Shuster, *Le médecin de soi-même* (Paris: Presses Universitaires, 1972).
L. J. Beck, *The Metaphysics of Descartes: A Study of the Meditations* (London: Oxford, 1965).
Y. Belavel, *Leibniz critique de Descartes* (Paris: Gallimard, 1960).

E. Bréhier, 'The Creation of the Eternal Truths in Descartes's System,' in W. Doney, ed., *Descartes* (Garden City: Doubleday (Anchor Books), 1967).

E. Gilson, *Etudes sur le rôle de la pensée médiévale dans la formations du système cartésien* (Paris: Vrin, 1930).

H. Gouhier, *La pensée religieuse de Descartes* (Paris: Vrin, 1924).

H. Gouhier, *Les premières pensées de Descartes* (Paris: Vrin, 1958).

R. Lefèvre, *Le criticisme de Descartes* (Paris: Presses Universitatires, 1958).

R. Lefèvre, *L'humanisme de Descartes* (Paris: Presses Universitaires, 1957).

G. Milhaud, *Descartes savant* (Paris: Alcan, 1921).

1. Letter to Elizabeth, May or June, 1645.
2. Rodis–Lewis, *L'oeuvre*, vol. 2, p. 429, note 16 (from Baillet, vol. 2, p. 450).
3. *Passions*, part 2, article 93.
4. Ibid., article 100.
5. Ibid., article 117.
6. Ibid., article 134.
7. 'Observations,' Alquié, *Oeuvres*, vol. 1, p. 48 (Adam & Tannery, vol. 10, p. 215).
8. *Passions*, part 2, article 90.
9. To Elizabeth, May, 1646.
10. Adam, *Vie*, p. 10.
11. Ibid., pp. 15 – 16.
12. Ibid., p. 15. Text in Alquié, *Oeuvres*, vol. 3, p. 1124.
13. Rodis-Lewis, *L'oeuvre*, vol. 2, p. 434, note 41 (Baillet, vol. 1, p. 16).
14. Adam, *Vie,* pp. 433 – 34, note c.
15. To Pollot, mid-January, 1641.
16. Adam, *Vie,* pp. 287 – 88, note 2 (Baillet, vol. 2, pp. 89 – 90).
17. Ibid., p. 20, note b (Baillet, vol. 1, p. 28, from Lipstorp).
18. To Balzac, 15 April, 1631.
19. To unknown correspondent, apparently Sept., 1638: Adam, *Vie*, p. 484, note b.
20. To Charlet, Oct., 1644. Gouhier, *Pensée religieuse*, pp. 128 – 32, 192 – 93.
21. To Charlet, 9 Feb., 1645. See also, to Charlet, August, 1646.
22. Gouhier, *Premières pensées*, pp. 29 – 30. Rodis-Lewis, *L'oeuvre*, vol. 1, pp. 31 – 37.
23. To Beeckman, 24 Jan., 1619; 23 April, 1619.
24. To Beeckman, 26 May, 1619.
25. 'Préambules,' Alquié, *Oeuvres*, vol. 1, pp. 45 – 47 (Adam & Tannery, vol. 10, pp. 212 – 15).
26. *Discourse*, part 1. The description of the dreams is from Baillet and appears in Adam & Tannery, vol. 10, pp. 217 – 19 in the original Latin, in French translation in Alquié, *Oeuvres*, vol. 1, pp. 52 – 61, and in English translation in Smith, *New Studies*, pp. 33 – 39. There is a thorough discussion in Gouhier, *Premières pensées*.
27. 'Meditation 3.' Haldane & Ross, vol. 1, p. 168.
28. Rodis-Lewis, *L'oeuvre*, vol. 1, pp. 35 – 37. G. Milhaud, *Descartes savant* (Paris, 1921) thinks the book basically taken from Zarlino.
29. Rodis-Lewis, *L'oeuvre*, vol. 2, p. 435, note 5.
30. Adam, *Vie*, p. 285.
31. To Plempius, 3 Oct., 1637.

32. To Mersenne, 14 April, 1648.
33. *Discourse*, part 2, Haldane & Ross vol. 1, p. 90. See Gouhier, *Métaphysique*, pp. 76 – 84, 84 – 90 (on Descartes' style).
34. *Discourse*, part 1, Haldane & Ross, vol. 1, p. 85; Alquié, *Oeuvres*, vol. 1, p. 574. See also *Rules for the Direction of the Mind*, rule 4, and the beginning of the *Search after Truth*.
35. *Discourse*, part 6, Haldane & Ross, vol. 1, pp. 129 – 30; Alquié, *Oeuvres*, p. 649.
36. To Vater, 22 Feb., 1638. To Pollot, 6 Oct., 1642.
37. To Mersenne, 10 Nov., 1629.
38. Adam, *Vie*, pp. 225, 262 – 63, 480, 482 – 83. Vrooman, pp. 195 – 96. To Mersenne, 17 May, 1638. To Van Foreest, 5 Jan., 1647.
39. Lefèvre, *Humanisme*, pp. 169 – 74, or Lefèvre, *Pensée*, pp. 130 – 35. *Discourse*, part 6: Haldane & Ross, vol. 1, pp. 119 – 20; Alquié, vol. 1, p. 634.
40. *Discourse*, ibid. To the Marquis of Newcastle, Oct., 1645. On Descartes' medicine, see Gouhier, *Pensée religieuse*, pp. 142 – 48, and Lefèvre, *Humanisme*, pp. 175 – 80.
41. To Mersenne, 15 April, 1630.
42. To Vatier, 27 Feb., 1638.
43. To Huygens, 4 Dec., 1637 (dated 1638 in Adam & Tannery). See also, to Mersenne, 9 Jan., 1639.
44. Adam, *Vie*, pp. 475 – 76, note 5. Vrooman, p. 194.
45. *Descartes' Conversation with Burman*, p. 51. Aziza-Shuster, chap. 1.
46. To Chanut, 15 July, 1646.
47. Baillet, vol. 1, pp. 196 – 97, as translated by B. Cohen, in the foreword to Descartes, *Treatise of Man*.
48. Gouhier, *Pensée religieuse* (letter of Nov. or Dec., 1632).
49. To Mersenne, 2 Nov., 1646. Adam, *Vie*, p. 495.
50. To Elizabeth, 9 Oct., 1649.
51. On Descartes' tendency to solitude and secrecy, see: De Sacy, pp. 30 – 37; Lefèvre, *Pensée*, pp. 112 –13. To Ferrie, 18 June, 1629. To Mersenne, 15 April, 1630; 9 Jan., 1639.
52. Adam, *Vie*, p. 122, note d.
53. Lefèvre, *Pensée*, p. 112.
54. To Mersenne, April, 1634. The motto is from Ovid, *Tristia* 3/25. De Sacy, p. 37.
55. To Vatier, 22 Feb., 1638. Gilson, *Rôle*, pp. 181 – 82. For his ambivalence in general, see Caton, pp. 197 – 202.
56. *Conversation with Burman*, p. 28.
57. *Passions*, part 3, article 159.
58. *Passions*, part 3, article 170.
59. To Mersenne, 11 Oct., 1638. See Gilson, *Rôle*, pp. 175 – 76.
60. *Le Monde*, chap. 7: Alquié, *Oeuvres*, vol. 1, p. 351.
61. Westfall, p. 59.
62. *Objections and Replies* to the *Meditations*, objections 3, Haldane & Ross, vol. 2, p. 39.
63. *Conversation with Burman*, p. 50.
64. *Objections and Replies*, reply to objections 5, Haldane & Ross, vol. 2, p. 226; reply to objections 6, ibid., p. 248.
65. To Mersenne, 15 April, 1630: Alquié, *Oeuvres*, vol. 1, p. 259.

66. Ibid: Alquié, p. 260.
67. On the creation of eternal truths, see Bréhier; Lefévre, *Criticisme*, p. 180, note; and Gouhier, *Métaphysique*, pp. 235 – 45. To Mersenne, 6 May, 1630.
68. *Principles of Philosophy*, part 1, principle 21, Haldane & Ross, vol. 1.
69. Gilson, *Discours*, pp. 340 – 42; *Rôle*, pp. 225 – 30. Beck, pp. 192 – 98.
70. To Chanut, 1 Feb., 1647: *Letters* Kenny, pp. 212 – 15; Alquié, *Oeuvres*, vol. 3, pp. 716 – 17.
71. *Passions*, part 2, articles 70, 76.
72. *The Search for Truth*, Haldane & Ross, vol. 1, pp. 307, 311; Alquié, *Oeuvres*, vol. 2, pp. 1109, 1112.
73. Bridoux, *Oeuvres et lettres*, pp. 1409, 1411.
74. Boyer, p. 379.
75. Herivel, pp. 42 – 53, 233 – 34. Koyré, esp. p. 79, note 2.
76. To Chanut, 6 June, 1647.
77. Adam, *Vie*, p. 70 (Baillet, vol. 2, p. 501).
78. Adam, *Vie*, pp. 336 – 37, 576 – 77.
79. *Passions*, part 2, article 147.
80. Adam, *Vie*, pp. 119 – 20.

Pascal: pp. 142 – 49

WORKS

Oeuvres complètes, ed. L. Lafuma (Paris: Seuil, 1963).
L'entretien de Pascal et Sacy: ses sources et ses énigmes, ed. P. Courcelle (Paris; Vrin, 1960).

Pensées, trans. J. Warrington (London: Dent (Everyman's Library), 1960).
Pensées, trans. A. J. Krailsheimer (Harmondsworth: Penguin Books, 1966). I have found this edition particularly convenient because it follows the order and, until close to the end, the numbering of the above edition of the *Oeuvres*. The numbers of the *pensées* in the notes below are those of the Lafuma edition I have used and of Krailsheimer. The numbers in parentheses are those of the widely used Brunschvicg edition.
Great Shorter Works of Pascal, trans. E. Caillet & J. C. Blankenagel (Philadelphia: The Westminster Press, 1948). I have used but sometimes modified translations from this book.

BIOGRAPHY

J. Mesnard, *Pascal*, 6th ed. (Paris: Hatier, 1967).
J. Steinmann, *Pascal* (New York: Harcourt, Brace & World, 1965).

1. 'La vie de Monsieur Pascal, écrite par Madame Périer, sa soeur,' *Oeuvres*, p. 18.
2. Ibid.
3. Ibid., pp. 18 – 19.
4. Steinmann, p. 7.
5. Ibid., pp. 14 – 20.
6. Ibid., pp. 20 – 27.
7. Ibid., pp. 27 – 30.

8. 'La vie,' *Oeuvres*, pp. 19 – 20.
9. *Shorter Works*, pp. 92 – 94; *Oeuvres*, pp. 279 – 80.
10. 'La vie,' *Oeuvres*, p. 20.
11. Ibid., p. 21.
12. Steinmann, p. 12.
13. 'La vie,' *Oeuvres*, p. 21.
14. Steinmann, p. 51.
15. Ibid., p. 56.
16. *Shorter Works*, p. 84; *Oeuvres*, pp. 275 – 79.
17. *Shorter Works*, p. 85.
18. Ibid., p. 86.
19. Ibid., p. 87.
20. Ibid., p. 91.
21. Steinmann, pp. 60 – 64.
22. 'La vie,' *Oeuvres*, p. 22.
23. *Pensées*, no. 913 (no Brunschvicg number).
24. *Shorter Works*, p. 216; *Oeuvres*, p. 282.
25. 'La vie,' *Oeuvres*, p. 25.
26. Ibid., p. 32.
27. *Pensées*, no. 688 (B 323).
28. 'La vie,' *Oeuvres*, pp. 30, 31.
29. *L'entretien*, pp. 30 – 37. Also in *Shorter Works* and *Oeuvres*.
30. *Pensées*, no. 680 (B 63).
31. *Pensées*, no. 687 (B 144).
32. *Pensées*, no 780 (B 62).
33. 'La vie,' *Oeuvres*, p. 28.

Spinoza: pp. 149 – 56

WORKS

Ethic, trans. W. H. White, rev. A. H. Stirling, 4th ed., (London: Oxford University Press, 1923). This is the translation quoted.
Spinoza's Ethics and On the Correction of the Understanding, trans. A. Boyle, (London: Dent (Everyman's Library), rev. ed. 1959).
The Chief Works of Benedict de Spinoza, vol. 1, *Tractatus Theologico-Politicus, Tractatus Politicus*, trans. R. H. M. Elwes, 2nd ed. (London: Bell & Sons, 1887).
The Political Works, trans. A. G. Wernham (London: Oxford, 1958).

LETTERS

The Correspondence of Spinoza, trans. A. Wolf (London: Allen & Unwin, 1928).

BIOGRAPHY

J. Freudenthal, *Die Lebensgeschichte Spinozas* (Leipzig: Von Veit & Co., 1899). A collection of basic documents.
D. Levin, *Spinoza* (New York: Weybright & Talley, 1970).
A. Wolf, *The Oldest Biography of Spinoza* (London: Allen & Unwin, 1927).

E. Altkirch, *Spinoza im Porträt* (Jena: Diedrich, 1913).

I. S. Revah, 'Aux origines de la rupture Spinozienne,' *Revue des Etudes Juives* (July–Dec., 1964).

I. S. Revah, *Spinoza et Juan de Prado* (Paris/The Hague: Mouton & Co., 1959).

A. M. Vaz Dias & W. G. van der Tak, *Spinoza Mercator & Autodidactus* ('S-Gravenhage/Paris/The Hague: Mouton & Co., 1959).

Y. H. Yerushalmi, *From Spanish Court to Italian Ghetto* (New York: Columbia University Press, 1971).

COMMENTARIES

M. Gueroult, *Spinoza*, 2 vols. so far (Hildesheim: Olms, 1968, 1974).

H. S. Wolfson, *The Philosophy of Spinoza*, 2 vols. (Cambridge, Mass., Harvard University Press, 1934).

H. H. Joachim, *Spinoza's* Tractatus de Intellectus Emendatione (London: Oxford University Press, 1940).

STUDIES

C. De Deugd, *The Significance of Spinoza's First Kind of Knowledge* (Assen: Van Gorcum, 1966).

H. G. Hubbeling, *Spinoza's Methodology* (Assen: Van Gorcum, 1964).

1. Revah, *Spinoza et Juan de Prado*, p. 27. On possible interpretations see Levin, pp. 180 – 82.
2. Ibid.
3. Yerushalmi, pp. 44 – 46, from Revah, op. cit., pp. 276f.
4. Revah, op. cit., pp. 29 – 30.
5. Ibid., p. 32.
6. *Ethic*, bk. 4, prop. 39, scholium.
7. Letter 18, *Correspondence*, pp. 141 – 42.
8. *Ethic*, bk. 4, prop. 38, scholium.
9. Bayle: *Lebensgeschichte*, p. 31, note 1.
10. Wolf, *Oldest Biography*, p. 166.
11. Ibid., p. 166.
12. Colerus, chap. 9: *Lebensgeschichte*, p. 60.
13. Bayle: *Lebensgeschichte,* p. 31., note 1. See also Colerus, chap. 9: *Lebensgeschichte,* pp. 60 – 61.
14. Colerus, chap. 9: *Lebensgeschichte*, p. 60.
15. *Ethic*, bk. 4, preface.
16. *Tractatus Theologico-Politicus*, trans. Elwes, chap. 20, p. 258.
17. Ibid, preface, p. 3.
18. *Ethic*, bk. 3, prop. 41, note.
19. *Ethic*, bk. 4, prop. 70.
20. Colerus, chap. 9: *Lebensgeschichte*, p. 62.
21. To Blyenburgh, 1665: letter 19, *Correspondence*, p. 148.
22. *Ethic*, bk. 3, prop. 38.
23. *Tractatus Theologico-Politicus*, chap. 19, p. 250.
24. Colerus, chap. 9: *Lebensgeschichte*, p. 62. See the relevant documents in *Lebensgeschichte*.

25. *Tractatus Theologico-Politicus*, chap. 18, p. 239. Ibid., chap. 20.
26. Altkirch, p. 52 (Masaniello's picture between pp. 52 – 53). Colerus, chap. 5, *Lebensgeschichte*, p. 56.
27. *Tractatus Theologico-Politicus*, chap. 20, in Wernham, *Political Works*, p. 239. See note 2 on translation.
28. Gueroult, vol. 1, p. 9.
29. *Ethic*, bk. 2, prop. 43 and scholium (end).
30. Gueroult, ibid.
31. To Albert Burgh: letter 76, *Correspondence*, p. 352.
32. *On the Correction of the Understanding*, sections 47 – 48, in *Spinoza's Ethics . . .* , trans. Boyle, pp. 240 – 41.
33. *Ethic*, bk. 4, prop. 22.
34. *Ethic*, bk. 4, prop. 20.
35. *Ethic*, bk. 5, prop. 3; bk. 5, prop. 2.
36. *Ethic*, bk. 5, prop. 42, demonstration.
37. Colerus, chap. 2, p. 37.
38. *Ethic*, bk. 3, prop. 31. Amores, 2/19.
39. *Ethic*, bk. 3, prop. 35.
40. *Tractatus Politicus*, chap. 11.
41. *Ethic*, bk. 3, prop. 38.
42. *Ethic*, bk. 3, preface.

Locke: pp. 156 – 65

WORKS

An Essay Concerning Human Understanding, ed. P. H. Nidditch (London: Oxford University Press, 1975).
Epistola de Tolerantia: A Letter on Toleration, ed. R. Klibansky, trans. J. W. Gough (London: Oxford University Press, 1968).
John Locke on Education, ed. P. Gay (New York: Teachers College, Columbia University, 1964).
Two Tracts on Government, ed. P. Abrams (London: Cambridge University Press, 1967).
Two Treatises of Government, ed. P. Laslett (London: Cambridge University Press, 1964).

BIOGRAPHY

M. Cranston, *John Locke: A Biography* (London: Longmans, 1957).
M. Cranston, *Locke* (London: Longmans (British Council), 1961).
K. Dewhurst, *John Locke (1632–1704), Physician and Philosopher* (London: The Wellcome Historical Medical Library, 1963).
W. N. Hargreaves-Mawdsley, *Oxford in the Age of John Locke* (Norman, Oklahoma: University of Oklahoma Press, 1973).

GENERAL STUDIES

R. I. Aaron, *John Locke*, 3rd ed. (London: Oxford University Press, 1971).
J. D. Mabbot, *John Locke* (London: Macmillan, 1973).

J. W. Yolton, *Locke and the Compass of Human Understanding: A Selective Commentary on the 'Essay'* (London: Cambridge University Press, 1970).

SPECIAL STUDIES

G. J. Schochet, 'The Family and the Origins of the State in Locke's Political Philosophy,' in J. W. Yolton, ed., *John Locke: Problems and Perspectives* (London: Cambridge University Press, 1969).

1. Cranston, *John Locke*, p. 13.
2. *Two Tracts*, introduction, p. 49.
3. Cranston, op. cit., p. 49.
4. Ibid., pp. 26, 27, 46, 69.
5. Ibid., p. 69.
6. Ibid., p. 17, note 1.
7. Ibid., p. 17.
8. *Hargreaves-Mawdsley*, pp. 99 – 100. Cranston, op. cit., pp. 38 – 38.
9. Cranston, ibid.
10. Cranston, op. cit., p. 43.
11. *Two Tracts*, introduction, p. 54; pp. 245 – 46.
12. Yolton, *Locke and the Compass of Human Understanding*, pp. 1 – 2.
13. *Two Tracts*, p. 119.
14. Ibid., p. 120.
15. Dewhurst, p. 5.
16. Cranston, op. cit., pp. 74ff., 92 – 93; Dewhurst, pp. 7ff. *Essay*, bk. 2, chap. 4, section 24.
17. Cranston, op. cit., p. 100.
18. Ibid., pp. 93 – 95.
19. Ibid., pp. 82, 11 – 13.
20. Aaron, pp. 50 – 55. Cranston, op. cit., pp. 140 – 41.
21. Cranston, op. cit., p. 114.
22. Ibid., p. 159.
23. Ibid., p. 221.
24. Ibid., p. 225.
25. Ibid., pp. 249 – 53.
26. Ibid., p. 263.
27. Cranston, *Locke*, pp. 17 – 18.
28. *Two Tracts*, introduction, pp. 91 – 98. *Letter on Toleration*, introduction, pp. 27 – 42. Mabbott, *John Locke*, pp. 103 – 23, 151 – 56, 165.
29. *Essay*, bk. 4, chap. 3, section 18; bk. 4, chap. 3, section 4.
30. Yolton, pp. 91 – 103, 162 – 72, 179 – 80.
31. Ibid., pp. 11 – 14, 49.
32. Dewhurst, p. 311.
33. Cranston, *John Locke*, p. 12.
34. *John Locke on Education*, section 35, p. 27.
35. Ibid., section 40, p. 29.
36. Ibid., section 95. p. 73.
37. Cranston, op. cit., p. 163.
38. *John Locke on Education*, section 197, p. 162.
39. Ibid., section 174, p. 137.

40. *Two Treatises:* 'Second Treatise,' section 42, p. 321.
41. Ibid., section 54, p. 322.
42. Ibid., section 55, p. 322.
43. Ibid., section 59, p. 525.
44. Ibid., section 61, p. 326.
45. Ibid., section 76, p. 336.
46. Ibid., section 66, p. 328.
47. Schochet, p. 95.
48. *Letter on Toleration*, preface, pp. xx – xxxi.
49. *Essay*, bk. 4, chap. 16, section 4.
50. *Letter on Toleration*, introduction, p. 16. Mabbot, p. 174.
51. *Letter on Toleration*, p. 135.
52. Cranston, op. cit. pp. 424 – 46.
53. Ibid., p. 76.
54. Aaron, p. 52.
55. *John Locke on Education*, sections 49 – 52, pp. 34 – 35.
56. To Collins, 17 Nov., 1703: Aaron, p. 45.
57. Cranston, op. cit., pp. 47 – 54.
58. Ibid., pp. 86 – 87, 121 – 22.
59. Ibid., pp. 215 – 18, 342ff.
60. Ibid., p. 461.
61. Aaron, p. 47.
62. Ibid., p. 48.
63. Ibid., p. 47.

Leibniz: pp. 165 – 74

WORKS

Neue Abhandlungen über menschlichen Verstand, French text with German translation, ed. & trans. W. von Engelhardt & H. H. Holz, 2 vols. (Frankfurt am Main: Insel Verlag, 1961).

P. Burgelin, *Commentaire du Discours de Métaphysique de Leibniz* (Paris: Presses Universitaires, 1959).

Confessio philosophi: La profession de foi du philosophe, text with translation by Y. Belaval (Paris: Vrin, 1961).

Philosophical Papers and Letters, trans. L. E. Loemker, 2nd ed. (Dordrecht: Reidel, 1969).

Selections, ed. P. Wiener (New York: Scribners, 1951).

The Political Writings of Leibniz, trans. P. Riley (Cambridge: Cambridge University Press, 1972).

Discourse on Metaphysics, trans. P. G. Lucas & L. Grint, corrected ed. (Manchester: Manchester University Press, 1961).

The Leibniz-Arnauld Correspondence, trans. H. T. Mason (Manchester: Manchester University Press, 1967).

BIOGRAPHY

G. E. Guhrauer, *Gottfried Wilhelm Freiherr von Leibniz,* 2 vols. (Breslau, 1846; reprint Hildesheim: Olms, 1966).

K. Müller & G. Krönert, *Leben und Werk von G. W. Leibniz: Eine Chronik* (Frankfurt am Main: Vittorio Klostermann, 1969).

W. H. Barber, *Leibniz in France: From Arnauld to Voltaire* (London: Oxford University Press, 1955).

C. Haase, 'Leibniz als Politiker und Diplomat,' in W. Totok & C. Haase, *Leibniz* (Hannover: Verlag für Literatur und Zeitgeschehen, 1966).

K. Müller, 'Gottfried Wilhelm Leibniz,' in Totok & Haase, op. cit.

W. Ohnsorge, 'Leibniz als Staatsbedienster,' in Totok & Haase, op. cit.

RELATIONS WITH OTHER PHILOSOPHERS

Y. Belavel, *Leibniz critique de Descartes* (Paris: Gallimard, 1960).

G. Friedmann, *Leibniz et Spinoza*, 3rd ed. (Paris: Gallimard ('Idées'), 1974).

STUDIES

Y. Belavel, *Leibniz: Initiation à sa philosophie* (Paris: Vrin, 1962).

G. Grua, *La justice humaine selon Leibniz* (Paris: Presses Universitaires, 1956).

G. Martin, *Leibniz: Logic and Metaphysics* (Manchester: Manchester University Press, 1964).

R. W. Meyer, *Leibnitz and the Seventeenth-Century Revolution* (Chicago: Henry Regnery Co., 1952).

A. Rivaud, *Histoire de la philosophie,* vol. 3 (Paris: Presses Universitaires, 1950), pp. 409 – 45.

L. J. Russell, 'Leibniz,' in P. Edwards, ed., *The Encyclopedia of Philosophy*.

1. Guhrauer, vol. 1, pp. 5 – 9.
2. Ibid., p. 3.
3. Ibid., vol. 2, p. 338. Müller & Krönert, p. 4.
4. Guhrauer, vol. 1, pp. 7 – 8. Müller & Krönert, p. 3.
5. Guhrauer, vol. 1, pp. 10 – 12. Müller & Krönert, p. 5.
6. Guhrauer, vol. 1, pp. 13 – 14.
7. *Philosophical Papers*, pp. 463 – 64.
8. 'On the General Characteristic,' *Philosophical Papers*, p. 222.
9. Barber, pp. 8 – 9. Guhrauer, vol 2, pp. 357 – 58.
10. Ohnsorge, p. 187.
11. Ibid., pp. 191 – 92. Guhrauer, vol. 2, p. 251.
12. Haase, p. 221.
13. *Leibniz-Arnauld Correspondence*, p. 158.
14. 'A New System,' *Philosophical Papers*, p. 455.
15. 'Considerations on Vital Principles,' *Philosophical Papers*, p. 588.
16. Müller & Krönert, p. 37.
17. Guhrauer, vol. 2, p. 336. Belavel, *Initiation*, p. 192.
18. Müller & Krönert, pp. 1 – 2. Guhrauer, vol. 2, pp. 338 – 41.
19. Guhrauer, vol. 2, pp. 341 – 42.
20. Ibid.
21. Ibid., p. 341.
22. Ibid., p. 337.
23. To Reymond, 10 Jan., 1714: *Philosophical Papers*, pp. 654 – 55.

24. *Nouveaux Essais*, chap 1: *Abhandlungen*, p. 6.
25. *Confessio philosophi*, pp. 27 – 28, 87 – 89 (88 quoted).
26. 'Felicity,' *Political Writings*, p. 84. See *Selections*, pp. 567 – 70.
27. *Philosophical Papers*, p. 280.
28. *Discourse on Metaphysics*, section 35, p. 59.
29. Ibid., section 35, p. 61.
30. *Monadology*, section 85, *Philosophical Papers*, p. 651. See Burgelin, pp. 304 – 305.
31. 'A New System,' section 14, *Philosophical Papers*, p. 457.
32. Belavel, *Leibniz critique*, pp. 537 – 37, 51, 67.
33. Friedmann, pp. 123 – 24.
34. Ibid., pp. 250 – 51, 285 – 86, 309 – 10.
35. Müller & Kronert, p. 96. Descartes, *Oeuvres philosophiques*, ed. Alquié, vol. 1 (Paris: Garnier, 1963), pp. 50 – 51.
36. Guhrauer, vol. 2, p. 347.
37. Belavel, *Initiation*, p. 193.
38. Müller, pp. 9 – 10.
39. Belavel, *Initiation*, p. 194. Guhrauer, vol. 2, pp. 355 – 56.
40. Guhrauer, vol. 2, supplement, p. 100.
41. Ibid., p. 364.
42. Ibid., pp. 364 – 66; supplement, p. 43.
43. Ibid., pp. 363 – 64.

Berkeley: pp. 174 – 82

WORKS

Principles, Dialogues, and Philosophical Correspondence, ed. C. M. Turbayne (Indianapolis/New York: Bobbs-Merrill, 1965).
The Works of George Berkeley, Bishop of Cloyne, ed. A. A. Luce & T. E. Jessop (London: Nelson, 1948–1957), vol. 1, *Philosophical Commentaries . . .* (1948); vol. 5, *Siris . . .* (1953).
Works on Vision, ed. C. M. Turbayne (Indianapolis/New York: Bobbs-Merrill, 1963).

BIOGRAPHY

A. A. Luce, *The Life of George Berkeley, Bishop of Cloyne*, rev. facsimile ed. (New York: Greenwood Press, 1968).
J. O. Wisdom, *The Unconscious Origin of Berkeley's Philosophy* (London: The Hogarth Press/The Institute of Psycho-Analysis, 1953).

GENERAL STUDIES

F. Copleston, *A History of Philosophy*, vol. 5 (London: Burns & Oates, 1959), pp. 202 – 57.
A.-L. Leroy, *George Berkeley* (Paris: Presses Universitaires, 1959).
I. C. Tipton, *Berkeley: The Philosophy of Immaterialism* (London: Methuen, 1974).
G. J. Warnock, *Berkeley* (Harmondsworth: Peguin Books, 1969).

SPECIAL STUDIES

H. M. Bracken, *The Early Reception of Berkeley's Immaterialism 1710–52* (The Hague: Nijhoff, 1966).

A. A. Luce, *The Dialectic of Immaterialism* (London: Hodder & Stoughton, 1963).

J. D. Mabbott, 'The Place of God in Berkeley's Philosophy' (*Journal of Philosophy*, Jan., 1931; reprinted in Berkeley, *A Treatise Concerning Human Knowledge*, ed. C. M. Turbayne (Indianapolis/New York: Bobbs-Merrill, 1970), pp. 100 – 128.

R. H. Popkin, 'Berkeley and Pyrrhonism' (*Review of Metaphysics* (1951 – 1952); reprinted in *Berkeley, A Treatise*, ed. Turbayne), pp. 201 – 24.

OTHER REFERENCES

P. Bayle, *Historical and Critical Dictionary: Selections*, trans. R. H. Popkin & C. Brush (Indianapolis/New York: Bobbs-Merrill, 1965).

D. Hume, *Enquiries*, ed. L. A. Selby-Bigge, 2nd ed. (London: Oxford, 1902).

1. Luce, *Life*, pp. 11 – 12.
2. Ibid., p. 27. Wisdom, pp. 109 – 10.
3. Luce, *Life*, p. 185, note 7.
4. *Philosophical Commentaries*, section 266.
5. Luce, *Life*, p. 29.
6. Luce, *Dialectic*, pp. 55 – 56.
7. Ibid., p. 59.
8. Ibid., p. 41.
9. Wisdom, p. 107.
10. Ibid., p. 12.
11. Ibid., p. 130.
12. *Siris*, section 119.
13. *Principles*, sections 94, 96.
14. 'Second Dialogue,' *Three Dialogues*, p. 154.
15. Wisdom, p. 108, from A. A. Luce, 'More Unpublished Berkeley Letters and New Berkeleiana,' *Hermathena* (Dublin, 1933). On deists, *Alciphron*, dialogue 5, section 13. See Luce, *Life*, pp. 132 – 3, 162 – 6.
16. *Philosophical Commentaries*, sections 373, 373, 375, 409. Wisdom, p. 35.
17. Warnock, pp. 205 – 12.
18. Wisdom, pp. 157 – 59.
19. *Philosophical Commentaries*, section 625.
20. Ibid., section 298.
21. Ibid., section 290.
22. Ibid., section 107.
23. Tipton, pp. 305 – 06.
24. *Alciphron*, section 14, in Tipton, ibid., pp. 188 – 89.
25. Bayle, 'Pyrrho,' *Dictionary*, p. 189.
26. Bayle, 'Zeno,' ibid., p. 374.
27. *Philosophical Commentaries*, section 279.
28. Tipton, pp. 275 – 78.
29. Bracken, pp. 40, 83.

30. Hume, *Enquiries*, section 12, part 1, p. 155, note.
31. Luce, *Life*, pp. 224 – 26, 111, 180 – 81. Wisdom, pp. 111 – 13.
32. Luce, *Life*, pp. 181 – 82.

Voltaire: pp. 182 – 89

WORKS

Mélanges, ed. J. Van den Heuvel (Paris: Gallimard (Pléiade), 1963).
Oeuvres historiques, ed. R. Pomeau (Paris: Gallimard (Pléiade), 1957).
Politique de Voltaire, ed. R. Pomeau (Paris: Armand Colin, 1963).
Romans et contes, ed. R. Groos (Paris: Gallimard (Pléiade), 1954).

The Age of Louis XIV and Other Selected Writings, trans. J. H. Brumfitt (New York: Washington Square Press, 1963).
Candide, trans. J. Butt (Harmondsworth: Penguin Books, 1947).
Philosophical Dictionary, trans. T. Besterman (Harmondsworth: Penguin Books, 1971).

LETTERS

Correspondance, ed. T. Besterman, 4 vols to date (Paris: Gallimard (Pléiade), 1963, 1965, 1975, 1978).
Select Letters of Voltaire, trans. T. Besterman (London/Edinburgh: Thomas Nelson, 1963).

BIOGRAPHY

W. H. Barber, *Leibniz in France: From Arnauld to Voltaire* (London: Oxford, 1955).
T. Besterman, *Voltaire* (London: Longmans, 1969).

GENERAL STUDIES

W. F. Bottiglia, ed., *Voltaire* (Englewood Cliffs: Prentice-Hall, 1968).
P. Gay, *Voltaire's Politics: The Poet as Realist* (Princeton: Princeton University Press, 1959).
R. Pomeau, *La religion de Voltaire* (Paris: Nizet, 1956).
R. Pomeau, *Voltaire par lui-même* (Paris: Seuil, 1955).
I. O. Wade, *The Intellectual Development of Voltaire* (Princeton: Princeton University Press, 1969).
I. O. Wade, *Voltaire and Candide: A study in the Fusion of History, Art, and Philosophy* (Princeton: Princeton University Press, 1959).

1. Besterman, *Voltaire*, p. 21.
2. Ibid., p. 22.
3. Ibid., p. 31. See Pomeau, *Religion*, chap. 1.
4. Pomeau, op. cit., p. 27.
5. To Thieriot, about 25 Dec., 1722.
6. To Thieriot, 26 Oct., 1726.

7. Besterman, *Voltaire*, p. 43.
8. Ibid., pp. 44 – 57; p. 51 quoted.
9. Ibid., p. 66.
10. Ibid., pp. 68 – 72.
11. Ibid., pp. 73 – 84.
12. Ibid., pp. 106 – 07.
13. Ibid., pp. 111 – 13.
14. *Lettres Philosophiques*, letters 13, 14, in *Mélanges*, esp. pp. 38, 56 – 58.
15. Besterman, *Voltaire*, pp. 161 – 62.
16. Pomeau, *Religion*, trans. in Bottiglia, p. 140.
17. Ibid., pp. 140 – 41.
18. Wade, *Voltaire and Candide*, chap. 6; and *Intellectual Development*, p. 400.
19. Besterman, *Voltaire*, p. 545.
20. To Thieriot, about Feb., 1729.
21. Besterman, *Voltaire*, p. 42.
22. Pomeau, *Religion*, pp. 121, 256, note 29.
23. Pomeau, *Voltaire*, pp. 85 – 86.
24. Pomeau, *Religion*, in Bottiglia, p. 141; Pomeau, *Voltaire*, p. 39.
25. Pomeau, *Voltaire*, p. 39. Besterman, *Voltaire*, p. 97.
26. 'Fanaticism,' *Philosophical Dictionary*, pp. 202 – 203.
27. Ibid., pp. 202 – 3.
28. Pomeau, *Voltaire*, p. 12.
29. Pomeau, *Religion*, p. 265.
30. 'Torture,' *Philosophical Dictionary*, p. 396.
31. Wade, *Voltaire and Candide*, chap. 6; *Intellectual Development*, pp. 676 – 77. Besterman, *Voltaire*, chaps. 27, 30. Pomeau, *Religion*, pp. 309ff; *Politique*, pp. 24ff.
32. Wade, *Voltaire and Candide*, chap. 6.
33. Wade, op. cit.
34. *Le philosophe ignorant*, quoted Besterman, *Voltaire*, p. 299.
35. Besterman, *Voltaire*, p. 200.
36. *Select Letters*, p. 176.
37. To Lally-Tollendal, 25 May, 1778: *Select Letters*, p. 177.
38. Wade, *Intellectual Development*, pp. 29 – 91, 268. Besterman, *Voltaire*, chap. 15.
39. Besterman, *Voltaire*, pp. 185, 350.
40. Ibid., p. 481.
41. Ibid., pp. 476 – 77.
42. Ibid., pp. 404 – 04.

Hume: pp. 189 – 97

WORKS

A Treatise of Human Nature, ed. L. A. Selby-Bigge (London: Oxford University Press, 1896).
Hume's Dialogues concerning Natural Religion, ed. N. K. Smith, 2nd ed. (New York: Social Science Publishers, 1948.)

LETTERS

The Letters of David Hume, ed. J. Y. T. Grieg, 2 vols. (London: Oxford University Press, 1932).

BIOGRAPHY

C. W. Hendel, 'The Ambitions and Concerns of a Lifetime,' *Studies in the Philosophy of David Hume* (Indianapolis/New York: Bobbs-Merrill, 1963), chap. 1.
E. C. Mossner, *The Life of David Hume* (Austin: University of Texas Press, 1954).
E. C. Mossner, 'Philosophy and Biography: The Case of David Hume,' in V. C. Chappell, ed., *Hume* (Garden City: Doubleday (Anchor Books), 1966.
N. K. Smith, *The Philosophy of David Hume* (London: Macmillan, 1941), chap. 24.

PSYCHOPATHOLOGY

H. Bruch, *Eating Disorders* (New York: Basic Books, 1973).
P. Federn, *Ego Psychology and the Psychoses* (London: Imago Publishing Co., 1953).
S. Freud, 'Notes upon a Case of Obsessional Neurosis' (Standard Edition, vol. 10).
C. Landis, *Varieties of Psychopathological Experience* (New York: Holt/Rinehart & Winston, 1964).
G. A. Talland, *Deranged Memory* (New York/London: Academic Press, 1965).
J. Wyrsch, *La personne du schizophrène* (Paris: Presses Universitaires, 1955).

GENERAL STUDIES

J. Noxon, *Hume's Philosophical Development* (London: Oxford University Press, 1973).

1. Mossner, *Life*, pp. 173, 174.
2. *Letters*, vol. 1, pp. 1 – 2.
3. Ibid., p. 16.
4. Mossner, *Life*, p. 84.
5. *Letters*, vol. 1, pp. 12 – 18.
6. To Gilbert Eliot of Minto, 18 Feb., 1751: *Letters*, vol. 1, p. 154.
7. Bruch, p. 154.
8. Ibid., pp. 154, 155.
9. *Letters*, vol. 1, pp. 16, 17.
10. Ibid., p. 16.
11. Ibid.
12. *Treatise*, p. 264 (book 1, part 4, section 7).
13. Ibid., p. 269.
14. Ibid., 'Introduction,' p. xx. See Noxon, pp. 1 – 2, 8 – 16, 148 – 52, for details and qualifications.
15. *Letters*, vol. 1, p. 7.
16. Mossner, *Life*, p. 217.
17. Ibid., p. 568.
18. Ibid., pp. 477, 512, 522, 529.
19. Ibid., pp. 81 – 85.

20. Ibid., pp. 214 – 15.
21. Ibid., pp. 449 – 55, 460 (quoted).
22. Ibid., pp. 566 – 67, 569.
23. To Sir John Pringle, 13 Aug., 1776: *Letters*, vol. 2, p. 356.

Rousseau: pp. 197 – 208

WORKS

Oeuvres complètes, ed. B. Gagnebin & M. Raymond, 4 vols. so far (Paris: Gallimard (Pléiade 1959 – 69). Vol. 1, *Les confessions, Autres textes autobiographiques*. Vol. 2, *La nouvelle Héloise, Théâtre-Poésie-Essais littéraires*. Vol. 3. *Du contrat social, Ecrits politiques*. Vol. 4, *Emile, Education-Morale-Botanique*.

The Confessions of Jean-Jacques Rousseau, trans. J. M. Cohen (Harmondsworth: Penguin Books, 1953).
The First and Second Discourses, trans. R. D. & J. R. Masters (New York: St. Martin's Press, 1964).
The Social Contract, trans. M. Cranston (Harmondsworth: Penguin Books, 1968).

BIOGRAPHY

G. de Beer, *Jean-Jacques Rousseau and His World* (London: Thames & Hudson, 1972).
G. May, *Rousseau par lui-même* (Paris: Seuil, 1961).
J. Starobinski, *J.-J. Rousseau: La transparence et l'obstacle, suivi de Sept essais sur Rousseau* (Paris: Gallimard, 1971).

GENERAL STUDIES

R. Derathé, *Le rationalisme de Jean-Jacques Rousseau* (Paris: Presses Universitaires, 1948).
R. Grimsley, *The Philosophy of Rousseau* (London: Oxford University Press, 1973).
C. W. Hendel, *Jean-Jacques Rousseau: Moralist*, 2nd ed. (Indianapolis/New York: Bobbs-Merrill, 1962?).
L. Millet, *La pensée de Rousseau* (Paris: Bordas, 1966).

POLITICAL PHILOSOPHY

R. Derathé, *Jean-Jacques Rousseau et la science politique de son temps* (Paris: Presses Universitaires, 1950).
R. D. Masters, *The Political Philosophy of Rousseau* (Princeton: Princeton University Press, 1968).
P. Arnaud et al, *Rousseau et la philosophie politique, Annales de philosophie politique* 5 (Paris: Presses Universitaires, 1965).

OTHER REFERENCES

The Letters of David Hume, ed. J. Y. T. Grieg, 2 vols. (London: Oxford University Press, 1932).
New Letters of David Hume, ed. R. Klibansky & E. C. Mossner (London: Oxford University Press, 1954).

1. *Confessions, Oeuvres*, vol. 1, pp. 7 – 8.
2. Ibid., p. 7.
3. Ibid., pp. 9 – 10.
4. Ibid., p. 8.
5. Ibid., pp. 10 – 11.
6. Ibid., p. 11.
7. Ibid., p. 12.
8. To M. de Belloy, March 12, 1770: ibid., p. 1550, note to p. 566.
9. Ibid., and note, pp. 124 – 41.
10. Ibid., p. 15.
11. Ibid., p. 19.
12. Ibid., p. 20.
13. Ibid., p. 32.
14. *Rousseau juge de Jean Jaques*, 2nd dialogue, *Oeuvres*, vol. 1, pp. 799 – 800.
15. *Ebauches des Confessions, Oeuvres*, vol. 1, pp. 1149 – 50.
16. Ibid., p. 1153.
17. Ibid.
18. *Confessions, Oeuvres*, Vol. 1, p. 656.
19. Ibid., book 4, p. 175; book 9, p. 446. *Rousseau juge . . . , 2nd dialogue, Oeuvres*, vol. 1, p. 860. *Correspondence générale*, edited P.-P. Plan, vol. 20, pp. 43 – 44, quoted in Starobinksy, p. 301.
20. *Les rêveries du promeneur solitaire*, 'Deuxième promenade,' *Oeuvres*, vol. 1, p. 1010.
21. *Oeuvres*, vol. 1, p. 1230 (note to p. 3).
22. *Les rêveries . . .* , 'Première promenade,' *Oeuvres*, vol. 1, p. 1001.
23. Ibid., p. 999.
24. To the Rev. Hugh Blair, 28 Dec., 1765: *The Letters of David Hume*, vol. 1, p. 530. To the Rev. Hugh Blair, 25 March, 1766: ibid., vol. 2, p. 314.
25. *Oeuvres*, vol. 1, pp. 1223 – 25 and notes. See Starobinsky, pp. 430 – 44.
26. *Confessions*, book 2, *Oeuvres*, vol. 1, pp. 643 – 44. *Confessions*, trans. Cohen, p. 594.
27. *Les rêveries . . .* , 'Première promenade,' *Oeuvres*, vol. 1, p. 1046.
28. *Discours sur l'origine et les fondements de l'inégalité*, part 2, *Oeuvres*, vol. 3, pp. 170, 161 – 62. Masters' translation, pp. 151 – 52, 140.
29. *Rousseau juge . . .* , 3rd dialogue, *Oeuvres*, vol. 1, p. 935.
30. *Du contrat social*, book 1, chap. 4, *Oeuvres*, vol. 3, p. 356. Cranston's translation, p. 55.
31. Ibid., chap. 7, p. 364. Translation, p. 64.
32. J. Plamenatz, 'Ce qui ne signifie autre chose sinon qu'on le forcera d'être libre,' in *Arnand et al.* pp. 150 – 51.
33. Derathé, *Rationalisme*, introduction and pp. 84ff. See *Emile*, end of book 3.
34. *Oeuvres*, vol. 1, p. 1748 (note to p. 976).
35. *Emile*, book 4, *Oeuvres*, vol. 4, pp. 499 – 500.
36. May, pp. 129 – 41.
37. *Oeuvres*, vol. 1, pp. 1406 – 07.
38. Ibid., p. 1422. The whole problem is summarized in pp. 1416 – 23.
39. Letter of 20 April, 1751: *Oeuvres*, vol. 1, p. 1431.
40. *Les rêveries . . .* , 'Neuvième promenade,' *Oeuvres*, vol. 1, p. 1087.

NOTES TO CHAPTER SEVEN

Kant: pp. 210 – 30

WORKS

Kants gesammelte Schriften (Berlin: Königlischen Preussischen Akademie der Wissenschafte, 1902 –).
Anthropology from a Pragmatic Point of View, trans. M. J. Gregor (The Hague: Martinus Nijhoff, 1974).
The Critique of Practical Judgement, trans. J. C. Meredith (London: Oxford University Press, 1952 (in 2 separate vols., 1928)).
Critique of Practical Reason and Other Writings in Moral Philosophy, trans. L. W. Beck (Chicago: Chicago University Press, 1949).
Immanuel Kant's Critique of Pure Reason, trans. N. K. Smith (London: Macmillan, 1933).
Kant on Education, trans. A. Churton, (Boston: Heath, 1906).
Lectures on Ethics, trans. L. Infield (New York/London: The Century Co, 1930).
The Metaphysical Elements of Justice (The Metaphysics of Morals, I), trans. J. Ladd (Indianapolis/New York: Bobbs)–Merrill, 1965).
The Metaphysical Elements of Virtue (The Metaphysics of Morals, II), trans. J. Ellington (Indianapolis/New York: Bobbs–Merrill, 1964).
Observations on the Feeling of the Beautiful and Sublime, trans. J. T. Goldthwaite (Berkeley/Los Angeles: University of California Press, 1965).
On History, ed. L. W. Beck (Indianapolis/New York: Bobbs–Merrill, 1963).
Réflexions sur l'éducation, trans. A. Philonenko (Paris: Vrin, 1966).
Religion within the Limits of Reason Alone, trans. T. H. Greene & H. H. Hudson (Indianapolis/New York: Bobbs–Merrill, 1964).

LETTERS

Briefwechsel, ed. O. Schöndörffer, 2nd enlarged ed., ed. R. Malter & J. Kopper (Hamburg: Felix Meiner, 1972).
Philosophical Correspondence 1759–99, trans. A. Zweig (Chicago: Chicago University Press, 1967).

BIOGRAPHY

E. Arnoldt, *Kants Jugend und die fünf ersten Jahre seiner Privatdozentur* (Königsberg, 1882), in E. Arnoldt, *Gesammelte Schriften*, ed. O. Schöndörffer (Berlin, 1908).
L. E. Borowski, R. B. Jachmann & A. C. Wasianski, in *Immanuel Kant: Sein Leben in Darstellungen von Zietgenossen*, ed. Felix Gross (Berlin: DeutscheBibliothek, 1912). A more recent reprinting (which I have not used) is *Wer war Kant?*, ed. S. Drescher (Pfullingen: Verlag Neske, 1974).
J. G. Hasse, *Lezte* [sic!] *Aeusserungen Kant's* [sic!], 2nd printing (Königsberg, 1804).
F. T. Rink, *Ansichten aus Immanuel Kant's Leben* (Königsberg, 1805).
J. H. W. Stuckenberg, *The Life of Immanuel Kant* (London: Macmillan, 1882).
K. Vorländer, *Die ältesten Kant-Biographien: Eine kritische Studie* (Berlin, 1918). An

estimate of the three old biographies, the best known of which, noted above, are by Borowski, Jachmann, and Wasianski. Borowski was asked by Kant to gather material for a posthumous biography. Kant himself read the first part of Borowski's memoir, which is nevertheless said to contain errors of fact. Jachmann lived with Kant no less than nine years, having free access to his house. Both friend and amanuensis, he knew Kant at the height of his fame. Wasianski heard Kant's lectures and afterward became his amanuensis. Years later, when a priest, he renewed the acquaintance. During Kant's last years he helped him considerably, and it is the old Kant he describes. The three memoirs were all published in a single volume in 1804.

K. Vorländer, *Immanuel Kant: Der Mann und das Werk*, 2 vols. (Leipzig: Felix Meiner 1924).

PSYCHOANALYSIS

D. Eicke, *Der Körper als Partner* (Munich: Kindler Verlag, 1973).

L. S. Feuer, 'Lawless Sensations and Categorial Defenses: The Unconscious Sources of Kant's Philosophy,' in C. Hanly & M. Lazerowitz, eds., *Psychoanalysis and Philosophy* (New York: International Universities Press, 1970).

R. D. Loewenberg, 'Kant's Self-Analysis,' in *American Imago* (1953), pp. 307 – 22; reprinted in *The Yearbook of Psychoanalysis*, vol. 10 (New York, 1955).

LEXICON

K. Eisler, *Kant Lexikon* (Hildesheim: Georg Olms, 1964; photo-reprint of ed. Berlin, 1930).

STUDIES

H. Mertens, *Kommentar zur Ersten Einleitung in Kants Kritik der Urteilskraft* (Munich: Johannes Berchmans Verlag, 1975).

H. Saner, *Kant's Political Thought* (Chicago: Chicago University Press, 1973).

J. Schmucker, *Die Ursprünge der Ethik Kants* (Meisenheim am Glan: Verlag Anton Heim, 1961).

H.-J. Vleeschauwer, *The Development of Kantian Thought* (London/Edinburgh: Nelson 1962).

1. Arnoldt, pp. 103ff.
2. Rink, p. 14.
3. Arnoldt, p. 110.
4. Borowski, in Borowski *et al.*, p. 21.
5. Wasianski, ibid., p. 247.
6. Arnoldt, p. 111, from Rink, pp. 14 – 15.
7. Borowski, op. cit. pp. 20 – 21.
8. Arnoldt, pp. 107, 109.
9. Borowski, op. cit., pp. 20 – 21.
10. Jachmann, 9th letter, ibid., pp. 170 – 71.
11. Wasianski, ibid., pp. 259 – 60.
12. Ibid.
13. Ibid., pp. 260 – 61.

14. Jachmann, 9th letter, ibid., pp. 260 – 61.
15. *Practical Reason*, pp. 258 – 59 (opening of 'Conclusion').
16. *Kant on Education*, p. 93; *Schriften*, vol. 9, p. 485.
17. *Kant on Education*, p. 51; *Schriften*, vol. 9, pp. 459 – 60.
18. *Kant on Education*, p. 50; *Schriften*, vol. 9, p. 466.
19. *Kant on Education*, p. 115; *Schriften*, vol. 9, p. 497.
20. Feuer, p. 19.
21. Wasianski, op. cit., p. 277.
22. *Kant on Education*, p. 73; *Schriften*, vol. 9, p. 473.
23. *Anthropology*, section 47; *Schriften*, vol. 7, p. 208.
24. Vorländer, *Immanuel Kant*, vol. I, pp. 372 – 74.
25. Ibid., p. 374.
26. K. Holgar, 'Results of the Work on Kant's Index of Persons,' in *Proceedings of the Third International Kant Congress*, ed. L. W. Beck (Dordrecht: Reidel, 1972).
27. *Critique of Judgement*, pp. 195 – 96 (section 53): *Schriften*, vol. 5, pp. 329 – 30.
28. Borowski, pp. 88 – 89; Jachmann, 10th letter, pp. 173 – 74, in Borowski *et al.* Stuckenberg, pp. 142 – 3.
29. Borowski, ibid., pp. 88 – 89.
30. Wasianski, ibid., pp. 284 – 85.
31. Jachmann, 9th letter, ibid., pp. 171 – 73.
32. Wasianski, ibid., p. 232.
33. From Johann Heinrich Kant, 3 July, 1773: *Briefwechsel*, p. 110.
34. From Johann Heinrich Kant, 21 Aug., 1789, 26 Jan., 1792: *Briefwechsel*, pp. 410 – 11, 551 – 52; *Philosophical Correspondence*, p. 185.
35. To Johann Heinrich Kant, 17 Dec., 1976: *Briefwechsel*, p. 720. Borowski, p. 69.
36. Stuckenberg, chap. 8. Arnoldt, pp. 144 – 56.
37. Borowski, op. cit., p. 68.
38. Borowski, pp. 68 – 69; Jachmann, 8th letter, pp. 164 – 65, ibid.
39. Wasianski, ibid., p. 81.
40. Jachmann, 8th letter, ibid., pp. 160 – 63.
41. Malter & Kopper, introduction to *Briefwechsel*, pp. lii-liii, lvi.
42. Ibid., pp. 1 – 1i. *Metaphysik der Sitten*, section 9 ('Kasuistische Fragen'), *Schriften*, vol. 7. To Maria von Herbert, early 1792: *Briefwechsel*, p. 564.
43. *To Reinhold, 21 Sept., 1791; to Beck, 27 Sept., 1791: Briefwechsel*, pp. 525, 529 – 30.
44. To Kästner, Aug. 5 [?], 1790: *Briefwechsel*, p. 467.
45. Saner, pp. 49 – 51.
46. Stuckenberg, pp. 192 – 93. Vorländer, *Altesten*, from an addition by Wasianski marked 'not for public.'
47. Wasianski, in Borowski *et al.*, pp. 253 – 54. Stuckenberg, pp. 192 – 93.
48. *Handschriftlicher Nachlass, Anthropologie, Erste Hälfte: Schriften*, vol. 15, p. 532.
49. Jachmann, 6th letter, p. 149.
50. *Streit der Fakultäten*, 3. Abschnitt: *Schriften*, vol. 7, p. 104. Stuckenberg, p. 102.
51. *Streit*, ibid., *Schriften*, vol. 7, p. 103. *Nachlass, Anthropologie, Erste Hälfte: Schriften*, vol. 15, p. 218.
52. 'Versuch über die Krankheiten des Kopfes,' *Schriften*, vol. 2, p. 266.

53. *Anthropology*, p. 83; *Schriften*, vol. 7, p. 212 (section 50).
54. To M. Herz, beg. April, 1778: *Briefwechsel*, p. 171.
55. *Anthropology*, p. 83; *Schriften*, vol. 7, p. 212 (section 50).
56. Jachmann, 9th letter, op. cit., pp. 192 – 94.
57. Jachmann, 15th letter, ibid., p. 202.
58. Jachmann, 14th letter, ibid., p. 194.
59. To M. Herz, end 1773: *Briefwechsel*, p. 113; *Philosophical Correspondence*, p. 77.
60. To M. Herz, 20 Aug., 1777: *Briefwechsel*, pp. 155 – 56; *Philosophical Correspondence*, p. 88.
61. Wasiansky, op. cit., p. 238.
62. Jachmann, 14th letter, ibid., p. 195. To S. T. Soemmering, 4 Aug., 1800: *Briefwechsel*, p. 806.
63 Wasianski, op. cit., pp. 241 – 42. To J. B. Erhard, 20 Dec., 1799: *Briefwechsel*, p. 792.
64. Jachmann, 15th letter, op. cit., p. 202.
65. Wasiansky, ibid., pp. 236 – 37.
66. *Streit der Fakultäten*, 3. Abschnitt, sections 5, 6, *Schriften*, vol. 7, pp. 110 – 12. Stuckenberg, pp. 103 – 04.
67. Jachmann, letter 6, op. cit., p. 150.
68. Ibid.
69. *Streit der Fakultäten*, 4. Abschnitt, *Schriften*, vol. 7, p. 109.
70. Ibid., p. 102. Loewenberg.
71. Jachmann, 15th letter, op. cit., pp. 196 – 98.
72. Wasiansky, ibid., pp. 299 – 39. Stuckenberg, pp. 170 – 71.
73. Wasiansky, op. cit., pp. 237 – 38. Stuckenberg, p. 433.
74. Wasiansky, op. cit., pp. 234 – 35. Stuckenberg, pp. 345 – 36.
75 Wasiansky, op. cit., p. 247.
76. Ibid., p. 27.
77. Hasse, pp. 15 – 16.
78. Ibid., pp. 28 – 29.
79. Stuckenberg, p. 466, note 133 (from T. G. v. Hippel, *Schlichtegroll's 'Nekrologie,'* vol. 1, p. 281).
80. Wasiansky, op. cit., pp. 278 – 79.
81. Ibid., p. 274.
82. Ibid., p. 310.
83. Ibid.
84. *Critique of Judgement*, p. 36 (introduction, section 10); *Schriften*, vol. 5, p. 195.
85. *Critique of Pure Reason*, p. 466 (A536, B564); *Schriften*, vol. 5, p. 195.
86. To Beck, July 1, 1794: *Briefwechsel*, p. 677.
87. *Anthropology*, p. 15; *Schriften*, vol. 7, pp. 133 – 34.
88. To J. G. Herder, 9 May, 1768; to M. Herz, beg. April, 1778: *Briefwechsel*, pp. 56, 171.
89. 'Open Letter on Fichte's *Wissenschaftslehre*,' 7 Aug., 1799: *Philosophical Correspondence*, p. 251. To Garve, 21 Sept., 1798: *Briefwechsel*, p. 799; *Philosophical Correspondence*, p.251.
90. Stuckenberg, p. 141. Borowski, p. 70. Wasiansky, p. 251.
91. 'Idea for a Universal History . . . ,' in *On History; Schriften*, vol. 8.
92. Saner, pp. 302 – 05.

93. From a note of 'Reflexionen zur Metaphysik,' in Saner, p. 306. See Vlee-schauwer, pp. 70 – 75, 94 – 98, 111 – 14.

94. *Religion within the Limits of Reason Alone*, pp. 27, 28, 32, 38.

95. *Metaphysik der Sitten*, section 49a: *Schriften*, vol. 6, p. 320; *The Metaphysical Elements of Justice*, p. 86.

96. *Metaphysik der Sitten*, section 49a, note: *Schriften*, vol. 6, p. 321; *The Metaphysical Elements of Justice*, p. 87, note.

97. *Metaphysik der Sitten*, section 49e 1: *Schriften*, vol. 6, p. 331; *The Metaphysical Elements of Justice*, p. 100.

98. *Metaphysik der Sitten*, section 49e 1: *Schriften*, vol. 6, p. 332; *The Metaphysical Elements of Justice*, p. 101.

99. Ibid.

100. *Metaphysik der Sitten*, section 49e 1: *Schriften*, vol. 6, pp. 334 – 35; *The Metaphysical Elements of Justice*, pp. 104 – 105.

101. *Metaphysik der Sitten*, section 49e 1: *Schriften*, vol. 6, p. 333; *The Metaphysical Elements of Justice*, p. 102.

102. *Metaphysik der Sitten*, section 7: *Schriften*, vol. 6, p. 425; *The Metaphysical Principles of Virtue*, pp. 85 – 86. See *Lectures on Ethics*, pp. 169 – 71.

103. *Critique of Practical Reason*, p. 135; *Schriften*, vol. 5, p. 24.

104. *Critique of Practical Reason*, pp. 135 – 36.

105. Ibid.

106. Ibid., p. 139; *Schriften*, vol. 5, p. 28.

107. *Foundations of the Metaphysics of Morals*, in *Critique of Practical Reason*, p. 114; *Schriften*, vol. 4, p. 460.

108. *Critique of Practical Reason*, pp. 220, 222; *Schriften*, vol. 5, pp. 116, 118. See Eisler, *Kant Lexikon*, 'Achtung.'

109. *Critique of Pure Reason*, p. 66 (A21, note). Mertens, pp. 144 – 50.

110. Schmücker names philosophers who influenced Kant's ethical thought, but says (pp. 393 – 94) that its main source was Kant's essential nature (*Ingenium*) and moral character.

111. *Critique of Judgement*, p. 38; *Schriften*, vol. 5, p. 196.

112. Ibid., p. 39; *Schriften*, vol. 5, p. 197.

113. Mertens, p. 109.

114. For Kant's triumph in The *Critique of Judgement*, see Vleeschauwer, pp. 135 – 37.

115. Jachmann, 7th letter, op. cit., pp. 150 – 51.

116. Hasse, p. 39.

117. *Observations on . . . the Beautiful and Sublime*, pp. 86 – 88; *Schriften*, vol. 2 (*Beobachtungen*, 3. Abschnitt).

118. Ibid., p. 89.

119. *Handschriftlicher Nachlass, Anthropologie, Erste Hälfte*: *Schriften*, vol. 15, p. 572.

120. *Handschriftlicher Nachlass, Bemerkungen zu den Beobachtungen über das Gefühl des Schönen und Erhabenen*: *Schriften*, vol. 20, pp. 472 – 73.

121. Ibid., pp. 3, 5, 11, 84, 116.

122. *Nachlass, Anthropologie, Erste Hälfte*: *Schriften*, vol. 15, pp. 557, 559, 560, 572.

123. Ibid., p. 575.

124. Vorländer, *Immanuel Kant*, vol. 1, pp. 131, 192 – 93. Stuckenberg, pp. 189 – 91.

125. Vorländer, ibid., p. 194.
126. Jachmann, 8th letter, op. cit., p. 169.

Hegel: pp. 230 – 42

WORKS

Werke in zwanzig Bänden (Frankfurt an Main: Suhrkamp Verlag, 1971)

The Difference Between Fichte's and Schelling's System of Philosophy, trans. H. S. Harris & W. Cerf (Albany: State University of New York Press, 1977).
Hegel's Philosophy of Mind, trans. W. Wallace & A. V. Miller (London: Oxford University Press, 1971).
Hegel's Philosophy of Right, trans. T. M. Knox (London: Oxford University Press, 1942).
Hegel: Texts and Commentary, trans. W. Kaufmann (Garden City: Doubleday (Anchor Books), 1966).
The Phenomenology of Mind, trans. J. B. Baillie, 2nd ed. (London: Allen & Unwin, 1931).

LETTERS AND DOCUMENTS

Briefe von und an Hegel, ed. J. Hoffmeister & R. Flechsig, 4 vols. (Hamburg: Meiner, 1952–60).
[*Dokumente zu Hegels Entwicklung*, ed. J. Hoffmeister (Stuttgart: Frommans Verlag, 1936).]

BIOGRAPHY

H. S. Harris, *Hegel's Development: Toward the Sunlight: 1770 — 1801* (London: Oxford University Press, 1972).
[R. *Haym, Hegel und seine Zeit* (Hildesheim: Olms, 1962) (photo-reprint of ed. Berlin, 1857).]
Hegel in Berichten seiner Zeitgenossen, ed. G. Nicolin (Hamburg: Meiner, 1970).
W. Kaufmann, *Hegel: A Reinterpretation* (Garden City: Doubleday (Anchor Books), 1966).
G. E. Müller, *Hegel: Denkgeschichte eines Lebendigen* (Bern/Munich: Francke, 1959).
K. Rosenkranz, *G. W. F. Hegels Leben* (Darmstadt: Wissenschaftliche Buchgesellshaft, 1971; photo-reprint of ed. Berlin, 1844).
F. Wiedmann, *Hegel in Selbstzeugnissen und Bilddokumenten* (Reinbek b. Hamburg: Rowohlt (Rororo), 1965).

PSYCHOPATHOLOGY

A. Künzli, 'Prolegomena zu einer Psychographie Hegels,' in G.-K. Kaltenbrunner, ed. *Hegel und die Folgen* (Freiburg: Verlag Rombach, 1970).

GENERAL STUDIES

H. Glockner, *Hegel*, vol. 2, *Entwicklung und Schicksal der hegelischen Philosophie* (Stuttgart: Frommanns Verlag, 1940).
R. Plant, *Hegel* (London: Allen & Unwin, 1973).

SPECIAL STUDIES

M. Green, *Hegel on the Soul: A Speculative Anthropology* (The Hague: Martinus Nijhoff, 1972).
H. Schmitz, *Hegel als Denker der Individualität* (Meisenheim/Glan: Verlag Anton Hain, 1957).

1. Wrong age: Harris, page 2, note.
2. Sister's letter: *Dokumente*, pp. 393 – 94; *Berichten*, pp. 15 – 16; trans. Kaufmann, *Hegel*, pp. 299 – 300.
3. *Phenomenology*, p. 477 (6 Aa). See Kaufmann, *Hegel*, pp. 17 – 18, 125 – 27.
4. *Phenomenology*, ibid.
5. Rosenkranz, p. 33.
6. From Hegel's 'Curriculum Vitae' : *Werke*, vol. 2, pp. 582 – 83.
7. Letter to sister of 20 Sept., 1825: Rosenkranz, p. 10; Müller, p. 13.
8. *Hegel's Philosophy of Right*, p. 265 (section 175, addition).
9. Ibid.
10. *Dokumente*, pp. 392 – 94, trans. in Kaufmann, *Hegel*, pp. 299 – 300; also *Berichten*, p. 3.
11. Rosenkranz, p. 6.
12. *Dokumente*, pp. 392 – 94, trans. in Kaufmann, *Hegel*, p. 300.
13. Haym, p. 22, Harris, p. 68.
14. Rosenkranz, p. 13.
15. Ibid., pp. 12 – 15. Harris, pp. 47 – 56.
16. *Dokumente*, pp. 7ff. Rosenkranz pp. 431 – 48.
17. *Dokumente*, pp. 7 – 8, trans, Harris *Hegel's Development*, pp. 7 – 10.
18. *Dokumente*, pp. 23 – 41, trans. Harris *Hegel's Development*, pp. 11 – 13.
19. *Hegel's Philosophy of Mind*, p. 57 (section 396, *Zusatz*).
20. Ibid., p. 60 (same *Zusatz*).
21. Ibid., p. 62 (same *Zusatz*).
22. Ibid., p. 55 (same *Zusatz*).
23. Ibid., p. 63 (same *Zusatz*).
24. See below, with references to Kaufmann, Müller, and Künzli.
25. 'Tübingen Fragment,' from Harris, p. 493 (slightly modified); *Werke*, vol. 1, p. 26.
26. Harris, p. 155.
27. *Dokumente*, p. 394, trans. Harris, *Hegel's Development*, p.258; also *Briefe*, vol. 1, p. 422, note to letter 22.
28. Harris, pp. 156, 258.
29. To Nanette Endel, 2 July, 1797: *Briefe*, vol. 1, p. 56, trans. Harris, *Hegel's Development* p. 264.
30. Diary of July – August, 1796, Rosenkranz, pp. 470ff. and *Dokumente*; trans. in Kaufmann, *Hegel*, pp. 309, 307.

31. To Windischmann, 27 May, 1810: *Briefe*, vol. 1, p. 314; trans. in Kaufmann, *Hegel*, pp. 328 – 29.

32. Harris, p. 265.

33. *Phenomenology*, pp. 251, 252 (4 B3).

34. To his bride, summer, 1811: *Briefe*, vol. 1, p. 368. To Niethammer, 9 June, 1821: *Briefe*, vol. 2, p. 272. To his sister, 12 Aug. 1821: *Briefe*, vol. 2, p. 286.

35. *Berichten*, pp. 497 – 99.

36. *Hegel's Philosophy of Mind*, pp. 136 – 39 (section 408, *Zusatz*).

37. *Hegel's Philosophy of Mind*, p. 92 (section 402, *Zusatz*).

38. Ibid, p. 123 (section 408).

39. Ibid., pp. 126, 128 (section 408, *Zusatz*).

40. Ibid., pp. 133, 134 (section 408, *Zusatz*).

41. To his sister, 9 April, 1814: *Briefe*, vol. 2, pp. 18 – 20; translated in Kaufmann, *Hegel*, p. 339. *Briefe*, vol. 4, p. 233. Hegel to Göriz, June 17, 1820: *Briefe*, vol. 2.

42. *Briefe*, vol. 1, p. 374, note to letter 228, giving the diagnosis made by Karl Schumm.

43. Rosenkranz, pp. 424 – 26.

44. *Briefe*, vol. 2, p. 486, note to letter 395.

45. *Phenomenology*, p. 476 (6 Aa).

46. Rosenkranz, pp. 424 – 26.

47. Ibid., pp. 352 – 60.

48. Künzli, p. 52.

49. Rosenkranz, pp. 361 – 62.

50. Künzli, pp. 52 – 53.

51. Rosenkranz, p. 360.

52. *Briefe*, vol. 4, p. 83.

53. *Briefe*, vol. 2, p. 403.

54. Rosenkranz, p. 360.

55. Ibid., pp. 16 – 17.

56. Heine, *Sämtliche Werke*, vol. 14 (1862), pp. 275 – 82; trans. in Kaufmann, *Hegel*, p. 366.

57. H. G. Hotho, *Vorstudien für Leben und Kunst* (Stuttgart/Tübingen, 1835), pp. 383 – 99; trans. in Kaufmann, *Hegel*, p. 359. Text in *Berichten*, pp. 245 – 56. For another vivid description of Hegel's voice production in lecturing, see *Berichten*, pp. 376 – 77.

58. *Phenomenology*, p. 396 (5 B2b).

59. From 'Differenz des Fichtischen und Schellingischen Systeme der Philosophie,' *Werke*, vol. 2, p. 20; trans. in Kaufmann, *Hegel*, p. 49. See *The Difference* . . . (quoted passages pp. 89, 91) for a complete translation and for introductions explaining the philosophic context.

60. Phenomenology, trans. Kaufmann, *Hegel: Texts,* p. 70 ('Preface,' 3, 3).

61. Hegel, *Sämtliche Werke*, ed. H. Glockner, vol. 1 (Stuttgart: Frommanns Verlag, 1927); in Müller, p. 195.

62. *Jensener Realphilosophie*, ed. J. Hoffmeister (Hamburg: Meiner, 1931); in Schmitz, pp. 62 – 65.

63. Schmitz, pp. 62 – 65.

64. Rosenkranz, p. 259.

65. *Texts*, pp. 91 – 95. Ludwig's letters, together with other documents, are to be found in *Briefe*, vol. 3, pp. 433 – 35, and vol. 4, pp. 121 – 36, 177 – 78. Hegel's side of the matter is unknown to us.

Schopenhauer: pp. 242 – 58

WORKS

Parerga und Paralipomena, ed. J. Frauenstadt, 2nd ed., 2 vols. (Leipzig: Brockhaus, 1916 (originally 1878)); part of *Sämtliche Werke*. The leading edition of Schopenhauer's works, which I have not had available, is now *Sämtliche Werke*, ed. A. Hübscher, 3rd ed. (Wiesbaden, 1972). The same editor has issued a critical edition of Schopenhauer's posthumous manuscripts, the following two volumes of which I have used: *Der handschriftliche Nachlass*, ed. A. Hübscher, vols. 4 – 1, 4 – 2 (Frankfurt am Main: Waldemar Kramer, 1974, 1975).

Essays and Aphorisms, trans. R. J. Hollingdale (Harmondsworth: Penguin Books, 1970).
The Fourfold Root of Sufficient Reason, trans. E. F. J. Payne (La Salle, Ill. : Open Court, 1974).
Parerga and Paralipomena, trans. E. F. J. Payne, 2 vols. (London: Oxford University Press, 1974).
The World as Will and Representation, trans. E. F. J. Payne, 2 vols. (Indian Hills, Col.: Falcon's Wing Press, 1958; reprinted New York: Dover, 1966).

LETTERS AND CONVERSATIONS

Schopenhauers Briefe, ed. E. Grisebach (Leipzig: Reclam, 1898).
Gespräche, ed. A. Hübscher (Stuttgart/Bad Cannstatt: Frommann/Günther Holzborg, 1971).

BIOGRAPHY

W. Abendroth, *Arthur Schopenhauer in Selbstzeugnissen und Bilddokumenten* (Reinbek bei Hamburg: Rowohlt (Rororo), 1967).
[O. Damm, *Arthur Schopenhauer: Eine Biographie* (Berlin: Reclam, 1912).]
W. v. Gwinner, *Schopenhauers Leben*, 3rd ed. (Leipzig: Brockhaus, 1910).
H. H. Houben, *Damals in Weimar! Errinerungen und Briefe von und an Johanna Schopenhauer* (Leipzig: Klinkhardt & Biermann, 1924).
[E. O. Lindner & J. Frauenstadt, *Arthur Schopenhauer* (Berlin, 1863).]
D. Raymond, *Schopenhauer* (Paris: Seuil, 1979).

PSYCHOANALYTIC

E. Hitschmann, 'Schopenhauer: Attempt at the Psychoanalysis of a Philosopher,' in E. Hitschmann, *Great Men* (New York: International Universities Press, 1956), pp. 35 – 125.

GENERAL STUDIES

F. Copelston, *A History of Philosophy*, vol. 8 (London: Burns & Oates, 1963), pp. 261 – 92.
P. Gardiner, *Schopenhauer* (Harmondsworth: Penguin Books, 1967).
A. Hübscher, *Denker gegen den Strom* (Bonn: Bouvier Verlag/Herbert Grundmann, 1973).

A. Rivaud, *Histoire de la Philosophie,* vol. 5, part 2 (Paris: Presses Universitaires, 1968), pp. 680 – 729.

1. Gwinner, pp. 11 – 12.
2. Ibid., p. 13.
3. Ibid., p. 14.
4. Ibid., p. 158.
5. Ibid., pp. 157 – 158.
6. 'Pandectae II,' no. 51, *Nachlass,* vol. 4 ÷ 1, p. 161.
7. Gwinner, p. 158.
8. Ibid., p. 159.
9. Ibid., p. 161.
10. Ibid.
11. *World as Will,* vol. 1, pp. 377 – 78 (section 67).
12. Gwinner, ibid.
13. Ibid.
14. Ibid., p. 48. Hitschmann, p. 43.
15. Gwinner, pp. 51 – 52. Hitschmann, pp. 43 – 44.
16. Gwinner, p. 68.
17. Ibid., p. 62. *Gespräche,* pp. 223 – 24.
18. Gwinner, pp. 75 – 77.
19. Ibid., pp. 85 – 86.
20. For the mother's family life and character, see Gwinner, pp. 8 – 9, 98 – 99 and all of Houben.
21. Gwinner, p. 92.
22. Ibid., p. 28. *Gespräche,* p. 223.
23. *Parerga,* trans. Payne, vol. 2, pp. 260 – 61 (section 131).
24. Gwinner, p. 93.
25. Gwinner, pp. 238 – 41. *Gespräche,* pp. 48 – 49.
26. Gwinner, p. 394. Hitschmann, p. 90.
27. Gwinner, p. 255.
28. Gwinner, p. 257.
29. 'Eis Heauton,' no. 22, *Nachlass,* vol. 4 – 2, pp. 116 – 17.
30. Ibid., p. 100, note 25.
31. Gwinner, p. 146.
32. Letter of 1807: Hitschmann, p. 47.
33. Gwinner, p. 59.
34. *Nachlass,* vol. 4 – 2, pp. 292 – 93. The passage is 'reconstructed' in the first person on pp. 121 – 22 of this volume of the *Nachlass.*
35. Gwinner, pp. 249 – 50.
36. Ibid., p. 250.
37. Ibid., p. 324.
38. *World as Will,* vol. 1, pp. 398 – 402 (section 69).
39. *Gespräche,* pp. 359 – 60.
40. Gwinner, p. 27.
41. *World as Will,* vol. 1, p. 191 (section 36).
42. Ibid., p. 193 (section 36). See vol. 2, pp. 400 – 401 (chap. 32).
43. Ibid., vol. 2, pp. 517 – 19, 521 – 23 (chap. 43).
44. Ibid., p. 517.
45. Ibid., pp. 523 – 24.

46. Ibid. (Orestes and Hamlet, pp. 521 – 22). *Gespräche*, pp. 129 – 30.
47. *Gespräche*, pp. 129 – 30 (Lindner & Frauenstadt, p. 204).
48. *World as Will*, vol. 2, p. 533 (chap. 44).
49. Ibid., vol. 1, p. 330 (section 60).
50. Hitschmann, pp. 50 – 51 (from O. Damm).
51. *Gespräche*, pp. 167, 115, 215, 220; and Hübscher, *Denker*, pp. 286 – 91.
52. Gwinner pp. 328 – 29. See also pp. 41, 59 – 60.
53. *World as Will*, vol. 1, pp. 255 – 67 (section 52). See vol. 2, pp. 445 – 47 (chap. 39).
54. Ibid., vol. 1, p. 186 (section 36).
55. Ibid., p. 190. See *Parerga*, ed. Frauenstadt, vol. 1, pp. 361 – 62 ('Von Dem was Einer ist').
56. *World as Will*, vol. 1, p. 190.
57. Ibid., p. 186 (section 36). On his theory of genius and its possible origins, see Hübscher, *Denker*, chap. 4.
58. *World as Will*, vol. 2, p. 463 (chap. 41).
59. Ibid., p. 507 (chap. 41).
60. Ibid.
61. Ibid., vol. 1, p. 314 (section 57).
62. Ibid., vol. 1, pp. 411 – 12 (section 71).
63. Gwinner, p. 11.
64. *Gespräche*, p. 131 (Lindner & Frauenstadt, p. 306).
65. *World as Will*, vol. 2, pp. 394 – 95 (chap. 31).
66. Gwinner, p. 11.
67. 'Senilia,' no. 25, *Nachlass*, vol. 4 – 2, pp. 8 – 9.
68. *Gespräche*, pp. 100 (Lindner & Frauenstadt, p. 170), 373.
69. *Parerga*, trans. Payne, vol. 2, p. 296 (section 153).
70. *Gespräche*, pp. 382, 170.
71. Ibid., p. 168 (Lindner & Frauenstadt, p. 9).
72. 'Senilia,' no. 102, *Nachlass*, vol. 4 – 2, p. 34.
73. *Parerga*, trans. Payne, vol. 1, p. 131 (section 14); ed. Frauenstadt, vol. 1, pp. 142 – 43.
74. 'Senilia,' no. 21, *Nachlass*, vol. 4 – 2, p. 8.
75. *Gespräche*, p. 324.
76. To the author of Damiron's Analysis, 21 Dec., 1829: *Briefe*, p. 55; Gwinner, p. 212.
77. Ibid.: *Briefe*, pp. 55 – 56; Gwinner, p. 212.
78. *Parerga*, trans. Payne, vol. 1, p. 135 (section 14); ed. Frauenstadt, vol. 1, pp. 146 – 47.
79. *Gespräche*, p. 326.
80. To the author of Damiron's Analysis: *Briefe*, p. 56; Gwinner, p. 213.
81. On this and on the subsequent controversy, in which Gwinner was charged with having plagiarized the notebook before its destruction, see *Nachlass*, vol. 4 – 2, pp. 288 – 93.
82. *Parerga*, trans. Payne, vol. 2, p. 615 (section 634); ed. Frauenstadt, vol. 2, p. 650.
83. *Parerga*, trans. Payne, vol. 2, p. 619 (section 369); ed. Frauenstadt, vol. 2 (section 382). *Gespräche*, p. 358.
84. Gwinner, p. 105.
85. To A. von Doss, 1 March, 1860: *Briefe*, p. 384.

86. *Gespräche*, pp. 350 – 51.
87. Ibid., p. 133 (Lindner & Frauenstadt, p. 270).
88. *Gespräche*, p. 133 (Lindner & Frauenstadt, p. 357). Hitschmann, pp. 56 – 57 (from O. Damm).
89. Raymond, pp. 46 – 52, from the *Jahrbuch der Schopenhauer-Gesellschaft*, vols. 55, 58. See also *Gespräche*, pp. 49 – 50, 193.
90. *Gespräche*, p. 133 (Lindner & Frauenstadt, p. 357).
91. *Gespräche*, pp. 151–52.
92. Gwinner, pp. 206 – 207, and note p. 207.

NOTES TO CHAPTER EIGHT

Mill: pp. 260 – 71

WORKS

The Philosophy of John Stuart Mill, ed. M. Cohen (New York: Random House (Modern Library), 1961).

Essays on Ethics, Religion and Society, ed. J. M. Robson, *Collected Works of John Stuart Mill*, vol. 10 (Toronto/London: University of Toronto Press/Routledge & Kegan Paul, 1969).

A System of Logic, 10th ed., 2 vols. (London: Longmans, Green & Co., 1897).

AUTOBIOGRAPHY

Autobiography, ed. J. Stillinger (London: Oxford University Press, 1971).

BIOGRAPHY

A. Bain, James Mill (London, 1882; reprinted New York: Augustus M. Kelley, 1966).
F. A. Hayek, *John Stuart Mill and Harriet Taylor* (London: 1951; reprinted New York: A. M. Kelley, no date).
B. Mazlish, *James and John Stuart Mill* (New York: Basic Books, 1975).
M. St. John Packe, *The Life of John Stuart Mill* (London: Secker & Warburg, 1954).

GENERAL STUDIES

K. Britton, *John Stuart Mill* (Harmondsworth: Penguin Books, 1953).
G. Himmelfarb, 'Introduction,' J. S. Mill, *On Liberty* (Harmondsworth: Penguin Books, 1974).
D. H. Munro, 'James Mill,' in the *Encyclopedia of Philosophy*, ed. P. Edwards.
J. C. Rees, 'Mill, John Stuart: Political Contributions,' in the *International Encyclopedia of the Social Sciences*, ed. D. L. Sills (New York: Macmillan/The Free Press, 1968).
J. M. Robson, *The Improvement of Mankind: The Social and Political Thought of John*

Stuart Mill (Toronto/London: University of Toronto Press/Routledge & Kegan Paul, 1968).

J. B. Schneewind, 'John Stuart Mill,' in the *Encyclopedia of Philosophy*, ed. P. Edwards.

1. Bain, p. 59.
2. Hayek, p. 286, note 28.
3. Mazlish, p. 315.
4. Packe, p. 76.
5. Bain, pp. 5, 9.
6. Bain, pp. 5, 9.
7. Bain, pp. 162, 334.
8. Mazlish, p. 66.
9. Ibid., pp. 71 – 72, 132. Packe, p. 16.
10. *Autobiography*, pp. 6, 9 (chap. 1).
11. Ibid., pp. 19 – 20 (chap. 1).
12. Ibid., p. 20 (chap. 1).
13. Ibid., p. 33, note 3, from early draft (chap. 2).
14. Ibid., pp. 32; 33, note 3.
15. Ibid., p. 33, note 3.
16. Ibid., p. 24, note 12, from early draft (chap. 1).
17. Packe, pp. 39 – 46.
18. Mazlish, pp. 201 – 202. Packe, pp. 66 – 68.
19. *Autobiography*, pp. 83 – 84 (chap. 5).
20. Ibid., p. 85 (chap. 5).
21. Ibid., pp. 86 – 87, 88, 89 (chap. 5).
22. *Autobiography*, pp. xii – xiv. Mazlish, pp. 259, 317 – 25, 438 – 39 (note 26).
23. Packe, pp. 108 – 11, 128 – 31, 348 – 56. Mazlish, pp. 282, 290, 314 – 17.
24. Hayek, p. 173.
25. Packe, pp. 205 (reaction to father's death), 356 (reaction to mother's death), 397 – 413 (reaction to Harriet's death). Mazlish, pp. 317, 324.
26. Packe, pp. 411 – 12.
27. Himmelfarb, p. 24. See also G. Himmelfarb, *On Liberty and Liberalism: The Case of John Stuart Mill* (New York: Knopf, 1975).
28. Stillinger, introduction to *Autobiography*, p. xix.
29. *Autobiography*, pp. 112 – 13 (chap. 6).
30. Robson, pp. 62 – 64. Mazlish, pp. 284 – 86. Packe, p. 130 (quoted).
31. Packe, pp. 313 – 14, 369 – 71. Robson, pp. 53 – 62 (59 quoted), 67 – 68.
32. Himmelfarb, pp. 27ff.
33. *Autobiography*, pp. 149 – 50 (chap. 7).
34. 'Bentham,' *Essays on Ethics* . . . , pp. 92 – 93, 95; in *The Philosophy of John Stuart Mill*, pp. 23 – 24, 26.
35. Robson, pp. 44 – 45.
36. 'Bentham,' in *Essays on Ethics* . . . , pp. 100, 93; *The Philosophy of John Stuart Mill*, pp. 33, 24.
37. Robson, p. 117 (quoted); 48 – 49, note 58. Packe, pp. 81, 90.
38. *Autobiography*, p. 101 (chap 5).
39. Ibid., p. 102 (chap. 5).
40. *System of Logic*, vol. 2, p. 427.
41. Ibid., p. 483.

42. 'Utilitarianism,' in *Essays on Ethics* . . . , p. 212; *The Philosophy of John Stuart Mill*, pp. 332 – 33.
43. 'On Liberty,' ibid., p. 260 (chap. 3).
44. 'On Liberty,' ibid., p. 281 (chap. 4).
45. 'On Liberty,' ibid., p. 187 (chap. 1, 'Introductory').
46. 'On Liberty,' ibid., p. 191 (chap. 1, 'Introductory').
47. Ibid., p. 197.
48. Robson, p. 193.
49. *Autobiography*, p. 159.
50. 'Grote's Plato,' in Robson, p. 191.
51. 'Bentham,' in *Essays on Ethics* . . . , p. 94; *The Philosophy of John Stuart Mill*, p. 25.
52. Robson, p. 192.
53. Entry of 26 March, 1854, in Mazlish, p. 328.
54. Mazlish, p. 300.
55. Ibid., pp. 300 – 302.
56. Ibid., p. 314.

Kierkegaard: pp. 271 – 76

WORKS

Concluding Unscientific Postscript, trans. D. F. Swenson & W. Lowrie (Princeton: Princeton University Press, 1944).
The Point of View for My Work as an Author, trans. W. Lowrie (New York: Harper & Row, 1962).

JOURNALS

The Last Years: Journals 1853 — 55, trans. R. G. Smith (London: Fontana, 1968).
The Journals of Søren Kierkegaard, trans. A. Dru (London: Oxford University Press, 1938).
[*Søren Kierkegaard's Journals and Papers*, trans. H. V. Hong & E. H. Hong, 7 vols. (Bloomington: Indiana University Press, 1967 – 1978), translated from *Søren Kierkegaards Papirer*.] At a late stage of my work I made use of vols. 5 and 6, which are autobiographical.

BIOGRAPHY

R. Grimsley, *Kierkegaard: A Biographical Introduction* (London: Studio Vista, 1973).
W. Lowrie, *A Short Life of Kierkegaard* (Princeton: Princeton University Press, 1944).

GENERAL STUDY

G. Malantschuk, *Kierkegaard's Thought* (Princeton: Princeton University Press, 1971).

SPECIAL STUDIES

S. Crites, 'Pseudonymous Authorship as Art and As Act,' in J. Thompson, ed., *Kierkegaard: A Collection of Critical Essays* (Garden City: Doubleday (Anchor Books), 1972).
J. Thompson, 'The Master of Irony,' in J. Thompson, ed., op. cit.

1. Lowrie, *Short Life*, p. 24.
2. Ibid., pp. 25 – 26.
3. Ibid., p. 25.
4. Ibid., p. 45.
5. Ibid., pp. 47 – 48.
6. Ibid., pp. 40 – 41.
7. *Point of View*, p. 76.
8. *Journals*, trans. Dru, entries 548 – 49, 670, 1288.
9. Ibid., entry 600.
10. Ibid.
11. Grimsley, pp. 53 – 55.
12. Lowrie, *Short Life*, pp. 65 – 66.
13. Malantschuk, pp. 37 – 38, from *Journals and Papers*, vol. 2, entry 1185 (*Papierer*, vol. 2, entry A 605). *Papierer*, vol. 2, entry A 603.
14. Grimsley, pp. 73 – 74. Malantschuk, pp. 44, 58 – 66, and 'Hegel' in index. *Concluding Unscientific Postscript*, p. 107.
15. *Concluding Unscientific Postscript*, p. 34, note.
16. Ibid., p. 271.
17. Lowrie, *Short Life*, pp. 108 – 109, 115 – 17.
18. Malantschuk, pp. 174 – 75. Lowrie, pp. 118 – 20.
19. Lowrie, p. 120.
20. Malantschuk, pp. 174 – 78.
21. Malantschuk, p. 13, from *Papierer*, vol. 4, B 1, p. 109.
22. Malantschuk, pp. 26 – 27, 31 – 32, from *Papierer*, vol. 5, entry B 147, and from *Stages on Life's Way*, trans. W. Lowrie (Princeton: Princeton University Press, 1940) p. 405.
23. Thompson. Crites. Malantschuk, p. 31.
24. Lowrie, pp. 201 – 209 (205 quoted).
25. *Point of View*, pp. 64 – 65.
26. Lowrie, *Short Life*, pp. 227 – 52 (p. 245 quoted)
27. *The Last Years*, p. 25, from *Papierer*, vol. 11 – 1, entry A 1.
28. Ibid., pp. 66 – 67, from *Papierer*, vol. 11 – 1, entry A 136. Lowrie, *Short Life*, pp. 27 – 28.
29. *The Last Years*, pp. 367 – 68, from *Papierer*, vol. 11, entry 3A 439.
30. Ibid., p. 104, from *Papierer*, vol. 11 – 1, entry A 256.

James: pp. 276 – 85

WORKS

Essays in Radical Empiricism (New York: Longmans, Green & Co., 1912).
A Pluralistic Universe (New York: Longmans, Green & Co., 1907).
Pragmatism (New York: Longmans, Green & Co., 1909).

BIOGRAPHY

G. W. Allen, *William James: A Biography* (New York: Viking, 1967).
F. O. Matthiessen, *The James Family* (New York: Knopf, 1947).
R. B. Perry, *The Thought and Character of William James, Briefer Version* (Cambridge, Mass.: Harvard University Press, 1948).
G. Santayana, *The Middle Span* (New York: Scribners, 1945).

GENERAL STUDY

H. S. Thayer, *Meaning and Action: A Critical History of Pragmatism* (Indianapolis/New York: Bobbs-Merrill, 1968).

SPECIAL STUDY

R. A. Hocks, *Henry James and Pragmatistic Thought: A Study in the Relationship between the Philosophy of William James and the Literary Art of Henry James* (Chapel Hill: University of North Carolina Press, 1974).

1. Matthiessen, p. 18.
2. Ibid., pp. 20 – 21.
3. Ibid., pp. 22 – 23.
4. Ibid., p. 37.
5. Ibid., p. 29.
6. Ibid., p. 169.
7. Allen, pp. 6 – 7.
8. Ibid., pp. 8 – 9.
9. Ibid., p. 17.
10. Matthiessen, pp. 161 – 66.
11. Allen, p. 10.
12. Perry, p. 3 (from a notebook of Emerson).
13. Allen, p. 21.
14. Ibid., p. 28.
15. Matthiessen, p. 69.
16. Allen, p. 53. For education see also Matthiessen, pp. 69 – 100.
17. Allen, p. 41.
18. Ibid., pp. 59 – 60.
19. Ibid., pp. 61 – 63.
20. Ibid., pp. 70 – 71.
21. Ibid., p. 94.
22. Ibid., p. 96.
23. Ibid., pp. 124, 122.
24. Ibid., p. 125.
25. Ibid., p. 128.
26. Ibid., p. 134.
27. Ibid., p. 138.
28. Ibid., p. 146.
29. Ibid., p. 149.
30. Ibid., pp. 150, 154.
31. Ibid., p. 163.

32. Ibid., p. 164.
33. Ibid., pp. 166 – 67.
34. Ibid., pp. 168 – 69.
35. Matthiessen, p. 127.
36. Ibid., p. 128.
37. Ibid., pp. 129 – 32. Allen, pp. 253 – 57.
38. Allen, p. 257.
39. Ibid., p. 254.
40. Perry, pp. 31 – 41. Matthiessen, pp. 184 – 87. Allen, p. xi.
41. Perry, p. 33.
42. Matthiessen, p. 139.
43. Perry, p. 386.
44. Perry, p. 295, presumably from *Pragmatism*. I have not succeeded in locating this quotation.
45. Perry, pp. 253 – 54.
46. Allen, p. 500.
47. *Pragmatism*, p. 69.
48. *A Pluralistic Universe*, pp. 309 – 311. See also pp. 28 – 31, 299.
49. *Essays in Radical Empiricism*, p. 78.
50. Matthiessen, p. 589.
51. Santayana, p. 166.
52. Matthiessen, pp. 317, 345. Hocks, p. 19.
53. Matthiessen, pp. 341 – 42. Hocks, pp. 20 – 22.
54. Matthiessen, p. 343. Hocks, p. 23.
55. Matthiessen, p. 344.
56. Ibid.
57. Ibid., p. 345.
58. Hocks, p. 3, from L. Edel, *Henry James, The Master: 1901–1916* (New York: Lippincott, 1972), p. 298.
59. Hocks, p. 3. J. Barzun, in the *New York Times Book Review* (6 April, 1972), p. 36. See the continuation of the exchange in the *Times Literary Supplement* (fall, 1972).
60. Hocks, p. 15, from Edel, op. cit., p. 295.
61. Hocks, pp. 87, 89.
62. Matthiessen, pp. 591 – 94. Hocks, p. 215.
63. Matthiessen, pp. 587ff. Hocks, pp. 215 – 38.
64. Allen, pp. 214 – 20.
65. Ibid., pp. 33 – 40. Matthiessen, pp. 272 – 85.
66. Allen, p. xii.

Nietzsche: pp. 285 – 97

WORKS

Werke in drei Bänden, ed. K. Schlechta, 6th ed. (Munich: Hanser Verlag, 1969).
Werke, Kritische Gesamtausgabe, ed. G. Colli & M. Montinari (Berlin: De Gruyter, 1967ff.). Of this edition, much of which is identical with earlier ones, I have used primarily *Ecce Homo*, which is contained in vol. 6 – 3 (1969), and two volumes of fragments, which contain much of the material assembled in *The*

Will to Power. These two are: *Nachgelassene Fragmente: Herbst 1887 bis März 1888* (1970), and *Nachgelassene Fragmente: Anfang 1888 bis Anfang Januar 1889 (1972)*.

Basic Writings of Nietzsche, trans. W. Kaufmann (New York: Random House (Modern Library), 1968).
The Gay Science, trans. W. Kaufmann (New York: Random House (Vintage Books), 1974).
The Portable Nietzsche, trans. W. Kaufmann (New York: Viking, 1954).
The Will to Power, trans. W. Kaufmann (London: Weidenfeld & Nicolson, 1968).

LETTERS

I have most usually used the letters in Schlechta's edition, listed above, but also the following:
Nietzsche in seinen Briefen und Berichten der Zeigenossen, ed. A. Baeumler (Leipzig: Kröner, 1932).
Nietzsche: Briefwechsel, Kritische Gesamtausgabe, ed. G. Colli & M. Montinari, vols. 1 – 1. 1 – 2, 1 – 3, 2 – 1, 2 – 2 (Berlin; De Gruyter, 1975–1977).
Selected Letters of Friedrich Nietzsche, trans. C. Middleton (Chicago: Chicago University Press, 1969).
Nietzsche: A Self-Portrait from His Letters, trans. P. Fuss & H. Shapiro (Cambridge, Mass.: Harvard University Press, 1971).
Friedrich Nietzsche, Paul Rée, Lou von Salomé: Die Dokumente ihrer Begegnung, ed. E. Pfeiffer (Frankfurt am Main: Insel, 1970).

BIOGRAPHY

L. Andreas-Salomé, *Lebensrückblicke* (Frankfurt am Main: Insel, 1968).
G. Bianquis, *Nietzsche devant ses contemporains* (Monaco: Editions du Rocher, 1959).
R. Binyon, *Frau Lou* (Princeton: Princeton University Press, 1968).
R. Blunck, *Friedrich Nietzsche: Kindheit und Jugend* (Munich/Basel: Ernst Reinhardt, 1953).
E. Förster-Nietzsche, *Der junge Nietzsche* (Stuttgart: Kröner, 1912).
R. J. Hollingdale, *Nietzsche: The Man and His Personality* (London: Routledge & Kegan Paul, 1965).

GENERAL STUDIES

R. J. Hollingdale, *Nietzsche* (London: Routledge & Kegan Paul, 1973).
K. Jaspers, *Nietzsche* (Chicago: Henry Regnery, 1965).
W. Kaufmann, *Nietzsche*, 4th ed. (Princeton: Princeton University Press, 1974).
S. Kofman, *Nietzsche et la métaphore* (Paris: Payot, 1972).

SPECIAL STUDIES

Nietzsche aujourd'hui?, 2 vols. (Paris: Union Générale d'Editions (10/18), 1973).
K. Schlechta & A. Anders, *Friedrich Nietzsche: Von den verborgenen Anfängen seines Philosophierens* (Stuttgart/Bad Cannstatt: Frommann (Günther Holzboog), 1962).

1. Mother and father: Blunck, pp. 22 – 30.
2. *Werke*, ed. Schlechta, vol. 3, p. 13.
3. Förster-Nietzsche, p. 9.
4. Ibid., p. 18.
5. Ibid.
6. Ibid., pp. 17 – 18.
7. *Menschliches, Allzumenschliches*, aphorism 379, *Werke*, ed. Schlechta, vol. 1, p. 647.
8. Blunck, p. 32.
9. Ibid., pp. 34 – 36.
10. Ibid., p. 47.
11. Ibid., pp. 36 – 38. Bianquis, pp. 24, 25 (from E. Förster-Nietzsche, *Der junge Nietzsche* (Leipzig: Kröner, 1912)), pp. 28, 36.
12. C. von Gersdorff to P. Gast, 14 Sept., 1900: Blunck, p. 73. Bianquis, p. 32, attributes the letter to P. Deussen, *Errinerungen an Friedrich Nietzsche* (Leipzig: Brockhaus, 1901), p. 14.
13. Kelterborn, cited in Bianquis, p. 221.
14. Letter to his mother, 27 April, 1863, in Blunck, p. 91.
15. *Werke*, ed. Schlechta, vol. 3, pp. 13, 39, 90, 107, 117, 149 – 53.
16. Ibid., pp. 14, 15 – 16.
17. Ibid., p. 16.
18. Ibid., p. 17.
19. Ibid., p. 18.
20. Ibid., pp. 18 – 19.
21. Ibid., p. 117. See also pp. 105 – 106.
22. Ibid., pp. 117 – 18. See also p. 149.
23. Ibid., p. 151.
24. Ibid., p. 148. Blunck, pp. 217 – 19.
25. *Werke*, ed. Schlechta, vol. 3, p. 151.
26. To G. Krug & W. Pinder, April 27, 1862: *Briefwechsel*, vol. 1 – 1, p. 202.
27. Förster-Nietzsche, pp. 152 – 55.
28. Blunck, pp. 116 – 20. Förster-Nietzsche, pp. 48 – 49.
29. Förster-Nietzsche, pp. 155 – 57.
30. To C. Gersdorff, 18 Sept., 1897: *Briefwechsel*, vol. 2 – 1, pp. 226 – 27; ed. Schlechta, *Werke*, vol. 3, p. 1045.
31. Blunck, pp. 155 – 60. Schlechta & Anders, pp. 50 – 59.
32. Förster-Nietzsche, pp. 212, 223.
33. See, e.g., letter to E. Rohde, 11 (?) April, 1872: *Werke*, ed. Schlechta, vol. 3, pp. 1063 – 64.
34. To C. Gersdorff, Aug. 4, 1869: *Briefwechsel*, vol. 2 – 1, p. 36; *Werke*, ed. Schlechta, vol. 3. p. 1013
35. To E. Rohde, 25 Oct., 1872: *Werke*, ed. Schlechta, vol. 3, p. 1075.
36. *The Case of Wagner*, in Kaufmann, *Basic Writings*. R. W. Gutman, *Richard Wagner* (Harmondsworth: Penguin Books, 1971), pp. 444 – 51, 496 – 509, 604 – 612. See Gutman, p. 507, who explains that Nietzsche may have been angry at Wagner because of Wagner's suggestion to Nietzsche's doctor that Nietzsche was suffering from excessive masturbation.
37. Health in earlier years: Blunck, pp. 48, 101 – 104. Later years, e.g., *Werke*, ed. Colli & Montinari, vol. 4 – 4, *Nachbericht zur vierten Abteilung* (1969), pp. 73, 90. For a compact summary of earlier studies, see W. Lange-Eichbaum & W. Kurth, *Genie, Irrsinn und Ruhm*, 6th ed. (Munich: Ernst Reinhardt Verlag, 1967),

pp. 485 – 92. For a brief survey, see Kaufmann, *Nietzsche,* pp. 69 – 71, and for a longer one, Jaspers, *Nietzsche,* pp. 88 – 115.

38. *The Merck Manual,* 12th ed. (Rahway, N.J.: Merck Sharp & Dohme, 1972), p. 1014. See also 13th ed. (1977), p. 1762.

39. P Deussen, *Errinerungen an Friedrich Nietzsche* (Leipzig: Brockhaus, 1901), pp. 91 – 93.

40. To Wagner, 27 Sept., 1876: *Werke,* ed. Schlechta, vol. 3, p. 1127.

41. To O. Eiser, an eye specialist, Jan., 1880: *Werke,* ed. Schlechta, vol. 3, p. 1162. Nietzsche's correspondence is said to show that he consulted more than thirty doctors and physiologists.

42. To F. Overbeck, 5 Aug., 1886: *Werke,* ed. Schlechta, vol. 3, p. 1242.

43. *Ecce Homo,* 'Why I Am So Wise,' section 8: *Basic Writings,* p. 690.

44. *Werke,* ed. Schlechta, vol. 3, p. 38.

45. Lou Salomé said, 'He sought God in the most diverse forms of self-divinization': Binyon, p. 149, from Lou Salomé's *Friedrich Nietzsche in seinen Werken* (Vienna, 1894), p. 39.

46. To F. Overbeck, 25 June, 1881: *Werke,* ed. Schlechta, vol. 3, p. 1169.

47. *Zarathustra,* book 1, section 21, *Portable Nietzsche,* p. 185.

48. *Ecce Homo,* 'Why I Am So Clever,' section 3, *Basic Writings,* p. 699.

49. Ibid., section 2. *Basic Writings,* p. 697. *Genealogy of Morals,* 'Preface,' section 5, *Basic Writings,* p. 455.

50. *Menschliches, Allzumenschliches,* 7, aphorism 381, *Werke,* ed. Schlecta, vol. 1, p. 647.

51. Ibid., aphorism 381.

52. Ibid., aphorism 386, *Werke,* ed. Schlechta, vol. 1, p. 648.

53. *The Gay Science,* p. 83 (book 1, section 9).

54. *Zarathustra,* book 2, 'On the Tarantulas,' *Portable Nietzsche,* p. 212.

55. *The Gay Science,* p. 210 (book 3, section 216).

56. *Zarathustra,* book 2, 'On Priests,' *Portable Nietzsche,* p. 203.

57. Ibid., *Portable Nietzsche,* p. 204.

58. *Genealogy of Morals,* 3rd essay, section 15, *Basic Writings,* p. 562.

59. *The Antichrist,* book 1, section 10, *Portabl*⋅ *Nietzsche,* p. 576.

60. *Will to Power,* p. 89 (book 2, section 139). *Werke,* ed. Colli & Montinari, *Fragments 1888–1889,* p. 168 (14 [189]), differently punctuated.

61. *Ecce Homo,* 'Why I Am a Destiny,' section 7, *Basic Writings,* p. 788.

62. Ibid., section 8, *Basic Writings,* pp. 790 – 91.

63. Ibid., 'Why I Am So Wise,' section 2, *Basic Writings,* p. 678.

64. Ibid., section 2, *Basic Writings,* p. 680.

65. Ibid., section 3, *Basic Writings,* p. 682.

66. Ibid., section 4, *Basic Writings,* p. 683.

67. Ibid., section 5, *Basic Writings,* p. 687.

68. Ibid., 'Why I Am So Clever,' section 2, *Basic Writings,* p. 697.

69. Ibid., 'Human All-too-Human,' section 4, *Basic Writings,* p. 743.

70. *Will to Power,* p. 290 (book 3, section 533). *Werke,* ed. Colli & Montinari, *Fragmente 1887–1888,* p. 51 (9[91]). The connection and therefore the contextual meaning of the paragraphs is different here, the section above, number 533, following the section numbered 552 in *The Will to Power.* Section 533 is, we see, part of an attack on determinism and Kantianism (the notion of the 'thing-in-itself'). Truth, says Nietzsche, is not there to be discovered, but is actively *created.*

71. To F. Overbeck, shortly before mid-September, 1882: Pfeiffer, p. 229. For

his desire that Lou inherit him see the letter of about mid-July, 1882, to Malwida von Meysenbug (Pfeiffer, p. 157).

72. Elisabeth to P. Gast, Feb. 10, 1883: Pfeiffer, p. 229; Binion, pp. 103 – 104. See *Werke*, ed. Schlechta, vol. 3, pp. 1372 – 73.

73. To F. Overbeck, rec. 11 Feb., 1883: Pfeiffer, p. 299; *Werke*, ed. Schlechta, vol. 3, p. 1200.

74. Feb., 1884: Pfeiffer, p. 351.

75. Suicidal urge: e.g., letter to L. Salomé and P. Rée, mid-Dec., 1882: Pfeiffer, pp. 269 – 70; *Werke*, ed. Schlechta, vol. 3, pp. 1196 – 97. 'Step by step': to F. Overbeck, rec. 28 Aug., 1883: Pfeiffer, p. 344; *Werke*, ed. Schlechta, vol 3, p. 1213.

76. *Zarathustra*, book 1, 'On Chastity,' *Portable Nietzsche*, p. 167.

77. *Beyond Good and Evil*, first words of preface, *Basic Writings*, p. 192.

78 Baeumler, from K. Strecker, *Nietzsche und Strindberg* (1921), p. 41f.

79. Bianquis, pp. 133 – 34, from P. Deussen, *Errinerungen an Friedrich Nietzsche*, pp. 91 – 93.

80. To Seidlitz, 12 Feb., 1888: *Werke*, ed. Schlechta, vol. 3, p. 1276.

81. Kaufmann, *Nietzsche*, pp. 455 – 57, summarizes the situation and translates the passage. For the German see *Werke*, ed. Colli & Montinari, *Ecce Homo*, pp. 265 – 66 ('Warum ich so weise bin,' section 3).

82. F. Overbeck to P. Gast, Jan. 15, 1889: *Selected Letters*, trans. Middleton, p. 353.

83. Hollingdale, 1965, p. 295, from E. F. Podach, *Der Kranke Nietzsche* (Vienna: Bermann-Fischer, 1937), p. 141.

84. *Selected Letters*, p. 355. See Bianquis, pp. 167, 171 – 72, 178 – 79, from Podach, op. cit., pp. 46, 29, 220 – 21, 233, 67.

85. *Werke*, ed. Colli & Montinari, *Fragmente 1888–1889*, p. 284 (16 [*24*] dated spring – summer, 1888).

Santayana: pp. 297 – 303

WORKS

Selected Critical Writings of George Santayana, ed. N. Henfrey, 2 vols (London: Cambridge University Press, 1968).
Poems (New York: Scribners, 1923).
Realms of Being, one-vol. ed. (New York: Scribners, 1942).
Scepticism and Animal Faith (New York: Scribners, 1923).
Soliloquies in England and Later Soliloquies (New York: Scribners, 1922).

AUTOBIOGRAPHY

Persons and Places: The Background of My Life (New York: Scribners, 1944).
The Middle Span (Persons and Places, vol. 2) (New York: Scribners, 1945).
My Host the World (Persons and Places, vol. 3) (New York: Scribners, 1945).
'A General Confession' and 'Apologia Pro Mente Sua,' in *The Philosophy of George Santayana* (See below).
'The Idler and His Works,' *The Saturday Review* (15 May, 1954). [Reprinted in *The Idler and His Works and Other Essays*, ed. D. Corey (New York: Braziller, 1957).]

PORTRAIT

B. Russell, *Portraits from Memory* (New York: Simon & Schuster, 1956). Russell's hostile portrait of Santayana is to be compared with Santayana's hostile portrait of Russell in *My Host the World*, pp. 26 – 31.

GENERAL STUDY

W. E. Arnett, *George Santayana* (New York: Washington Square Press, 1968).

SPECIAL STUDIES

The Philosophy of George Santayana, ed. P. A. Schilpp (Evanston/Chicago: Northwestern University (The Library of Living Philosophers), 1940.

1. *Persons and Places*, pp. 30 – 45.
2. Ibid., pp. 44, 46.
3. Ibid., p. 14.
4. 'A General Confession,' *The Philosophy of George Santayana*, p. 5.
5. Ibid.
6. *Persons and Places*, pp. 14 – 16.
7. Ibid., p. 23. *My Host the World*, p. 134. 'A General Confession,' pp. 10, 4.
8. 'A General Confession,' p. 4.
9. 'Apologia,' *The Philosophy of George Santayana*, p. 602.
10. 'A General Confession,' p. 4. *Persons and Places*, p. 17.
11. *Persons and Places*, p. 28.
12. 'A General Confession,' p. 6.
13. *Persons and Places*, pp. 7 – 8.
14. Ibid., pp. 120 – 21.
15. Ibid., p. 119.
16. Ibid., p. 9.
17. Ibid., p. 75.
18. Ibid., pp. 78, 84, 85, 88.
19. Ibid., pp. 87 – 89.
20. Ibid., p. 88. *My Host the World*, p. 10.
21. *My Host the World*, p. 10.
22. *The Middle Span*, p. 109. 'To W. P.,' *Poems*.
23. *My Host the World*, p. 8.
24. *The Middle Span*, p. 109. *My Host the World*, pp. 13, 14.
25. *My Host the World*, p. 7.
26. Ibid., p. 7.
27. 'Apologia,' p. 602.
28. *My Host the World*, pp. 134 – 35.
29. Ibid., p. 135.
30. 'A General Confession,' p. 10.
31. *Scepticism and Animal Faith*, pp. 61, 72 – 73.
32. *My Host the World*, p. 13.
33. Indian philosopher: *Realms of Being*, pp. 168 – 80. Plato: 'Apologia,' pp. 542 – 49. Spinoza: *Realms of Being*, pp. 160 – 62; *Persons and Places*, pp. 244 – 45. 'The One or the Absolute': *Realms of Being*, p. 739.

34. 'The Idler and His Works,' p. 9.
35. 'Apologia,' p. 500.
36. *Realms of Being*, pp. 727 – 28.
37. 'The Idler and His Works,' *The Saturday Review* 15 May, 1954) p. 7
38. Ibid., p. 50.

Russell: pp. 303 – 18

WORKS

The Basic Writings of Bertrand Russell, ed. R. E. Egner & L. E. Denonn (New York: Simon & Schuster, 1967).
The Collected Stories of Bertrand Russell, ed. B. Feinberg (New York: Simon & Schuster, 1972).
Human Knowledge: Its Scope and Limits (New York: Simon & Schuster, 1948).
Russell's Logical Atomism, ed. D. Pears (London: Fontana/Collins, 1972).
Selected Papers of Bertrand Russell (New York: Random House (Modern Library), 1927).

AUTOBIOGRAPHY

The Autobiography of Bertrand Russell: 1872–1914 (London: Allen & Unwin, 1967).
The Autobiography of Bertrand Russell: 1914–1944 (London: Allen & Unwin, 1968).
The Autobiography of Bertrand Russell: 1944–1967 (London: Allen & Unwin, 1969).
'My Mental Development,' in *The Philosophy of Bertrand Russell*, ed. P. A. Schilpp (Evanston/Chicago: The Library of Living Philosophers, 1944).
My Philosophical Development (London: Allen & Unwin, 1959).
Portraits from Memory (New York: Simon & Schuster, 1956).

BIOGRAPHY

R. W. Clark, *The Life of Bertrand Russell* (New York: Harcourt Brace Jovanovich, 1975).
R. Crayshaw-Williams, *Russell Remembered* (London: Oxford University Press, 1970).
C. Malleson, 'Fifty Years: 1916–1966,' in *Bertrand Russell: Philosopher of the Century* (see below).
Ottoline at Garsington: Memoirs of Lady Ottoline Morrell 1915–1918, ed. R. Gathorne-Hardy (London: Faber & Faber, 1974).
M. L. Ross, 'The Mythology of Friendship: D. H. Lawrence, Bertrand Russell, and The Blind Man,' in S. P. Rosenbaum, ed., *English Literature and British Philosophy* (Chicago: Chicago University Press, 1971).
[D. Russell, *The Tamarisk Tree* (London: Elek/Pemberton, 1975).]
G. Santayana, *My Host the World* (New York: Scribners, 1953).
G. Santayana, *The Middle Span* (New York: Scribners, 1945).
K. Tait, *My Father Bertrand Russell* (New York: Harcourt Brace Jovanovich, 1975).
A. Wood, *Bertrand Russell: The Passionate Sceptic* (London: Allen & Unwin, 1957).

GENERAL STUDIES

A. J. Ayer, *Russell* (London: Fontana/Collins, 1972).
R. Jager, *The Development of Bertrand Russell's Philosophy* (London: Allen & Unwin, 1972).

SPECIAL STUDIES

Bertrand Russell: A Collection of Critical Essays, ed. D. F. Pears (Garden City: Doubleday (Anchor Books), 1972).
Bertrand Russell: Philosopher of the Century, ed. R. Schoenman (London: Allen & Unwin, 1967).

1. *Autobiography*, vol. 1, pp. 15, 17.
2. Clark, p. 25.
3. *Autobiography*, vol. 1, p. 22.
4. Ibid., pp. 19, 20, 30, 31.
5. Ibid., p. 31.
6. 'My Mental Development,' pp. 3, 5.
7. M. St. John Packe, *The Life of John Stuart Mill* (London: Secker & Warburg, 1954), p. 434.
8. *Autobiography*, vol. 1, p. 15.
9. 'My Mental Development,' p. 4.
10. *Autobiography*, vol. 1, p. 16.
11. Ibid., p. 15.
12. *Portraits from Memory*, p. 2. 'My Mental Development,' p. 6.
13. *Autobiography*, vol. 1, p. 22.
14. Ibid., p. 20.
15. Ibid., p. 22.
16. 'My Mental Development,' p. 5.
17. *Autobiography*, vol. 1, p. 28.
18. Ibid., p. 26.
19. Ibid., p. 21.
20. Ibid., pp. 31, 38.
21. Ibid., pp. 38, 40.
22. Ibid., p. 46.
23. Ibid., pp. 38, 40.
24. Ibid., p. 36, 42, 43.
25. 'My Mental Development,' p. 8. *Autobiography*, vol. 1, p. 67.
26. *Autobiography*, vol. 1, p. 82.
27. Ibid., p. 84.
28. Ibid., pp. 85 – 86.
29. Ibid., p. 126.
30. Ibid., p. 30.
31. Clark, pp. 84 – 87.
32. *Autobiography*, vol. 1, p. 146.
33. Ibid., p. 46.
34. Ibid., pp. 152 – 53.
35. Ibid., vol. 2, p. 21.
36. See M. L. Ross, 'The Mythology of Friendship.'

37. Wood, p. 38.
38. C. Malleson, 'Fifty Years: 1916–1966,' p. 17.
39. Wood, p. 61.
40. Wood, in Russell's *My Philosophical Development*, p. 270.
41. Santayana, *My Host the World*, p. 27.
42. Crawshay-Williams, p. 8.
43. Ibid., pp. 9, 25.
44. Ibid., p. 26.
45. Ibid., p. 109.
46. Tait, pp. 96, 67, 187.
47. *Autobiography*, vol. 2, p. 159.
48. Ibid., vol. 3, p. 220.
49. Ibid., vol. 1, p. 13.
50. 'The Study of Mathematics' (1907), quoted in *My Philosophical Development*, p. 211.
51. *Collected Stories*, p. 26.
52. *My Philosophical Development*, p. 36.
53. 'My Mental Development,' p. 19.
54. Ibid., p. 7.
55. *Autobiography*, vol. 1, p. 25.
56. Ibid., pp. 19 – 20.
57. Ibid., pp. 152 – 53.
58. *My Philosophical Development*, p. 79.
59. W. V. Quine, 'Remarks for a Memorial Symposium,' in *Bertrand Russell: A Collection of Critical Essays*, p. 4.
60. *Autobiography*, vol. 1, p. 204.
61. To Constance Malleson, 29 Sept. 1916: *Autobiography*, vol. 2, p. 75.
62. 'The Perplexities of John Forstice,' *Collected Stories*, pp. 29, 32.
63. D. Russell, *The Tamarisk Tree*.
64. Clark, p. 22. Tait, pp. 99, 97, 128, 131–32.
65. To C. Malleson, 5 July, 1918: *Autobiography*, vol. 2, p. 87.
66. 'My Mental Development,' p. 19.
67. *Portraits from Memory*, p. 52.
68. Jager, p. 428.
69. On neutral monism, see A. Quinton, 'Russell's Philosophy of Mind,' in *Bertrand Russell: Philosopher of the Century*, pp. 95 – 100, 105.
70. *My Philosophical Development*, p. 27.
71. *Selected Papers*, p. 16.
72. Jager, p. 498.
73. *Autobiography*, vol. 1, pp. 76, 147. 'My Mental Development,' p. 10.
74. *Human Society in Ethics and Politics*, p. 26, as quoted in Jager, pp. 479 – 80.
75. *Religion and Science*, p. 232, as quoted in Jager, p. 480.
76. *Autobiography*, vol. 3, p. 220.
77. Ibid., vol. 2, p. 38.
78. From Russell's journal entries of 21 Nov. 21, 1902, and 8 April, 1903, in Clark, pp. 91, 97.
79. *Ottoline at Garsington*, p. 273.
80. Clark, p. 532.
81. Tait, pp. 107, 43.
82. Clark, p. 88.

83. Ibid., p. 426.
84. *Autobiography*, vol. 1, pp. 84 – 85, 148 – 49.
85. Clark, p. 30, citing the entry for Jan. 14, 1904, in a private journal kept by Russell.
86. *Autobiography*, vol. 1, p. 26; vol. 2, pp. 153 – 54.
87. Santayana, *The Middle Span*, pp. 72 – 73.
88. Tait, p. 190.
89. Conrad Russell, 'My Father—Bertrand Russell,' in the *Illustrated London News* (14 Feb, 1970): Clark, p. 630.

Wittgenstein: pp. 318 – 34

WORKS

The Blue and Brown Books, 2nd ed. (Oxford: Blackwell, 1969).
Notebooks 1914–1916, German with trans. by G. E. M. Anscombe (Oxford: Blackwell, 1961).
On Certainty, German with trans. by D. Paul & G. E. M. Anscombe (Oxford: Blackwell, 1974).
Philosophical Investigations, German with trans. by G. E. M. Anscombe (Oxford: Blackwell, 1967).
Tractatus Logico-Philosophicus, German with trans. by D. F. Pears & B. F. McGuiness, 2nd corr. impression (London: Routledge & Kegan Paul, 1963).
Vermischte Bemerkungen (Frankfurt am Main/Oxford: Suhrkamp/Blackwell, 1977/1978).
Zettel, German with trans. by G. E. M. Anscombe (Oxford: Blackwell, 1967).

TRANSCRIBED CONVERSATIONS AND LECTURES

Lectures and Conversations on Aesthetics, Psychology & Religious Belief, ed. C. Barrett (Oxford: Blackwell, 1966).
Ludwig Wittgenstein und der Wiener Kreis, recorded by F. Waismann (Oxford: Blackwell, 1967).
'Wittgenstein's Lecture on Ethics,' transcribed by F. Waismann, *Philosophical Review* (Jan., 1965; reprinted *Philosophy Today No. 1*, ed. J. H. Gill (New York/London: Macmillan/Collier-Macmillan, 1968).

LETTERS

P. Engelmann, *Letters from Ludwig Wittgenstein, with a Memoir* (Oxford: Blackwell, 1967).
Briefe an Ludwig von Ficker (Salzburg: Otto Müller Verlag, 1969).
Letters to C. K. Ogden (Oxford/London: Blackwell/Routledge & Kegan Paul, 1973).
Letters to Russell, Keynes and Moore (Oxford: Blackwell, 1974).

BIOGRAPHY

A. Ambrose, 'Ludwig Wittgenstein: A Portrait,' in A. Ambrose & M. Lazerowitz, *Ludwig Wittgenstein: Philosophy and Language* (see below, in Special Studies).

W. W. Bartley III, *Wittgenstein* (Philadelphia/New York: Lippincott, 1973).

R. W. Clark, *The Life of Bertrand Russell* (London: Cape/Weidenfeld & Nicolson, 1975).

M. O'c. Drury, *The Danger of Words* (London: Routledge & Kegan Paul, 1973).

K. T. Fann, ed., *Ludwig Wittgenstein* (New York: Dell, 1967).

F. A. Hayek, 'Unfinished Draft of A Sketch of a Biography of Ludwig Wittgenstein,' written in 1953 for private circulation; with some later insertions and corrections.

A. Janik & S. Toulmin, *Wittgenstein's Vienna* (New York: Simon & Schuster, 1973).

N. Malcolm, *Ludwig Wittgenstein: A Memoir*, with a Biographical Sketch by G. H. von Wright (London: Oxford University Press, 1958).

G. E. Moore, *Philosophical Papers* (London: Allen & Unwin, 1959).

F. Pascal, 'Wittgenstein: A Personal Memoir,' *Encounter* (August, 1973).

B. Russell, *The Autobiography of Bertrand Russell: 1914–1944* (London: Allen & Unwin, 1968).

S. Toulmin, 'Ludwig Wittgenstein,' *Encounter* (January, 1969).

H. Wittgenstein, in B. Leitner, *The Architecture of Ludwig Wittgenstein: A Documentation with Excerpts from the Family Recollections by Hermione Wittgenstein* (Halifax, Canada/London: The Press of the Nova Scotia College of Art and Design/Studio Publications, 1973).

K. Wuchterl & A. Hübner, *Wittgenstein in Selbstzeugnissen und Bilddokumenten* (Reinbek b. Hamburg: Rowohlt (Rororo), 1979).

LETTERS TO PERIODICALS

Encounter (Dec., 1973), from G. R. ffennell.

Times Literary Supplement (16 Nov, 1973), from G. E. M. Anscombe; (7 Jan, 1974), from G. E. M. Anscombe; (11 Jan, 1974), from W. W. Bartley III; (18 Jan., 1974), from W. Miller, B. McGuiness; (8 Feb., 1974), F. A. Hayek, W. W. Bartley III, R. Koder; (22 Feb., 1974), from M. O'c. Drury, I. Strickland.

GENERAL STUDIES

G. E. M. Anscombe, *An Introduction to Wittgenstein's 'Tractatus'* (London: Hutchinson, 1959).

P. M. S. Hacker, *Insight and Illusion: Wittgenstein on Philosophy and the Metaphysics of Experience* (London: Oxford University Press, 1972).

A. Kenny, *Wittgenstein* (London: Allen Lane, The Penguin Press, 1973).

N. Malcolm, 'Wittgenstein,' in *The Encyclopedia of Philosophy*, ed. P. Edwards, vol. 8.

SPECIAL STUDIES

A. Ambrose & M. Lazerowitz, *Ludwig Wittgenstein: Philosophy and Language* (London: Allen & Unwin, 1972).

W. W. Bartley III, 'Theory of Language and Philosophy of Science as Instruments of Educational Reform: Wittgenstein and Popper as Austrian Schoolteachers,' (Boston: *Boston Studies in the Philosophy of Science*, vol. 14).

F. B. Greenwood, 'Tolstoy, Wittgenstein, Schopenhauer: Some Connections,' Encounter (April, 1971).

Understanding Wittgenstein, Royal Institute of Philosophy Lectures, ed. G. Vesey vol. 7, 1972/73 (London: Macmillan, 1974).

OTHER REFERENCES

L. Tolstoy, *A Confession, The Gospel in Brief, and What I Believe*, trans. A. Maude (London: Oxford University Press, 1940).

1. Hayek, pp. 1 – 2. Janik & Toulmin, p. 170. Engelmann, p. 138. Bartley, *Wittgenstein*, p. 17. Ficker, pp. 48 – 49, which draws on two obituary articles published in the *Neue Freie Presse* of 21 Jan., 1913. I have also used unpublished material kindly given to me by Professor W. W. Bartley, III.
2. Hayek, p. 2.
3. *Vermischte Bemerkungen*, p. 122 (1947).
4. Ibid., p. 163 (1950).
5. Janik & Toulmin, p. 171. Engelmann, p. 138. Bartley, *Wittgenstein*, p. 41. Disciple of Freud: *Lectures and Conversations*, p. 51; Malcolm, pp. 44 – 45.
6. H. Wittgenstein, *Architecture*, p. 17.
7. Anscombe, 'Introduction.'
8. Von Wright, in Malcolm, p. 5, note 1.
9. Hayek, p. 6, from David Pinsent's diary.
10. Janik & Toulmin, p. 173. Bartley, Wittgenstein, p. 43.
11. Hayek, pp. 2 – 3.
12. H. Wittgenstein, p. 17.
13. Hayek, p. 3.
14. H. Wittgenstein, p. 18.
15. Clark, pp. 171 – 72.
16. Ibid., pp. 191, 203.
17. Ibid., p. 192.
18. 21 Jan., 1913: *Letters to Russell*, p. 21.
19. H. Wittgenstein, p. 18. Engelmann, pp. 140 – 42.
20. Bartley, *Wittgenstein*, p. 44.
21. Engelmann, pp. 140 – 42.
22. To Russell, 12 June, 1919: *The Autobiography of Bertrand Russell*, vol. 2, pp. 117 – 18; *Letters to Russell*, pp. 69 – 70.
23. One version: Bartley, *Wittgenstein*, p. 42. Another version: Janik & Toulmin, p. 173. Hayek, p. 2, says his soldiers 'refused to obey orders.'
24. H. Wittgenstein, p. 19.
25. Malcolm, p. 61.
26. H. Wittgenstein, p. 19.
27. Hayek, p. 29. H. Wittgenstein, pp. 19 – 20. Bartley, 'Theory of Language,' and Bartley, *Wittgenstein*, pp. 83 – 123.
28. Bartley, *Wittgenstein*, pp. 124 – 35; 'Theory of Language,' pp. 317 – 19.
29. Bartley, *Wittgenstein*, p. 33.

30. Von Wright, In Malcolm, *Ludwig Wittgenstein*, p. 20.
31. 'Salvation' : N. Malcolm, 'Wittgenstein,' in *The Encyclopedia of Philosophy*, ed. P. Edwards, vol. 8, p. 327. Logic and Suicide: *The Autobiography of Bertrand Russell*, vol. 2, p. 99.
32. Clark, p. 204.
33. Nov. or Dec. 1913: *Letters to Russell*, p. 44.
34. Jan. 1914: Ibid., p. 47.
35. Letters of 16 Nov., 1919; 26 Jan., 1920; 21 June, 1920; 2 Jan., 1921; 23 Oct., 1921: Engelmann, pp. 21, 27, 33 – 34, 41, 47.
36. James: Drury, p. 68; *Letters to Russell*, p. 82; Hayek, p. 7. Tolstoy: *Letters to Russell*, ibid., p. 82; H. Wittgenstein, p. 19; *Briefe an Ludwig von Ficker*, p. 28 (letter of 24 July, 1915); Engelmann, pp. 79 – 81.
37. Notebooks, p. 51.
38. Ibid., pp. 72 – 73.
39. Ibid., p. 74.
40. Ibid., p. 78.
41. Ibid., p. 77.
42. Ibid.
43. Ibid., p. 80.
44. Ibid., p. 91.
45. Malcolm, 'Wittgenstein,' ibid. (see note 29).
46. Pascal, pp. 33 – 34. See also G. R. ffennell's letter to *Encounter*.
47. Pascal, pp. 26, 32.
48. Malcolm, *Ludwig Wittgenstein*, pp. 61, 62. See also Von Wright, in Malcolm, pp. 18, 19. On tensions in friendship in relation to honesty see his letters to Russell proposing a full and then a qualified break (letters of Jan. or Feb. 1914 and 3 March, 1914: *Letters to Russell*, pp. 50 – 51, 53 – 54).
49. Ambrose, p. 15. Carnap, in Fann, p. 34, and in P. A. Schilpp, *The Philosophy of Rudolf Carnap* (La Salle, I11., Open Court, 1963), pp. 25 – 28. Britton, in Fann, pp. 56 – 57.
50. Malcolm, *Ludwig Wittgenstein*, p. 27.
51. Ibid.
52. Ibid., p. 26. Ambrose, p. 15.
53. Moore, p. 256.
54. Malcolm, *Ludwig Wittgenstein*, pp. 27 – 28.
55. Drury, p. xiv.
56. Malcolm, *Ludwig Wittgenstein*, p. 63; and 'Ludwig Wittgenstein' (see note 29).
57. Britton, in Fann., p. 61. Von Wright, in Malcolm, *Ludwig Wittgenstein*, pp. 1 – 2.
58. Malcolm, *Ludwig Wittgenstein*, p. 58.
59. Von Wright, in Malcolm, *Ludwig Wittgenstein*, p. 2.
60. Ramsey to his mother, 20 Sept., 1923: *Letters to C. K. Ogden*, p. 78.
61. Ambrose, p. 13.
62. Gasking & Jackson, in Fann, p. 50. See also Mays, in Fann.
63. Letter of 5 Dec., 1919: *Briefe an Ludwig von Ficker*, p. 39.
64. Ibid., p. 35. Translation in Engelmann, pp. 143 – 44.
65. Malcolm, *Ludwig Wittgenstein*, p. 31.
66. Drury, pp. 67 – 68.
67. Mays, in Fann, p. 80.
68. *Vermischte Bemerkungen*, p. 53 (1933 – 1934).

69. Drury, p. xiv.

70. Drury, in Fann, pp. 67 – 68. See *Notebooks*, p. 86 (21.10.16): 'And the beautiful *is* what makes me happy'.

71. Moore, pp. 312, 315. *Wiener Kreis*, p. 116; translated in 'Wittgenstein's Lecture on Ethics,' pp. 15 – 19.

72. *Wiener Kreis*, p. 115. 'Wittgenstein's Lecture on Ethics,' p. 19.

73. *Wiener Kreis*, pp. 118, 117. 'Wittgenstein's Lecture on Ethics,' pp. 18 – 19.

74. *Blue Book*, pp. 59 – 68. Ambrose, p. 18. Hacker, pp. 64 – 66, 70 – 75.

75. Hacker, pp. 201ff., 223, 262. Moore, p. 311. Ambrose, p. 19. Kenny, pp. 167 – 79. J. Teichman, 'Wittgenstein on Persons and Human Beings,' and R. Bambrough, 'How to Read Wittgenstein,' in *Understanding Wittgenstein*.

76. Malcolm, *Ludwig Wittgenstein*, p. 33.

77. *Vermischte Bemerkungen*, p. 129 (1948).

78. Ibid., p. 138 (1948).

79. Ibid., p. 124 (1947).

80. Ibid., p. 60 (1937).

81. Engelmann, p. 19.

82. Malcolm, *Ludwig Wittgenstein*, p. 23.

83. Pascal, p. 26.

84. Ibid., pp. 62, 63.

85. F. Fransella, *Personal Change and Reconstruction: Research on a Treatment of Stuttering* (London/New York: Academic Press, 1972), pp. 21, 27, 310 – 16.

86. *Vermischte Bemerkungen*, p. 30 (1931).

87. Ibid., p. 90 (*c.* 1945).

88. Ambrose, p. 19. *Blue Book*, p. 54.

89. Malcolm, *Ludwig Wittgenstein*, pp. 62, 32.

90. Ibid., pp. 56 – 58.

91. *Vermischte Bemerkungen*, p. 91 (1946).

92. Ibid., p. 75 (1939–1940).

93. Ibid., p. 43 (1931).

94. Pascal, pp. 28 – 29, 31.

95. Malcolm, *Ludwig Wittgenstein*, pp. 17 (by Von Wright), 38. Pascal, p. 39.

96. *Vermischte Bemerkungen*, p. 88 (1944).

97. Drury, p. 136.

98. Childlike innocence; 'Intolerable!'; 'Genuine?': Pascal, pp. 37, 26, 25.

99. Drury, p. 69. Malcolm, 'Wittgenstein,' p. 329 (see note 29 above).

100. Tolstoy, 'Preface,' *The Gospel in Brief*, p. 118. *Notebooks*, p. 75; *Tractatus*, p. 147 (6.4311).

101. Tolstoy, ibid. *Notebooks*, p. 73.

102. Tolstoy, op. cit., subtitles of chaps. 5, 7, 10, 12; pp. 172, 199, 235, 253.

103. Hayek, p. 30. Bartley, *Wittgenstein*, pp. 133 – 35. H. Wittgenstein, p. 20.

104. H. Wittgenstein, p. 21.

105 *Vermischte Bemerkungen*, p. 67 (1937).

106. Ibid., p. 63 (1937).

107. Ibid., p. 143 (1948).

108. Notebooks, p. 86 (20.10.16). *Tractatus*, p. 149 (6.44). Malcolm, *Ludwig Wittgenstein*, p. 70. *Wiener Kreis*, pp. 68 – 69; 'Lecture on Ethics,' p. 9. Compare A. Schopenhauer, *The World as Will and Representation*, vol. 2, trans. E. F. J. Payne (New York: Dover, 1966), p. 170f.

109. See, e.g., my earlier pages on Wittgenstein's style (pp. 67 – 73) and my earlier remarks in the present section on *On Certainty* pp. 328 – 31.

110. Bartley, *Wittgenstein*, pp. 33, 46 – 54. See the ensuing controversy in the *Times Literary Supplement*. The dates of the letters are listed in the bibliography to this section, on Wittgenstein.
111. Letter of Irina Strickland, recording a conversation of 1952, and printed in the *Times Literary Supplement* of Feb. 22, 1974.
112. Malcolm, *Ludwig Wittgenstein*, p. 45.
113. Wuchterl & Hübner, pp. 66 – 67.
114. Pascal, p. 25.
115. Bartley, *Wittgenstein*, pp. 33 – 36.
116. Malcolm, *Ludwig Wittgenstein*, p. 100.
117. Ibid., p. 34.

Sartre: pp. 335 – 44

ANNOTATED CHRONOLOGICAL BIBLIOGRAPHY

M. Contat & M. Rybalka, *Les écrits de Sartre* (Paris: Gallimard, 1970).

WORKS

L'être et le néant (Paris: Gallimard, 1943).
L'idiot de la Famille: Gustave Flaubert de 1821 à 1857 (Paris: Gallimard, 1971).
Being and Nothingness, trans. H. Barnes (New York: Washington Square Press, 1966).
Critique of Dialectical Reason, trans. A. Sheridan-Amity (London: NLB, 1976).
Nausea, trans. R. Baldick (Harmondsworth: Penguin Books, 1965).
The Problem of Method, trans. H. E. Barnes (London: Methuen, 1963).

AUTOBIOGRAPHY

Les mots (Paris: Gallimard, 1964).
The Words, trans. B. Frechtman (New York: Fawcett World Library, 1966).
Situations, X: Politique et autobiographie (Paris: Gallimard, 1976).

BIOGRAPHY

S. de Beauvoir, *The Prime of Life* (Harmondsworth: Penguin Books, 1965).
S. de Beauvoir, *Force of Circumstance* (Harmondsworth: Penguin Books, 1968).
S. de Beauvoir, *All Said and Done* (London/New York: André Deutsch/Weidenfeld & Nicolson/Putnam's, 1974).
F. Jeanson, *Sartre dans sa vie* (Paris: Seuil, 1974).

GENERAL STUDIES

H. E. Barnes, *Sartre* (London: Quartet Books, 1974).
W. Desan, *The Marxism of Jean-Paul Sartre* (Garden City: Doubleday (Anchor Books), 1966).
W. Desan, *The Tragic Finale: An Essay on the Philosophy of Jean-Paul Sartre* (Cambridge Mass.: Harvard University Press, 1954).
P. Thody, *Sartre* (London: Studio Vista, 1971).

SPECIAL STUDIES

V. Brombert, *The Intellectual Hero: Studies on the French Novel 1880–1955* (Chicago: University of Chicago Press, 1964).

B. T. Fitch, *Le sentiment d'étrangeté chez Malraux, Sartre, Camus et Simone de Beauvoir* (Paris, 1964).

1. *The Words*, p. 52; *Les mots*, p. 66.
2. Contat & Rybalka, p. 34.
3. Ibid., pp. 36, 40.
4. *The Words*, pp. 102, 52.
5. De Beauvoir, *All Said and Done*, p. 52.
6. *Situations, X,* p. 146.
7. *The Words*, p. 10.
8. Ibid., p. 11; *Les mots*, p. 11.
9. *The Words*, p. 55; *Les mots*, pp. 70 – 71.
10. *The Words*, p. 16.
11. Ibid., p. 34, note.
12. Ibid., p. 28.
13. Ibid., pp. 79 – 80.
14. Ibid., pp. 65 – 66.
15. Ibid., p. 136.
16. Ibid., p. 136.
17. Ibid., p. 20.
18. Ibid., p. 25.
19. Ibid., p. 28.
20. Ibid., pp. 30 – 31, 37.
21. Ibid., pp. 39 – 43.
22. Ibid., pp. 45 – 47.
23. Ibid., p. 59.
24. Ibid., pp. 61 – 63.
25. Ibid., pp. 64 – 65.
26. Jeanson, p. 21.
27. *The Words*, pp. 87 – 91.
28. Ibid., pp. 120, 122.
29. Contat & Rybalka, p. 22. Jeanson, p. 292.
30. Jeanson, pp. 289 – 90, 294.
31. Ibid., p. 235, from a 1965 interview.
32. De Beauvoir, *The Prime of Life*, pp. 30 – 31, 42.
33. Ibid., p. 135.
34. Ibid., pp. 43, 127 – 28.
35. Ibid., pp. 129, 208.
36. Ibid., pp. 208 – 209, 220.
37. Ibid., p. 250. Contat & Rybalka, p. 26.
38. Fitch, chap. 2. Brombert.
39. *Nausea*, pp. 9 – 10, 21, 22.
40. Ibid., p. 145.
41. Ibid., pp. 148, 184 – 88, 192.
42. Ibid., p. 248.
43. Ibid., pp. 252 – 53.
44. Brombert, pp. 144 – 45, 181, 201.

45. *Being and Nothingness*, p. 755.
46. Ibid., pp. 758 – 59.
47. Ibid., p. 761.
48. Ibid., pp. 762 – 63.
49. Ibid., pp. 764 – 65.
50. Ibid., p. 767.
51. *Problem of Method*, pp. 173 – 74.
52. Desan, *Marxism*, pp. 83 – 85.
53. Barnes, *Sartre*, pp. 114ff.
54. *L'idiot*, p. 8.
55. Jeanson, p. 262.
56. *Situations*, X, pp. 134 – 35.
57. Jeanson, p. 231 (May, 1965).
58. Jeanson, pp. 235 – 36 (July, 1965).
59. *Situations*, X, p. 197.
60. Jeanson, pp. 235 – 36 (July, 1965); corrected by *Situations*, X, p. 191.
61. Jeanson, pp. 161 – 65.
62. *Situations*, X, p. 146.
63. Ibid., p. 210.
64. Ibid., p. 226.

NOTES TO CHAPTER NINE

A Tabular Summary, with Tentative Generalizations: pp. 345 – 54

1. It does not help much to read that in traditional French or English villages under the *ancien régime* 'a good tenth of all children under six years old' had lost either father or mother, most usually the father, while 'the loss of both parents was surprisingly infrequent.' P. Laslett, *in Encounter* (March, 1976), p. 82. Laslett refers to his article in *Population Studies* (Autumn, 1974) and to *Family Life and Illicit Love in Earlier Generations*, forthcoming from Cambridge University Press.

2. J. Radford & A. Burton, *Thinking: Its Nature and Development* (New York: Wiley, 1974), p. 226.

3. A. M. Wilson, *Diderot* (New York: Oxford University Press, 1972). See 'Diderot, Denis, relations with his father' in the index.

4. R. Handy, 'Hans Vaihinger,' in *The Encyclopedia of Philosophy*, ed. P. Edwards.

5. W. Kluback, *Wilhelm Dilthey's Philosophy of History* (New York: Columbia University Press, 1973), pp. 70 – 88.

6. H. B. Biller, 'Paternal Deprivation, Cognitive Functioning, and the Feminized Classroom,' in A. Davids, ed., *Child Personality and Psychopathology: Current Topics*, vol. 1 (New York: Wiley, 1974), pp. 23, 24, 25, 30.

7. R. Grimsley, *The Philosophy of Rousseau* (London: Oxford University Press, 1973), pp. 70 – 88.

8. H. Spiegelberg & B. Q. Morgan, eds., *The Socratic Enigma* (Indianapolis/New York: Bobbs-Merrill, 1964). S. Kierkegaard, *Concluding Unscientific Postscript*, trans. D. F. Swenson & W. Lowrie (Princeton: Princeton University Press,

1944), p. 185. W. Kaufmann, *Nietzsche*, 4th ed. (Princeton: Princeton University Press, 1974), pp. 391 – 411. For Diderot see A. M. Wilson, op. cit., index ('Diderot, Denis, self-identification of, with Socrates').
9. J. Noxon, *Hume's Philosophical Development* (London: Oxford University Press, 1973), pp. 74 – 75.
10. *The Philosophy of Karl Popper*, ed. P. A. Schilpp, vol. 1 (La Salle; Open Court, 1974), p. 41.
11. L. Wittgenstein, *Briefe an Ludwig von Ficker* (Salzburg: Otto Müller Verlag, 1969), p. 33.
12. K. Rosenkranz, *G. W. F. Hegels Leben* (reprint Darmstadt: Wissenschaftliche Buchgesellschaft, 1971), pp. 347, 350; and Hegel's *Vorlesungen über die Asthetik*, part 3, chap. 2, sections 1, 3c.
13. V. Zuckerkandel, *Man the Musician* (Princeton: Princeton University Press, 1973) esp. chaps. 18, 19.

The Challenge of Death: Nietzsche, Camus, and Jaspers: pp. 355 – 57

1. D. Winnicott, *Playing and Reality* (London: Tavistock, 1970), pp. 47 – 55. M. Balint, *Thrills and Regressions* (London: The Hogarth Press/The Institute of Psycho-Analysis, 1959), p. 151. S. Z. Klausner, ed., *Why Man Takes Chances* (Garden City: Doubleday, 1968), 'Foreword.' E. Wyschograd, 'Sport, Death, and the Elemental,' in E. Wyschograd, ed., *The Phenomenon of Death* (New York: Harper & Row, 1973). See also R. M. Linder, 'The Psychodynamics of Gambling,' in J. Halliday & P. Fuller, *The Psychology of Gambling* (London: Allen Lane, 1974).
2. David Brower, cited in C. S. Houston, 'The Last Blue Mountain,' in S. Z. Klausner, op. cit., p. 53.
3. C. Bonington, *Annapurna Faces South* (Harmondsworth: Penguin Books, 1973), pp. 37, 38.
4. John Harlin, as cited in C. S. Houston, op. cit., p. 58.
5. For Berkeley see A. A. Luce, *The Life of George Berkeley, Bishop of Cloyne* (New York: Greenwood Press, 1968), p. 223.
6. E. Husserl, *Philosophie Première*, trans. A. L. Kelkel (from *Erste Philosophie (1923—1924)*, Zweiter Teil) (Paris: Presses Universitaires, 1972), pp. 29 – 30 (p. 22 of German original).
7. N. Malcolm, *Ludwig Wittgenstein: A Memoir* (London: Oxford University Press, 1958), pp. 68, 55.
8. To O. Eiser, Jan., 1880: Friedrich Nietzsche, *Werke in drei Bänden*, ed. K. Schlechta, vol. 3 (Munich: Hanser Verlag, 1969), p. 754.
9. Overbeck to Gast, 1883: R. Binion, *Frau Lou: Nietzsche's Wayward Disciple* (Princeton: Princeton University Press, 1968), p. 109.
10. To G. Brandes, April 10, 1888: *F. Nietzsche, Werke in drei Bänden*, ed. K. Schlechta, vol. 3, p. 1287.
11. A. Costes, *Albert Camus et la parole manquante* (Paris: Payot, 1973), chap. 10.
12. A. Camus, *The Myth of Sisyphus*, trans. J. O'Brien (London: Hamish Hamilton, 1960), pp. 11, 48.
13. 'Krankheitsgeschichte,' in K. Jaspers, *Schicksal und Wille: Autobiographische Schriften* (Munich: Piper & Co., 1967).
14. Ibid., p. 109.

15. Ibid., p. 142.
16. 'Karl Jaspers: An Autobiography,' in *The Philosophy of Karl Jaspers*, ed. P. A. Schilpp (New York: Tudor, 1957), pp. 84 – 85.

NOTES TO CHAPTER TEN

On Words, Especially 'Yes' and 'No': pp. 361 – 63

1. A. R. Luria & F. I. Yudovich, *Speech and the Development of Mental Processes in the Child* (Harmondsworth: Penguin Books, 1971).
2. R. A. Spitz, *No and Yes: On the Genesis of a Human Communication* (New York: International Universities Press, 1957), pp. 94, 99.
3. P. Farb, *Word Play* (New York: Bantam, 1975), p. 233.
4. D. Morris, P. Collett, P. Marsh & M. O'Shaughnessy, *Gestures: Their Origin and Distribution* (London: Cape, 1979), pp. 162 – 68. See also D. Morris, *Manwatching* (London: Cape, 1977); and I. Eibl-Eibesfeldt, 'Similarities Between Cultures in Expressive Movement,' in R. A. Hinde, ed., *Non-Verbal Communication* (Cambridge: Cambridge University Press, 1972), pp. 303 – 304.
5. Eibl-Eibesfeldt, op. cit., p. 304.
6. For a survey of the state of cognitive dissonance theory and research about a decade ago, see R. B. Zajonc, 'Cognitive Theories in Social Psychology,' in G. Lindzey & E. Aronson, *The Handbook of Social Psychology*, 2nd ed., vol. 1 (Reading, Mass.: Addison Wesley, 1968), pp. 359ff.
7. S. Ulam, *Adventures of a Mathematician* (New York: Scribners, 1976), p. 120.

Precocious Intellectuality: pp. 363 – 65

1. C. J. Newman, C. F. Dember & O. Krug, 'He Can But He Won't: A Psychodynamic Study of So-Called "Gifted Underachievers," ' in *The Psychoanalytic Study of the Child*, vol. 38 (London: Hogarth Press/Institute of Psycho-Analysis, 1973). See also, M. A. Wallach & N. Kogan, *Modes of Thinking in Young Children* (New York: Holt, Rinehart & Winston, 1965), esp. pp. 140 – 42, 301 – 303.
2. A. Freud, *Normality and Pathology in Childhood* (London: Hogarth Press/Institute of Psycho-Analysis, 1966), p. 221.
3. M. Klein, *Contributions to Psychoanalysis 1921–1945* (London: Hogarth Press/Institute of Psycho-Analysis), p. 15.
4. Ibid., pp. 21 – 22.
5. Ibid., p. 24.
6. K. Kelly, 'A Precocious Child in Analysis,' in *The Psychoanalytic Study of the Child*, vol. 25 (London: Hogarth Press, 1970), pp. 134, 144.
7. H. Wider, 'Intellectuality, Aspects of its Development from the Analysis of a Precocious Four-and-a-half-year-old Boy,' in *The Psychoanalytic Study of the Child*, vol. 21, (1966), p. 297.
8. Ibid., pp. 300, 301, 302.

9. Ibid., pp. 305, 309.
10. Ibid., pp. 309, 315.

The Bodily Clumsiness of Philosophers: pp. 366 – 68

1. 'Of Presumption,' in D. M. Frame, *The Complete Works of Montaigne* (Stanford: Stanford University Press, 1957), pp. 486 – 87 (book 2, essay 17).
2. A. C. Wasianski, in *Immanuel Kant: Sein Leben in Darstellungen von Zeitgenossen*, ed. Felix Gross (Berlin: Deutsche Bibliothek, 1912), p. 248.
3. W. Kaufmann, *Hegel: A Reinterpretation* (Garden City: Doubleday (Anchor Books), p. 300.
4. J. S. Mill, *Autobiography*, ed. J. Stillinger (London: Oxford University Press, 1969), pp. 23 – 24, note 12.
5. R. Crawshay-Williams, *Russell Remembered* (London: Oxford University Press, 1970), p. 33.
6. *The Philosophy of C. D. Broad*, ed. P. A. Schilpp (New York: Tudor/Library of Living Philosophers, 1959), pp. 50, 34, 35, 67.
7. N. Wiener, *Ex-Prodigy* (Cambridge, Mass: M.I.T. Press, 1964), pp. 74 – 75.
8. H. Yukawa, *Creativity and Intuition* (Tokyo: Kodansha, 1973), pp. 26, 29.
9. K. Dewhurst, *John Locke (1632–1704), Physician and Philosopher* (London: The Wellcome Historical Medical Library, 1963), pp. 30, 49, 163; 13 – 14, 20.
10. Letter of Harriet Taylor, 23 Nov., 1856: F. A. Hayek, *John Stuart Mill and Harriet Taylor* (1951; republished New York: A. M. Kelley, no date), p. 183.
11. 'The Idler and His Works,' in G. Santayana, *The Idler and His Works and Other Essays* (New York: Braziller, 1957).
12. *The Philosophy of Karl Popper*, ed. P. A. Schilpp, vol. 1 (La Salle, Ill.: Open Court/Library of Living Philosophers, 1974), pp. 26 – 27.

Precociously Intellectual Philosophers: pp. 368 – 70

1. T. S. Knight, *Charles Peirce* (New York: Washington Square Press, 1965), pp. 4 – 5.
2. R. G. Collingwood, *An Autobiography* (London: Oxford University Press, 1939), p. 1.
3. *The Journals of Søren Kierkegaard*, ed. & trans. A. Dru (London: Oxford University Press, 1938), entry 155 (Sept. 4, 1837).
4. Ibid., entry 42 (March, 1836).
5. Ibid., entry 318 (Sept. 11, 1839).
6. S. Kierkegaard, *Journal, Extraits, 1854–1855*, trans. K. Ferlov & J. J. Gateau (Paris: Gallimard, 1961), pp. 244 – 46 (11–2, A 128) (1854). S. Kierkegaard, *The Last Years: Journals 1853–55*, trans. R. G. Smith (London: Fontana, 1968), p. 251.
7. Ferlov & Gateau, p. 255 (11–2, A 147) (24 Nov., 1854). Smith, p. 262.

Paradoxical Philosophers: pp. 370 – 75

1. What I say obviously reflects the 'double-bind' theory of schizophrenia, formulated by Bateson, Jackson, Haley, and Weakland, in 'Towards a Theory of Schizophrenia,' republished in G. Bateson, *Steps to an Ecology of Mind* (London:

Paladin, 1973), pp. 173 – 98. Like other current theories of schizophrenia, the 'double-bind' theory has not proved very tractable in research. For examples of 'double bind' see P. Watzlawick, J. H. Beavin, & D. D. Jackson, *Pragmatics of Human Communication* (London: Faber & Faber, 1968), pp. 91 – 93; or the whole of R. D. Laing, *Knots* (Harmondsworth: Penguin Books, 1971).

2. *Vorlesungen über die philosophische Religionslehre*, as cited in the introduction to Kant's *Religion within the Limits of Reason Alone*, trans. T. M. Greene & H. H. Hudson (New York: Harper & Bros., 1960), p. lix.

3. To Garve, 21 Sept., 1798: *Philosophical Correspondence*, trans. A. Zweig (Chicago: Chicago University Press, 1967), p. 252. On Kant's antinomies, see L. W. Beck, 'Antinomy of Pure Reason,' in *Dictionary of the History of Ideas*, ed. P. P. Wiener; and N. Hinke, 'Antinomie,' in *Historisches Wörterbuch der Philosophie*, ed. J. Ritter.

4. *Hegel's Science of Logic*, trans. A. V. Miller (London: Allen & Unwin, 1969), p. 190 – 91 (book 1, chapter 1, part a, section 2, remark 2).

5. Ibid., p. 439 (book 2, section 1, chapter 2, part c, C, remark 3).

6. S. Kierkegaard, *The Point of View for My Work as an Author*, trans. W. Lowrie (New York: Harper & Row, 1962), pp. 76, 77.

7. S. Kierkegaard, *Concluding Unscientific Postscript*, trans. D. S. Swenson & W. Lowrie (Princeton: Princeton University Press, 1944), p. 267.

8. S. Kierkegaard, *Philosophical Fragments*, trans. D. S. Swenson (Princeton: Princeton University Press, 1946), p. 29.

9. E. g., letters to F. Overbeck, rec. 11 Feb., 1883; to F. Overbeck, 22? March, 1883; to Lou Salomé and Paul Rée, mid-Dec., 1882; Overbeck to Gast, 31 July, 1883: Friedrich Nietzsche, Paul Rée, Lou von Salomé: Die Dokumente ihrer Begegnung, ed. E. Pfeiffer (Frankfurt am Main: Insel, 1970) pp. 269 – 70, 299, 331.

10. *Friedrich Nietzsche, Paul Rée, Lou von Salomé: Die Dokumente ihrer Begegnung*, ed. E. Pfeiffer (Frankfurt am Main: Insel, 1970), pp. 260 – 66; R. Binion, *Frau Lou* (Princeton: Princeton University Press, 1968), p. 101.

11. To Lou Salomé, prob. 16 Sept., 1882.

12. 17 – 18 Feb. and 17 – 18 March, 1913, in F. Kafka, *Briefe an Felice* (Frankfurt am Main: Fischer Verlag, 1967).

13. Overbeck to Gast, 31 July, 1883: Pfeiffer, op. cit., pp. 330, 331; Binion, op. cit., p. 106, note.

14. Pfeiffer, op. cit., p. 336; Binion, p. 107.

15. 'Schopenhauer als Erzieher,' *Unzeitgemässe Betrachtungen*, in F. Nietzsche, *Werke in drei Bänden*, ed. K. Schlechta, vol. 1 (Munich: Hanser Verlag, 1969), pp. 317 – 18. In *Ecce Homo*, Nietzsche, reviewing 'Schopenhauer as Educator,' says that he inscribed in it his innermost history, his *becoming*, and above all, his promise.

16. *Beyond Good and Evil*, *Basic Writings of Nietzsche*, trans. W. Kaufmann (New York: Random House (Modern Library), 1968, sections 200, 225.

17. *Twilight of the Idols and the Anti-Christ*, trans. R. J. Hollingdale (Harmondsworth: Penguin Books, 1968), p. 44 ('Morality as Anti-Nature,' sec. 3).

18. *The Will to Power*, trans. W. Kaufmann (London: Weidenfeld & Nicolson, 1968), sections 510, 512.

19. Ibid., sec. 513.

20. Ibid., sec. 516.

21. Ibid.

22. Ibid., sec. 515; *Werke*, ed. Colli & Montinari, *Fragmente 1888–1889*, (Berlin: De Gruyter, 1972) pp. 125 – 26 (14 [152]).

23. *The Will to Power*, trans. Kaufmann, sec. 517.

24. J. Granier, *Le problème de la vérité dans la philosophie de Nietzsche* (Paris: Seuil, 1966); and J. T. Wilcox, *Truth and Value in Nietzsche* (Ann Arbor: University of Michigan Press, 1974).

Philosophy and Pathology: pp. 375 – 77

1. W. Goldfarb, 'Therapeutic Management of Schizophrenic Children,' in J. G. Howells, *Modern Perspectives in International Child Psychiatry* (Edinburgh: Oliver & Boyd, 1969), pp. 693 – 94.

2. M. S. Mahler, *On Human Symbiosis and the Vicissitudes of Individuation*, vol. 1 (London: Hogarth Press/Institute of Psycho-Analysis, 1969), p. 59.

3. P. Lomas, *True and False Experience* (London: Allen Lane, 1973), pp. 61 – 62.

4. *The Autobiography of Bertrand Russell: 1872–1914* (London: Allen & Unwin, 1967), p. 150.

5. E. G. Mishler & N. E. Waxler, *Interaction in Families: An Experimental Study of Family Processes and Schizophrenia* (New York: John Wiley, 1968), pp. 164, 188.

6. E. Jacobson, *Psychotic Conflict and Reality* (London/New York: Hogarth Press/New York Psychoanalytic Institute, 1967), e.g., p. 38.

7. G. E. Gross & I. A. Rubin, 'Sublimation: The Study of an Instinctual Vicissitude,' in *The Psychoanalytic Study of the Child*, vol. 27 (London: Hogarth Press, 1973), pp. 351 – 52.

8. Ibid. See also F. S. Klaf, *Strindberg: The Origin of Psychology in Modern Drama* (New York: Citadel Press, 1963); H. Nagera, *Vincent van Gogh: A Psychological Study* (London: Allen & Unwin, 1967); and A. J. Lubin, *Stranger on the Earth: A Psychological Biography of Vincent van Gogh* (New York: Holt, Rinehart & Winston, 1972).

9. On 'anxious grandiosity' see H. Kohut, *The Analysis of the Self: A Systematic Approach to the Psychoanalytic Treatment of Narcissistic Personality Disorders* (New York: International Universities Press, 1971), p. 20.

10. Letter to Arnold Künzli of 28 Feb., 1943, in C. G. Jung, *Letters, Vol. I: 1906 — 1950* (Princeton: Princeton University Press, 1973), pp. 331 – 32. See also the letter of 16 March, 1943, p. 333, in which Jung imagines a sounder, less strident Nietzsche.

Philosophical Psychotics: pp. 377 – 79

1. M. Maclane, *The Story of Mary Maclane*, in B. Kaplan, ed., *The Inner World of Mental Illness* (New York: Harper & Row, 1964), pp. 264 – 65.

2. M. Rokeach, *The Three Christs of Ypsilanti: A Psychological Study* (New York: Random House (Vintage Books), no date (copyright 1964)).

3. Ibid., pp. 6 – 7.

4. Ibid., p. 107.

5. Ibid., pp. 207, 254, 256, 258, 317.

6. D. P. Schreber, *Memoirs of My Nervous Illness* (London: William Dawson & Co., 1955). J. Custance, *Wisdom, Madness, and Folly* (New York: Farrar, Straus & Cudahy, 1952). See excerpts from these and other writings in B. Kaplan, op. cit.

(note 1). M. Sechehaye, *Autobiography of a Schizophrenic Girl* (New York: Grune & Stratton, 1951) is particularly remarkable. Most, though not all, of the psychiatrists who have considered the case of Swedenborg have regarded him as insane. I say this because of the summary of their views in W. Lange-Eichbaum & W. Kurth, *Genie, Irrsinn und Ruhm* (Munich/Basel: Ernst Reinhardt Verlag, 1967), pp. 539 – 41.

Philosophers: p. 379

1. A. Moszkowski, *Conversations with Einstein* (London: Sedgwick & Jackson, 1972), p. 4.
2. L. Wittgenstein, *Vermischte Bemerkungen* (Oxford: Blackwell, 1978), p. 124 (1948).
3. K. R. Eissler, *Talent and Genius* (New York: Quadrangle Books, 1971), p. 263. H. Kohut, op. cit. ('Philosophy and Pathology,' note 9), p. 316.

NOTES TO CHAPTER ELEVEN

Trivialization? pp. 380 – 84

1. *Immanuel Kant's Critique of Pure Reason*, trans. N. K. Smith (London; Macmillan, 1953), p. 334 (A 50), I. Kant, *Prolegomena to Any Future Metaphysics* (Manchester: Manchester University Press, 1953), p. 129 (section 59).
2. K. Ward, *The Development of Kant's View of Ethics* (Oxford: Blackwell, 1972), p. 166.
3. 'Attempt at a Self-Criticism,' section 5, *The Birth of Tragedy*, in *Basic Writings of Nietzsche*, trans. W. Kaufmann (New York: Random House (Modern Library), 1968), p. 23.
4. *The Antichrist*, section 62, in *The Portable Nietzsche*, trans. W. Kaufmann (New York: Viking, 1954), p. 655.
5. W. Kaufmann, *Nietzsche* (Princeton: Princeton University Press, 1974), chap. 12.
6. *Minutes of the Vienna Psychoanalytic Association*, ed. H. Nunberg & E. Federn, vol. 2 (New York: International Universities Press, 1962), pp. 31 – 32; as quoted in P. Roazen, *Freud and His Followers* (New York: Knopf, 1975), p. 199. For Freud's reaction to Nietzsche, see also his essay, 'On the History of the Psychoanalytic Movement,' section 2.
7. For Nietzsche's psychology, see, e.g., "Second Essay" and "Third Essay" in *The Genealogy of Morals*. For his praise of himself as a psychologist, see, e.g., "Genealogy of Morals," *Ecce Homo*, in *Basic Writings of Nietzsche*, op. cit., p. 768.

Fruitfulness? pp. 384 – 92

1. For Kant's great influence, positive and negative, on Frege, see J. D. B. Walker, *A Study of Frege* (Oxford: Blackwell, 1965), p. 165.
2. L. E. J Brouwer, 'Intuitionism and Formalism,' in P. Benacerraf & H. Putnam, eds., *Philosophy of Mathematics* (Englewood Cliffs: Prentice Hall, 1964), p. 69.

3. J. Agassi, *Faraday as a Natural Philosopher* (Chicago: University of Chicago Press, 1971), pp. 28, 86 – 87, 90 – 91. Y. Elkana, *The Discovery of the Conservation of Energy* (London: Hutchinson, 1974), p. 189.

4. D. Bohm, 'Heisenberg's Contribution to Physics,' *New Scientist*, 12 Feb., 1976.

5. The evidence was given by Max Talmey, who was familiar with Einstein at the time in question. See R. W. Clark, *Einstein: The Life and Times* (New York: Avon, 1972), p. 33.

6. A. Einstein & M. Born, *Briefwechsel 1916–1955* (Reinbek bei Hamburg; Rowohlt, 1972), p. 19 (letter no. 5, probably of 1917 or 1918).

7. M. Born, *Natural Philosophy of Cause and Chance* (New York: Dover, 1964), p. 228.

8. W. Heisenberg, *Physics and Philosophy* (New York: Harper, 1962), pp. 88 – 92.

9. R. H. Robins, *A Short History of Linguistics* (London: Longmans, 1967), pp. 174 – 78. E. Cassirer, *The Philosophy of Symbolic Forms*, vol. 1 (New Haven: Yale University Press, 1953) pp. 155 – 63.

10. The authority in question is L. Bloomfield, as quoted in N. Chomsky, *Cartesian Linguistics* (New York: Harper & Row, 1966), p. 86, note 36.

11. From *Uber das vergleichende Sprachstudium in Beziehung auf die verschiedenen Epochen der Sprachentwicklung*, as trans. in M. Cowan, *Humanist without Portfolio* (Detroit: Wayne State University Press, 1963), p. 240.

12. R. H. Robins, op. cit., p. 176, note 8.

13. J. von Uexküll, 'A Stroll Through the World of Animals and Men,' in C. H. Schiller, ed., *Instinctive Behavior* (New York: International Universities Press, 1957). K. Lorenz, *Studies in Animal and Human Behaviour*, vol. 2 (London: Methuen, 1971), pp. 273 – 77. H. Gipper, *Bausteine zur Sprachinhalts-forschung* (Düsseldorf, 1963). T. A. Goudge, 'Uexküll,' in P. Edwards, ed., *Encyclopedia of Philosophy*.

14. K. Lorenz: 'Methods of Approach to the Problems of Behaviour,' in Lorenz, op. cit., p. 252; 'Kant's lehre vom Apriorischen im Lichte der gegenwärtigen Biologie,' in *Blätter für Deutsche Philosophie* 15 (1941), p. 100; *Behind the Mirror* (London: Methuen, 1977), pp. 8, 15 (quoted), 63.

15. L. A. Coser, *Masters of Sociological Thought* (New York: Harcourt Brace Jovanovich, 1971), pp. 21, 155, 201 – 202, 292, 444.

16. See S. Lukes, *Emile Durkheim: His Life and Works* (London: Allen Lane, 1973), esp. pp. 55, 415; and E. Wallwork, *Durkheim: Morality and Milieu* (Cambridge, Mass. : Harvard University Press, 1972), pp. 33 – 34, 36 – 38, 152 ff.

17. E. Durkheim, *Les formes élémentaires de la vie religieuse*, 4th ed. (Paris: Presses Universitaires, 1960), pp. 12 – 28, 616 – 38.

18. E. G. Boring, *A History of Experimental Psychology*, 2nd ed. (New York: Appleton-Century-Crofts, 1950), p. 249. W. S. Sahakian, *History and Systems of Psychology* (New York: Wiley, 1975), p. 190.

19. J. Piaget, *Insights and Illusions of Philosophy* (London: Routledge & Kegan Paul, 1971), pp. 57 – 58.

20. H. Spiegelberg, *Phenomenology in Psychology and Psychiatry* (Evanston: Northwestern University Press, 1972), pp. 201, 302.

21. S. Freud, 'The Unconscious' (1915), section 1, *Standard Edition*, vol. 14.

22. Both Freudian and Kantian terms often changed, at least in emphasis, in the course of time, and they often have an indeterminate fringe of possible

meanings. To find my way I have used J. Laplanche & J.–B. Pontalis, *The Language of Psycho-Analysis* (London: Hogarth Press/Institute of Psycho-Analysis, 1973) and R. Eisler, *Kant-Lexikon* (Berlin, 1930; photographic reprint Hildesheim: Olms, 1964). I have used the terms as simply and generally as possible.

23. Letter to M. Bonaparte, 21 Aug., 1938, in E. Jones, *The Life and Work of Sigmund Freud*, vol. 3 (New York: Basic Books, 1957), p. 466.

24. C. G. Jung, *Memories, Dreams, Reflections* (New York: Pantheon Books, 1963), p. 70.

25. Ibid., p. 74.

26. Ibid., p. 99. Jung's reaction to Nietzsche, ibid., p. 102.

27. C. G. Jung, *Psychological Types*, 2nd ed. (Princeton: Princeton University Press, 1971), pp. 304, 305.

28. C. G. Jung, *Memories, Dreams, Reflections*, pp. 350 – 52.

? pp. 394 – 5

1. *Select Fragments, The Works of Aristotle*, ed. D. Ross, vol. 12 (London: Oxford University Press, 1952), p. 37 (from Cic. *Tusc.* 3.28.69).

2. Ibid., p. 117 (from *Vita Arist. Marciana*, p. 44. 10 – 15 (Rose)).

Index